BCh - 3rd ed.

THE ECONOMICS OF SELLERS' COMPETITION

Model Analysis of Sellers' Conduct

THE ECONOMICS OF SELLERS'
COMPETITION

Model Analysis of Sellers' Conduct

by

FRITZ MACHLUP

Baltimore: The Johns Hopkins Press

0941545   ~~69783~~

By the Same Author
Books in English

The Stock Market, Credit, and Capital Formation (1940)
International Trade and the National Income Multiplier (1943)
The Basing-Point System (1949)
The Political Economy of Monopoly (1952)
The Economics of Sellers' Competition (1952)
An Economic Review of the Patent System (1958)
The Production and Distribution of Knowledge in the United States
   (1962)
Plans for Reform of the International Monetary System (1962)
Essays on Economic Semantics (1963)
International Payments, Debts, and Gold (1964)
International Monetary Arrangements: The Problem of Choice (1964)
Involuntary Foreign Lending (1965)
Remaking the International Monetary System: The Rio Agreement and
   Beyond (1968)

Also nine titles in German, and nine in French, Italian, Japanese,
Russian, and Spanish

Copyright © 1952 by The Johns Hopkins Press
Baltimore, Maryland 21218
All rights reserved
Manufactured in the United States of America

Standard Book Number 8018-0414-0

Originally published, 1952
SECOND PRINTING, 1956
THIRD PRINTING, 1960
FOURTH PRINTING, 1964
FIFTH PRINTING, 1969

Author's Preface

ALTHOUGH a clear and readable style of writing has been one of my major objectives, I doubt that this book will make suitable reading for the raw beginner in the study of economics, unless he is very smart. I shall be very happy if I have succeeded in writing a book suitable for both the intermediate and advanced student and also for the expert in the field.

I realize that an expert gets easily bored if he has to trudge over wide stretches of familiar ground. But to publish only for the expert—jumping over everything that he may be expected to know well—is nowadays a luxury that professional journals can afford, but not the publishers of books. The writer of a book must address a somewhat wider audience and must go over much of the ground that less advanced students have to cover if they are to comprehend the entire discussion. But often a fresh approach to a subject, starting from first principles, may hold new insights even for the most jaded specialist.

If I have succeeded in my endeavours, this book should be useful in many courses in intermediate and advanced economics. Its sub-title, *Model Analysis of Sellers' Conduct,* is not meant to advertise it as a model of analysis, but to indicate that it emphasizes the method of analysing economic problems by constructing and manipulating well-designed models of relevant human conduct. This emphasis, I hope, will be useful far beyond the subject matter of this book and may make its study worth while even in courses in which "competition and monopoly" is only a small portion of the agenda.

Although I recognize the power of mathematical arguments and the usefulness of geometric aids in economic analysis, I have made little use of them. The 26 graphs and the one page of algebra that are included in this book are not part of the text and thus can be skipped with the greatest of ease. While this may please the majority of readers, I shall perhaps be chided for it by my critics. But it has been my aim to keep the book as far as possible within the confines of literary economics.

[v]

The plan of the book is probably clear from the table of contents: an introductory Part I, offering a discussion of the methodological issues pertinent to the "theory of the firm" and of the concepts basic for the analysis of sellers' competition, is followed by
six parts whose titles indicate the system of organization of the
analysis: "Many Sellers," "More Sellers," "Many and More Sellers," "Few Sellers," "Few but More Sellers," and "One Seller."
That the last part, on "One Seller," consists of only one chapter,
while the part on "Few Sellers" extends over five chapters, will
probably be found to be indicative of my judgment of the relative
importance of the respective topics.

The relationship of the present book to some of my other actual, planned, or announced publications on the subject of competition and monopoly may be briefly explained. This book, together
with its companion volume, published under the title *The Political Economy of Monopoly: Business, Labor and Government
Policies*, takes the place of the previously announced book "On
the Economics of Competition and Monopoly." Questions of governmental economic policy with regard to monopoly and competition, the institutional sources of monopoly power, the various
types of monopolistic business practices, the effects of monopolistic wage policies, the attempted measurements of the degree of
business monopoly, and several other issues concerning the political economy of monopoly are discussed in the companion volume. The present book is confined to the economic theory of competition in selling, though it cannot cover all of it: for example,
the analysis of discriminatory pricing is deferred to a separate
book on "The Economics of Price Discrimination," planned for
publication in future years.

Some sections of the present book have been published elsewhere. Large parts of Chapters 2 and 3 were contained in my article on "Marginal Analysis and Empirical Research," published in
the *American Economic Review*, Vol. XXXVI (1946), pp. 519–
554. An Italian translation of the bulk of Chapter 4 was published
under the title "Tipi di concorrenza nella vendita" in the *Giornale
degli Economisti*, Vol. XIX (New Series Vol. III, 1941), pp. 129–
150. Most of Chapters 7 and 8 was published as an article under
the title "Competition, Pliopoly and Profit" in *Economica*, New

Series Vol. IX (1942), pp. 1–23 and 153–175. A part of Chapter
10 is being published in a German translation under the title
"Volkswirtschaftliche Scheinverluste beim Zustrom neuer Wettbe-
werber," in *Ordo*, Vol. V (1952). Chapter 11 was published as an
article entitled "Characteristics and Classifications of Oligopoly,"
in *Kyklos*, Vol. V (1952), pp. 145–163; and a section of Chapter
13 under the title "Oligopolistic Indeterminacy" in the *Weltwirtschaftliches Archiv*, Vol. 68 (1952), pp. 1–19.

The number of my intellectual creditors is too great to permit
a full accounting of my indebtedness. But it would be most ungrateful not to acknowledge the great impact on my thinking of
the writings of Joan Robinson, Edward H. Chamberlin, and Frank
H. Knight. Footnote references to their published work, however
numerous, cannot possibly suffice to show how much of theirs
reappears in this book. In the development of my views on methodology I owe much to Alfred Schutz, social philosopher of the
New School of Social Research. For friendly criticism of earlier
parts of my manuscript I am indebted to John D. Sumner, of the
University of Buffalo, who read Chapters 4 to 10; Arthur Smithies,
of Harvard University, who read Chapters 6 and 7; and a good
many students in my courses at the University of Buffalo, Stan-
ford University, and the Johns Hopkins University. My greatest
debt is to Edith Tilton Penrose, of the Johns Hopkins University,
who read the entire manuscript and suggested countless improvements.

I also acknowledge gratefully financial aid, for editorial and
clerical expenses, from the Lessing Rosenthal Fund for Economic
Research at the Johns Hopkins University.

FRITZ MACHLUP

Baltimore, Maryland, July 1952

Table of Contents

[ix]

Chapter

Analytical Table of Contents

Chapter

Chapter

Chapter

List of Graphs

PART I—THEORY OF THE FIRM AND TYPES OF COMPETITION

CHAPTER 1

Model Analysis and Observation: Prices and Costs

A Note on Model Analysis: Abstractions, Constructs, Models · Theoretical and Descriptive Economics · Models in the Theory of Price

The Economy, the Industry, the Firm: The Selection of Models · The Comparison of Prices · The Profits of Enterprise

The Lack of Actual Price and Cost Data: The Selling Price · The Dating of the Data · Total Cost of Production · The Average Cost of the Actual Output · The Marginal Cost of the Actual Output · Hypothetical Price and Cost Schedules

CONCERNED ONLY WITH certain aspects of human action, economists do not look at the "whole man" but rather at man as consumer, worker, employer, tenant, landlord, saver, investor, buyer, seller. This book deals only with the seller, indeed only with the "seller for profit."

The seller for profit is customarily called a business firm and the analysis of sellers' conduct is usually treated under the heading "theory of the firm," although this is a rather big name for so narrow an aspect of business behavior. We shall have a good deal to say in these early chapters about the deliberate narrowness of the theory of the firm as a part of the "theory of relative prices" and of the "economics of competition and monopoly."

"Price" and "selling" are concepts that necessarily go together: there can be no sale without a price, and there can be no price without a sale—at least, without a sale in mind. Economic analysis of selling prices calls for comparisons between different prices and for comparisons of prices with "costs." Costs and prices are indispensable data in any theoretical or empirical study of competition and monopoly. Prices and costs are the most essential objects of "observation" and the most essential parts of the "analytical models" employed in micro-economic inquiry. Almost naturally, therefore, will prices and costs be the subjects of discussion in Chapter 1 of this book. But first let us settle some preliminaries.

A NOTE ON MODEL ANALYSIS

Discussion in economics abounds with references to analytical models. In the chapters that follow we shall encounter such references almost continually. The chances of misunderstanding this word are so great that we should not grudge the time for a few comments on "model building" that may allay the fears of some readers who dislike newfangled words and distrust abstractions that have proceeded so far that the feeling of familiarity is lost.

Abstractions, Constructs, Models

Every one of us thinks almost exclusively in abstractions, only the degree of abstraction varies. When we come to speak of classes or types of things or events, abstraction has already gone a considerable way. For as soon as we group several single things or events into classes or types, we have abstracted from many of their individual attributes and have to that extent deprived them of some of their individuality or uniqueness. As long as the "type" contains still enough of the attributes and features which we know in individual specimens, we retain a feeling of familiarity and regard the abstraction as relatively "realistic." But for purposes of analysis we must often go much further and abstract from still more of the familiar features of the thing or event or whatever it is we are thinking about. Eventually, what is left is merely a phantom of the real thing, a mental construction that may contain more things that we have not noticed or perceived in reality than things that we have. Now, if our abstraction or mental construction contains several parts in whose interaction and interrelationships we are interested and which we may in our imagination combine in several ways to derive different "results" we speak of an analytical model.

The economic theorist is, of course, not alone in the business of constructing analytical models. Anybody at all who thinks about causal relationships, about "how things work," builds himself a "model." And he does not even have to be a theorist by profession or avocation. The man in the street who describes for himself or for others how something has happened does this by using a mental model. And so does every historian, every lawyer, every scientist. We think with the aid of models, whether we know it or not. If we do not know it, we are like the unschooled upstart who did not know that he knew how to speak prose.[1] Of course, there is no need to use the word "model." Other words have been used in the same sense—for example, "construct" and "schema"—and most people can get along without any such term, because they feel it unnecessary to explain to others or to themselves the processes and techniques they use in their thinking.

Theoretical and Descriptive Economics

Many economists are not conscious of the use of analytical models unless these models are made out of algebraic functions or geometric curves or some other fancy building material. It is true that the econometricians or the addicts to geometric analysis talk more about models than do other economists. But there is no reason why models cannot be described entirely in plain words, and indeed most models are. We can take any book of economic history or institutional economics and find analytical models on almost every page. And I am not referring to "pure" fictions, like pure competition; I am referring to constructions that are needed for the description of business practices, government policies, legal provisions, or historical events. For example, "price leadership," "collusion," "restraint of trade," "price discrimination," "concentration," "consumer deception," "foreign exchange control," "support prices for potatoes"—every one of these matters implies the use of analytical models.

All theorizing involves model building. Does then the fact that some of our work in economics is "theoretical" while some is "descriptive" indicate that models play a greater part in the former than in the latter? The answer is "no." The difference is merely that in our theoretical work we construct new models, adapt old ones,

---

[1] Molière, *The Bourgeois Gentleman* (1670).

modify this or that part of a model, manipulate or "operate" models to examine and re-examine various combinations of assumptions, whereas in our descriptive work we use ready-made models and the results of previous (conscious or unconscious) model analysis without necessarily being aware of the amount of "theory" that is involved.

There are, to be sure, wide differences in degree. For example, in my book on *The Political Economy of Monopoly* the chapters on monopolistic wage determination are "more theoretical" than the chapters on monopolistic business practices. But this is chiefly because the theoretical foundation on which business practices can be discussed is much firmer than that on which a discussion of labor practices can be placed. Thus, we are able to *apply* theory to the one discussion, while we have to *make* or *examine* theory in the other. But there should be no mistake about the amount of theory, good or bad, that goes into so-called "purely descriptive" economics. Anyone reading with a critical mind the description of a law case, for example, a case involving discriminatory pricing techniques or restrictive patent licensing, must realize that the argument rests largely on economic theories developed by means of model analysis—sometimes sound, sometimes unsound, but always of a degree of abstraction much higher than may have been apparent to the lawyers who presented or examined the argument.

Models in the Theory of Price

Some of the models in economic theory are designed for a degree of generality that can be attained only by a level of abstraction which is incompatible with realistic details. It is customary to divide the theory of relative prices into three parts, or three "levels of analysis": the theory of the firm, the theory of the industry, and the theory of the whole system. The first two are "partial equilibrium" analysis, the third is "general equilibrium" analysis, where "equilibrium" stands by and large for "initial position" and for "end result" of the operation of assumed "forces" or conditions.[2]

---

[2] The equilibrium concept in economics is primarily a tool for the explanation of *movement:* we "explain" a movement by pointing to "causes"

The division into the three levels is a matter of methodological convenience because different kinds of assumptions are made for the basic models used. Our conception of "how the economy works" is greatly aided by the construction of these basic models which schematize some of the interrelationships that we think exist between various phenomena.

The models of the firm, the industry, and the whole system that are used in price theory are so "shockingly" unrealistic that a few comments might be added to give the reasons for it. The purpose of an analytical model is to demonstrate the operation of the factors considered most relevant for the problem under examination. In order to be most useful for such a purpose the model should omit everything held to be of small or no relevance for the particular problem. Any part of a model that merely serves to make it look more realistic becomes an unnecessary burden in the use of the model. Of course, one must distinguish two kinds of protest against lack of realism: first, that certain realistic assumptions were omitted in the construction; second, that the assumptions made were unrealistic. The answer to the first of these protests is that realism in a model constructed for purposes of analysis is undesirable if it reduces its simplicity, and may cause confusion by "cluttering up" the model with irrelevant details. People who are superficial, who prefer to "look" rather than to "think" and are more interested in the outer trappings than in the inner workings of things, are wont to complain about models that are "unrealistic" in this sense. But a complaint of unrealism in this sense should be taken seriously only if the critic can prove that the missing parts in the model essentially change the end results of its operation and

---

that are responsible for a departure from one position and an approach to another one. These two positions are idealized as positions of *rest*, an "initial" equilibrium and a "new" equilibrium. The movement is thus "understood" as an adjustment to a "disequilibrating" change. We need the assumed "balance of forces" in the *initial* position in order to isolate the disequilibrating change, that is, in order to make sure that nothing else has occurred and that the movement exhibited by the operation of the model can be attributed without any doubt to the specified disturbance. We need the assumed "balance of forces" in the *new* position in order to make sure that the adjustment is complete and all effects of the disequilibrating change have been fully recorded. But let no one make the mistake of interpreting the "equilibrium theorist" as trying to detect equilibrium positions in reality.

that a "more complete" model yields results much more closely conforming to generally observed or experienced reality.

The second kind of protest can be answered only by an invitation to provide a substitute model with more realistic assumptions which nevertheless does all that the rejected model can do. Models are not selected chiefly for their input of assumptions but for their output of results. We know what we want to have explained, and then construct models that can aid in explaining it. Of all the models that might explain the result, we choose the one that works with the assumptions that we believe conform most closely to observed reality. Models with "more realistic" assumptions but not yielding results conforming to observed reality are disqualified.[3]

The models now generally used in the theory of relative prices —generally used because the results appear to conform to our observations and the assumptions seem the most plausible—are certainly unrealistic. The model of the individual firm does not bear any close resemblance to anything that we in the real world know as a firm; the model of an industry is quite dissimilar to what is popularly understood to be an industry or what the statisticians understand by that term; and least of all does the model of the economy as a whole look like any picture that a close observer of reality may ever have drawn for himself.[4]

THE ECONOMY, THE INDUSTRY, THE FIRM

The fact that economic theorists engaged in price analysis have constructed models of the firm, the industry, and the economy as a whole does not mean that they need all these models for every

[3] We hear sometimes suggestions to the effect that we should *begin* with realistic assumptions. This suggestion overlooks the fact that observation provides *millions* of *realistic* assumptions for each "case" or "problem," but no guide for selecting the relevant ones. One must work backward from the result that is to be explained, and construct models with constellations of assumptions which would approximate the result. These alternative models then provide several sets of possibly *relevant* "causes"; finally one selects the model whose assumptions appear most *plausible* on the basis of observed reality.

[4] No more does the model of a magnetic field which the physicist constructs for his analytical work look like anything anybody has ever "seen" in the real world; nor has any physicist ever "observed" a neutrino; nor a biologist a gene.

problem of price theory. The selection of models in each case is a matter of relevance and convenience.

The Selection of Models

For some problems of the interdependence of economic magnitudes in the economy as a whole, we can do without the models of the firm or the industry. For example, we often feel that a "solution" based on the assumption of pure competition may serve as a reasonable "approximation." But for the theory of an economy in which all firms operate under pure competition it is unnecessary to spend much time on the theory of the individual firm, because the relationships are so simple that no separate models of the individual business unit are needed to demonstrate them. Even more frequently can we dispense with the model of the industry. On the other hand, there may be problems for which the model of the whole system would be an unnecessarily clumsy thinking aid and which can more simply be analysed with the help of the theory of the industry. Needless to say, there is more than one model of the firm, of the industry, and of the whole economy. Economists have constructed whole sets of models for each and select the ones they think are most handy for tackling the particular problem that they may wish to analyse.

Assume for example we wish to analyse the effects of a cartel agreement on the output of the commodity concerned. We shall first find it convenient to examine how an imaginary individual firm will adjust itself to the change in selling conditions. We do this by selecting two models of firms, one of a producer acting under conditions of unregulated competition, another of a producer with the same cost conditions acting under the cartel restrictions imposed upon him and with the knowledge of similar restrictions imposed on the other suppliers of the "same" commodity. We can thus compare the equilibrium output of "the" firm in the two models. Then we ask ourselves what the possibilities are of new firms taking up business in the same field. If no such possibilities exist, we are satisfied with the results indicated by the theory of the firm. If the possibility of new firms entering the field is open, we shall resort to an industry model, analyse the profit rates a newcomer might expect to obtain if he started production, compare the profit rates with those obtaining elsewhere, and examine the combined effects of the output restrictions by the insiders and the new production by newcomers. We may be satisfied with these results, or we may decide to go further if we believe that we can fruitfully analyse the indirect repercussions of the changes which have resulted from the operations of the models up to this point.

Taking another example, let us assume that we wish to analyse the effects of an import quota on the price and output of a certain commodity. If the number of domestic producers is large, we may decide that the assumption of pure competition, unrealistic as it is, will yield sufficiently close results. We shall then skip experimenting with models of the individual firm and start immediately with an industry model, making assumptions about the supply by domestic producers and about the total domestic demand for the commodity. Depending on our assumptions about the case of entry of new firms into the industry, the assumed supply will include or exclude the potential output of potential newcomers.

Let us refer, as a third example, to a problem that I have discussed elsewhere,[5] the effects of a pay raise obtained by a trade union for the workers of a particular industry. Depending on the number and size of firms in the industry, we shall either begin with individual firm analysis or immediately proceed to industry analysis. But we shall probably not be satisfied with studying the effects upon prices and production of the commodities made by the industry directly affected. We shall need to go into the further repercussions on other industries, other commodities, other worker groups. The kind of repercussions studied will be suggested to us by a general-equilibrium model, a model of the economy as a whole.

The Comparison of Prices

In each of the models prices play a major role. But as we move "up and down" the various levels of analysis the meaning of price may often undergo slight variations. For example, as we shall see

[5] Fritz Machlup, *The Political Economy of Monopoly: Business, Labor and Government Policies* (Baltimore: Johns Hopkins Press, 1952), Chapter 10.

in Ch. 9, the subjective price expectations of the individual firm may be translated into a definite price "given" to all firms as we move "up" from the theory of the firm to the theory of the industry. Or the prices paid by the consumer, as assumed for the demand curve in an industry model, will call for several translations as we "move down" to the model of the individual firm and its expected average net revenue. Yet, although we might be strict and not forget to shift methodological gears as we ascend or descend between the different levels of analysis, we shall for many problems be permitted to neglect such exactitude and, for the sake of simplicity, assume that the price to the firm is the same as the price to the industry.

Simplifications of this sort presuppose another "unrealistic" kind of assumption, the assumption of homogeneous commodities and homogeneous factors of production. Let no one believe that a critic who proves that there are wide differences between labor and labor has demolished economic theory where homogeneity of labor is often assumed. Economic theory is equipped to deal with any number of different factors of production; indeed, if it were proved that no two hours of labor, or no two tons of coal, were alike, economic theory could proceed on the assumption that the relative efficiencies of all the different factors, the substitutabilities of one for another, were given. But things would certainly be more complicated and, hence, regardless of how different or alike the various units in a class of productive factors are in reality, we must first learn how to operate models in which "homogeneity" is assumed.

This assumption, that the various units of what we call one factor of production are perfectly alike, is a great help in the theory of monopoly. For example, if we say that a restriction of entry may allow the price of a productive service employed within a field to remain above the price of the *same* services elsewhere, we certainly imply that the excluded ones are just as good, in every respect, as the ones employed. That is, we affirm (or complain) that they receive different prices although they are theoretically interchangeable. Of course, before one can apply this theory to a case where monopolistic restrictions are suspected, one would have to make a judgment about the extent to which the productive factors within and outside the "industry" are really the same. This judgment involves much more than technological substitutability; it involves views about the changeability of social, political and economic institutions.

Assume two pieces of land, exactly the same size and possessing the same physical and chemical quality of soil, and in the same climate, but located in different parts of the country, or merely at different distances from a particular city, railroad station, river, or harbor. No one will doubt that location is an important quality of such resources and therefore that their productive services are different, no matter how alike they are in all other respects. No one will be surprised if the two pieces of land command different prices and no one will blame monopolistic restrictions for it.

Assume now two groups of workers, exactly alike in physical makeup, in personal characteristics, in skill, industry, ambition, willingness and capacity, but located in different parts of the country. If they receive different prices for their services, shall we also accept this as a necessary consequence of the difference in location? We are not inclined to do so, for while we accept the immobility of land as natural and inevitable, we do not so accept the immobility of labor. The difference in the location of labor is not a part of its quality as it is of land. Any lack of mobility that exists with regard to labor may possibly be due to monopolistic restrictions. For example, closed-shop contracts between industries and local unions may prevent the movement of workers. On the other hand, the workers' failure to move may be due to other circumstances. There may be, on the part of the workers, an unwillingness to move. Both groups may be equally unwilling to move, but one of them may have the good luck to be in the location with superior job opportunities. Surely we cannot in this case attribute the difference in wages to monopoly restraints. But how shall we judge the situation if it is lack of information that explains the failure of the workers to move to the better-paying jobs? And how, if they know about the better jobs and would like to move, but lack the necessary funds and cannot borrow them? Are we to regard the two worker groups as the "same" factors of production, whose movements are impeded by institutional impediments to competition, or as factors as different from each other as the two pieces of land at different locations?

The difficulty is not one of theory but of judgment and appraisal. The theorist can deal with the situation equally well as a competitive one involving different productive resources or as a monopolistic one involving the same resources. It is not the price difference that indicates the presence of monopolistic restrictions, for an examination of the nature of any impediments to mobility and substitutability is necessary before we can decide whether the resources whose prices are compared are to be regarded as the same or different resources.

The Profits of Enterprise

While it is easily said that the presence of monopoly profits indicates the presence of monopoly, it is not easily said what monopoly profits are and how they can in concrete cases be distinguished and separated from normal profits, from profits due to differential managerial ability, to differential exposure to uncertainty, or to mere windfalls.

Those who regard "enterprise" as a factor of production, and profit as the income earned by this factor, have a particularly difficult time disentangling differences in the "quality" of this factor from differences in monopolistic position when differential profits in different firms or industries are to be compared. Other models of the economic system, reserving the concept of productive factor to physically measurable things, avoid this particular difficulty, but the task of dissecting the business profit as computed by the accountant, and of sorting its various parts into different boxes, labeled "resources cost," "windfalls," "monopoly profits," etc., remains formidable.

In any case, it is helpful to understand that this important phase of the discussion of cost-price relationships is part of the theory of the transfer of enterprise and resources between different fields of activity. That is, it is part of the theory of the industry, part of the theory of open or barred access. We shall come back to these issues when we deal, in Chapter 7, with the theory of profit and newcomers' competition. The trouble with most of the analysis of the industry is that its concepts are so highly abstract that they cannot be made practically operational. That is, we cannot find for them any counterparts in the real world that could be objects of statistical measurement.

One should think that we are much better off in this respect when we come to the theory of the firm. Unfortunately we shall find that matters there are not a great deal better as far as the availability of data is concerned.

THE LACK OF ACTUAL PRICE AND COST DATA

Everybody—except lawyers and economists—knows what a price is. Most people know how to find out what prices they would have to pay if they wanted to buy certain things. Very few people, however, would know what to do if they had to find out about "the price" of any particular product in the country.

The Selling Price

Does a product have "a" price in the country? Can one call it "a" product if it is at different places? Differences in location, in quality, in the size of the order, in the terms of delivery and payment, in the type, place or function of the buyer and of the seller —these are some of the difficulties in the way of defining "the" product and ascertaining "the" price.

Quite apart from locational or other differences between different sellers, it is difficult to say even for one seller alone what his selling price is. Differences in product quality and in specification, discrimination between customers, and changes of data from one moment to the next present the worst of the difficulties. It may be no way out of these difficulties to try to calculate "average receipt per unit of product" in lieu of "price," because the composition of the physical product may be varying. The average revenue, or average price, per yard, square foot, or pound may be meaningless if the product varies in width, substance, caliper, shape, density, smoothness, color, finish, specific weight, or what not. For example, from one week to the next the average sales proceeds of a cardboard mill may have risen per ton of product, but declined per sheet or square foot, if the second batch of deliveries included a bigger portion of thinner calipers; and similarly contradictory findings concerning the average price per "unit" would be obtained in several other industries in which alternative units, such as weight, length, square measures, cubic measures, etc., are used and the composition of the output varies. But even with relatively great homogeneity within a few classes of products, the speed of delivery, the size of the single shipment, the size of the whole order, the terms of payment, the risks of credit, etc., may be so different that the average revenue per relevant unit of output of one period is hardly comparable with that of another.

These difficulties are serious and they gravely complicate empirical research on prices. But they do not make such research impossible. With sufficient care it is possible to achieve comparability of price data. Price lists, accounting records or any other unadjusted data will not do for our purposes; explanations by the men in charge of selling and the men in charge of production are needed before the "raw data" can be properly corrected for all disturbing variables and, with the aid of competent interpreters, transformed into findings of so-called facts.

The Dating of the Data

In taking average sales revenue in lieu of price we slide over the fact that the sales contracts, the production, shipment, and receipt of the sales proceeds for a given lot of goods occur at different times. In industries where production is not for stock but on specification under particular orders we may get four different answers in our search for the average price; the average price of the orders received by the sales department during a certain week will not be the same as that of the orders executed in the same week by the production department or by the shipping department; and the collections of the week would yield a still different average price. Where the sales department keeps good records, it may be possible to analyse the orders received and ascertain an average selling price (estimating and taking account of all cost differentials for different specifications in order to make the individual prices comparable). Accounting data will usually refer to the shipments of the week (with numerous corrections of the data needed to take account of cost differentials and, especially, freight costs if delivered prices are charged). Needless to say, the shipments of the week may be on orders received last year, last month, or last week, and the average price may be the result of several different prices obtained during the past year.

This raises, of course, the problem of the appropriate dating of the data. This is important for the calculation of price data as such. It is still more important if the object of the calculation is to compare prices with costs. Should the orders or the shipments in a particular month be compared with the purchase contracts or the actual outlays of the same month? Are not many outlays more properly allocated to the finished product of a later period? On the other hand, may not today's outlay be for a product the price of which was contracted several months ago? But, in some firms, may it not be for a product the price of which will be agreed upon only several months from now? Should we assume a lag of selling prices behind costs or a lag of costs behind selling prices?

If costs as well as prices would do us the favor of staying put for a sufficiently long time, and then one of them would start moving, and then the other, the significant time lags would show up in the data. But this is too much to expect from "reality." What we "see" in reality is a more or less continuous motion of most costs and prices, and we can have little hope that the data will reveal the "actual" leads and lags. Nor is there any reason for the leads and lags in one year to hold for other years when many conditions may be different. No general rule can help us here; how a researcher will date the data will depend on the kind of data at his disposal and on the kind of question to which he addresses himself.

Total Cost of Production

Almost all obstacles which stand in the way of getting an unambiguous figure for the selling price of a product are equally troublesome in finding the production cost of the product; differences in quality and specification, changes of conditions through time, etc., present the same vexing questions. But in addition to these questions several special puzzles are involved in production cost calculations.

Quite apart from the problems of calculating the unit cost of production, the mere adding up of expenses to obtain a relevant *total cost* figure contains many controversial issues. It may be easy to add the total outlays made over the life time of a firm; but if a shorter period is taken it is difficult to decide how much of the past outlays should be charged to the period in question, how much of the outlays during the period should be charged to future periods, and how much of future outlays should be charged to the production of the given period.

Fixed investment, its depreciation, repair and maintenance, and the interest on the capital invested, are at the bottom of many cost-calculation problems. There is a long history of legal and economic arguments about these problems; they have been especially prominent in litigations arising out of government regulation of railroad and public utility rates. The endless debates about the valuation of property, about historical cost vs. reproduction cost vs. "prudent" investment, about contractual interest vs. fair return on the whole investment, etc., have brought out that there is no single answer to these complex questions. From the point of view of the investor, concerned with the return on his individual investment, the actual historical cost he has incurred is the interesting thing; from the point of view of the lawyer, concerned with a "fair" return, the thing to look for is not the actual cost of investment but the cost of "prudent" investment; from the point of view of the economist, concerned with the utilization and allocation of resources, the cost of reproduction of the service is the significant thing in the long run. (In the short run and for a declining industry the value in alternative uses, if any, of the given equipment would be the significant basis for determining the investment cost.)

This means that the value of assets on the books of the firm will rarely be the correct basis for determining the interest charges and depreciation charges relevant for problems of competitive resource allocation. For example, if the cost of construction and the prices of equipment are higher than they were at the time the investments were actually made, depreciation charges made on the basis of book values are too low and the accounting profits, therefore, too high. (That is, the books show as profit what should be regarded as cost.) The net worth of the firm reflecting the undervaluation of the assets will likewise be too low. Since, before economic profit is calculated, "imputed" interest on the equity capital has to be added to the normal interest on borrowed funds, the undervaluation of the assets will result in an understatement of the interest charges just as it does in an understatement of the depreciation charges. The opposite, of course will be true if the book values of assets are higher than the present cost of the construction or equipment now required for the production of the output of the firm. Depreciation and interest charges will then be overstated from the point of view of an evaluation of competitive resource allocation. If firms have large excess capacity, neither the depreciation nor the interest charges for the unused assets are a part of the economic cost of production of the actual output.

From these considerations one must conclude that accounting records will hardly ever provide complete data for calculating the total cost of production. Substantial corrections will usually be necessary and will require intensive consultations and careful analysis. (The "actual" total cost of production obtained from such analysis, is, of course, the cost of the actually produced output, not a cost schedule for a series of alternative outputs.)

Another type of difficulty arises from changing inventory values. If a loss from inventory depreciation is written off as soon as prices fall, the calculation of the current cost of production will be different from what it would be if the earlier high price of materials were charged against current production until the expensive inventory stocks are worked off.[6]

The problems mentioned here are only a small sample of those

[6] The significance of accounting practice in this respect is illustrated by the following: "Because of the sharp increase in the level of raw material prices and the uncertainty of future price trends, the Company is considering changing this year the accounting method of valuation of its major domestic inventories from the "Average Cost" method which has been used in the past, to the "last-in, first-out" (LIFO) method. The LIFO method tends to eliminate from taxable profit the gains and losses due to increases and decreases in the market value of inventories. If adopted in this fiscal year it could have the effect of reducing net profit as much as $10,000,000." Procter & Gamble Co., *Earnings Statement for nine months ended March 31, 1951* (April 26, 1951).

connected with the calculation of production costs. The production cost relevant for an analysis of the "cost-price relationship" and for the evaluation of monopoly positions seems to become more puzzling the more closely it is examined.

The Average Cost of the Actual Output

For some problems of monopoly the total cost of the output actually produced can tell the story as well as, or better than, cost per unit of output could. For example, in the analysis of the effects of monopolistic obstacles to the entry of new enterprise into an industry, total economic profit, the excess of total sales revenue over total cost, will be at least as revealing as average profit per unit of output would be. And if the output is not entirely homogeneous, but consists of different qualities or sizes, substances, shapes, finish, etc., the calculation of average revenue and average cost is an unnecessary complication of the problem. There are, however, problems for which the knowledge of a firm's total cost of production is not enough. In the belief that the concept of average cost is useful in the solution of their problems, economists, accountants, and business administrators have spent vast efforts on the techniques of calculating average costs under varying conditions.[7]

We must again distinguish between the cost of output actually produced and a cost schedule for a series of possible outputs. At the moment we are concerned only with the former. Even this gives us more than enough complications. For all attempts to ascertain an unambiguous average cost of the output actually produced come to grief over the treatment of fixed costs, common costs, and joint costs, that is, when costs must be arbitrarily allocated if they are allocated at all.

In attempting to include a part of fixed costs in the average cost per unit of output we should distinguish historically fixed

---

[7] We mean average cost per unit of output, that is, total cost divided by the quantity produced. Cost may also be averaged over time, as we shall see later. For example, if the price of raw material fluctuates daily, or if the price of fuel fluctuates seasonally, these material or fuel costs may be averaged. But this is a separate matter. Average costs per unit of output are calculated even if all individual expense items are constant.

costs from economically fixed costs. Economically fixed costs are costs that are independent (as a total) of the volume of output, but they need not remain the same over time; they may vary with other things than output. Historically fixed costs are simply outlays made in the past. Often costs are historically fixed as outlays but not as economic production costs, in which case the cost accounts of the firm show economically incorrect figures.[8]

Several different methods are used by cost accountants and analysts for the allocation of fixed costs over annual outputs. Some follow the practice of spreading the entire annual fixed cost (including depreciation charges calculated by one of several alternative methods) over the actual output of the year. Others have adopted a "standard cost" procedure of charging a constant burden per unit of output in order to avoid charging the entire cost of unused capacity to the actual output.[9]

Sometimes no account is taken of the fact that a lack of homogeneity in the product might justify a very different allocation of fixed costs. If the productive equipment has a lower capacity for certain qualities, substances, or shapes than for others, it is misleading to charge a uniform overhead per unit of output regardless

[8] For example, the annual rent of the leased premises of the factory may be contractually fixed; but the charge to current production cost might well have to be higher or lower. If rental values have generally increased, the cost of using these premises for the particular production is equal to their value for alternative uses, i.e., higher than the contractual rent. The obverse holds if rental values have fallen. Other examples are the interest costs on bonded indebtedness, the depreciation charges on fixed assets, etc.

[9] The following example will illustrate the differences: Assume that 1,200,000 tons per year could be produced most efficiently with the existing equipment, which has a value of $12,000,000 and is expected to have a service life of ten years. Assume further that the firm had expected to produce at least 800,000 tons per year, that is, it had counted on earning an annual amortization of $1,200,000 with an annual production of 800,000 tons, or $1.50 per ton. Assume finally that the output over a certain two-year period was only 1,200,000 tons, instead of the expected 1,600,000 tons. If the firm uses a standard cost technique, it will consistently figure with *$1.50* as depreciation cost per unit of output. If the firm uses straight-line depreciation and spreads it over the actual output of each year, the average cost will depend on when the 1,200,000 tons were actually produced. If all of it was produced in the first year and nothing in the second, the depreciation per unit of output would have been calculated at *$1.00* per ton. If 600,000 tons were produced each year, depreciation would be *$2.00* per ton.

of its composition. For this reason, the allocation of the fixed cost is sometimes made by adding it as a percentage of the direct cost. This, however, may substantially fail to take care of the problem because the differences in the direct cost of the different qualities (substances, shapes) may be unrelated to the differences in the "cost of capacity" due to the fact that a given plant may be capable of producing more of one quality than of another.[10] Whatever system of allocation is chosen, the result is largely arbitrary.

The same problem arises in connection with the common costs of two or more different products made by the same firm. This is hardly surprising since there is no clear border line between different qualities of the same product and different products. Nevertheless, it is conventional to give separate emphasis to the multi-product firm and its problem of allocating the common cost of the different products. This common cost may be fixed (management, engineering, buildings, machines) or variable with output (labor, fuel, power, materials). The most widely used methods of allocating the common cost are (a) by adding fixed percentage margins to the direct and clearly allocable cost, (b) by distributing the common cost in proportion to the sales proceeds of the products, or (c) by a standard cost procedure worked out with reference to some norm or long-run plan. Needless to say, the result does not help us to know "the" average cost of each of the products.

For reasons not relevant to the calculation of average costs, "truly joint costs" are often distinguished from other common costs in multi-product firms. Products are "truly joint" if they must be produced together and in constant proportions. Truly joint costs are variable costs. They vary (as a total) with the output of the entire set (fixed combination) of joint products. There is no basis for allocating joint costs among the joint products in an attempt to calculate the average cost of each of them. Any formulas that accountants devise for the "solution" of this problem is neither

[10] For example, in the production of mechanical wood pulp, the labor and fuel cost of white groundwood is lower than of brown pulp, but the power cost is higher. That is to say, the tonnage produced of white groundwood with the existing plant and equipment (water power installations, turbines, grinders) is smaller, which would call for a higher allocation of fixed costs per ton of white pulp—if the accountants knew about it.

more nor less arbitrary than the methods designed to "find" what share of any other common cost should "properly" be charged to the average cost of a given product.

Somewhat similar to the problems of "costing" in a multi-product firm are the average cost problems arising in multi-plant firms and in multi-process firms. There is no need for us to go into these matters. The only point to remember is that in none of these situations is there such a thing as an "actual" average cost that could be found or ascertained by empirical research or any technique of analysis. There are, of course, various accounting practices which firms may choose to adopt and which yield various numerical results they may wish to regard as "the" average costs of their products. And empirical research may attempt to establish what figures the firms have developed along such lines. But these figures are purely subjective in nature since they are based on the accountants' personal preferences for one formula or another and on a number of similarly arbitrary assumptions prerequisite to their calculations. While there may be an "objective estimate" of the total economic costs of a firm for its entire production, there is nothing that may be called an objective calculation or estimate of average cost. There is no "actual" average cost.

The Marginal Cost of the Actual Output

Most of the obstructions in the way of an unambiguous notion of average cost do not hinder the development of an unambiguous idea of marginal cost. The marginal cost of the actual output of a particular product is the difference between the total cost of producing that actual output and the total cost of producing a little less, for example, one unit less. The nice thing about it is that this difference can usually be ascertained even without knowing or finding the total cost of the actual and of the smaller output. Neither the total cost—which is ascertainable but with great trouble—nor the average cost—which is not ascertainable at all in any unambiguous sense—needs to be known for the marginal cost to be determined.

For the determination of marginal cost no theories, formulas or rules concerning the allocation of fixed, common or joint costs are needed. For example, it does not matter at all how the depreciation of fixed assets is calculated and how much of it is included in total cost. For, ordinarily, depreciation would not be changed either way if a slightly smaller output were produced. (If, with a smaller output, the wear and tear on the equipment should be noticeably less, one can estimate how much this would amount to if one has an idea only of the cost of the equipment and the physical effect of using it; one need not first make an estimate of the total annual depreciation or of the average depreciation per unit of output.) It does not matter either, for marginal cost, how interest on bonded debt or on equity capital is treated in total-cost or average-cost findings, since the interest burden (paid out or imputed) probably would not in the least be affected by a slight reduction in the output of the firm. The only items that in all probability would be affected are the payroll, the use of materials, the use of power, perhaps certain excise or other taxes. In exceptional cases the calculation may be more difficult, for example, if the reduced output could be more economically produced with different machinery or different production methods. But these complications, treated under the heading of "long-run marginal cost," need not concern us at this point.

Common costs present no more of a problem to the estimation of marginal cost than do fixed costs. It is not much trouble to find out what difference the difference in output would make to all possible expenditure items. Not even truly joint costs create complications for the calculation of marginal cost. The output of one product out of a set of truly joint products cannot be reduced, it is true, without reducing at the same time the output of the other products in the set. Hence, the difference in outlays between producing the smaller and the larger output will be partly offset by a difference in revenues from selling the joint products. Thus, taking beef and hides as our example of truly joint products, the marginal cost of beef would be the difference in the total cost of raising a herd of, say, 200 heads rather than merely 199, minus the sales proceeds from selling the hide of that extra steer. These calculations may become more complicated if the selling prices of the joint products are not constant but vary as their quantities are changed. The principle, however, is clear and unambiguous. The marginal cost of any one product of a set of joint products is equal to the cost of increasing the output from x — 1 to x, minus the additional revenue from selling the increased output of the by-products.[11]

It has sometimes been said that marginal cost cannot be calculated for a product produced by a multi-product firm, because the problem of allocating the common cost cannot be solved. This is a sad misunderstanding, for in such cases the marginal cost is the only cost that can be unambiguously ascertained, while neither the total cost nor the average cost can be established (without resort to completely arbitrary rules of the game of cost accounting). For the calculation of total cost and of average cost, some arbitrary share of the common fixed and common variable cost must be

---

[11] A numerical illustration may help clarify the principle. A, B, and C are joint products, produced in fixed proportions from the same raw materials. There are joint fixed costs for management and plant, joint variable costs for labor and material needed in producing the joint products, separate fixed costs for finishing plants, and separate variable costs for labor and material needed in finishing each of the three products. Assume output per period is 214 thousand units of A, 428 thousand units of B, and 642 thousand units of C, and that changes in output can be made only in round lots of a thousand units of A, two thousand of B, and three thousand of C. We are asked to estimate the marginal cost of A.

In order to produce 214 rather than only 213 thousand units of A it is technologically necessary and economically desirable to produce 428 rather than 426 thousand units of B and 642 rather than 639 thousand units of C. What differences are involved for outlays and revenues? Let us assume the following figures:

Difference in joint fixed cost		$ nil
Difference in joint variable cost of ABC		2765
Difference in fixed cost of finishing plants		nil
Difference in finishing cost of A		1250
Difference in finishing cost of B		1825
Difference in finishing cost of C		930
Total difference in total costs of A, B and C		$6770
Difference in revenue from sales of B	$3000	
Difference in revenue from sales of C	1800	
Total difference in total revenue from B and C		4800
Net difference attributable to last thousand units of A		$1970

Marginal cost of A at present output.... $1.97 per unit.

In cases of truly joint products we may not be much interested in the separate marginal costs of one of the set. But in reality the proportions of products are seldom rigidly fixed and then the separate marginal costs of each of the products are significant. They can be calculated by an analogous technique.

allocated to the particular product. This is not so for the calculation of marginal cost. Fixed costs are irrelevant for marginal cost
and the correct share in the difference in common variable cost is
conditioned by the technological and market situation.[12] The engineer can tell how much of each factor of production is needed
to change the output from x — 1 to x; the purchasing expert can
tell the expenses required; the salesmen can tell the revenue from
the sale of by-products.

We conclude that the "actual" marginal cost can be established,
if only by research and analysis, and that assertions to the contrary
are incorrect. It is a different matter, however, if it is asserted that
marginal costs are in fact not estimated or are of little significance
in business practice. This is something that we shall have to consider carefully.

It is, however, appropriate to state at this point that the marginal cost of the actual output cannot be determined from accounting records. Accounting records reflect changes over time and to
estimate marginal cost by attempting to eliminate such changes
from the records would be more cumbersome and less accurate
than to estimate it by "ad hoc" methods using engineering data,
current factor prices and current factor opportunity costs. To be
sure, current factor opportunity costs are essentially subjective.
An "objective outsider" cannot well know the values which the
available resources would have in alternative uses. These are things
in the minds of the men in charge of operations and it is difficult
to substitute the knowledge of the most astute outside expert for
that of the experienced inside practitioner.

Hypothetical Price and Cost Schedules

Economic theory is seldom concerned with "actual" prices and
costs of an "actual" output. Most problems of price theory call for
whole schedules of prices and costs for a range of outputs, because
an "explanation" of actual price, cost, and output logically implies
a demonstration of why price, cost, and output are not different
from what they are. Of many possible prices, many possible costs,

---

[12] Where an increase in output makes it necessary or desirable to expand
productive capacity, certain costs that are "fixed" otherwise become variable
and the changes in these costs are, of course, included in marginal cost.

many possible output volumes—what caused any existing ones to be the chosen ones? We need to have an idea of the prices at which different outputs *could* be sold and the costs at which they *could* be produced, before we can say much about why prices, costs, and outputs are what they are.

These hypothetical prices and costs of different outputs are customarily presented in the form of schedules, curves, or functions.[13] These schedules, curves or functions do not always mean the same things in different contexts. Indeed, their meanings at different levels of economic analysis are necessarily different, both with regard to the nature of the quantitative relationships they express and with regard to the assumptions concerning whether other things are equal or changed.

It is customary to say that *one* point on a demand or cost schedule is "actual," namely, the price at which the product is actually sold and the cost at which it is actually produced, while all other points are hypothetical. However, it is perhaps better if we free ourselves entirely of the idea of anything actual, for as soon as anything is actual it is a matter of the past. The relationships with which the economist is chiefly concerned are expected, anticipated; they are a matter of the future. If the theory of the firm is developed in order to demonstrate important factors in the decisions of producers about the prices at which they will sell or the outputs they will produce of certain products, *every* point on the schedules is hypothetical. *Every* point refers to relationships anticipated, even if one point may conform to actual experience and may *become* actual, provided that the anticipations turn out to be correct. This is essentially what is meant when the *"ex ante"* character of the schedules (curves, functions) is stressed.

[13] It is logically impossible to provide direct *empirical* tests to establish the correctness of *hypothetical* relationships. "Direct empirical tests" would mean that the figures are no longer hypothetical but have become "actual"; yet, at one time only *one* value for each variable can be actual; to take the actual values at different times for the hypothetical values at one time implies a confidence in the invariability of conditions over time which is not justified by our experience. This does not mean that the work done on "statistical" cost and demand curves is worthless, but only that it rests so much on "plausible" assumptions and "working hypotheses" that one must not create a false contrast between an "empiric-realistic" approach and a "purely theoretical" one, since the former is based on the latter and includes it.

CHAPTER 2

The Theory of the Firm: Marginal Analysis of Prices, Inputs, and Outputs

Conduct Models of the Firm · The Marginalist Way of Thinking · The "Determination" of Prices, Output and Input · Subjectivity of Cost and Revenue · The Omission of Important Variables · The Range of Price and Output Variations · The Time-Range of Anticipation · The Numerical Definiteness of the Estimates · The "Extreme. Difficulty of Calculating" · The Analysis of Change Needs no Exactness · Non-Pecuniary Considerations · Maximum Profit versus Security · Maximum Profit versus Most-Favored Odds

W HAT ECONOMISTS USUALLY call the theory of the firm is a part of the theory of relative prices and has been developed in order to explain the determination of prices, inputs and outputs by business units under various competitive and monopolistic conditions.[1] Of course, any models of the individual firm that are constructed for the specific purposes of price theory may be utterly unsuitable for other purposes. For example, for a theory of the growth of the firm, where we are not interested in the why's of decisions concerning prices and outputs of particular products but of decisions concerning the investment of available funds or the increase of the power of management, the traditional theory of the firm is all but useless.[2] A model can seldom serve very many

---

[1] We must distinguish between explanation and evaluation as two different objectives of price theory. For example, the effects of an excise tax upon price and output may be explained without being evaluated. The former is causal analysis, the latter is welfare analysis. We shall not deal here with welfare economics, except in occasional comments.

[2] This is clearly shown in an unpublished study of the growth of the size of the firm by Edith Tilton Penrose of Johns Hopkins University as part of a project financed by the Merrill Foundation and jointly conducted by G. Heberton Evans, Jr., and myself.

purposes and never all purposes. This methodological principle, which I like to call the "relativity of the relevance of models," is fundamental to all analysis.

Conduct Models of the Firm

We have mentioned that growth theory and price theory call for very different models of the conduct of the firm. But even within the purview of price theory there is a variety of models from which to choose. The choice will depend on the problem at hand and on the working habits of the analyst. Of several models that could be used for the analysis of a particular problem the analyst may prefer the one with which he is most familiar. On the other hand, he may not wish to choose the simplest possible one if this would involve too much changing of models while an only slightly more complicated model could be adapted to a larger number of problems.[3]

The most general model of the decision-making of the business firm concerning prices, inputs and outputs has three sets of basic "data":

(a) the possibilities of buying productive services,
(b) the possibilities of transforming them into products, and
(c) the possibilities of selling the products.

Expressed as schedules of quantitative relationships the three

---

[3] A few examples may serve to make clear what all this means. For the analysis of pure competition the simplest possible model can do without the concept of marginal revenue. Such a model, however, would not serve for the analysis of other market positions. It will therefore be preferable, in order to avoid changing models, to use a "more complicated" one which includes the marginal revenue concept. On the other hand, the model of the multi-product firm, although very much more realistic than that of the firm producing only one homogeneous product, is unnecessarily complicated for most price problems. For example, the general effects upon price and output of an excise tax, of a wage rate reduction, of a decline in demand, etc., can be treated, at least in first approximation, without bothering with the interrelated demands for or costs of the various products made by each firm. Likewise, although many firms have the alternative of disposing of increased quantities of product either by reducing their selling price or increasing their selling effort, there are so many problems for which this is of small relevance that it will be preferable to use a simpler model from which variations in selling costs are omitted.

sets of "possibilities" are usually referred to as (a) the factor supply functions, (b) the production functions, and (c) the product demand functions. If there are many different factors of production and many different products within the horizon of the firm, the number of functions will be large and the model unwieldy. Several devices are employed to simplify the model. We shall list them here briefly and discuss them later in greater detail.

1. The factor supply functions are changed into simple relationships between the prices to be paid per unit of each factor and the quantities of each factor that would be available to the firm at these prices. Other variables influencing the buying possibilities of the firm, such as special buying efforts for materials, superior working conditions and welfare schemes for labor, are either abstracted from, or assumed to be constant, or assumed to be part of the average cost per unit of the factor.

2. The product demand functions are made into simple relationships between the prices charged per unit of each product and the quantities of each product that could be disposed of by the firm at these prices. Other variables influencing the selling possibilities of the firm, such as special selling efforts, advertising, superior facilities and extra services for customers, are either abstracted from, or assumed to be constant, or assumed to be deducted from the average revenue per unit of product.

3. While the various possibilities of buying, transforming, and selling that the firm anticipates are always uncertain, but some are more uncertain than others, any differences in the certainty or uncertainty of these anticipations are either abstracted from or somehow accounted for without complicating the comparability of the alternative possibilities.

4. Any anticipation of future changes in the quantitative relationships described in any of the functions are either abstracted from or somehow accounted for, usually in such a way that the functions of the model are assumed to reflect fully the entire relevant future as anticipated by the decision makers.

5. The number of products is reduced for the "joint-product" case to two, and otherwise to one product.

6. Since this would still leave the model with a whole set of factor supply functions, one production function, and one product

demand function, a preliminary operation is employed to reduce the factor supply functions and the production function to a single production cost function, which can then be set into juxtaposition with the product demand function.[4]

7. The firm is assumed to be interested in maximizing money profits.

8. The firm is assumed not to be influenced by any considerations not accounted for in the functions that reflect its buying, transforming and selling possibilities.

These are truly remarkable simplifications and while some of them are harmless and aid merely in the exposition of essential ideas, others may well vitiate any "solutions" that are obtained with the help of the simplified model. Whether this is the case or not will depend on the problem at hand. Where a simplifying assumption is found to be unsafe, it must either not be allowed or the results must be qualified accordingly. But so many misunderstandings are abroad about allegedly illegitimate assumptions in the theory of the firm that we must embark on a more detailed discussion of the crucial issues.

The Marginalist Way of Thinking

From the assumption that the firm is interested in a maximum of profit ensues the usefulness of "marginalism" as a dominating principle in the theory of the firm. Indeed, this makes the theory of the firm consistent with other portions of economic theory as a system of propositions about human conduct oriented toward the objective of using limited resources to satisfy as many as possible of practically unlimited aims. Marginalism, as the logical process of "finding a maximum," is clearly implied in the so-called *economic principle*—to achieve with given means a maximum of ends.

To use marginalism in the theory of the firm it is not necessary

---

[4] Alternatively, if it is intended to focus attention not on volume and price of *output* but rather on volume and price of a particular *input*, the product demand functions, the production function and the supply functions of all factors except the one in question are combined and reduced to a "net revenue productivity function" of the particular input, which can then be set into juxtaposition with the supply function of this input to determine its price and quantity employed.

to assert that firms attempt to maximize money profits only nor to deny that a goodly portion of all business behavior may be non-rational, thoughtless, blindly repetitive, deliberately traditional, or motivated by extra-economic objectives.[5] It merely presupposes that the "rational-economic" portion of business conduct is by and large sufficiently important to affect what is going on in the world to an extent large enough to warrant analysis; and that the substitution of money profits for a composite of pecuniary and non-pecuniary rewards simplifies the analysis so much that the gain in expediency far exceeds the loss in applicability.

The concepts of marginal revenue, marginal cost, marginal productivity are tools for the operation of the marginal calculus in the theory of the firm. They serve to express the difference it makes to the total receipts or the total costs of the firm if output or input is increased by a small amount, ideally by "one unit."

The use of these tools simplifies our thinking enormously. Often it is impossible to calculate average revenue and average cost, and difficult to calculate total revenue and total cost, but quite feasible to calculate marginal revenue and marginal cost. This was said before with regard to "actual" revenues and costs, but it holds equally with regard to the hypothetical revenues and costs of various hypothetical outputs. (One can of course always compute marginal revenue and marginal cost figures if one knows or assumes only a few consecutive total or average figures, while the op-

---

[5] "Economics in a narrow sense is confined to such aspects of conduct as can be explained with reference to the principles of maximizing satisfaction, income, or profit. Under definitions of this sort any deviations from the marginal principle would be extra-economic. Yet, to refuse to deal with any type of business conduct that cannot qualify by the strict standards of marginalism may justly be regarded as a lazy man's excuse. If certain types of business conduct can be found in reality with regularity and consistency, it is undoubtedly desirable to analyse them regardless of their 'economic rationale.' And if some of these allegedly 'non-economic' aspects of conduct can be explained within the conceptual framework of economics, one may prefer definitions which admit behavior types not strictly subject to marginal analysis among the proper subject matter of economic theory." Fritz Machlup, "Marginal Analysis and Empirical Research," *American Economic Review*, Vol. XXXVI (1946), p. 519. The argument in the rest of this chapter and the next is largely identical with that contained in the article, partly because I included there several sections I had drafted for this chapter, partly because I am reproducing now several sections that I developed for the article.

posite is not true.) Yet, if we know or assume merely the marginal figures, the effects of a business decision upon the profits of the firm are fully determined. If the marginal revenue of an increased output is greater than the marginal cost, it will pay to produce the increased output; if the marginal revenue at a given output is smaller than the marginal cost, the production of a smaller output would be more profitable; if they are equal, neither an increase nor a reduction of output can increase the profit (or reduce the loss) and therefore the profit is as high as it could be.[6]

There can be no doubt about the fact that in reality, to arrive at business decisions about prices or production, the men in charge rarely bother to compute total revenue and total cost, but they do usually think about the *changes* which their decision is likely to effect in revenue and cost. This marginalist way of thinking is so natural, so self-evident to anybody who thinks at all rationally about the possible effects of what he does or may do, that it is hard to understand how the teachers of economic theory and business administration have succeeded in presenting it in such a fashion that it appears artificial and fanciful to the very people who practice it continually.

I am convinced that the portion of all business decisions that are based upon a marginalist way of thinking is sufficiently large to justify the economist's use of the marginal calculus in his model of the firm as a description of the *process* by which businessmen reach their decisions on prices and outputs. But even if this were not so, if most businessmen in reality were thinking in very different ways or were thoughtlessly applying rigid rules of thumb, it might still be possible for the application of the marginal calculus in the theorist's model of the firm to yield *results* more closely in conformance with the observed actions of reality than the results obtained on the basis of any other postulate. This would fully warrant the use of the marginal calculus in the theory of the firm, even if it were never used in the practice of firms. Of course, one would not be fully satisfied and would anxiously search for an

[6] Equality of marginal cost and marginal revenue may also indicate a minimum—smallest rather than largest profits—namely, if the marginal cost curve cuts the marginal revenue curve from above rather than from below. This may be noted as an exception.

alternative, more plausible principle. But only after such a principle were discovered that would, in the operation of a theoretical
model, give the same or better results would marginalism be
dropped from the theory of the firm.

Perhaps it is necessary to mention that the theory of the firm,
although concerned with the "individual" firm—in the sense of an
action-model of a decision-making unit as distinguished from an
interaction-model of several such units as members of an "industry"—is not concerned with any "particular" firm in the real world.
It is not claimed that the conduct of any particular firm in our
economy can be explained by marginal analysis. All that is necessary for the theory to be relevant and applicable is that *enough*
firms act in such a way that the results of their actions broadly correspond with those inferred from the model.

The "Determination" of Prices, Output and Input

The theory of the "equilibrium of the single firm" is not as ambitious as is often believed. It does not attempt to give all the
reasons why a given firm makes the type or quality of product
that it makes; why it produces the output that it produces; why it
employs the workers that it employs; or why it charges the prices
that it charges. It is probably an understatement of the importance
of the historical situation when economists remark that "there is
usually some element in the prices ruling at any time which can
only be explained in the light of the history of the industry." [7]
The phrase "usually some element" does not do justice to the part
played by historical antecedents in the determination of product,
output, employment, and prices. The role of the past in shaping
the actual conditions under which the firm operates, in developing
the routine of its responses to changes in conditions, and in im-
pressing it with experiences which have taught it to size up and
anticipate these changes as the basis for its decisions—this role
is by no means denied by marginal analysis. The role of the past
in the process of adjusting the present to the anticipated future
is essential in all theory of human conduct. It is implied in the

[7] R. L. Hall and C. J. Hitch, "Price Theory and Business Behavior," *Oxford Economic Papers*, No. 2 (1939), p. 33.

very attempt to construct a pattern of behavior of the single firm.

Instead of giving a complete explanation of the "determination" of output, prices, and employment by the firm, marginal analysis really intends to explain the effects which certain *changes* in conditions may have upon the actions of the firm. What kind of changes may cause the firm to raise prices? to increase output? to reduce employment? What conditions may influence the firm to continue with the same price, output, employment, in the face of actual or anticipated changes? Economic theory, static as well as dynamic, is essentially a theory of adjustment to change. The concept of equilibrium is a tool in this theory of change; the marginal calculus is its dominating principle.

Subjectivity of Cost and Revenue

The proposition that the firm will attempt to equate marginal cost and marginal revenue is logically implied in the assumption that the firm will attempt to maximize its profit (or minimize its loss). It should hardly be necessary to mention that all the relevant magnitudes involved—cost, revenue, profit—are subjective, that is, perceived or fancied by the men whose decisions or actions are to be explained (i.e., the businessmen) rather than "objective," that is, calculated by disinterested men who are observing these actions from the outside and are explaining them (statisticians and economists as theorists—not as consultants).

The marginal cost that guides the producer is the addition to his total cost which he expects would be caused by added production. An outside observer, if he had expert knowledge of the production techniques and full insight into the cost situation of the producing firm, might arrive at a different, "objective" figure of the firm's marginal cost; but what the observer thinks is not necessarily the same as what the producer thinks. The producer's actual decision is based on what he himself thinks; it is based on "subjective" cost expectations.

One may perhaps assume that the producer is intensely interested in knowing his cost and that, in general, he has the experience which enables him to know it. Yet, one must not assume that all producers really "know" their cost in the sense in which an efficiency expert would determine it; several of them may lack the interest or experience; they may not find it worth their while to dig too deeply into the mysteries of their business. (After all, we know that there are good businessmen and bad, and that the majority are somewhere between good and bad.) But this does not invalidate the proposition that the producer is guided by marginal cost.

The same thing is true with regard to price expectations and sales expectations. It is the "demand as seen by the seller" from which his revenue expectations stem. The increase in demand that is relevant in the analysis of the firm need not be "the real thing"; it may precede an "actual" increase in demand, lag behind it, or be entirely imaginary. Likewise, the elasticity of demand that is relevant is not the one estimated by you or me; what counts is the businessman's view of the possible responsiveness of his market. We may think that he is wrong and that a price reduction could bring him far more business than he believes; but this is not relevant for the explanation of his actions. The businessman does what he does on the basis of what *he* thinks, regardless of whether you agree with him or not.

Thus—in contrast to the economics of the industry or the economic system as a whole—marginal analysis of the firm, as a part of the theory of economic change and adjustment, should not be understood to imply anything but subjective estimates, guesses, expectations and hunches. Obviously, therefore, we must also have a theory of how these subjective data are affected by objective changes in the businessman's environment. For example, if we wish to examine the possible effects of a freight-rate increase upon the prices charged and outputs produced by a typical firm, we must assume that the "fact" of the high freight rates becomes known to the men concerned. But this is surely a more than plausible assumption to make. It is so obvious that we ordinarily do not stop to spell it out. We are sure that the changes which we "objectively" observe will be more or less readily noticed and translated into corresponding changes of the subjective cost or revenue estimates by the firms. Ordinarily there may be no harm in skipping some steps in the analysis, but occasionally it is well to remember that the translation of a change noticed by the observer into a change noticed by the actors is a necessary part in the explanation of human action.

To guard against misunderstandings, let me repeat that the subjective nature of the cost and revenue estimates which "determine" an *initial* equilibrium position of "the firm" differs in one important respect from the subjective nature of the change in estimates that determines an *adjustment* by "the firm." The former —the estimates behind the initial position—need not conform to anything that we economists observe from the outside, that is, they may be contrary to "objective facts"; [8] but the latter—the changes in the estimates that cause the firm to move—should conform to our observations, and can easily do so because the observed events are so patent that they are most likely to impress themselves upon the consciousness of most of the decision makers whose conduct—or, rather, the results of whose conduct—we are trying to explain or to predict.[9]

[8] Of course, emphasis on the subjectivity of the cost and market conditions means one thing in the *explanation* of action, but another in the *appraisal* of action. When we say that the subjective cost estimates of the businessmen are what counts, even where they are manifestly incorrect in comparison with objective findings, this should be acceptable within the "economics of adjustment," but not within the "economics of welfare." In the latter, even when we make the distinction between social cost and private cost, we usually assume that the businessman makes his private cost estimates in full conformance with the objective facts of the situation that confronts him. Any failure on the part of the businessman to do that may increase or conceivably reduce the discrepancy between private and social cost.

[9] My emphasis on this methodological "subjectivism" has been widely criticized. One of my critics believes that "refuge in subjective interpretations of the cost and revenue functions . . . leaves theory saying that businessmen do what they do because they do it." R. A. Gordon, "Short-Period Price Determination in Theory and Practice," *American Economic Review*, Vol. XXXVIII (1948), p. 287. This is a misunderstanding. The businessman in the model acting upon marginal principles will react, say, to an increase in the price of fuel oil, not just by doing anything that may come to his mind, but by making some "typical" adjustments in his production, input, output and prices. The point is that, in order to predict or explain the type of adjustment, we do not have to know the subjective whims and guesses that may have influenced his initial position. For, happily, the direction of the "equilibrating" (adjusting) action is to a large extent independent of the exact position of "equilibrium" from which we assume the businessman has been pushed by the "disequilibrating" change.

The Omission of Important Variables

It is clear to most businessmen that there are several ways of increasing the physical volume of sales. They can, as a rule, sell more of a product (a) if they reduce the selling price, (b) if they improve the product quality, or (c) if they increase their selling efforts. These four variables—output, price, quality, and selling effort—can be immediately treated in one consistent general theory, but with the disadvantage that the beginning student has a harder time and that two-dimensional geometrical treatment is excluded. For didactic purposes, therefore, the theorist decides provisionally to omit two of the variables: quality and selling effort. He can re-introduce them later, either in separate, more complicated, models or by re-interpreting the two-dimensional function of his provisional model in a way that permits the merging of price and selling cost into net revenue. (See Chapter 6, pp. 179 ff. and 189 ff.) The advantage of simple curves—connecting points in a system of only two coordinates—for purposes of exposition is so great that it easily compensates for the disadvantage of having to break up an observed *ensemble* of variables and to omit some of them for the time being.

The same reasoning holds for the question of multi-process, multi-plant, and multi-product firms. The belief of some critics of marginalist theory that this theory cannot deal with such complicated situations is without foundation. A general marginalist theory of the conduct of the firm with regard to prices and production can deal with any number of production processes, production stages, productive plants, and products. But it can be stated only in algebraic formulation, which is not suitable for the teaching of students who have little training in mathematics; hence the decision to begin with the case of the single-product firm with one or more plants in a single location and not to bother with different or separate production processes. More complex models, notwithstanding the fact that most firms in reality are multi-product firms, are needed only for the analysis of special problems. A very extensive body of theory can be developed with the simple set of cost and revenue curves for the single product.[10]

[10] A terminological remark concerning "cost" and "revenue" curves versus

The Range of Price and Output Variations

Beginning students of economics who watch their instructor draw demand and cost curves covering half the blackboard may be misled into believing that the businessman is supposed to visualize the possibilities of producing and selling amounts of output ranging from almost zero up to two or three times the amounts that he is currently producing and selling; that the businessman is supposed to figure out how much he might be able to sell at prices several times as high as the current price, and how much at prices only one-half or one-third as high. The curve draftsman, indeed, seems to ascribe extraordinary powers of imagination to the business wizards.

Misunderstandings of this sort, and erroneous criticisms of marginal analysis, could be avoided if it were made clear to the students that the length of the curves, i.e., the wide range they cover, was chiefly designed to enable those in the back rows of the classroom to make out what goes on on the blackboard; and to permit them to practice curve analysis on paper and in their notebooks without using magnifying glasses. The range of possibilities —prices, sales, outputs—which a businessman may have in mind is probably quite narrow. Rarely will a businessman bother pondering the probable effects of a price increase or cut by 50 percent;

"supply" and "demand" curves may be appropriate. The latter set of names is sometimes carried from the theory of the industry into the theory of the firm with rather confusing results for the beginning student. In the theory of output determination of the firm one should avoid speaking of a supply curve; the quantities of product the firm will supply cannot be shown by a curve or function of price, except in the special case of pure competition. In recognition of this fact the term "cost curve" has generally replaced the former "supply curve." (Of course, the supplies of productive factors to the firm can properly be expressed as "supply curves" or "factor cost curves.") The name "demand curve" can be retained in the theory of output determination of the firm, provided one emphasizes that it is "demand as seen by the seller." The term "sales curve" has been proposed to take the place of "demand curve" for the product of the firm. But there is a lack of symmetry between sales curve and cost curve, the former pointing to the physical quantities saleable at various dollar prices, the latter pointing to the dollar cost of various physical quantities of product. For the sake of symmetry one should use "revenue curve" in lieu of demand or sales curve. Both revenue and cost refer to dollar figures as functions of the physical quantity, and both can be expressed as total, average, and marginal values.

but he may easily think about what a 10 or 15 percent price change might do to his sales; or what discount it might take to land some additional orders.

The principles of analysis are not altered by the realization that the alternatives which businessmen weigh concerning prices or production volumes cover a much more moderate range than the curves which teachers of economics draw to depict the pattern of marginal calculus.

It should also be obvious that all potential changes in price and output, however small, are not infinitesimally small, but instead are changes by finite magnitudes. This fact may be forgotten when we draw smooth, continuous curves, and it may be well to make it clear that the curves merely serve the purpose of guiding the eye conveniently over the separate points that indicate the revenue or cost figures for different output volumes.[11]

The Time-Range of Anticipations

In view of the known attempts to derive statistical cost curves from accounting data—which of necessity refer to conditions of the past—it is important to recall that the marginal cost and marginal revenue concepts in the analysis of the price and output decisions of the firm refer to expectations of future conditions. To be sure, past experience is always in the background of anticipation of the future, and past accounting records may form a firm point of departure for evaluating prospective and hypothetical cost and revenue figures. But anticipations alone are the relevant variables in the marginal calculus of the firm.

What is the time-range of the significant anticipations? How far into the future do they reach, and what period, if any, is given

[11] There have been people who wondered about the "proper" drawing of cost curves at the point where the absolute limit of capacity is reached: Should the cost curve "break off" at that point or should it "shoot up" vertically toward infinity? The answer, of course, is that this will not make any difference to anybody who understands what it is all about. A cost curve may be defined alternatively as the locus of the lowest cost figures at which various outputs can be produced or as the locus of the largest output figures that can be produced at various cost levels. Take the first definition and the curve will break off where no more can be produced; take the second and the curve will rise vertically.

special emphasis? Is tomorrow more important than next year or several years hence? Is it the "short run" or the "long run" which controls current action?

When a firm wishes to increase production, it usually has a choice of expanding the equipment and productive capacity of its plant or of stepping up the output of the existing plant with unchanged equipment. If productive capacity is already well utilized, the marginal cost of producing larger outputs will be higher in the existing establishment with unchanged equipment than in an establishment with adjusted, increased equipment. If several degrees of adjustment in the productive equipment are possible, several marginal cost functions will be "given" and several different outputs will be "the equilibrium output" under given sales expectations.

To cope with these problems economists have made the distinction between the "short period," assuming no adaptation of equipment, and the "long period," assuming complete adaptation of equipment. Students often believe that the latter period is called "long" because it takes a long time to expand the plant. This need not be the case. A better understanding of the concepts might be achieved by associating the degree of planned plant adjustment with the length of time for which the changed production volume is expected to be maintained. If an increased demand is expected to prevail for a short period only, it will not pay to invest in plant expansion, and "short-run cost" will determine output. On the other hand, if demand is expected to continue at the higher level for a sufficiently long period, an expansion of the establishment will be considered a profitable investment, and output will be determined by "long-run marginal cost"—which, of course, includes the investment outlays needed for the appropriate expansion of capacity, that is, the cost elements which will later become fixed (and will then be no part of short-run marginal cost). Many "intermediate periods," that is, several degrees of plant adjustment with different marginal cost conditions, may exist.

It is, therefore, a misunderstanding to argue that short-run cost is of controlling influence on the ground that we always live and work in the short period. The duration for which demand conditions are expected to prevail will determine the relevant "period" of cost anticipations. Of course, this relevance is again subjectively determined by the businessman, not objectively by the economist.

The time-range of the anticipations with regard to the demand and selling outlook is subject to similar considerations. It is a mistake to think that the relevant "period" for demand and marginal revenue expectations is determined by the length of time it takes for today's production to reach the market.[12] If a price reduction is apt to spoil the market for a long time to come, or a price increase to harm customer loyalty, the effects on future profits will hardly be neglected in considering current actions. If a firm were to regard a certain price change as a desirable step for the time being, but feared that a later reversal might be difficult or costly, it would weigh this anticipated future cost or loss against the short-run benefit.[13]

Anticipations of this sort complementary or competing with one another, are not exceptions to marginal analysis but are part and parcel of it. Of course, if someone insists on formulating a theory that covers only the "short run," whatever this may mean, and on dealing with all longer-term anticipations by way of qualifications, he may do so; the difference is chiefly terminological. I would not know, however, how to delimit such a "short period" and set it apart from "future periods." For this reason I prefer a formulation of the theory that allows firms to think as far ahead as they care to. To be sure, when an instructor teaches graphical analysis, he will do well to abstract from complicated cost and revenue anticipations and to concentrate on those that can be neatly packed away in geometric curves.

[12] Richard A. Lester, *Economics of Labor* (New York: Macmillan, 1941), p. 181.

[13] Robert A. Gordon, after distinguishing two possible approaches of theory to the case "where the businessman's horizon extends beyond the short period of price theory," namely, a multi-period analysis and a single-period analysis, states with regard to the latter: "Single-period analysis has three alternatives: (a) it can ignore all anticipations relating to future periods; (b) it can include anticipations only insofar as they relate to future effects of present action; or (c) it can include all anticipations, both those mentioned in (b) and also anticipations as to future change which are independent of present action." *Op. cit.*, p. 280. But Gordon concludes with charging that the "doctoring" of the "functions of the present period for changes expected to occur in the future" is "misleading and tautological."

The Numerical Definiteness of the Estimates

The geometric curves and arithmetic schedules by which the instructor presents marginal cost and marginal revenue of the firm seem to leave no room for doubt that these anticipations take the form of estimates of definite numerical values. While this may be necessary for teaching purposes, it should not mislead the student into believing that every action of the businessman is in fact the result of a conscious decision, made after careful calculations of differential revenue and cost.

Businessmen do not always "calculate" before they make decisions, and they do not always "decide" before they act. For they think that they know their business well enough without having to make repeated calculations; and their actions are frequently routine.[14] But routine is based on principles which were once considered and decided upon and have then been frequently applied with decreasing need for conscious choices.[15] The feeling that calculations are not always necessary is usually based upon an ability to size up a situation without reducing its dimensions to definite numerical values.[16]

The businessman who is persuaded to accept a large order with a price discount or some other concession usually weighs the probability that he will have to make the same concession to his other customers. This is one of the considerations included in his "calculation" of marginal revenue. In order to explain this to the student, or to reduce it to curves and schedules, the economics teacher makes "exact" calculations; in order to make up his mind whether to take or reject the order, the businessman ordinarily needs no arithmetic, mental or written, and indeed needs no con-

[14] See George Katona, "Psychological Analysis of Business Decisions and Expectations," *American Economic Review*, Vol. XXXVI (1946), p. 53.

[15] Discussing the difference between "routine behavior" and "genuine decisions," Katona explains with regard to routine actions that "principles, well understood in their original context, tend to be carried over from one situation to another." *Ibid.*, p. 49. Genuine decisions are made when expectations "change radically." *Ibid.*, p. 53.

[16] Although I do not know either the width or length of my automobile, I am quite capable of making adequate comparisons between these magnitudes and the space between two parked cars, which I estimate again without thinking of feet, inches, or any numbers.

crete figures. Yet his reasoning or his routine behavior is most conveniently analysed in terms of marginal revenue.

Where the marginal revenue is negative, that is to say, where gross receipts after accepting the additional order (with the price concession) would be smaller than without it, no further consideration is necessary. But if the dollar volume of sales can be increased by accepting the order (taking full account of all repercussions on future marketing possibilities), the businessman must take another step in his reasoning: will it pay to make more sales in view of the additional cost of producing the larger output? If conditions have not changed, he will not have to make new calculations; if changes have occurred or are expected, some figuring may be required. But it is a type of figuring for which usually no accounting records are consulted, no memoranda prepared and of which no records are made. Often the businessman can do this "figuring" in his head; if not, he may take a piece of scrap paper, jot down a few round numbers, reach his conclusion, and throw the paper in the waste basket.

The contention that such reasoning is typically based either on additional cost or on total cost—and hence most conveniently described in terms of marginal cost—is contradicted by certain empirical researchers who claim that most businessmen calculate on the basis of average cost even if they lose money by doing so. With this contradiction we shall deal later.

The objection is sometimes made that the figuring implied in the marginal calculus is much too difficult for most businessmen. Especially the estimate of the "marginal net revenue productivity" of a productive factor, on which the decision to employ or not to employ is supposed to be based, seems to be very complicated. It involves as many as seven separate "steps" and at least as many, but probably more, variables.[17] If this analytical pattern were taken

[17] The seven steps are as follows:
(1) Determine by how much a given physical volume of production, x, is increased if the employment of a particular factor is increased slightly (e.g., by one unit), and call the output increase the factor's "marginal physical product."
(2) Determine the selling price at which the marginal physical product can be sold.
(3) Multiply the two in order to obtain the "value of the marginal physical product."

as a realistic description in photographic likeness of the actual reasoning of the typical employer, the employer would have to be endowed with talents which only few possess in reality.

An analogy may explain the apparent contradiction.

The "Extreme Difficulty of Calculating"

What sort of considerations are behind the routine decision of the driver of an automobile to overtake a truck proceeding ahead of him at slower speed? What factors influence his decision? Assume that he is faced with the alternative of either slowing down and staying behind the truck or of passing it before a car which is approaching from the opposite direction will have reached the spot. As an experienced driver he somehow takes into account (a) the speed at which the truck is going, (b) the remaining distance between himself and the truck, (c) the speed at which he is proceeding, (d) the possible acceleration of his speed, (e) the distance between him and the car approaching from the opposite direction, (f) the speed at which that car is approaching; and probably also the condition of the road (concrete or dirt, wet or dry, straight or winding, level or uphill), the degree of visibility (light or dark, clear or foggy), the condition of the tires and brakes of his car, and—let us hope—his own condition (fresh or tired, sober or alcoholized) permitting him to judge the enumerated factors.

Clearly, the driver of the automobile will not "measure" the

---

(4) Determine whether the quantity x has to be sold at a lower price because of the sale of the marginal physical product; if so, multiply this price reduction by x and obtain the "revenue loss on sales because of price cut."

(5) Deduct the "revenue loss on sales because of price cut" from the "value of the marginal physical product" in order to obtain the "marginal gross revenue product."

(6) Determine whether the production of the marginal physical product was connected with increased or decreased outlays for any other complementary or substitutable means of production (materials, fuel, lubricants, labor of any sort, capital funds, wear and tear of equipment, etc.), exclusive of the factor in question, and call them (positive or negative) "incidental expenses."

(7) Deduct the "incidental expenses" from the "marginal gross revenue product" in order to obtain the "marginal net revenue product."

variables; he will not "calculate" the time needed for the vehicles
to cover the estimated distances at the estimated rates of speed;
and, of course, none of the "estimates" will be expressed in numerical values. Even so, without measurements, numerical estimates or
calculations, he will in a routine way "size up" the total situation.
He will not break it down into its elements. Yet a "theory of overtaking" would have to include all these elements (and perhaps
others besides) and would have to state how changes in any of the
factors were likely to affect the decisions or actions of the driver.[18]
The "extreme difficulty of calculating,"[19] the fact that "it would be
utterly impractical"[20] to attempt to work out and ascertain the
exact magnitudes of the variables which the theorist alleges to be
significant, show merely that the *explanation* of an action must
often include steps of reasoning which the acting individual himself does not *consciously* perform (because the action has become
routine) and which perhaps he would never be *able* to perform in
scientific exactness (because such exactness is not necessary in
everyday life). To call, on these grounds, the theory "invalid," "unrealistic" or "inapplicable" is to reveal failure to understand the
basic methodological constitution of most social sciences.

Imagine an empirical researcher attempting to test by a naive
questionnaire method the "theory of overtaking," questioning hundreds of drivers about their ability to estimate distances and speed,
and to calculate the relevant time intervals and the degrees in
which a small change in any one of the variables affected the result. Would he not obtain a most hopeless assortment of answers?
Would not these answers support the conclusion that the assumptions of the theorists had been wrong and that one must look for
other explanations? Yet I can hardly believe that any sensible person would deny the relevance of the enumerated variables and
would contend, for example, that speed and distance of the ap-

[18] Very cautious drivers are apt to operate with safety margins so wide
that small changes in the "variables" may not affect the actions. Timid souls
may refuse to pass at all when another car is in sight.
[19] Richard A. Lester, "Shortcomings of Marginal Analysis for Wage-
Employment Problems," *American Economic Review*, Vol. XXXVI (1946),
p. 72.
[20] Lester, *ibid.*, p. 75.

proaching automobile could not have been taken into account by the driver passing the truck, because he was not good in mathematics.[21]

The Analysis of Change Needs No Exactness

The businessman who equates the marginal revenue and marginal cost of output (or marginal net revenue productivity and marginal factor cost) when he decides how much to produce (or how many to employ) need not engage in higher mathematics, geometry, or clairvoyance. Ordinarily he would not even consult with his accountant or efficiency expert in order to arrive at his decision; he would not make any tests or formal calculations; he would simply rely on his sense or his "feel" of the situation. There is nothing very exact about this sort of estimate. On the basis of hundreds of previous experiences of a similar nature the businessman would "just know," in a vague and rough way, whether or not it would pay him to hire more men.

The subjectivity of his judgments is obvious. Just as different drivers may reach different conclusions about the advisability of passing another car under given "objective" conditions, different businessmen will have different "hunches" in a given situation. The subordinates or partners of the man who makes a decision may sharply disagree with him; they may see the situation quite differently. They may be more optimistic about the possibilities of obtaining more orders with only slight price concessions or through increased sales efforts (which would raise both the marginal revenue and marginal productivity curves drawn by the theorist to characterize their considerations). Or they may be more certain about the technical possibility of achieving a larger output by certain production methods (which would lower the marginal cost curve, and could raise or lower the marginal productivity curves). Some decision, usually a routine decision without debate, is made, or at least some action is taken; and the decision or action is neces-

[21] Driving at night, when he has nothing to go by except the size and brilliance of the headlights of the approaching cars, the experienced driver becomes conscious of the fact that in daytime he has better ways of sizing up their speed and distance. With reduced visibility he will "calculate" with greater safety margins.

sarily affected by the businessman's conjectures concerning sales possibilities and production possibilities.

The way in which changes in the essential variables will affect the probable decisions and actions of the businessman is not much different if the curves which the theorist draws to depict their conjectures are a little higher or lower, steeper or flatter. These curves are helpful to the students of economics in figuring out the probable effects of change—in learning in what direction output, prices and employment are likely to be altered, and under what circumstances increases or decreases are likely to be drastic or negligible. Better markets, for example, or higher costs, will in general affect businessmen even of different vision or daring in much the same way; and any differences can be conveniently "typed" in terms of shapes, positions and shifts of the curves into which the theorist condenses the businessmen's conjectures.

Non-Pecuniary Considerations

Most marginal analysis of the equilibrium of the single firm rests on the assumption that the business firm attempts to maximize its profits. To make this assumption is not to deny that the men who run a business may be motivated also by other considerations.

That a businessman is motivated by considerations other than the maximization of money profits does not necessarily make his conduct "uneconomic." The economic theorist finds no difficulty in fitting into the pattern of "economic" conduct (that is, into the conceptual scheme of consistent maximization of satisfaction within a given preference system) the householder and consumer who makes donations to friends or the church; or the seller of labor services who chooses a badly paying but less strenuous job in preference to one that pays more but calls for more exertion. Likewise, there is nothing essentially "uneconomic" in the conduct of a businessman who chooses to pay higher prices for raw material purchased from a fraternity brother, or to sell at a special discount to members of his church, or who refrains from embarking on a promising expansion of his business because he prefers an easier life.

There are economic theorists who would include considerations of this sort among the data for the marginal calculus of the firm. The satisfaction from favoring his friends through higher purchase prices or lower selling prices is a special reward or "revenue" to the businessman; he may ask himself how much it is worth to him, and we may conceivably add it to his revenue curve. To give up an easier life, expend greater efforts and increase his worries are among the businessman's "costs" when he considers an expansion of his business; we may conceivably add it to his "cost" curve. Any number and type of non-pecuniary sacrifices and rewards could thus be included, at some sort of "money equivalent," among the costs and revenues that make up the profits of the firm: the marginal calculus of the firm would become all-inclusive—that is, it would include any kind of rational considerations, no matter how much of a sacrifice of money profits they might call for.

If *whatever* a businessman does is explained by the principle of profit maximization—because he does what he likes to do, and he likes to do what maximizes the sum of his pecuniary and non-pecuniary profits—the analysis acquires the character of a system of definitions and tautologies, and loses much of its value as an explanation of reality. It is necessary to separate the non-rational elements of business conduct from the rational ones. And it is preferable to separate also the non-pecuniary from the pecuniary ones.[22]

The issue whether or not it is methodologically "sounder" not to reduce the various non-pecuniary satisfactions and dissatisfactions (utilities and disutilities) of the businessman to money terms, and not to make them part of the profit-maximization scheme, is not so important as some writers believe. For not much of the result depends on whether non-pecuniary considerations of the business-

---

[22] For example, we may well distinguish the political and the economic ambitions of a man if we wish to explain his conduct in running his business. If he sacrifices potential money profits for the sake of obligating some political bosses to him and thereby furthering his political ambitions, his actions are of course perfectly rational, but might not fit into the pattern of business conduct designed to make the most money. On the other hand, political means may further economic ends, even pecuniary profits. If political power is used to further the financial ends of a firm, this "political activity" is really economic in design; paying for a lobby to obtain favorable legislation may be not different in nature from paying for advertising. But all this is not of any great relevance to the ordinary theory of the firm as a part of price theory.

man are translated into money terms or, instead, treated as exceptions and qualifications in the explanation of typical business conduct. The purpose of the analysis of the firm is not to explain all actions of each and every firm in existence; we are satisfied if we can explain certain strong tendencies in industry or in the whole economy. The chief aim of the analysis, moreover, is to show the probable effects of certain changes; if the direction in which output or price is likely to move as a result of a certain change in "data" is not affected by the existence and strength of non-pecuniary factors in business conduct, their inclusion in or exclusion from the marginal analysis of the firm is not a crucial matter. These non-pecuniary factors, important as they may be, are not likely to affect the typical reactions to typical changes; they are more in the nature of "constants," significant in determining any given *position,* but irrelevant in the determination of a *change* of position.

To be sure, the nature, strength and effects of non-pecuniary considerations in business behavior are problems that need to be investigated. One may presume that producing larger production volumes, paying higher wage rates, or charging lower product prices than would be compatible with a maximum of money profits may involve for the businessman a gain in social prestige or a certain measure of inner satisfaction.[23] It is not impossible that considerations of this sort substantially weaken the forces believed to be at work on the basis of a strictly pecuniary marginal calculus.

During the war we were able to observe that patriotism was a strong force in the production policy of American business. There can be no doubt that many firms produced far beyond the point of highest money profits. To be sure, they made large profits, but in many instances they could have made still more money without the last, particularly expensive, portions of output. Their conduct

---

[23] A gain in social prestige may sometimes increase the good will of a firm on which it expects to cash in later. If such a gain is an aim of the firm's policy, it should be treated as a part of its pecuniary considerations. For example, a firm may grant extraordinarily high wage rates as a part of its selling and advertising expense; that is to say, it may hope that its "generous labor policy" will make its products more popular. A portion of current labor cost of the firm would then properly be allocated to future rather than current output.

was not defined by the principle of maximization of money profits.[24]

Another of the possibly important qualifications in the analysis of the firm refers to the conflict of interests between the hired managers and the owners of the business. The interest of the former in inordinately large outlays or investments may be capable of description in terms of a pecuniary calculus, but it is not maximization of the firm's profits which serves here as the standard of conduct. Maximization of salaries and bonuses of professional managers may constitute a standard of business conduct different from that implied in the customary marginal analysis of the firm. The extent to which the two standards would result in sharply different action under otherwise similar conditions is another open question in need of investigation. At this juncture we know only that qualifications must be made, although it is chiefly the theory of the expansion of the firm, not so much the theory of the price and output policy of the firm that would be affected. How much the qualifications on account of the divergent interests of managements and ownership may modify the results of marginal analysis of the single firm as a price and output adjuster we do not know.[25]

[24] Observance of laws and regulations presents a special problem for the analysis of business conduct. It will depend on business morals whether prohibited, unlawful alternatives may be regarded as definitely excluded and therefore non-existent; or whether they may be considered as possibilities subject only to certain peculiar risks. Assume, for example, that a price ceiling is fixed for the sale of a product, and fines are provided for violations. To the businessman who is unconditionally law-abiding the ceiling price is the only possible price, regardless of how insistently some of his customers may tempt him with higher bids. To the businessman, however, who abides by the law only because of the risk of being found out and fined, "demand prices" above the ceiling are real possibilities and the risks of penalties are additions to cost or deductions from revenue. If the sanctions for violations include jail sentences, the risk becomes largely non-pecuniary and it is up to the potential violator, or to the theorizing economist, whether or not that risk will be "converted" into money terms. Black-market prices are in part the result of such risk conversions.

[25] On the basis of his studies on business motivation, Katona holds that "ego-centered motives may be responsible for the executive's thinking but they do not detract from his identification with the firm," and that "the current widespread split between ownership and management functions does not provide valid arguments against the role assigned to the profit motive in our economy." George Katona, *Psychological Analysis of Economic Behavior* (New York: McGraw-Hill, 1951), p. 197.

Maximum Profit versus Security

For teaching purposes it is usually expedient provisionally to abstract from "uncertainty" and to assume that all alternative possibilities—revenues and costs of all outputs—are equally certain. When the assumption of uncertainty is introduced all serious complications can be avoided by employing the trouble-saving device of correcting each uncertain value to its "certainty equivalent." The more uncertain the expectation of a revenue the more of a safety margin must be deducted, and the more uncertain the estimate of a cost the more of a safety margin must be added, in order to make all revenue and cost expectations comparable. These procedures avoid or evade difficulties either by defining them away or by assuming them resolved. It is only permissible, however, to do this after one has satisfied oneself that the simplified model remains useful for the explanation of a real world in which information is very incomplete, uncertainty very large, and the willingness to bear uncertainty very different as between different persons and different periods.

Some overly anxious to discard or reform "old" theory have quickly assumed it to be necessary in a very direct and explicit way to take account of the presence of uncertainty and the aversion to risk. They have proposed to do it by postulating a "security motive" operating separately from the "profit motive." Business conduct is then assumed to be oriented toward two separate goals, maximum profits and security, with the former severely limited by the importance the latter has for the survival of the business firm. According to this view, since firms are willing to sacrifice profit opportunities for the sake of greater security, it is misleading, or even patently incorrect, to base the theory of the firm upon the postulate of profit maximization.

It is highly questionable whether the separation of profit and security as quasi-independent goals is a useful device in the analysis of business conduct. Will not any move that promises profits without risks increase security *pari passu* with profits? Will not any move that involves great risk, imply as great a risk to profits as it does to security? Is it not the risk of loss that creates the danger to security? Is it possible or sensible to talk about profit expectations and consistently exclude the possibilities of loss?

The old proverbial inequality [26] stating that a bird in hand is better than two in the bush or ten in the wood well illustrates the point that "profit maximization" does not mean what its narrow interpreters contend it means. The bird catcher who wishes to maximize the number of birds in hand, but prefers one safely in hand to two potential victims in the bush, implicitly admits that his confidence in his catching ability is not great; he may catch two, one, or none, but apparently the chance of getting two does not compensate him for the risk of getting none. The distribution of possible outcomes in the case of the ten birds in the wood overlaps with that of the second choice in that it includes the possibilities of getting two, one, or none; but it also includes several other possibilities—up to a catch of ten birds. But the probabilities of such a lucky catch are deemed to be low and the bird catcher prudently resigns himself to the safe possession of one bird in hand. This, after weighing all the odds and chances, is obviously the maximum he expects he will have. It would be rather silly to say that the pursuit of the maximization principle would make him go after the ten birds and that it is the quest for security that causes him to pass up the "better" opportunities. No one, to change the example, attempting to maximize his profits will knowingly prefer a chance in a lottery promising a prize of a million dollars to one in a lottery promising only half a million if in the first case the chance is one in a million while it is ten in a million for the second.

To be sure, the optimist and the pessimist, the gambler and the timid soul, the man with large reserves and the one without, may have different inclinations toward taking chances. The risk of a loss that could endanger the survival of a firm is very different from the same risk of the same loss if the men in charge could stand it without batting an eye. But does this imply that it is easier to analyse business conduct by separating the profit motive from the security motive? All it does imply is that for certain problems—

---

[26] "A bird in hand is worth two in the bush." Miguel de Cervantes, *Don Quixote*, Ch. 4. "Better one byrde in hand than ten in the wood." John Heywood, *Proverbes*, Part I, Ch. 11.

by no means for all or many—it may be expedient to develop a model with a "preference function" for risk bearing, so that the propensity to take chances can be set against the opportunity of making profits and losses with various distributions of the odds.[27]

Again indulging in my penchant for analogies, I wish to caricature the dilemma of an automobilist wavering between the goals of attaining maximum speed regardless of risk—which might mean for him to drive at 120 miles per hour—and maximum safety—which might mean to stand still, perhaps at home in his garage. If the goal, however, is maximum speed (minimum time) in getting to his destination, he will surely weigh the risks and drive at varying speeds depending on circumstances. Admittedly, it may be pertinent to add other motives—enjoying the countryside, chatting or petting with his passenger, avoiding the tension of high-speed driving, etc.,—if one is to explain the conduct of particular drivers in particular situations. But for an explanation of the effects which various typical occurrences are likely to have upon a driver's conduct—for example, a narrow S-curve, a bumpy stretch of the road, heavy traffic—we shall not go wrong if we take maximum speed (minimum time) in getting to his destination as the only basic assumption. The typical driver knows that he will not get there at all if he takes the curves too fast or if his car breaks down after hitting too vehemently the bumps in the pavement. In short, the postulate of maximum speed comprises the risks of delays and suffices for the explanation of the most typical responses of automobile operators. Similarly, the postulate of maximum profit comprises the risks of losses and suffices for the explanation of the most typical responses of business operators.[28]

Maximum Profit versus Most-Favored Odds

Those who revolt against the single rule of the principle of profit maximization but are willing to recognize it as one of two

[27] See, for example, Leonid Hurwicz, "Theory of the Firm and of Investment," *Econometrica*, Vol. XIV (1946), p. 110.

[28] About the special significance of the "security motive" in the theory of oligopoly see Chapter 13.

or more governors of business conduct still recognize that the principle as such makes sense and, to some extent, works. Other revolutionaries are more radical and want the principle to be thrown out altogether. They deny that "profit maximization" makes any sense as a guide to action where there is uncertainty.[29]

Where foresight is uncertain, each action that may be chosen is identified with a "distribution" of potential outcomes—not with a unique outcome—and these distributions are overlapping. There is no such thing as "maximizing" a distribution of possible outcomes. At best, the actor may select among the alternatives that action whose "outcome distribution" is *optimal* according to his preference scheme.[30]

All this may or must be granted. Yet, the conclusions are not those that the critics have drawn. All that follows, in my opinion, is that the expression "profit maximization" should be understood to stand for "selection of the action with the optimum distribution of potential outcomes" according to the businessman's outlook and preferences. This reinterpretation of the maximum as an optimum —which still is a maximum in non-pecuniary terms—does no harm to the theory of the firm as an output and price adjuster. It neither reduces the theory to "empty tautologies" nor vitiates the generalizations derived from it.

Those who raise the cry "empty tautologies" apparently have in mind the impossibility for an outside observer to establish the exact risk-aversion preference scheme and the risk-distribution estimates of a businessman, and the resulting impossibility of testing the theory through "concrete cases." They forget that the outside observer would not have much more positive information about profit expectations in "concrete cases" if businessmen were "absolutely certain" about their revenue and cost estimates. They also forget that it is not the purpose of the theory of the firm to

[29] Gerhard Tintner, "The Theory of Choice under Subjective Risk and Uncertainty," *Econometrica*, Vol. IX (1941), pp. 298–304; Armen A. Alchian, "Uncertainty, Evolution, and Economic Theory," *Journal of Political Economy*, Vol. LVIII (1950), pp. 211–21. Alchian states that "where foresight is uncertain, 'profit maximization' is meaningless as a guide to specifiable action" (p. 211).

[30] Armen A. Alchian, *op. cit.*, p. 212.

predict the prices or outputs a particular firm would decide upon in an objectively described situation. The real purpose is to explain the general effects upon prices and outputs that particular kinds of changes of the data would tend to have. The model of the firm faced with uncertainty is neither more nor less "empty" than the model without the accessories for uncertainty. It merely is more consistent with our knowledge of the way businessmen think.

Those who believe that the generalizations about price and output which we derive from the theory of the firm are "vitiated" by the recognition of the significance of uncertainty in the decision-making of the businessman would have a point if one or both of the following possibilities were shown to be likely: (a) if the changes of data whose effects are analysed were to affect the businessman's propensity to bear uncertainty significantly and in an haphazard, unpredictable way; (b) if they were to change the distribution of potential outcomes of alternative moves significantly and in an haphazard, unpredictable way. Neither of these possibilities, however, is at all likely to occur in connection with events of the type ordinarily analysed. For example, the imposition of an excise tax would neither substantially change a firm's willingness to take chances, nor would it affect the probability distribution of net-revenue opportunities in an unpredictable way.[31] Likewise, an increase in the price of a productive factor, or an increase in the demand for the product, would tend to affect these probability distributions in definite directions and ordinarily in determinate degrees; and there is no reason for assuming that these changes would seriously reshape the risk-aversion preference scheme of the businessman. Hence, it is unnecessary to know just what this preference scheme was like in the first place, or just what the distribution of the net-revenue opportunities relating to all the alternative moves was before the change in data. The theory is to explain how the change may affect prices and outputs, not what they were before and will be afterwards. This explanation is accomplished by "assuming" an initial equilibrium position and "determining" intermediate or final equilibrium positions in

---

[31] Exceptions are conceivable and in such a case one would have to admit that little or nothing can be said about it.

accordance with the assumed changes in data. This is how models, mental or physical, are supposed to work.[32]

[32] The reader may feel that I have made this point sufficiently clear in earlier passages and would not have needed to repeat it. A survey of the literature in the economic journals, however, will convince him of the necessity of repetition; too many fail to grasp the idea and too many forget it in the course of their argument. Of course, not everything that is sound for the Economics of Adjustment is equally sound for the Economics of Welfare. The difference in aims and claims dictates a difference in some basic methodology.

CHAPTER *3*

The Practice of the Firm: Empirical Evidence and Counter-Evidence

Economists' Vocabulary and Business Language · Rationalizations of Decisions or Actions · Averaging Fluctuating Costs and Prices · Actual versus Potential Average Costs · Average-Cost Pricing as the Lawyer's Ideal · Average-Cost Pricing as the Accountant's Ideal · Average-Cost Pricing as a Cartel Device · Average Cost as a Clue to Long-Run Demand Elasticity · Reasons and Variables · Research on Actual Pricing Methods · The Absence of Numerically Expressed Estimates · The Evaluation of Empirical Evidence · A Re-evaluation of the Claims · Who Can Afford to Pass Up Profits? · The Break-Even Chart · Theory and Practice

W E LET THE DISCUSSION of "The Theory of the Firm" be followed by a chapter on "The Practice of the Firm" because the suspicion is strong that business practice contradicts the assumptions of the theory so flagrantly as to cast grave doubt on its validity. There is not as yet available any large amount of material derived from systematic empirical research on the business conduct of the single firm. But almost everybody interested in these questions has had occasional conversations with businessmen, and the impressions gained from such inquiries into the businessmen's experiences often form an empirical basis for the doubts which so-called "realistic" critics entertain of "theoretical" analysis.

I submit that the few systematic and the many casual researchers have often been misled by pitfalls of semantics and terminology and by a naive acceptance of rationalizations in lieu of genuine explanations of actions.

Economists' Vocabulary and Business Language

The vast majority of businessmen have never heard of expressions such as elasticity of demand or supply, sloping demand curves, marginal revenue, marginal cost. If they do not know the words or the concepts, how can they be supposed to think in these terms? A scattered few of the men may have been exposed to such words and ideas in half-forgotten college courses, but they have found in practice that they have no use for a vocabulary unknown to their associates, superiors, subordinates, and fellow businessmen. Thus the most essential terms in which economists explain business conduct do not exist in the businessman's vocabulary. Does this not prove that the explanations are unrealistic or definitely false?

Only an inexperienced researcher could draw such a conclusion. The technical terms used in the explanation of an action need not have any part in the thinking of the acting individual. A mental process in everyday life may often be most conveniently described for scientific purposes in a language which is quite foreign to the process itself.

To ask a businessman about the "elasticity of demand" for his product is just as helpful as inquiring into the customs of an indigenous Fiji Islander by interviewing him in the King's English. But with a little ingenuity it is possible to translate ideas from the businessman's language into that of the economist, and *vice versa*. Questions such as "Do you think you might sell more of this product if you cut the price by 10 per cent?" or "How much business do you think you would lose if you raised your price by 10 per cent?" will evoke intelligent answers in most cases provided the questions are readily reformulated and adapted to the peculiarities of the particular man and his business. Often it will be necessary to know a good deal of the technology, customs and jargon of the trade, and even of the personal idiosyncrasies of the men, before one can ask the right questions. A set formulation of questions will hardly fit any larger number of businessmen in different fields and, hence, questionnaires to be filled out by them will rarely yield useful results.

Rationalizations of Decisions or Actions

Psychologists will readily confirm that statements by interviewed individuals about the motives and reasons for their actions are unreliable or at least incomplete. Even if a person tries to reconstruct for himself in his memory the motives and reasons for one of his past actions, he will usually end up with a rationalization full of afterthoughts that may make his actions appear more plausible to himself. Explanations given to an interviewer or investigator are still more likely to be rationalizations in terms that may make the particular actions appear plausible and justified to the inquirer. In order to be understood (and respected) the interviewed person will often choose for his "explanations" patterns of reasoning which he believes to be recognized as "sound" and "fair" by others. Most of these rationalizations may be subjectively honest and truthful. It takes an experienced analyst to disentangle actual from imaginary reasons and to separate relevant from irrelevant data, and essential from decorative bits of the information furnished. Written replies to questionnaires are hopelessly inadequate for such purposes.[1]

Questions of business policy are particularly difficult objects of inquiry because the businessman usually is anxious to show by his answers that he is intelligent, well informed and fair. The standards of fairness and business ethics to which he wishes to conform are often those which he believes are accepted by his lawyers, accountants, customers, competitors, fellow citizens, economists, and others. Only through detailed discussions of different situations and decisions, actual as well as hypothetical, will an investigator succeed in bringing out the true patterns of conduct of the individual businessman.[2]

[1] Cf. George Katona, *Price Control and Business* (Bloomington, Ind.: Principia Press, 1945), p. 210. He states that "only detailed interviews can probe into the motives behind business decisions."

[2] For further comments on the difficulties of good empirical research on business conduct, see my paper "Evaluation of the Practical Significance of the Theory of Monopolistic Competition," *American Economic Review*, Vol. XXIX (1939), p. 233. After discussing the policies of my former business partners I concluded (p. 234): "An investigator who would have based his findings on their answers to questionnaires or even on personal interviews, would have come to erroneous results. An investigator who could have seen all the actually or potentially available statistics would have come to no results at all. The only possibility for a fruitful empirical inquiry into these problems lies, I think, in the more subtle technique of analyzing a series of single business decisions through close personal contact with those responsible for the decisions."

One of the recent conclusions of casual or systematic empirical research on the business firm is that businessmen do not pursue a policy of maximizing profits, and of pricing according to the marginal cost and marginal revenue principle, but instead follow rules of pricing on the basis of average cost calculations even where this is inconsistent with profit maximization. I shall attempt to reinterpret the findings of systematic research along these lines. For this purpose we must first clear up some misunderstandings which appear to have contributed to the support of the average-cost theory of pricing.[3]

Averaging Fluctuating Costs and Prices

In discussions with businessmen I have found that two different types of averages must be distinguished: averages over time and averages as a function of the volume of output.

Selling prices frequently fluctuate over time, not only cyclically and seasonally but during the week or the day. In calculations for investment, cyclical price fluctuations will be taken into account and average prices will be estimated. In planning the production of seasonally demanded goods—summer dresses, swimming suits, winter sport clothes, Christmas toys, etc.—price discounts for off-season sales will be counted into the average selling price. Hotels in resorts may charge preferential rates for guests arriving on Tuesdays and leaving on Thursdays; wholesale grocers will dispose of over-ripe fruit and vegetables at reduced prices; public utilities may charge lower rates to industrial off-peak customers; in all these cases the firms may wish to figure out their average revenue or average price over time.

---

[3] According to accepted theory, price will equal average cost (inclusive of normal profit) chiefly under the pressure of competition. The individual firm will charge a price above or below average cost depending on the situation and in line with the marginal calculus. However, when price has risen above average cost, other firms will expand production and new firms will enter the industry, and their competition will tend to reduce price to the average cost level. Thus it is not the price policy of the individual firm but the pressure of actual or potential competition which will make prices equal to average cost. In contrast with this, the theory advanced by the critics of marginal analysis asserts that firms set their prices according to average cost regardless of the state of competition and regardless of the market situation.

Costs may show similar fluctuations over time. Raw materials and fuel prices may vary cyclically and seasonally, electric power rates even over different hours of the day. Seasonal changes of the weather will often cause cost differences in several technical processes: natural instead of artificial heat for drying when wind, temperature and humidity are favorable; hydroelectric instead of steam-generated power when rivers carry sufficient water; and so on. These and hundreds of other reasons call for calculations of average costs by the affected business firms.

The average revenues and average costs that must be calculated to take care of such variations over time are not in the least inconsistent with the marginal revenue and marginal cost principles. Indeed, a firm considering an increase in output or an expansion of capacity will certainly anticipate variations in revenue and cost. The marginal revenue, the change in revenue attributable to the increase in output, may be made up of low-price sales and high-price sales; they are "averaged" when marginal revenue is estimated. The marginal cost may be made up of high-price purchases and low-price purchases, good technical performances and bad; these varying cost items are "averaged" when marginal cost is estimated. This averaging is a necessary part of the marginal calculus and has nothing to do with average-cost pricing.

Actual versus Potential Average Costs

The absence of the expressions "marginal cost" and "marginal revenue" from the businessman's vocabulary, and the fact that he usually explains his price policy in terms of "average cost," account for a good part of the skepticism of the empiricists. In the economist's jargon, the businessman who considers taking more business is supposed to say to himself: "At the increased volume of output, marginal cost will be this much and marginal revenue that much." (Statement I.) In a literal translation into everyday language, he would say, "The increase in production will cost me this much and will bring in that much." (Statement II.) He could say it also in a different version: "The increase in business will raise total costs from this to this much, and total receipts from that to that much." (Statement III.) These statements are absolutely equivalent, all expressing the marginal calculus of variations.

The same thing can also be expressed in a fourth, much more complicated way: "The increase in business will change average cost from this to this much, and average price from that to that much: it will, therefore, change profits by changing the margin of so and so much, times an output of this much, to a margin of so and so much, times an output of that much." (Statement IV.) With all its complications the statement is still equivalent to the former ones. It is a bit foolish to divide total costs and receipts by the output figures just in order to multiply afterwards the differences again by the output figures; but it is not incorrect. The average-cost figures as such are, of course, irrelevant in the calculation.[4]

The average-cost figures, in spite of their prominent place in our businessman's complicated statement, had no place in his actual decision. The decision was based on the profitableness of the added business. When not only the current but also the potential average cost—that is, the average cost at a different production volume—and also the change in total receipts are considered, then the reasoning is true marginal calculus, not average-cost reasoning as some mistakenly believe.

Average-Cost Pricing as the Lawyer's Ideal

Generations of lawyers have accepted and proclaimed the fairness of the average-cost standard of pricing. Decades of regulatory

---

[4] This can be easily illustrated by assuming any set of figures. Assume that the firm considers taking new orders for 1,000 tons of product, reducing its average price. Statement IV might read: "The increase in business from 10,000 tons to 11,000 tons will raise total cost from $80,000 to $86,900 and, hence, will reduce average cost from $8.00 to $7.90; it will raise total receipts from $99,500 to $107,800 and, hence, will reduce average price from $9.95 to $9.80; it will, therefore, raise profits by changing a margin of $1.95 times an amount of 10,000, i.e., $19,500, to a margin of $1.90, times an amount of 11,000, i.e., $20,900. Let's take the business."

Statement III would read under the same circumstances: "The increase in business will raise total costs from $80,000 to $86,900, that is by $6,900, and will raise total receipts from $99,500 to $107,800, that is by $8,300. Let's take the business."

Statement II on the same situation would read: "The increase in production will cost me $6,900 and will bring in $8,300. Let's take the business."

Statement I, finally, would read: "At the increased volume of output, marginal cost will be $6.90 and marginal revenue $8.30. Go ahead."

experiments and arguments, and a long history of court decisions, have emphasized the average-cost principle as the just basis of pricing. Is it then surprising that businessmen try to explain their pricing methods by average-cost considerations?

Corporations in regulated industries are sometimes caught in their official price justifications: a change in the market situation may make it wise and profitable to change the selling price, but that price has been anchored to an average-cost calculation which it is now difficult to disavow. The companies cannot very well submit to their regulatory commissions revised average-cost calculations every time market conditions change. They have to put up with relatively inflexible prices which, were it not for the regulatory authorities, might be as much against their own interests as against those of the consumers.

More often, however, the businessman is not conscious of the fact that he uses average-cost considerations merely as rationalizations or justifications. Selling with high profit margins might indicate monopoly and "squeezing of the consumer"; selling below cost might indicate unfair competition and "cutting the throat of the competitor." As a good citizen the businessman wishes to avoid both these wicked practices. As long as he can justify his prices as covering "average cost plus a fair profit margin" he can say, to others as well as to himself, that he is living up to the accepted standards of law and decency. If this "fair profit margin" is at times a bit generous and at other times rather thin, he can still justify his price. (That such variations betray his "explanation" of this pricing method as incomplete or untenable may escape his attention as well as that of his questioners.)

Average-Cost Pricing as the Accountant's Ideal

Selling price must cover average cost inclusive of overhead and fair profit margin if the business enterprise is to survive and to prosper. A good accountant regards it as his duty to watch over the soundness of the firm's pricing methods and to warn against prices below full cost.

Practical and academic accountants have sometimes attacked the marginal-cost principle as a fallacy conducive to practices that are liable to result in business losses. They have reasoned that a general application of differential cost considerations might mean that firms forget that they ought to recover their overhead in *some* part of their business.

Reasoning of this sort reveals a twofold misunderstanding of the marginal principle. (a) That marginal cost does not "include" fixed overhead charges need not mean that it will always be below average total cost; indeed, marginal cost may equal or exceed average cost. (This will always be true for volumes of output at or beyond "optimum capacity" of the firm.) (b) To use marginal cost as a pricing factor need not mean that price will be set at the marginal cost level. Indeed, this will never be done. In the exceptional case of pure competition, price cannot be "set" at all but is "given" to the firm and beyond its control; and marginal cost will be equal to price not because of any price policy but only because of adjustments in the firm's production volume. In the normal case of non-pure competition, the firm will never charge a price as low as marginal cost; it will charge a price at which marginal revenue is equal to marginal cost, and this price must therefore be above both.

It is a misunderstanding to believe that the use of marginal cost in the businessman's pricing technique implies an advice that selling price should be set at the marginal-cost level.[5] Marginal cost and marginal revenue are exactly what a businessman is considering when he asks himself: "Could I get some more business and would I want it under the conditions under which I could get it?"

The idea, held by some accountants, that pricing on the basis of the marginal principle would sacrifice profits is the opposite of the truth—except in one very special sense: where the average-cost rule has been used as a monopolistic device, resort to the marginal principle might be taken to mean abandonment of a

---

[5] We are not talking here about "marginal-cost pricing," the much debated pricing principle advocated for public monopolies subsidized out of general revenues of the government. Under marginal-cost pricing, price is in fact set at the marginal-cost level. But under the marginal principle of pricing, where marginal cost and marginal revenue are equated, price is necessarily above marginal cost.

cartel arrangement in the industry and "outbreak" of unrestricted competition.

Average-Cost Pricing as a Cartel Device

In times of depression businessmen often discover that it is wiser to lose only a part rather than all of their overhead cost; that it is better to sell at prices below full cost than to stick to prices which would cover all costs but at which they cannot sell. They usually deplore these deviations from the full-cost principle of pricing and argue that nobody would *have* to sell below cost if nobody *did* sell below cost.

Price fixing among producers or official price codes may in such situations succeed in the maintenance of a monopolistic level of price in spite of strong temptations for competitive price cutting. Tacit understandings to observe average-cost rules of pricing sometimes constitute an alternative way of achieving price maintenance in a declining market. Moral suasion in the direction of "good accounting" and of "sound pricing" on the basis of "full cost" may be an effective device of domestic price cartels (through trade associations or in the form of tacit understandings).

Outright price fixing, just as any other cartel agreement, is a device to affect the estimates of revenue conditions for the products of the individual firms. Only if demand as seen by the individual seller is effectively changed through his anticipations of serious reactions on the part of his competitors and fellow cartel members will he find it advantageous to restrict his output to the extent necessary for the maintenance of the agreed price. The essential effect of the agreement is upon the elasticity of the expected demand.[6]

---

[6] The application of the traditional cost and revenue curves to the situation of a firm in a cartelized industry is not very satisfactory. In the case of the unconditional adherence of the firm to a straight price-fixing agreement, the economist may depict the average revenue curve of the firm as a horizontal line, at the fixed price level, breaking off abruptly at the largest volume of output which the faithful cartel member thinks he can sell. Thus the relevant elasticity, infinite for smaller ranges of outputs, suddenly becomes zero. If, on the other hand, the firm does not unconditionally observe the

The general adoption of an average-cost rule is in effect a price agreement among the members of the particular industry. Where a trade association announces a representative "average cost," the announced value need not tally at all with the average cost of an individual firm. Where cost conditions are believed to be very similar throughout the industry, the understanding may be informal and tacit. It may be made entirely a matter of "business ethics" not to sell below average cost plus fair profit margin. For the firm that strictly observes this ethical code the average cost calculation performs the same function as a fixed cartel price and thus determines the average ($=$ marginal) revenue curve—which breaks off abruptly at the output it can sell at that price.

If a businessman believes that the best policy for him in the long run is to stick to the cartel, this does not necessarily mean that he disregards the marginal principle. On the contrary, the feared consequences of breaking away from the cartel, its probable effects upon long-run revenue, may dictate his continued adherence. Likewise, if violations of the ethical code of average-cost pricing are feared to have adverse consequences, continued membership in this "ethical cartel" may not be a departure from the marginal principle. The average-cost rule and the sanctions for violating it have the same sort of effects upon demand elas-

---

agreement, but instead compares the advantages of compliance with those of contraventions, the geometric apparatus becomes difficult to operate. The firm may have to weigh the probabilities of various consequences of its potential contraventions; e.g., the firm may not be found out by its cartel partners and may succeed in selling a substantially increased output at reduced prices; it may be caught and fined, and thus realize very low net revenues from its additional sales; or it may cause its competitors to break away from the cartel and to cut their prices in retaliation. Each of these possibilities might be translated into separate average and marginal revenues; but how much sense it makes to draw curves for the certainty-equivalents of the distribution of all these chances and risks for various outputs is an open question. It does make sense to express the effect of the cartel agreement by saying that demand (average revenue) as seen by a cartel member who considers price cutting in contravention of the agreement as a practical alternative becomes—compared with the situation without agreement—less elastic owing to the risks of penalizing or retaliatory actions. In any event, that it may become inopportune to use curve analysis is one thing; it would be another to find that the general theory of the firm provides no suitable framework within which to analyse the typical conduct of cartel members. See, however, below, Chapter 15, especially pp. 481–86.

ticity and marginal revenue that other types of price agreements have been shown to have.[7]

Average Cost as a Clue to Long-Run Demand Elasticity

Even without any ethical or unethical code prescribing an average-cost rule of pricing, average cost may be the most important datum for the estimate of long-run demand elasticity. The elasticity of demand for any particular product is determined by the availability of substitutes. In order to estimate how much business it may lose if it raises its price, a firm will consider whether existing or potential competitors can supply competing products at the particular price. The elasticity of supply from competing sources determines the elasticity of demand for the firm's product. The supply from competing sources will depend on their actual or potential cost of production. And usually the best clue that a firm has to the production cost of competitors is its own production cost, corrected for any known differences of conditions.

Assuming that competitors have the same access to productive factors, materials, and technology, their production cost cannot be much different from that of a particular producer who may be considering a price increase. In the absence of any cartel arrangements he will have to count on his competitors expanding their business at the expense of his if he ventures to raise his selling price above average cost. Where he need not fear existing competitors, but entry into the industry is relatively easy, he will have to reckon with newcomers' competition if he makes the business too attractive by allowing himself too generous a profit margin above average cost. Under such circumstances he will know that he stands

[7] The theory of the firm cannot, of course, explain the determination of the cartel price, unless the cartel is organized as a central selling syndicate which (under certain, though unusual, conditions) may be considered as a single firm. Otherwise the formation of the cartel price calls for an apparatus other than that employed in the analysis of the individual firm. All that the theory of the firm can contribute to the economics of the cartel price is an explanation of the decisions by a member firm to stick to the agreed price or to depart from it. This is completely misunderstood by Henry M. Oliver, Jr., when he blames marginal analysis of the firm, among other things, for its failure to explain cartel prices. "Marginal Theory and Business Behavior," *American Economic Review*, Vol. XXXVII (1947), pp. 375–83.

to lose too much business and had better stick fairly closely to a price based on average cost.

Notwithstanding any rationalizations of this price policy, the reasons for it lie in the competitiveness of the industry resulting in a high elasticity of demand visualized by individual sellers.[8] To "explain" this price by reference to some emotional attachment to the average-cost principle is to miss the mark. The role of average cost in the firm's pricing process in this case is to aid in gauging the elasticity of the long-run demand for its product.

Reasons and Variables

Seeing how many different roles average cost may play in the pricing process without in the least contradicting the statement that (changes in) marginal cost and marginal revenue determine (changes in) output and price, one should realize the dangers of attempts to use utterances of businessmen as evidence against the correctness of marginal analysis.

Businessmen's answers to direct questions about the reasons for charging the prices they are charging are almost certainly worthless. Every single fact or act has probably hundreds of "reasons"; the selection of a few of them for presentation to the inquirer is influenced by the prejudices or old theories which the informant had impressed upon him by school, radio, newspapers, etc.

Except in the case of a genuine decision leading to a recent change of policy, one may say that an approach much more fruitful than that of asking about reasons *for* some policy is to ask about reasons *against* its alternatives. Instead of asking for explanations of the price actually charged or the output volume actually produced, questions about "why not more" and "why not less" are likely to yield more revealing results. But even these answers must be checked and double-checked through a network of cross-examina-

---

[8] Where the average-cost rule is a cartel device, the elasticity of demand will be small or zero from the actually realized point on *downward*. When average cost is a clue to size up potential competition, the elasticity of demand will be high from the actually realized point on *upward*. The former prevents price reductions, the latter price increases.

tion,[9] segregating and isolating certain variables in a manner familiar to the scientist working with the calculus of variations and with the determination of partial derivatives.

Research on Actual Pricing Methods

On the basis of marginal analysis of the firm and the industry, we should expect for most industries that price in the long run would not deviate too much from average cost, yet that the firm would attempt to get better prices when it could safely get them and would not refrain from cutting prices when it believed that this would increase its profits or reduce its losses.

Now let us compare with this the findings of one of the empirical research undertakings which shook the researchers' confidence in the marginal principle and convinced them that businessmen followed the "full-cost principle" of pricing regardless of profit maximization. An inquiry was made by interviewing 38 entrepreneurs.[10] "A large majority" of them explained that they charged the "full cost" price. Some, however, admitted "that they might charge more in periods of exceptionally high demand"; and a greater number reported "that they might charge less in periods of exceptionally depressed demand." [11] Competition seemed to induce "firms to modify the margin for profits which could be added to direct costs and overheads." [12] Moreover, "the conventional addition for profit varies from firm to firm and even within firms for different products." [13]

This is precisely what one should have expected to hear. Do these findings support the theory of the average-cost principle of pricing? I submit that they give little or no support to it. The margins above average cost are different from firm to firm and, within firms, from period to period and from product to product. These

[9] For an excellent exposition of sound principles of "survey research" see the last chapter of George Katona's *Psychological Analysis of Economic Behavior* (New York: McGraw-Hill, 1951).

[10] R. L. Hall and C. J. Hitch, "Price Theory and Business Behavior," *Oxford Economic Papers*, No. 2 (1939), p. 12.

[11] *Ibid.*, p. 19.

[12] *Ibid.*, p. 19.

[13] *Ibid.*, p. 20.

differences and variations strongly suggest that the firms consult other data besides or instead of their average costs. And, as a matter of fact, the reported findings include some that indicate what other considerations were pertinent to the price determinations by the questioned businessmen.

Of 24 firms which gave reasons for not charging higher prices, 17 were tabulated as admitting that it was "fear of competitors or potential competitors" and a "belief that others would not follow an increase." Another two stated that "they prefer a large turnover." [14] To me the 19 answers indicate that these businessmen were estimating the risk of losing business if they raised prices or, in other words, that they were concerned about the elasticity of demand.

Of 35 firms which gave reasons for not charging lower prices, 4 firms explained that they were members of price-fixing combinations; 2 stated that it was "difficult to raise prices once lowered"; and 21 referred directly or implicitly to their estimates of demand elasticity. (Nine firms: "Demand unresponsive to price"; one firm: "Price cuts not passed on by retailers"; eleven firms: "Competitors would follow cuts.") Only 8 firms gave reasons other than price fixing or price elasticity considerations; these 8 were listed as having "quasi-moral objections to selling below cost." [15] Unfortunately the interviewers did not find out what these conscientious objectors to price cutting thought about the responsiveness of demand; and whether they would remain adamant if they were sure that a small price concession would produce a large increase in sales. I suspect that a cross-examination would have brought out the fact that the moral or quasi-moral views on price maintenance were regularly coupled with a very strong opinion that a price reduction would not produce sufficiently more business and, thus, would constitute useless sacrifice of profits.

In any event, there is little or nothing in the findings of this inquiry that would indicate that the businessmen observed an average-cost rule of pricing when such observance was inconsistent with the maximum-profit principle. On the other hand, there is plenty of evidence in the findings that the businessmen paid much

[14] *Ibid.*, p. 21.
[15] *Ibid.*

attention to demand elasticities—which to the economist is equivalent to marginal revenue considerations.

The Absence of Numerically Expressed Estimates

Why should others in the face of this evidence have come to the conclusion that the marginal principle was not applied and profit maximization not attempted by the group of businessmen studied? How could others have failed to be impressed by the facts just recited?

It seems that their confidence in the conventional analysis was lost when they found to their surprise that the businessman had no definite numerical estimates of the magnitudes relevant to the application of the marginal principle. They had assumed that a businessman should "know" the elasticity of demand for his product, and now they were shocked to find "that the great majority of entrepreneurs were in profound ignorance with regard to its value." [16] A student who had expected to find exact estimates must indeed have been disappointed when most of his informants "were vague about anything so precise as elasticity." [17]

The inquirers found the same vagueness with regard to marginal cost estimates. While the entrepreneurs usually computed direct cost and total overheads "with some pains at accuracy," [18] they could not furnish any data on marginal cost. He who expected that marginal cost and marginal revenue were equated on the basis of precise calculations must feel frustrated. The student who had to do homework computing marginal cost and revenue figures to the second or third decimal point may feel fooled when he learns that the businessman does not do anything of the sort. But to conclude from the absence of definite numerical estimates that the magnitudes in question were irrelevant in the conduct of the firms is a *non sequitur*. On the basis of the previous discussion of this subject (see above pp. 42 ff.) we should understand that the con-

[16] R. F. Harrod, "Price and Cost in Entrepreneurs' Policy," *Oxford Economic Papers*, No. 2 (1939), p. 4. Concerning this discovery Harrod remarks emphatically: "This, indeed, must be regarded as one notable result of our inquiry."
[17] R. L. Hall and C. J. Hitch, *op. cit.*, p. 18.
[18] R. F. Harrod, *op. cit.*, p. 4.

struction of a pattern for the analytical description of a process is not the same thing as the actual process in everyday life; and we should not expect to find in everyday life the definite numerical estimates that are part of the scientific pattern.

Apart from the absence of numerical estimates of marginal revenue and marginal cost it is difficult to see what other findings of the inquiry could have persuaded the researchers that they had disproved the theory of marginalism in the conduct of the firm. There is not a single proposition in the tabulated results of the inquiry that cannot be fully harmonized with marginal analysis. The "Analysis of Replies to Questionnaire on Costs and Prices," which the researchers presented as an appendix to their report,[19] contains a wealth of illustrative material—illustrative, as I see it, of the application of the marginal principle to business decisions of the single firm.

The Evaluation of Empirical Evidence

Will direct empirical research alone ever furnish irrefutable evidence forcing a decision in the controversy about the relative merits of the "full-cost pricing" theory and the "maximum-profit pricing" theory? The main difficulty lies in the possibility that in a very large number of concrete cases the two theories yield just about the same results and the "findings of fact" would therefore fit both theories. It would be an expensive task to dig up and investigate a large number of cases where the "data" are such that the two pricing rules would call for drastically different prices: where a price based on average cost would definitely imply a sacrifice of profit in the long run and where a price yielding maximum long-run profits would definitely be below average cost or exceed it by an unusually large margin. I have no doubt whatsoever that such research, if ever undertaken, would yield overwhelmingly more evidence of presumably profit-oriented not-cost-plus pricing than of profit-sacrificing cost-plus pricing.

But is it really necessary to undertake this research? Is not the existence of cartels, fair-trade laws, minimum-price laws, bans against selling below cost, etc., indirect, but conclusive evidence

[19] Hall and Hitch, *op. cit.*, pp. 33–45.

of the fact that the incentive to sell more cheaply than at "average cost plus fair profit" must at times be very strong, and not only on the part of a few but indeed of hundreds of thousands of firms? Does not the existence of maximum prices enforced by a most extensive and expensive governmental machinery infallibly attest to the fact that at times there must be an almost irresistible temptation for firms to charge prices with an allegedly excessive margin above full cost? What other testimony is needed to demonstrate that there must indeed be millions of pricing decisions every year that are not based on the average-cost rule?

No doubt there are also instances in which firms follow the average-cost principle even where it involves a sacrifice of profit. Apart from cases of governmental price regulations and controls, where average-cost pricing is forced upon the business firms, we can well conceive of instances of strictly traditional conduct, routine behavior and rule-of-thumb decisions based upon some accepted full-cost standard. But these instances of sticking to the full-cost standard where it costs money to do it are probably rare exceptions.

Those who do not accept the indirect evidence suggested above and choose to wait for direct evidence culled from empirical research in the pricing practices of firms will probably never be able to make their choice between the alternative theories. There are not likely to be masses of observations explainable by only one of the theories and incompatible with the other. For when there is an apparent conflict between observations and the theory they are supposed to test, the observations can usually be disqualified as of uncertain reliability; and, where this will not do, the conflict can usually be reconciled by means of auxiliary hypotheses, that is, by particular assumptions that can explain the deviations. Where the observations can neither be dismissed as unreliable nor reconciled with the theory on the basis of special circumstances, then at last, "negative empirical evidence" against the theory exists. But if neither of the theories claims universal applicability and both assert merely "tendencies" and likelihoods, the negative evidence leaves the theories unscathed.

A Re-evaluation of the Claims

Perhaps a re-evaluation of the claims of the competing theories can help in this dilemma. The adherents of the full-cost theory claim that businessmen "normally and ordinarily" do not employ the marginal calculus, but instead pursue a simple cost-plus rule of pricing (adding a fair profit margin to the average total unit cost of output). It is not denied that this pricing rule may incidentally maximize the profits of the firm, indeed there is a strong suggestion that this is actually the case in the long run. The adherents of the marginalist theory claim that businessmen will adjust their prices and production to changes in cost or market conditions in ways conveniently depicted and analysed in terms of incremental revenue and incremental cost. It is not denied that the businessmen themselves may think in terms of average cost, nor that they may in the absence of marked changes in cost or market conditions follow routine practices which do not produce a maximum of profit.

These claims, it seems to me, are not diametrically opposed to each other; indeed, they seem to have different aims and to refer to different situations: the one aims at a description of how businessmen think about their prices most of the time when they are not pressed or provoked to readjust to change; the other aims at an analysis of what businessmen do about their prices when conditions markedly change. Perhaps it is legitimate to conclude from this re-evaluation of claims that the full-cost theorists are right most of the time while the marginalist theorists are right only occasionally, namely, *at the strategic moments that are relevant for economic analysis.*

This statement illustrates the significance of the indirect evidence to which I previously referred, the governmental and syndicalist interventions to keep firms from departing from the ideal of full-cost pricing. The interventions against "selling below cost" are supposed to be needed in times of depression and stagnation, the interventions against "profiteering" in times of boom and inflation; in "normal" times businessmen apparently do not have to be told to charge full-cost-plus-fair-profit-margin. This indicates that a significant change in demand will cause businessmen to stray from the average-cost standard, and that their moves will call for an explanation with reference to their desire to avoid losses or to make more money than the ordinary full-cost pricing allows. In other words, the conduct of firms, when demand changes markedly, becomes inconsistent with the average-cost theory of pricing but can be explained in terms of marginalist theory. In "normal" times, however, when things just "go on" as they have before, the average-cost theory seems to work well. But the marginalist theory, even if it should not provide an accurate description of conscious business thinking, still yields results which are *approximately* in conformance with the observed results of actual conduct. Thus, while the average-cost theory is manifestly out of tune with the observed facts in times of change, the marginalist theory gives good results in times of change and approximate ones in times of relative stability. This recognition should decide the issue for anybody familiar with scientific method.[20]

Who Can Afford to Pass Up Profits?

Another point seems worth making. It has been contended that certain firms in certain industries have been following the full-cost principle of pricing for many years and have not attempted to maximize their profits. If this is really true—and I do not know— one must first ask whether this was really a sacrifice of profit opportunities in the particular instances, inasmuch as adherence to the full-cost price may incidentally have resulted in the highest possible profits. On the other hand, if firms have actually refrained from making the profits they could have made, the contention implies that the firms have enjoyed very sheltered monopoly positions. A firm that foregoes profit opportunities for several years and still makes profits is undoubtedly in a position of considerable monopoly power.

According to the model of perfect competition a firm that maximizes its profits will just succeed in avoiding losses. (To earn "normal" returns on investment is to earn zero economic profit.)

[20] This decision is of course only for the time being. If someone some day should present a new theory that works better in all situations, such new theory may well replace the one now accepted.

If a good deal of natural "friction" should keep actual and potential competitors from pressing it too hard, a firm sparing no efforts and using its best may perhaps make some modest profits. But if a firm passes up chances for greater profits, and still makes handsome profits, it is undoubtedly in a well protected monopolistic position. Nothing but such a position, with the safe profit margin that it provides, can explain how a firm can afford, year in and year out, to disregard the marginal principle of business conduct.

The same conclusion is reached from another avenue. It was said above that businessmen may pursue a mechanical full-cost standard of pricing when they are not pressed or provoked to readjust to change. Under active and vigorous competition, however, businessmen are always pressed and provoked to adjust and, when they are not pressed and provoked, they are pressing and provoking others to continuous adjustments. The competitive businessman is always under pressure; if not from without, then from within, from his own ambition. The absence of change, the stability over long periods of time, which are part of the climate in which full-cost pricing can prevail and endure, are incompatible with a high degree, or even a moderate degree, of competition.[21]

The Break-Even Chart

A new fad in recent years, widely propagandized, is the break-even chart. On a diagram two lines are shown, one representing total revenue, the other total cost, with the sales volumes on the horizontal dimension and the dollar figures on the vertical. The sales volume at which the two lines intersect is the break-even

---

[21] This seems to be recognized by the critics of marginalism. For example: ". . . marginalism does postulate continuous readiness to change. It is not logically compatible with . . . an easy-going or complacent attitude out of which a business man must be shocked into alertness . . ." Or: "Business men, for the most part, do not appear to be either as avaricious or as dynamic or as logical as marginal theory portrays them; probably most of them are too little money-loving, or too lazy, or too irrational seriously to attempt the prescribed marginal calculations." Henry M. Oliver, Jr., *op. cit.*, pp. 381–82. Although I believe that these statements show an overestimation of the claims of marginalist theory as well as an underestimation of the qualities of businessmen, they do characterize a state of lame, inactive, or non-existent competition.

point, total revenue being equal to total cost. The cost curve begins at a point above the origin to show fixed cost, and proceeds as a straight line sloping up to the right to indicate constant variable costs per unit of output. The revenue curve begins at the origin and likewise slopes up to the right as a straight line indicating a constant selling price per unit of output. If the price is higher than variable unit cost ("direct cost") the lines must cross. At sales below the break-even point, the revenue does not cover the fixed cost; at sales above the break-even point, profit is obtained.

What is the use of such charts? Since total cost and total revenue are represented by straight lines, they relate only to situations in which not only the average variable cost but also the selling price is constant. Thus, they abstract from the existence of "demand" for the product, of the possibility that sales may be influenced by the price charged. The price is given, and the chart then shows how many dollars will be obtained when varying amounts of product are sold. A similar multiplication is done for costs. Thus, the charts are nothing but glamorized multiplication tables, doing a bit of simple arithmetic which a person of average intelligence could have learned to do in his head.

As far as I know, the most important practical use of the charts is as "target posters." Sales personnel who have no say about the selling price and no control over cost, that is, sales people who have the task of selling as much as they can at a given price, are sometimes given such charts so that they may better visualize the minimum sales they must achieve if any profit is to be had.

But what has all this to do with our discussion of the marginal calculus? Strangely enough, the fact that businessmen use the "break-even chart technique" has been mentioned by some as evidence that businessmen think in terms of average cost and pursue a full-cost principle of pricing instead of a profit-maximizing pricing technique. Why a device for presenting simple arithmetic by means of "graphical art" should be regarded as evidence in the controversy about pricing practices is difficult to understand—except as just another misunderstanding.

Theory and Practice

Complaints that a certain theory does not conform to reality or will not work in practice are probably as old as the oldest theory.[22] There has perhaps never been a theory against which no such complaints have been directed. In the majority of all cases the complaints were justified and faulty theories were eventually replaced by better ones.

The theory of the firm which economists have developed in order to explain price changes and price relationships has been the target of violent criticism. Much of the criticism was well taken, since the theory was often badly or carelessly formulated and needed to be amended. Moreover, exponents of the theory have sometimes exaggerated its relevance and applicability. Criticism may then be sobering and healthy.

But too much of the criticism is based on sheer ignorance of what a theory is supposed to do. Some believe a theory should be realistic in the sense that it features all the things that everybody can plainly see. Some criticize a general theory because it says too little about specific cases. Some reject a special theory because they think it is disproved by a concrete case—to which it does not apply. Too often the dissatisfaction with a theory is due to the inability of the critic to understand exactly what it says and means, what it aims to explain, and where it can be applied. Much of the dissatisfaction with the theory of the firm is of this kind.

[22] Cf. Immanuel Kant, "Concerning the Popular Expression 'That May be True in Theory But Will Not Do in Practice,'" in H. W. Hastie, *Kant's Principles of Politics, including his Essay on Perpetual Peace. A Contribution to Political Science* (Edinburgh: T. T. Clark, 1891).

CHAPTER 4

Types of Competition in Selling

This chapter is in some respects a "preview" of the rest of the book: most of what is contained in the sections on Polypoly, Oligopoly, Pliopoly, and Monopoly will be either summarized or elaborated in the later chapters. There will, however, be no discussion of the Perfect Market other than that contained in this chapter.

N O ONE EXPECTS A single definition to suffice for a term that has several meanings. While this is obvious regarding outright equivocations or homonyms, it is true also where a word has several interrelated meanings whose common core is too vague or general to be made the criterion for a catch-all definition. "Competition" is the name for a large family of meanings whose family resemblance is not always strong. Even "competition in the economic sense," indeed, even "competition in selling," refer to a number of very different phenomena and thus confound attempts at definition. Moreover, because economic institutions change and also the light in which we see economic processes changes, the old meanings of the term change and new meanings are added all the time. Hence, frequent reconsiderations of the content and use of the concept "competition" are in order.

COMPETING CONNOTATIONS OF "COMPETITION"

The various effects, good and evil, which have been ascribed to economic competition in general and to competition between sellers in particular could not possibly all be the effects of one and the same set of phenomena. It is sometimes useful to reverse the logical procedure and "deduce" from the alleged results the assumptions which an author must have made implicitly when he started from the condition of "competition among sellers." Such an examination reveals that the "competition" which eliminates excessive profits is something else than the "competition" which makes a producer produce an output at which his marginal cost is equal to his selling price; that the "competition" which gives the purchaser more freedom of choice so that he is "not subjected to the alternative of either turning to one single purveyor or else doing without" [1] is not the same as the "competition" which "weeds out the inefficient"; that the "competition" which prevents different prices for the same commodity from prevailing at one time in a market is something else than the "competition" which forces a small firm to give up its independence; that the "competition" which leads to an increase in advertising outlays in an industry is not the same as the "competition" which reduces the price differentials between different localities to the cost of transport, and those for different "future" transactions to the cost of storage; that the "competition" which leads to continual improvements in the qualities of products is something else than the "competition" which makes earnings proportionate to efficiency.

[1] F. W. Taussig, *Principles of Economics,* Fourth edition (New York: Macmillan, 1937), p. 61.

Qualifying Adjectives

Writers have tried to differentiate between various connotations of the term by employing qualifying adjectives. To the vocabulary employed in business language, such as *fair, sharp, keen, fierce, brutal, unfair, destructive, ruinous,* and *cut-throat* competition, economists have added (to mention the better known) *free, atomistic, pure, perfect, effective, unrestricted, simple, complete, homogeneous, rigorous, unmitigated, restrained, restricted, limited, incomplete, modified, cautious, considerate, cooperative, intermediate, hybrid, monopolistic, imperfect, heterogeneous, friendly, civilized, oligopolistic, controlled, regulated, discriminatory, predatory, potential,* and *workable* competition. There is little agreement concerning the use of the combined terms. The student of economics has thus no occasion for memorizing any definitions; none would take him through the writings of many authors. The only way to avoid confusion is to acquire a thorough understanding of the problems and of the purposes of a discussion and of the terminology, however awkward, of one's partners and opponents.

Competing Goods and Competing Sellers

The first distinction which we should make in order to gain more insight into the problems is this: we should distinguish competition between sellers from competition between their products.

If Mr. A. has been producing a certain product, say A-peaches, and Mr. B. is starting the production of B-peaches, the supply of B-peaches, may compete with A-peaches no matter whether Messrs. A and B know of each other or not. This competition between goods is not confined to commodities of the same kind; of course, the more similar the goods the greater is the substitutability (rivalry) between them; but, in the end, the most different products compete with one another for the consumer's dollar. (Peanuts compete with comic magazines; rugs compete with refrigerators; neckties compete with bill folds.) If the various products compete with one another only in this general way, competition can hardly mean "personal" competition between sellers. But even competition between very close substitutes, like our

A-peaches and B-peaches, may remain entirely impersonal, that is, it need not involve anything of which the sellers are conscious or from which rivalry among sellers arises.

That competition between closest substitutes sold in one and the same market need not have anything to do with competition between sellers can be readily seen. The extreme of "rivalry" between goods is, of course, the perfect substitutability that exists between homogeneous products. If Mr. A has regularly sold 100 pounds of peaches and if now another 100 pounds of peaches of exactly the same kind and quality are offered for sale, the second hundred pounds will compete with the first hundred pounds (and also with many other things offered in the market) no matter whether it is Mr. B or Mr. A himself who sells the second lot. The increment of output of a producer competes with his original output.

In this sense competition between all products and competition between all parts of the output of any one product will exist regardless of whether there is only one seller or a large number of sellers in the market. The only difference is that not all sellers are equally conscious of this sort of competition. The more conscious a seller is of the competition of any increment of output with the other parts of his output, the more reluctant will he be to produce it. But this is another matter which will occupy us under another heading.

Here it suffices to state this. That goods compete with one another for a place in the consumers' system of preferences and for a place in the consumers' budgets implies little concerning competition between the sellers of these goods. It is appropriate to make this rather obvious statement because one can find authors who declare that monopoly can never exist because of the ever-present competition of products for the consumers' dollar. Competition between goods and competition between sellers are very different things.

The Seller's Methods of Getting Business

When sellers' competition is regarded as an action, or as the totality of actions, by which sellers try to secure more business or, in particular, more sales of a given product, one will be impressed with the wide range of methods that are used for that purpose. A seller, in order to push his sales, may reduce his selling price; improve the quality of his product; render supplementary services to buyers; publicize the availability and quality of his product and strengthen its appeal by more advertising; accommodate his customers by delivering his product without charging the full cost of delivery; grant them more favorable terms of credit; increase his selling efforts in many other ways; exaggerate or lie about the excellent qualities of his product; disparage the quality of his competitors' products; inconvenience or intimidate buyers who patronize his competitors; obstruct competitors' operations, for example, reduce their capacity to produce, either in quantity or in quality, by restricting their access to required materials or equipment; resort to costly "predatory" devices to drive competitors out of business.

This enumeration is not supposed to be exhaustive, but merely illustrative of different kinds of competitive actions. They can be classified in several ways, but broadly they may be divided into two categories: one where the seller does something that increases the attractiveness of his own offerings to buyers, the other where the seller does something that detracts from his competitors' offerings. While of course both kinds of competitive action are supposed to put the seller's own product ahead of his competitors', actions of the first category are, in a sense, *positive* in that they add something to the seller's service to customers, giving them more for their money or at least making them think so, whereas actions of the second category are, in the same sense, *negative* in that they take away from the competitors' services to customers, either actually or in the customers' view. By actions of the first category a seller tries to make his product cheaper, bigger, better, or more appealing to the buyer. By actions of the second category a seller tries to make his competitors' products more expensive, less serviceable, less available, or less appealing to the buyer.

Competitive actions of the negative kind, efforts to reduce the saleability or availability of competitors' products, are usually regarded as "unfair competition." Their role is confined to instances of "oligopoly," a type of sellers' competition to which we shall have to give much space in this book. From the point of view of economic analysis "unfair competition" offers few fascinating problems and we cannot blame economists for giving it a rather cursory treatment. Sellers' competition of the positive kind is customarily classified into three groups: competition through reduced price, through improved quality, and through increased selling effort. Selling effort may or may not result in additional benefits of significant value to the buyers; the fact that the seller incurs more cost need not ensure that the buyer derives a positive benefit.[2]

The Buyer's Choice of Sellers

That more than one seller offer a certain commodity and that the consumer thus has a choice not only of the kinds of goods he can buy but also of the sellers from whom he can buy them, may be considered a distinct contribution to the consumer's freedom of choice. The presence of several sellers competing for the consumer's patronage does not necessarily contribute to greater efficiency, higher quality, better service, or lower prices; indeed, sometimes the opposite effects may result from the presence of a multitude of sellers catering to a limited group of consumers. Yet, the feeling that they have a large range of alternatives, and that they can compare the services of various sellers before deciding to favor one with their patronage, is for many consumers an advantage which they would not like to miss.

It is possible that many a consumer treasures the presence of several alternative sources of supply only because he has been impressed, by textbook and newspaper talk, with the alleged benefits of "competition." Perhaps many consumers would gladly forego their greater freedom of choice if they believed that they might be served more cheaply by one single distributing agency. On the other hand, a number of consumers would still prefer competition between sellers in the sense of a greater choice of sellers even if

---

[2] For example, if the seller's advertising misrepresents his product but induces people to buy it, they will hardly be benefited, particularly after they find out. On the other hand, competition of the negative sort may conceivably benefit the customer by pointing out real defects of the competitors' products.

they had to pay for it in terms of higher prices; they might hate the feeling of being dependent on "one single purveyor."

This sense of competition between sellers implies little or nothing about any real rivalry between the sellers, or about their way of acting, or about the size of their supply or the rate of their profit. Competition between sellers in this sense means only the buyer's freedom to select from among numerous sellers the one from whom he buys.

POLYPOLY

A state of mind of buyers was the essence of the concept of sellers' competition discussed in the preceding paragraphs. A state of mind of sellers will occupy us now; the state of mind of him who feels that he is merely "one among very many" selling in the same market.

A Seller Among Very Many

The feeling of a seller that he is "competing" with heaven-knows-how-many has important consequences for his conduct. If he knows that there are many others who sell the same or similar service or product, and that there is no particular one among them who watches him, his competitors are then "colleagues" to him rather than "rivals." To be sure, they all strive for the same objective: sales at good prices. But if there are very many and if no one of them has any special "importance," each single seller may have the feeling that the others would not care about what he does. This absence of real rivalry or rival-consciousness is the essence of the form of competition which is called "competition in a market of very many sellers" or, shorter, *polypoly*. (In Greek "many" is *polloi*, and "to sell" is *polein*, hence *polypoly* for the market position of one of "many sellers.") [3]

The term polypoly is by no means a novel creation, or a "newfangled" word. It was used as early as 1662, and it is now found regularly in German, French, Italian, and, though less frequently,

[3] The sameness of poly for "many" and poly for "selling" is only apparent: in Greek the two words have different o's, one an omikron, the other an omega.

in English works on competition. It has not always been used exactly in the meaning proposed here; to some it meant "too many sellers," or the condition of an overcrowded trade;[4] to others it meant "monopolies in every commodity," or the condition of universal monopoly;[5] again to others it meant "several sellers," or the condition now ordinarily called oligopoly.[6] But in recent years the meaning of polypoly as competition among very many sellers has been unambiguous.

If there are only a few sellers in the market (or in a certain part of the market), the sellers will be rival-conscious; that is to say, they will make guesses about each other's reactions to their own actions. These actions and reactions are typically concerned with changes in price, quality, selling efforts, etc. The sellers will, before they act, think of what the others might think and do about their actions; and this forethought will influence them in their decisions. This is not so where there are very many sellers, none of whom is important. *A polypolist is a seller who is unconcerned about rivals' reactions because he has too many competitors (or colleagues) to consider any one of them as his rival.* The polypolist is aware of his small share in the market and he knows or thinks that none of his competitors would feel any tangible affect of his actions. Thus he will not anticipate any reactions by them.

It is not inconsistent with this model of conduct if the seller knows that he can secure more sales at the expense of other sellers, as long as he believes that the others will hardly notice it. If there are some 10,000 such competitors in a certain line, and one of them, stealing business from the others, succeeds in boosting his sales by 50 percent, the loss of business to each of the rest will average .005 percent. If there is no reason to expect a very uneven distribution of that loss among the other sellers, the individual seller will not expect that his "competitors" will take notice of his actions.

---

[4] Johann Joachim Becher, *Politische Discurs* (Frankfurt, 1st ed. 1662, 3rd ed. 1688), pp. 112–116.

[5] Umberto Ricci, *Dal protezionismo al sindicalismo* (Bari: Laterza, 1926), p. 131.

[6] Erich Schneider, *Reine Theorie monopolistischer Wirtschaftsformen* (Tübingen: Mohr-Siebeck, 1932), p. 132. In his later writings, however, Schneider uses the term polypoly in the same sense as we do.

Of this type of seller one has to distinguish two species because of differences in their state of mind which lead to different patterns of conduct: the polypolist who has practically unlimited sales opportunities but no choice of prices and the polypolist who has some such choice but is limited in his sales outlets.

The Polypolist Without Choice of Prices

A seller may feel that he has absolutely no say in the matter of selling price; that he has to accept the market price or make no sales—not because somebody dictates the price that he must charge, not because any contract or regulation forces him to sell only at that price—but simply because the market price, for reasons unknown to the seller (unless he has been told something about "supply and demand") is what it is and the seller feels he could not do anything about it.

The position of such a seller has been called one of *pure competition;* if this position is considered the "pure" form of competition, one should note that it certainly is pure from any element of "competitive strife." No feelings of personal competition or rivalry will sway the "pure competitor"; he is the extreme form of a polypolist.

The basic idea is this. Each single seller knows that there are so many other people selling exactly the same commodity that his own supply simply "does not matter." He feels that it does not make any difference to the price which rules (or will rule) on the market whether he sells much or little or nothing; and that it will not make any difference to his so-called "competitors"—to him they are just "other sellers"—how much he decides to sell.[7]

The seller's feeling of his complete lack of influence upon sell-

[7] I have elsewhere characterized the state of mind of this seller under "pure competition" by the answers he gave as a witness testifying in an imaginary hearing. See Fritz Machlup, *The Political Economy of Monopoly: Business, Labor and Government Policies* (Baltimore: Johns Hopkins Press, 1952), pp. 15 ff. The repeated reference to the seller's "state of mind" is designed to emphasize the methodological individualism and subjectivism appropriate to most analyses of social conduct. I do not propose, however, to stop with the "psychological" determination of conduct as if the thinking of the actors were independent of the real facts of the situation. Of course, they act in a certain way, because they think in a certain way, but *how* they

ing price is, apart from the absence of agreements, conventions or collusion, based on two circumstances. First, the seller knows that his supply represents such an exceedingly small part of the total market supply that changes of his supply would not count. Second, the seller knows that he sells exactly the same good as all the others, undifferentiated by quality or service or anything else so that there is nothing by which he could keep any customers if he charged more than "the" price. The first condition, that there are a great many sellers in the market, is necessary in order to give the single seller the feeling of unimportance. The second condition, that the goods sold by these many sellers are standardized and undifferentiated in all respects, is necessary in order to give the single seller the feeling that he would, at a stroke, lose all sales if he tried to ask more than the market price. As a matter of fact, products do not necessarily have to be physically homogeneous to be economically perfect substitutes. Goods may be perfectly substitutable for one another if there are certain differences, provided these differences are physically measurable and subject to definite and constant evaluation by a considerable group of users who are indifferent as to whether they have a given amount of one or a certain (though different) amount of the other. In this case the two goods will be economically perfect substitutes at a given price ratio. Examples may be gold of different fineness, fuel of different caloric content, wood pulp of different water content, certain chemicals of different strength.

Under polypoly of standardized products (pure competition) the seller in fact does not usually charge a price; the price is given to him and all he can do is to sell or not to sell. Such a position can perhaps be best visualized if we think of somebody who wants to sell a small amount of Government bonds which he has been holding. Could he insist that the Government bonds which he offers are bigger and better than those of other people? Could he charge $104.50 when the price for the type he offers is only $103.25?

---

think is in turn conditioned by their experiences with situations judged to be "like" the one that confronts them. Hence, the "real" situation may be taken as the "ultimate" determinant of their conduct. It is always the *actor's* judgment of that "real" situation that counts; but it can be safely assumed that most businessmen are "sensible" people capable of adequately appraising the market situation in which they operate.

Clearly not. If he wants to hold out for a higher price, he may decide not to sell now; or he may, if he needs some money and does not wish to borrow, sell only a part of his holdings now and keep the rest. But he would not even dream of "charging a price." The price is given to him; he may take it or leave it.

We know, of course, that (under given demand conditions) the market price will fall if more is offered for sale. The seller probably knows it too; but he does not imagine that it is *his* (relatively unimportant) supply that would depress the price. If nobody else tried to sell more at the same time, the price would probably not recede in spite of his sale; and if many others tried to sell more, the price would fall even if he refrained from selling. Hence he concludes that he cannot influence the price in the least. The price would be the same whether he sold little or much; in other words, the demand as seen by this individual seller would be "perfectly elastic." [8]

Horizontal Demand Curves

The elasticity of demand in the market for a commodity as estimated by a market expert or an econometrician, or merely imagined by an economist, is one thing. The elasticity of the demand for a single seller's products as estimated, imagined or expected by the individual seller and taken into consideration when he makes his decisions is another thing. The total market demand for the products of a whole industry is by no means the sum of the imagined demands for the products of the individual firms which compose the industry. It makes no sense to "add up" the imaginations or expectations that different sellers have concerning the possible

[8] The question arises whether this perfect elasticity of demand should be taken as the *criterion* or as the *consequence* of pure competition. Some writers appear to do the latter and to define this position in terms of its conditions, the large number of small sellers and the standardization of the commodity. But they fail to specify how large the number of sellers has to be, how small any single seller must be and what degree of homogeneity of the commodity is required. Instead, they state that the number must be *so* large, and each seller *so* small, and the commodity *so* little differentiated, that the single seller will not have any choice of price. This amounts to saying that the perfect elasticity of demand as seen by the seller is really the criterion. See Chapter 5 for further discussion of this criterion in the definition of pure polypoly.

doings of the buyers; the "sum" of these mutually incompatible expectations would certainly not show anything relevant to what the buyers actually would do. The sum of the demand curves (sales expectation curves) of all single sellers would not be the "actual" demand curve for the total product of the industry.

To make this clear let us assume that an observer estimates that 400,000,000 bushels of potatoes could be marketed at 60 cents a bushel (this is, then, one point on the "market demand curve"); let us assume further that there are some 400,000 farmers who grow potatoes and that there are no restrictions or regulations concerning their production; let us assume finally that farmer John Doe is just making up his mind about the planting of potatoes. If John Doe expects a potato price of 60 cents per bushel and considers whether he should arrange for an output of 1000 bushels or only 800 bushels or perhaps 1200 bushels, he can and will in all these cases calculate with the 60-cent price. That is, he will think of 800 bushels to be sold at 60 cents, or 1000 bushels at 60 cents, or 1200 bushels at 60 cents. The student of economics who has to picture John Doe's sales expectations by a "demand curve" will draw a horizontal straight line at the height where the scale of the ordinate (y-axis) reads "60 cents." And since all possible outputs of our farmer are considered saleable at this one price, the student will speak of an "infinite" elasticity of demand. But neither the student nor John Doe will expect that the price of 60 cents would be obtainable if all 400,000 farmers tried to sell 1200 bushels each. Indeed it is known that the market demand for potatoes is not very elastic, so that 480,000,000 bushels might be saleable only at a price of 40 or 45 cents.

Is it perhaps ignorance on the part of John Doe, our polypolistic seller of a standardized product, or is it stupidity, that makes him expect one and the same price for an output varying by some 40 percent? By no means. John Doe is not thinking of the total potato crop; he leaves this forecasting job to the market experts (who probably had some ideas about it when they advised Doe to calculate with a 60-cent price); Doe is thinking only about his own output, and he is perfectly right in his belief that 200 bushels up or down will not have any noticeable effect on the potato price. The notion here is that of the "demand as seen by the seller."

There is, by the way, an analogous problem of the "supply as seen by the buyer." Will consumer Mrs. Smith think that the potato price would rise should she decide to buy a larger quantity of potatoes? Indeed not. To her the supply of potatoes is perfectly elastic, although for the total market more potatoes might be available only at a higher price. But we must not linger over this analogy, since we are not now concerned with the state of mind of the buyer while we have so much more to say about the seller.[9]

Pure Competition and Its Synonyms

This particular (and probably rare) type of seller—the seller who feels that he can do absolutely nothing about the price but that he can sell any quantity he cares to sell at that price—occupies a prominent place in economic theory because of the important consequences of his state of mind. These consequences concern the volume of his production.

The determination of the output of the seller under "pure competition" will be discussed in more detail in the next chapter. At this point we note only briefly that, although the model of pure competition implies that output will be pushed up to the point where marginal cost is equal to the selling price, there is nothing in the concept that would lead to a determination of output at the so-called "lowest-cost level" and nothing that would lead to an elimination of abnormal profits. Another concept of competition will have to be introduced and employed in conjunction with the concept of pure competition if "optimum output" and "normal profit" are to be deduced.

A variety of terms, besides *pure competition,* have been suggested to denote the position of our "polypolist without a choice of prices." *Atomistic competition* is a very descriptive designation. *Perfect competition* is frequently used in the same connotation, but has been employed also with other meanings. This can result in ambiguities and misunderstandings if the reader is not sufficiently alert. Other terms synonymous with pure competition

[9] An appendix to this chapter deals with "Types of Competition in Buying." See below pp. 126–32.

are *homogeneous competition, polypoly of standardized products, undifferentiated polypoly,* or *perfect polypoly.*

The Polypolist with a Choice of Prices

We have seen that the polypolist with unlimited sales opportunities and without a choice of prices is a seller of standardized products. His products are in no respect different from those marketed by a large number of other sellers; the absence of any difference (in quality, appearance, service, convenience, etc.) explains the complete absence of the seller's choice of price.

If there are any differences in the product or service offered which allow the seller to believe that some of his buyers are attached or loyal to him or prefer him for any reason to other sellers of the "same" (read: similar) goods, the seller may have a choice of possible selling prices. For him the question is no longer "to sell or not to sell" at the one, given price, but rather "to sell more at a lower or less at a higher price." The seller may count on some of his customers staying with him if he raises his selling price. And he cannot hope to sell any quantity he cares to sell at a given price, but he will find instead that his sales are definitely limited and that an increase in sales is obtainable, if at all, only through price reductions or increased selling costs.[10]

If the number of sellers offering these similar goods or services is still so very large that the sellers are not concerned about one another's reactions, we must still speak of polypoly, but this time not of polypoly of standardized products but of differentiated products. Since the seller has a choice of prices and may, like a "monopolist," select the price at which he hopes profits will be greatest, his market position has been called one of *monopolistic competition.*

The range of prices within which a seller of this type can choose will often be rather narrow. The existence of a large number of other sellers who offer almost the same good or service may make the demand, as the individual seller faces it, very elastic.

---

[10] There may be cases, especially in retailing, where price reductions are forbidden by contract or by regulation. Then it is only through increased selling costs, if at all, that more business can be secured.

True, the slight difference between his particular service and that of the "competitors" would save him from losing, at a stroke, *all* customers, if he raises his prices; but he would expect to lose a good many. Thus, the demand as seen by this seller (though not perfectly elastic as it would be under pure competition) is still of high elasticity. But a generalization on this point is not permissible: there are probably positions of differentiated polypoly in which the price range within which the seller can choose is considerable.

The very large number of sellers in a market of slightly differentiated goods is apt to exclude—as in undifferentiated polypoly —any feeling of rivalry between the individual sellers. We have found that it is characteristic of polypoly that the share of each seller in the total market is so small that he does not expect that his output would "matter." While the polypolistic seller of the slightly differentiated good knows that the volume of his sales and the height of his prices are interdependent, he does not believe that his sales and his prices will substantially affect the business of the "competitors" (who are to him merely "other sellers"). Even if he secures more sales at the expense of other sellers, the latter will hardly notice it: there are too many.

This model of competition pictures the state of mind of a seller who believes that his sales can be expanded only at a lower price (or with higher selling costs), but does not believe that a reduced price (or increased sales effort) on his part will arouse particular reactions on the part of other sellers in the market. He thus feels that he has very many "competitors" from whom he might gain, or to whom he might lose, some business, but that he has no "rivals" whose reactions he would have to heed.

The terms employed to denote this concept are used, unfortunately, also for other concepts. *Monopolistic competition* has been used for competition among few sellers and is now most often employed in a wider sense to include both competition among sellers of differentiated products and competition in markets where sellers are few. *Imperfect competition*, sometimes reserved to indicate a sloping rather than horizontal demand curve, is often employed in a different sense with reference to factor mobility, entry into a field, super-normal profits. *Polypoly of differentiated products* is a combination of terms that has as yet escaped promiscuous usage. Atomistic-monopolistic competition and *atomistic hetero-poly* have been suggested; *differentiated polypoly, imperfect polypoly,* and *monopolistic polypoly* are other unambiguous designations.

Illustrations

It is often useful for analytical studies to construct models or "types" of men or of behavior even if such men or such behavior do not exist in reality in full likeness. However, the types of sellers as they have been described in this section, the polypolist of standardized products and the polypolist of differentiated products, do exist in reality, or are closely approached, though perhaps only rarely.

Examples of polypolies of standardized products are usually taken from agricultural markets. The production plans of farmers and their decisions to sell their produce are as a rule (except in cases of "organized marketing schemes" or other restriction plans) made without any idea of influencing the price or of choosing between several possible prices. When the farmer decides on how much wheat to grow or how much cotton to sell he does not "charge" a price, he does not lower or raise his price, but he simply figures on the basis of the price that he expects to rule or that is quoted or offered to him. This expected or quoted price holds good for any quantity which he may care to sell.

Examples of polypolies of differentiated products may be found in various retail trades in large cities. The big department stores, however, or some shops in particular districts do not belong in this category. They watch their rivals and know that they are watched by their rivals and, therefore, they heed well the possible reactions to their own moves before they make them. But there are, for instance, the tailors, the milliners, the dress repair shops, and other such businesses in densely populated districts of large cities. Each man's business is strictly limited, not by his decision to "produce" this and this much, but simply by his limited clientele. If he raised prices he would lose some business; if he lowered prices he would gain some business. But he would not think that his price policies would evoke important reactions on the part of his "competitors" or that such reactions need be taken into account.

It should be noted—and this refers not only to the types of seller just discussed but also to all types analysed later—that we may find several, different types in one man. A certain seller may be a polypolist in one respect and another type of seller in another respect. No single model can be expected to fit one man in all his activities; different situations and different actions of a person may require different models for their interpretation.

Tilted Demand Curves

The differences in product or service which help a seller to retain some of his customers at a higher selling price, and which prevent a seller from acquiring a deluge of customers upon the slightest price reduction, need not be conspicuous. The outside observer may fail to detect any difference, and even many customers may be absolutely indifferent to the alleged differences between the products and to the obvious differences between the sellers. It suffices that *some* customers have preferences for certain products or certain sellers, and that these preferences are of different intensities. Then a seller can expect that he will experience a merely gradual loss of sales or gradual gain of sales as he increases or reduces his selling price. The geometry-minded economist can then depict the sales expectations of the individual seller by saying that the demand as seen by the seller is represented by a sloping curve.

Again, as under perfect polypoly, the various demand curves as seen by the individual sellers must not be added together if one wishes to arrive at a total demand curve for the industry as a whole. The expectations of the individual sellers are incompatible with one another. The sales expectation curve of each single seller will usually be much more elastic than the total demand curve for the product of the industry. This is easily understood: the industry as a whole can at lower prices sell to customers who would not buy, or would not buy so much, at higher prices; each individual seller, however, can hope to acquire not only these sales which are "new" for the industry, but also sales he takes away from his competitors and which are thus not new sales from the point of view of the entire industry. Hence, the demand curve as seen by the seller is usually more elastic than the demand curve which the economist may conceive for the industry as a whole. Parenthetically it should be noted that, when the products of the "industry" are differentiated, it will sometimes make little or no sense to speak of a demand curve for the product of the industry as a whole, particularly when there are substantial price differentials between different qualities.

Limited Sales Opportunities for Differentiated Products

The differentiation of one seller's product from the products of other sellers may be the result of deliberate efforts on the part of the producers. Design, shape, color, wrappings, trade-marks, brands, and similar devices may create differences which would not exist otherwise, and advertising and sales talk may widen the gap between the thus differentiated products. The differentiation may lie merely in the service extended by the seller. Delivery, terms of credit, and other conveniences for the buyer, courtesy of the sales force or merely personal attractiveness of, or attachment to, the seller may make the differences that tilt the demand curve with which the seller is faced.

If the selling price is "given" to the seller (i.e., beyond his control) not by the anonymous forces of pure competition, but rather by convention, agreements, or enforcement,[11] the demand as seen by the seller may not be represented by a tilted curve but by a horizontal curve of definitely limited length. The retailer who sells an article with a fixed price (price cuts being prevented by sanctions on the part of the manufacturer or by provisions of some so-called "fair trade" legislation) will expect a certain amount of sales at the prescribed price and will not have any sales expectations at any other price, other prices being ruled out. The demand curve, horizontal up to the quantity which is expected to be sold, will at that point break off. If, however, more sales might be secured through additional selling costs (e.g., improvements in the store,

---

[11] Cases of this sort, however, are usually not polypolistic but rather oligopolistic, because the conventions or agreements in question ordinarily make the seller conscious of reactions, on the part of some competitors, to any contraventions on his part.

employment of a more expensive sales force, etc.) we could, in drawing our curves deduct the additional selling costs from the revenue which they secure and, thus, obtain again a sloping net demand curve, or more correctly, a sloping average net revenue curve (i.e., average revenue net of selling expenses).[12]

One of the most important differentiating factors lies neither in the quality or appearance of the product nor in the service of the seller, nor in the person of the seller, but in the distance from the consumer when the market is not centralized. If all sales take place in a centralized polypolistic market at prices f.o.b. market center, the different distances of producers from consumers will not differentiate sellers in the eyes of the buyers or *vice versa*. The transport cost from the producer to the market will be of concern to the producer only, the transport cost from the market to the consumer will be a matter for the consumer only. With prices set f.o.b. market the consumer will be indifferent to any particular seller—at least transport cost will not differentiate the sellers. In the absence of a centralized market, however, what would otherwise be perfect polypoly may easily become imperfect polypoly because the distance between producer and buyer may differentiate the otherwise identical products of different sellers.

Oligopoly

The Seller Conscious of Rivals' Reactions

Transport costs may not only differentiate the products of different sellers, but may break up a seemingly large market into regional markets shared by only a few sellers. This would make the sellers rival-conscious. They could not believe any longer that all of their actions (concerning selling prices, selling efforts, etc.,) would remain unnoticed and unopposed by the other sellers. Catering to a relatively limited market, each seller would know that any substantial gain of customers must imply a substantial loss to the few other sellers, and reactions on the part of the latter would be

[12] This is elaborated below in Chapter 6, pp. 189 ff. In this and other discussions I use the phrases demand curve, sales opportunity curve, or sales expectations curve to mean the curve of maximum average revenue that the seller expects to obtain for various amounts of output.

the natural thing to expect. If an action is expected to bring about reactions, these reactions and their consequences will obviously be among the things considered before the action is taken.

The model of the state of mind of such a rival-conscious seller is much more complicated than that of the polypolist, the seller heedless of rivals' reactions. Since fewness of sellers in the (partial) market is among the main causes of their rival-consciousness, this market position is called "competition among few sellers" or *oligopoly*. (In Greek "few" is *oligoi* and "to sell" is *polein*, hence oligopoly for the market position of "few sellers.")

Oligopoly has in common with polypoly of differentiated products that the seller may have a choice of prices (or average net revenues) at which he might sell his goods or services. The difference lies in the mental process of choosing the selling price. Sales expectations at the various possible prices are among the essential factors in the seller's decision. The character of these sales expectations is fundamentally different under oligopoly, on the one hand, and differentiated polypoly, on the other. Under the latter the reflection "How much more shall I be able to sell if I lower the price by five percent?" is concerned only with buyers' reactions. Under oligopoly the same reflection is concerned also with rivals' reactions: indeed, buyers' reactions cannot be guessed without a simultaneous guess with regard to the most probable reactions of rivals.

One-Way Demand Curves

The demand curve, the economist's device for dealing with sales expectations, becomes a very awkward thing to handle in the theory of oligopoly. It has, of course, nowhere been suggested that in actual fact sellers draw demand curves or think of demand curves. All that is assumed is that sellers, as a rule, think before they act; or at least, before they make changes in their policies; and demand curves are usually a handy method of picturing some of the sellers' thoughts.

This is certainly so with regard to the demand as seen by the seller under pure polypoly; there a horizontal line expresses conveniently the idea that the seller believes he could sell at one certain price regardless of the quantity that he considers selling. The tilted curve as a picture of the sales expectations of the polypolistic seller of differentiated products is already somewhat "forced," because it gives the impression of exactness where vagueness prevails in reality. A vague guess concerning sales possibilities at a few different prices is pictured as an exact curve running over a wide range of prices. Yet, this does not invalidate the results since it is principles and not concrete cases that are involved. The sloping demand curve under differentiated polypoly pictures the seller's thoughts about the behavior of his actual and potential customers. At lower prices our seller might sell more to his old customers and also attract new customers, drawing some of them away from other sellers; but who these other sellers were he would hardly know, and still less would he expect them to come back at him by one measure or another. The selling prices of the polypolist are supposed to influence only customers but not competitors.

The oligopolist, on the other hand, expects that his selling prices will also affect the policies of his rivals. In speculating by how much he might be able to increase his sales at a somewhat reduced price (or by increased selling efforts) he asks himself first whether, when, and to what extent his rivals would follow suit (or retaliate by other methods). How many new customers can be attracted (and old customers retained) depends then not merely on the reduced price of our oligopolist but on the combined influence of all price changes (the primary, i.e., his own, plus the induced, i.e., his rivals' price changes). Indeed, if rivals were apt to slash their selling prices more radically than the seller who started to cut, the price reduction might bring him not increased but diminished sales.

All this does not yet impair the usefulness of demand curves for picturing the combined effect of price changes on possible sales. If the prices charged by the rivals were a definite function of our seller's prices and if his sales were a function of both, our seller's sales could still be expressed as a function of his own selling prices. The multiplied vagueness and uncertainty of the seller's expectations need not cause additional difficulties. True, the seller may float in a sea of doubt as to whether the rivals would meet his price cut in full or only by two-thirds or only by one-half; and this may, of course, widen the range of his estimates and guesses regarding potential sales. Yet there will probably be one (perhaps conservative) estimate or guess on which the considerations and final decisions of the oligopolist will be based—and this is what the student of economics (theoretically) plots as a point on the "demand curve."

The real difficulty lies in the fact that some of these demand curves (more than under other market positions) are good only for one-way considerations: the expected reactions of rivals to a price rise from $4.75 to $4.99 may be totally different from what they might be to a price cut from $4.99 to $4.75. The rivals may, for instance, be expected to follow suit in the case of a price cut, but to stay put in the case of a price advance. This would have to be pictured either by two different one-way curves or by one demand curve with a sharp corner at the point at which the seller happens to stand and from which two one-way courses start: a flat up-hill walk and a steep down-hill fall.[13]

This, of course, is only one of many possibilities and should not be taken as the "typical" situation prevailing under oligopoly. Especially in the rather frequent cases of "organized" or "cooperative" oligopoly—where understandings among the sellers make the "guessing" of the competitors' behavior very simple—the situation will be altogether different. In these cases a rival-conscious seller, if he should ever be out of step with the others, will be concerned chiefly about their possible retaliations for his uncooperative conduct.

The consequences of the peculiar psychology of the rival-conscious seller for his price and output policies will be dealt with in several chapters entirely devoted to a discussion of oligopoly.

To Watch and To Be Watched

The rival-consciousness which was found to be the criterion of oligopoly implies not merely the seller's awareness of the existence of rivals or his adjustment to their actions. Also the polypolist

[13] See the note by Paul M. Sweezy, "Demand under Conditions of Oligopoly," *The Journal of Political Economy*, Vol. XLVII (1939), pp. 568–73.

of differentiated products is fully aware that he has competitors and he will probably look around to find out what prices they charge and what selling policies they employ. Only if he does this will he reach a sound judgment about his own sales possibilities at various prices and under various policies. But that he watches the others does not imply that he is conscious of being watched by them and of having to watch his step because of possible counter-moves.

The difference between watching and being watched or, still better, between watching-the-others and watching-oneself-be-cause-of-one's-being-watched-by-others, should be clear. It is only with the latter that the model of the oligopolistic seller is con-cerned. Situations which appear oligopolistic at first sight may on closer inspection be found to be polypolistic. This may be the case in some instances of price-leadership. Small firms may watch the leader and orient their prices to those of the leader, but they need not in all cases think that their own actions will arouse any reac-tions on the part of the leader or on the part of the other "followers." Their actions are then most appropriately explained by the model of polypoly. The reasoning of the leading firm may also in some exceptional cases be similar to that of a monopolistic polypolist. If there are, however, two or three leading firms in the industry, their situation becomes clearly oligopolistic with regard to the in-terrelationship of their policies.

It is possible that firms during the course of the business cycle move back and forth between positions of polypoly and oligopoly with regard to one and the same product. The shifts in the demand for their product in relation to their existing productive capacity may make them act polypolistically (i.e., unconcerned about rivals' reactions) at one time and oligopolistically at another. It is even conceivable that they are polypolists in their short-run considera-tions and oligopolists in their long-run considerations (i.e., in their expansion and investment plans).

Many, Few, Two, One

We started our classification of market positions of sellers with the position of the seller who felt that he was only one among very many sellers: *polypoly*. There we distinguished the seller with unlimited sales opportunities but no choice of prices—the perfect polypolist—from the seller who had a choice of possible prices but was limited in his sales outlets—the monopolistic polypolist (or polypolist of differentiated products). We proceeded then to the position of the seller who felt that he was one among few; few enough to make him concerned about reactions to which rivals might be induced by his actions. This position, *oligopoly*, includes, of course, the case of two rivals: *duopoly*.

It would seem reasonable to discuss now the position of the seller who feels that he is the only one in the market: the position of *monopoly*. Yet, we are not fully equipped for such a discussion before we have dealt with quite a different concept of competition: the concept of "easy entry" into the industry. This "competition from newcomers," as I like to call it, has important implications for all possible market positions, especially oligopoly and monopoly.

PLIOPOLY

Many Sellers and More Sellers

The idea of easy entry into an industry presupposes that the concept of an industry makes sense. Since some deny that it does, we shall later (Chapter 7) take the time to justify the use of the concept and explain its meaning and significance in the analysis of our problems. At this point, however, we must merely warn against mistaking the concept of an industry as a theoretical model for price analysis with the statistical concept of an industry defined by technological criteria as used, for example, in connection with an index of concentration. For our present purposes the concept of the industry comprises all firms whose operations affect one another's selling opportunities and sales revenues so definitely that we must not neglect taking account of them.

Competition in the sense of easy entry into the industry and competition in the sense of many sellers in the industry are frequently confused with each other, or are even confounded. This is understandable; where there are *many* sellers already, why should there not easily be *more* sellers when profits lure? In actual practice easy entry into a trade and large numbers in the trade go well together. It may seem strange to think of a polypolistic industry into which entry is not free. But even if a *large* number of sellers and an *augmentable* number of sellers seem to be closely associated in reality—although exceptions can be found—logically the two things are completely divorced from each other. And, as will be seen, the concepts of polypoly and of easy entry are very different in nature.

The criterion of polypoly is not simply "large numbers" but it is, instead, a state of mind and a type of behavior usually associated with large numbers of sellers in a market. Polypoly is present if the sellers have certain ideas concerning their position in the market and concerning the saleability of their goods. Thus a subjective attitude or way of thinking of certain individuals is the essence of the concept of polypoly.

Easy entry, on the other hand, is a probability concept, which is primarily in the mind of the outside observer, although it may also become an expectation of the sellers themselves. It interests us first in its objective aspect.[14] The observer, *viz.*, the economist, asks himself what probability there is of more producers entering an industry where profits have increased. The judgment of the economist concerning the degree of this "competition from newcomers" is based not on his observation of the existing sellers in the industry but on his belief that others are likely to hear about, and be attracted by, the handsome profits made in the industry; and on his judgment that the setting up of new establishments in the industry can be achieved without too many obstacles and without too much delay. The objective probability (i.e., in the judg-

[14] The problem of subjective vs. objective judgments is not simple. A sensible distinction between "subjective" and "objective" for purposes of this analysis can be made by distinguishing between the status of the person making a judgment. The judgment of the seller or any other acting person who is the *subject* of the economist's observation is always "subjective," whereas the judgment of the observing economist may be called "objective" as long as he is a disinterested ("scientific") *observer* only. Subjectivity and objectivity in this sense have nothing to do with the smaller or greater probability of the judgment being "correct."

ment of disinterested observers) of some firms entering a certain field is the essence of this type of competition.[15]

Competition in this sense of a ready and unhampered movement of entrepreneurial resources in the direction of highest prices and profits has sometimes been termed *free competition,* sometimes *perfect competition.* Both these terms are also used with different meanings. Free competition often refers to freedom from state intervention; perfect competition is often used as a synonym for perfect polypoly. Attempts to reserve "perfect competition" as designation for the phenomenon of the ready inflow of firms into profitable industries have not been successful; the terminological confusion has persisted.[16] Obviously the solution is to coin a new

[15] This concept is "subjectivized" as soon as the probable appearance of newcomers becomes a consideration of a seller operating in an industry. We shall see later that such subjective expectations of "new" competition are of significance in the theories of oligopoly and imperfect monopoly.

[16] Edward H. Chamberlin in *The Theory of Monopolistic Competition* (Cambridge: Harvard University Press, 1931) wants *pure* competition to denote the conditions of many sellers offering a homogeneous product, while *perfect* competition should be "concerned with other matters as well: mobility of resources, perfect knowledge, etc." (p. 25). On the other hand, according to Joan Robinson's *Economics of Imperfect Competition* (London: Macmillan, 1932), *perfect* competition "prevails when the demand for the output of each producer is perfectly elastic" (p. 18) without regard to mobility of resources and possibilities of entry into the industry. At one place, for example, she deals with the case of "a perfectly competitive industry into which firms do not enter in response to abnormal profits" (p. 289). Inconsistently, however, she states at another place that "under competition average cost is equal to price" (p. 144). For Nicholas Kaldor, *free* competition denotes "freedom of entry into a trade or industry," while *perfect* competition is characterized by the horizontal demand curve for the single firm. "Market Imperfection and Excess Capacity," *Economica,* New Series, Vol. II (1935), p. 34. Frank H. Knight, in a very different type of analysis, expands his concept of *perfect* competition to comprise perfect knowledge, including knowledge of the future without any uncertainties. *Risk, Uncertainty and Profit* (New York: Houghton, Mifflin, 1921), Chaps. III and VI.

The college textbooks, likewise, follow different practices. George J. Stigler lists three conditions as constituting *perfect* competition: smallness of the economic units, absence of restraints, and complete knowledge. *The Theory of Price* (New York: Macmillan, 1946), p. 21. According to Kenneth E. Boulding, the assumptions of *perfect* competition are "many firms," "perfect markets" and "free entry," with the perfect markets characterized by perfectly elastic demand curves for the individual firms. *Economic Analysis* (New York: Harper, 1941), pp. 410–13. Albert L. Meyers follows Chamberlin in denoting the conditions resulting in perfect elasticity of

word.[17] In order to contrast the notion of *more* sellers entering the market with the notion of *many* sellers in the market, the term *pliopoly* might serve. (In Greek "more" is *plio[n]*, "to sell" is *polein*, hence *pliopoly* for the ready appearance of "more sellers" in the market.) The expression *newcomers' competition* may be used as an equivalent for the new term.[18]

Contrasting the Logical Nature of the Concepts

The different logical nature of the two concepts of competition, polypoly and pliopoly, can be further elucidated.

(1) The economist who states that polypoly exists in a cer-

---

demand (as seen by the individual seller) by the term *pure* competition, while a "perfect market" is something else, which together with free mobility of the factors of production makes for *perfect* competition. *Modern Economics, Elements and Problems* (New York: Prentice-Hall, 1941), pp. 109 and 127. Lorie Tarshis, on the other hand, follows Mrs. Robinson in that he uses the term *perfect* competition for the conditions resulting in infinite elasticity of the average revenue curve. *The Elements of Economics* (Boston: Houghton Mifflin, 1947), p. 136. To Frederic Benham *perfect* competition is the same thing as to Mrs. Robinson, but the "perfect market" is something else; it means availability of complete information on prices and price offers and the possibility that any buyer can deal with any seller, and *vice versa*. *Economics* (London: Pitman, 1938), pp. 25 and 206.

[17] It is with serious apprehension that I suggest the use of a newly coined word. I am fully aware that the majority of readers dislike the practice of coining new words for old concepts. At an open hearing in a Congressional committee the following remarks were made after terms like oligopoly, monopsony and others had been explained:

The Chairman (Senator O'Mahoney): I am inclined to think that it is an unfair competitive practice so far as the understanding of economics is concerned. It is designed on the part of the economist to exclude the common people like myself from understanding what we are talking about.

Mr. Frank: As I understand it, Mr. Chairman, that is frequently the function of economists. They vie with lawyers in that respect.

The Chairman: Using language to conceal thought.

Investigation of Concentration of Economic Power, Hearings before the Temporary National Economic Committee, Part 5 (Washington: 1939), p. 1742.

I plead not guilty on the charge of wishing to conceal thought. My objective is to have a word which can identify a thought and distinguish it clearly from other thoughts. If people have been using one term ("competition" or "perfect competition") to denote four or five different things, there is only one way out of the confusion: to give them new names.

[18] See, however, below, p. 131.

tain industry believes that a certain state of mind exists on the part of all or most sellers in the industry; polypoly is the observing economist's picture of a type of (sales) *expectations of the (observed) sellers* in the industry. The economist who states that pliopoly exists in a certain industry expects that more people will join the industry if profits are high; pliopoly is here essentially an *expectation of the (observing) economist.*

(2) The economist who states that polypoly exists in an industry is concerned with *certain* people (however anonymous), namely, all or the majority of the sellers in the industry; the economist expects almost *everyone* of them to behave in a certain way. The economist who states that pliopoly exists in an industry is concerned not with certain people, but with quite *unknown and undefined ones,* namely some few enterprising men or firms who may become newcomers to the industry; the economist expects *some* people (but by no means everybody), hitherto outside the industry, to behave in a certain way.

(3) The economist who states that polypoly exists in an industry thinks of a situation which is present at any *moment of time* and explains everyday actions of the sellers. The economist who states that pliopoly exists in an industry thinks of a process which he expects to take place in the *course of time* and which would explain a future situation at the completion of the process. (Polypoly has thus meaning in both the short and the long run; pliopoly essentially in the long run.)

(4) The economist who states that polypoly exists in an industry relates the conditions expressed by this term to the analysis of the *equilibrium of the individual firm,* that is, to an analysis dealing chiefly with variations in size and output volume of an individual member of the industry. The economist who states that pliopoly exists in an industry relates the conditions expressed by this term to the analysis of the *equilibrium of the industry,* that is, to an analysis dealing chiefly with variations in profits and in the number of firms in the industry.

(5) The statement that polypoly exists in an industry may, conceivably at least, be subject to *immediate empirical verification.* One can, for example, imagine that all sellers in the industry are asked, and reliable reports are obtained, about the character

of their price and sales expectations, about their feelings toward "competitors," and about their influence upon the competitors' policies. No immediate empirical verification is conceivable concerning the statement that pliopoly exists in an industry. If higher selling prices or lower costs increase the profit margin in an industry, the facts which constitute pliopoly or "newcomers' competition" will not be observable before a *considerable period of time* will have passed. It may take years before newcomers will have sufficiently spoiled the good business in the industry.

Pre-Conditions of Newcomers' Competition

A statement about the existence of pliopoly in an industry is really a *forecast* to the effect that any higher profit margins which may arise would soon disappear because of the emergence of new firms in the industry. Forecasts are usually based on the observation of certain things or circumstances which are considered the necessary and sufficient condition for the predicted events. What are the necessary conditions of pliopoly?

Knowledge of the high profits which can be made in the industry must spread to those outside. (The spreading of such knowledge will frequently be due to officers and employees of the unusually prosperous firms.) Some of the people or firms who obtain the knowledge of the unusually fine prospects must possess the courage and versatility to turn to a field which might be entirely foreign to them. (It may again be with the help of former employees of existing firms that the new firms overcome the obstacles connected with a lack of specialized experience.) Specialized equipment, tools, materials, skills, and the use of the production processes must be available to the new firms without excessive cost. (Licence fees, rentals, or royalties for patented machinery or protected processes, refused access to necessary materials or means of transportation, etc., may well prevent new producers from starting business in the lucrative industry.) Plants, machines, tools and organization must be sufficiently divisible to permit modest additions to the productive capacity of the industry with modest initial investments. (If only large production units are economical and if the initial investment is large, prospects will appear doubtful or, at least, too uncertain.) Money capital needed for the new enterprises must be available at normal cost. (This may not be the case if the initial investment is large or if the risk estimates of investors are exaggerated or if the capital market is closely controlled by opponents of the new ventures.) State interference against new competition in the industry must be absent. (In many countries and fields the authorities try to prevent "overcrowding" or pretend to "protect" the public from "incompetent" or "undesirable elements" by setting up all kinds of barriers against newcomers.) Threat and any sort of restraint by those in the field against would-be intruders must be absent. (The threat of cutthroat competition or of violent actions may help to keep new competitors out.) There are probably other things the presence or absence of which are among the necessary conditions for pliopoly. Each of the conditions may be necessary while none by itself is sufficient; all of them have to be satisfied or pliopoly will not be "perfect."

This very cursory review of the conditions of pliopoly must have convinced us that there is nothing absolute about the whole matter. Spreading information about the high profits was mentioned as the first condition; how long must there have been higher profits for people to gain the impression that an industry is particularly promising? how long until the information reaches the right people? The same question arises with respect to all other conditions: the advent of the enterprising spirits, the raising of the necessary funds, the overcoming of resistance and red tape, the building up of the production apparatus, etc.; how much time may all this take? From the rise of the profit margins in the industry to the opening of the business by the new firms, time must undoubtedly elapse; but how much time may elapse under perfect pliopoly? Where does perfect newcomers' competition end and imperfect newcomers' competition begin? Is one year, a year and a half, two years the "right" time to allow for overcoming the "frictions" if pliopoly is to be regarded as perfect? Or is it three months for hot-dog stands but three years for airplane factories?

The forecasts involved in statements about the existence of pliopoly display, thus, not only the usual vagueness of all predictions and the added vagueness of predictions in the social sciences but the third-degree vagueness which is connected with an absence of any conventional standard of comparison. Even if there were full agreement about the predicted facts (for instance, that high profits in necktie making would be wiped out within a year because of new firms taking up that line) there would still remain the open question whether or not the case deserved to be called one of perfect pliopoly.

Entrance and Exit

Whereas "perfect competition" is often understood to refer to both easy entry into and easy withdrawal from the industry, the term pliopoly refers to entry only. The reason for a conceptual separation of the ease of inflow and the ease of outflow of entrepreneurial resources lies in the lack of correlation between the two movements. In many cases entry of new firms into an industry may be easy (hence, pliopoly present) whereas the disappearance of firms from the industry may be difficult and slow. In other cases the situation may be the opposite.

Pliopoly may be absent or very imperfect whereas withdrawal from the industry may be achieved without delay in some trades where admission is artificially restricted but investment is relatively small or resources relatively versatile. A modest sunk investment may be readily relinquished, or nonspecialized machines and skills quickly transferred to other fields, when profits fall below normal. State interference or barriers set up by the industry may, however, prevent new firms from entering when supernormal profits would attract them.

More frequent, it seems, is the combination of easy entry with slow exodus. That machinery and other durable equipment is constructed more rapidly than it is used up is probably the most important reason for this "one-sided perfect competition." The difference between construction period and utilization period may, thus, account for the fact that supernormal profits often have a shorter life than subnormal profits. Pliopoly wipes out the former. But whereas more sellers may come in thick and fast when business is good, the reduction of the number of sellers in bad times and, hence, the restoration of normal profits in an ailing industry may be a slow (and painful) process.

It should be noted that easy withdrawal of capital from industries is by no means a necessary condition for the existence of pliopoly. Even if no "new" money capital were available and the funds sought for a profitable field must first be withdrawn from other industries, slow amortization would not necessarily impede the financing of the new firms or the new ventures of firms hitherto outside the industry. If no very large initial investment is required, the capital could readily be furnished out of the vast sum of replacement funds currently liquidated in the economy as a whole even if the flow of replacement funds in each single industry were thin and slow.

The concepts of pliopoly and of profit are logical correlatives. It will depend on the profit concept employed whether one prefers to say that pliopoly tends to wipe out "supernormal" profits or that it tends to cause "zero" profits. An analysis of these problems with a brief discussion of the theory of profit will be attempted in Chapter 7. Only this much should be stressed in this preview: while statements concerning output, marginal cost, and price are linked with the concepts of polypoly, oligopoly and monopoly, statements concerning profit, average cost, and price are linked with the concept of pliopoly.

The Seller Conscious of Potential Newcomers

The probability of new firms entering a profitable industry may become a consideration for the firms operating in the industry and may motivate them in their actions concerning production, prices, and sales. This is surely not possible in the case of polypoly. Where there are so many sellers that the single seller is not concerned about how his existing competitors react to his doings, he would not be much concerned about potential new competitors. Of course, the sellers in almost all industries complain that the field is overcrowded; they may try to dissuade would-be newcomers from entering; and they may call for concerted action to keep would-be newcomers out of the industry. But the price, production and selling policies of any one seller would not be influenced by the thought of potential new competition. What could he do single-handed? He is too unimportant a part of the market for his actions to have any substantial effect.

But in the case of oligopoly the thought of newcomers' competition may affect the policies of the rival firms. The oligopolist would then not only consider reactions of existing rivals but also the probability of attracting new rivals. The latter consideration, however, would be of substantial influence only if sellers were *very* few. Only if the single seller has a substantial share of the market will it pay him to forego present profits in order to diminish the attractiveness of his trade to possible newcomers and thus to maintain his "control."

If the seller has almost full control of his market, that is to say, if he does not think of anybody as a rival, then he may be seriously concerned about preserving his position by reducing the lure which his profitable industry may have to outsiders. The policy of a monopolist may be greatly influenced by any pliopolistic possibilities that might exist.

Monopoly

That pliopolistic possibilities are rather remote, if not entirely absent, is one of the characteristics of a monopoly position. Absence of oligopoly is another characteristic; and absence of polypoly is a third.

Where the appearance of rivals is a possibility that cannot be disregarded, one may speak of imperfect monopoly. Where pliopoly is entirely absent, monopoly can be perfect.[19]

The implications of the triple criterion of monopoly—absence of polypoly as well as of oligopoly and pliopoly—seem rather ob-

[19] When I attempt here to construct a model of a "monopoly position" and of a perfect or imperfect "monopolist" I am using these words in a much narrower sense than I have done elsewhere, and especially in my book on *The Political Economy of Monopoly*. There I spoke of "monopolistic" and of "monopoly power," or of the "degree of monopoly," in a sense which included everything that was not pure and perfect competition. The "degree of monopoly" (in that general sense, e.g., measured by any sorts of cost-price gaps) may in the case of an oligopolist be much greater than the "degree of monopoly" in the case of a "perfect monopolist" (in the sense of the present analysis).

vious. Absence of polypoly and oligopoly means that the seller is the only one in the market; absence of pliopoly means that he is likely to remain the only one. (In Greek "alone" is *monos*, "to sell" is *polein*, hence, *monopoly* for the position of the seller who is the only one in the market.) But we shall presently find that not only the application of the model but even the testing of its logical consistency is beset with difficulties.

The Seller Without Competitor

Absence of oligopoly is common to the position of the monopolist and the polypolist. Each feels that he does not have to worry about the sellers' reactions to his own actions, though for different reasons: the polypolist is unconcerned about rivals because he has too many, the monopolist because he has not any.

This sounds simple as long as we have the statistical industry concept in the back of our minds. But we have to disown it for purposes of price theory because it would make the market position of a firm depend on the way the Census Bureau chooses to classify firms and delimit industries. A firm may be the only seller in the "industry" as long as a narrow classification is used; it may be one of hundreds of firms in the "industry" according to a wider classification. The industry concept in price theory, to be sure, is also arbitrary, but the arbitrariness is designed to fit the theoretical problem involved: an attempt is made to group together for particular problems those firms whose selling opportunities and sales revenues are so interdependent that they must not be neglected when the effects of price, output and investment decisions are analysed (either by a firm or by an outside observer). To apply this industry concept consistently is difficult because it constantly runs counter to deeply ingrained habits of thought.

A firm may be the only producer of a certain commodity in the customary sense of the word and yet be very much aware of the competition of substitute products offered by other firms in the same market (i.e., to the same group of buyers). For example, we can imagine that a sole producer of aluminum regards the copper cartel as a close competitor whose reactions to his own price policy he must anticipate. If so, the model of oligopoly, rather than that of monopoly, will fit the case. Or, we may imagine that there is only one producer of margarine in the country or in the world; yet he cannot fail to be aware of the most direct substitutability between his product and the products of thousands of producers of other fats, oils, and butter. There is no good reason for regarding him as a monopolist; he should be regarded as an oligopolist if he considers some particular producers his direct rivals, or as a monopolistic polypolist if he sees them as an anonymous group of direct competitors. The monopolistic polypolist does not know from which particular seller he will "steal" business if he reduces his prices or increases his selling efforts; he merely knows the group of sellers at whose expense he can gain, i.e., the "industry." The monopolist, however, does not know even that much. He knows that he will gain (lose) trade at lower (higher) prices or with increased (reduced) selling efforts, but he cannot identify the group of sellers from (to) whom he will gain (lose) it.

Let us try to put the distinction into a generalized form. If the demand for any particular seller's product is of an elasticity greater than zero, this can be attributed to substitution between this product and others. If the substitutability is particularly great between his product and the products of a small number of identifiable rival producers, he will be in the position of oligopoly. If the substitutability is particularly great between his product and the products sold by many other producers who can be identified only as a group, we call the group an industry and our seller a polypolist. If no particularly marked substitutability between a seller's product and other products is obvious (to the seller, perhaps also to the observer), if, instead, the substitutability is so widely dispersed over goods and services "in general" that one will not find it worth while to single out any of them as close substitutes, then we can say that our seller has no competitor, that he is a monopolist. In brief, a monopolist is a seller who competes for the consumer's dollar but does not know either the individuals or the products that he competes with.

The Demand Curve for the Monopolist's Product

One may be inclined to assume that the demand as seen by a monopolist will be less elastic than the demand as seen by a monopolistic polypolist. This, however, is not necessary. At the output volumes and selling prices chosen by sellers who try to maximize their profits, the elasticity of demand will always be greater than unity, and there is no reason why, at the "optimum point" chosen by the seller, the elasticity should be greater under monopolistic polypoly than under monopoly. There may, however, be a difference in the length of the range of outputs for which the demand is relatively elastic. The fact that there are many other sellers offering close substitutes implies the existence of a large potential clientele for the monopolistic polypolist. Relatively modest price changes may succeed in switching this clientele to and from the particular seller. There may be no such large potential clientele for the monopolist. The range for which the demand remains relatively elastic in response to price reductions may therefore be considerably shorter in the demand curve for the monopolist's product.

The same thought may be expressed in terms of the range of selling prices among which the seller can choose. There is a presumption that the possible price range in which the monopolistic polypolist may move is smaller than that of the monopolist. This does not mean that the monopolist will *want* to use the wider leeway that he has for experimenting with higher and lower prices; indeed, he may find price reductions less attractive than the polypolist. It merely means that the demand curve is likely to cover a wider price range in a shorter range of alternative volumes of output.

All this, however, is very speculative and the presumptive differences in the sales opportunities must not be taken as distinguishing features between monopoly and monopolistic polypoly. We shall find such a distinguishing feature in the seller's attitude toward newcomers' competition.

No Entry

That the monopolist can keep his prices above average cost and reap his profits undisturbed from intruders is the third characteristic of his position. This absence or remoteness of pliopoly may have a variety of causes and it is worth examining whether the barriers against newcomers are "natural" or "artificial," permanent or temporary, inevitable or removable. This will be discussed partly in Chapter 8, dealing with pliopoly, and partly in Chapter 17, dealing with monopoly.

Since the monopolist has no competitor, pliopoly—the emergence of one or more competitors, that is, of sellers offering direct substitutes for his product—would transform the monopolist into an oligopolist. Recalling that the existence of pliopoly is primarily a judgment of the economist, but may sometimes be an important consideration of a firm, we shall find it necessary to discuss whether our criterion, absence of pliopoly, means that the economist believes a particular seller is relatively safe from intruders or whether it means that the seller thinks so himself. This question becomes relevant in instances in which the probability of competition from newcomers is "misjudged" by the seller.

In the analysis of imperfect monopoly—that is, of monopoly situations in which the appearance of competitors is a possibility that cannot be disregarded—we shall have occasion to wonder whether a valid distinction can be made between an oligopolist, concerned with existing rivals, and an imperfect monopolist, concerned with potential rivals. We shall find that the difference is sufficiently great to warrant the distinction.

The seller's ideas about the possible consequences of pliopolistic developments can, incidentally, serve as a test for the distinction between polypoly and monopoly. The entrance of another firm into the same "industry" would probably leave a polypoly situation unchanged from the point of view of the old firms, whereas the appearance of a competitor would put an end to a monopoly situation. Let a seller who is unconcerned about reactions and retaliations of other sellers—and who for that reason might be a polypolist or a monopolist—picture for himself what it would mean to him if another firm started offering a substitute of the product that he sells. The polypolist would, of course, not be enthusiastic about the prospect of further "overcrowding" of his field, but he would not single-handedly make sacrifices to prevent it. The monopolist, on the other hand, would be willing to make considerable sacrifices if this could keep out the would-be intruder. Thus *the attitude toward a potential newcomer can distinguish monopoly from monopolistic polypoly.*

Perfect Market

The confounding of different ideas in one concept often acts as an obstacle to clear thinking. If certain notions are different and independent, it is bad practice to call them by the same name or regard them as integral parts of one concept. The logical divorce of polypoly from pliopoly, which we pronounced earlier, should help matters considerably. But still another divorce is called for. The notion of the "perfect market" should be separated from those of perfect polypoly and perfect pliopoly.[20]

Perfection of a Market

While perfect polypoly refers essentially to the individual seller—the *firm*—and perfect pliopoly to a group of sellers—the *industry*—, perfection of the market refers to the interactions within a group of sellers and buyers—the *market*. Perfection of the market is some quality of the mechanics or organization of the

[20] The present confusion is partly conceptual—mixing up different and independent abstractions in one compound but vague concept regardless of how it is named—and partly merely terminological—inconsistent use of terms for different concepts by different authors or even at different places in one work. Here is a sample of the terminological situation concerning the perfect market. Arthur Robert Burns, in *The Decline of Competition* (New York: McGraw-Hill, 1936), uses the term *perfect market* to denote infinite elasticity of the demand for the product of a firm, although he sometimes uses the term "perfect competition" interchangeably with it. Likewise, Boulding sees the criterion of a *perfect market* in the perfect elasticity of the "individual demand curve" for the firm, but this "perfect market" is seen as one of three conditions of "perfect competition"; yet at other places he says perfect competition when he means nothing more than that the demand curve is horizontal (*op. cit.*, pp. 410–12). This horizontality condition is termed "pure competition" by Chamberlin, who however states that there may be pure competition on an *imperfect market*. As an illustration he refers to the wheat market and the individual wheat farmer, and states: "The market, though a very imperfect one, is purely competitive" (*op. cit.*, p. 6). The "imperfection" of this market for Chamberlin lies in the imperfect knowledge of the future on the part of sellers and buyers of wheat, which results in serious deviations of the "actual price of wheat" from its "normal price." To most other authors the wheat market is one of the examples of a *perfect market* because of its organization which secures a maximum of intercommunication and mobility, resulting in simultaneous uniformity and intertemporal flexibility of prices.

The confusion has been repeatedly protested, but thus far to no avail.

market. There are several qualities of a market which may deserve to be isolated as useful abstractions for the theoretical description of the market mechanism. Not all of these may turn out to be sufficiently clear for purposes of analysis. Five such concepts will be listed here as possible candidates for the award of the term "perfect market." [21]

The first two of the five concepts of a perfect market are defined by certain *effects* which it is supposed to accomplish, the other three by certain *conditions* which are supposed to be essential for its functioning. [22]

Concept A. A perfect market is one that secures (i) uniformity and (ii) flexibility of price. (i) A standardized commodity (i.e., one of which any specimen is perfectly substitutable for any other specimen) cannot be sold at different prices at the same time, but must sell at a uniform price (subject to differentials for transportation costs to different parts of the market). (ii) This uniform price must sensitively reflect any changes in market demand and supply.

Concept B. A perfect market is one that secures prompt attainment of equilibrium of supply and demand, so that effective

---

Henry L. Moore said that ". . . confusion exists in current economics" when ". . . perfect competition is confused with a perfect market." Henry L. Moore, "Paradoxes of Competition," *Quarterly Journal of Economics,* Vol. XX (1906), p. 215. Among the few who carefully distinguished between *perfect competition* and *perfect market* was Joseph A. Schumpeter, *Business Cycles* (New York: McGraw-Hill, 1939), pp. 46 and 60.

[21] It is not attempted here to prescribe to others how they should use certain terms. Freedom of choice should not exclude free choice of words and terms. But one may appropriately plead that wasteful uses of terms be avoided if some significant concepts are thereby deprived of any name at all. If an author has found a term to denote, for example, the position of the individual seller whose sales curve is perfectly elastic, why should he assign a second term—"perfect market"—to the same concept while several other concepts concerning certain qualities of a market are in want of terms by which to call them?

[22] Even if perfection is described in terms of conditions, that is, in terms of the organization and mechanics of the market, rather than in terms of the results produced by the operation of these conditions, there is an implicit assumption that certain results will be produced. If we were to find out that the conditions described are not sufficient to produce these results, we would probably restate the conditions to make them adequate for the task. As a rule it is nevertheless preferable to take the conditions rather than the results as criteria of the definitions.

supply will be completely cleared and no effective demand will be left unsatisfied. A situation in which the quantity for sale at the actual price exceeds or falls short of the quantity demanded at that price cannot endure in a perfect market. The price in such a market must change until it accomplishes equality of quantity supplied and quantity demanded. The quantity sold is, of course, always (by logical necessity) identical with the quantity bought, since every sale is also a purchase. But the quantity which people *wanted* to sell at the price at which actual sales took place is not always equal to the quantity which people *wanted* to buy at that price. Such an inequality constitutes "market disequilibrium" and, in a perfect market, equilibrium will be promptly restored through changes of the market price: an excess demand will be eliminated through a price increase, an excess supply through a price decline.

Concept C. A perfect market is one in which three institutional conditions are fulfilled, conditions which pertain to (i) knowledge, (ii) accessibility, and (iii) absence of restrictions. Expressed in briefest form, (i) all buyers and sellers have complete knowledge of prices and price offers, (ii) every buyer may buy from any seller, and every seller may sell to any buyer, and (iii) no restrictions are imposed upon sellers or buyers as to the prices which they may accept or as to quantities for which they may contract.[23]

Concept D. A perfect market is one in which the three basic requirements listed in Concept C are satisfied and, in addition, no individual seller or buyer is big enough to exert any perceptible influence upon the market, i.e., upon other sellers or buyers.

Concept E. A perfect market is one in which all conditions of Concepts C and D are fulfilled and, in addition, every individual seller or buyer acts on the assumption that he can sell or buy at the market price any quantity he cares to sell or buy, respectively. That is to say, every seller regards his own selling possibilities, and every buyer regards his buying possibilities, as infinitely elastic.

[23] In addition to the three institutional conditions the general condition of economic motivation of the parties concerned must be fulfilled: it must be assumed that sellers prefer to make more money rather than less and that buyers prefer to get more for their money rather than less.

Comparison of the Concepts

There is no difference between Concepts A and B if price flexibility is defined by "prompt attainment of equilibrium between supply and demand." If flexibility is defined by other characteristics, A need not be the same as B.

It is apparent that some of the five concepts relate only to homogeneous or, at least, exactly specified commodities. Otherwise there would be no sense in talking about price uniformity in Concept A and no possibility of having perfect elasticities of demand or supply for every seller or buyer, respectively, in Concept E. As we formulated Concept B it would also be confined to a standardized commodity. For with differentiated products it is difficult to attach unambiguous meaning to the concept of "effective supply," and the postulate that sellers can sell all they want to sell at the actual prices would not be realized. Only with some strain could Concept B be so reformulated that it would fit also a market in which the commodity is traded in different, though highly substitutable, qualities, shapes, brands, etc.

The other two concepts, however, are not limited to standardized commodities. According to Concept C the organization and mechanics of the market must permit a potential seller (1) to know what prices are being paid or offered, (2) to have access to any buyers who offer these prices and to find them as willing to buy from him as from any other source, and (3) to ask or accept any price he wishes to ask or accept, and to dispose of any quantities of his goods or services that he wishes to dispose of at the prices he can obtain. Conversely, a potential buyer must be able (1) to know what prices are being accepted or asked, (2) to have access to any sellers who ask these prices and to find them as willing to sell to him as to any other buyer, and (3) to offer or pay any price he wishes to offer or pay, and to acquire any quantities that he wishes to acquire at the prices at which he can get them.

Knowledge

The "knowledge" necessary for market perfection in this sense is by no means knowledge of the demand and supply schedules either of the total market or of any buyers and sellers dealing in the market. All that is necessary is that the buyers and sellers know of all transactions actually taking place and of all current "asked or bid" quotations.[24] It is not necessary that anybody knows what quantities the market would provide or absorb at different prices. Still less is perfect knowledge of the future—perfect foresight—required for the perfection of the market. Perfect foresight without any uncertainty would be necessary only for that much more comprehensive state of perfect competition which would eliminate any possibility of profits in a changing economy.[25] The perfect market for a specified service or product is a much less ambitious concept and, accordingly, the "knowledge" required for it is a very limited one: of prices accepted, offered, and asked.

Accessibility

The "access" necessary for market perfection is not the access of all firms to all means of production, or the access of all owners of productive factors to all fields of occupation or employment, or even the easy entry of newcomers into a particular trade or industry. All these are conditions essential for certain types of competition, but not for the model of a "perfect market" for a particular service or product. Free access of everyone to everything is an assumption relevant to the general equilibrium of the *economy as a whole*. Free entry of productive resources and entrepreneurship into a particular industry is an assumption relevant to the equilibrium of that *industry*. But for the equilibrium of a particular "perfect" *market* all that is needed is access of buyers and sellers to one another. Exaggerations in enumerating the conditions necessary for the analysis of a particular problem are just as misleading as are omissions from such an enumeration.

[24] "Every potential buyer of a good constantly knows and chooses among the offers of all potential sellers, and conversely." Frank H. Knight, *op. cit.*, p. 78. "All buyers and sellers are in full communication with each other, so as to constitute really one market." Edward H. Chamberlin, *op. cit.*, p. 31.

[25] See below, Chapter 7, pp. 228–31.

Absence of Restrictions

In a perfect market there must not be any restrictions concerning the quantities which sellers may sell or buyers may buy, or concerning the prices which they may agree to accept or to pay. In a perfect market any disequilibrium must lead instantaneously to a change of price, and only price variations are supposed to restore equilibrium. Whenever any part of the supply cannot be disposed of at a certain price, sellers must be permitted to ask, and buyers must be permitted to pay, lower prices. Whenever any demand is left unsatisfied at a certain price, buyers must be permitted to offer, and sellers must be permitted to accept, higher prices. Restrictions on price movements may sabotage their equilibrating function in the market. Absence of price restrictions is therefore a necessary condition for the existence of a perfect market.

Where price restrictions are imposed by the government it is easy to see how they may create a market disequilibrium and/or obstruct the attainment of equilibrium in a market in which an excess demand or excess supply appears. The same interference with the market mechanism can be seen where price restrictions are imposed upon members of a trade or industry by some self-government established in their field—cartels, associations, unions, code authorities, etc. The question becomes delicate when price restrictions are self-imposed in the sense that a would-be seller for some reasons resolves to resist temptations to reduce his price offer, or a would-be buyer resolves to resist temptations to raise his price bids, even if abiding by such resolutions should make it impossible for them to sell or to buy, respectively, as much as they would like to. Will such self-imposed restrictions interfere with the "equilibration" of the market? What is the difference between self-imposed price limits and the "ordinary" willingness and unwillingness of a buyer or seller to go above or below certain prices?

Reservation Prices

The existence of "reservation prices" on the part of buyers and sellers is usually not regarded as an imperfection of the market.

A potential seller may resolve: "I shall not sell below this price, but will hold out until I can get at least this much." A potential buyer may resolve: "I shall not pay more than that price even if I have to go without the commodity." Should such reservations be considered incompatible with a "perfect market"? The answer to this question is significant because on it may depend the possibility of divorcing the concept of the market mechanism from any concept involving the conduct of individual sellers and buyers.

One may be inclined to make a distinction on the basis of the purposes of the reservation prices. Where the motive is to exert an influence upon the market, and where there is power to exert such an influence, the existence of reservation prices may be regarded as inconsistent with the notion of a perfect market. This would be so according to Concept D, which requires that no individual seller or buyer be able to influence the market. But if one is concerned with the mere mechanics of the market and thinks of its "perfection" according to Concept C, the existence of influential sellers or buyers need not make the market imperfect.

This is not acceptable without qualifications. While Concept C of a perfect market allows self-imposed price reservations even of influential sellers or buyers, and while Concept D allows self-imposed price reservations of sellers or buyers provided none of them can individually exert influence upon the market, neither concept takes account of the possibility of "uniform price reservations" of large groups of small sellers or buyers. Such *uniformity of reservation prices* can hardly be the consequence of independent tastes and preferences of individuals, or of independent cost calculations of individual business firms. On the other hand, they need not be the result of a "rule" imposed by an outside power or a collective body regulating the market conduct of its members. They may be the result of recommendations by some agency, of generally adopted codes of behavior, or of strict adherence to customary practice. In any event, such uniformity of reservation prices is the equivalent of imposed price restrictions and incompatible with a perfect market under any definition.

The Comparison of the Concepts Resumed

It is now possible to resume the comparison of the concepts of a perfect market, and to appraise their usefulness. The concepts defined by "effects accomplished" are less useful than the concepts defined by "conditions satisfied." Of the latter concepts, E is the narrowest because it requires besides the institutional conditions of Concept C that every seller is a perfect polypolist and every buyer a perfect polypsonist.[26] Concept D is not quite so narrow. It still calls for polypoly and polypsony, but there may be differentiation among the various sellers or the various buyers so that they will not regard their individual selling or buying opportunities as infinitely elastic. Concept C is not concerned with the positions individual sellers or buyers enjoy in the market, but is confined to the mechanics of the market.

Any one of these three concepts has its use and, hence, we need names for all three. If there is only one term—"perfect market"—available, it would be best to employ it for the concept with the smallest number of criteria and to use supplementary terms to denote the other concepts which require more conditions. The "perfect market" would thus be the one defined by Concept C. Concept D would be called a perfect market in which all sellers are polypolists and all buyers polypsonists. Concept E would be called a perfect market with perfect polypoly and polypsony.

The selection of Concept C as the one to which the name "perfect market" is given has the advantage that the institutional conditions of market organization are conceptually separated from the characterization of the positions of individual sellers and buyers in the market. This permits several combinations and permutations of different assumptions. For example, even a market in which all sellers are oligopolists will function differently according to the degree of its perfection in terms of knowledge, accessibility, and absence of imposed restrictions. Thus, according to this termino-

---

[26] Polypsony prevails if a buyer believes that his purchasing policy will not produce any reactions on the part of other buyers. Pure polypsony prevails if the buyer assumes that he will be able to purchase at a given price any quantity that he may care to purchase.

logy, there could be oligopoly on a perfect market.[27] By contra-distinction, there could be perfect polypoly of the sellers in a market made imperfect through specific restrictions. Likewise, existence, absence, or imperfection of pliopoly in an industry may be entirely independent of the perfection or imperfection of the market in which its products are sold.

SUMMARY

I cannot claim that all analytically significant types of competition in selling have been reviewed in this chapter. If any interesting market position or market conduct cannot be explained or interpreted with any of the models constructed so far, new models are needed. It is not surprising that in an ever-changing economy models which have been constructed for the explanation of older forms of competition may not fit the newer forms; nor is it surprising that, as we find out more about the facts in certain markets or industries, we may discover that some old models have really never fitted the phenomena they should explain.

The last twenty years have seen several successful efforts to construct new models for the explanation of market behavior. Some results of these studies have been embodied in our survey and an attempt has been made to disentangle mixed concepts and to isolate their diverse elements. The following notions of "competition" were distinguished: competition between goods irrespective of the sellers' actions or positions (substitution); competition between sellers, each acting to increase the attractiveness of his own offerings or to detract from the offerings of others (positive and negative competitive actions); competition as the existence of alternatives for the buyer in selecting his suppliers (buyers' choice among sources of supply); competition as a state of mind of a relatively small seller surrounded by very many others (polypoly); competition as the position of a seller with practically unlimited selling opportunities and no choice of selling prices

[27] This conforms to Schumpeter's terminology. He discussed the case where "supply in a perfect market . . . is controlled by firms that are in a position to influence . . . price by their individual action," and specifically mentioned oligopolists and duopolists selling in a perfect market. *Op. cit.*, p. 60.

(perfect polypoly); competition as the position of a relatively small seller among very many sellers of slightly differentiated products (imperfect or differentiated polypoly); competition between a few sellers conscious of each other's reactions (oligopoly); competition from newcomers entering an attractive field (pliopoly); competition for the consumer's dollar, undisturbed from particular rivals or groups of competitors (monopoly); competition as the condition for the equilibrating price mechanism in an organized market (market perfection).

Different Classifications

These various concepts (types, models) may be classified according to several different principles. If one wishes to classify according to the point of view from which the concepts have meaning, those which depict certain states of mind of *sellers* might be separated from those which refer to opinions of *buyers* and from those which refer to judgments of the disinterested *observer*. The concepts of competition which refer to the sellers' position in the market have sometimes been separated into *pure competition* on the one hand and *non-pure competition* on the other hand; this would make standardized polypoly stand alone in its class and would contrast it with another class containing differentiated polypoly, oligopoly and monopoly. A classification of sellers' positions which I once suggested [28] contrasted *sellers conscious of their rivals' reactions* with *sellers heedless of rivals' reactions*. This distinction put oligopoly (and duopoly) with standardized or differentiated products into one class, and polypoly (both standardized or differentiated) and monopoly into the other class. The choice between different classifications, emphasizing one distinguishing idea or another, will be dictated by the particular problems one sets out to analyse. If no analysis is intended, one classification is probably as good as any other.

[28] Fritz Machlup, "Monopoly and Competition: A Classification of Market Positions," *American Economic Review*, Vol. XXVII (1937), pp. 445–51.

Types of Competition in Buying

Polypsony: Perfect Polypsony · Imperfect Polypsony
Oligopsony: The Supply as Seen by the Rival-Conscious Buyer · Illustrations
Pliopsony: The Profitable Industry
Monopsony: Three Criteria · Each Firm Deals in Many Markets

VARIOUS MODELS OR types of competition in selling which were developed in the preceding chapter will be further elaborated in the subsequent chapters and put to work in an analysis of the conduct of business firms and of processes in industry. Almost all the types of competition in selling discussed have their counterparts in analogous types of *competition in buying.*[1] These types or models should be briefly surveyed here in order to make sure that we shall not encounter terminological or conceptual trouble when the occasion arises to make use of them.

POLYPSONY

What polypoly is in selling, *polypsony* is in buying. Literally it stands for the market position of one of "many buyers."[2]

---

[1] Since labor services are among the most important objects of purchase by business firms, we must keep in mind that "buying" stands also for "hiring." It also stands for "leasing."

[2] To denote the position of the sole buyer in a market Mrs. Joan Robinson coined the word *monopsony.* Unfortunately her advisers on the Greek language sold her a word—*psonein*—which in classic Greek means not "buying" in general, but "buying fish" or other edibles for sale on the fish market. (In modern Greek the fishy connotation is no longer attached to the word.) Mrs. Robinson's terminological suggestion was quickly adopted by professional economists, and the word monopsony has become the accepted term for the position of a sole buyer. The word polypsony was then the logical term to denote the position of one of many buyers.

[126]

Polypsony is the state of mind (or expectations) of a buyer who is convinced of his own unimportance in the market for the commodity or service that he demands and who is, therefore, unconcerned about reactions of competing buyers to his own actions. There are so many buyers in the market and he constitutes such a small share of the total demand that, in his opinion, no one of the other buyers would feel any tangible effects of his actions. Thus the polypsonist does not anticipate any reactions from other buyers.

We can distinguish between perfect and imperfect (or differentiated) polypsony. The former implies unlimited buying opportunities at a given price; the latter, limited buying opportunities with a choice of buying prices or of other terms and conditions.

Perfect Polypsony

Under perfect polypsony the seller feels that he has absolutely no influence upon the price at which he can buy and that he can buy at that price as much as he wishes. If he offered a lower price, he would not be able to obtain any of the good or service he wants. On the other hand, he would not have any commercial reason for paying a higher price, since he can buy all he wants to buy at the given price.

The criterion of perfect polypsony is that the supply to the individual buyer—the supply as seen by the buyer—is perfectly elastic. The meaning of this horizontal supply curve is that the buyer could buy small or large amounts but could not expect to affect thereby the price that he has to pay. He feels a complete lack of influence upon the price for two reasons. First, the buyer knows that his demand represents only an exceedingly small part of the total market demand (so that changes in his own demand would not matter). Second, the buyer knows he is to the sellers neither better nor worse than any other buyer, and has nothing to offer that would differentiate him from other buyers (so that he could not obtain any of the supply if he offered less than "the" price).

Alternative terms used for perfect polypsony are "pure competition in buying" or "perfect competition in buying."

Imperfect Polypsony

If there are any differences between buyers causing sellers to prefer some buyers to others, the buyers cannot be perfect polypsonists. A differentiated polypsonist need not fear that he would be without any supply if he offered a slightly lower price. He expects he can still find sellers willing to sell to him even at a reduced price. On the other hand, he cannot expect to be able to buy practically unlimited amounts of the good or service at a given price. He finds his possible purchases definitely limited and can obtain increased supplies, if at all, only at higher prices or through other attractions.

This buyer is still a polypsonist as long as he does not expect that his purchases or price bids will seriously affect other buyers and cause them to "come back" at him. But this buyer, being differentiated from others in the sellers' opinion, may have a choice of buying prices and may be able, like a monopsonist, to select the price he considers best for his business. For this reason, the market position of this buyer has been called *monopsonistic competition.* But in order to make sure that this position is clearly distinguished from that in which a small number of buyers, conscious of potential reactions of rival buyers, devise their strategic buying policies, the terms *differentiated polypsony* or *imperfect polypsony* are preferable.

The monopsonistic element in the polypsonistic position lies in the fact that the supply of the good or service in question to the individual buyer is not infinitely elastic, or at least not over the entire relevant range. This need not always mean that the supply curve to the firm slopes upwards, indicating that higher prices have to be paid if larger amounts are to be obtained. There may be restrictions upon price, preventing the buyer from attempting to procure increased amounts by paying higher prices. In other words, the supply curve to the firm may be horizontal over some range—too narrow a range for the appetite of the firm— and then break off. Where price competition for a "scarce" good or service is ruled out, there may be competition through other attractions—for example, in the case of labor, competition through better working conditions. If this additional buying cost is added to the price paid, a rising average factor-cost curve (supply curve) may picture the situation even in instances where the price itself is fixed.

Oligopsony

Where buyers are few, they will be conscious of the effects of their buying policies upon one another and of the possible reactions to any changes in their buying policy. The position of the buyer concerned about his rivals' reactions to his own actions is called *oligopsony*. This model includes, of course, the situation involving only two competing buyers: *duopsony*.

The Supply as Seen by the Rival-Conscious Buyer

The supply curve depicting the buying opportunities of the individual buyer will not reveal whether he is a differentiated polypsonist or an oligopsonist. In both situations the curve will be either rising or horizontal but too short. Only the state of mind of the two types of buyer distinguishes them. If before offering or agreeing to pay a higher price a buyer feels he should consider the possible reactions of other buyers, his conduct is that of an oligopsonist. In deciding whether an increase in the price he pays for a good or service would procure him an increase in the amount that he can obtain, he first asks himself whether other buyers will also offer higher prices (or "retaliate" in any other way) or whether they will not make any changes in their buying policies. It is possible that an oligopsonist has different expectations regarding the reactions of rival buyers to price increases, on the one hand, and to price reductions, on the other. Such a situation can be pictured by conspicuous discontinuities in the slope of the supply curve to the oligopsonist and may have strange effects upon his policies.

Some distinctions between various forms of oligopsony should be made. Oligopsony may be unorganized—with the buyers engaging in guessing games, bluffing games, or even price wars—or cooperative—with understandings among the allegedly competing buyers.

Illustrations

Illustrations of oligopsonistic situations will be found chiefly in raw materials markets—tobacco leaves, for example—and in labor markets. In the latter, the analysis becomes especially difficult if the oligopsonists are "opposed" by a monopolist: a strong labor union.[3]

PLIOPSONY

The term *pliopsony* may be used to denote the presence of a high probability that more buyers of particular means of production will readily appear on the scene when an "industry"—a group of firms—that uses these means of production becomes especially profitable. Where the "industry" happens to be the same group of firms in the analysis of selling and in the analysis of buying, the emergence of "more sellers" (of a product) is identical with the emergence of "more buyers" (of a means of production). As a rule, however, the delimitation of the "industry" will have to be very different for the analysis of different problems. It is most unlikely that the group of firms which we can expediently call "industry" and isolate from the rest of the economy when we discuss the production, sale, and price of a particular *product* should be the same as the group of firms which we call "industry" when we discuss the employment, purchase, and price of a particular *means of production*.[4] Hence, although both pliopoly and pliopsony relate to the ease of entry into an "industry," the word industry will usually refer to different groups of firms, neither of which may tally with any Census classification.

The Profitable Industry

Pliopsony—the ready appearance of *more* buyers—is independent of polypsony—the position of one of *many* buyers. The exist-

[3] On the legitimacy of speaking of labor monopolies and on the economic effects of monopolistic and monopsonistic wage determination see my book on *The Political Economy of Monopoly*, Chapters 9 and 10.

[4] These statements, which to some readers may sound rather obscure at this point, will be further elaborated in a section on the concept of the "industry" in Chapter 7 dealing with "Pliopoly."

ence of the one does not imply the existence of the other. For example, a group of firms may act, not as polypsonists, but rather as oligopsonists and yet the conditions may be such that new firms will readily take up businesses using the same materials or services whenever such use appears extraordinarily profitable. On the other hand, there may be many buyers, each of them acting as a polypsonist, and yet some barrier may exist which prevents the entry of new buyers of the materials or services in question.

The concept of pliopsony, just as that of pliopoly, is closely linked with the concept of profit. The only difference is that "profit" refers to the production and sale of a certain product when we speak of pliopoly, while it refers to the purchase and use of a certain means of production when we speak of pliopsony.

The pre-conditions of pliopsony are practically the same as those of pliopoly. And there is also the same lack of conventional standards concerning the length of time within which under perfect pliopsony the profits in the "industry" must be wiped out.

There are no alternative terms which denote exactly the same thing that pliopsony is designed to denote. *Easy entry* as well as *newcomers' competition* adequately describe the general idea without, however, distinguishing between the buying and selling ends of the business. There are problems (regional wage differentials, for example) for which pliopsony refers to an altogether different group of firms than pliopoly.

MONOPSONY

"Monopsonistic," as an adjective, modifies nouns that denote positions other than monopsony itself. It means that there is "something pertaining to monopsony" involved in competition or in polypsony—and this "something" is usually the possibility of choosing among different buying policies. *Monopsony* itself may mean more than merely that.

Three Criteria

We make the definition of monopsony analogous to that of monopoly by selecting as its criteria (1) absence of polypsony,

(2) absence of oligopsony, and (3) absence of pliopsony. The first two criteria mean that the firm acts as the only buyer in the market; the third criterion means that the firm is likely to remain the only buyer in the market even if it is in the enviable position of making supernormal profits.

Each Firm Deals in Many Markets

It is important to understand that a firm may enjoy a monopoly position without having a monopsony position with respect to any of the things or services that it buys. Conversely, a firm may enjoy a monopsony position without having a monopoly position with respect to any of its products. Moreover, a firm may at one and the same time be in very different market positions with regard to the different things or services that it buys. It may be a perfect polypsonist with regard to one raw material, an oligopsonist with regard to another, a differentiated polypsonist with regard to one type of labor and a monopsonist with regard to another. Any number of combinations of these situations is possible. After all, the firm deals in as many different "markets" as there are things or services that it buys and products that it sells. And there is little reason why its position in these different markets should be the same.

PART II—MANY SELLERS

CHAPTER 5

Perfect and Imperfect Polypoly

The Characteristics of Polypoly: The Criteria · Three Reminders

Perfect Polypoly: The Volume of Output under Perfect Polypoly · Two Problems: Subjectivity and Time · The Volume of Output and the Size of the Firm · The Size of the Firm under Perfect Polypoly

Imperfect Polypoly: The Volume of Output under Imperfect Polypoly · Restricted Production · The Size of the Firm under Imperfect Polypoly

Transport Costs: Differentiation through Transport Costs · Centralized Market · Location and Competitive Position · Transport Cost and Plant Size

CLASSIFICATIONS SOMETIMES serve no other purpose than that of storing away an accumulated mass of knowledge in some orderly fashion. There may not be much substantive meaning in those classifications. Other classifications, however, are designed to aid in the analysis of the classified material. Our classification of market positions is meant to be one of the latter sort. The distinction between polypoly, oligopoly, monopoly, and pliopoly is not suggested for decorative purposes or as a mere plaything or in sheer pedantry. I believe that this set of models helps in explaining things—such as changes in production volumes, selling prices, product qualities, plant capacities, profit rates. The present chapter and the next will be devoted to the analysis of polypoly.

THE CHARACTERISTICS OF POLYPOLY

Polypoly is the market position of a seller who is unconcerned about any competitors' reactions to his own actions, ordinarily because he thinks there are so many other sellers in the market, and his own share is relatively so small, that none of the others would feel any effects of what he could do.

The Criteria

If polypoly were defined simply as "a market of many sellers" some insoluble problems would be encountered. What is a market and what is the relevant extension of the market? Is the street, the district, the region, the country, or the world the relevant market area? Is the market confined to one perfectly homogeneous product or do "similar" (how similar?) products belong to the same market? How much is "many"? Where does "a few" end and "many" begin? Are 75 sellers few or many sellers?

If the statement were made that where sellers are many they will act without much rival-consciousness, one would have the choice of recognizing such a statement either as false in the majority of cases or as true by definition. The statement would be false in the majority of cases if we took "market" and "commodity" in the every-day meaning of the words and made "many" start arbitrarily at one hundred or any such number. For there is little doubt that one could find plenty of rival-consciousness among these "many sellers in one market." On the other hand, the statement would be of little use for an analysis of actual cases if we regarded it as true by definition. This could easily be done by declaring that in all cases where rival-consciousness is found sellers must not be called many and that the result of counting a large number was erroneous because of a failure to break market or commodity down into sufficiently narrow entities. (There may be 300 drug stores in the city but only four drug stores on the corners of Main and North Streets; the storekeepers are conscious of each other's reactions; hence, there are only a few in "the market.")

This sophistry is avoided if polypoly is defined as the market position (or the state of mind) of sellers who know that they have competitors, but, in making up their minds about changing their selling or production policies, do not ponder over what their competitors' reactions might be. Wherever polypoly exists it will *most likely* be the result of a large number of sellers offering the same or very similar service. For only when the seller can believe that the other sellers will not seriously feel the effects of his actions will he be able to expect that they will not react to them. Thus, one may appropriately say that polypoly is usually due to a large number of sellers, whereas it is not appropriate to turn the statement around and say that a large number of sellers results in polypoly or, indeed, constitutes polypoly. In other words, a large number of sellers is, with few exceptions,[1] a necessary but not a sufficient condition of polypoly.

The only sure way of finding out whether or not polypoly is present in a given trade or industry is to interview the sellers. Of course, there may be sufficient clues in the situation to convince us, without much questioning, that a certain trade is polypolistic. (We have not canvassed the farmers or the tailors of our illustration in Chapter 4; but one can put oneself in their situation and then analyse one's state of mind.)[2] The clues will as a rule be concerned with the number of sellers sharing some more or less limited market or sub-market. But incidental circumstances may be important. To give an example, it is quite likely that women's specialty shops with prices shown in their windows are oligopolistic while similar upper-floor shops may be polypolistic. The less conspicuous the competitive action and the less apparent the incidence of its effects (that is to say, the more difficult it is to identify the competitors who may lose by the action) the more likely will the case be one of polypoly.

Three Reminders

A recapitulation of a few points may help to avoid misunderstandings about the characteristics of polypoly. (1) It is not the large number of sellers *per se* that is a criterion of polypoly; the

---

[1] An exception, for instance, is the case of gold production under a gold standard. Since the monetary authorities provide an infinitely elastic demand for gold, the position of the gold producers would be the same as under pure polypoly even if there were only a few sellers of gold. We shall take this up under the heading of "quasi-perfect polypolies."

[2] The applicability of this method, which might be called "imagined introspection"—an essential feature of what is called "Verstehen" in German sociology—is confined to the social sciences. Marschak made the excellent statement that "it would be a pity if we should not avail ourselves of that type of hypothesis provided by our insight—however imperfect or ambiguous—in the behavior of our fellow-men. This is our only advantage against those who study genes or electrons: they are not themselves genes or electrons." Jacob Marschak, "A Discussion on Methods in Economics," *Journal of Political Economy*, Vol. XLIX (1941), p. 445.

criterion is a certain state of mind of sellers, which is frequently *due* to the presence of a large number of sellers. (2) To describe polypoly as competition without rival-consciousness might be going too far, because consciousness of the existence of rivals and their actions is fully compatible with polypolistic behavior; only the concern about rivals' *re*actions is ruled out. The seller who watches the rival may still be a polypolist; only if he were self-conscious because he thought himself watched would he be an oligopolist. (3) That the seller must be an exceedingly small part of the market, too insignificant to influence the price, is not a requirement of polypoly; all he needs to have is the feeling that he is too insignificant to affect substantially the business of others.

The last of these three points was made in order to emphasize that the concept of polypoly comprises "competition" in standardized as well as in differentiated products, but excludes oligopolistic competition. There is, of course, the important distinction between the polypolist who has practically unlimited selling opportunities with no choice of price, and the polypolist who offers a differentiated product and thus is limited in his sales opportunities, opportunities which may involve a choice of several possible prices, qualities, varieties, or sales techniques. The consequences that the two types of polypolistic thinking are likely to have for volume of output, size of establishment, and other matters will now be analysed.

PERFECT POLYPOLY

Perfect or undifferentiated polypoly is the position of a seller who feels that he can do nothing about the price, but that he can sell any quantity he cares to sell at that price.

The Volume of Output under Perfect Polypoly

If a seller of this type wants to make as much money as his business can bring, he will push his production up to a volume where the expense of a *further* increase in output would exceed the selling price. Since he expects that he *can* sell at the given price any quantity he cares to sell, he *will* care to produce and to sell any quantities whose additional costs of production and handling would be below the price.

The accepted technical language for this situation is that the marginal revenue equals the selling price (because total proceeds are increased by an amount equal to the selling price of the additional unit of output); and since the highest possible profit is obtained at the volume of output where marginal cost is equal to marginal revenue (because at smaller output volumes additional cost would still be below additional revenue, and profit, therefore, not yet maximized), the firm seeking to maximize profit will push its output up to the point where marginal cost is equal to selling price (or below it by the smallest possible margin).

Those who like to express such propositions in a shorter way by using symbols may say this: With P standing for selling price, MR for marginal revenue, and MC for marginal cost, we can deduce that

(1) if the seller wants maximum profit, he must produce an output whose $MC = MR$;

(2) if he sells under perfect polypoly, his $MR = P$; hence,

(3) he will produce an output whose $MC = P$.

The conclusion that the seller will produce an output whose $MC = P$, must not be understood to mean that he makes his price equal to marginal cost, as is sometimes foolishly said. Under perfect polypoly the seller cannot set a price; he can only accept a price and decide on the output which he will produce. By varying the output, he makes his marginal cost equal to price.

That marginal cost is equal to price indicates nothing about the relation between average cost and price and, hence, nothing about the amount of profit. To say that the output is produced at which profits are greatest is not to imply that profits are high or even positive, nor that profits are "normal." There is nothing in the concept of perfect polypoly that would rule out abnormal profits, and nothing that would require a determination of output at the so-called "lowest-cost level." The only thing necessarily implied in the concept is that the chosen outputs cannot lie in a range in which marginal costs are falling, because if it is at all profitable to produce, it would then always be more profitable to produce more. Hence, the chosen output must lie in a range in which marginal costs are rising. Since there is by definition no limit to the saleability of output, the fact that *some* volume of output is being chosen (in preference to a still larger one) can be explained only by a limit set through increasing marginal costs: to produce more would not pay, because the additional costs would exceed the selling price of the increased output.

The maximum profit which the polypolistic producer of standardized products (just as any other producer) tries to make need not be made by producing the output that could be produced with the lowest average unit cost. If the market price rises, a larger output will be produced at a higher cost and with a higher profit. It is an entirely different type of competition—pliopoly—which operates against higher profits. Perfect polypoly and pliopoly together tend to ensure production at the lowest possible average cost. But this cannot be discussed until later. (Chapter 9.)

Two Problems: Subjectivity and Time

The adjustment of output to achieve equalization of marginal cost to selling price involves two problems which we have discussed earlier: first, the subjectivity of cost and price and, second, the time element in the adjustment of output.

The marginal cost is an expected cost, and the price is an expected price. How long into the future the expectations reach will depend on the problem in question—for example, on whether the adjustment involves only an increase of production with given equipment or also an increase in productive capacity—and on environmental and personal factors. While the subjective character of the demand curve has often been stressed with regard to the monopolistic seller, the "given price" (that is, the horizontal demand curve) under perfect polypoly is in principle no less subjective. This "given" selling price need not be the one that has been established in the market (and can be recorded by the observer) although, of course, experience with past prices of the product will usually determine what future price can be expected.

When market prices have been fairly stable or when they have been oscillating consistently around some "normal," then the expected price will probably be the same as that stable or normal price. After irregular fluctuations of the market price, however, one cannot tell what price will be expected by the producer. He may expect the last price to continue or he may expect the "trend" of price change to continue or he may expect the "trend" of price change to reverse itself. He will, necessarily, calculate with *some* price, though perhaps only vaguely and with a wide safety margin; but *which* price forms the basis of his calculation is not any "objective" datum which the observer can find in any records.

We need not add here to what was said in Chapter 2 about the subjectivity of the relevant cost and price data, or about the time-range of these expectations. But there is also another sort of time coefficient inherent in our problem: the reaction time of the producers. When experiences of some sort cause a change in the producer's cost or price expectations, the "equilibrium of the firm" is, at that moment, disturbed: marginal cost is not equal to marginal revenue, and a change in the production plan is required in order to adapt it to the changed situation. Adjustments take time. It takes time to "wake up" and start adjusting; it takes time to make "provisional" adjustments; it takes still more time to complete final adjustments.

To realize the time element in the adjustment of production plans is to realize that the propositions about "output determination" are not mere tautologies—which must be "true" at any moment of time—but that they are statements of probable tendencies in the real world, provided there are in the real world producers approximately corresponding to the types and models that we construct.

The Volume of Output and the Size of the Firm

What is the mechanism by which an increase in the market demand for a commodity brings about an increase in the output produced by existing firms in the industry? The first reaction in the market is, under perfect polypoly, a rise in the price of the product. The higher price will be an inducement to step up production on the part of those producers who (1) know about the price rise, (2) expect the higher price still to prevail when an increased output would be ready for sale, and (3) think they can increase output at a marginal cost fully covered by the increased price. When the higher price is not expected to last long, and if output is produced only in large "lots" or a larger output cannot be produced with the given equipment—that is, "in the short run" [3]—the firm will not increase its production. But these (rare) obstacles to increased output in the short run are not likely to be effective in the long run, that is, with plant and equipment adequately adjusted.

The adjustment of fixed productive equipment to the production of larger outputs will be undertaken only if the producer believes the higher price will be lasting. For only then could he calculate that an investment in plant expansion would pay. Naturally, long-run marginal cost is relevant for adjustments of this sort. The expansion of the productive facilities of a firm may mean *larger plants* or *more plants,* depending on technological and organizational conditions. In either case will the size of the firm be increased.[4]

It is obvious that small outputs are more economically produced by small firms, and large outputs by large firms. If for each possible volume of output the relatively most suitable size of the "firm" is chosen, it is probable that there is one certain volume of output for which the unit cost of production will be lowest. This would be the "optimum output" produced in the firm of "optimum size." It is, however, quite possible that the unit cost of production will be the same for many different scales of production. We should then have

[3] The reader who is versed in the geometry of value theory will observe that the cost condition mentioned in the text would be represented by a short-run marginal cost curve that rises in steps rather than continuously or even one that rises vertically, the absolute limit of plant capacity having been reached (i.e., the elasticity of short-run supply having become zero).

[4] It is well to remember that the firm in this context is only a model of an economic unit of control engaged in the production of "the" product (or set of joint products) whose price and output is analysed. Thus, when we speak of the size of the firm being adjusted to a price increase of the product we must not make the mistake of thinking of the large diversified corporations we "see" in the real world and which control the production of hundreds of products in dozens of establishments. They have attained their size, not in adjusting to the cost and demand conditions of given products, but by expanding into ever new lines, chiefly, in adjusting to the management's propensity to grow. In other words, the firm in the models of price theory must not be confused with the firm in the models of growth theory. (I am indebted to Edith T. Penrose, whose analysis of the growth of the firm demonstrated to me the need for this warning.)

a range of *constant* long-run costs of the individual firm and, consequently, an *optimum range* of sizes of the firm or of scales of production. Very small outputs can probably not be produced at low unit cost, owing to the fact that some instruments of production are "indivisible" (i.e., not available in smaller sizes at proportionately smaller cost); and sometimes very large outputs cannot be produced by the firm at low cost owing to diseconomies of large-scale production.

The Size of the Firm under Perfect Polypoly

Does the concept of perfect polypoly imply anything concerning the size of the firm? The concept does rule out the choice of uneconomically small sizes.[5] Since the firm under perfect polypoly is, by definition, not limited regarding the saleability of its products at the given price, there would be no reason for building and operating an "undersized" plant if a larger one could secure lower costs. Unless the firm is limited as to the availability of investment funds —limitations which might again be expressed in rising cost curves —there is no reason why the firm should not expand up to (or beyond) the point where further expansions would result in higher unit cost.

On the other hand, there is nothing in the concept of perfect polypoly inconsistent with the growth of a firm beyond the optimum size or beyond the range of optimum sizes. If high selling prices (that is, selling prices which are expected to remain high over a long period) make it profitable to increase output, capacity may be expanded beyond the optimum size just as output with given capacity may be stepped up beyond the optimum volume. It is another type of competition, pliopoly, which in conjunction with perfect polypoly operates against oversized firms. But, again, this is reserved for later discussion.[6]

But although perfect polypoly and *oversized* firms are not in-

[5] Yet there may exist at any time "uneconomically small" *plants* which were built in the past, and "uneconomically small" *firms* which have been slow in their adjustment.

[6] One ought to guard against possible confusions between the size of the plant and the size of the firm. Large plants call for large firms, but large firms are possible without large plants.

compatible, perfect polypoly and *large* firms are in a sense incompatible. This apparent paradox resolves itself when the meaning of "large" and "oversized" is clarified. A firm may be "oversized" in relation to some optimum size and yet small in relation to the total production of the industry. Undersized and oversized are used here with reference to the lowest-cost size; if the lowest-cost size is very small, an oversized firm may still be small; on the other hand, the lowest-cost size may be so large that a firm can be very large, even giant, and yet undersized in comparison with the optimum. "Large" can mean in this context at least two things. A firm may be large according to some standard customarily applied to the whole economy (e.g., firms with a capitalization of many million dollars, or firms with more than several thousand employees) or it may be large in relation to the size of the market in which it sells. It is in this latter sense (that is, where "large" refers to the portion which the firm contributes to the market supply) that large firms are not compatible with the condition of perfect polypoly. For, as a rule, perfect polypoly presupposes the coexistence of very many sellers of a standardized product, each of the sellers offering only a small share of the total market supply.

It follows that perfect polypoly can exist (with few exceptions) only in industries in which the optimum size of the single establishment is very small in relation to the industry as a whole. Where the optimum size of the establishment is large, the number of firms in the industry is probably small; polypoly must then give way to oligopoly, to the market where sellers are few and rival-conscious.

IMPERFECT POLYPOLY

Imperfect or differentiated polypoly [7] is the market position of sellers whose offerings are slightly differentiated from those of

[7] One may object to the term "differentiated polypoly," since the adjective here is supposed to modify not the noun "polypoly" but should apply instead to the polypolistic seller or his product. The products or services of the many sellers are differentiated from one another; or, at least, differentiating features exist which cause some buyers to prefer one seller to another and which result in limited sales opportunities of any individual seller. Thus, the phrase "differentiated polypolist" fits the situation while "differentiated polypoly" does not. Nevertheless, the latter term will be used interchangeably with imperfect or monopolistic polypoly.

other sellers and who can, for this reason, choose among a few possible prices, product varieties, or promotion techniques to influence the sales of their goods or services, but who are not concerned about arousing any reactions on the part of their competitors.

We shall leave competition through product quality and selling efforts for later discussion, and deal first with price competition. That a polypolistic seller has a choice of possible selling prices at which he might sell limited quantities is expressed in the sloping demand curve with which the economist pictures the seller's sales expectations. The sloping demand curve brings out a specific difference between polypoly of differentiated products and polypoly of standardized products (the latter position characterized by a "practically unlimited" horizontal demand curve). The knowledge on the part of the individual seller that larger quantities could be sold only at reduced prices (and this is what is exhibited by the sloping demand curve) is a decisive point in his considerations concerning the output which he will produce.

The Volume of Output under Imperfect Polypoly

The undifferentiated polypolist was pictured as trying to bring his output up to a volume where his marginal cost was equal to the selling price. Such a volume of output would be found unprofitably large by a polypolist of a differentiated product.

The perfect polypolist was able to sell as much as he wanted. If he sold only a limited quantity it was because he did not want to produce more (his limited production capacity resulting in increasing costs of increased outputs). The polypolist of a differentiated product is not able to sell as much as he would like to sell at the given price; his business is definitely limited; additional business is obtainable, if at all, only at lower prices; and this may not pay.

Additional output, in extreme cases, may bring no (or no positive) addition to gross receipts (the lower prices not leading to sufficiently greater volume). In no event will additional output, under differentiated polypoly, bring in an addition to gross receipts as high as the price fetched by the additional sale. For, obviously, the reduction in selling price means that the "former" (smaller) output will now bring smaller revenue, a decrement for which the additional output is responsible, so to speak. The addition to total revenue, the marginal revenue, that can be had from the additional sale consists, thus, of a positive and a negative item. The positive item is the price received for the "new" sale, the negative item is the cut taken on "old" sales (that is, on the smaller quantity that could have been sold at a higher price). As long as the negative item is smaller than the positive one, marginal revenue will still be positive; but the presence of the negative item will always cause marginal revenue to be smaller than the selling price. In short, if the demand as seen by the seller is less than perfectly elastic, i.e., if the elasticity of demand is less than "infinity," then the marginal revenue from increased business must always be less than the price at which that business volume can be secured.[8]

It remains valid that profits are maximized, or losses minimized, at a volume of output at which a *further* increase in production would secure an addition to total revenue just equal to, or less than, the addition to total cost. Since for the polypolistic seller of differentiated products marginal revenue is lower than the selling price, the marginal cost of the chosen output will likewise be below its selling price.

Using the symbols which we used before, that is, P for selling price, MR for marginal revenue and MC for marginal cost, and writing f for the "price-loss-sales-gain ratio," [9] our deduction reads as follows:

[8] In the above exposition the words "former" or "old" output refer to hypothetical outputs at an identical time. The use of the "former—now" and "old—new" comparisons reproduces, however, the process of thinking and choosing. In choosing among alternatives the individual passes in review, one after the other, the various hypothetical outcomes.

Where the word "sales" is used in the text the "physical quantity sold" is meant; the money proceeds are called gross revenue or receipts.

It is assumed throughout the discussion that the seller is unable to charge discriminatory prices, that is, to sell additional output at reduced prices without reducing at the same time the price on the "old" sales volume.

[9] This ratio (the relative price change divided by the relative change in quantities sold that results from the price change) was once termed "price flexibility" in the literature. The phrase "price flexibility" is now employed with quite another meaning, namely, to denote the fact that prices are not rigid but move freely in response to changed market situations. With the old term gone, a new term had to be coined.

(1) if the seller wants maximum profit, he must produce an output whose $MC = MR$;

(2) if he is a polypolist of differentiated products, his $MR = P - P.f$; hence,

(3) he will produce an output whose $MC = P - P.f$.

The new symbol, f, looks like a stranger to us but it is only an old acquaintance in a new guise: it is the elasticity of demand turned upside down. If e stands for the elasticity of demand, the price-loss-sales-gain ratio, f, is simply $\frac{1}{e}$. (In the Appendix to this chapter a very easy algebraic exposition of these relationships will be attempted.)

The greater the price-lost-sales-gain ratio (i.e., the ratio of the relative price cut to the relative increase in sales which can be thereby secured) or (which is the same thing) the smaller the elasticity of demand, the greater will be the deviation between marginal cost and selling price. With an infinite elasticity of demand the deviation will disappear; with a very high elasticity the deviation will be very small. The existence of the deviation implies that the chosen output falls short of the output that would be chosen (at the same selling price and in otherwise equal circumstances) if the seller or his product were not differentiated. Under undifferentiated polypoly it was only the increasing marginal cost that caused output to be limited (since its saleability was not limited); under differentiated polypoly it is also the necessary reductions of selling price and, thus, the diminishing additions to total revenue that lead the producer to restrict his output.

In the discussion of perfect polypoly it was stated that there was nothing in that concept that would rule out abnormal profits and nothing that would require that the competing firms produce the "lowest-cost output." The concept of polypoly of differentiated products does not contain any such implications either. Neither the absence nor the existence of profits, neither the full utilization nor the under-utilization of productive capacity can be deduced from the concept. Another concept of competition, pliopoly, will have to join forces with the one under consideration in order to permit inferences concerning profits or excess-capacity.

There was one negative implication contained in the concept of perfect polypoly: that the chosen output could not lie in a range in which marginal costs were decreasing (because nothing would then prevent the seller from producing a larger output). This negative implication is not contained in the concept of differentiated polypoly. Here the incentive for stepping up production when marginal cost is decreasing may be effectively offset by the incentive for restricting production when marginal revenue is decreasing faster. But this must not be interpreted to mean that the choice of an output short of the "lowest-cost level" or even in a range of decreasing marginal cost is a necessary corollary of "monopolistic competition." A volume of output may well be chosen in a range at which not only marginal cost but also average cost is increasing. (Only the simultaneous effects of perfect pliopoly and imperfect polypoly will lead to a choice of output in a range in which average costs are still decreasing.)

Restricted Production

That the expectation of reduced average receipts from larger business will result in "output restriction," is a statement which can easily be misleading. One should beware of the unqualified conclusion that "production under monopolistic competition is smaller than under pure competition." All that the tendency toward output restriction means is that in the case of a differentiated product the output produced will be smaller than the output at which marginal cost would equal price. But it does not mean that production under differentiation must be smaller than it would be if the same products were standardized. For one cannot legitimately assume that the cost conditions in all firms and the demand conditions in the markets would be the same for a standardized commodity as for a differentiated commodity.

Comparisons between the two will have no meaning if it is quality that differentiates the products. Often the "unit" of product has lost its physical identity through the change in quality so that comparisons of prices make little sense. And is it not highly probable that cost conditions in the production of a standard quality would be different from what they are in the production of different qualities? And is it not very likely that the consumers' demand will be greater if some of the qualities represent an improvement over what otherwise would be the standard quality? But, incidentally, how can an aggregate of consumers' demand be measured if the quantities demanded refer to different qualities and the demand for each single quality depends on the prices of all other qualities? [10]

Merely in order to point to the possibilities contained in the dynamics of product differentiation let us imagine the transition from a perfect to a differentiated polypoly. Let us assume that the perfectly homogeneous products of a large number of small producers become differentiated through trade-marks, fancy names, or what not. (The illustration is not realistic, because trade-marks advertising, etc., are more likely to be features of oligopolistic markets.) The essential idea in the transition to "monopolistic competition" is, of course, that the demand curves which picture the individual sellers' sales expectations will become tilted and that each of these sellers will find it profitable to produce less than before. But can one not imagine that the commodity with its many brands would now become more popular and find its market enlarged? Then, instead of reducing their output volumes, producers would increase them. And, allowing our imagination to carry us still farther, the growing size of the industry may secure for it some external economies (i.e., economies which an individual producer cannot bring about by his own actions); and the reduced cost may permit reductions of selling prices and further expansions of output.

The differentiation of the product, in this example, results in increased total output compared with the previous standardized production. Many illustrations can be thought up to show how changes in cost or demand, incidental to standardization or differentiation, can result in output changes opposite to those which are commonly expected when products become more standardized

[10] If the consumers' demand curves for all different qualities of a product were known, the "aggregate" demand curve for the product might still be indefinable. Only for very particular problems does it make sense to construct such an aggregate demand curve. For one would have to assume that the prices of all qualities always rise or fall by an identical percentage and that the shares of all different qualities in the total sales always remain the same.

or more differentiated. Another of these illustrations will be given later (in the discussion of transport costs) in order to make it apparent that the "restricted outputs" of differentiated products (restricted to a volume at which price is above marginal cost) may exceed the "unrestricted outputs" of the same products with the differentiation eliminated.

Thus, "restriction of production under differentiated polypoly" does not necessarily mean less production than under pure competition, but it means only less production than might be socially warranted under existing cost-price relationships. The addition to total cost that would be caused by additional production could be fully covered by the *price* at which the extra output could be sold, while it could not be covered by the additional *revenue* which the extra output would produce (the additional revenue being smaller because of the lower price of the whole output). The "extra output" remains, therefore, unproduced. And this fact is "regrettable" from a very plausible point of view concerning social welfare. Some output remains unproduced although the prices paid would suffice to cover the extra cost of producing it.

The Size of the Firm under Imperfect Polypoly

Imperfect polypoly has the same "restrictive" effects on the size of the firm as it has on output.[11] After all, there is nothing changed in the basic reasoning as we substitute long-run marginal cost for short-run marginal cost. Perhaps it is more difficult for most of us to imagine how one arrives at investment decisions than it is to imagine how one decides on changes of output in a firm of unchanged size.

[11] We must again warn against forgetting the limitations imposed by our model, which basically relates to a single-product firm. The results of this analysis are applicable, at best, to real-world firms producing a given set of products and not expanding their fields of activities, or to single, specialized departments of real-world firms. In any event, we are not concerned here with the theory of growth, which alone can explain the size of the business firm and its limits (if any), taking account of the dynamics of entrepreneurship, retained earnings, industrial research, etc., and including the processes of expansion through vertical integration and through diversification which are ruled out by the model of the firm that is employed in the theory of price and output determination.

In the discussion of the size of the firm under perfect polypoly the argument ran in terms of expected selling price and the length of time for which it was expected to prevail. We must now substitute expected "demand conditions" or "sales expectations" for "selling price."

Under perfect polypoly, we concluded, a firm in equilibrium would never be less than "optimum size" (although it could be larger). Under imperfect polypoly a firm in equilibrium may be less than optimum size; that is, it may find it unprofitable to expand to the size at which it would produce at the lowest possible long-run average cost. In other words, the firm may fail to expand in spite of decreasing long-run cost, because the lower prices of larger sales—the diminishing marginal revenue—would check the expansionist tendency. Not always, however, will firms under imperfect polypoly be undersized in equilibrium; they may even expand beyond the optimum. This will depend on the combined effects of imperfect polypoly and perfect or imperfect pliopoly. (See Chapter 10.) All that can be said about the effects of imperfect polypoly on the size of the firm is that it will check the tendency to expansion: at a certain selling price the firm would not find it profitable to be as big as it would be if the elasticity of demand were perfect, that is, if the firm could sell as much as it cared to sell at that price.

It should be noted in this context that firms may possess excess capacity and at the same time be "undersized." There may be a smaller-than-optimum volume of output produced in a firm of smaller-than-optimum size; hence, utilization as well as expansion of capacity may be restricted. Imperfect polypoly in which undersized firms with unused capacity prevail are often found in trades overcrowded with small firms run personally by their owners. In these cases underdeveloped firms and excess capacity, far from being inconsistent with each other, may be two aspects of one thing. The firm as well as the scale of its operations are too small in relation to the capacity of the management, or in other words, the capacity of the management (which is indivisible) is too large in relation to the size of the firm and the scale of its operations.[12]

[12] It might be worth pointing out in what respects firms may be "undersized." In all cases the expression means that larger volumes of output could

Whether the optimum size of the firm is very small or large in relation to the size of the industry is of cardinal importance. If the optimum size is very large so that the possible internal economies act as strong expansionist forces within the firms, smaller firms must grow large or disappear; the number of firms in the industry will decrease and oligopoly will emerge. (The firms may not actually reach their optimum size but they will approach it to the extent that the industry is confined to fewer competitors.) On the other hand, if the optimum size were extremely small, all practical differences between products might disappear, and undifferentiated polypoly emerge. The latter consideration is merely academic because, even if all other productive factors were infinitely divisible, the "managerial factor" cannot easily be divided below one man. And this indivisible factor may be sufficient to account for the technological, personal or locational differentiations of the products.[13]

---

be produced in larger firms at lower unit cost. This might be so for several reasons. (1) Smaller firms may not be able to employ profitably certain processes, machines, specialists or types of organization, which are employed to great advantage in bigger firms. (2) Smaller firms may not be able to obtain their supplies as economically as bigger plants. (3) Smaller firms may have to employ certain machines, appliances or organizational units in a size smaller but not proportionately cheaper than those employed in bigger firms. (4) Smaller plants may have to employ for their smaller output the same expensive machines, appliances, specialists or organizational units as are employed in bigger plants for much larger outputs. (For a more detailed exposition see below, Chapter 10.)

All these causes of "decreasing long-run cost of production" have in common that they arise out of some sort of indivisibility (or imperfect divisibility) of productive resources which either prevents these resources from being used for small-scale production or requires that the cost of these resources be borne by smaller outputs. Where "management" of single-ownership-firms is their most significant fixed resource, the higher-than-optimum unit costs may show themselves merely in high "normal" profit margins (high per unit of output) rather than in the expense accounts of the firms; and the establishments in question may be "undersized" only in that the capacity of management is insufficiently utilized.

[13] At the risk of exposing the subtlety of the argument—that indivisibility is at the root of product differentiation—to ridicule, we ought to explain that "perfect divisibility" would mean for example, hundreds of microscopic drug stores on each corner, so that locational differentiation between the competing sellers would disappear. The argument was first presented by Nicholas Kaldor, "Market Imperfection and Excess Capacity," *Economica*, New Series, Vol. II (1935), p. 42. But it was not taken seriously by Chamberlin, *The Theory of Monopolistic Competition* (Cambridge: Harvard University Press,

TRANSPORT COSTS

Locational differentiation of goods and services is perhaps one of the chief reasons why, in the real world, perfect polypoly is so rare. Distance between seller and customer will necessarily differentiate personal services and will often differentiate transportable goods. This is more obvious for services than for goods.[14]

Differentiation Through Transport Costs

For transportable goods, distance or, more correctly, transport costs may easily become an element of product differentiation and cause a tilt in the demand curve for the product of the polypolistic seller. If the buyers have to bear transport costs (in terms of money or convenience) that are different for different sellers, their preferences for neighborhood sellers as against distant ones will be obvious; and the individual sellers will rightly expect that such preferences can be offset by the height of their selling prices f.o.b. mill. A higher selling price will probably result in the loss of more distant customers while it need not drive away the neighborhood patrons: a lower selling price will probably succeed in gaining sales to buyers whom distance would otherwise have kept away.[15]

Centralized Market

The organization of a centralized market can overcome the differentiating effects of transport costs. If sellers pay the cost of

---

Fifth Edition, 1947), pp. 198–200. See also J. M. Cassels, "Excess Capacity and Monopolistic Competition," *Quarterly Journal of Economics*, Vol. LI (1937), pp. 426–43.

[14] The delivery of personal services usually requires personal contact between producer and customer: not the service but either the servicing or the serviced person must be transported to the location of the other party. The expense of this transport (in terms of money or convenience) may be considerable. Thus, the location factor alone, apart from "personal" factors, necessarily makes personal services to consumers differentiated products.

[15] If the seller absorbs the transport costs, a uniform "delivered" price would mean graduated net prices (i.e., prices net of transport costs) with additional sales to more distant destinations bringing diminished average revenue. The downward slope of the "demand curve" (in terms of the net revenue received by the seller) is thus apparent. This case involves price discrimination inasmuch as the seller accepts from more distant buyers lower net revenues than from buyers close-by.

transport from the production place to a central market, and buyers pay the cost from the market to their places, locational differentiation is eliminated; each seller gets one net price for all his sales no matter where the buyers are located, and each buyer pays one market price no matter where the sellers are located.

Centralization of the market, by eliminating or reducing locational differentiation, can secure higher elasticities of demand for the products of the individual sellers. If transport cost no longer differentiates the products of different sellers, their substitutability for one another is greatly enhanced. Centralization of a market, incidentally, also increases demand elasticities in other ways, particularly by facilitating comparisons of qualities and prices. Naturally evolved or artificially created institutions have existed at all times and places to provide market centralization wherever practicable. One may think here of examples from ancient times, of the oriental bazaars, of the produce markets of our times, or of the whole streets or districts in many of our cities which are occupied by particular trades or industries (such as the auto repair shop districts in nearly all American cities, the leather goods streets, the book seller streets, the garment makers streets in New York City).

However, the fact that products, not different in any other respects, can be standardized by eliminating locational differentiation, and competition thus be made pure, need by no means imply that prices paid by the consumer would then be lower and outputs larger. For, underlying the locational differentiation there is a saving of transport costs that would be lost by standardization through centralized marketing. True, dealing in a central market, each seller would be confronted with practically unlimited saleability of his product at the given market price; true, therefore, he would not restrict his output below, but would rather bring it up to, the volume where his marginal cost equaled the price received. But the net price received by the seller would be drastically pared down by transport costs. For, (1) the uniform market price may already be weakened by the transport costs which consumers would have to pay from the market to their places; and (2) out of that weak market price the seller would have to defray the transport cost from his shipping place to the market. Hence, the given and uniform market price may at the same time mean increased delivered prices to the buyers and reduced mill prices (farm prices) to the sellers.

In other words, when polypoly is made perfect by means of centralized marketing, with sellers and buyers paired at random, and cross-hauls thus made necessary, sellers may receive lower net prices, and buyers may have to pay higher delivered prices, than under polypoly rendered monopolistic through locational differentiation under which sellers and buyers are paired in such a way that transport cost differentials are taken into account and cross-hauls avoided. As a result, output may be greater under locational differentiation than under locational standardization. The "restricted outputs" of the locationally differentiated products (restricted to a volume at which price is above marginal cost) may then be well in excess of the "unrestricted outputs" of the locationally undifferentiated products.

Location and Competitive Position

In order to isolate the effect of location upon competition one has to abstract from all other factors which may differentiate the products or keep down the number of producers. How does the locational distribution of producers and consumers then affect competition among the "very many" sellers of an otherwise "undifferentiated" product?

Even if there is a centralized market, or several (regional) centralized markets,[16] for a standardized commodity, it is by no means certain that all sales will be made in these central markets.

[16] The existence of several centralized regional markets is compatible with a state of undifferentiated polypoly as long as the single seller feels that he can dispose of all his output (i.e., of any quantity he may care to sell) in the market that suits him best, at the price which rules or is expected to rule in that market, and without noticeably affecting this price. It goes without saying that the price differences between these regional centralized markets can never be greater, and may be smaller, than the cost of transporting the commodity from one market to the other. Arbitrage would prevent price differences from exceeding the cost of transportation between the markets. Where each market is served by a sufficiently large number of producers located nearer to that market than to any other, it may happen that the price differences are smaller than the cost of trans-shipments and, hence, that trans-shipments are unnecessary.

A few producers and a few consumers may be so located with respect to each other that they know they can make savings by avoiding cross hauls, that is, by not dealing in the central market. In these circumstances the product of the near-by producer may become locationally differentiated from the (otherwise perfectly substitutable) product available in the central market. It will be unlikely that the sellers who serve their conveniently located customers will be able to sell at one f.o.b. mill (or f.o.b. farm) price any amount of their product that they care fo sell. They will probably have a choice of prices, serving only their near-by customers if they charge higher f.o.b. prices, serving also those farther away if they charge less.[17]

Restating the simple point which bears on this general discussion we may say: When the individual seller of a product, which is standardized in every respect but location, finds that he cannot sell at one given f.o.b. mill price (f.o.b. farm price) any quantity he may care to sell, the elasticity of demand for his product is not infinite, that is to say, competition is not "pure." The seller may still feel that he shares the market with so many others that changes in his output will not make any noticeable difference to any of his competitors and that his price policy will not result in any reactions on their part. The seller has then still the attitude of a polypolist. If, however, transport costs and distance become very considerable factors, the total market will be broken up into several overlapping and decentralized regional markets. While very many sellers may share the total market, fewer sellers share each regional market. What superficially appears to be polypoly with respect to the total market may be an oligopoly with respect to the regional markets.

We are, thus, led to recognize that either large local agglomerations of people—producers or consumers—or extremely low transport costs are among the necessary conditions of perfect polypoly.

---

[17] In certain (not infrequent) cases they may be able to discriminate between near-by and more distant customers by charging lower mill-net prices to the latter than to the former, perhaps in the less conspicuous form of quoting delivered prices. This case of discriminatory pricing was called the "let-him-pay-more" type of discrimination. Fritz Machlup, *The Political Economy of Monopoly: Business, Labor and Government Policies* (Baltimore: Johns Hopkins Press, 1952), Chapter 5.

Agglomeration of producers implies that a large number of sellers are in the same location relative to all consumption points, close-by as well as distant; in competing for the "best" business they reduce the returns from all business to the same mill-net (or farm net) price.[18] Agglomeration of consumers creates a large uniform "market" at the consumption point, which will leave producers who are located at differently distant points with different mill prices net of transportation cost. But any one producer, if he has no better outlet for his wares, will be able to sell all he cares to sell in the same market, so that transport costs will be "constant" for him and will leave him with one mill-net price per unit of output for all his business. In the absence of agglomeration of producers or consumers, extremely low transport costs may reduce any differences in net returns due to dispersion of producers or consumers to negligible size and thus result in practically equal net prices for the entire business of any one producer. If neither producers nor consumers are agglomerated and if transport costs are not extremely low, there will be deviations from perfect polypoly. It will depend on the locational distribution of sellers and buyers, and on the relative importance of transport costs, whether what might otherwise be perfect polypoly will in fact, because of the location factor, become imperfect polypoly or a group of overlapping oligopolies.

Transport Cost and Plant Size

Again in this analysis of polypoly have we crossed the border into the analysis of oligopoly. First the discussion of optimum plant sizes and now the discussion of transport costs and regional markets have called for this advance payment of attention to the oligopoly type of seller. We may take the occasion to point here to the logical correlation between "large" and "small" optimum

---

[18] For example, all wheat farmers in Saskatchewan are in the same relative position in the sense that no single farmer has a better outlet for his produce than any other. If the farm net prices obtained from shipments to a particular destination point were higher than those from the rest, every seller would attempt to grab all the good orders until all net prices were equalized.

plant size, "high" and "low" transport costs, and "small" and "large" number of establishments sharing a market.

The optimum plant size is often called small if it takes a large number of such plants to supply the market; it is called large if a few of such plants can provide what the market demands. But the size of this market depends on the relative height of transport costs: lower transport costs will mean a larger area, higher transport costs a smaller area to be served. Hence, a given optimum plant size may appear "large" if transport costs are relatively high, and "small" if transport costs are relatively low. This statement, however, can be reversed with equal validity. Transport cost of a given height per mile and unit of product will appear relatively high if the optimum plant size is large and each plant thus has to serve a large area and ship the product over many miles; the same transport cost per mile will appear relatively low if the optimum plant size is small and each plant thus has to serve only a small area and ship only over short distances. It seems that the principle of relativity prevails here as elsewhere.

In a less "tautological" formulation, using less interdependent standards for judging the size of plants and the height of transport costs, the following generalization about the probability of polypoly, perfect or imperfect, seems to be permissible. Polypoly can exist in fields where the economical size of the producing unit is very small, where the transport costs are very low, or where the agglomeration of producers or consumers is very dense. All three conditions together will usually make for a "large market with many sellers." Any two of the conditions may possibly compensate for the absence of the third. For example, high transport costs (high in relation to the value of the product) need not interfere with polypoly (that is to say, need not create oligopoly positions) where the settlement of consumers is so dense and the economical plant size so small that long transports are not called for. Sparse settlement of consumers need not rule out polypoly if the plant size is small and low transport costs reduce differences of distance below magnitudes that count. Or, high transport costs and dispersion of consumption points may still be compatible with polypoly if the plant size is small and producers are agglomerated in one or more particular regions rather than dispersed all over the map.

Marginal Revenue and Elasticity of Demand

Notations:

Higher price . . . p_1; quantity saleable at p_1 . . . q_1;
lower price   . . . p_2; quantity saleable at p_2 . . . q_2;
price-elasticity of demand . . . e;
"price-loss-sales-gain" ratio . . . f.

Argument:

Total revenue at higher price	$= p_1\,q_1$;
total revenue at lower price	$= p_2\,q_2$;
marginal revenue (first form)	$= p_2\,q_2 - p_1\,q_1$;
positive item of revenue change, or "sales gain"	$= p_2\,(q_2 - q_1)$;
negative item of revenue change, or "price loss"	$= q_1\,(p_1 - p_2)$;
marginal revenue (second form)	$= p_2\,(q_2 - q_1) - q_1\,(p_1 - p_2)$;
price-elasticity of demand,	$= \dfrac{q_2 - q_1}{q_1} \div \dfrac{p_1 - p_2}{p_2} = \dfrac{p_2\,(q_2 - q_1)}{q_1\,(p_1 - p_2)}.$

Thus, while marginal revenue is "sales gain" minus "price loss," elasticity of demand is "sales gain" divided by "price loss"; and the "price-loss-sales-gain" ratio, $f = \dfrac{q_1\,(p_1 - p_2)}{p_2\,(q_2 - q_1)}.$

Assumption:

Sales increase is just one unit, i.e., $q_2 - q_1 = 1$.

Argument continued:

This assumption reduces several of the above formulas. Thus, marginal revenue (second form) $= p_2 - q_1 (p_1 - p_2)$; and the "price-loss-sales-gain" ratio, $f = \dfrac{q_1 (p_1 - p_2)}{p_2}$;

multiplying both sides of this equation by p_2, we obtain

$p_2 f = q_1 (p_1 - p_2)$;

substituting this in the reduced formula for marginal revenue, we come to the

Conclusion:

Marginal revenue $= p_2 - p_2 f =$

$$= p_2 (1 - f) = p_2 \left(1 - \frac{1}{e}\right).$$

Geometric Representation:

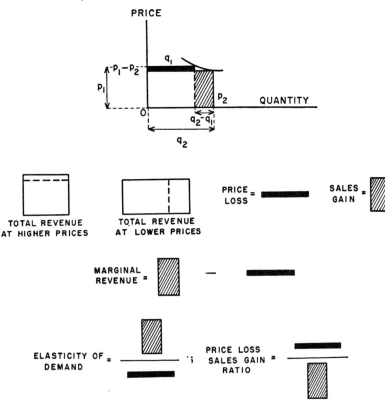

Fig. 1.

CHAPTER 6

Polypolistic Nonprice Competition and
Other Forms of Non-Perfect Polypoly

Polypolistic Nonprice Competition: Institutional Pricing Factors · Oligopolistic Considerations · Competition Invigorated or Weakened · Standardization, Differentiation and Price Maintenance · The Degree of Competition through Quality Differences

Polypolistic Quality Competition: The "Measurability" of Quality · Quality Determination with Variable Selling Prices · Quality Determination
and Demand Elasticity · The Effects of Improvements upon Demand ·
Quality Determination with Fixed Selling Prices

Polypolistic Competition Through Selling Effort: Selling Effort vs. Im-
proved Quality · Relationship between Selling Cost and Demand · The
Effect of a Given Selling Effort · Variable Selling Efforts and Variable
Prices · Selling Costs vs. Production Costs · Determination of Selling
Effort with Fixed Selling Prices

Quasi-Perfect Polypoly: The Limit of the Horizontal Range · The Causes
of the Horizontality · The Demand for the Product of the "Follower" · Unlimited Offers to Purchase

The Rise or Decline of Polypoly: Empirical Findings · Growth of Size of
Firms and Markets

Imperfect Polypoly and General Equilibrium: Price and Sales Expectations · Objective Changes and Subjective Expectations

W HEN ECONOMISTS SPEAK of competition and use no modifying
adjective or other qualification, they usually mean price
competition. But, of course, they all realize that sellers compete
also in other ways, for example, by offering better qualities or engaging in various kinds of promotional activities. We must, inquire into the nature of polypolistic nonprice competition and try
to examine what determines a polypolist's decisions to improve
product quality or increase his selling efforts. This discussion,
which will take most of this chapter, will be followed by com-

ments on a few other problems connected with "quasi-perfect" and imperfect polypoly.

POLYPOLISTIC NONPRICE COMPETITION

Institutional Pricing Factors

There are numerous fields in which a very large number of firms sell to a densely settled consumer population a fairly well standardized product or service with only trivial locational differentiation—hence, fields which would have just about everything that is needed for polypolistic competition—but where *trade associations, state intervention,* or *custom and tradition* have created conditions which reduce the model of the polypolistic seller to limited applicability. For, if there are uniform list prices, open prices, or price recommendations of a trade association, or prices fixed by the public authority or by custom, a rather fundamental change of the seller's pattern of thought and conduct is to be expected.

The undifferentiated polypolist would accept the market price as the result of "the anonymous forces of supply and demand," not susceptible to his influence; the differentiated polypolist, able to choose his price but still convinced of his own unimportance in his field, would feel that he did not have to care about what his competitors thought of him or how they reacted to his price making; but the seller who is faced with the institutional pricing factors mentioned may think and act differently even if he is "one out of very many" in the market. Any one of these institutional pricing factors is apt to introduce into the mind of the seller considerations of possible sanctions, retaliations and other reactions—considerations which are foreign to strictly polypolistic pricing.

Oligopolistic Considerations

It is a matter of terminological strategy whether such a seller under organized or regulated price making should be treated as a special type of polypolist or a special type of oligopolist or perhaps as a separate category. There may be a large number of small sellers in the trade and no one of them may think of any particular rival or rivals when he weighs the advantages and disadvantages of price maintenance versus price cutting. This element of impersonal competition would make these sellers differentiated polypolists, especially if their individual sales efforts and other acts of nonprice competition were carried out in the spirit of gaining business without knowing exactly from whom and without expecting or considering any rivals' reactions. On the other hand, the model of polypoly would here be of little service in the explanation of selling prices. And, furthermore, in his considerations concerning price maintenance versus price cutting the individual seller would be definitely "reaction-conscious," although these reactions would be expected to come from collective agencies or groups rather than from particular rivals.

There seems to be little doubt that organized, regulated or custom-bound price making occurs in fields which would otherwise be polypolistic as well as in fields which would in any event be oligopolistic. For an analysis aiming at nothing but the principles of *price* determination, there would be little point in distinguishing between various patterns of thinking if this thinking had been pushed into the background by institutional factors which had become the prime causes of the price situation of the particular trade or industry. However, the "background" may begin to be important in certain circumstances and may temporarily neutralize the institutional forces,—which amounts to saying that even the strictest rules, regulations and customs are sometimes violated. Still more significant is the fact that price making is only one of the possible forms of competition; while the scope of price competition may be seriously restricted, nonprice competition may be practised in several forms and may follow a definitely polypolistic or definitely oligopolistic pattern. Hence, if the analysis of competition is to be more than price analysis, the distinction between patterns of competitive thought continues to be useful.

Competition Invigorated or Weakened

Selling effort and quality improvement are the two main elements of competition other than price competition. Between the

restriction of price competition and the practice of nonprice competition the following relationships are conceivable: (1) Nonprice competition is practised more vigorously *because* of existing
restrictions of price competition and is, thus, the way in which
the forces of competition, checked on one front, assert themselves
on another. (2) Nonprice competition is practised more vigorously *in order to* avoid price competition and plays, thus, a part in
the elimination or restriction of price competition. (3) Nonprice
competition would have been practised in the same forms and
to the same extent even if price competition had not been restricted. (4) Nonprice competition is mitigated or restricted along
with price competition by the same or parallel devices.

The expression that nonprice competition is a "substitute" for
price competition is correct, but it does not tell whether the practice of nonprice competition in a particular case serves to increase
the degree of competition or to reduce it. The degree of competition was *increased* in the first of the above four possibilities, when
nonprice competition was resorted to after and because price competition had been restricted. But the degree of competition was
reduced in the second of the above possibilities, when nonprice
competition was a means of abstaining, and persuading the rivals
likewise to abstain, from price competition.

The conclusion suggests itself that the latter function of nonprice competition is more characteristic of oligopoly and the former
of polypoly positions. In a trade or industry which is polypolistic
in character nonprice competition is likely to strengthen the forces
of competition and to afford them another outlet if price competition is institutionally restricted. In oligopolistic positions, on
the other hand, nonprice competition is likely to weaken the
forces of competition in that the practices of nonprice competition
permit rivals to refrain from the price cutting to which they would
otherwise be more easily inclined.

Standardization, Differentiation, and Price Maintenance

In many discussions of recent years there has been an inclination to treat product standardization as a factor always making
for a higher, and product differentiation as a factor always making

for a lower, degree of competition. These generalizations do not hold for all situations. It is true that standardization increases the substitutability of many sellers' products for one another and therefore tends to increase the elasticity of demand as seen by the individual seller. It may thus lead to positions approaching, or actually constituting, perfect polypoly. Conversely, it is true that differentiation of products decreases the substitutability between the products of different sellers and therefore tends to reduce the elasticity of demand as seen by the individual seller. It may thus lead to higher prices and lower outputs than would prevail if demand elasticities were greater. Yet, on the other hand, it must not be overlooked that standardization of products and services may facilitate price agreements and price maintenance, while differentiation of products and services may either make it harder to conclude and enforce price agreements or, as was pointed out before, may constitute a fairly effective competitive practice in fields in which price competition is institutionally restricted.

The fact that standardization may aid in reducing rather than increasing the degree of competition can be observed even within one and the same industry with respect to certain of its services of varying degrees of standardization. For example, there may be twenty different automobile repair shops in the district where you live. If you drive in to have the brakes of your car relined or the piston rings replaced and ask for estimates of the repair cost, all twenty (save the one or two who miss the right line or page in their fat and heavy price book) will quote an identical price. But ask them for an estimate for straightening out that dent in your fender and they will give you quotations differing by 100 and more per cent. The necessary labor time will vary from shop to shop just as widely in the case of the replacing of a standard part as it will in the case of the non-standardized repair. However, the repair cost of any standard trouble on your automobile can be easily fixed by agreement or recommendation, whereas the repair cost of differentiated trouble cannot.[1]

[1] Of course, where the new parts which have to be installed in the automobile make up a large portion of the repair bill, and the labor time therefore only a small portion, the estimates and bids cannot deviate so widely from one another as they would if almost all cost were labor. But even apart from the price of the parts, the cost of their installation can be and largely

Standard products and standard services are thus the ones which can be most easily subjected to price fixing, price control and price maintenance schemes. Price uniformity, sometimes naively believed to be "evidence" of effective competition, is the simplest way of arranging for the elimination of price competition; but price uniformity by "compliance" can be maintained only if the products are fairly standardized. The greater the differences between the products are, the harder will it be to obtain compliance with a uniform price or to agree on "price differentials" and enforce them once they have been agreed upon.

Standardization and differentiation are not opposites in every respect. One speaks of differentiation, not where products are fundamentally very different, but only where they are fairly similar. This similarity implies then that the products may be "standardized" in some respects and "differentiated" in others. If they are by nature sufficiently standardized to make price fixing schemes workable, *differentiation may become a competitive factor* reducing the rigidity of the price fixing scheme, no matter whether the price fixing is the result of a "monopolistic" conspiracy, of trade association practices, of governmental interventions or of custom and tradition.

The Degree of Competition through Quality Differences

Flexibility in quality will ordinarily not compensate for inflexibility of price.[2] But there is no *a priori* reason for this and

---

is the result of price fixing, while the cost of non-standardized repair jobs is not. To say this is not necessarily to complain about it. The consumer who needs repair service in an outlying region, where he can find only one or two shops to take care of his emergency, may benefit from the price fixing as much as the consumer in a large city, who would be able to shop around for the cheapest place, may lose. And, inasmuch as the particular market is rather imperfect and would offer plenty of opportunity for price discrimination against the unversed, easygoing, or isolated customer, the price fixing scheme may possibly be regarded more as a protection for the consumer than as a conspiracy for his exploitation.

[2] Rarely will competition through quality differentiation of the product or service compensate the *consumer* for what he may have lost through the price fixing (which in turn was made possible through the relative homogeneity or standardization of the product or service). The differentiation may offer the consumer some sorts of quality improvements or some additional

there are exceptions in which quality competition is probably as keen as price competition could ever become. The comparison between the two may conceivably be made in terms of the seller's sacrifice necessary to gain an increase in the volume of sales, the sacrifice being, on the one hand, the price cut and, on the other hand, the expense of the quality improvement. Measured in these or in similar terms, there are undoubtedly cases where a set of fixed prices with quality competition (i.e., competition through product differentiation) are no less "competitive" than a set of standard qualities with price competition could be. Exactly this seems to be the situation in several industries with "conventional price lines." In these industries, of which the women's apparel and women's dress industries are the best-known examples, "manufacturers and wholesale buyers . . . have come to accept these [price] lines as virtually immutable" and "as a result the focus of competition becomes the character of the garment which can be offered at the accepted price and not the price at which some specific garment should be quoted." [3] While many manufacturers

services which he would not have bought had he had the choice between these improved products or services at the regular price and unimproved products or services at non-regulated, competitive prices. Many consumers get, under the price fixing scheme, a luxury kind of product or service which is out of proportion to their ordinary standard of living. (For example, men in lower income brackets might prefer a 50-cent hair cut in simple barber shops without electric massage, hot towels, hair lotion and what not, to a one-dollar hair cut with all these fancy services. Or, they might much rather themselves clean the windshields and check the radiators of their cars and pay less for gasoline.) The point that the luxury type of service which is supplied in consequence of certain price fixing schemes if out of line with the standard of living of many consumers was made in another context by Thurman W. Arnold, *The Bottleneck of Business* (New York: Reynal S. Hitchcock, 1940).

[3] *Price Behavior and Business Policy*, Monograph No. 1, written by Saul Nelson and Walter G. Keim for the Temporary National Economic Committee. The quoted passages in the text are from pp. 70 and 55. The following appraisal, on p. 102, is noteworthy: "Price lines do not involve any constant wasteful redirection of competitive effort. Even in the absence of price lines, such factors as quality and style would necessarily play major roles in the apparel market. In fact, the existence of price lines, instead of complicating the problems of choice facing the buyer . . . , actually simplifies them somewhat. The number of variables between rival offers is reduced. The buyer can accept price as a constant and concentrate his attention upon comparing other elements such as quality or style. To the seller some economy is achieved in the problems of business planning."

make several qualities, selling at several price lines (though the producer of cheap products would rarely sell also at the very high price lines), there are some manufacturers who sell only at one price line, maintaining this price line for many years (for example a "$10.75 house" in the women's dress industry before the war) thus competing exclusively through quality and style.

This competition through offering the "better and bigger value" at the conventional price instead of offering the conventional product at "lower prices and better terms" can, of course, be oligopolistic as well as polypolistic, just as price competition can be. If the producer, while he considers the wisdom of adding some frills or fringes, or of skimping in material or labor, reflects on what his rivals might do when they learn about his change of quality or style, then he is clearly an oligopolist. His decision will be influenced not only by the anticipated reactions of his customers but also by the anticipated reactions of his rivals. "Why should I spend good money on that frill or gadget if Jones Bros. and Smith & Co. are likely to answer by spending the same, or even more, thus depriving me of much or all of the potential sales advantage?" Of this sort would be the reasoning of the oligopolist. The polypolist, on the other hand, is not concerned about any of his rivals' reactions to his quality improvement or deterioration. He does not believe that his moves are closely watched, or immediately copied or countered by his competitors and he is only concerned about the impression he can make on the buyers. It seems that most of what was stated concerning polypolistic price competition holds true also for polypolistic nonprice competition. (It goes without saying that polypoly stands here always for *differentiated* polypoly; any conscious price competition as well as nonprice competition is outside the realm of *perfect* polypoly.) But a more detailed analysis of polypolistic quality competition is in order.

POLYPOLISTIC QUALITY COMPETITION

Although "quality competition" may be practised in industries in which price competition is completely eliminated, the two may well be practised together. Can a theory of "quality determination" in the individual firm be formulated similar to the theory of output determination? Steps toward such a formulation will be attempted here, first for the case where both price and quality are variable, then for the case where only quality is variable while the price is fixed. A few preliminary observations on the problem of "measurability" of quality are necessary.

The "Measurability" of Quality

It would be tempting to formulate a theory of quality determination under polypoly in the same elegant fashion as the theory of output determination under polypoly was formulated. Unfortunately, this cannot be done. Statements about the relationship between the cost of *output increase* and the corresponding sales expectations were facilitated by the physical measurability of the quantity produced. (Both marginal revenue and marginal cost thus referred to physical units of output.) Statements about the relationship between the cost of *quality improvement* and the corresponding sales expectations are complicated by the fact that "quality" cannot be physically measured. It may be possible to give physical descriptions of different qualities and measure some of the physical constituents of quality (e.g., weight, size, brilliance, flexibility, durability), but it is not possible to say, for example, that quality B is 25 percent "better" than quality C. There are physical units to measure the *quantity* produced, but there are no physical units to measure the *quality* produced.

The construction of an arbitrary quality index—a "hedonic index of quality," as it was once called in a study of automobile qualities—is perhaps, for certain problems, the best way out: one can imagine a scale of physically describable qualities (grades A, B, C, Models 120, 130, 140 or something of the sort) which may permit some meaning to be attached to the idea of cost and revenue resulting from slight quality changes. Other methods that may suggest themselves, such as to express quality in terms of cost, or in terms of the required labor or other factors of production, or in terms of consumers' preference, will often lead into blind alleys. For, in the first place, neither money cost, nor labor cost, nor sales proceeds are linear functions of output (that is to say, neither are average costs always constant nor are average receipts or prices constant for all volumes of outputs) and, therefore, if quality were measured in terms of any of these values, one physically identical quality would, at different outputs, appear as so many different qualities.[4] Secondly, if the most profitable quality (just as previously the most profitable quantity of output) is to be *determined* by marginal cost and marginal revenue, there is little sense in *expressing* quality in cost or in revenue.

[4] It has been suggested, in order to obtain a continuous function, that we express the quality of the product in terms of factors of production employed, assuming that each additional unit of factor, when most wisely applied to a given product, makes for a higher quality. "Quality" becomes then almost indistinguishable from quantity: a larger factor input makes for a larger value product. This "quality" will have no definite relationship to weight, or strength of material, or purity of ingredients, or technical efficiency of the product, or whatever is commonly regarded as constituting quality. Adding a certain amount of factors in order to obtain the quality improvement of 12,000 units of output will certainly mean something very different from adding the same amount of factors for the quality improvement of 13,000 units of output (unless a single investment in fixed equipment or something of the sort can do the trick). Also, adding a certain amount of factors per unit of output for the quality improvement of 12,000 units of output will probably mean something different from adding the same amount of factors per unit of output for the quality improvement of 13,000 units of output (unless a constant outlay per unit of output, independent of the scale of production, can do the trick). The cost, in terms of factors of production, of a certain, physically described quality improvement is probably neither "fixed" nor "constant" and thus a translation of quality in terms of technical cost into physically describable quality becomes impossible.

A further shortcoming of expressing quality in terms of expended factors of production becomes manifest in the analysis of changes in production technique. When the producer finds better ways of producing improved qualities —a change that would be most sensibly expressed in terms of reduced cost —a theorist who chose to express quality in terms of expended factors of production would have to state instead that "the demand has increased." (Because the *same* "quality" in terms of expended factors would, with the new technique, probably mean a better quality in the everyday sense of the word.)

Matters may become still worse if quality is expressed in terms of money cost. To the disadvantages mentioned before would have to be added the calamity that any change in factor cost would be displayed in a shift of the demand curve for the "given quality." For example, higher material prices would mean that any "given quality" in terms of cost becomes an inferior quality in the everyday sense, and the demand prices of the inferior quality are, of course, likely to be lower. However, for certain problems, especially where the cost of improvement is constant per unit of output, no errors need be involved in the technique of expressing quality improvement in terms of the money cost incurred for it. See below, pp. 179–82.

Quality Determination with Variable Selling Prices

Those who are used to diagrammatic representations of cost and revenue relationship will either use their usual graphs of cost and demand curves with a separate set of curves for each quality under consideration (i.e., quality would be the parameter of a whole series of curves); or they will resort to a three-dimensional graph where output is shown on one axis, total receipts and total costs on the second, and quality on the third axis. But since qualities are discrete properties of the products, points along the quality axis have ordinal, not cardinal, meaning, and continuous curves along the quality axis are, therefore, of little use. Hence, the three-dimensional device is really nothing other than all the two-dimensional sets of curves put one behind the other, thus facilitating the comparisons. (See Fig. 2.)

If for each quality a two-dimensional set of cost and demand curves shows the output and the selling price which secure the highest profit, a whole series of maximum profits is obtained and the choice of quality will be determined by the maximum of all these maxima (the so-called *maximum maximorum*). The three-dimensional diagram would help to find the maximum difference between total receipts and total costs and, thus, the best combination of output and quality. If quality changes could, by means of some index method, be conceived as measurable and continuous, the "marginal cost of quality" at the optimum combination would have to be equal to the "marginal revenue of quality," just as the marginal cost of output has to be equal to the marginal revenue of output.[5]

It should be noted that the simple cost curves and revenue

[5] I am indebted to Arthur Smithies, who saved me from the error of elaborating upon the marginal cost and revenue of quality and, at the same time, insisting on the non-measurability of quality. If my concept of quality does not permit the assumption of continuity or quasi-continuity of the effects of "slight changes," the highest possible profit can be found only by comparing all differences of total revenue and total cost, but not by the short-cut method of comparing marginal values. The technique of the marginal calculus is a help in finding the maximum (minimum, optimum) only because of the "slight changes" which show whether further movements in the same direction will lead nearer to or away from the desired position.

curves can do their usual service only if it is assumed that, for some reason, only one quality at a time is to be produced and sold. For multi-product or multi-quality firms the apparatus becomes more complicated because of the related costs (joint costs:

DETERMINATION OF PRODUCT QUALITY

I. *Imperfect Polypoly, Price and Quality Competition*

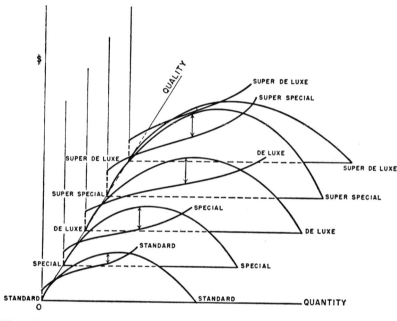

FIG. 2. Total Revenue and Total Cost Curves for Several Qualities.

The producer is assumed to have a choice of producing any one of five different qualities. The qualities are marked "Standard," "Special," "DeLuxe," "Super-Special," and "Super-DeLuxe." For each quality the total revenue and total cost curves are drawn, one set of curves behind the other; revenues as well as costs are assumed to be higher for the better qualities. Note that the cost curves begin above the base, which indicates the existence of fixed costs. Maximum profit for each alternative is shown by the greatest distance between the total revenue and the total cost curve. Comparison of the five maxima shows that the highest maximum, the "maximum maximorum," can be obtained by producing the "DeLuxe" quality.

technical complementarity or substitutability of the "products" in their production) and the related demands (complementarity or substitutability of the products in the selling market). It is not intended here to burden the reader with the algebraic or geometric solutions of this problem.

Quality Determination and Demand Elasticity

Would the degree of deviation from perfect elasticity of demand influence the *determination of quality* just as it does the determination of output? Does the producer's choice of quality, just as his choice of quantity of product, depend on the imagined demand elasticity and, derived from it, on his so-called "degree of monopoly"? In order to reason this out, we shall first assume a case of undifferentiated polypoly and then compare with it the results obtained for a case of differentiated polypoly.

Under perfect polypoly, the producer may have a choice of various qualities he may produce (although each quality would have to be standardized) but has no choice of prices at which he can sell any given quality. (See Fig. 3.) The price of each quality is "given" to him and is independent of his output. In other words, the undifferentiated polypolist feels that he could sell of any quality at its market price any quantity he might care to produce. The demand curves to him would all be horizontal lines— at different levels for different qualities—and, hence, the marginal revenue of output would always coincide with the corresponding demand curves. A change in quality would mean a movement from one given price to another given price, independent of the output produced. There would most likely be different marginal cost curves for different qualities, and the output volumes at which these marginal costs would equal the prices obtainable for the respective qualities would probably also be different. We may assume (having excluded multi-quality firms) that the producer will choose to produce that quality for which his profits would be greatest. With the saleability of any one quality unlimited at its respective market price, cost and price considerations alone would determine the most profitable choice of quality. Only cost and price comparisons—not any ideas about the responsiveness of the

II. *Perfect Polypoly, Choice among Standardized Qualities, Saleable in Unlimited Quantities at Given Differential Prices*

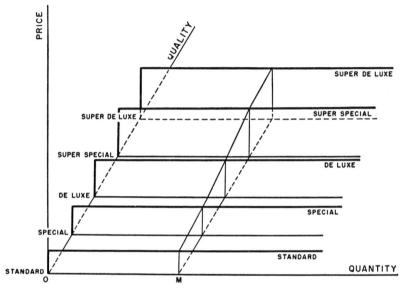

FIG. 3. Average Revenue Curves for Several Qualities.

The producer is assumed to have a choice of producing any one of five different qualities of his product, each of which is also produced in exactly the same specifications by several hundreds of other producers and sold in a centralized, perfect market. Hence, our producer can sell any volume of output that he cares to produce at the market price of the quality he chooses to make. The graph shows the demand curves as seen by the seller: perfectly elastic for each of the five qualities, the prices (= average and marginal revenues) being higher for the better qualities. To illustrate the rates of change of marginal revenue as we move up to superior qualities, a thin line is drawn connecting the marginal revenue values for a quantity OM. Cost curves are not shown. If marginal cost curves were drawn for each quality, their intersections with the horizontal demand (= marginal revenue) curves would indicate the outputs of each quality that would yield maximum profits, and the producer would choose to produce that quality for which the maximum profit would exceed all other maximum profits.

market—would count in the decision whether or not a superior quality should be produced.

Things are different if polypoly is not perfect. The qualities among which the producer chooses are now not only different from one another but also somewhat differentiated from those offered by other producers. The latter type of differentiation may be one of quality proper or of location, incidental service, reputation, or what not. In any case, for none of the qualities that he may offer can the seller visualize an unlimited market, that is, an infinitely elastic demand. Of each of his qualities he could sell smaller quantities at higher prices or larger quantities at lower prices; that is to say, all demand curves, picturing his sales opportunities, are sloping; the demand curves for better qualities, of course, may lie higher and more to the right than those for inferior qualities. (See Fig. 4.) But there is nothing that would make these various demand curves equally elastic at given quantities; thus, the marginal revenues at given outputs of various qualities would not be proportional to the prices of these qualities at the respective outputs. Hence, to change from one quality to another is not likely to affect the marginal revenues of given outputs in the same degree as the selling prices, and thus the choice of the most profitable quality will not be solely determined by the relation between production costs and market prices, but will be affected by the seller's ideas about the demand elasticities for the various qualities.

In order to illustrate our point, let us suppose a producer finds out that he can make a better quality product at a unit cost not much higher than his present cost, provided he can produce and sell a large output. While the thought whether or not it will be possible to sell a larger output would not plague the perfect polypolist (provided, of course, the better quality product is also a standard product) it will gravely concern the seller under differentiated polypoly. He may expect to be able to obtain a higher price for the superior product, but perhaps only for a small quantity, and his views of the elasticity of the demand for the improved product may be such that he does not expect so sell enough of it except with a price reduction which would unnecessarily endanger his present profit position. In this case he will obviously not attempt the improvement of his product. If the elasticity of demand for the

III. *Imperfect Polypoly, Price and Quality Competition*

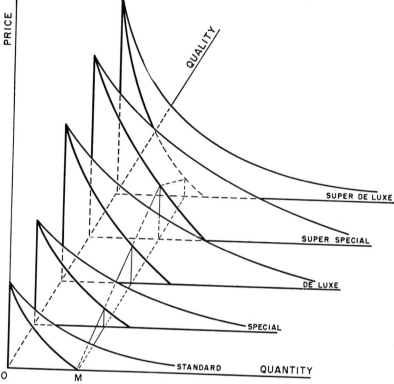

FIG. 4. Average and Marginal Revenue Curves for Several
Qualities.

The producer is assumed to have a choice of producing any one of five
different qualities of his product, all of which are differentiated from competitors' products. The graph shows the demand curves for each of the five
qualities and also the corresponding marginal revenue curves. To illustrate
one of the main points of the case, the marginal revenue values for a quantity
OM are shown and connected by a dotted line, exhibiting the fact that the
marginal revenue for this quantity of the best quality is lower than that of
two inferior qualities. Cost curves are not shown. If marginal cost curves were
drawn, their intersections with the marginal revenue curves would indicate
the outputs yielding the highest profits. A comparison of these maxima would
then show which is the largest and which of the five qualities could be most
advantageously produced. There is no presumption that the gap between
price and marginal cost is either smaller or greater for the chosen output of
the chosen quality than for the same or for the most profitable quantity of
any other quality.

improved product were greater, so that the producer could easily expand the business to the extent necessary to "get the cost down," then, but only then, would it pay him to go ahead with the quality improvement.

In other words, the elasticity of demand which the seller anticipates for his improved quality may not be large enough to induce him to undertake the large-scale production of this quality; to produce the improved quality on a small scale may leave him, because óf high production cost, with less profit than he can make by the production of the inferior product. The quality improvement may remain untried. Thus, paradoxically, product differentiation by different sellers—by causing the elasticities of demand for their products to be lower—may be seen to be a factor hampering product improvements by each individual seller.[6]

The Effects of Improvements upon Demand

The result of this analysis must not lead us to unwarranted generalizations. First of all, in our hypothetical example we assumed a relatively small elasticity of demand for the improved product and a condition of decreasing cost. Hence, for small outputs the cost was too high and for larger outputs the price obtainable was too low; consequently, the better quality was not produced. These assumptions, however, were not dictated by a judgment based on observed facts of any real situations; they were chosen merely in order to show that insufficiently high demand elasticities—such as *may* prevail under differentiated polypoly—*could* stand in the way of quality improvements. But it is entirely possible that quality improvements may effectively change the elasticity of demand for a product in such a way that the production of improved qualities would be greatly encouraged.

The effects of quality improvements upon the demand for a product may be classified according to the way in which the

---

[6] "The conclusion seems to be warranted that just as, for a given 'product,' price is inevitably higher under monopolistic than under pure competition, so, for a given price, 'product' is inevitably somewhat inferior." Edward H. Chamberlin, *The Theory of Monopolistic Competition* (Cambridge: Harvard University Press, 1932), p. 99.

demand curve for the product shifts.[7] The product may gain in higher-class appeal (by an "esotericizing" or "refining" quality improvement) or in mass appeal (by a "vulgarizing" quality improvement) or it may gain in general appeal with all income classes (by a "popularizing" quality improvement). The "esotericizing" improvement would account for low demand elasticities and, therefore, permit charging very high prices for relatively small quantities. The "vulgarizing" improvement would account for high elasticity of demand and, therefore, encourage the seller to look for a rapidly enlarged sales volume at slightly reduced prices. The "popularizing" improvement would expand demand but would be neutral as to its elasticity.[8]

It appears plausible to assume that producers might search for new improvements of their products which could affect demand in certain desired ways. The comparison of the "incentives to improve" under perfect polypoly on the one hand and differentiated polypoly on the other is to a certain extent self-contradictory, because we cannot well assume an improvement which is, at the same time, novel and yet supplied by a large number of small producers.[9]

The existing differentiation of products between different producers, which may operate as an *obstacle* to *potential* (further) improvement of products, is probably often the *consequence* of *actual* (previous) product improvements. There could perhaps be more nearly perfect polypoly if every producer produced only the identical, standard quality. But if also superior qualities are wanted, their production, given the minimum or optimum scales of production for any one quality, may be possible only if producers

---

[7] I acknowledge my indebtedness to Arthur Smithies, upon whose advice this paragraph was inserted. He read the manuscript of this chapter (July 1941) and suggested the ideas embodied in the next sentences.

[8] The criterion of this classification may either be sought in independently discernible facts of consumer psychology or in the respective effects of the quality improvements upon the price elasticity of demand. Using the former criterion, we would be able to state the matter as empirical proposition of more or less satisfactory probability value; the second criterion would yield merely statements of a tautological character.

[9] There is, of course, the possibility that improvements are imitated so rapidly that a situation approaching perfect polypoly can be quickly restored.

can specialize in particular qualities. The supply of better qualities may, therefore, necessitate a differentiation of the products as between different producers in the industry. With given minimum or optimum scales of production, the increased degree of monopoly which may be implied in the increased differentiation (imperfection) of polypoly is the price we must pay for the improvement of product qualities.

Quality Determination with Fixed Selling Prices

Of special interest is the determination of quality in the peculiar case of differentiated polypoly with fixed price, no matter whether this price is fixed by regulation, agreement, or custom. (See Fig. 5, A.) We referred above to the practice of quality competition in industries with fixed price lines; the example of the single-price house in the women's dress industry, competing only through quality, can bring the problem most sharply into focus. The distinguishing conditions in this case are: (1) the selling price is definitely fixed; (2) the demand, however, is limited, so that the horizontal demand curve breaks off abruptly at a certain volume; (3) any slight quality improvement may increase sales, that is, prolong the horizontal part of the demand curve; (4) quality improvements are likely to involve a prime-cost differential which is constant per unit of output (such as adding a decorative button to each dress, costing one cent a piece for labor and material).

The theoretical solution of the problem of finding the "optimum quality" of the firm can be obtained by several methods. The most pedestrian method is, of course, arithmetical calculation, as it is made by the businessman. The geometric method, of comparing the various sets of cost and demand curves, is also unnecessarily laborious in this case.[10] A simplified geometric solution for cases with constant cost differentials can be obtained in this manner: instead of drawing separate sets of cost curves and demand curves (where the higher cost curves would correspond to the longer

[10] If the cost differentials for different qualities are not constant per unit of output but depend on the volume of production, separate cost curves for each quality must be drawn. For an example of a graph with cost curves for two different qualities see Chamberlin, *op. cit.*, p. 79.

IV. *Imperfect Polypoly, Quality Competition at a Fixed Price*

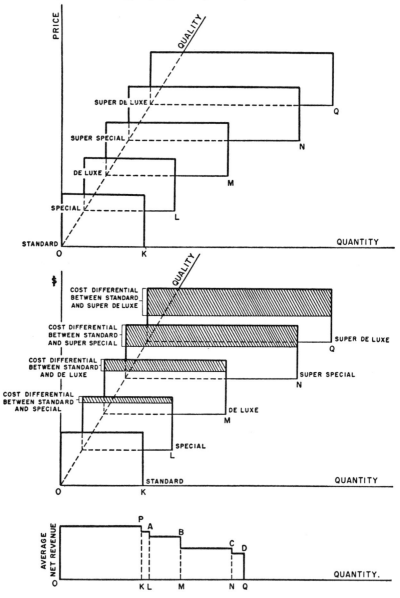

FIG. 5. A. Average Revenue Curves for Several Qualities Saleable at Fixed Price. B. Average Revenue Curves Net of the Quality Cost Differentials. C. Composite Average Net Revenue Curve.

horizontal demand curves, because the larger outlays for better qualities secure larger sales volumes) we can do with a single cost curve, namely, that of the cheapest quality, and deduct the unit cost differentials of better qualities from the fixed selling price at which the larger quantities of the better qualities are sold. Thus we obtain for different sales volumes average revenues net of the respective unit-cost differentials. These decreasing average revenues with increasing sales make this position fully analogous to that of price competition under differentiated polypoly. (See Fig. 5, B and C.)

The role of the price-elasticity of demand is taken here by the quality-elasticity of demand. (Since the unit cost of quality im-

---

FIG. 5

The producer can sell only at a fixed price, but at this price he has a choice of several qualities. The better the quality of his product, the larger his sales volume. Figure 5 A shows the horizontal demand curves of limited range: horizontal, because the price is fixed; limited range, because the market will take only limited quantities.

The better qualities cost more to produce, but this extra cost is constant per unit of output. The cost differential between "Special" and "Standard" quality is deducted from the fixed price (= average gross revenue) of "Special"; the cost differential between "De Luxe" and "Standard" is deducted from the fixed price (= average gross revenue) of "De Luxe"; and so forth. Figure 5 B shows these extra-cost deductions (shaded areas), leaving average net revenues (net of the quality cost differentials). Figure 5 C shows the composite average net revenue curve derived by this process. It indicates that the firm would be able to sell a quantity OK of "Standard" quality at a net price of KP, or a quantity OL of "Special" quality at a net price (average revenue net of cost differential) of LA, or OM of "De Luxe" at MB, or ON of "Super-Special" at NC, or OQ of "Super-De Luxe" at QD.

Since the average net revenue curve is a "stepped" curve, the corresponding marginal revenue curve would be quite erratic at the steps, but would coincide with the average net revenue curve at the horizontal stretches. Where quality can be improved by many small steps, almost continuously, a sloping average net revenue curve will be approached. The cost of "Standard" is not shown in the graph. The intersection of the marginal cost curve of "Standard" with the composite marginal revenue curve (corresponding to the curve of average revenue net of quality cost differentials) will indicate the volume of output and the grade of quality at which profits are highest. Where the marginal revenue curve is very erratic and will, therefore, be intersected several times, the alternative profit opportunities will have to be compared in order to determine the quality yielding the highest profit.

provements is assumed here to be constant, we are justified this
time in expressing quality by unit cost differentials.) A certain
percentage increase in the quantity saleable at the fixed price is
brought about by a certain percentage increase in unit cost through
improved quality or, alternatively expressed, by a certain percentage decrease in average revenue net of improvement cost. The
greater the quality-elasticity of demand expected by the producer,
the higher will be the "marginal revenue of quality" and the farther will he go in the improvement of the quality. The less the
expected elasticity of demand with respect to quality, the lower
will be the "marginal revenue of quality" and the less will be done
by way of quality improvement.

POLYPOLISTIC COMPETITION THROUGH SELLING EFFORT

The technologist and the moralist will usually insist on treating
selling costs separately from the cost of quality improvement, and
so will the economist for certain problems. But there is less reason
for our present purposes to separate the analyses of increased selling effort and of improved product quality. Indeed, it will be seen
that, apart from technological or moral criteria, there is no very
firm basis on which to draw a dividing line between these two
major forms of nonprice competition.

Selling Effort versus Improved Quality

Full-page advertisements in daily papers and weekly magazines, or big signs and posters on the roadside along the highways,
pose no problems of classification: they come clearly under the
heading of "selling effort." Equally simple is it to put new technical
gadgets, stronger materials, or more effective ingredients under
the heading of "quality improvement." But as soon as we come
to differences of color and design, fashion and style, to the things
which satisfy and appeal, flatter and distinguish, to the matters
which make buying more agreeable and convenient, we should,
as unbiased economists, give up any attempt to group them as
selling effort on the one hand or quality improvement on the other.
Only he who assumes the right to make value judgments—for

example, whether the quality is "really" improved or improved only in the "mistaken belief" of the buyer—or who is impressed with merely technological matters—for example, whether labor was applied directly to the object of sale (color or design) or only to other things conducive to increased buyers' appreciation (printing an advertisement; air-conditioning the store)—would feel entitled to draw a line. The economist has no strong ground on which he could do it.[11]

Selling efforts involve the incurring of cost and are supposed to increase revenue. Exactly the same statement holds for quality improvements. Quality improvements as well as selling efforts (and, of course, all the things in the middle group constituting both) vex the economic theorist because of their physical nonmeasurability. Some theorists have tried to distinguish price policy, quality policy, and promotion policy as the three determinants of sales. Others have tried to distinguish quantity of output, quality of product, and selling effort as the three independent variables resulting in costs and revenues. In both these systems, "promotion" and "quality," in contradistinction to price and output, suffer from the absence of homogeneous units of measurement.

Relationship between Selling Cost and Demand

In the case of selling effort (promotion) it is still more tempting than in the case of quality improvement to "measure" it either in terms of costs or in terms of efficiency as a revenue producer. Those who yielded to this temptation soon sadly discovered that the important mutual independence of cost and demand curves was lost. They found that the greater the selling cost, the greater the demand; and they believed that selling costs offered a very special problem in value theory. Yet, exactly the same dilemma would be found if one were measuring output not in physical units, but in terms of production costs (assuming, of course, always the most efficient production methods). Cost and demand would then no longer be independent of each other, since increased production cost would bring forth increased receipts. Only if output is physi-

---

[11] Of course, as a citizen or government official he may, and sometimes must, make such decisions.

cally described can the demand function be independent of the cost function. If an additional ten tons of output is produced and sold, the additional production cost is determined independently of the additional sales proceeds. Now, on the same footing, if selling efforts are physically described, the respective cost and revenue functions are equally independent of each other. The cost of erecting a large neon sign or of hiring beauty queens as sales girls is determined independently of the additional receipts which it is expected to produce.[12]

The diagrammatical economist [13] will be deeply grieved. While the system of real numbers was available for the description of the scale of output, and the makeshift of alphabetical grading might be resorted to for the description of the scale of quality, the scale of "promotion" has to be adorned with a detailed description of every single variety of selling effort and every possible combina-

---

[12] That it jeopardizes the mutual independence of demand and cost is only one of the drawbacks of expressing selling efforts in terms of costs. Other disadvantages lie in the fact that "selling costs of 100,000 dollars" do not define any definite promotion policy, not even if the best possible use of the expended money is postulated. The "best possible use" of the selling cost itself is ambiguous: does it mean that the best policy will bring the highest price for the given output or the highest sales volume at the given price, or how else should the effect be divided between customer loyalty and sheer quantity? Furthermore, if we agreed that the "best possible use" should be defined by the horizontal shift (not the upward shift) of the demand curve, would not for various points of a demand curve, that is, for various price levels, different types of promotion effort be the "best"? While advertisements in *Fortune* magazine might recommend themselves as the best method of pushing sales at a high price, posters and handbills may be more effective in moving the good at a low price. After all, what impresses the buyers and brings the sales is not the amount of money spent for promotion but rather the methods and devices adopted. Moreover, if the rates for newspaper ads are changed, the amount of advertising that can be bought for 100,000 dollars will, of course, change. With selling efforts expressed in terms of cost, the change in newspaper rates, which implies a change in the amount of advertising obtained at that cost, would instead express itself in different positions of the demand curve. If, on the other hand, selling effort were physically described, a change in the cost of advertising with given effects of advertising would determine the most profitable changes both of the form and the amount of promotion.

[13] This is not meant in any disparaging sense. The pedagogic and expository value of curve analysis has been proven beyond doubt. Exercises in curve analysis are an almost indispensable part of the training of an economist.

tion thereof, omitting only the definitely inferior combinations; or, perhaps, instead of one axis for selling effort we should have as many different axes as there are different sorts of selling efforts.[14] (Just as a production function cannot be graphically shown where there is a multitude of factors of production, the "selling effort function" also resists geometrical representation.)

This picture of the difficulties involved in a graphical analysis of selling efforts has perhaps been drawn in too dark colors. There are many problems which may not yield to all the exactitude of such a technique but can be tackled with a sufficient degree of approximation if much simplified expressions for selling efforts are used. For some problems the analysis will not be invalidated even if selling effort is expressed in terms of cost, provided it is well understood that the selling costs stand for the physical things or services for which they were incurred, and that these physical things or services are the link between the selling costs themselves on the one side and the demand or revenue functions on the other.

The Effect of a Given Selling Effort

The effect of a certain kind and amount of selling effort expended on behalf of a given quality of product can be described in at least two ways: (i) by the increase in the quantity that can be sold at a given price, and (ii) by the increase in price at which a given quantity can be sold. The former of the two measurements appears much more realistic, because sales promotion is so often practiced in fields in which price competition is largely eliminated, and increased sales at a given price are then the only objectives of selling efforts. It is hard to find, in actual business, a case in which advertising or other selling efforts are used for the definite purpose of obtaining higher prices for given quantities of output, though it should not be too hard to imagine such a situation. Starting from a given point on the demand curve (sales opportunity curve) for the product of a firm, the one effect of selling effort would be pic-

---

[14] The axes along which selling effort is to be plotted would have to be marked with the amount of half-page or full-page ads in various types of papers and magazines, the number of shop windows, the types of delivery service, and many other things still less amenable to quantification.

tured by a horizontal move to the right, the other by a vertical move upward. (See Fig. 6.)

Although it calls for some strain of one's imaginative faculties, one may visualize the horizontal moves of all possible points of a

---

THE EFFECT OF A GIVEN SELLING EFFORT

I. *Sales Opportunities at Various Prices With and Without Selling Campaign*

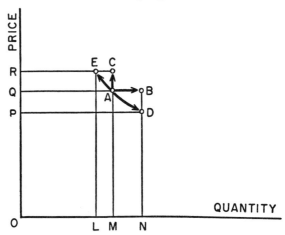

FIG. 6. Effects of Price Changes and Selling Effort Upon Saleable Quantity.

Assume A to be a point on the demand curve, indicating that a quantity OM is sold at a price OQ. All points except A are "hypothetical." Point B indicates the expectation that a larger quantity, ON, could be sold at the unchanged price, OQ, if a certain selling effort were made. The same quantity, ON, could be sold also without selling effort if the price were reduced to OP. (This expectation is indicated by Point D.) Point C indicates the expectation that a higher price, OR, could be obtained for the quantity OM if the selling effort under consideration were made. Without selling effort only a smaller quantity, OL, could be disposed of at the higher price OR. (This expectation is indicated by Point E.) Points B, C, D, and E are expected results of different hypothetical departures from A. Point B would apply if the selling effort were made without a change in price; Point C, if the selling effort were made without a change in output; Point D, if the price were reduced, without the selling effort; Point E, if the price were raised, without the selling effort.

demand curve that are expected to result from a given selling effort; and likewise visualize the vertical moves of all possible points of the same demand curve resulting from the same selling effort. (See Figs. 7 and 8.) Assuming reversibility of all demand curves, the new curve derived from the horizontal shift—increased

THE EFFECT OF A GIVEN SELLING EFFORT

II. *Effects of Selling Effort on Demand Prices and Quantities Demanded*

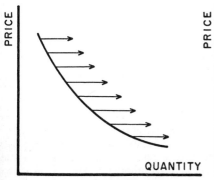

FIG. 7. Larger   Quantities   at   FIG. 8. Higher Prices for
Given   Prices.   Given   Quantities.

The horizontal or vertical shifts are probably not by equal amounts at different points. Hence the shape of the new curve may be different from that of the old. Whether or not the new curve that shows the increased quantities saleable at given prices will be the same as the new curve that shows the increased prices obtainable for given quantities will depend on assumptions and definitions. (See text and Figs. 9 and 10.)

quantities at given prices—would be identical with the new curve derived from the vertical shift—increased prices for given quantities. (See Fig. 9.) That the supposedly different effects of a given selling effort upon sales at given prices and upon prices for given quantities should result in one and the same increased demand curve can be explained in two ways. It may be regarded as a corollary of the postulate of economic statics, namely, that time is elimi-

III. *Dynamic or Time-Sequence Analysis of Effects of Selling Campaign*

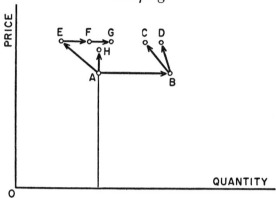

FIG. 9. Different Effects of Different Timing of Price Changes and Selling Campaign.

The assumption of "reversibility" of all movements along demand curves implies, among other things, that the net result of an advertising campaign and of a price increase would be the same no matter in what order the two steps were taken. This would be in accord with the postulates of "static analysis." In dynamic analysis matters may be otherwise. The result of the sequence "advertising—price increase" may be different from that of the sequence "price increase—advertising" and, moreover, the results may differ according to different time intervals between the steps. This is graphically shown in Figure 9. Starting from Point A, a certain amount of continuous advertising without price change increases the quantity sold and we move to Point B; a subsequent price increase reduces the quantity and we end up in Points C or D, depending on whether little or much time was allowed to pass between the beginning of the advertising and the price increase. If, on the other hand, we make the same price increase before starting to advertise, the quantity sold drops sharply and we move to Point E; now starting to advertise we may raise sales and move to points F or G, depending on whether much or little time was allowed to pass between the price increase and the advertising. None of the final points, C, D, F, or G, need to be identical with point H which indicates the price at which the original quantity could be disposed of after the advertising.

Static analysis abstracts from all these complications: Points C, D, F, G, and H would all coincide. Static analysis, of course, should not be used where the indicated differences are of the essence. But most of the problems of traditional value theory are of such a degree of generality that the static approach suffices.

nated as a variable and time sequences do not affect the results of a process. Or it may be regarded as a requirement implied in the concept of a demand curve—the locus of maximum prices obtainable for given quantities or of maximum quantities saleable at given prices—forcing us to neglect all inferior sales possibilities. This requirement involves, for example, where the sequence "advertising—price increase" would give better end-effects than the sequence "price increase—advertising" the latter should be considered irrelevant for the analysis of economic conduct. (See Fig. 10.) This device, therefore, takes account of dynamic effects, but it presupposes that we always know where we start. There would be different demand curves for different initial selling prices.

Variable Selling Efforts and Variable Prices

Even if the effects of a *given* kind and amount of selling effort can be reduced—as has just been shown—to a single increased demand curve, there remains the terrifying fact that the number of *alternative* promotion policies might be enormous, if not infinite, and that to each of these alternatives would correspond a different increased demand curve. Thus, the problem of determining the selling effort chosen by the firm in conjunction with the selling price, if both are variable and must be compared with variable selling cost and variable production cost, looks quite formidable. There is, however, no need to attempt the solution of this problem with such a forbidding array of alternative demand curves and alternative selling cost curves in confusing combination with production cost curves. The problem of the *optimal selling effort* can be solved independently of production cost, just as the problem of the optimal production technique is ordinarily solved independently of demand and revenue considerations.

The point is that we can immediately eliminate from consideration all selling techniques which yield net prices—i.e., average revenues net of selling expenses—below the maximum obtainable. For example, if a firm can sell a certain quantity of product either at a price of $25 with a selling cost of $10 per unit or at a price of $20 with a selling cost of $4 per unit or at a price of $14 without

IV. *Demand as Schedule of Maximum Prices or Maximum Quantities Obtainable by Any Sequence of Steps*

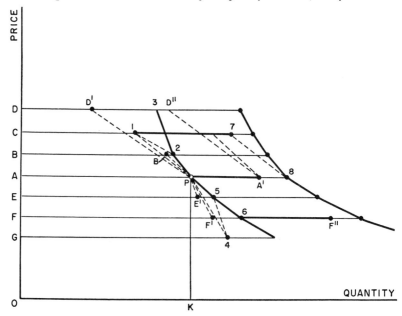

FIG. 10. The Relevant Demand Curves Pass Only Through Maximum Points.

A demand curve is defined as the locus of maximum prices obtainable for given quantities or of maximum quantities saleable at given prices. This implies that all points short of a maximum attainable must be neglected, even if the maximum, under dynamic assumptions, is reached only by a detour. For example, in Fig. 9, the points F, G, H, and C would all be off the relevant demand curve and only D would qualify. This principle permits the derivation, in Fig. 10, of various points of two demand curves, one without advertising, the other with a given advertising expense, starting from a given price.

Starting point is P, where a quantity OK is sold at the price OA. If without advertising the price were raised directly to OD, sales would fall off much more drastically than if this price were reached in three steps: 1, 2, 3. Hence, point D' is neglected, as are points E' and F' for the reduced prices OE and OF, because better results can be had through different procedures; in the latter case by steps 4, 5, 6.

With advertising (in a given amount) and without price change point A' could be reached, but would be rejected as less advantageous than the sales achieved by the steps 1, 7, 8. Similarly, points D'' and F'' are rejected for the "demand curve with the given selling expense" because larger sales at the respective prices can be achieved by other sequences of steps.

any selling cost, it will discard the first and the third alternative, and choose the second. The "net prices," or average revenues net of selling expenses, would be $15, $16, or $14, respectively. Only the $16 figure is relevant. The demand curve (sales opportunity curve) can conveniently be conceived in terms of net prices (i.e., as an average net revenue curve), that is, as the locus of the *maximum* average *net* revenues obtainable for different quantities of product.[15] Selling techniques resulting in average net revenues below the highest possible for given outputs are irrelevant for the concept of the sales curve.

There are several methods of deriving one single "net" demand curve, or an average revenue curve net of selling expenses, from the practically infinite number of "gross" demand curves that correspond to the practically infinite number of alternative selling efforts. (1) For each quantity of product all gross prices obtainable through all possible selling techniques are plotted vertically, and from each of these gross prices the expense of the selling effort (per unit of sales) incurred for the sake of obtaining the particular price is deducted. The highest of the resulting "net prices" is the one that counts as the demand price for the particular quantity. (Figs. 11 and 12.) (2) For each selling price all quantities saleable through all possible selling techniques are plotted horizontally, and from the selling price the expenses of the respective selling efforts (per unit of sales) are deducted, yielding a variety of "net prices" obtainable for a variety of quantities. For each net price the largest saleable quantity counts as the quantity demanded at the particular net price.[16]

---

[15] This is analogous to the production cost curve, which is the locus of the *minimum* costs at which varying quantities of product can be produced. Production techniques resulting in costs above the lowest possible for given outputs are not relevant for the concept of the cost curve.

[16] The graphical representation of this construction is more cumbersome, because the alternative selling efforts at each particular selling price yield different sales quantities as well as different average net revenues. Whether the resulting points are optimal cannot be ascertained before a very large number of combinations of alternative selling efforts at all possible prices has been tried.

I. *Alternative Selling Prices With Different Selling Costs and Resulting Average Net Revenues*

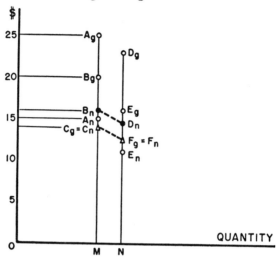

Fig. 11. Average Gross and Net Revenues for Two Output Volumes Saleable under Three Alternative Selling Techniques.

The seller can dispose of an output *OM* by using three different selling techniques: Technique *A* yields a selling price (average gross revenue) of *MAg*, causes selling costs of *AnAg* per unit, and therefore leaves an average net revenue of *MAn*. This is more than the average revenue obtained by using Technique *C*, which does not cost anything but brings only a selling price of *MCg*. Technique *B* brings the best results; the selling price obtained is *MBg*, which is less than *MAg*, but the selling cost is only *BnBg* per unit, which leaves an average net revenue of *MBn*. This is the maximum obtainable. (All these points correspond to the numerical illustration given in the text on p. 742. The subscripts *g* and *n* denote gross and net, respectively.)

An analogous set of comparisons is made for the output *ON*, again with three selling techniques, *D*, *E*, and *F*. Technique *D* is the best, the average net revenue *NDn* being the maximum obtainable.

The demand curve without any selling cost passes through the points marked by surrounding triangles; the curve of average net revenues with optimal selling techniques passes through the points marked by solid black circles. This is the curve relevant for our purposes.

II. *Maximum Average Net Revenue or Demand Prices With the Cost of Optimal Selling Techniques Deducted*

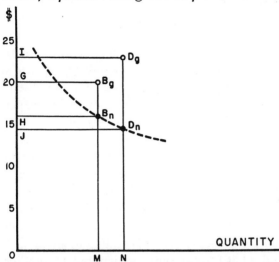

FIG. 12. Curve of Maximum Average Net Revenues; Areas of Total Gross Revenues and Total Selling Costs of Optimal Selling Techniques.

The curve of average revenues net of the expenses of the optimal selling techniques, as derived in Fig. 11, is drawn, the same process presumably having been employed for deriving the highest obtainable average net revenues for all possible volumes of output. The areas representing total gross revenue, total selling expenses, and total net revenue are shown for the two quantities OM and ON, marketed with the optimal selling techniques. For quantity OM, gross revenue is $OMBgG$; selling expenses are $HBnBgG$; and net revenue is $OMBnH$. For quantity ON, gross revenue is $ONDgI$; selling expenses are $JDnDgI$; and net revenue is $ONDnJ$.

Selling Costs versus Production Costs

To deal with selling costs by treating them not as additions to production costs but as deductions from gross receipts has several advantages. It avoids the entanglement of selling cost with

[193]

production cost and with questions of technological efficiency in production; it permits separation of the problem of optimal promotion policies from the problem of determining price and output of the firm; it substitutes a single demand curve (in terms of net prices) for an infinite number of demand curves (in terms of gross prices); and it overcomes the apparent interdependence of cost and demand curves.[17] At the same time it conforms to good—although not very common—accounting practice. For the sake of comparability of productive efficiency, selling expense should not be included among production cost; and for the sake of comparability of markets and marketing efficiency, selling expense should be directly deducted from gross sales receipts.[18]

It is possible to subdivide selling expenses according to their variability as a function of physical sales or as a function of gross revenue; and according to their character as "active" costs, designed to promote sales, or "passive" costs, varying with sales without affecting them.[19] For some specific problems it may be expedient to add certain kinds of selling expenses to production cost and deduct others from sales revenue. Distinctions are made for specific purposes and what fits one purpose may not fit another. The distinction between selling costs and production cost that is useful for the analysis of the conduct of individual firms under polypolistic competition may not be the same as a distinction suitable for the theory of the industry or for problems of welfare economics. It is therefore doubtful whether the "distinction between the two

---

[17] Chamberlin was seriously handicapped by his belief that selling costs along with production costs "must be included in the cost curve." *Op. cit.*, p. 129. Abba P. Lerner was, as far as I know, the first to suggest treating selling costs as "reductions in price." See his article "The Concept of Monopoly and the Measurement of Monopoly Power," *Review of Economic Studies*, Vol. I (1934), p. 173.

[18] In discussions of marketing and business management it is sometimes mentioned that the seller has a choice between (a) selling to distributors at lower prices and leaving it to them to pay for promotional efforts, and (b) selling at higher prices but defraying the selling costs himself. The decision is made in terms of receipts net of selling costs. See, for example, Arthur Stone Dewing, *The Financial Policy of Corporations*, Third Ed. (New York: Ronald Press, 1934), p. 277.

[19] Erich Schneider, *Einführung in die Wirtschaftstheorie, II. Teil* (Tübingen: J. C. B. Mohr–Paul Siebeck, 1949), pp. 89, 109–10, 118–20.

types of costs" is really, as has been asserted, "fundamental for value theory." [20]

It will be often difficult to decide whether certain expense items should be regarded as selling cost or production cost. For some purposes one decision, for other purposes the opposite decision will be appropriate, and often the question is altogether irrelevant. Thus we can expect little help from rules designed to determine the "correct" classification of expense items. For example, the statement that "of all the costs incurred in the manufacture and sale of a given product, those which alter the demand curve for it are selling costs, and those which do not are costs of production," [21] suffers from the ambiguities inherent in the concept of the demand curve. Demand as seen by the individual seller is one thing, demand for the product of an "industry" is another. What alters the one demand curve need not alter the other. Moreover, unsuccessful advertising, since it does.not alter the demand curve, would become production cost. Improvements of the product, if they increase the demand, would be selling costs. Several other "tests" for the distinction between selling and production cost have been suggested,[22] but many of them are ambiguous and few are pertinent to the analysis of the conduct of the individual firm.

It goes without saying that, as a practical matter, selling efforts will never be made under perfect polypoly. Under perfect poly-

[20] Chamberlin, *op. cit.*, p. 125.

[21] *Ibid.*, p. 123.

[22] Chamberlin made several other such suggestions. For example, "costs of selling increase the demand for the product on which they are expended; costs of production increase the supply." (*Ibid.*, pp. 125–26.) Or, the costs "made to adapt the product to the demand are costs of production; those made to adapt the demand to the product are costs of selling." (*Ibid.*, p. 125.) In another version, selling costs are the costs of *altering* the consumers' demands while the costs of *satisfying* them are production costs; or the *creation* of "a new scheme of wants" is the purpose of selling costs while want *satisfaction* is the purpose of production costs. (*Ibid.*, pp. 120, 123.) These distinctions have their place in the analysis of problems of welfare economics, but they are of little use for problems of the individual firm. For considerations of an individual seller it is not relevant whether a change in his sales opportunities is due to a *response* of consumers' conduct without alteration of their preference schedules (schemes of wants) or rather a *change* of their preference schedules.

poly, the saleability of any desired volume of product is not doubted by the seller, hence no special selling efforts need be made. If Mr. Smith wishes to sell $500 or $5000 or $50,000 worth of Government bonds, he will neither have to erect neon signs, nor air-condition his office, nor advertise in *Fortune* magazine in order to secure or improve the market for his offerings. Likewise, the wheat farmers or the small milk producers will not make any individual selling efforts on behalf of their products. The big wheat flour mills, however, and the larger distributing dairies are likely to engage in advertising and other forms of selling efforts. It is in differentiated polypoly, as well as oligopoly and monopoly, that selling efforts play a role.

Determination of Selling Effort with Fixed Selling Prices

Of special interest again, as it was with the costs of quality improvements, is the problem of determining the most profitable amount of selling expenses in the extreme case of differentiated polypoly with a fixed selling price. For this problem the retail store which offers goods under resale price maintenance (enforced by the so-called "fair trade" laws) is a good illustration. Since the minimum price is fixed (and price competition, therefore, ruled out) and also quality is fixed (and certified by brand or trade-mark as the standard quality) and location of the store is given (the location being the primary factor making for differentiation), selling efforts remain as the only real "variable" among the lot. Now, assuming all the conditions are present that were stated earlier for the case of quality competition—except that the selling costs, instead of constant per unit of output, are fixed as lump sums and are thus regressive per unit of output—we can easily find the most profitable amount of selling costs from the effects they are expected to have upon the sales volumes.[23]

[23] The justification for now taking up the "determination of *selling effort* with fixed selling prices" after having discussed (p. 179) the problem of "*quality* determination with fixed selling prices," may be questioned in view of my previous statement that the distinction between quality improvement and selling effort is often arbitrary. The justification lies chiefly in the different assumptions concerning the shape of the cost function. The previous assumption was *constant* cost per unit of output; the assumption now is *fixed*

Again it would be possible to draw the whole series of curves and to compare the various sets of cost and demand curves (where the cost curves containing larger selling expenses would correspond to longer horizontal demand curves). But again there will be simpler methods. For example, we can do with the one cost curve containing the absolute minimum of selling effort and deduct any additional selling costs from the fixed selling price. Thus we obtain for different sales volumes average revenues net of the respective average extra selling cost. Since the average selling cost need not increase with increasing total selling cost, we may not for all ranges have decreasing average revenues with increasing sales. But soon decreasing average revenues must set in and the case, once again, becomes analogous to that of price competition under differentiated polypoly.

This time, in analogy with price-elasticity and quality-elasticity of demand, we may speak of the promotion-elasticity of demand. A certain percentage increase in the quantity saleable at the fixed price is brought about by a certain percentage increase in unit cost (through higher selling expenses) or, alternatively expressed, by a certain percentage decrease in average revenue net of selling expenses. The greater the promotion-elasticity of demand expected by the seller, the higher will be the marginal revenue of promotion and the farther will he go in his selling efforts. The less the expected elasticity of demand with respect to promotion, the lower will be the marginal revenue of promotion and the less will be done by way of selling efforts.

Quasi-Perfect Polypoly

Several times, in this chapter and in others, perfect elasticity of demand as seen by the seller was mentioned as a criterion of perfect polypoly. Two kinds of distinctions are necessary concerning this "horizontal demand curve," one according to the limit of the horizontal range, another according to the causes of the horizontality.

---

cost. For instances of constant rather than fixed selling cost the solution given under the heading of quality determination will be applicable.

The Limit of the Horizontal Range

No demand curve could possibly remain horizontal over *absolutely* unlimited ranges of quantities of goods or services. It is easily possible that a seller believes he might sell twice the amount he is actually selling and still obtain the same price; and it is conceivable that he believes he could sell ten times as much and would still not have to accept a lower price. But the demand curve must somewhere stop being horizontal; it cannot go endlessly into space. This, however, is irrelevant for the models we have been discussing. If the limit of the horizontality is beyond the practical range of activity of the seller, it is pointless to ask *where* the limit might be. Relevant for the analysis of this type of seller's conduct is only whether or not the demand curve remains horizontal over a *practically* unlimited range. It would be practically unlimited if it covered the quantities which the particular seller might care to sell under given, technologically or organizationally determined cost conditions.

The demand curve may reach the end of its horizontal course before reaching the end of the range of potential activity of the seller. The seller may then have a choice of disposing of smaller or larger quantities at a given price, but there is a limit to his selling opportunities before he has reached the limit of his producing capacities. If this seller, for one reason or another, has no practical choice of selling price—the price being fixed by one device or another—the demand curve will be perfectly elastic up to a certain point, at which it breaks off. (The elasticity of this demand—prior to its limit—would be called "perfect" or *infinite* because, up to the limit of saleability, *finite* changes in quantity sold are divided by *zero* changes in price.)

Perfect elasticity of demand can be regarded as practically *unlimited* if the horizontal demand curve is intersected by the increasing marginal cost curve of the firm; for then it is only the cost situation that limits the firm's expansion of output or capacity. The range of perfect elasticity of demand will have to be regarded as definitely *limited* if the horizontal demand curve comes to an end while marginal cost is still below the price; in this case it is only the demand situation that limits the firm's expansion.

The Causes of the Horizontality

Demand which is infinitely elastic over only a *limited* range may be visualized by a seller either in an oligopoly position or in a position of differentiated polypoly. It will generally be a case of a "fixed" price. The seller may be bound to sell at the particular price by (a) governmental price regulation (price "ceilings" and "floors," (b) price agreement with other sellers or with an association of sellers (cartels, etc.), (c) price agreement with a supplier (resale price maintenance demanded by manufacturer or wholesale distributor), (d) tacit understanding with other sellers (fair prices, live-and-let-live prices, etc.), (e) generally accepted trade practices (customary price lines, the value of popular coins, such as the nickel or the dime, etc.).

Demand which is infinitely elastic over a practically *unlimited* range may be anticipated by a seller in a position of perfect polypoly or quasi-perfect polypoly. These positions imply practically unlimited opportunities to sell at a given price. They may be due to (a) the fact that the seller is one among a very large number of relatively small suppliers of a standardized product, (b) the fact that the seller is a very small "follower" of relatively large price leaders, or (c) the fact that a purchasing agency, usually of the government, stands ready to purchase any amount of the product at a stipulated price. The first of these three cases is called perfect polypoly because the price is not set or fixed by any one seller in the market, but rather determined by anonymous market forces ("supply and demand"). The other two cases may be called quasi-perfect polypoly. The price is fixed in the one case by the price leader, in the other by the (governmental) purchasing agency.

The practically unlimited opportunity to sell at a given price was explained for perfect polypoly as the consequence of two circumstances: the large number of sellers (making the share of each in the total market exceedingly small) and the standardization of their product (entailing the latent threat of a complete loss of any seller's sales at his slightest attempt to charge more, and permitting the substitution of any amount of his product for the product of any other seller).

Now we are faced with two cases in which there is perfect elasticity of demand over a practically unlimited range without there being a large number of sellers. One might have misgivings about using without qualification a term in a sense which conflicts with its literal meaning. It is for this reason that "quasi-perfect polypoly" is proposed to denote these circumstances.

The Demand for the Product of the "Follower"

Price leadership is a phenomenon of oligopolistic markets. Usually the leaders as well as the followers are typical oligopolists in the sense that they are conscious of being watched and careful to consider all possible rival reactions to their own conduct. But there is the possibility that an industry contains, besides the big leaders and a few large or medium-sized followers, some very small firms. In spite of the fewness of sellers in the market, the share of the little ones may be exceedingly small. In this case, if neither quality nor location differentiates the product sufficiently, it may happen that the price set by the leaders becomes for the little ones a definitely "given" market price, not perhaps because of fear of any dire consequences of disobedience or for any other reasons of "price policy," but simply because of the typical feature of perfect polypoly: namely, because the little firms would not be able to sell anything above the "given" price while they have no difficulty in selling whatever they offer at that price.

The output of these small-scale producers is limited by their productive capacity, that is to say, by their increasing production costs. These small firms are often the remnants of a past era, the last representatives of an outgoing production technique, so that a multiplication of their number is not to be expected. For only under these circumstances, that is, if there is little likelihood either that the small firms increase their production to more significant volumes or that the number of such small firms rises substantially, will the larger producers be prepared to neglect the competition from the "small fry." With their small outputs the small-scale producers are not felt by anybody as "disturbing" elements in the market, and the oligopolists in the industry, the larger and medium-sized firms, who watch each other and know that every one of their moves is watched, can afford to pay no attention to the little fellows; thus the latter can assume the position of quasi-perfect poly-polists.

Examples of such quasi-perfect polypolies within otherwise oligopolistic industries can probably be easily found by empirical industry studies, if these studies include also the small firms which "do not count" either as to their production volume or their market influence. The mechanical wood pulp industry can provide illustrations.

Unlimited Offers to Purchase

Government purchases of unlimited quantities can "artificially" create an infinitely elastic demand for a product which may be offered by a few sellers only. Any one of these few sellers would then be in the position of quasi-perfect polypoly.

The declared and undoubted willingness on the part of the monetary authority under the gold standard in its various forms to buy gold at a fixed price can make a quasi-perfect polypolist out of every gold producer, regardless of the fewness of such producers. The foreign-exchange markets, which under the gold standard display infinite elasticities of demand on the part of gold arbitrageurs, may even in the absence of any gold-standard legislation exhibit at least temporarily these perfect demand elasticities if there are efficiently operating exchange stabilization funds. Governmental purchasing at fixed prices may achieve the same thing in other markets and may be found to be, under certain circumstances, a possible method of demonopolizing or deoligopolizing certain industries. It is quite possible that oligopolists who have been severely restricting their outputs may choose to accept the relatively low prices offered by a governmental purchasing agency for anything they care to produce; these producers would thus be transformed from high-price oligopolists into low-price quasi-perfect polypolists.[24]

[24] The practical applicability of this idea will depend on the degree of unused capacity. If the outputs, under full utilization of productive capacity, are so large that the public's demand at a price that covers average cost is not sufficient to take the whole output ("decreasing cost industries"), the governmental purchasing agency would either accumulate increasing surplus stocks of the product or incur constant losses in reselling to the public.

This idea of using "standing offers" of the government to purchase unlimited amounts of product at a stipulated price, thereby making the demand elasticities perfectly elastic and removing the producers' incentives to restrict output, has been recently proposed under the name "governmental counterspeculation." It is not intended here to discuss the practical merits of adopting such a plan to cope with the problem of monopolistic deviations from the economic use of resources. There are many reasons for believing that the practical, political and administrative difficulties of operating the device of "counterspeculation" would be overwhelming and might cause a waste of resources greater than that involved in the monopolistic restriction of production. Only on a level of theorizing which provisionally abstracts from many factors of practical politics can the possibility of using the device for transforming differentiated polypoly and oligopoly into quasi-perfect polypoly be accepted.[25]

THE RISE OR DECLINE OF POLYPOLY

Empirical Findings

The frequency of the occurrence of polypoly positions in the real world is difficult to estimate and impossible to measure. It has been mentioned once before that there is only one sure way of

[25] The last paragraph was inserted into the text after the appearance of Abba P. Lerner's *Economics of Control* (New York: Macmillan, 1944). Lerner describes the scheme as follows (p. 55): "The government through a special board estimates what would be the price of the good that would make demand equal to supply if there were no restriction of the kind we wish to abolish. It then guarantees this price to all the sellers in the case of a seller's restriction or to all buyers in case of a buyer's restriction. The buyers (or sellers) then know that the price will not move against them if they buy or sell more and that they will not get a better price if they restrict their dealings. The Board of Counter-speculation then buys in the free market what it has promised to sell to buyers at the guaranteed price or sells in the free market all that it has undertaken to buy from the sellers at the guaranteed price. The Board of Counter-speculation will make a profit or a loss if it makes a mistake and these may be expected roughly to cancel out. With experience it will be able to estimate more and more accurately and to guarantee for longer periods. By this means the benefits of an optimum allocation of goods may be brought about when the natural forces of competition fail to do this."

ascertaining whether or not polypoly exists in a certain line: to ask the sellers such questions as would clearly reveal their states of mind, their patterns of thinking, of pricing, and of planning their production and their plants. Nevertheless, without interviews or questionnaires, merely by studying the conditions prevailing in the field and in its various sectors one may with imagination also obtain an impression of the actual market position. ("Actual" re- fers, of course, to the subjective point of view of the producer and seller.)

The results of this imagined introspection can, as long as we are concerned with present-day conditions, be cross-checked with the results of an inquiry by interview. If it is stated, for example, that in the manufacturing of knit goods, women's apparel, house- hold equipment, china ware, furniture, etc., the positions of many or most firms are polypolistic in character, these statements will be subject to verification. But similar statements referring to the past are not subject to verification and, therefore, assertions about a rise or decline of polypoly can be regarded, at best, as "more plausible" or "less plausible."

Growth of Size of Firms and Markets

Assertions about a rise or decline of polypoly are precarious because, among other things, the relative significance of the vari- ous industries (in the ordinary sense of the word) has changed through time. Industries exist now which did not exist in the past, and industries may have both oligopolistic and polypolistic sectors at the same time. Very generally, however, one may say this: (1) the growth of the optimum size of firms in most industries, that is, the drift toward large-scale production, has worked to reduce the number of firms in active competition with one another; but (2) the parallel growth of total effective demand, the simultaneous growth of the market area consequent upon cheaper and quicker transportation, and the increased density of the consumer popula- tion in certain places have all worked in the opposite direction. The latter forces, making for an increase in the number of firms actively competing in the same market, possess probably a com- bined strength which has exceeded that of the oligopolizing forces.

The conclusion that the frequency of *polypoly* has probably increased, and not decreased, during the last century need not be regarded as contradicting the widely held thesis of the "decline of *competition*." Competition means many things and we are not always quite sure what it is intended to mean in a particular context. It may mean ease of entry of new firms and, as such, it may have declined in spite of the rise of polypoly; or it may mean the absence of price agreements or other price fixing schemes, and such schemes may not be altogether incompatible with the rise of polypoly. Indeed, it is very likely that the compass of price fixing schemes, trade association practices, and similar conspiracies has grown in response or as a reaction to the increase of polypolistic competition.

The rise of polypoly during the last century appears plausible chiefly in view of the growth of the city and of the supersession of relatively isolated, local markets by large regional or national markets. The small village, which in its earliest beginnings probably fostered positions of pure monopoly in several lines, soon becomes a fertile ground for the development of duopoly and oligopoly positions; these may well change into polypolies when the place grows into a town or city. Similarly, the expansion of a local market first into a regional and later into a national market, an expansion made possible through improved transportation facilities, may make competition increasingly impersonal and anonymous, hence less oligopolistic. It goes without saying that such a development has by no means been universal; in many fields the growth of the size of firms for technical or tactical reasons has unmistakably led to the oligopolization of the market. And these fields with their sometimes spectacular history have attracted most of the public and professional attention.

IMPERFECT POLYPOLY AND GENERAL EQUILIBRIUM

Economic theorists who do not confine themselves to analyses of the single firm or the single industry, but work on the elaboration of the general equilibrium system, have almost a vested interest in the prevalence of polypoly and, if possible, perfect polypoly. The beauty and usefulness of a model depends on its simplicity. The complicated mass of interdependences between the various magnitudes in the whole economic system should be reducible to a small number of variables and the results must be determinate. The assumption of perfect polypoly was felt to be of utmost importance because it enabled the model builder to do with no more than three sets of variables: the tastes and preferences of the individuals, the technical coefficients of production, and the available productive resources. From these three sets of data or independent variables (indifference functions, production functions, and resources) all economic action could be derived. Particular "imaginations" of producers and sellers were not among the data, for this was unnecessary thanks to the assumption of perfect polypoly, which meant that the producers and sellers would always believe they could sell all they wanted at the prices formed in the free market.

Price and Sales Expectations

To be quite exact, perfect polypoly as we defined it would not fully satisfy all these postulates. In our definition, perfect elasticity of the demand as seen by the seller was the characteristic feature of undifferentiated or perfect polypoly, but the "given" price was not necessarily the one that happened to rule at the moment in the market. We allowed our type of seller the freedom to expect another price to rule when the product would be ready, provided this price was not subject to his control and was believed to be independent of his supply. If we insist on our pattern of a perfect polypolist, then the general equilibrium theorist needs, besides his three sets of data, a set of price expectations of producers and sellers. And, in order to get not only determinate movements but also a determinate ultimate equilibrium position, certain laws of change of expectations would have to be assumed.

That positions of perfect polypoly are rare, has been pointed out almost *ad nauseam*. Most of the polypolistic industries or trades that exist show sufficient differentiation of product or service to make the market of each single seller limited and expansible only through price reductions, quality improvements, or increased selling efforts. If modest price reductions (quality improvements, selling efforts) can secure considerable sales increases, then the deviations of the conduct of the differentiated polypolist from the pattern of conduct of the perfect polypolist will not be large enough to worry the general equilibrium theorist. If, however, the elasticities of demand, as seen by the sellers, are not that large— as in actual fact they are not—it becomes less defensible to rule out the differentiated polypolist any longer from the model which is constructed for the explanation of the economic world.

The admission of the differentiated polypolist into the general equilibrium model need not yet wreck it, in spite of the fears of some most distinguished economists.[26] The fourth set of data, which became necessary when we permitted the perfect polypolist to have price expectations, becomes only slightly more complicated when the differentiated polypolist is introduced: price expectations become sales expectations, or horizontal demand curves become sloping demand curves in the producers' or sellers' anticipations. The difficulty for the model and for the safe arrival at a determinate, ultimate equilibrium position lies only in the laws of change of the sales expectations. Sales expectations will have to be revised if other data change. There is no reason why the laws of these revisions should not be such as to secure the unimpeded functioning of the model.

Objective Changes and Subjective Expectations

If sales expectations changed without any rhyme or reason and if the revisions of expectations, which become necessary whenever sellers find their past expectations disappointed, were without any recognizable relationship to changes in the objective data, then economic equilibrium analysis would indeed be of little use. We should never be able to state the probable consequences of certain changes in consumers' demand or certain changes in production technique, because everything would depend on the wild and unpredictable imaginations of the sellers. If we can, however, assume that the revision of sales expectations will, by and large, proceed in an orderly fashion and according to intelligible principles—and it

[26] See, for example, J. R. Hicks, *Value and Capital: An Inquiry into Some Fundamental Principles of Economic Theory* (London: Oxford University Press, 1939), pp. 83–84.

seems to me that such an assumption is not too extravagant—then the general equilibrium theorist need not give up and can make his peace with the differentiated polypolist. Whether or not such an appeasement will also be possible in the case of the oligopolist remains to be seen.

Another assumption, also of fundamental significance for the general equilibrium model, is that of the free and easy entry of new firms and resources into profitable industries. This assumption, usually lumped with others in the alleged catch-all "competition," concerns the theorist not merely in connection with general equilibrium analysis but also with the analysis of the equilibrium of the industry. This phase of "competition" will be the subject of the next chapters.

PART III—MORE SELLERS

CHAPTER 7

Pliopoly: Newcomers to a Profitable Industry

The Nature and Prerequisites of Pliopoly: The Distinctions Recapitulated
· The Pre-Conditions Summarized

The Industry: Limiting the Scope of Interdependence · The Boundaries
of the "Industry"

Profit: Business Profit versus Economic Profit · Transitory and Long-Run
Profits · Fixed Resources and Normal Profit · Supernormal Profits and
Entry · Subnormal Profits and Exodus

Entrepreneurship and Uncertainty: The Quality of Entrepreneurship
Managerial Services · Uncertainty · The Safety-Margin in Profit Estimates

Indivisibility and Immobility: Indivisibility · Indivisibility and Uncertainty Combined · Immobility · Profits versus Imputed Rents · The Case
of Cheap Resources

IN THE DISCUSSION OF the various types of competition—in Chapter 4—it was shown that the existence of *many* sellers in an
industry and the entry of *more* sellers into the industry are two
different things. The consequences of these two types of "competition" were often unconsciously, and not to advantage, thrown
together in theoretical analysis. A clean-cut separation of the two
concepts is advisable and will obviously be facilitated by the use
of different terms for the two different notions. *Polypoly* has been
the accepted term for the status of "many sellers" in one field.
Pliopoly is the term proposed to denote the probability of "more
sellers" entering a field.

THE NATURE AND PREREQUISITES OF PLIOPOLY

The Distinctions Recapitulated

The logical nature of the two concepts was contrasted above.[1]
The following differences were found to be significant:

---

[1] Chapter 4, pp. 105–107. The formulation in Chapter 4 is less sketchy
than the recapitulation.

(1) Polypoly is concerned with the state of mind of the sellers in a certain field; pliopoly is concerned with the probability—seen primarily by the observing economist—that new sellers will break into the field when it appears profitable.

(2) Polypoly is concerned with a definite group of people, namely the businessmen engaged in the field under consideration; pliopoly is concerned with some indefinite, perhaps still unborn, individuals who may desire to take up that business when it becomes profitable.

(3) Polypoly is concerned with a situation present at any moment of time; pliopoly is concerned with a process expected to be started only by certain stimuli and to take place in the course of time.

(4) Polypoly is concerned with the analysis of the equilibrium of the individual firm; pliopoly is concerned with the analysis of the equilibrium of the industry (although it will affect the individual firms in the industry).

(5) Polypoly is concerned with everyday conduct which conceivably can be ascertained by immediate empirical inquiry; pliopoly is concerned with processes which can only occasionally be empirically tested and only over considerable periods of time.

The Pre-Conditions Summarized

Among the pre-conditions of pliopoly the following were enumerated: [2]

(1) Spread of knowledge of the profit opportunities existing in a field.

(2) Existence of versatile and venturous entrepreneurs.

(3) Access to necessary equipment, materials, facilities, funds, and skills.

(4) Absence of restraints, public or private, legal or illegal, barring the entry into the field or prohibiting the use of adequate production methods.

(5) Adequate divisibility of the necessary productive elements and facilities.

[2] The previous enumeration (Chapter 4, pp. 107 ff.) was more exhaustive and elaborate.

Ease of entry into a field and ease of exodus from it are not necessarily associated with each other. The above conditions relate only to entry. The concept of pliopoly, or newcomers' competition in selling, is not concerned with the withdrawal of firms from an industry that has become unprofitable.[3]

Analogous to the concept of pliopoly, which relates to the selling end of the business, is the concept of pliopsony, relating to the buying end. While both are "newcomers' competition," the newcomers, on the one side, will be new sellers of certain products and, on the other, new buyers of certain means of production. The "industries" which they enter may be different groups of firms; that is to say, a firm may compete with one group in the sale of products and with another group in the purchase of productive means.[4]

THE INDUSTRY

After having used the concept of "the industry" innumerable times, and before embarking on a discussion for which this concept is fundamental, we are compelled to attempt a definition. The use of the expression "entry into the industry" presupposes that there are borderlines of some sort between one industry and another. Yet we know that often in reality there are no such borderlines of any sort. Upon what grounds should one decide that a certain group of firms producing a certain set of products constitute "an industry," distinct and disconnected from other groups? If it is understood that the products of different firms are generally not identical but different, what degree of similarity or dissimilarity or, more concisely, what degree of substitutability would justify us in speaking of the "same" industry or of "different" industries?

Limiting the Scope of Interdependence

The economist's concept of the industry is an abstraction for the purpose of limiting the scope of problems of interdependence. In the last analysis, everything in the economy hangs together;

---

[3] See above, Chapter 4, p. 109.
[4] See above, Appendix to Chapter 4, p. 130.

but not all interdependence is substantial or even definite as to its direction. It saves time and effort in analysis to assume certain variables as constant or, what often comes to the same thing, to disregard them; and it is quite legitimate to do so if changes of these variables are negligible for the particular problem or if the direction of the relationship is uncertain. The concept of the industry is nothing but an expedient device for ruling out negligible or too uncertain interdependence.[5]

Interdependence is conveniently expressed by *cross-elasticities* of demand and supply (or cost). Cross-elasticity of demand is the ratio which the relative change in the quantity of product sold (at a given price) by A bears to the relative change of price charged by B (which is causing the change in A's sales). Cross-elasticity of supply is the ratio which the relative change in the quantity of factor available (at a given price) to A bears to the relative change of price offered by B (which is causing the change in supply to A). In other words, these cross-elasticities show the influence of B's price bids and offers upon A's sales and purchases. In some cases another variety of elasticity expression is preferable, showing the influence of B's quantities (of products sold or of factors bought) upon A's prices (obtainable for a given amount of product or to be paid for a given amount of factors). Using the term cross-elasticity for both types of relationships we might advance the following statement as something approaching a definition of an industry. *Firms related through cross-elasticities of the demands for their products or of the supplies of their factors may be said to constitute an "industry" if these cross-elasticities are either so important or so definite that they could not be neglected without impairing the considerations of the firms or the analysis of the economist.*[6]

[5] Robert Triffin, *Monopolistic Competition and General Equilibrium Theory* (Cambridge: Harvard University Press, 1940), has come to the contrary conclusion. He states (p. 89): "In the general pure theory of value, the group and the industry are useless concepts."

[6] This statement should probably be qualified by the warning that a very wide extension of the "industry," by taking in too many "repercussions," may render inapplicable one of the most fruitful tools of industry analysis: mutually independent demand and cost functions. The mutual independence of demand and cost functions—wherever these tools are made use of—would require an upper limit to the extension of the industry concept. (For this qualification I am indebted to Arthur Smithies.)

The simultaneous attention to cross-elasticities of demand for the products and cross-elasticities of factor supply or cost makes for more variables, i.e., for a larger extension of the "industry," than we should like to handle. Hence, it will be better to concentrate either on demand relationships or on cost relationships but not to intertangle them, although this means that the "industry" from the point of view of *product relationship* (demand conditions) will usually be another group than the "industry" from the point of view of *factor relationship* (cost conditions). For the purposes of the present discussion, which deals more with the sales aspect than with the cost aspect of production, we had then better confine ourselves to product relationships.

Related demand may mean substitutability or complementarity of products; the cross-elasticities of demand will be positive in the case of competing products and negative in the case of complementary products. It is a matter of taste whether or not the relationship of complementarity should be excluded from the definition of the industry. When one speaks, for example, of the "construction industry," he does take complementarity as the principle of classification. But for the purposes of the present discussion it is more appropriate to include only positive substitutability in the definition of industry. The criterion of belonging to (or entering into) an industry would then be the definitely adverse effect of the increased (or newly started) operations of a firm upon the sales conditions of other firms.

This effect need not be of a particular magnitude if only it is definite and certain in its direction. As one may wish to say, the "qualitative effect" may be taken as a sufficient criterion if the "quantitative effect" is negligible. The *degree* of change in the sales conditions of, say, agricultural producers which may be caused by the added output of one more farmer is probably not noticeable, but the *direction* of change is certain; thus they can be said to belong to the same industry.

The Boundaries of the "Industry"

The proposed definition of an industry as the "relevant group" of firms is so flexible that it prevents the formulation of meaningful generalizations about the industry. Such generalizations can be formulated only for clearly delimited industries, and this requires the construction of specific industry models.

The best-known and most-used model is that of a group of firms producing products that are perfectly substitutable for one another. There is no problem, regarding this model, as to the meaning of "within" and "outside," or "entry" and "exodus." This industry model is logically related to the conduct model of perfect polypoly, but does not fit the model of imperfect polypoly. To achieve this consistency, that is, to make it permissible to group together firms who sell differentiated products, a model has been constructed on the principle that a "marked gap" in the degree of substitutability may surround the products sold by the firms in question. The differentiated products offered by the members of the "industry" are much more easily substituted for one another than for any product sold by anybody else. The gap in the "chain of substitutes" delimits the industry.[7]

The usefulness of this model has been attacked on the ground that the "boundary" may be different with respect to each individual producer.[8] Although there may be for each producer a marked gap in the chain of substitutes—beyond which his sales opportunities will not be noticeably sensitive to changes in the prices of other products—these gaps may be different for every product. And, in this case, the group of firms (called an "industry") would be relevant only from the point of view of an individual producer. The economist analysing problems other than those of the individual firm would not be able to isolate any group of firms relevant for any problem common to all its members.

Although this objection may be justified in many instances, there is no doubt that a model that assumes a common boundary of high substitutability for the products of all firms in the group is useful, not only for the derivation of intermediate theorems serving as first steps in the analysis of the more complex relationships pertaining to more realistic models, but also for more or less direct application to problems of the real world. If we recall the

[7] Joan Robinson, *The Economics of Imperfect Competition* (London: Macmillan, 1932), p. 5.

[8] Nicholas Kaldor, "Mrs. Robinson's 'Economics of Imperfect Competition,'" *Economica*, New Series, Vol. I (1934), pp. 339–40.

practical-political problems of governmental restrictions of entry into particular trades or professions, we become aware of the economic significance of "groups" where the boundaries are clear enough to render gratuitous our sophisticated inhibitions on account of the shifting gap in the chain of substitutes. The very fact that a number of firms, operators, or practitioners act as groups, bringing political pressures to obtain protection against newcomers, indicates that they recognize a common boundary line. The theorist has no need to be squeamish about models that assume that industries can be delimited.[9]

The effects may be visualized by the firms themselves or only by the economist. Both points of view may be significant. The judgment of the firms will have bearing on problems of oligopoly and monopoly proper. But for the problem of the probability of the appearance of newcomers attracted by profits and of the disappearance of the profits because of the competition by the newcomers, it will be the point of view of the economist that determines what should be included in the "industry." For different problems one and the same firm will be regarded as belonging to different industries, differing both as to composition and size. "Industry" is merely a short expression which stands here for all firms whose operations affect one another's selling opportunities and sales revenues so definitely that we must not neglect taking account of them.

PROFIT

Repeatedly have the terms profit and supernormal profit been mentioned in this discussion without an attempt at definition. A digression on the profit concept seems indispensable. Indeed, the

[9] It is interesting that Robert Triffin, despite his rejection of all "group" and "industry" concepts for economic analysis, continues to use the concept of "entry." He distinguishes "free entry"—the appearance of new firms producing the same goods under the same cost conditions—"homogeneous entry" —the appearance of new firms producing the same goods, though not at the same cost—and "heterogeneous entry"—the appearance of new firms producing imperfect substitutes. Triffin, *op. cit.*, p. 120. For a concurring opinion on my industry concept see Andreas G. Papandreou, "Market Structure and Monopoly Power," *American Economic Review*, Vol. XXXIX (1949), p. 887.

concepts of newcomers' competition—pliopoly and pliopsony—cannot be defined without reference to profit. It is profit which is said to attract new competitors to an industry; and it is perfect competition from newcomers which is said to wipe out profit. Unless the meaning of profit is made clear the concept of pliopoly cannot have any clear meaning.

It is not surprising that profit means different things for the accountant and for the economist since the purposes for which their concepts are used are different. Even within the scope of economic theory the meaning of profit will have to change according to the character of the problem in question.

Business Profit versus Economic Profit

The accounting or business concept of profit comes nearest to what the economist sometimes calls the residual net income of a firm. The accountant usually starts from "total sales," i.e., the receipts for products and services sold, and deducts direct manufacturing (and distributing) cost, such as wages paid and raw material used up, in order to get what is sometimes called gross profits, sometimes "net earnings from operation" or something of the sort. From this amount the accountant deducts general expenses or overhead costs, such as interest on the firm's debts (bonds or mortgages), rents on leased property or equipment, administrative expenses (executives' salaries), etc., in order to arrive at net profits.[10] (Depreciation of buildings and machinery is sometimes treated as part of manufacturing costs, sometimes as part of overhead cost.)

Yet, net-profit figures thus arrived at would not tell anything about the profitability of the firm even if the cost figures employed by the accountant were more than merely "past history." In all cases the cost and net-profit figures of the accountant reflect the ownership situation in the particular firm. And there are, first of all, differences in the "capitalization" of the firms, due to the different ways in which they have raised their capital. Corporations

---

[10] We neglect here "other income" or "income from other sources," such as interest received from government bonds, or dividends collected from corporate stock, held by the firm.

with greater bond issues and smaller capital stock will have, of course, smaller total net profits in the accounting sense. More generally, the greater the proportion of the resources employed by a firm which are owned by it (or furnished by it at no contractual cost), the higher will be its residual income; the greater the proportion of the resources hired, leased or borrowed, the greater will be costs paid out and the smaller will be residual income, or the accountant's net profit figure.[11]

Businessmen who ask themselves how they fared last year will be interested in their residual income. Businessmen, however, who ask themselves whether or not they should enter a new, supposedly lucrative field will be interested in another matter. They will examine whether total receipts are likely to be above the total costs of all required resources, no matter whether these costs would be contractual income paid to others or opportunity costs of the resources which they own themselves and might use elsewhere. Net profits would be found to exist only after all opportunity costs of all factors, owned or hired, are covered.

The economist, in a discussion of competition and the allocation of resources, takes a similar view. The cost of a productive service is the value of its best alternative use, or, in other words, the "opportunity" which must be foregone when the resource is employed for a given purpose. Any number of potential applications "compete" for the use of the productive services. Losses arise when resources are allocated to fields in which the "value product" is below the values that could be produced by using the resources in other fields. These latter values, the sacrificed opportunities, are the costs of using the resources, or their productive services, in the given field. To find a field where the produced value is above the cost of the necessary productive services—that is to say, to find a field with economic net profits—means that a reallocation of resources, namely their entry into the "profitable" industry, is indicated. Newcomers' competition is supposed to bring this about. If it were done perfectly, there could be no net profit in the long run.

[11] The accountant's net profit comprises non-contractual costs such as interest on the firm's own capital, risk premiums on insurable but self-borne risks, and, in some cases (other than in corporations), wages of management and rent on real property owned by the owners of the firm.

Transitory and Long-Run Profits

Newcomers' competition, or pliopoly, is essentially a long-run concept. The long run is usually defined as the time interval sufficient to allow completion of adjustments of plant capacities, fixed equipment, and the number of firms. This definition should be handled with caution lest we "infer" from it that in the long run pliopoly must, of logical necessity, be perfect; a barrier which prohibits entry into a profitable industry and, thus, precludes "adjustment" of the industry, would "by definition" perpetuate the short run *ad infinitum.* In order to avoid such useless tautologies,[12] the concept of "long run" will have to assume something of a "normative" character and the frictions that delay adjustment will have to be appraised as either "natural" and "normal" or "artificial" and "excessive."

With perfect pliopoly at work, that is to say, with no artificial or excessive frictions interfering with entry, net profits are zero or tend to fall back to zero whenever they have become positive. But since adjustments to new situations must take some time even where there are no excessive frictions, positive net profits can exist in transition periods.[13] Where pliopoly is absent because of excessive obstacles to entry, surpluses of receipts over long-run cost may endure. These "remainders" after all costs are paid may have the character either of monopoly rent or of profit.

Fixed Resources and Normal Profit

The fact that some of the resources employed in the enterprise are relatively immobile and relatively specialized—which makes their quick transference to other uses difficult or even impossible— in addition to the relative durability and indivisibility of resources, forces us to think of them in the short run as the *fixed resources* of the firm. They are fixed in contrast to the variable factors of production, which can be acquired as they are needed for the cur-

[12] The concepts "long run" and "perfect pliopoly" would express the identical idea.

[13] It may be well to repeat that the spreading of the knowledge of profit opportunities is one of the many factors included in the catch-all "frictions" —normal or excessive.

rent production of output, and of which varying quantities are used if varying amounts of output are produced.[14] Capital funds owned or borrowed by the firm; real property, plant and equipment owned or rented by the firm; managerial ability and specialized skill hired on long-term basis or furnished by the owners of the firm; these and other things are examples of "fixed resources" of the firm. Once they are acquired (by long-term contract or for ownership) the cost of these resources to the firm is fixed and independent of the exact output chosen in the short run. Anything that can be earned will help defray the "overhead" and will be gladly accepted. If the fixed resources are quite immobile or quite specialized, they are available for service, in the short run, even if they earn nothing. Whatever they earn (that is, any surplus of total receipts over the total of variable costs) is a *quasi-rent* to the firm.

If this quasi-rent is so large that it can take care of all the contractual charges for the hired fixed resources and of the deprecia-

[14] The classification of costs into variable and fixed is usually taken for granted without analysis of the causes which make some costs fixed over a certain period. The two basic causes, *immobility* and *specificity*, are of equal weight. If mobility were perfect (i.e., if transfer and transport costs were zero) but if the resource in its present form were absolutely specific (i.e., if it were of no use elsewhere), its continued use by the firm would be no (variable) cost of production. If the resource were highly versatile and equally valuable for many other uses (i.e., not specialized) but if it were not mobile (i.e., if the cost of transferring it equaled or exceeded its value at the alternative place of employment), the continued use of the resource by the firm, again, would be no (variable) cost of production. The element of *durability* enters because only in the case of durable resources are large "stocks" of the productive services bought in advance. (The durable good *is* a stock of future services.) If the resources are not durable, inventories or contracts for future delivery will prejudice the firm only for moderate periods. To the extent of existing inventories and contracts even non-durable materials (if they have only the specific use and no other valuable application, or if they can be transported only under forbidding costs) may result in a "fixed supply" to the firm and their continued use would be no (variable) cost of production. The fourth element making for fixed costs, *indivisibility*, needs, at this point, no further explanation. But it might be mentioned that indivisibility may be created by institution where it is physically absent. If a firm were compelled to hire a minimum number of workers on a yearly basis—annual wages—that portion of labor cost would be no (variable) cost of production. In summary, immobility, specificity, durability and indivisibility are the four properties responsible for the problems of fixed resources and fixed cost.

tion and depletion of the owned fixed resources, and still leave something above all this, there will be profit in the business sense. But this business profit might be less than what the businessman would have received for the services of his own fixed resources, had he devoted them to some other purpose. In this case his "economic profit" would be negative. *If the quasi-rent is exactly sufficient to cover all opportunity costs of all the fixed resources (owned and hired) which would be needed to establish the enterprise if it did not exist, then the quasi-rent is called "normal."* This normal remainder after covering the direct costs is often called the *normal profit* of the industry.

Normal profit would be in its entirety *profit in the business sense* if all the fixed resources were owned by the firm; otherwise it exceeds profit in the business sense by the contractual payments made to owners of hired fixed resources. On the other hand, normal profit, being equal to the opportunity cost of all the fixed resources (including management) that would be required to reproduce the services of the enterprise, is equivalent to *zero profit in the economic sense.*

Supernormal Profits and Entry

The danger of making tautological propositions is considerable in discussions of the concept of normal profits. Because supernormal profits seem to invite newcomers to an industry and subnormal profits seem to drive away those who are in an industry, some writers are inclined to define normal profits as the earnings of the fixed resources in an industry which neither grows nor declines in size or number of firms. It should be clear that such a definition is useless: it muddles together attractiveness and actual afflux, desirability of entry and ease of entry, zero profits and monopoly rents.

To say that an industry which is not easy to enter will have "high normal profits" is to conceal the essence of the problem. The essential question is whether resources, however scarce, are allocated to the industry when their cost can be earned by the industry, or whether they are not so allocated in spite of the fact that their cost can be earned by the industry. The scarcity of resources is one thing; the ease of their entry into the industry is another. "*Normal* profits" will be high if the opportunity cost of the fixed resources required by the industry is high; profits will be *abnormally* high if resources, perfectly substitutable for those used by the industry, are available at less than they could earn in the industry but find their entry into the industry obstructed.[15]

Subnormal Profits and Exodus

The connection between subnormal profits and decline of an industry is rather complicated. It can be shown that the level of subnormal profit that will cause the exodus of an enterprise depends on several factors, the most important of which are: the net opportunity cost of the fixed resources in their present form; the unexpired service-life of the durable fixed resources; the timing of replacement requirements.

If the fixed resources of the enterprise are not very specific and not very immobile, a modest decline in revenue may result in a withdrawal of the resources from the industry. Plant and machinery may be withdrawn in bulk, in their present form, and managerial ability may likewise be transferred to other uses. The more specific and immobile the fixed resources are, the less likely will there be such withdrawals and the more important will be the questions concerning the duration of contracts, the service-life of equipment, the timing of replacement requirements.

Let us confine our consideration to the role which plant and equipment play in this connection. Assume them to be exceedingly specific and immobile, and of high durability. Their opportunity cost in their present form, the present salvage value, will be very low and, therefore, only a very drastic fall in revenue will lead to the immediate disappearance of the enterprise. How long the firm will continue to operate if the fall in revenue is not quite so drastic, will depend on the requirements for maintenance and replacement of outworn equipment. If the fall in revenue is considerable,

[15] I can merely point in passing to the problem which arises from the fact that the opportunity cost of each resource, i.e., its value in the best alternative use, may in turn be affected by conditions of entry into alternative fields. This complicates but does not, I think, invalidate the attempt to deduce normal profits from opportunity costs.

it may happen that the first substantial replacement requirement finishes the enterprise. In this case, the opportunity cost of the productive resources (which would be needed for the replacement of fixed equipment) in relation to the value produced in the industry would be too high to permit the allocation of the productive resources to the industry.

On the other hand, it may happen that the various parts of the firm's equipment come up for replacement in so small installments that the reinvestment always seems warranted. If the outlay which can secure continued operation of the enterprise is small enough in comparison to the revenue (however reduced), then it may, again and again, pay to incur the cost of replacement. It is conceivable that a considerable part of the equipment of an enterprise is replaced in spite of decidedly subnormal profits—indeed, in spite of heavy losses in the accounting sense—if only the replacement requirements arise little by little, in sufficiently small doses at a time.[16]

However, if large replacement requirements arise simultaneously, the enterprise may be condemned to extinction even with a revenue which is much less short of normal than in the case of the staggered replacement bills. A complete and simultaneous replacement of all the fixed resources of the enterprise would not pay even with the smallest deficit of earnings below normal, that is to say, with earnings below the level at which the full opportunity cost of all the services needed for reproducing the fixed resources can be covered.

Thus it seems that there is not one but a multitude of levels of profits of sufficient subnormality to cause the exodus of an enterprise. This, however, is not so significant in an industry that consists of a goodly number of establishments. Among a large number of establishments there will probably always be one that is confronted with substantial maintenance and replacement requirements. This will be the marginal establishment, or perhaps the marginal firm, going out of business when profits fall below

---

[16] The marginal productivity of reinvestment may be very high while the average productivity is negative. In simpler words, a firm may steadily lose money and yet the replacement of a broken screw may constitute an investment with a rate of return of over a million percent.

normal. The exodus-level of earnings in an *industry as a whole* (consisting of many establishments) may, therefore, be said to be determined by the total-reproduction cost of the necessary fixed resources, and not by the lower partial-replacement cost or even salvage value of existing equipment. These lower levels would determine only the exodus of a *particular firm*.

It is understood that exodus from the industry takes place, by definition, in the "long run"; and it should also be understood that the calendar-time involved in these developments may be very long.

ENTREPRENEURSHIP AND UNCERTAINTY

The Quality of Entrepreneurship

It is often said that the existence of economic profit is due to a scarcity of "entrepreneurial ability," and that the different profit levels in different industries are due to the different qualities of "entrepreneurship" required for particular lines. According to this view the level of profit and the ease of entry into an industry are not linked with the idea of perfect competition from newcomers. For, it is said, normal profits will be high in "trades which require unusual personal ability," and low in trades which require less of it and are therefore easy to enter.[17]

In order to clarify the issue it is necessary to inquire into the meaning of the "quality of entrepreneurship" and "personal ability of the entrepreneur." It seems appropriate to distinguish between the function of choosing, initiating and venturing an enterprise and, on the other hand, the executive function within a given, existing enterprise. In many respects, to be sure, the difference is only one of degree. No sharp lines, for example, can be drawn between the ability to start new enterprises, the ability to start new ventures in established enterprises and the ability to make some minor innovations in running existing establishments. All these are concerned with decisions which are risky in view of the uncertain future in an ever-changing world. But in one respect

[17] Joan Robinson, "What is Perfect Competition?", *Quarterly Journal of Economics*, Vol. XLIX (1935), p. 107.

two functions, the strictly entrepreneurial and the managerial, are fundamentally different: the latter can be expressed in physically measurable terms, such as the labor-time, the full working time, of a manager; the former, the strictly entrepreneurial function, is not reducible to any physically distinguishable units.[18]

In the theory of income distribution it is one of the prime postulates of logical procedure that the resources (factors, productive agents or services, whichever terminology is preferred) can be expressed in physical units.[19] If rent of land or wage of labor is explained on the basis of efficiency, and if this efficiency is measurable in physical terms, the logic of the explanation is unobjectionable. If the efficiency does not show itself in the quantity of physical product, but only in quality or in the amount of saved incidental expenses or in something of the sort, efficiency may still be compared in value terms. A comparison between the efficiency of various factors or the qualities of resources will be possible as long as the resources or factors, such as the piece of land or the unit of labor, are well defined in physical terms. One acre of land per year or one worker's labor per hour can be said to produce a revenue of so and so many dollars if marginal analysis shows that this is the increment or decrement of revenue resulting from the application or non-application of that additional unit of factor.

If, however, neither units of factor nor units of product can be expressed in physical terms, the relationship between efficiency and "value" of the resources loses its explanatory significance. It is sheer circularity of reasoning to say that 100 dollars worth of "uncertainty-bearing" or 100 dollars worth of "entrepreneurial ability" have an efficiency of 100 dollars and have, therefore, a value (or derive an income) of 100 dollars. The "entrepreneurial

[18] Frank H. Knight's work on *Risk, Uncertainty and Profit* (New York: Houghton, Mifflin, 1921), is the classical analysis of the problems discussed in this chapter. Knight describes the manager as the man who gives the orders, and the entrepreneur as the one who chooses the man who gives the orders.

[19] The argument produced in this section was previously presented in my essay on "The Meaning of the Marginal Product," in *Explorations in Economics* (New York: McGraw-Hill, 1936), pp. 250–63, reprinted in *Readings in the Theory of Income Distribution* (Philadelphia: Blakiston, 1946), pp. 158–74.

ability" must not be defined and measured by the profit which it supposedly explains at the same time.[20]

Managerial Services

Managerial service has its measurable units: man-hours or man-years. Managerial services can be bought and contracted for. Managerial ability, either hired on a long-term basis or furnished by the owner of the firm, has its value which is derived from its general productivity in general lines of production or from its specific productivity in one special line. The income of the managers will accordingly be wage or rent.[21]

If the "entrepreneurship" which is said to be required by certain industries is, in fact, managerial ability, whose services might just as well be secured from hired men, then the high "profit" made by the entrepreneur who performs these services himself is really nothing but an implicit wage or an implicit rent. (It will be wage if the services would be of equal usefulness to other industries; it will be rent to the extent that the specific value of the services to the particular industry exceeds their opportunity cost.) Surely, the implicit wage of men of high ability has no more to do with perfect or imperfect competition from newcomers than has implicit rent of land of high fertility.[22] These resources obtain high prices no

[20] Knight's distinction between insurable, or at least measurable, risk and non-measurable uncertainty is based on the principle discussed above. If risk is measurable, the exposure to risk, that is "risk-bearing," is measurable too. Uncertainty, on the other hand, is not measurable, nor is uncertainty-bearing; thus there can be no unit of uncertainty-bearing and, a fortiori, no value of such a unit of uncertainty-bearing. A. C. Pigou attempted to construct "efficiency units of uncertainty-bearing." *Economics of Welfare* (London: Macmillan, 4th edition, 1938), p. 772.

[21] In modern theory not only land but any sort of factor earns rent when its income is in excess of its "minimum supply price," that is, of the lowest price at which its services can be secured, which, as a rule, is its opportunity cost.

[22] After I had published my article "Competition, Pliopoly and Profit" in *Economica*, New Series, Vol. IX (1942), R. G. Hawtrey published a criticism of my views on newcomers' competition and profit in a brief article on "Competition from Newcomers" in *Economica*, New Series, Vol. X (1943), pp. 219 ff. He argues that I have "neglected the opportunity cost of the entrepreneur's own services" (p. 220); that "in a sense big business incomes might be classified as wholly rent of ability (except for the very considerable ele-

matter whether it is in the form of contractual or in the form of residual incomes.[23] The high prices of valuable resources would never prevent more firms from entering the industry when profits —that is, revenues in excess of the costs of these and all other needed resources—appear or increase. If managerial ability is scarce and the industry can grow only by attracting managerial ability of higher opportunity value or of lower efficiency, the managerial ability in the existing firms will earn differential rents. But if new managerial talent of higher value (or lower efficiency) is available and yet is not moving into the industry despite the fact that the industry could earn their prices, the earnings of the existing firms will contain *more* than "differential rents of ability." The quick and easy appearance of more firms in the industry, and hence the quick disappearance of profits in the economic sense,—and, conversely, the failure of newcomers to appear and profits to disappear—must depend on other things than on managerial ability and differences in its required quality.

Uncertainty

If by "entrepreneurial ability" (which is said to be required by industries) is meant foresight, initiative, and the willingness to bear serious uncertainty (in a non-measurable degree) then the conclusions will be different.[24] Profits can be said to be due to en-

ment of luck)"; and that "the rent of ability is the excess over a normal income, and the normal income is the opportunity cost of the profit-maker who makes the choice between business enterprise and other vocations as a source of income" (p. 222). I have no quarrel whatsoever with these statements if they relate to the services of management, their opportunity costs and differential rents. Hawtrey, however, refuses to recognize a difference between management and enterprise, and insists on explaining "*profit*" as the opportunity *cost* and *rent* of ability of "the entrepreneur," whose essential attribute is seen in "selling power." If Hawtrey sees only costs and rents as the components of the "remuneration of entrepreneurship," he is surely not consistent when he ridicules the notion that, in general equilibrium, profits (in the sense of *surpluses over costs and rents*) are zero.

[23] Of course, residual incomes are profit in the business sense. But they need not be, and are not in this case, profit in the economic sense.

[24] Foresight combined with "self-knowledge and self-confidence or initiative" and "knowledge of, and willingness to trust, other men's powers of judgment" are, according to Knight (*op. cit.*, p. 287), the essential factor in entrepreneurial ability.

trepreneurial ability if this ability consists in venturing what not everybody ventures or, better still, in venturing what only a few venture in this world where almost everything is uncertain.

In order to isolate uncertainty as a factor making for profits let us assume that there are no other barriers against the flow of resources and that none of the resources is indivisible; furthermore, let us argue *a contrario* and assume for a moment that full certainty, instead of uncertainty, prevails about our future. In particular, let us assume that the gross receipts of every enterprise are expected with fullest certainty. Profits can obviously not exist under these conditions. When the gross receipts from enterprise should exceed the sum of all prices of all the resources that are needed to produce the gross receipts, nothing would prevent more people from turning entrepreneur and buying or hiring (borrowing, leasing) more of the "cheap" resources. The demand for resources would stop rising only when the prices of the resources had increased enough to exhaust the full value product.[25]

On the other hand—abandoning now the assumption of full certainty—if the expected gross receipts are felt to be uncertain, nobody would be willing to buy or hire (borrow, lease) resources whose prices fully exhaust the uncertain proceeds. With the outcome uncertain, entrepreneurs calculate with safety-margins. They buy or hire resources only at prices which add up to an amount that falls short, by a safety-margin, of the expected gross receipts. In other words, not the full value produced is imputed to the resources but only a value discounted for the uncertainty with which it is expected. If actual gross receipts then happen to come exactly up to expectations, they will not only cover all costs of all resources, variable and fixed, hired and owned, but they will leave a remainder equal to the safety-margin: economic profit.

The Safety-Margin in Profit Estimates

This does not mean that he who calculates with the greatest safety-margins will reap the highest profits. On the contrary, he will stay out of the industry and thus make no profits, while those who are more courageous and enter into the venture may profit

[25] Frank H. Knight, *ibid., passim.*

from the effect of the uncertainty that holds back the conservative.

Uncertainty makes enterprisers hesitant; it reduces the demand for resources, the demand that is derived from the uncertain demand which the enterprisers expect for their products; in consequence, uncertainty will lower the prices of the resources.[26] But uncertainty is not equally strong in all fields of enterprise. The greater the uncertainty with which most of the enterprising men anticipate the future that will bear on the success of a venture, the rarer will be the men of sufficient entrepreneurial drive to dare the venture. And the rarer the men who dare the venture, the less will be the demand for (or the "competition" in buying) the necessary productive factors and the supply of (or the "competition" in selling) the product. Hence, the greater will be the difference between average cost and selling price.[27]

To repeat the gist of the argument: Grave uncertainty makes most entrepreneurs calculate with conservative safety-margins; when they figure with these wide safety-margins, the enterprise will not show high profit prospects and will not appear attractive to many; hence, the safety-margins deemed necessary by many may eventually procure profits to the few, more enterprising, who enter the industry with such uncertain prospects.

In a world of perfect mobility, divisibility and foresight, and without any uncertainty about the future, pliopoly would be general and perfect. Such a world would know no economic profits. In a world of uncertain change, newcomers' competition in general cannot be perfect and profits will arise. Yet, in some fields where uncertainty is considered slight, entrance competition may approach perfection; pliopoly may then be said to exist in industries in regard to whose prospects "entrepreneurs" entertain little doubt. In most fields some degree of uncertainty is likely to exist and to

[26] Perhaps it should be made clear that "uncertainty" in the sense of unforeseeableness will create losses as well as profits; "uncertainty" in the sense of a feeling inducing entrepreneurs to apply conservative discounts to their best guesses will always reduce factor prices and thus can make only for profits, provided the guessing is not bad and the discounts are sufficient.

[27] Smaller "competition" in buying the factors and selling the product may, but need not, mean absence of polypoly in the respective markets. It is sufficient that total demand for factors and total supply of product are smaller than they would be otherwise (that is, if entrepreneurs were less uncertain).

operate against too ready an inflow of more sellers. The more uncertain the prospects appear in an industry, the more imperfect
will entry be and the greater may be the profits of the firms established in the industry, sheltered by the deterrent uncertainty.[28]

INDIVISIBILITY AND IMMOBILITY

Indivisibility

Just as uncertainty can explain profits in a world of perfect mobility and perfect divisibility, indivisibility (in the acquisition of
resources) can explain profits in a world of perfect mobility and
absolute certainty about the future.

The term indivisibility is used for a variety of concepts, two
of which are of particular importance in the theory of production
and distribution: "indivisibility in acquisition" and "indivisibility
in use." The fact that a certain component of a productive combination is indivisible in the sense that it can be *obtained* only in
a certain minimum size ("lump") is one thing. It is another that
often this "lump" or "fixed factor" has to be *used* in combination
with given minimum amounts of other factors if these other factors
are to be efficiently employed, that is to say, if the use of smaller
amounts of "variable factors" with the "fixed factor" would imply
operation under increasing returns (i.e., be inefficient). It may be
preferable to reserve the term *indivisibility* for the second concept
—the "indivisibility in use," resulting in increasing returns to variable factors—and to denote the first concept—the "indivisibility
in acquisition," resulting in substantial discontinuities of growth—
by the term *lumpiness*. But since the latter term is less pleasing
to the ear and most writers have been using the term indivisibility
to cover both notions, which are not too difficult to keep apart, no
effort will be made here always to say lumpiness when indivisibility in acquisition is meant.

The indivisibility (in acquisition) which prevents perfect ad-

---

[28] It has been pointed out to me that the existence of other barriers to
entry may reduce uncertainty in the sheltered industry. This is quite true;
yet, we are not interested here in the problem of uncertainty as such but
only in uncertainty that operates as a deterrent to entry into otherwise un-
protected fields.

justment may be that of human resources, natural resources, or man-made resources. One cannot very well employ half an engineer, a third of a chemist, a fifth of a mechanic or an eighth of a manager. (Various arrangements for the temporary hire of skills, such as the institution of consulting experts, have the function of reducing the effects of the indivisibility of human resources.) One cannot economically work with miniature blast furnaces, baby strip mills, and midget paper machines; one cannot build motors, engines or turbines of much less power at proportionally smaller cost; one cannot work with half a conveyor belt or a quarter of a rail transport system; most machines can be made half-size only at more than half the cost and/or with less than half the efficiency.

Indivisibilities can cause serious obstacles to pliopoly. The establishment of new firms in an industry where efficient equipment comes only in large units cannot be an easy matter. That it may take some time to erect and equip the new plants is perhaps the least serious of the obstacles. The most direct effect of the non-existence of small units at proportionate cost and with proportionate efficiency is that all increases in productive capacity are "lumpy" or discontinuous.

Let us again assume for a moment absolute certainty of expectations on the part both of entrepreneurs actually established in an industry and of those contemplating entering it. Assume, furthermore, that the industry concerned consists of large, indivisible units. And assume finally that all firms are of optimum size, produce the optimum output, and make only normal profits. If now demand increases, production will be increased by employing more variable factors with the given fixed resources. Even if the higher proceeds from the larger sales are expected to last permanently and without any doubt, they may not be high enough to permit the installation of another fixed production unit. The receipts will then leave a remainder above all costs. This remainder or profit will endure because it is not sufficiently high to make an entry of additional fixed resources pay. If demand increases still more and profit is pushed still higher, so that an additional set of fixed resources can be employed on a paying basis, then profit may be wiped out again. The indivisibility of important resources allows the industry to expand in jumps only; if demand increases by amounts which do not correspond to these "jumps," profits can arise even if all other conditions of easy entry are fulfilled. (The question whether these profits are better called rents will be discussed later.)

The indivisibility need not be technological in the narrow sense of the word, but may refer to organizational and institutional matters. Certain manufacturing industries cannot be operated with less than a full-fledged sales and servicing organization on a national scale, others cannot do without intensive national advertising.[29] The lump which the optimum size of an automobile manufacturing plant constitutes may not by itself appear forbiddingly large to newcomers, but the establishment of the apparatus for the nationwide distribution of the new cars under the exclusive dealer arrangements which are condoned by the law may represent an obstacle that cannot be easily overcome. The lumpiness of the sales apparatus may effectively exclude pliopoly in the industry.

Indivisibility and Uncertainty Combined

Indivisibility, while it may itself be a direct cause for absence of pliopoly, may also indirectly create conditions adverse to the possibilities of pliopoly. Indivisibility may operate indirectly through the element of uncertainty (which was assumed away in the above consideration only in order to show the logical independence between indivisibility and uncertainty). Uncertainty is seriously increased if indivisibility of factors permits industrial expansion in large jumps only. For while the market for a relatively small increase of an industry's output may be comparatively easy to predict, expectations concerning demand elasticity in the face of a *substantial* increase of output cannot be but highly uncertain.

Indivisibility will be the most serious barrier to entry if the "industry" has been operating only its first unit of lumpy resources.

---

[29] Advertising outlay is very imperfectly divisible if it is supposed to achieve acceptance of and loyalty to a. product in a nationwide market. If in the United States the three largest cigarette manufacturers each spend between 8 and 15 million dollars annually for national advertising of their brands, new entries into the field are made impractical. On the effectiveness of advertising in excluding newcomers' competition in the cigarette industry see William H. Nicholls, *Price Policies in the Cigarette Industry* (Nashville: Vanderbilt University Press, 1951), pp. 187–203.

For in this case the addition of a second unit would imply a doubling of the industry's productive capacity; a jump of one hundred percent will usually appear most daring. The importance of lumpiness as a barrier to entry may decrease with increasing numbers of indivisible units already in the industry, because further additions (undertaken by newcomers or insiders) will then mean smaller and smaller percentage increases in capacity. For example, the obstacles to the establishment of a second paper mill in a small market are much greater than those to the establishment of a sixth paper mill in a larger market. For, ordinarily, a one hundred percent increase in capacity is a more courageous venture than a twenty percent increase. For example, the first paper mill in a small country (provided it is protected from outside competition by high tariffs or transport costs) will enjoy a fairly safe monopoly position, allowing it to make handsome profits, before demand increases sufficiently to justify erection of a second mill.[30]

Indivisibility is probably one of the most important elements in the *de facto* "monopoly" positions of firms operating the first units in the area. (The positions are monopolistic only in the sense that profits can endure.) These firms will usually guard their positions by avoiding a price policy which through conspicuously excessive profits might arouse the attention of the public and the interest of outsiders. (On these positions of imperfect monopoly see Chapter 17.) One of the typical strategies of such firms, whose (imperfect) monopoly positions are protected by nothing but by the lumpiness of their productive organization, will be to expand ahead of the demand for their products.[31] The strategic use of

[30] The effects of lumpiness on pliopoly and profit are by no means confined to manufacturing industry. The opening of a second dentist's office in a village is likely to appear as a more difficult undertaking than that of a 26th office in a town. Apart from obstacles of a sociological nature, the former undertaking implies that the demand for dental services must have approximately doubled since the time the first dentist found it just worth his while to move in. Only a four percent increase in demand would be called for in the other case, where the newcomer is about to provide the 26th "lump" and could probably make a living even if he had to share with the established competitors a clientele that had not increased at all.

[31] If it were not for the safeguarding of its position, the paper mill of our previous example would postpone the acquisition of a second machine until output increased to a point where its production on one machine would be more expensive than on two machines. Where the breaking in of out-

lumpiness would call for expansion at such a rate that the "lumps" would always be insufficiently utilized and outsiders would not see any profit in a plan to move in with another such lump of productive capacity.

The combined effect of indivisibility and uncertainty is further enhanced by the fact that that very indivisibility may give rise to large investment requirements for expansion of and entry into the industry. The effect of uncertainty is likely to be stronger the larger the investment which has to be exposed to the uncertainty. The obstacle which uncertainty presents to pliopoly may, therefore, become more forbidding if the investment requirements of an entry into the industry become larger owing to the large minimum or optimum size of establishment.[32]

Three ways have thus far been shown in which indivisibility of productive resources offers resistance to perfect pliopoly and offers an opportunity for insiders to make profits. (1) Indivisibility, by preventing gradual growth of the industry, may, if demand for the products rises by less than what would warrant the acquisition of another unit of the lumpy resources, lead to lasting profits even in the absence of uncertainty. (2) Indivisibility, by reducing predictability, increases the uncertainty of expectations and, thus, the

---

siders must be warded off, the firm will build the second machine at a much earlier point.

[32] With equal mathematical risk expectations per invested dollar (supposing that uncertainty can be quantified) small investments may find funds over night while large investments may not be undertaken at all. If the productive unit, and hence the initial investment is small, a slight increase in the profit margin observed over a moderate period of time may attract new competitors. If the productive unit, and hence the investment, is large, only a considerably higher profit margin observed over a conservatively long time may attract new entrants to the industry. Thus, even if competition is "free" in any other respects, newcomers' competition will rarely be "perfect" if the necessary investment for setting up new firms in the industry is very large. Yet, generalizations are dangerous here as elsewhere. The largest investments, indeed, if there is much "phantasy" in them, may quickly catch the investors' interest, and people may go in for these enterprises in a big way. Economic history furnishes sufficient evidence for surprisingly rapid entries of new firms into industries where the initial capital requirements were enormous. Thus, it cannot be said that a large optimum size of plant is *a priori* incompatible with pliopoly. But since the statement that perfect pliopoly prevails in a particular industry is largely a forecast, its probability-value becomes small for industries where initial investments are large.

profits that may arise thanks to the deterring effects of that uncertainty. (3) Indivisibility, by making investment requirements larger, may aggravate the effects which uncertainty of any given degree is apt to have.

There may be still other, more indirect, ways in which indivisibility of resources can curb entry and protect profits in the industry. As has been shown elsewhere, polypoly cannot exist where the optimum plant size is large: such an industry will consist of only a few firms. Out of the oligopolistic position of the industry circumstances may develop which act as an effective check to the entry of newcomers. For example, the danger of price wars and of cutthroat competition may deter potential entrants and, thus, add to the forces that preclude pliopoly.

Immobility

Uncertainty, indivisibility, and immobility are usually mentioned together when "imperfections" of newcomers' competition are discussed. We have just shown the roles of uncertainty about the prospects of a business and of indivisibility of needed resources in the explanation of profit: both uncertainty and indivisibility can prevent the profit-removing allocation of additional resources to an industry. Has immobility of resources the same effect and should it therefore be added to the "causes" of profit and of the absence of pliopoly?

Immobility of resources may effectively differentiate resource which would otherwise be homogeneous and perfectly substitutable for one another. Resources which are immobile will often not qualify for certain uses for which they could qualify if they were mobile. Their opportunities are more limited and their opportunity cost, therefore, may be lower. Two consequences are possible. (1) The immobile resources with low opportunity cost may be hired for a use in which they create a value in excess of their cost: firms hiring the resources may profit from the cheap factor cost. (2) The immobility, by preventing resources from competing with better-located resources, makes the latter scarcer and, thus, more valuable than they would otherwise be: firms owning the scarcer resources may profit from the high value product.

In the one case firms *hire* resources which are cheaper because of their immobility. In the other case firms *own* resources which are more valuable because of the immobility of potential substitute resources. Are the higher earnings of the firms in the two cases profit in the economic sense? and what are the relationships between these earnings and the competitive position of the respective firms?

Profits versus Imputed Rents

Let us look first into the second case, the case of "profits" derived from the ownership of scarce resources, and its connection with immobility. Immobility of owned resources is often given as a rather obvious explanation of the continuance of losses of a firm through extended periods. For it explains why certain fixed resources cannot move out of an industry that has become a loser (either through the fall in the value product or through a rise in current cost). If immobility of resources that have been devoted to a certain line of production and cannot easily move out can explain persistent losses to the firms concerned, one should think that immobility of resources, preventing their moving into a line of production which could well earn their costs, can also explain persistent profits in this line. Yet, economic theory has preferred not to use the term profit in this connection. The "losses" and "profits" in point are mere accounting losses and profits, respectively, or *ex post* comparisons of historical valuations with current earnings.

The current earnings of the owned resources can, owing to the immobility of potential substitute resources, be higher than they would be otherwise, and, of course, higher than are the earnings of the outside immobile resources. But these surplus earnings are regarded, by economic theorists, as *rents* rather than as pure profits. And this is not unreasonable, because it will depend chiefly on the actual ownership of the resources whether the rents are paid out as "costs" or retained as "business profits" of the firm.

If the scarce resources—which are scarcer than they would be if all existing resources of the kind were able to move in—are owned by the firms, all the rent income will be business profit; if the scarce resources are currently hired or acquired by the firms, the rent income will probably be paid out to the owners. (If the firms have hired the scarce resources on long-term contracts before the value of the product rose, parts of the rent will for the duration of the contracts be business profits.) The fact that in any case the earnings can be *imputed to the scarce resources* justifies us to speak here of rents and not of pure profit. Immobility may create rents, not pure profit.

The label which is put on the earnings in question does not, however, save us from inquiring whether the specific rents earned by owned resources may not have resulted, in part at least, from the competitive position of the firm or industry concerned. We may find, for instance, that the immobility of potential substitute resources was artificially created and subject to institutional control. With artificially increased scarcity of the resources, the specific rents earned by these resources may well be characterized as *monopoly rents.* And the concept of pliopoly is thus seen to be linked not merely with the phenomenon of pure profit but also with that of specific rents.[33]

If all this sounds too "abstract," it can be made more concrete by way of illustrations. Assume that some special skill is the scarce resource. Assume that a "certificate of skill" or "permit" by public authorities, trade associations, or unions is a condition of exercising the skill in a given area; this creates immobility of the scarce resource if the certificate is not issued freely and without discrimination. The scarcity of the skilled labor is thus artificially increased. If the certified specialists run their own business, their scarcity value will show up in business profits; if they are hired and draw a wage or salary, their scarcity value will be a business expense. In both cases we can regard the respective incomes as monopoly rents.

In this illustration of an artificial immobility of skilled labor, *imputation* of the monopoly rent to the scarce resource is clearly

---

[33] This statement has a bearing on the problems of measuring "profit rates": since monopoly rents may be imputed to certain assets which appear in the books of the firm, the comparison of earnings with capitalization need not show high profit rates. Hence, high monopoly rents need not imply high profit rates. Only pure profits, which cannot be imputed to any asset, would result in high statistical profit rates.

possible (though perhaps not in exact amount). But, except in a slave economy, there is not likely to be any corresponding item among the assets in the books of the business firm, not even if the firm and the skill are owned by the same person. Now assume that licences are required to operate a certain business in a certain area, and that these licences are issued only to a limited number of firms, but are freely transferable (negotiable, saleable). In this case the monopoly rents of the business will be *capitalized* in the value of the licence, and this licence may be an item among the assets of the business firm. Thus we see that monopoly rent, created through artificial immobility of resources, can appear in different guises: as business profit, as business expense, or as a normal return from a business asset.

The Case of Cheap Resources

We have still to examine the other case of immobility, the case of firms profiting from acquiring or hiring resources which are low-priced because immobility reduces their opportunities. These resources are perhaps not cheap relative to their productivity, and in this event a firm could not really profit from acquiring or hiring them. If the resources are, however, really cheap for the uses that can be made of them, that is to say, if their efficiency-cost is low in comparison with the efficiency-cost of like resources elsewhere, then the question arises why not more firms try to set up their businesses at the location where the cheap factors can be had. Why would not other firms move to the cheap-factor location? why would not new firms enter the "industry" and settle at the favorable location? [34]

We see that immobility in this case, far from explaining the existence of profits or the failure of new firms to appear as buyers of the cheap resources, can obviously have its supposed results only if newcomers' competition is absent for other reasons. What may these reasons be?

One reason, and probably the most common in cases of the sort, is indivisibility. The economic plant size in the industry that em-

[34] This is an instance where the "industry" is a group of firms using certain means of production.

ploys the cheap factors may be such—in relation to the supply of these factors—that another plant at the same location would not pay. Another plant at that location may require more of the cheap factors than are available, so that any entrepreneur considering the proposition would know that he must not count on obtaining cheap factors in sufficient amounts. Or, another plant at the location may not pay because of limitations on the sale of the product, that is to say, because demand conditions in the region may not warrant the high jump in output that would be involved in the erection of another plant. Thus it would be indivisibility of the economical plant size that would prevent the gradual expansion or entry of firms which through competition in buying the factors (and in selling the product) would eliminate abnormal profits.[35] Indivisibility, rather than immobility, would thus be

[35] Competition in buying the cheap factors may mean two things: (1) that the demand for factors will continue to rise, owing to the entry of new firms, until no profit can be made from the use of the factors, i.e., until the price of the factor is equal to its average productivity; or (2) that the factor price is believed to be independent of the individual firm's demand so that the firm continues to buy factors up to the point where their marginal productivity is equal to the price of the factor. The first type of competition in the buying market is *pliopsony,* the second is perfect *polypsony.* Absence of competition in buying the cheap factors may mean accordingly (1) that no more buyers enter the market and that the factor price fails to be driven up to the factor's average productivity, or (2) that the buyer or buyers think that the factor price would be higher the more they employ, and that they accordingly restrict employment below the point at which the factor's marginal productivity would have decreased to the level of the factor price.

The second type of "absence of competition" (which can be pictured by upward sloping curves of the factor supply as seen by the buyer) need not be implied in what is said in the text above. Assume, for example, that there are 1000 laborers of a certain type in a remote valley. A firm settles in the valley and employs 800 of the 1000 men. The firm assumes it would be able to get more (than 800) men at the given (low) wage rate (i.e., the supply of labor to the firm is felt to be perfectly elastic), but with the given plant size it would not pay to hire more (i.e., the marginal productivity of a greater crew would be below the wage rate). The wage rate is low, the average productivity of labor is higher, but no second plant moves into the valley, because in the particular industry smaller plants, employing less than 600–800 men, are not economical, and only 200 men are available without outbidding the existing plant; the wage rate will therefore stay low.

Should the existing firm believe that the wage rate could be reduced when employment was restricted below 800 men, the firm would perhaps cut down its operations: monopsonistic restriction of employment. In this case both types of buyers' competition would be absent.

the ultimate explanation of the profits, which, incidentally, would be pure profits inasmuch as they are not imputable to any resource or right or asset of any sort. In view of the "protected" situation of the firm, one may prefer to speak here of *monopoly profits* (as distinguished from monopoly rents).

Other reasons for the absence of newcomers' competition, that is, for the exclusion of other firms from the use of the cheap, immobile resources, may go back to existing property rights or privileges of one kind or another; the firm may own a patent protecting the technical process which uses the cheap resources; the firm may control the local supply of a complementary means of production (say, fuel); the firm may own all the land in the region, thus controlling all potential sites for additional plant; the firm may enjoy a governmental privilege (licence, tax-exemption, or the like) that is not available to newcomers; etc. In all these cases the business profits that are supposedly "due" to the immobility and cheapness of resources can be imputed to the specific right or resource which, by excluding would-be competitors, secures to the firm maintenance of the favorable position.[36] The earnings in question will be rents "derived" from the scarce resource that protects them: the patent rights, the fuel deposit, the land property, the governmental privilege. These rents can properly be regarded as monopoly rents.

[36] The favorable position need not imply a "monopsonistic position," as was pointed out in the preceding footnote. The favorable position may, but need not, mean that the price paid to the factor is lower than the marginal productivity of the factor; it is sufficient that it is lower than its average productivity. But in any event the whole difference will be imputed to the right or resource which keeps newcomers out.

CHAPTER 8

Pliopoly: Profits, Rents, and Artificial Scarcity

Advance Calculations of Profits: Rents and Profits, Ex Ante and Ex Post ·
Discrepancies in Profit Calculations · The Relevant Profit Calculations ·
Advance Calculation and Prospectus · Accounting and Economic Concepts

Costs, Rents, and Profits: The Distribution of Total Revenue · Profits as
Seen by Outsiders, Insiders, and Economists

Supernormal Profits and Their Causes: Positive Profits Seen by the Outsider · No Profits Seen by the Outsider · The Economist's Dissenting Calculation · Monopoly Rents in the Form of Factor Costs

Artificial Scarcity: Natural and Artificial Scarcity · Monopolistic Barriers

THE DISCUSSION OF the "causes" or preconditions of economic profit in the preceding chapter calls for elaboration in several respects. It is necessary to distinguish more clearly between profits and rents; between anticipated earnings and realized ones; between accounting concepts and economic concepts; between profit calculations by firms within the industry, by firms outside, and by disinterested economists; and, finally, between natural and artificial scarcity.

ADVANCE CALCULATIONS OF PROFITS

Rents and Profits, Ex Ante and Ex Post

Splitting up the excess of receipts over all costs, explicit or implicit, into rents and pure profits may appear like splitting hairs. The separation seems particularly subtle (and useless) because the dividing line will shift evasively with the point of view that is taken. It will be different looking backward or looking ahead, starting a new business or continuing an old, taking account only of actual expenditures or also of foregone opportunities, considering short periods or indefinitely long ones, and so on.

Yet, as usual, the problem under consideration dictates the point of view that should be taken. Our problem is the probability of entry into an "industry" and, hence, the attractiveness of starting a new business or rebuilding an existing one. This settles the question of what must be considered as cost in our analysis: not historical cost (*ex post* cost) but anticipated cost (*ex ante* cost); not contractual cost but opportunity cost; not the cost for a short period but the cost for a period in which the investment is expected to "pay for itself."

The anticipated excess of receipts over costs in this sense may be either (1) net-earnings which *can be imputed* to a specific resource, which thus has to the enterprise a value in excess of its value in alternative uses, that is to say, in excess of its opportunity cost, or (2) net-earnings which *cannot be imputed* to any resource or asset of the enterprise. The first of the two types of net-earnings is specific rent, the other is pure profit.

The net-earnings (expected by the entrepreneur who is entering an industry) that are explained by the economist as the result of uncertainty, holding back other businessmen from entering *en masse* the same industry, cannot be imputed to any asset or resource owned by the one who starts the business. The same is true for the net-earnings that are explained as the result of indivisibility of certain of the resources needed in the industry. If the indivisible resources can be easily replaced, they cannot acquire a value above the cost of replacement. Thus, the net-earnings that are due to indivisibility preventing further expansion or entry cannot be imputed to the indivisible resources. These net-earnings are not imputable to any asset, and are therefore called pure profit (though they may, in some instances, be called "monopoly profit").

The criterion of being non-imputable may not hold for the "profits" of an existing enterprise. If the net-earnings of an existing enterprise are protected against pliopolistic pressure either by uncertainty which deters potential newcomers or by indivisibility of resources which makes new entries unprofitable, the anticipated profit may be imputed to an intangible: to the fortunate market position of the firm. One may speak of the "good will" of the firm. This good will—anticipated profits capitalized—is usually paid for in case the ownership of the firm passes into other hands. To the new proprietors, who will have paid for the intangible good will, pure profits may then take on the aspect of rent.

But this should not confuse the issue. For the problem of pliopoly, or newcomers' competition, the relevant point of view is not that of one who acquires an existing business but rather that of one who starts a new one or adds a new line to his firm, or perhaps also of one who completely rebuilds or replaces all the resources necessary for the production of the services in question.

Discrepancies in Profit Calculations

How hard it is to keep apart the different points of view—different both as to the persons concerned and as to the direction of their views—can be seen when we look once again into the uncertainty explanation of profit. Two distinct effects of uncertainty have so far been left unseparated. There is, in the first place, the uncertainty of "others," the uncertainty which prevents these others from going into the venture and thus makes it possible that *ex ante* profits may show up in the advance calculations of those who calculate with smaller safety-margins. There is, secondly, the "own" uncertainty of those who do enter the business; their own uncertainty which makes them calculate *ex ante* earnings net of some (smaller) safety-margins and which thus makes it possible that, when the expectations come true, modest *ex post* profits will appear where *ex ante* profits had been zero, and considerable *ex post* profits will appear where *ex ante* profits had been modest.[1]

But whose profit estimates are relevant for the interpretation of pliopoly, that is, of the statement that "profits in an industry" will call forth new entry, which in turn will eliminate the "profits"? We must distinguish (1) profits as seen by the economist; (2) profits as seen by those engaged in the business; and (3) profits

---

[1] The uncertainty of "others," who are thereby deterred from entering a field, is obviously greater than the uncertainty of those who have already entered it. But even the latter, the insiders, may have different feelings of uncertainty with regard to further expansion and to mere continuation of their operations.

as seen by those contemplating entering the business; and they need not be equal. If the results of the advance calculations of potential newcomers look much less favorable than the results calculated by the insiders or the disinterested observers, new entries will not take place. This forces us to analyse the causes of the possible discrepancies between the insiders', outsiders', and economists' estimates of profit.[2]

That a certain industry has been profitable for several years need not imply absence of pliopoly if the profits in question are merely *ex post* results of low valuations of resources in the past. If the resources needed for the industry are now relatively scarcer, the industry will not be profitable in an *ex ante* sense.

And again, that profits in a certain industry have been zero and are expected to remain zero need not yet indicate that perfectly pliopolistic conditions prevail. As was pointed out above, resources employed by the existing firms may possess an artificially created scarcity, and the rents earned by these resources may have the distinct character of monopoly rents. If these rents are not paid out as cost but are part of the net-earnings of the firms, the scarce resources may be among its assets and their valuation may be a full capitalization of their earnings. The statistical "profit rate"—the rate of income to capitalization—may then appear as "normal."

The Relevant Profit Calculations

Relevant to the problem of easy entry into an industry are, as seems now fairly clear, both *ex ante* profits and *ex ante* rents, calculated, on the one side, by prospective entrants and, on the other side, by insiders continuing in the industry, both calculations checked against the "objective" calculation by the economist, and, of course, made on the basis of periods sufficiently long to warrant the investment.[3] At first thought one might suppose that the ad-

---

[2] An insider's estimate of the profits from an expansion of his operations may be different from that of the profits from operations on the existing scale. The latter is relevant for our comparison because the analysis of entry hinges on the *current* profits of insiders being safe or unsafe from encroachment by newcomers.

[3] This long-period aspect has the advantage of avoiding the arbitrariness

vance calculation of the prospective entrant is all that matters. Yet, for a significant evaluation of the situation it is essential to compare the potential newcomer's prospects with the insiders' prospects. For, after all, if the advance calculations of outsiders look unattractive, we can speak of impeded entry, or absence of pliopoly, only after ascertaining that the insiders' advance calculations come out with a nice excess of receipts over all costs. And where rents assume the character of cost to the individual firm, a final evaluation will require an "objective" check by the economist.

The profit situation in an industry may often be such that an outsider, if his advance calculation were as promising as those of the insiders, would take up the business. But there may be "something" making the outsider's calculation unsatisfactory. This may be due, as we have seen, to several circumstances: (1) to a deterring degree of uncertainty, which may force the potential newcomer to calculate with excessive safety-margins while the insider may feel much less uncertain about the future prospects; (2) to the indivisibility (in acquisition) of large productive units, making the prospects for "another" production unit appear unsatisfactory while the prospects for the existing amount of production facilities may be unusually bright; (3) to the scarcity of some productive resource, privilege, or right not available to the would-be newcomer (or available only under forbidding conditions) though available to those who carry on in the industry. In very popular language, putting oneself in the place of an encouraged or discouraged candidate for entry, pondering over his own advance calculation and reflecting on the situation of the insiders, he would ask: "What have they got that I haven't got?"

Such advance calculations are made every day by scores of businessmen, either for themselves when they are making up their minds about the prospects of a contemplated business venture, or for potential partners or lenders when such are invited to consider participation in or financial commitments to the enterprise. It will aid us in the clarification of the problem of *ex ante* profits and rents if we study the pattern of these advance calculations.

---

which the concept of *realized* profits of any brief period (such as a year) must have owing to the arbitrariness of asset valuations.

Advance Calculation and Prospectus

At the risk of committing the offense of misplaced concrete-ness, let us try to understand the pattern of advance calculation, investment decision and, in particular, decision to enter an industry, by working on an illustration which, though made-up and simplified for our purpose, gives some appearance of realism.

There is proposed, let us say, the erection of a small paper-board mill for the production of a special sort of paper-board, made chiefly from chemical and mechanical pulp. A small ground-wood-pulp mill is to be connected with the paper-board mill and to supply a part of the necessary groundwood (mechanical pulp). After careful comparisons of the best locations and most economical plant sizes—in full consideration of the cost of water-generated and steam-generated power, the cost of pulpwood (spruce, balsam fir, or poplar) and of the purchased raw stock, the cost of labor, the cost of construction and equipment, the tax situation, the freight situation, etc., etc.—it is proposed to build the mill in Maine (near spruce forests and on a river site with good water-power). The hydraulic power plant is planned for 1250 h.p., the paper-board mill for a production of about 60 tons in 24 hours. (Paper mills usually operate continuously except week-ends.)

The capital requirements of the firm are estimated as follows:

Fixed Capital

Land and Hydraulic Power Construction	$160,000
Buildings	400,000
Machinery and Equipment	650,000
	$1,210,000

Working Capital [4]

Wood (for average of 6 months' requirement)	50,000
Raw stock and other supplies	85,000
Goods-in-process (ca. 1 month's production)	55,000
Finished goods on stock (ca. 2 months' production)	120,000
Accounts receivable (ca. 1½ months' production)	105,000
Cash (for contingencies)	20,000
	435,000
Total capital required	$1,645,000

[4] Large items in manufacturing expense may of course be negligible items

Of this amount the proponents plan to raise $500,000 through
a bond issue (at 6 per cent) from a group of financiers, while the
rest is to be raised as share capital among themselves and various
friends. Their negotiations and considerations are based upon a
confidential prospectus with advance calculations as follows:

"Paper-board in the quality we are planning to produce has
sold at $95.00 a ton (and higher) during recent years, which
means approximately $90.00 f.o.b. mill. We are calculating con-
servatively with an average price of only $80.00 f.o.b. mill. Our
plant and equipment is contemplated for an output of 60 tons in 24
hours, which in 255 working days per year would make a yearly
production of 15,300 tons. Allowing for temporary stoppages,
breakdowns, etc., we shall count only on 50 tons daily and
250 working days, hence on a yearly production of 12,500 tons.
On these total sales of 12,500 tons @ $80.00, that is, $1,000,000,
we figure a deduction of $40,000 for discounts, allowances and bad
debts, which seems sufficiently conservative since none of the
investigated firms in similar position has in any year had more
than 3 percent of such deduction. On this conservative estimate
our yearly sales should be at least $960,000. This is the figure used
in our statement below.

[Comment of the economist: Up to this point several contributions to the safety-margin have been provided. The potential production of 15,300 tons at a price of $90.00 would bring a gross
revenue of $1,377,000 minus 3 percent for deductions, that is
$1,336,690. Of course we must not think that all the excess over
the $960,000, which appear in the calculation, are safety-margin
—i.e., $376,690—because the operating expenses are calculated
below on the basis of the smaller production. The safety-margins
in the expected selling price ($10.00 per ton) and in the extra
deduction from gross sales (1%) amount to $135,000. The further
safety-margin through the reduced estimate of annual output
would amount to 2800 tons times the net profit margin per ton.]

"The largest item in our manufacturing expenses is raw stock.
We calculate on the basis of an input of 60 percent chemical pulp,

(or none at all) in a list of working capital requirements and *vice versa.*
Working capital requirements refer to inventories, etc., and their size may
depend on many other things than the rates of input.

to be bought from various sources, and 40 percent mechanical pulp, half of which will be bought, the other half produced in our own groundwood mill out of pulpwood grown in the State (spruce and balsam fir). We calculate with prices of raw stock and pulpwood 15 percent above the highest prices of the past ten years, and with a loss of fibre of 10 percent (instead of the customary 5 percent). The estimates for the expenses for felts, wires and screens, belting, lubricants and other supplies are all very conservative, and the estimates in fuel cost include not only a margin for possible price increases of 20 percent above present prices but also average consumption figures of 15 percent above the ones guaranteed by the firms which submitted bids for boilers, steam-engines, drying-cylinders, etc. The estimate for wages is conservative both as to number of men and wage rates. It is based on the largest crew in any of the investigated mills and on wage rates 20 percent above the union wages in comparable establishments.

[Comment of the economist: There are again several supposedly generous "reserves" in all the figures used in the calculation of the direct manufacturing expenses. Whether or not the safety-margin will turn out, in the future, to be ample is of course unpredictable.]

"Among the general expenses we have figured administration expenses, insurance premiums, taxes, etc., on the basis of careful estimates. For depreciation and obsolescence we allow 4 percent per year for buildings (corresponding to a service life of 25 years) and 10 percent for machines and equipment (corresponding to a service life of 10 years). Among the fixed charges appear $30,000 for 6 percent interest on a $500,000 bond issue.

[Comment of the economist: The uncertainty involved in estimates of the service life of fixed assets is too great to permit any judgment concerning the safety-margin included here. The physical life of machines is generally much longer than ten years but the length of their economic life depends on the rate of technical progress, current interest rates, and other changes in the production or selling end of the industry. He who counts on having his investment in machines pay for itself within ten years usually entertains the silent hope that they will actually render useful service for several years after their amortization. This is then another item under the heading "safety-margin." Besides the conservative estimate of service life, the initial cost of the fixed assets may be calculated with more or less caution, thus providing an extra cushion. However, while the investing firms regularly think that they add a sufficiently large reserve for possible excesses of construction cost over the bids and estimates of contractors and construction firms, very frequently these margins turn out to be too narrow. But what counts here is the expectation, not the afterthought. There is no depreciation allowed on water-power and land. This implies that they maintain their value indefinitely. The cost of the use of these fixed resources appears not as a separate item in the profit and loss account or cost calculation but merely as a part of the normal return expected on aggregate investment.]

"An abbreviated statement of the estimated profit calculation follows:

Sales per year (12,500 tons @ 80.00)		$1,000,000
Less discounts, allowances, bad debts		40,000
		960,000
Direct manufacturing expenses per year		
Raw stock and materials	415,000	
Felts, wires, screens, belting, lubricants, etc.	25,000	
Fuel, oil and coal	80,000	
Wages	170,000	
Total		690,000
Income from operation		$270,000
General expenses and charges per year		
Administration expenses, general expenses, etc.	45,000	
Insurance	6,000	
Taxes	15,000	
Depreciation on buildings (4%)	16,000	
Depreciation on machinery (10%)	65,000	
Interest on 500,000 bonds (6%)	30,000	
Total		177,000
Net income		$ 93,000
Normal return on share capital (6% of $1,145,000)		68,700
Profit or surplus above normal return		$ 24,300

"A 6 percent return on our investment seems therefore amply secured. The net income, in the above statement, amounts to 8.12 percent of our share capital, but both sales proceeds and costs have been calculated with such conservative margins that under normal circumstances the actual net income may well be many times the one shown above. A calculation based on present prices of product and materials, on present wage rates, on construction costs according to actual bids and estimates, on guaranteed fuel expenditure and normal loss of fibre, and on full utilization of capacity would result in a 40 percent return on our capital. In other words, with good luck in all respects, our investment would pay for itself in two and one-half years and, on the other hand, would seem warranted even under very adverse circumstances."

[Comment of the economist: The confidential prospectus shows no more than the usual optimism. Of course, with a smaller dose of optimism the "investment opportunity" would vanish. A fall in the price of the product from the $90 at which it supposedly sells at present to $70 is nothing unheard of, yet it would wipe out the whole net income. A longer strike, a defect in the power plant, or similar work stoppages may easily turn a year's profit into heavy losses. To be sure, calculations of investment returns take the "year" only as a convenient accounting period; the relevant period may be ten or twenty years, that is, no less than the time in which the investment is expected to pay for itself under adverse conditions.[5]]

[5] The relevant period is not determined by the length of the life of the most durable resource employed in the enterprise—which would be infinity for land or 25 years for the buildings in the above illustration. For a product which is expected to meet only a very temporary demand the relevant period is determined solely by the expected duration of the demand, no matter how long the physical life of the fixed resources is. In this case the investment must be expected to pay for itself in the short period during which the demand is believed to last—or the investment will not be undertaken. Of course, the cost of the fixed resources is then the cost of their acquisition or construction minus an eventual salvage value. (A favorite example of such a case is the construction of a "grand stand" for a one-day street procession or celebration. The investment must pay for itself on the one day, even if the structure potentially might last many years.)

Accounting and Economic Concepts

It is often a useful exercise to relate cost-accounting figures to the concepts that matter in theoretical economics. A few questions concerning the economic interpretation of the above profit and cost items shall be discussed here.

(1) Are the "direct manufacturing expenses" of the above statement identical with short-run variable costs? They are not, though the two bear a close relationship to each other. The calculation was prepared for the consideration of investment plans, hence for long-run considerations (and all costs are variable in the long run, that is to say, in a planning stage); that all items in the calculation were expressed in per-year figures was only a matter of convenience. Yet, one may imagine that some time after the investment has been undertaken the management makes up its production plans and budget estimates for a period ahead, without contemplating any changes in fixed resources; then these direct manufacturing expenses will be the major part of short-run variable cost. Some portions of some other items that appear under general direct expenses will probably also be variable with output and, therefore, will have to be added. For example, user cost (that is, the difference between depreciation and maintenance of idle plant and depreciation and maintenance of plant utilized in various degrees) will be a short-run variable cost. Or, general expenses, taxes, etc., may contain parts that are variable with the amount of business transacted. Or, the amount of working capital invested in inventories of all sorts, and thus interest charges on working capital as well as insurance premiums on inventories, may be variable with output. (The variable interest cost of working capital will perhaps be negligible if the interest that can be saved, or earned through short-term investment of liquid funds, is little.) But the main point to be understood is that the "direct manufacturing expenses" of the above statement refer to one particular output, whereas "variable costs" are essentially a series or schedule of cost figures referring to several alternative volumes of output.

(2) Can the "income from operations," as shown in the above statement, be identified with quasi-rent? It cannot for all the reasons given for the non-identity of direct manufacturing cost and

short-run variable cost. Quasi-rent will fall short of income from operations by all those items by which short-run variable cost exceeds direct manufacturing cost.

(3) Can "general expenses and charges" be identified with fixed costs? Of course not, as follows logically from our answers to the first question. It bears repetition that in an advance calculation for investment plans *all* items are by definition variable, though some of the items will in the future, after the investment has been made, become fixed charges due to unavoidable depreciation or fixed commitments.

(4) Is the "net income" shown in the statement "profit" in the economic sense? Certainly not. The residual income of the firm still contains the cost of the owned resources, in the particular case the interest on the owned capital.

(5) Is there no rent for the use of water-power and land? Rent payments for water-power and land were capitalized in the purchase price (and construction cost) of these fixed resources. The cost calculation contains therefore no explicit item for rent; instead, the interest charges on the respective investment—either contractual interest paid out or normal return of the owned capital—comprise the "rent" for these resources. A separate item for rent would involve double counting, unless the value of land and water-power were not included in the aggregate investment on which a normal return must be earned.—If the fixed resources in question had a greater value to the particular firm than to other potential users, so that the purchase price did not capitalize the full rent, then the specific rent (which would be equal to the difference between rent earned and rent paid) would be no cost element to the firm but would be a part of the surplus above normal returns.

(6) Is the "profit or surplus above normal return" pure profit in the economic sense? Not necessarily, because this final net remainder may just as well consist of nothing but specific rents, that is, income items attributable to specific resources. (On the other hand, some such specific rent items may have been switched into cost, for example, if administration expenses contain salaries above the "opportunity values" of the particular human resources.)

To the extent that the surplus in question is economic *ex ante* profit, it may result (apart from the effects of indivisibility) from the effects of uncertainty upon the masses of outsiders, that is to say, from the lack of foresight, daring and enterprise of potential competitors; but, on the other hand, it may result from unwarranted over-optimism and errors of judgment on the part of the proponents preparing to take up the business. Will the future tell which of these two factors was more important in the particular case? Will this perhaps be revealed many years later, when *ex post* earnings come up to, or fall desperately short of, the expectations which have induced the investors to undertake the enterprise? This question is more than a fortune-teller, not to speak of an economist, can answer. For who should say which developments were foreseeable and which not? If all developments conformed exactly to the "potentials" from which the "safe" estimates in the advance calculations were derived, and, if consequently, the eventual *ex post* profits exceeded the estimated profits by the full safety-margin, then perhaps we would be permitted to say that these profits were the result of the entry-repelling feeling of uncertainty and of nothing else. But where the situation has altered, where prices, costs, and production volumes have undergone various changes, it would be ridiculous to try to dissect eventual *ex post* profits and to attribute certain positive or negative portions to the effects of unforeseeable change, of entry-repelling uncertainty, or of outright errors of judgment and calculation.

COSTS, RENTS, AND PROFITS

The Distribution of Total Revenue

The discussion of the nature of net revenue, rent and profit may gain in focus by a schematic "map" tracing the "distribution" of the prospective gross revenue of the business enterprise. This distribution map does not show the actual money flow. For, in reality, costs are usually defrayed before proceeds are received and, when proceeds are received, the funds may go into debt payments, short-term investment, or idle liquidity reserves, although of course the most normal use of the greater part of the funds is reinvestment in repetitive cost outlays. The map is to show how gross revenue is expected to cover direct costs, contractual expenses, and sunk investment, normal returns and supernormal returns of several sorts. The "Remainders" after deducting the various cost items are named merely by numbers rather than by the customary but ambiguous terms which accounting and business language employs in too many meanings.

Although other interpretations are not ruled out, the period over which revenue and costs are estimated is preferably the shortest of the long periods over which the investment seems warranted. Over these long periods there arise fewer of the awkward problems of proper depreciation charges: the total cost of most of the durable but wasting (exhausting) fixed resources acquired as initial investment must be completely amortized and no valuations at intermediate degrees of deterioration are called for. In other words, the investment in wasting fixed assets (machinery, equipment) is "sunk" as a whole and, instead of annual depreciation percentages, one hundred per cent of it is put down as the cost of acquired fixed resources.[6] Where the services of specialists (management) are secured by long-term contracts, where the use of plant or machinery is secured in long-term leases, or where capital funds are raised through bond issues, mortgage loans, or other long-term contracts, the contractual salary, rent, and interest payments are entered under the cost of hired (leased, borrowed) fixed resources. Both the cost of acquired wasting fixed resources and the cost of services from hired fixed resources appear here under the heading of *"pre-committed"* cost.

In contradistinction to these costs to which the firm commits itself at its birth (or at the beginning of the new undertaking) the *direct costs* are of a "pay-as-you-go" character. They are the costs of resources which you buy or hire as, if and when you use them.

Remainder I—sales minus direct cost of the goods sold—is analogous to what some accountants call "net income from operation" (analogous but not equal, because the one is an anticipated, the other a realized remainder). We have seen before that Remainder I is not analogous to quasi-rent, because the latter may be minus some variable parts of the precommitted cost of final

---

[6] For a brief discussion of the nature of "fixed resources" see above, footnote 14 on page 221.

resources, particularly in the form of user cost (depreciation through use).[7] Remainder I is of course not analogous to the "net income from operations" for those accountants who want this income to be net of depreciation.

Remainder II is net of all costs in the accounting sense. It is, thus, the (anticipated) residual income of the firm and is analogous to the accountant's (realized) "net income" or "profit." It still contains the opportunity cost of all the services which are (so to speak) gratis at the disposal of the firm: before all, its equity capital. The opportunity cost of investment funds, that is, their potential return in other uses or, in customary language, the "normal return of capital" is usually the only cost item not included in the cost accounts of the corporations. In single ownership or partnership firms other gratis services may also be important. For example, "normal compensation" for the owners' activities in the firm, and perhaps "normal rentals" for land or premises owned by the owners of the firm and used but not paid for by the firm, may be among the opportunity costs to be deducted from Remainder II.

Remainder III is net of all costs, both in the accounting and in the economic sense. It is this Remainder III which is the chief subject of analysis in the theory of newcomers' competition, the theory of pliopoly. A positive Remainder III is equivalent to "supernormal profits." Since it may consist of rents and of pure economic profit, both being defined as some sort of surplus above all costs, the word "net surplus" may be the best synonym for Remainder III. (Of course, this net surplus has little to do with, and must not be confused with, the accounting term "surplus.")

Cases where pliopoly is absent are most often characterized, as was pointed out before, by a typical discrepancy between the calculations of insiders and those of outsiders, with a positive Remainder III for insiders and a negative or zero Remainder III for outsiders. This discrepancy, however, is sometimes largely a matter of how our concepts are used. Assume, for a drastic ex-

---

[7] The variability of depreciation allowances, which is dictated by the fact that wear and tear through use may exceed depreciation through mere lapse of time, means only an *earlier* exhaustion of the fixed resource; what varies is the time-distribution of depreciation but of course not the amount of total depreciation over the lifetime of the asset. This explains why the cost of the use of a fixed resource may be "variable" in the short period.

Costs, Rents, and Profits

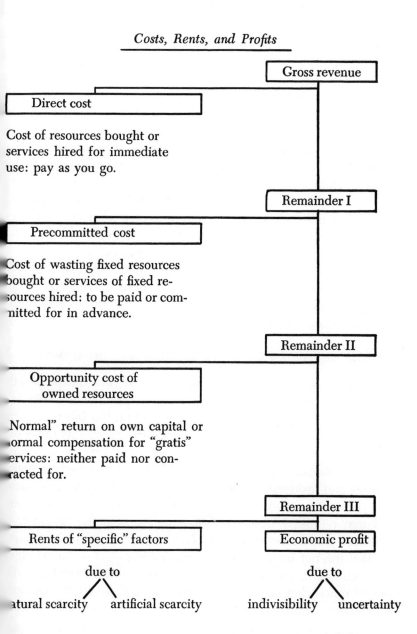

Gross revenue

Direct cost

Cost of resources bought or
services hired for immediate
use: pay as you go.

Remainder I

Precommitted cost

Cost of wasting fixed resources
bought or services of fixed resources hired: to be paid or committed for in advance.

Remainder II

Opportunity cost of
owned resources

"Normal" return on own capital or
normal compensation for "gratis"
services: neither paid nor contracted for.

Remainder III

Rents of "specific" factors   Economic profit

due to   due to

natural scarcity   artificial scarcity   indivisibility   uncertainty

ample, that would-be newcomers are kept out of a lucrative trade by threats of violence. Two alternative ways of describing the profit estimates of the outsiders are possible. According to the one, the advance calculations of the would-be entrant will show a very tempting Remainder III, but in spite of it he will stay away for he will not dare ignore the threats of the racketeers in control of the trade. According to the other way of speaking, the advance calculation of the would-be entrant will show a negative Remainder III if full account is taken of the costs and damages which may arise from intruding into the "protected" business. The second way of stating the matter may be preferable from many points of view, but can be used only for those cases where the barrier against entry into the trade (or the getting over or around the barrier) is reducible to a dollars-and-cents expression.

A catalogue of typical cases of consistent and inconsistent profit estimates by outsiders, insiders, and economists, with the most likely implications concerning newcomers' competition, may help in organizing our thoughts on the subject.

Profits as Seen by Outsiders, Insiders, and Economists

Outsiders, as we have used the term here, are the potential newcomers to an industry (trade, business, profession), that is, the enterprising people who consider taking up the business if it appears worth while. Their profit calculations as well as those of the insiders (that is, of those who have been operating a going concern in the industry) are of course "subjective," inasmuch as both outsiders and insiders are the "actors," motivated by their wishes and expectations. Calculations by the economist, on the other hand, may be called "objective," inasmuch as he is the "observer," disinterested and merely curious.[8] His "objective" calculation may be called for, not because of any superior foresight or knowledge of the economist, but chiefly because of the inherent relativity of cost and rent: what may be cost to the single firm may be rent for the "industry," and monopoly rent at that. In those cases where

---

[8] The economist's calculation is called objective if he is "not practically but only cognitively interested" in the question. The quoted clause is taken from an article by Alfred Schütz, "The Problem of Rationality in the Social World," *Economica*, New Series, Vol. X (1943), p. 134.

monopoly rents assume the nature of cost to the individual firm, the net surplus may be zero in the outsiders' calculations as well as in the insiders'; but the economist must not omit these cases from his analysis of pliopoly. (In the catalogue which follows these cases of "cost to the firm, rent to the industry" would come under Type D.)

SUPERNORMAL PROFITS AND THEIR CAUSES

Type	Remainder III or "Net Surplus"	Calculated by	Possible Causes
A	positive zero (or negative)	outsider insider	(1) Error of judgment, sometimes resulting in overcrowded trade with high mortality rate.
B	positive positive	outsider insider	(1) Temporary disequilibrium, terminated by entry into industry. (2) Barrier against entry, without possibility of transforming it into cost items or capital items.
C	negative (or zero) positive	outsider insider	(1) Uncertainty affecting outsider, reflected in his higher estimates of costs and lower estimates of proceeds. (2) Indivisibility of resources, making for poor prospects for "another" production unit in spite of good prospects for existing facilities. (3) Barrier against entry (of enterprise or resources), constituting a cost item or capital item to new entrant but not to insider.
D	zero (or negative) zero positive	outsider insider economist	(1) Barrier against entry (of enterprise or resources), transformed into cost items or capital items of all firms.

Positive Profits Seen by the Outsider

A positive "net surplus" (Remainder III) may simply be due to error or over-optimism on the part of a particular "calculator." If he is an outsider, while other calculators at the same time—insiders in particular—obtain no favorable results, a malinvestment is likely to occur. This case, listed as Type A, is probably not very important. It is said, however, that there are certain trades in which consistent over-optimism and errors of judgment on the part of outsiders are typical, with the result that these trades are constantly overcrowded and that there is a quick turnover in entrepreneurship: easy entry of unenlightened newcomers and hasty exodus of disillusioned enterprisers. Retail stores in large cities are cited as examples.

A positive net surplus, expected by both outsiders and insiders, may be a matter of a short-lived "disequilibrium," a temporary situation, created through improved sales or cost conditions, to which enterprising people are just about to react to an extent sufficient to terminate it. The sequence is this. The advance calculations with positive net surplus reflect attractive investment opportunities; these are being seized upon; the newcomers' demand for factors of production and supply of products affect cost and sales conditions in the industry in such a way that in due time further potential entrants will not find their advance calculations attractive; no longer will Remainder III in outsiders' calculations be positive. Newcomers' competition will have "worked."

It will be clear that this case, listed as Type B (1), is the model of perfect pliopoly, provided of course that the time lags involved are not excessive. (Case A is also a pliopolistic one; indeed, entry might be considered "too" easy in the trades with excessive birth rates and corresponding mortality rates.) Just what time lag may be called normal and what excessive, or, in other words, how long a "temporary disequilibrium" in a "pliopolistic industry" may last before it is in danger of being regarded as an "under-investment equilibrium" of a "non-pliopolistic industry," is a matter for the economist's judgment. Such judgment will preferably be in terms of various degrees of pliopoly, rather than in terms of "presence" or "absence" of pliopoly.

Type B (2) is non-pliopolistic. Some sort of barrier to entry prevents elimination of a positive net surplus for outsiders as well as for insiders. This barrier, however, must be of that peculiar sort, mentioned before, which is not reflected in the cost or investment figures of the (contemplated or existing) firms: a barrier that is not reducible to a dollars-and-cents expression. The outsider is attracted to the industry by handsome profits, but he cannot get in; the obstacle that bars his entrance is not removable for money; the fortunate insiders cannot ascribe their sheltered position to any possession that can figure as an asset in their books; hence, insiders as well as outsiders continue to find that the particular business is blessed with a supernormal profit rate.

Cases in point are firms operating under a franchise or licence if the franchise or licence was not acquired for money or money's worth [9] and cannot be transferred for money or money's worth, and if those without franchise or licence cannot obtain one for money or money's worth. The positive net surplus, anticipated by the insider, will in this case be a rent income, for it can be imputed to the franchise or licence that protects his business against newcomers' competition. Hence, the franchise or licence may be very valuable; but it cannot be an asset on the books of the insider, because it has neither a cost nor a market value.

Another illustration of Type B (2) was mentioned above: the case where potential newcomers were kept out by threats of violence. In this case there is nothing that could possibly become the asset to which the insiders' net surplus might be attributed; and the anticipated violence against intruders may not be reducible to expense items in advance calculations of the latter. Thus, both insiders and outsiders will envisage handsome profits, but the outsiders will prefer to stay out.

No Profits Seen by the Outsider

The most general constellation is that of type C, where long-run supernormal profits are secured by insiders, not in spite but

[9] I have been asked why I use this clumsy phrase instead of the single word "purchased." The answer is that the acts of "appreciation and friendship" by which businessmen sometimes secure licences from the authorities are not normally called "purchase."

because of the absence of similar profit expectations on the part of potential newcomers. The zero or negative net surplus calculated by outsiders is the condition for the endurance of a positive net surplus for insiders.

C (1) is the case in which uncertainty and caution force the potential newcomer to calculate costs and proceeds with safety-margins so large that no positive net surplus results from his advance calculation. The case has been discussed and illustrated above. Uncertainty as the industry's protection against new competition is effective on the cost as well as on the selling side of the calculation. Indeed, in some instances it may not be easy to distinguish the two. If an outsider shrinks from entering an industry whose products are in unusually heavy demand, his staying out may be explained either by conservatively low estimates of proceeds or conservatively high estimates of cost. (Perhaps amortization cost; an outsider, lacking confidence in the continuance of the good market, may calculate either with reduced selling prices in the future or with a shorter economic service life of his fixed investment.) The insider will then reap the profits, undisturbed by intruders; furthermore, to the insider many items, especially on the cost side of production, will appear less uncertain than to outsiders and will require much smaller safety-margins.

Indivisibility, or more correctly imperfect divisibility, of certain fixed resources (such as a plant of economic size) is listed under C (2) as another protection of the industry against new competition. To be sure, it will hardly be possible to separate in practice the effect of this factor from that of uncertainty. But it seems fair to state that, in actual fact, imperfect divisibility of certain resources (natural, human, or man-made) is effective in almost all local industries, trades, and professions, and probably more effective than uncertainty. One general store, one barber shop, and one restaurant may be profitable in almost every village, but there may not be enough business for a second such enterprise. The potential newcomer, therefore, foresees no profit from the particular undertaking and stays away, while the one who has come first, the insider, can thrive under the protection of imperfect divisibility.

The same is true in many lines of industrial production where a number of firms share a market at profitable prices, whereas another firm with its substantial addition to the product supply would have to face a price collapse or even a price war. If the addition to supply were negligible, no such price collapse would threaten; but the imperfect divisibility of plant would necessitate a large output and thus involve the danger of a smashing price reduction and even cut-throat competition. The newcomer, taking this possibility into account, will find the whole proposition unattractive. He will give up the idea of entering the industry; and the insiders' profits will be secure. The "lump" responsible for confining entry to huge business units or excluding it altogether may be a technologically unnecessary "factor of production," required merely as a result of trade practices. For example, national advertising may have become a prerequisite of consumer acceptance and its cost may be such that it can be borne only by such an enormous sales volume as only an established firm can have and no newcomer can anticipate for himself. These examples and the ones given before will suffice to impress us with the paramount importance which imperfect divisibility of the productive unit has for the explanation of limitations of pliopoly and the continuance of supernormal profits in the long run.

Under C (3) another type of obstacle to entry is listed, which, as in the two preceding cases, results in insiders' net surplus protected by the outsiders' lack of profit expectations, but with the qualification that the "profits" or surpluses have the character of rents. An example is the possession by insiders of valuable patent rights securing them exclusive use of certain processes or the exclusive production of certain articles. If the patent rights have no cost value to the holders and thus cannot constitute assets in their books, there will be no corresponding cost item and no capital item in their calculations. Outsiders, on the other hand, will be faced with higher production cost (by paying royalties for the use of the patented process or by using other, more expensive processes) or with lower proceeds from an unpatented, less popular product. Thus, no positive net surplus will attract newcomers, while a positive net surplus, imputable to the patent rights and, therefore, of the nature of monopoly rent, may be counted on by the insiders.

More examples are perhaps appropriate. Insiders may have

secured important tax exemptions when they started the industry. (Many American communities have granted such exemptions; various European countries have built up new national industries under the attraction of tax remissions.) Similar tax privileges are often not available to later entrants. Hence, potential newcomers will have to figure with higher tax expenditures than the fortunate insiders. The differential advantage of the insiders may be maintained for a long time.

Insiders may have formed an association which secures them certain advantages not available to a newcomer. Or, newcomers would have to become members of that association by payment of high initiation fees. Insiders may operate under licences or permits or certificates of skill, once acquired at no cost. Newcomers would have to acquire those licences, permits, or certificates at a cost, for instance, through payment of fees or bribes. In all these and similar cases we might find that no positive net surplus is anticipated by outsiders, because they must calculate with the cost of overcoming the barrier to entry; at the same time the insider may reckon with a handsome rent, attributable to the right or privilege that protects him against newcomers' competition.

The Economist's Dissenting Calculation

The only difference between cases under C (3) and cases under D lies in the insiders' calculation. In the insiders' calculations of Type D the positive net surplus is made to disappear through a transformation of the specific rents either into business expenses or into normal return on business assets. The rent character of the respective part of the total revenue can then be revealed only by an "objective" analysis of all expense and capital items, which is to ascertain that no item exceeds the opportunity cost of the really necessary resources to which it refers.

An easy illustration is provided by adapting the patent-right example of Type C (3) to the present constellation. Let the patent rights be owned by another person or firm, for example, by one of the stockholders or by a holding company, and let the producing firm be licensed by, and pay royalties to, the patentee; the net surplus, as calculated by the insider, may no longer be positive. The specific rent earned through the exclusion of new competitors is transformed into a business expense. The tentative calculation by the outsider yields no surplus, because he is barred from using the patented method or from making the patented product. The calculation by the insider yields no surplus either, because he must pay royalties for the use of the patent. But the economist's calculation will yield a net surplus over the sum of all opportunity costs of all the necessary resources used.

The same effect which is achieved by transforming a specific rent into a business expense can be achieved by capitalizing it into a business asset. Still using our patent case as an example, let the producing firm purchase the entire patent rights at their full value, which is of course nothing but the capitalized rent income; the patent rights will become an asset in the books of the firm, that is to say, the investment of the firm will include an amount which is not "opportunity cost of necessary fixed resources" but merely "capitalization of expected rent"; by calculating "normal return" on this investment just as on all the other invested funds, the "cost" figures of the enterprise will be raised by an amount which equals the monopoly rent; the net surplus over normal returns will have disappeared. The ratio of net income to capital will no longer be supernormal according to the insider's calculation, though it will still be supernormal in the economist's computation. The economist, primarily interested in the surplus above the opportunity costs of necessary resources, will still see the net surplus that is earned in the enterprise thanks to the barriers against new competition.

Monopoly Rents in the Form of Factor Costs

Barriers may be erected against the entry of new *enterprise*, as is the case with patent rights, legal monopolies, franchised or licensed firms, etc., or they may be against the entry of needed *resources*. The difference should be obvious: a barrier against more firms entering the industry may create a "scarcity value" of the product in excess of the combined values of all resources used in its production; a barrier against more of certain resources entering the industry may create greater scarcity of the product along with, and consequent upon, the increased scarcity of the resources the entry of which is obstructed.

Examples would be trade unions shutting out competing labor groups and maintaining a wage rate in excess of the opportunity cost of the particular quality of labor; trade associations excluding competing materials or instruments; professional associations restricting the admission to professional schools or the granting of certificates or occupational licences; organized pools regulating the supply of certain raw materials for certain purposes. All these and similar devices can create an artificial scarcity of the labor, material, instrument, or skill in question, thereby raising the value which these factors or resources have to the industry above their respective opportunity costs. The payments for the scarce resources or services will be costs in the calculations of outsiders as well as of insiders. These payments, however, are "excessive" in comparison with what the services or resources in question could earn in other uses and in comparison with what would have to be paid for substitute services or resources if these were not artificially kept out; in recognition of this, the economist will consider these payments not as *cost* but rather as *rent*.

That such apparent cost items of the firms concerned are essentially monopoly rents may be more obvious in the case of resources owned by the producing firms themselves or by some of its stockholders or by an affiliated company. The price paid for a scarce metal purchased from an affiliated company is clearly cost in the bookkeeping sense and may absorb any possible net surplus of the processing firm. If that price is in excess of the opportunity cost of the metal, or in excess of the opportunity cost of the services needed for its extraction, it contains rent. This rent may be largely due to artificial restriction of the use of the metal in the industry, and therefore may have the character of monopoly rent.

Where firms own natural resources and calculate among their cost the depletion of these resources, and where this depletion is based upon a valuation of the resources which in turn is derived from the scarcity value of the extracted material, the cost in question may contain a generous admixture of monopoly rent.[1]

[10] Cf. Joe S. Bain, "The Profit Rate as a Measure of Monopoly Power," *Quarterly Journal of Economics*, Vol. LV (1941), pp. 285–86.

Hence, without positive net surpluses resulting from outsiders' or insiders' calculations, the economist's computation will have to exhibit a net surplus; a net surplus, or rent, that will be attributable to resources which are scarce by nature but possibly made still scarcer by restrictive policies.

ARTIFICIAL SCARCITY

In the last analysis, pliopoly is to be understood in a wider sense than that referred to in the outset, namely not merely connoting easy entry of enterprise but also absence of artificial restrictions to entry of (natural, human, or man-made) resources. With pliopoly absent, *economic profits, monopoly rents,* and *excessive factor prices* can arise and last over extended periods. All three are earnings in excess of opportunity costs.

Natural and Artificial Scarcity

All rents are the result of scarcity and are earnings in excess of opportunity costs, but not all rents are monopoly rents. On what grounds may certain rents be called "monopoly rents"? It seems most reasonable to choose the element of *human control* as the criterion distinguishing artificial scarcity from natural scarcity. This is by no means a clean-cut distinction, especially since the effects of "institutional factors of old standing" may be considered "artificial" as well as "natural," depending on one's point of view. Here seems to be one of those issues where value judgments enter into what might be thought of as judgments of fact. The dividing line between the natural and the artificial can perhaps be set by means of a mental experiment, asking what type of action (or omission) would be capable of remedying the situation, that is, in the particular case, of decreasing the scarcity of the resource in question. If we had to imagine a change in the tastes and idiosyncrasies of consumers or workers, a change in the knowledge of the technical arts, discoveries, or indeed an act of God as the only ways of removing or reducing a scarcity—then we should not hesitate to consider it "natural." On the other hand, if we thought that the supply of the scarce resource could be readily increased

by something like a "cease-and-desist" order or by the removal of
some "interference" or "restriction" or "privilege"—then the scarcity would seem "artificial." Of course, we may often find it hard
to come to a decision.

Let us for purposes of illustration take the case of a special
skill. The men who possess it receive a high price for their labor.
Outside of the particular industry there is no use for the special
skill and its owners could not earn more than the price of common
labor. Thus, the earnings of the skilled men in the particular industry contain an ample amount of specific rent because the price
of the labor is in excess of its opportunity cost. If all men who
possess the skill can find employment in the industry that can use
it, and if men who are capable of acquiring the skill are not restrained from doing so, then the rent of the scarce resource is not
a monopoly rent. The scarcity is a natural one. If, however, men
who possess the skill are kept out of the industry that may have
use for it (if only at slightly reduced wage rates) and thus must
work elsewhere at much lower wages—while the men who do find
employment in their trade continue to earn high wages—, or if
men who are capable of acquiring the well-paid skill are restrained
from doing so, then the high price paid for the skilled work contains monopoly rent. The scarcity is artificially increased.

Monopolistic Barriers

The criterion is, thus, that perfectly substitutable resources
would be available at lower prices were it not for certain barriers;
barriers which were probably deliberately erected and could probably be removed by appropriate anti-monopoly measures. In the
majority of cases such measures, designed to ease entry of resources
into better-paid uses (jobs), are not popular; vested interests are
too firmly intrenched and are defended by well-sounding slogans,
such as "safeguarding against inferior services," "preserving the
jobs for the local people," "keeping out unreliable elements, stran-
gers, aliens," "protecting the living standard of the profession,"
"selecting only the best material," etc. But even if the interests of
the insiders are deemed to be worthy of protection, or if such
protection is deemed to be in the interest of the consumer or the

community or nation, it remains a monopolistic position and should be called so—unless one prefers to call monopolistic only those positions which he dislikes and to avoid the term for positions which he favors.

The term "monopolistic" has now been used as the opposite of "pliopolistic." Previously, in other contexts, it has been used as an opposite of "perfectly polypolistic" and again in other places as an opposite of "oligopolistic." This is a rather unsatisfactory state of terminological affairs but there seems to be no way out. The absence of what we called here pliopoly—or a low degree of it—has always been called "monopolistic" and it would be useless to crusade against this usage. All that can be hoped for is increased consciousness of the various connotations of "monopolistic." *Non-pure competition* (imperfect polypoly and oligopoly) is one thing and *obstructed entry* (non-pliopoly) is another. The idea common to both is that the allocation of resources to a certain use, either within a firm or within an industry, falls short of what is considered the competitive norm.

PART IV—MANY AND MORE SELLERS

CHAPTER 9

Polypoly and Pliopoly Combined, When Both Are Perfect

Group Equilibrium and Marginal Units: Simultaneous Equilibria · Different Meanings of Marginal

Perfect Polypoly and Perfect Pliopoly: Maximization and Equalization of Profit Rates · The Danger of Equivocation · The Adjustment of Price Expectations · A Model Sequence of Price Adjustment · The Dispersion of Expected Prices During Transition Periods · The Adjustment of Cost Conditions · Average Cost Inclusive of Rent · The Transformation of Implicit Rent into Money Cost

Capacity Output and Optimum Size: Lowest-Cost Output and Size of the Firm · Quasi-Rent and Scarcity Rent

THE PRESENCE OF many sellers in a market can create a certain state of mind in an individual seller, a type of thinking and acting which has no concern for rival reactions: *polypoly.* Easy entry can make it probable that more sellers will appear in an industry that has become especially profitable: *pliopoly.* To speculate about the typical position of the members of an industry where there are many sellers and where more sellers readily appear when profits arise, that is, to inquire into the consequences of a coincidence of polypoly and pliopoly, has been one of the chief tasks of the theory of competition. In this chapter we shall deal with perfect polypoly combined with perfect pliopoly, and with the implications of this combination for the output and size of the firms concerned. Other combinations, where either polypoly or pliopoly or both are imperfect, will be discussed in the next chapter.

GROUP EQUILIBRIUM AND MARGINAL UNITS

Simultaneous Equilibria

The synthesis of the theories of polypoly and pliopoly is a combination of propositions about the equilibrium of the individual firm with propositions about the equilibrium of the industry. The term "group equilibrium," which has been used for this combination, is felicitous in that it conveys the necessity of postulating *simultaneous equilibria* of the individual group members as well as of the group as a whole. The firm is in equilibrium if it makes as much profit as it possibly can under given circumstances—the principle of the maximization of profit. The industry is in equilibrium if supernormal profits are wiped out—the principle of the equalization of the rate of profit, or elimination of excess profits. The dangers of the combination of the respective theories lie in possible confusions due to equivocal concepts with slightly different meanings on the two levels of analysis; in a possible neglect of different time coefficients and of the distinction between momentary positions and processes in time; and in illegitimate generalizations of statements which hold, if at all, only for the "marginal firm."

Different Meanings of Marginal

"Marginal" can mean different things in different contexts. The marginal principle may refer either to homogeneous units or to heterogeneous units arranged in a certain order. Marginal revenue, marginal cost, marginal product, and similar concepts refer to the effects of a change in the number of homogeneous units of output produced or factors employed. Marginal land, marginal producer, marginal firm, and similar concepts refer to heterogeneous units arranged in a certain order, to wit, to physical or human or institutional units of different qualities or capacities. There is also another important difference between various types of marginal magnitudes: they may refer, firstly, to subjective estimates which the economist presumes are being made by individual firms as the bases for their current actions; they may refer, secondly, to subjective estimates which the economist expects will be made by individual firms in the future under the impression of circumstances which he expects to arise; or they may refer, thirdly, to objective estimates made by the economist in analysing probable or potential developments.

The marginal land, the marginal producer, the marginal firm (and most of the other marginal concepts referring to heterogeneous units) are concepts of the third type, because they constitute the economist's ideas about the supply of productive or entrepreneurial capacity, ranked from high to low fertility or efficiency, or from low to high cost of production, and they serve to explain the points at which certain production units, according to the economist's expectations, would be put into or withdrawn from operation.

Marginal revenue, marginal cost, and marginal product may be either of the first or of the second type of marginal concept. In the analysis of the equilibrium of the individual firm, the firm's "actual" subjective estimates of revenue, cost, and productivity are "data" which are assumed by the economist currently to determine the amounts of output produced or factors employed. In the analysis of the ultimate group equilibrium, however, it is not the "actual" (current) subjective estimates by the individual firms that are the data that the economist assumes will determine the (ultimate) outputs and employments; instead, the economist assumes that the subjective estimates are subject to certain (predicted) changes under the pressure of events the emergence of which he expects on the basis of his analysis of the probable entry or exodus of productive and managerial capacity. Thus we see that the second type of marginal concept is the result of the combination of ideas belonging to the first type on the one hand, and to the third type on the other. If this statement sounds rather obscure at this point, it will, I think, become clear as we proceed.

PERFECT POLYPOLY AND PERFECT PLIOPOLY

Maximization and Equalization of Profit Rates

The principle of *profit maximization in the firm* requires that each firm produce an output the marginal cost of which is equal to or just short (by the smallest possible margin) of marginal revenue. Under perfect polypoly, marginal revenue is equal to the expected selling price, hence output and size of the organization are chosen such as to equate marginal cost to the expected selling price ($MC = P$). The principle of the *profit-rate equalization in the whole economy* requires that the rates of return in all industries are equal, hence, that—with "normal" returns counted as cost—profits are eliminated.[1] Under perfect pliopoly, excess profits lead to more entries into the particular industries, hence to an increased supply of the products of these industries, with the result that selling prices are depressed until profits are reduced to zero ($P = AC$). These two lines of reasoning lead to the apparently inevitable inference that marginal cost and average cost, both being equal to selling price, must be equal to each other; and this, of course, implies [2] that the firms under these conditions always produce the lowest-cost output and are of the lowest-cost size.

The exposition of this argument is usually supplemented by geometrical representation of cost and demand functions. The corollary of perfect polypoly ($MR = P$) is exhibited by the *horizontality* of the demand curve visualized by the seller. The corollary of perfect pliopoly ($P = AC$) is exhibited by the *tangency* of the demand curve with the average cost curve. Since average cost curves regularly are, for certain well-known reasons, U-shaped curves, a horizontal tangent must touch the average cost curve at its lowest point. (Fig. 13.)

The Danger of Equivocation

The whole argument seems convincing and foolproof. However, one must beware of the most common trap in the social sciences: equivocation. The same terms in the various parts of the argument may have slightly different meanings, and inferences

[1] The discussion of normal profits, in the preceding chapter, should have made it clear that a firm which earns only the "normal profit rate" (or normal rate of return on investment) makes no economic profit at all.

[2] Marginal cost is equal to average cost at the lowest point of the latter, because as long as MC is below AC, AC is still falling, and as soon as MC is above AC, AC must be rising.

Tangency of Horizontal Demand Curve With Average Cost Curve

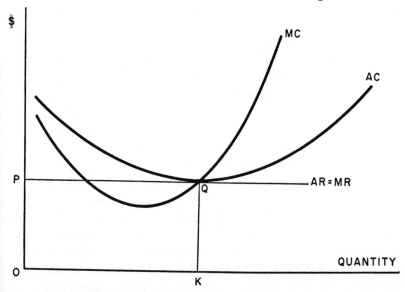

FIG. 13. Horizontal Average Revenue Curve Tangent to Average
Cost Curve; Output at Lowest-Cost Volume.

Equilibrium of the firm requires that an output is produced whose marginal cost is equal to marginal revenue. Perfect polypoly implies that the elasticity of demand as seen by the seller is infinite and, therefore, that the marginal revenue curve, *MR*, coincides with the (horizontal) demand or average revenue curve, *AR*. Hence, marginal cost will in this case be made equal to average revenue, or price ($KQ = OP$).

Equilibrium of the industry with free entry requires that only normal profits are earned. Normal profits being included in cost, the absence of supernormal or subnormal profits implies that average revenue neither exceeds nor falls short of average cost. That is, average revenue, or price, will be equal to average cost ($KQ = OP$).

It follows that marginal cost, marginal revenue, average revenue, and average cost must all be equal at the equilibrium output. Since marginal cost equals average cost at an output, *OK*, at which average cost reaches its lowest point, production of the lowest-cost volume of output is implied.

based upon their identity would then be faulty. The equilibrium condition of perfect polypoly is equality of marginal cost and price. The equilibrium condition of perfect pliopoly is equality of price and average cost. Does "price" in both statements refer to an identical magnitude and do the "marginal cost" and the "average cost" in the two statements refer to an identical cost schedule?

The price to which marginal cost is said to be equated under conditions of perfect polypoly is an expected price, expected by every single one of the supposedly large number of producers. It is anything but certain that all the different producers in the industry should always entertain exactly the same price expectation upon which they base their decisions. Thus, the "price"—a subjective expectation—may be different for different producers. It will often be different for different considerations of even the same producer, for instance, in considerations based upon short-run expectations, on the one hand, and in those based on long-run expectations, on the other; or, the degree of certainty with which a price is expected will often vary according to the length of the relevant period, and thus the price upon which the decision concerning output volume in a given plant is based may be different from the price upon which decisions concerning plant extensions are based. Now, after having questioned that the "given" price is identical for different considerations of any one producer or for analogous considerations of different producers operating in a certain industry, one can hardly assume that it is again the identical price which the outsider and potential new entrant into the industry will employ in his investment calculations. And, of course, the potential newcomers' price expectations are the relevant factors in the equilibrium of perfect pliopoly.

The same ambiguities are inherent in the cost concepts of the theories combined here. Unless differential rents are considered as cost items, cost conditions cannot (except in simplified illustrations used for teaching purposes) be assumed to be identical for all producers in an industry and, still less, identical for different degrees of plant adjustment of any one producer. But regardless of the sameness or disparity of these cost calculations, that the cost calculations of the existing producers should be the same as those of the potential newcomers to the industry is more than questionable. Yet, it is the outsiders' cost calculations which are relevant to the "average cost" in pliopoly theory, whereas the insiders' cost calculations are relevant for the "marginal cost" in polypoly theory.

To recognize all these ambiguities and possible fallacies is not to condemn the theories in question. It is necessary, however, to inquire into the factors which may determine the size of the probable error, into the forces which may tend to reduce or hold it down, and into the ultimate limitations of the applicability of the theory.

The Adjustment of Price Expectations

That every one of a large number of producers of a standardized product *may* have a different expectation concerning the most probable selling price means little if it can be shown that substantial discrepancies are unlikely to prevail or, at least, that a frequency distribution of the prices expected by the different producers would most likely exhibit a considerable uniformity of expectations in the overwhelming majority of cases. The existence of this uniformity can be shown to be highly probable. This is so because past experience is the most important single factor shaping future expectations, and past experiences, at least the more recent ones, concerning level and movement of price are, of course, common to the individuals concerned. Major discrepancies in the ways of interpreting past experiences may occur, but not usually in a sufficiently large number to disturb the general uniformity.

This uniformity of price expectations will be especially marked if the past experience has been one of long-lasting stability of price or one of fairly regular oscillations of prices around some level that has come to be considered as normal. Save a few incurable optimists, men will not indefinitely, undisturbed by ever-repeated disappointments, continue to expect a price of $1.50 for a product that has always sold at or around one dollar. Gradual revision of expectations after a series of disappointments will, in the "regular" cases, bring expected prices into line with actual prices.

Adjustment and uniformity of price expectations will not be probable in situations where very irregular price fluctuations per-

mit the wildest guesses and the most conservative suppositions to
have just about the same chance of coming true. It stands to reason, however, that what appear as irregular fluctuations in the short
run would be "averaged out" for considerations extending over
longer periods. It is quite likely that in these situations the long-
run plans of established producers and of the marginal newcomers
are built upon relatively uniform price expectations.

The real problem within the scope of a theory of competition
is the adjustment of subjective price expectations to such changes
of market price as are expected by the economist to result from
certain changes in market demand or cost conditions and from the
subsequent entries (or exits) of firms into (or from) the industry.
In other words, the relevant problem at this point is the adjustment
of subjective price expectations as a part of the whole process of
adaptation which is supposed to lead eventually to the equilibrium of the industry, that is, to the above-mentioned "group equilibrium."

Let us try to illustrate this by sketching the first steps of a
model sequence of positions which firms and industry have to pass
through in a process of adaptation to a permanent increase in
market demand, under the assumptions of perfect polypoly and
pliopoly.

A Model Sequence of Price Adjustment

1. Under the impact of increased demand the market price
is increased.

2-A. Producers who believe that the price will quickly recede
to its former ("normal") level, that is, producers with unchanged
price expectations, will not change their plants or their outputs.
They will reap merely "windfall profits"; their expected future
profits remain unchanged.

2-B. Producers who believe that the price will stay for some
time, but not for very long, at the higher level, that is, producers
expecting an increased short-run price but an unchanged long-
run price, will increase production in their plants but leave their
productive capacities as they are. They will produce at increased
average costs and still more increased marginal costs; their ex-

pected profits will, of course, be higher than those of producers A (who are not stepping up their production).

2-C. Producers who believe that the price will permanently stay at a higher level (even if not at the level reached by the first impact of the increased demand), that is, producers expecting both short-run and long-run price to be higher than before (though perhaps lower than the current market price, and perhaps the long-run price lower than the short-run price) will immediately step up production in their existing plants and will also plan plant extensions or even new plants. Average cost of the increased output will be increased because of production above normal capacity, and average cost of the still larger output in the enlarged or augmented plants will also be increased (though to a lesser extent) owing to diseconomies of size. Expected profits will be substantially increased.[3]

2-D. Producers who believe that the price will rise still higher, that is, producers expecting both short-run and long-run price not only to be higher than the initial price but also higher than the current market price, will raise production and will plan plant extensions and additions at a scale exceeding that of producers C. The increases in costs as well as in expected profits are greatest for producers D.

3. Increased volumes of output coming onto the market cause the market price to drop from the highest level reached in phase 1. If the price is now still above its initial level, the expectations of various producers may be affected in the following way: Some producers of group A become more optimistic and some of group D become less optimistic, so that the former join the rank of those who increase production, while the latter reduce their outputs and cut their expansion plans to more modest scales.

4. The increased price and news and rumors about larger production figures, new investment plans, and higher earnings of the

[3] The existence of diseconomies of size follows from the assumption of perfect polypoly, which implies that firms have reached optimum size and can expand only under increasing costs. If one denies that diseconomies of size can exist, one denies implicitly that perfect polypoly can exist. This would reduce the analysis in the text to mere exercise or to a preliminary step for a more complex model. I do not question, however, that diseconomies of size exist in certain fields.

existing firms attract outsiders—first of all, producers of technologically related products—who, expecting that the new price or,
at least, a price in excess of the initial one, will persist, take up the
production of the particular product.

5. Increased outputs from the enlarged plants as well as the
new production from the new establishments coming onto the
market cause another price recession. The effect upon price expectations is likely to be in the nature of a damper on optimism.
Current production volumes will be reduced, investment plans
which have not yet led to large outlays may be tabled, and plant
expansions or new plant already under construction will perhaps
be changed to smaller dimensions.

6. No further entries into the industry seem warranted now.
Whether at this juncture the actual market price is above or below
or just at its initial level will depend on the degree to which plant
capacities and production volumes were increased during the described phases and on the degree to which the market can absorb
the quantities supplied: in other words, on the comparative elasticities of supply and demand.

The sequence of transition phases will go on much longer in
the case of an overexpansion of the industry, because this would
call for an adjustment by way of a painful and long-drawn-out
process of weeding out some of the excess capacity—unless demand increases further and catches up with the expansion of the
industry. The more gradual the expansion the more likely will overexpansion have been avoided.[4]

To retrace some of the steps that were undertaken to increase
production in plants with unchanged capacity is, of course, much
simpler. The extent to which the old producers, under pressure
of the downward movements of market price, will have to revise
their price expectations, and thus their production scales, will de-

---

[4] Overexpansion is meant here in terms of the existing cost conditions and
of the given increase of demand by which it was stimulated. The excess capacity is created under the stimulus of a price rise that is caused by the first
impact of the demand increase but not maintained. The price expectations
which are responsible for the expansion turn out to be exaggerated in comparison with the ultimate equilibrium price. Thus we see that, if expected
prices were always exactly equal to current prices, the adjustment process
leading to a long-run equilibrium would be very much longer, if not endless.

pend, on the one hand, on the degree of their previous optimism and, on the other hand, on the amount of new capacity that was added to the industry. New entries are, of course, not merely a matter of the price expectations of the actual and potential newcomers but also of their cost calculations. If these outsiders have figured with higher cost than the insiders—which is one of the factors behind an increasing long-run cost curve of the industry and also the chief factor behind the economist's idea about the entry of the "marginal producer"—new entrants will have been less numerous and the ultimate price will be above the initial one. With subjective price expectations fully adjusted, the output volumes of the individual producers would then be higher than before the change in demand, and their profits (in the business sense of the word) would also be higher.

If newcomers can work under exactly the same cost conditions as the established firms, the ultimate price will be back at the initial level, with the outputs of the individual firms also back at the original figures, provided they have adjusted their price expectations to the final market price level and have not expanded their production capacity—an expansion that would turn out to be a bad investment.[5] This is the famous model case of increasing costs of the individual firm (a necessary condition for the assumption of perfect polypoly) but constant costs of the industry as a whole (availability of any and all needed resources, inclusive of managerial capacity, at the same prices and the same quality).

The Dispersion of Expected Prices During Transition Periods

In the sequence of positions outlined above no uniformity of price expectations was assumed during the earlier phases of adjustment. For the second phase we assumed no less than four different types of expectations in reaction to a current price change and there could be any number of divergent sets of prices within each type. Hence, even if the equality of marginal cost and expected

---

[5] If they have expanded their capacity (at increasing costs, of course) the price at the close of the expansion period would not be the final equilibrium price—though it may be the equilibrium price for a very long "short period"—because the withdrawal of capacity from the industry would still have to be accomplished if nothing else changes in the years to come.

price were always observed by each individual firm, there would have prevailed a conspicuous inequality of prices expected by different firms. However, the dispersion of price expectations during earlier phases of transition periods does not disturb the theorist who simultaneously postulates the *maximum*-profit equation of perfect polypoly ($MC = P$) and the *no*-profit equation of perfect pliopoly ($P = AC$); for it is clear that the latter of the two equations is not meant to hold for transition periods, but only for the termination of a long-lasting process of adjustment.

In later phases a gradual downward revision of previously increased price expectations is "observed," an adjustment of expectations which brings about an increasing degree of uniformity. This downward revision is forced about by the pressure upon market price that is exerted by the larger quantities of product supplied, among others, by newly opened establishments. This gradual reduction of the price with which the individual firms calculate is, so to speak, "in the cards," that is to say, it is seen as a necessary development by the economist as he counts on new entries into the industry when price rises high enough to promise profits to newcomers. The price recession cannot, however, go farther ultimately than to the point (or points) where entries stop and exits would begin. Hence, the economist implicitly predicts the ultimate price expectations entertained within the industry by predicting the price expectations which neither attract new firms nor repel old ones. This is the real link between the theories of "pure" and "perfect" competition, or perfect polypoly and pliopoly.

The adaptation of subjective price expectations to current prices is a necessary part of the theory of group equilibrium, but it should be emphasized that this adaptation must be slow and gradual if the group equilibrium is to be reached quickly, with a minimum of frictions. A fast and full adaptation of expected prices to current prices would lead to "wrong" investment decisions, which would have to be corrected afterwards in a slow and painful process before group equilibrium could be reached. If we choose to call a slow and imperfect adjustment of subjective price expectations an element of "friction," then we must recognize that the existence of frictions is a necessary condition for the attainment of group equilibrium.

Ultimately, however, that is, for later phases in the equilibrating process, the adjustment and uniformity of expected prices was not only postulated but also shown to be a fairly reasonable assumption (at least for cases where data did not change again before a certain degree of adjustment could be reached). And this would rehabilitate the simultaneous validity of the two equations, $MC = P$ and $P = AC$, as far as the identity of price is concerned.

The analogous task of showing that the marginal cost and the average cost in the two equations refer to an identical cost schedule still remains to be done. Can it be done?

The Adjustment of Cost Conditions

Under conditions of perfectly free and easy entry into, and exodus from, an industry, the marginal producer is a zero-profit producer.[6] For if he made less than zero profits he would not stay in the industry, and if he made more than zero profits he could not remain the marginal producer as more producers would come in. Thus, if the zero-profit equation holds for the marginal producer by definition, and if the maximum-profit equation holds for him as for every other firm in the industry, the equality of the marginal and average cost of production is established for the marginal firm. But if intramarginal firms are defined as firms that could stand also a lower price, that is to say, firms that produce under more favorable cost conditions, it follows clearly that their average cost, lower than that of the marginal firm, cannot be equal to but must be lower than their marginal cost.

According to this line of reasoning, the profits, or net surpluses, of low-cost producers are not only maximized but also positive; thus, the cost schedule of these producers cannot be the same as that of the producers with no profit. In other words, the cost schedule which results in zero profits cannot be the same schedule

---

[6] Robert Triffin proposed that the term *free entry* be reserved for the case where all actual and potential producers are faced with exactly the same cost conditions. *Monopolistic Competition and General Equilibrium Theory* (Cambridge: Harvard University Press, 1940), p. 120. His proposal has not been adopted.

which, with the same selling prices, is relevant for the determination of output and size of an intramarginal firm.

This argument, which seems definitely to establish the nonidentity of the relevant cost schedules, is based upon "given" cost conditions. However, just as the selling conditions were shown to be subject to change in the process that leads to the group equilibrium, the cost conditions of the members of the group may not be frozen either. Does not the cost schedule with which the firm calculates take part in the adjustment process just as the demand schedule [7] of the firm? Is, in other words, the cost of production in an individual firm independent of the changes in the size of the industry, or must we not rather expect that entries of new firms into the industry will cause an upward movement of the cost figures of each single firm?

The model sequence which was sketched above did not contain anything about cost adjustments. It concentrated upon the adjustment of price expectations and left adjustments on the cost side of the firms' calculations out of the picture. This omission must now be repaired.

A cost schedule for a firm, in an industry that consists of many firms, is usually constructed on the basis of given prices of all factors of production. (Just as the firm in the position of perfect polypoly calculates under the supposition that it could sell larger amounts of product at the same price at which it expects to sell smaller amounts, the firm in the position of perfect polypsony calculates under the supposition that it could buy larger amounts of factors at the same prices at which it expects to buy smaller amounts.) Changes in factor prices would, of course, change the cost schedule. It is quite likely that the increased demand for factors in an expanding industry affects the supply of factors to individual firms: the prices of factors may rise in the course of the expansion process of the industry.

An upward movement of the cost schedules of the firms, brought about by the increased production and employment in existing, enlarged, and newly erected plants, is the "natural"

[7] Under perfect polypoly this demand curve is, of course, a horizontal line at the level of the expected price.

counterpart of the downward movement of selling prices that follows from the same causes. The profit margin created by the initial price increase, which resulted from the increased market demand, is again "squeezed out" in the process leading to the new group equilibrium, squeezed out from between the downward pressure of selling price and the upward pressure of production cost. The fact that theory places, in general, more emphasis upon price adjustment than on cost adjustment is easily comprehended: the industry model—the "group" whose equilibrium is studied—is usually defined by its product rather than by its factors of production. If the "industry" uses the same factors of production that are used by many other industries, and uses only a small portion of the entire factor supply, then the influence of the particular industry's demand for factors upon factor prices may be neglected, whereas the effect of the industry's supply of product upon product prices is the very reason why the particular group is distinguished from other groups as a separate "industry."

The upward adjustment of the prices of variable factors of production and, thus, the upward adjustment of the cost calculations of the individual firms may or may not be included in the model sequence leading to the new group equilibrium, depending on the assumed conditions of factor supply to the industry. But even if an increasing scarcity of variable factors in the industry causes upward adjustments of cost calculations in all individual firms, marginal and intramarginal, this upward adjustment would not eliminate the cost differentials between marginal and intramarginal firms. Even if the prices of factors which the firms employ in variable amounts are increased throughout, differences between low-cost producers and high-cost producers will remain. The upward adjustment of the cost of variable factors does not assimilate the production cost in intramarginal firms to that to which the zero-profit equation of perfect competition refers.

However, such a process of "full adjustment" (or assimilation) of cost is postulated by those who take full account of all changes in the "implicit valuation" of the "fixed resources" of the firms and include differential rents in the full cost of production. The concept of "average cost inclusive of rent" is the device employed for this purpose.[8] The specific resources or factors to which cost advantages are due are, of course, sources of rent incomes; if all productive resources, the fixed ones as well as the variable, are credited with their full value when the cost account is set up, then costs are automatically "adjusted" to any change in demand and to any other change as well. (See Fig. 14.) It goes without saying, then, that the "average cost inclusive of rent" must for all intra-marginal firms be the same as the average cost of the marginal firm, the "no-rent" firm. But the question suggests itself whether this full adjustment of average cost through the artificial device of including differential rents in cost is merely an empty tautology or whether it has meaning in the interpretation of reality.

Average Cost Inclusive of Rent

If differential rent is the difference between the cost of the low-cost producer and the cost of the no-rent firm; and if "cost inclusive of rent" is the cost of the low-cost producer plus the differential rent; then it is evident that "average cost inclusive of rent" is a tautological expression standing for "average cost of the no-rent firm," or even standing for "selling price," if the absence of rent means that there is no margin between average cost and selling price. In this case, price is not made *equal* to average cost through certain forces operating in the real world, but average cost (inclusive of rent) is, by definition, made *identical* with price. This seems to be a rather useless play with words.

The device of the "average cost inclusive of rent" can have real meaning, however, if this rent can assume the aspect of cost, either from the point of view of the firms in question or from the point of view of the observer-economist. A transformation of differential rent into cost from the economist's standpoint will take place in his reasoning about the optimum allocation of resources. In comparing alternative uses of resources, the full imputation of specific rent incomes to the respective factors is necessary in order to obtain and compare correct opportunity costs and thus to avoid "uneconomical" applications of undervalued resources. But

[8] See the instructive exposition in Joan Robinson, *The Economics of Imperfect Competition* (London: Macmillan, 1932), Ch. IX, pp. 120–29.

Tangency of Increased Demand Curve With Average Cost Curve Secured Through Rent Increase

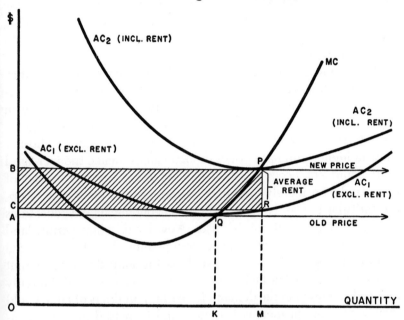

FIG. 14. Price Increase Raises Rent and Lifts Average Cost Inclusive of Rent to New Position of Tangency.

At the old price OA ($= KQ$) this perfect polypolist has been a marginal producer, earning no rent: his average cost (without rent) at output OK equals the price where his marginal cost equals his marginal revenue, (all KQ). Assume now that an increase in demand sends the price up to OB ($= MP$). At this new price our producer finds it best to increase his output to the volume OM, where his marginal cost again equals his marginal revenue. His average cost, exclusive of rent, of this output is MR; hence, his average revenue, MP, exceeds his average cost by RP. This is his "average rent"; his total rent is $CRPB$, the shaded area. If rent is included in cost, his average cost including rent ($MR + RP$) must of course be equal to average revenue, MP. If the new average cost curve including rent is drawn (by spreading the total rent over the output and adding it to the average cost without rent), this curve, AC_2, must of necessity have its lowest point in P and thus be tangent to the new demand curve.

this, more normative than explanatory, cost concept finds its real counterpart in the actual cost calculations of the firms, if only enough time is allowed for implicit rents to become explicit rentals and for implicit valuations to become market values. There is, in actual fact, a tendency for differential rents to become in time actual costs to the buyers or employers of the factors in question, provided the particular resources can institutionally become objects of sales, rental or wage contracts.

Let us imagine for a moment that land, owing to some fancy legal institutions, could not be rented, sold, or mortgaged. If certain products of land were more heavily demanded and rose in price, the increased rents from the use of land could not be reflected in higher rentals, and the increased land values could not show in higher purchase prices or loan values; hence the increased rents could not become actual money costs. Any cost aspect of rent would be merely "implicit," although a neglect of this opportunity cost of land might result in uneconomical land allocations among its various alternative uses. Now let us again permit land to be rented, sold, or mortgaged, and assume that the traditional frictions in land transactions (such as the long duration of rent contracts, personal attachment to land, etc.,) are substantially reduced. Changes in the demand for certain products of land would then soon show in increased rentals and increased market valuations for land. For farmers would not merely try to hire more help and to buy more fertilizer and equipment, but they would also try to acquire more land, as tenants or as buyers; the rentals and prices for land might react to the increased demand more readily than the wages of farm hands or the prices of fertilizer or equipment. Thus the "fixed cost" of agricultural production would rise quickly.

If all land were operated by tenant farmers and if all rent contracts were for a year only and were let by public auctions, the cost character of rent would probably be more explicit than that of the price of equipment. Differential rents for better land would clearly and unquestionably be parts of the cost of production, calculated by every individual producer. The expression "average cost inclusive of rent" would not strike us any longer as artificial or philosophical, but rather as unnecessary because self-evident. The full adjustment of the average cost of production on intramarginal land to the average cost of production on marginal land would not be the (tautological) result of the theorists' definitions and conventions, but rather the (empirical) result of generally observed market phenomena. Observation would reveal that some farmers pay in increased rent what, compared with others, they save paying for labor and material.

The Transformation of Implicit Rent into Money Cost

The transformation of implicit rent into actual money cost is, in most lines of production in the real world, slow and imperfect. The speed and perfection of this transformation depends on several factors, most of them of an institutional nature. The larger the number of independent firms in the industry, the quicker and more complete, as a rule, will be the transformation of implicit rent into explicit cost. But almost never will this transformation be simultaneous for the whole industry; it will take place only gradually as rent and wage contracts in individual firms come up for renewal and as the property in question changes hands through sale in a competitive market. Thus, while a number of firms reckon already with adjusted prices of fixed resources, other firms in the industry continue to calculate on the basis of their historical costs. The actual average cost calculations of different firms are, therefore, not of great relevance and the theorist's device of speaking about "average cost inclusive of rent" appears as a legitimate attempt to make average cost figures more significant by anticipating the cost adjustments which may be expected actually to take place in due time.

This forwardation by the theorist of a cost adjustment which the firms (provided market conditions remain as they are) would make at some time in the future will probably not lead the theorist into serious error; for the supposed adjustment refers only to average cost and not to marginal cost, the basis of the firms' decisions and actions.[9] It is the fixed resources whose cost adjustment is delayed; but since fixed costs do not enter into marginal cost, it does not matter if the theorist pictures these fixed costs as adjusted

---

[9] On the question whether or not businessmen really use the marginal calculus, see above, Chapters 2 and 3.

while in reality the cost accountants of most firms still compute their averages with unadjusted figures. The marginal costs of production are the same whether they are calculated on the basis of the old or the revised average total cost figures or even without any fixed costs at all. As far as investment decisions are concerned —decisions about new, therefore at the moment *still variable,* commitments concerning what will *later* be *fixed* costs—the underlying considerations will include new purchases of, or new contracts about, fixed resources and, therefore, the "long-run marginal cost" will probably comprise already adjusted values of these fixed resources.

CAPACITY OUTPUT AND OPTIMUM SIZE

Having satisfied ourselves that there is some measure of justification in our reasoning in terms of "average cost inclusive of rent," we must cautiously note that this justification is probably restricted to particular problems and not extensible to all problems dealing with average cost. We must ascertain whether or not this justification extends fully to the case before us, whether or not all inferences based on propositions about "average cost inclusive of rent" in the theories of perfect polypoly and pliopoly are safe and meaningful. The most crucial of these inferences is the famous statement that, under perfect polypoly and pliopoly, all firms will be of such a *size* as will permit the lowest possible cost of production, and that they will actually produce the lowest-cost volume of *output.*

Lowest-Cost Output and Size of the Firm

The "lowest-cost" volume of output (often called the capacity output, although it may be less than the technical maximum) refers to average total cost of production in a firm of given size; in the customary graphs this output is shown by the abscissa of the lowest point of the short-run average total cost curve.[10] If the short-

[10] "It is generally agreed that, since the absolute technical upper limit of the output obtainable from the fixed factors is likely to lie far beyond the realm of practical economic operations, their capacity output should be taken

run cost curves for all possible sizes of the firm are drawn and
for each quantity of output the lowest possible average cost is
marked out—i.e., the unit cost of each quantity as if it were produced in the most adequate arrangement (with the most perfectly adapted number and sizes of plants)—the series of these
lowest possible unit cost figures constitutes the long-run average
total cost curve. (See Fig. 15.) This curve may have one lowest
point, or perhaps a lowest stretch of points, constituting the absolute minimum cost of production. The issue in question is whether,
if polypoly and pliopoly are perfect, exactly that size of firm (i.e.,
size and number of plants operated by the firm) and exactly that
output volume which permit realization of the lowest of all possible unit costs will actually be chosen by all firms.[11]

The examination of this issue seems simpler if we separate
for the moment the short-run problem (determination of output
in a firm with given plant and equipment) from the long-run problem (determination of both the whole structural arrangement of
the firm and its volume of output). We can assume, for example,
that there is only one practically possible plant arrangement so
that there is no other problem than that of output determination.
The output at which the unit cost of the firm (or farm) is lowest
is called, as was mentioned before, production at full "capacity."
The implication is that the production of a smaller output signifies
"unused capacity." This concept of capacity is not a technological

---

as that at which the average full costs of production are at their minimum."
J. M. Cassels, "Excess Capacity and Monopolistic Competition," *Quarterly
Journal of Economics,* Vol. LI (1937), p. 428.

[11] Statements about the size of the firm are easily confused with statements about the size of the plant. This makes, of course, no difference in the
case of single-plant firms. In this case the size of the plant with the supplementary organization "implies" the size of the firm and vice versa. As far as
multi-plant firms are concerned the situation is different. The long-run cost
curve of a firm is the locus of the lowest possible unit costs of all outputs
produced in any number or sizes of plants. Since plants are not perfectly divisible, small outputs would have to be produced (if they were produced) in
uneconomically small plants, and the same might be true for certain output
volumes which are not the exact multiple of the capacity output of the plant
of the most economical size. Multi-plant firms are more economical than
single-plant firms whenever diseconomies of larger scale, or locational limitations, of the individual plant are in the way of *plant* expansions, while indivisibilities of important factors in the overhead organization permit economies of larger *firms.*

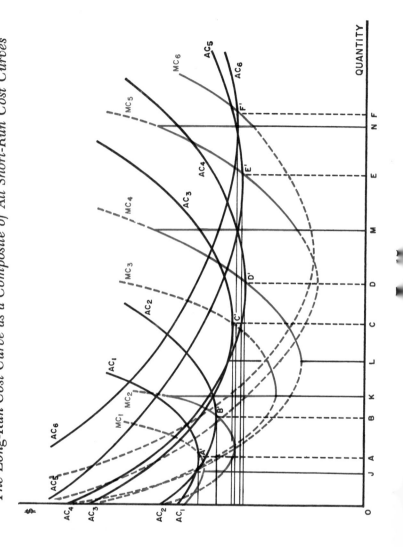

concept. Simple reflection shows that changes of prices of factors of production will change the average cost curve of the plant and probably shift its lowest point. The "capacity" of an absolutely unchanged plant is then "automatically" decreased if through the change of the unit-cost curve its lowest point is shifted to the left,

---

Fɪɢ. 15. Set of Six Short-Run Average and Marginal Cost Curves for Output Produced in Differently Sized Firm.

A short-run cost curve connects the points showing the lowest cost at which each possible volume of output can be produced in the firm with fixed productive equipment. The long-run cost curve connects the points showing the lowest cost at which each possible volume of output can be produced in the firm with plant and organization ("size") at every point optimally adapted to the output volume. Hence, the long-run cost curve is a composite of those parts of the series of short-run curves that are not "undercut" by any part of any other short-run cost curve. While each curve is a locus of minimum costs—namely, each lowest cost of each output—every average cost curve may have a minimum point—namely, the lowest one of all average costs of all the outputs shown on the curve. In Figure 15, A', B', C', D', E', and F' are the minima of the six short-run average cost curves. Whether or not the minimum point of a short-run average cost curve qualifies as a point on the long-run average cost curve depends on whether or not the next-larger size firm is too large to produce the particular output any cheaper, that is, whether it will be to the right or to the left of that minimum point that the short-run curve is intersected by the short-run curve pertaining to the next-larger size firm. For example, A', the lowest point of AC_1, is not relevant in the long run and lies off the long-run curve, because OA, the lowest-cost output in firm size 1 can in the long run be more cheaply produced in firm size 2. On the other hand, B', the lowest point of AC_2, does lie on the long-run curve, because OB, the lowest-cost output in firm size 2, cannot be produced at any cost lower than BB' in any other arrangement. The parts of the short-run curves that compose the long-run curve are shown by heavier lines.

Note the kinks, jumps and drops of the long-run marginal cost curve. Where a short-run average cost curve is intersected by the "next" one while it still descends—such as AC_1 and AC_3—the long-run marginal cost curve will exhibit a sudden drop; where that intersection occurs in the ascending part of the short-run average cost curve, the long-run marginal cost curve will show a drastic rise followed by a precipitous fall at the output for which the next size becomes appropriate.

Where firms can adapt themselves by small changes (rather than by "jumps" from one size to another) the discontinuities of the long-run curves disappear. Each short-run curve will then contribute only one point to the long-run curve, which will smoothly envelop the infinite number of short-run curves.

and increased if the lowest point is shifted further to the right.

Now, if we recall that the relevant unit-cost curve includes not only the cost of variable factors of production but also the values (rents) of fixed resources, we realize that "plant capacity" will change automatically with every change in the product price that changes the values (rents) of fixed resources. If there are any fixed resources whose supply is not infinitely elastic, the values of these resources will rise whenever the demand for the product rises, and fall whenever the demand for the product falls. One and the same production volume that constitutes, at a certain level of selling price, "operation of the plant at its full capacity" would imply "operation beyond full capacity" if the price of the product fell (because in this case decreased rent would shift the lowest point of the cost curve to the left), and it would imply "unused capacity" if the price of the product rose (because in this case increased rent would shift the lowest point of the cost curve to the right). Hence the proposition that all firms, under the "full equilibrium" conditions, operate at full capacity means, if anything, something very much different from what an "unenlightened" reader would gather from the technological connotation of the term "capacity." He would probably charge the economist with gross misuse of words if he were given to understand that in the case of a scarce supply of fixed resources (say, mineral resources) the large output volumes at high selling prices and the small output volumes at low selling prices may both be regarded as "production at full capacity," because "capacity" (of the unchanged mining establishment) is, in the sense used by the economist, a function of the value of the fixed resources, which in turn is a function of the selling price of the product.

Before we try to evaluate the meaning and significance of this shifting concept of the capacity of a plant, we must recognize that the concept of the optimum size of the firm (lowest-cost size of the firm) is subject to the same relativity. This is quite obvious now that it has been made clear that the cost curves will shift with changing values of variable as well as fixed factors of production and that changing product prices will change the values of all scarce resources including the "entrepreneurial and managerial set-up" of the firms. Thus, if any of the productive factors or resources are scarce, that is, not available in perfectly elastic supply, the optimum or lowest-cost size of firm will not be any definite, technologically determined size; but, instead, its physical dimensions will depend upon the price at which the product sells. When the product price is low, a smaller firm will be the "lowest-cost firm"; when the product price rises, a larger firm will become "lowest-cost firm." [12]

Quasi-Rent and Scarcity Rent

We must become increasingly apprehensive of any unhealthy growth of a system of apparently tautological phrases and slogans. What can be the use of saying that each firm, seeking maximum net revenue, will organize itself in the most economical size and will produce at full capacity—if neither "capacity" nor "most economical size" is a definite magnitude, uniquely determined under given technological conditions but if, instead, both vary with selling price and net revenue of the firm? Yet, things are not so bad as they sound.

First of all, the embarrassing ambiguity or relativity of "capacity" and "optimum size" is present only in cases where the supply of resources to the industry is scarce. In all other cases, that is, in those not infrequent cases where additional quantities of resources (variable, fixed, and entrepreneurial) are available to the industry at constant prices, productive capacity and optimum size of firm are definite and independent of the price at which the product sells.

Secondly, where some productive resources are scarce, it makes rather good sense that the scarce resources should be utilized more intensively as more product is demanded and, thus, that we ought to regard the economic capacity of these scarce resources as increased and an enlarged firm—which would have been uneconomically large for a smaller demand—as the most economical size.

[12] We must be careful not to confuse the concept of the firm in the sense in which it is used above, and in price, cost, and output analysis in general, with other concepts of the firm, for example, in the theory or history of the growth of business enterprises or in legal or sociological discussions. In the present context a firm may "in fact" be just one of the several divisions of a corporation which is engaged in numerous "industries."

298   MANY AND MORE SELLERS

These two points, reassuring us about the significance of propositions concerning capacity production and optimum size of firm,
are rather different in character. The first of the points has an empirical foundation; it refers to probable developments in the real
world. The second one contains a strongly normative element; it
refers to the adequacy of interpretation in the light of desirable
standards of performance.

The first point maintains that there are in reality enough instances where the industry has access to increasing quantities of
all its productive factors and resources without boosting their
prices or values. In these cases the cost functions, and therefore
the magnitudes of the lowest-cost output and lowest-cost size of
firm, are independent of the demand for the product. When demand rises, the net surplus earned by existing producers will rise
only temporarily; no increased rents, only increased quasi-rents,
will be created. For one cannot permanently impute higher values
to fixed resources which can be reproduced at given, constant costs.
(It would make little sense to speak of "average cost inclusive of
quasi-rent.") Firms which are persuaded, by the improved selling
market, to expand in size will be disappointed. The larger size of
the firm will not be economical, because new firms can and will at
given, constant costs duplicate what has been the optimum size
of the productive arrangement and the product price will recede
again to its former level. It will not pay to operate larger firms than
those which had been the most economical ones, nor will it pay to
operate the existing firms permanently at a larger scale of output.
The entry of new firms and the easy reproduction of all productive facilities at constant costs will (provided full adjustment
can be achieved) force all perfect polypolists again to produce
capacity outputs in firms of lowest-cost size, with capacity and
economical size meaning exactly the same technological realities
as before.

The second point means to justify propositions about capacity
and size in instances in which they do not refer to the same technological realities. Without any change in the technical conditions
of production, an uneconomical size of firm can become the most
economical size simply because a greater demand for the product

calls for a more intensive use of a scarce resource.[13] But this stamp of approval upon economizing a scarce resource by operating a larger firm, this recognition of the enlarged firm as the most economical because it uses the scarce resource—perhaps managerial talent—more intensively, can be given in good faith only if it is certain that the scarcity of that resource is natural and not artificial. (See Chapter 8.) This means, however, that the economist's judgment as to the natural or artificial scarcity of resources in an industry will be decisive in the question of what should be considered the capacity output and the economical size of the firm.

If artificial restrictions of entry create a high rent of certain resources, a cost curve inclusive of this rent cannot be accepted as the one that determines the most economical output and the most economical size of the firm. Only rents due to natural scarcity can be admitted into the cost calculations relevant for the determination of the "lowest-cost" volume of output and the "lowest-cost" size of firm. Artificial scarcity rents must be eliminated from these calculations.

At this point, however, we hit again upon a piece of tautological argumentation. For, when the assumption of *perfect pliopoly* was made, artificial restrictions of entry and, thus, artificial scarcity rents of resources were excluded by definition. The judgment whether or not the elasticity of the supply of resources to the industry is artificially low precedes the whole argument. For that the "natural" elasticity of supply has not been interfered with, is presupposed when the synthesis of the theories of perfect polypoly and perfect pliopoly is entered upon. Hence, any rents that are increased or decreased by changes in the demand for the product are accepted here as "legitimate" because, by assumption, they are due only to natural scarcity. The justification of the postulate that scarce resources must be economized, and capacity output and optimum size of the firm should be considered as increased when product demand rises, appears thus to be implied in the assumption of perfect pliopoly.

[13] "Potential output [i.e., capacity output] is conditioned in most cases by economic circumstances and must be interpreted as being the optimum output from the economic point of view." Cassels, *op. cit.*, p. 443.

CHAPTER 10

Polypoly and Pliopoly Combined, When Either or Both Are Imperfect

Perfect Polypoly and Imperfect Pliopoly: Concrete Examples and Theoretical Models · Excessive Size and Excessive Outputs

Imperfect Polypoly and Perfect Pliopoly: Under-utilized Capacity in an Undersized Firm · Price, Cost, and Sales Expectations · The Adjustment of Sales Expectations · The Predicted Equilibrium Position

Excess Capacity under the Tangency Rule: The Four Interpretations · The Limits of Applicability · The Differential Rent of Differentiated Polypolists · Implications Concerning Unused Capacity and Potential Economies

The Wastes of Newcomers' Competition: Product Variety at Higher Cost · Nine Reasons for Higher Cost of Smaller Scale · The Significance of the Nine Points · Three Other Reasons of Higher Costs · Weighing the Losses and Benefits

Imperfect Polypoly and Imperfect Pliopoly: Product Differentiation as a Barrier to Entry · A Common Cause for Both Imperfections · Political Interference with Entry · The Effects upon Total Output · Low Price Policy to Prevent Entry

IN THE PRECEDING chapter the combination between perfect polypoly and perfect pliopoly was examined. Now imperfections of the one or the other type of competition must be analysed. We turn first to the combination of perfect polypoly with imperfect pliopoly.

PERFECT POLYPOLY AND IMPERFECT PLIOPOLY

That polypoly should be perfect and pliopoly absent or imperfect, is perhaps regarded as a peculiar, utterly academic combination. But, as a matter of fact, several realistic examples can be found for this combination.

Concrete Examples and Theoretical Models

Restrictions of areas under cultivation for agricultural production are cases in point. An artificial reduction of the employed acreage raises rent, induces a greater economy in the use of the now "scarcer" land, that is to say, it "calls" for more intensive methods of production (more labor and capital per acre of land); in other words, it leads to an increase of what appears as the optimum volume of output, the "capacity," per unit of land. But, since land is not "really" scarce, its intensive use cannot be considered as economical. Output per acre is, in view of the comparative "natural" scarcities of land and the other employed factors of production, uneconomically large.

Examples from industrial rather than agricultural production cannot be easily found, because perfect polypoly is hardly possible in industry. But decisive for the worth-whileness of a detailed discussion is not the frequency or infrequency of the actual occurrence of the situation in question, but rather its usefulness for the attainment of analytical principles, principles necessary for the explanation or evaluation of observed situations which may be somehow related (perhaps only by contrast) to the discussed one. The position of perfect polypoly in actual fact is rare indeed. Yet, the insight gained from the analysis of this position is not affected by its rareness.

Excessive Size and Excessive Outputs

The principle that is elucidated by combining the assumptions of perfect polypoly and imperfect pliopoly is the resulting tendency toward uneconomically large output volumes and organizational structures of the individual firms. The fact that the number of firms or production units (or the quantity of certain fixed resources) is artificially prevented from growing, or from growing sufficiently, as the demand for the product rises, will increase the output and the size of the single firm beyond the respective optimum dimensions.

Perfect polypoly implies that marginal cost in each firm is made equal to price ($MC = P$). Imperfect pliopoly implies that price is not pressed down to average cost $(P > AC)$. Hence, marginal cost is higher than average cost, and average cost must be rising and, therefore, must be in excess of its lowest-possible value. This amounts to saying that plants produce above full capacity and firms are oversized.

It goes without saying that "price" in the two propositions, if conclusions drawn from them are to be valid, must be an identical magnitude and that the two "cost" functions must be correlated with each other. There is, however, no need to repeat here what has been said before about the adjustment of price expectations. Here, as before, we are dealing with perfect polypoly, hence, with cases where the imagined sales possibilities are nothing but the expectations of "the" probable market price of the standardized product. We may, with little compunction, accept the theory that the price expectations on the part of most persons concerned will become adjusted and uniform.

As to the meaning of "cost" in the two propositions the reasoning must be somewhat different here from that which was employed above in the discussion of the adjustment of cost conditions under perfect pliopoly. For it is exactly the failure of cost to undergo the upward adjustment which explains why the average cost of the chosen outputs can remain below the ultimate price—and this enduring gap between average cost and price is, of course, the essence of imperfect pliopoly. There must be a reason for the economist's refusal to promote the net surpluses (earned by the firms in the industry sheltered against newcomers' competition) to the rank of costs. These net surpluses—which are the main theme of the assumption that pliopoly is absent or imperfect—are either incapable of being imputed to specific resources used by the firms (that is to say, net surpluses would have to be pure profit rather than rent) or, if they can be imputed (and thereby assume the character of rent) they are regarded as "rent due to artificial scarcity." In neither case will the net surplus be included in "average cost." (If it were included, the "average cost inclusive of profit and monopoly rent" would be equal to price—and the inequality expressed by the second proposition, $P > AC$, would not be possible.)

We may add that the unit cost which is supposed to remain

lower than price need not be the one calculated by insiders nor the one calculated by frustrated candidates for entry, but may merely be one calculated "objectively" by the economist. (See Chapter 8, pp. 258–67.) For it may happen that the monopoly rent is transformed into a cost item in the accounts of the established firms and that the barrier against entry likewise figures as a cost item in the advance calculations of the outsiders. (This is Type D of the list given on p. 259.) Only in the computation by the economist, dissenting from the points of view of the interested parties, will then the artificial costs of entry and the monopoly rents of the firms operating in the industry be excluded from the unit-cost figure relevant for the inequality under consideration $(P > AC)$. But since the marginal cost schedule relevant for the profit maximization equation $(MC = P)$ will not be affected by the inclusion or exclusion of rent elements from average cost calculations, the correspondence between the cost terms of the two propositions is not seriously jeopardized.

If the restriction of entry refers to resources other than "entrepreneurial talent," that is, if it refers not to the number of independent firms but rather to some factors employed by firms (for instance, land in the above illustrations) the effect will not be seen in overly large production scales or excessive size of the individual firms but, instead, in an uneconomically large production per unit of the resource that has been made artificially scarce. On the other hand, where the entry of new enterprise is obstructed, the effect will manifest itself in a larger volume of output per firm and a larger size of the firm itself.

It should be noted that the absence or imperfection of pliopoly is not said here to "prevent" the attainment of group equilibrium. Group equilibrium is reached when there is no further inherent tendency for change or adjustment in the group or among its members. Obstructed entry of firms allows the industry to reach an equilibrium with positive profits or artificial rents, with oversized firms and with outputs in excess of "economic capacity."

In a geometrical representation of this case the corollary of perfect polypoly $(MR = P)$ is exhibited by the horizontality of the demand curve, as visualized by the individual seller. The corollary of imperfect pliopoly $(P > AC)$ is exhibited by the fact that the demand curve is not reduced to tangency with the average cost curve. (See Fig. 16.) The demand curve is likely to intersect the average cost curve in two points, but neither of them will be chosen by a firm that tries to maximize profits. The equilibrium of the firm requires equality of marginal cost and marginal revenue and, therefore, a volume of output larger than the lowest-cost output and smaller than the output at which average cost, in the rising part of the average cost curve, is equal to price. At the chosen output average cost is below the selling price but above the lowest possible cost level.

IMPERFECT POLYPOLY AND PERFECT PLIOPOLY

The combination of the assumptions of imperfect polypoly and perfect pliopoly was one of the outstanding achievements of the pioneers of monopolistic competition theory.[1] For purposes of exposition simplified assumptions were often made and the methodological complications of dropping them in favor of more "realistic" assumptions were not always fully appreciated. For example, it was sometimes assumed without sufficient qualifications that the subjective sales *expectations* of the individual firms and their "*actual*" sales possibilities in the market were identical; sometimes it was assumed also that the sales expectations of the *different firms* in the industry were all identical and that their selling prices were identical; and often it was assumed that the *cost conditions* in all different firms were identical.

Under-utilized Capacity in an Undersized Firm

With all these assumptions certain inferences are obvious and sound inescapable. The principle of the maximization of profit by the individual firm requires the choice of a size structure and volume of operations at which marginal cost is equal to marginal revenue. Under conditions of differentiated polypoly, where firms anticipate that they could sell larger outputs only at reduced prices, marginal revenue is smaller than selling price. Hence, marginal cost must likewise be below the selling price ($MC < P$). The

[1] Chiefly Joan Robinson and Edward S. Chamberlin.

No Tangency of Horizontal Demand Curve and Average Cost Curve

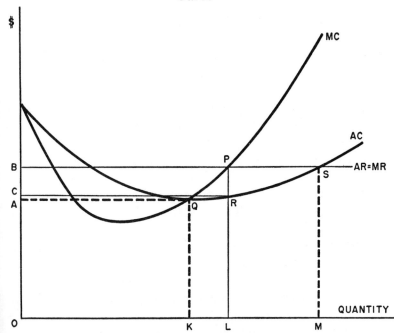

Fig. 16. Average Revenue Curve Not Reduced, Average Cost Curve Not Lifted, Profits Supernormal, Output Above Lowest-Cost Volume.

Since polypoly is perfect, marginal revenue is equal to average revenue (= price) and the firm will produce an output, *OL*, whose marginal cost will be equal to price, *LP*. But since pliopoly is imperfect, price may be above average cost. At the chosen output, average cost is *LR*, average monopoly rent *RP*, total monopoly rent *CRPB*.

The lowest possible cost would be *KQ* at output *OK*, but the firm prefers to produce more, because at that output its marginal cost would be below marginal revenue. Equality between average cost and price would be achieved at output *OM*, but the firm prefers to produce less, because at that output its marginal cost would be above marginal revenue. At the output at which profit is maximized, average cost, *LR*, is lower than the price, but higher than the lowest possible cost.

The average revenue curve is not pressed down toward tangency with the average cost curve, because entry is barred and no newcomers appear to encroach on the business of the firm. The average cost curve is not lifted up toward tangency with the average revenue curve, because the profit or rent is due to artificial barriers, not to any real scarcity of resources, and therefore cannot be counted as a cost.

principle of the equalization of the profit rate in the whole economy requires that extra profits and artificial rents are eliminated.
Under perfect pliopoly excess profits lead to more entries into the
particular industry, with the result that prices are depressed until
profits are reduced to zero ($P = AC$). Now, if according to the
first proposition, marginal cost is below price but, according to
the second proposition, price is equal to average cost, it follows
that marginal cost must be below average cost; this implies that
average cost is decreasing and, therefore, still above its lowest
possible value. Hence, the size of the firm and the volume of
operations obviously fall short of optimum size and optimum output, respectively. Firms, under differentiated polypoly and perfect pliopoly, are undersized and have unused capacity.[2]

This argument is usually supplemented by a geometrical representation. (See Fig. 17.) The presence of differentiated polypoly
is exhibited by the downward slope of the demand curve. The presence of perfect pliopoly is exhibited by the tangency of the demand
curve to the average cost curve. A downward sloping demand curve
can touch a U-shaped average cost curve only at the left of the lowest point of the average cost curve, hence, at a point signifying an
output and a size of firm falling short of those magnitudes that
would permit production at lowest possible unit costs.[3]

Price, Cost, and Sales Expectations

Before we can accept this inference as a correct and meaningful statement, we must again check the premises with regard to
possible equivocations and with regard to their empirical significance. And this time we are in a much worse predicament than
we encountered in the case of perfect polypoly. For, under conditions of differentiated polypoly, the assumption that all selling
prices of all the differentiated products (that is, of the differentiated products of the many existing sellers as well as those of the
potentially attracted new sellers) are the same, cannot well be

[2] Let us not relent in our effort to bear in mind that the firm of our
model is a one-product firm.

[3] The geometrical proof is identical for the output and for the size of the
firm: the short-run cost curve demonstrates for output what the long-run
cost curve demonstrates for size.

Tangency of Sloping Demand Curve With Average Cost Curve

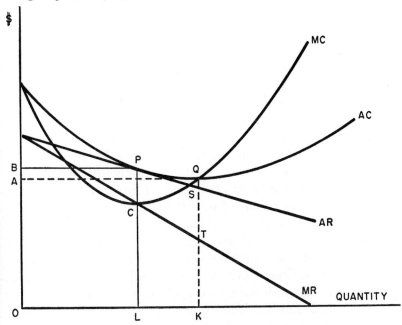

FIG. 17. Sloping Average Revenue Curve Tangent to Average Cost Curve, Output Below Lowest-Cost Volume.

Equilibrium of the firm requires output *OL* to be produced, where marginal cost is equal to marginal revenue, *LC*. Since polypoly is imperfect and larger outputs can be sold only at reduced prices, marginal revenue is lower than price or average revenue, *LP*. Since pliopoly is perfect and no supernormal profits can endure, equilibrium of the industry requires that average revenue is equal to average cost, *LP*.

The lowest possible average cost would be *KQ* at output *OK*, but the firm will produce less, because at that output marginal cost, *KQ*, would be far above marginal revenue, *KT*, and indeed the firm would lose money, since that output could be sold only at a price *KS*, which is less than *KQ*, the average cost of this lowest-cost volume of output. There is only one output at which the firm can break even: *OL*.

Note that at this output the two average curves are tangent to each other and the two marginal curves intersect each other.

maintained. Hence, if "price" in the first proposition refers to individual existing sellers and "price" in the second proposition refers chiefly to potential newcomers, the two will hardly be the same. Similarly, the assumption of identical costs cannot well be granted when differentiated products are produced. But if none of the terms in the two premises are common or correlated with each other, we can deduce nothing.

On the other hand, the terms of the two propositions cannot be altogether unrelated or we would have been foolish to think here of a "group" of firms, an "industry" which new firms may wish to enter or old firms may wish to leave.[4] It is the purpose of the concept of the industry to emphasize and isolate the effects of the operations of firms on each other's sales possibilities. And it is definitely a reasonable assumption that the sales possibilities of any one firm in the industry will be adversely affected by an increase in the operations of other existing firms, and by the commencement of operations of new firms, producing similar goods or services. This adverse effect will involve a disappointment of past sales expectations of the firm under consideration and will probably induce the firm to a revision of its sales expectations.

Thus, the influence of new entries and of newcomers' competition upon the insiders' sales expectations need not, and cannot, be questioned. But the "adjustment" of these expectations to the gradual change in the market conditions (with which the individual firm can be expected to be confronted) is much more complicated than a mere adaptation of an expected price to an actually ruling market price. For, under differentiated polypoly, there is no such thing as a uniform market price, but instead there are a variety of prices at which similar goods or services are sold; the individual firm has a choice as to the price that would be to its best advantage. The change in the sales possibilities of the firm becomes apparent not, as is the case under perfect polypoly, through a fall of the market price which the firm has to accept if it wishes to make any sales at all, but rather through a decline in actual sales, and the firm does not have to accept this decline as inevita-

---

[4] At least one author holds that it really is foolish or useless to think of groups or industries within the economy as a whole. See Robert Triffin, *Monopolistic Competition and General Equilibrium Theory* (Cambridge: Harvard University Press, 1940), pp. 88–89.

ble, but can influence its sales volume by changing the price that it charges. The seller will have to make up his mind about the probable elasticity of the changed demand for his product (that is, of the demand that is *reduced* in consequence of the newcomers' competition which has emerged as a result of the positive profit expectations which, in turn, were an effect of the *increased* demand for the products of the industry). There is nothing that would ensure (1) that the demand elasticity, as the seller imagines it, will ever be a "correct" estimate of his actual sales possibilities at various prices, and (2) that the elasticity of the reduced demand, correctly or incorrectly imagined by the seller, will induce him to make price concessions rather than price advances.

The Adjustment of Sales Expectations

The problem of "incorrect" estimates of demand is a very delicate one and raises a number of fascinating questions of a methodological nature. May anything legitimately be regarded as correct or incorrect if a test of the correctness or incorrectness is inconceivable? Demand in the schedule sense is never "actual" but is merely a series of hypotheses. As a rule, only one point of a demand curve (sales expectations curve) can ever be or become actual: the point showing the actual quantity sold at the actual price. All the other points are essentially fictitious: *if* the price were that-and-that rather than this, sales *would* be so-and-so rather than thus. But since at one and the same time only one price can be charged to the group to which the demand function refers, only one price-quantity pair can be observed; the demand curve need not remain unchanged over time. Only if it could be assumed that the demand in the schedule sense remained absolutely unchanged over a considerable period of time, and were not in the least affected by speculative or other reactions to experimental price changes, only then would it be possible to test and verify a demand curve for a number of points.

But even if one decides that one may legitimately speak of correct and incorrect guessing of the demand (in the schedule sense), the mechanism of adjustment of the sellers' incorrect guesses to their "actual" sales possibilities is very crude and for certain situations completely absent. Wrong estimates, for example, may have been made with regard to sales at all different prices except the one actually chosen; this would amount to an incorrect estimate of the elasticity of demand and, if the seller knew better, he might prefer to charge a different price; but, ignorant of the "correct" demand elasticity, the seller regards his actual price as the best possible, which he thus has no incentive to change. He may never find out and never revise his estimates.

The correction of mistaken sales expectations is further encumbered by the incapacity of sellers to distinguish between a disappointment in consequence of an incorrect guess and a disappointment resulting from a sudden decrease in demand. A seller who, confident about the low elasticity of the demand for his product, has raised his price and finds that his sales shrink much more than he has anticipated, can either blame himself for an optimistic underestimation of the elasticity of demand or, just as well, blame the "bad times" and the "weaker market" for a slackening of demand.

Perhaps it does not matter a great deal whether sellers attribute the disappointments of their sales expectations to bad guessing or unforeseeable changes of the market conditions, if only their disappointments force them to make appropriate adjustments. But even if it is fairly certain that, consequent upon a disappointment, sales expectations will be revised as to the quantities saleable at the price hitherto charged, it is by no means certain that the revision will comprise the elasticity of demand. If the elasticity of demand had been underestimated by a seller, who therefore charged a higher price than he would have done in cognizance of the correct elasticity, and if the seller attributes every decline in sales to a reduced demand for his products but does not change his estimates of elasticity, he will stick to his high price and fail to obtain the volume of sales that he might get at a reduced price. Needless to say, his net revenue will be lower than it might have been if he had correctly estimated the demand and set his selling price accordingly.[5]

[5] I refer again to the reservation which I made above concerning the questionable legitimacy of judging the "correctness" of a seller's estimate in view of the fact that nobody can test it. If a businessman evaluates a certain market position one way and an economics professor disagrees and evaluates it differently, who is to say who is right and who is wrong since neither can prove his case?

The Predicted Equilibrium Position

So much is certain, we cannot safely assume that the sales expectations of the seller under differentiated polypoly will undergo that compelling process of gradual adjustment that has been described for the perfect polypoly case. Hence, the economist who combines the theories of imperfect polypoly and perfect pliopoly and pictures the equilibrium position of the individual firm after group equilibrium is reached, is on much shakier ground than he was in the case of perfect polypoly. There the economist's judgment concerning the cost conditions of the new (marginal) firms taking up the business did imply also a prediction of the ultimate market price and, thus, a prediction of the ultimate demand curve as it would, in due time, have to be in the minds of all (or most) individual sellers. Nothing of the sort seems to hold when the products of the different producers in the industry are differentiated. The fullest knowledge of the newcomers' cost conditions (and even of their selling prices) does not equip the economist to predict the ultimate demand curves and selling prices of the individual firms operating in the industry.

Under these circumstances statements about the ultimate group equilibrium of differentiated polypolists under perfect pliopoly are of uncertain, limited scope. The limits of the applicability of the theory will depend on the interpretation that it is given. Different interpretations are possible. They differ considerably as to the truth value or probability value of the chief proposition of the theory, which claims *equality of the selling price to average cost at a point at which the sloping demand curve is tangent to the decreasing part of the average cost curve.* At least four different interpretations may be distinguished:

(1) The proposition will not hold in every case covered by the assumptions; expressing merely a general tendency, the proposition is only of moderate probability value.

(2) The proposition must hold in every case covered by the assumptions; the inclusion of differential rents into costs will move up the average cost curve by exactly the distance which the demand curve may have failed to come down.

(3) The proposition must hold in every case covered by the

assumptions; whenever the predicted results fail to arise, the con ditions must have been other than those assumed.

(4) The proposition is likely to hold in almost every case cov ered by the assumptions; the theory applies, however, only to prod ucts of highest mutual substitutability so that the particular de mands are highly elastic, the prices very uniform, and any change in particular demand that are caused by changes in competitiv supply will show themselves predominantly in changes in the pos sible range of selling price.

EXCESS CAPACITY UNDER THE TANGENCY RULE

The meaning of the "tangency rule" demands further elabora tion. The rule maintains that equilibrium will be reached at a pos: tion at which the (downward sloping) demand curve for th product of the firm is tangent to its (decreasing) average cos curve. Under two of the four interpretations which were distir guished, the proposition, or rule, is of a tautological characte₁ under the other two it has empirical significance. In our list, th first and fourth are the empirical, the second and third the tautc logical statements. The crucial issue is whether or not the "tangenc rule" means that we really know something about the shape an position into which the demand curve for the differentiate product of the polypolist will be forced by the working of pe₁ fect pliopoly. Let us restate the four ways of interpreting th tangency rule more clearly before we discuss its applicabilit limits.

The Four Interpretations

(1) No attempt is made to "predict" the imagined deman curves, either as to their shape or their exact position. All that i said is that newcomers' entry will *tend* to take any heavy profit and rents out of everybody's business in the industry. As long a firms in the industry are making considerable net surpluses, nev firms will be coming out with products similar to those whic the established firms have so profitably produced; the latter wi soon find their business spoiled by inroads on their sales; the will be restricted to smaller volumes and perhaps also forced t

reduce prices. Whether or not their profits and rents will be completely wiped out depends largely on the degree of substitutability of the new products for the old. (Hence, while pliopoly is credited with exerting a pressure upon the demand curve downward and to the left, one cannot be altogether sure that the pressure will be sufficient to result in the position of tangency of the demand curve to the given average cost curve.)[6]

(2) Again, no attempt is made to "predict" that the inroad of newcomers upon the market of the established firms will be sufficient to eliminate all net surpluses calculated on the basis of given costs. However, any such remaining net surpluses are now considered as differential rents of scarce resources and are added to cost, so that there cannot be any surplus left, and average cost must be equal to selling price. (In geometrical exposition, if the left-and-downward shift of the demand curve for the individual firm did not succeed in establishing its tangency to a given unit-cost curve, you would credit a specific factor of production with differential efficiency and differential earnings and, by adding the full value of this factor to total cost, you would raise the average cost curve to the position of tangency to the demand curve.)

(3) All cases where newcomers are not capable of stealing sufficient business from the established firms to wipe out all the net surpluses, are considered as cases of imperfect pliopoly. From this it "follows" that under perfect pliopoly prices "must" become equal to cost. This interpretation represents a type of tautological reasoning different from that of interpretation (2). Under interpretation (2) many more cases will be accepted as perfectly pliopolistic and

---

[6] This corresponds to Chamberlin's view. According to him, "the solution of tangency flows from certain heroic assumptions which are later dropped, and is to be regarded as of only limited direct applicability." *The Theory of Monopolistic Competition* (Cambridge: Harvard University Press, 5th ed., 1947), p. 195. After having dropped the assumption that "the differentiation of the product" is such that consumers' preferences are "evenly distributed among the different varieties" and that, therefore, the demand curves for the product of each firm in the group are identical (*op. cit.*, pp. 82–83), he modifies his "statement of the group problem . . . by recognizing that the demand curves are not adjusted uniformly to a position tangent to the cost curves." And he concludes that "some (or all) of the curves may lie at various distances to the right of the point of tangency, leaving monopoly profits scattered throughout the group . . ." *Op. cit.*, p. 113.

the predicted result (elimination of net surplus) is made to come "true" by promoting rents to the rank of costs. Under interpretation (3) the predicted result is made to come "true" by throwing out all cases where the result would be different, so that there would be considerably fewer cases of perfect pliopoly left. Whereas the tautological device of interpretation (2) deserves further discussion, the tautological character of interpretation (3) is quite absurd. Obviously it cannot be worth much having a theory which states that "perfect pliopoly must lead to the elimination of abnormal profits because where abnormal profits are not eliminated pliopoly cannot be perfect." [7]

(4) Polypoly and perfect pliopoly are likely to exist only when the differences between the products of the large number of firms —of those already established and also of those newly entering— are not very great. Indeed, it would be hardly conceivable that the differences between the products in the industry should be very important if the number of sellers is so large as to give each of them the feeling of relative unimportance and of not-being-watched by any of his competitors. Likewise, it would hardly be reasonable to assume that entry of new firms and resources into the industry is free and easy, yet that the new firms were not able to bring out products very similar to those of the established firms. Thus, while the products are *different enough* to set limits to the saleability of any one of them, that is to say, to prevent the demand for any one product from being perfectly elastic, they are still *similar enough* to make the demand for any one product so highly elastic that the seller has only *little* choice concerning the price he can charge. The more elastic the particular demand curves, the smaller will be the range of possible prices among which the seller can choose in any given situation. If the demand curves are shifted under the pressure of an increased supply of similar products and if they maintain their high elasticity (and I dare say there are good reasons for assuming the elasticities to be still further increased by the newcomers' competition) the adjustments of sales expectations will predominantly be adjustments of price. Therefore, "pre-

---

[7] In an attempt to avoid what is often called "tautological reasoning" or "implicit theorizing," we have insisted from the beginning on the probability character of the pliopoly concept. See Chapters 4 and 7.

dictions" of the ultimate selling price are, in such situations, not so unfounded as they seemed in the beginning.

The Limits of Applicability

Depending on which of the four interpretations of the tangency rule is chosen, the limits of its applicability will be very different. Under interpretation (3) the "rule" is merely a definition and its applicability can never be determined before "everything is over." The tangency rule here does not refer to a result to be expected from a certain, independently discernible constellation of facts; instead, it is merely the criterion of a definition and it permits the presence of the constellation, or the name by which it may be called, to be "concluded" from the result. "If you reach tangency after a short while, call the case one of perfect pliopoly," is all that is said according to interpretation (3).

Interpretation (2) does not seem to be much more helpful, because the general applicability of the tangency rule is obtained here by surrendering any determinacy as to whether it is a downward adjustment of demand or an upward adjustment of rents through which tangency is established. Yet, since we have found that reasoning along these lines made sense when perfect pliopoly was combined with *perfect* polypoly, we shall presently give further thought to this point in connection with our present concern, the case of perfect pliopoly combined with *imperfect* polypoly.

Turning from the tautological to the two empirical interpretations of the tangency rule, we find that interpretation (1) claims less than interpretation (4) and may therefore apply to a wider array of actual cases. The statement says no more than that inroads upon the business of established firms by newly starting firms are to be expected and that this will *tend* to reduce the utilization of the capacities of existing firms and to eliminate substantial net surpluses. This statement is sufficiently general and will apply to a fairly large sector of the real business world.

Interpretation (4) claims much more than that and can apply, therefore, only to a smaller sector of the real world. According to this interpretation, the cost conditions of the new entrants in

316 MANY AND MORE SELLERS

the industry will set the level for the prices of the products of the industry. Since the products are not standardized, the prices need not be identical; but since the products are similar and easily substitutable for one another, the prices cannot be so very different.[8] The demand curves with which the particular sellers will be confronted when group equilibrium is reached, will all be very elastic and the prices will be within a fairly narrow range. These selling prices cannot be much above the lowest production cost of the newcomers. As long as they are much above it further entries will follow and the supply of new products so similar to the old will continue to depress the price level at which existing producers find it practicable to sell.

In this last interpretation the results of combining the theories of *imperfect* polypoly and perfect pliopoly are not much different from those reached by the synthesis of *perfect* polypoly and perfect pliopoly. In the geometric representation, the difference is merely that the demand curves are *almost* horizontal rather than *perfectly* horizontal. The thesis of the combined theories, that the output produced will fall short of the capacity output, and the size of the firm will be below the optimum size, will hold true, but it will not be quantitatively important. The deviation from the optimum would amount to much only if the demands were not so highly elastic as we have concluded they must be for the tangency rule to apply at all, according to this, the most reasonable interpretation. With the highly elastic demands the deviations will be negligible. One can then readily understand why some outstanding economic theorists maintain that the assumption of perfect polypoly gives sufficiently close approximations, and therefore why they question the advisability of working with the more complicated assumptions of differentiated polypoly.[9]

The Differential Rent of Differentiated Polypolists

We must now go back to that other interpretation of the tangency rule—interpretation (2)—according to which tangency

[8] The products have to be sufficiently similar so that comparisons of price per unit makes sense.

[9] Cf. J. R. Hicks, "Annual Survey of Economic Theory: The Theory of Monopoly," *Econometrica*, Vol. III (1935), p. 12.

of the demand curve to the average cost curve is in part the result of including rent in cost.[10] We recall that this procedure was conceded as permissible in the discussion of perfect polypoly and perfect pliopoly, on the grounds that naturally scarce resources of greater efficiency (a) would command higher prices and, thus, cost more in competitive markets and (b) that they would, in any event, "cost" more in the "forgone-opportunity" sense of the word even if the specific scarcity values were not reflected in the current prices paid in the markets for productive resources and services.

The difficulty with this approach lies in the measurement of differential efficiency if the efficiency manifests itself not in the physical quantity of output produced or in the physical quantity of variable factors employed, but also, or only, in the *quality* of the product. If a certain type of land or a certain degree of managerial skill can secure a given (or larger) amount of *physical* product from a smaller (or given) amount of factors than can be obtained on other types of land or by other degrees of managerial skill, the differential efficiencies of these resources are comprised in the technical coefficients of production. If, however, the special qualification of a resource consists in its ability to turn out products of a quality different from those of other make, then its differential efficiency is a matter of market appeal and market position. Whether the earnings can be imputed to the specific resource and should be regarded as differential rent, scarcity rent, or monopoly rent is a moot question (if not a hairsplitting quibble).

Under undifferentiated polypoly and perfect pliopoly several circumstances help in ascertaining the non-monopolistic character of differential rents. First, the product sells at a price which is entirely beyond the control of the seller: the seller has absolutely no

[10] This was the procedure adopted by Joan Robinson in her *Economics of Imperfect Competition*. Kaldor commented on this point as follows: "Mrs. Robinson includes in her 'cost curves' such profits which are not competed away by the entry of new producers; and under the circumstances, her statement that 'demand curves will be tangential to cost curves' and that firms will be of 'less than their optimum size' is merely a statement of a tautology. It does not imply 'excess capacity' or anything of that sort." Nicholas Kaldor, "Market Imperfection and Excess Capacity," *Economica*, New Series, Vol. II (1935), p. 34.—Unfortunately I read Kaldor's excellent article only after I had written most of this chapter. I could have saved much independent effort if I had substituted more diligent reading for my gratuitous originality.

choice of prices. Second, the resource which excels in efficiency (measurable because of its purely technical character) has a definitely determined degree of substitutability for resources of lower efficiency; the differential earnings can be unambiguously imputed on the basis of physical productivity. Third, the resource of so high an efficiency may itself be the object of a competitive demand on the part of the many old and potential new firms, so that this scarce resource (perhaps a particular managerial skill) may have a competitive price or, at least, will be likely to have it eventually.

Under differentiated polypoly the first of these three circumstances is definitely absent: the product sells at an "administered" price, that is to say, the seller has some degree of control over price. The second of the circumstances may also be absent: the differential efficiency of the resource (perhaps a particular location, or the particular managerial skill referred to above) may consist, chiefly or exclusively, in the ability to differentiate the product from rival products. The third of the circumstances may still persist: the scarce resource may itself be in competitive demand throughout the industry (or other industries) and thus have (currently or eventually) its competitive price. This would mean that the ability to differentiate a product "efficiently" from rival products and to pursue with it a skillful price policy is recognized in industrial circles and thus comes to be valued correspondingly or even to command "its" price. But should this fact induce the economist to recognize the high value of this ability or talent as a *cost* factor in the firm that employs it? If the answer is "yes," the average cost curve will be raised to tangency to a demand curve that has failed to be pressed down by competitive forces—and the tangency condition of perfect pliopoly will appear as fulfilled. If the answer is "no," and the high value of the scarce resource is regarded as monopolistic in nature, then the raising of the cost curve would be "disallowed" by the economist and the tangency condition declared unfulfilled.

I doubt that a generally satisfactory answer can be given to this question. Value judgments—such as whether the product differentiation is held to be "useful" to the consumer—will probably influence the answer which most people would be inclined to give in particular cases. If "nobody else can make as good a product as Mr. X," then Mr. X's ability will probably be assigned a natural scarcity value. But if "shrewd advertising practices, claiming fictitious advantages for his product, secure Mr. Y an undeserved hold on the consuming public," then the value of Mr. Y's ability will probably be differently adjudicated. These would surely be arbitrary criteria. It is hardly the economist's task to decide which products are good and which are bad for the people. On the other hand, it may be considered the economist's task to find out whether something is scarce owing to the doings of certain men and to the aid or protection they find in certain controllable institutions, or whether it is scarce by nature. If Mr. Y is protected by a patent, or by his singular newspaper connections, or by the largeness and indivisibility of an investment in good will, or by other effective indivisibilities of necessary resources, or by the activities of hired gangsters—protected, that is, against other equally able men or firms entering his trade and offering effective substitutes—then the rent earned in Mr. Y's business is not due to his ability to offer a differentiated product but rather to the barrier or obstacle which prevents newcomers from effectively competing with him.

Although it seems like moving in circles, we come again to the solution that an appraisal of the perfection of pliopoly will imply whether or not the raising of the average cost curve to the position of tangency with the demand curve is "legitimate" in the case.

Implications Concerning Unused Capacity and Potential Economies

The curious thing is that this decision implies also a judgment concerning the extent to which the firm is undersized and its capacity under-utilized. For, if the differential earnings are *allowed* as a non-monopolistic differential rent, or "legitimate" value, of a resource scarce by nature, they will be included in cost and the average cost curve will have its low point more to the right. (See Fig. 18.) Thus the adjudication of the case as one of perfect pliopoly with the full right to a tangency position will carry with it the verdict of unused capacity and unused economies. (It will be remembered that the demand curve has a negative slope and

Imperfect Polypoly With Excess Capacity Depending on Inter-pretation of Rent

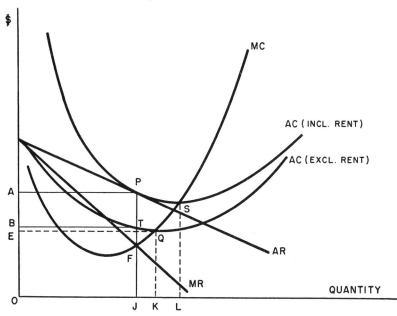

FIG. 18. Recognition of Rent as Cost Removes "Monopoly Profit" But Increases "Monopolistic Excess Capacity."

The most profitable output of the firm, under the conditions depicted here, is *OJ*, where marginal revenue equals marginal cost, *JF*, and the selling price is *JP*. Since, at that output, average cost without rent is *JT*, average rent is *TP* and total rent, *BTPA*. If this rent is regarded as monopoly rent due to artificial restrictions of entry, and therefore not recognized as cost, the relevant average cost curve remains well below the average revenue curve and the lowest possible cost, *KQ*, will be at output *OK*. If, however, the rent is regarded as due to natural scarcity and therefore recognized as cost of production, the relevant average cost curve (incl. rent) is raised to tangency with the average revenue curve—in point *P*—and the lowest possible cost, *LS*, will be at the larger output *OL*. The "excess capacity" due to "monopolistic *output* restriction" will be only *JK* in the case of "monopolistic *entry* restriction" and large "monopoly profit," or "monopoly rent," but will be *JL*, or about twice as large, if entry is regarded as free and profit as normal.

the point of tangency must therefore be on the descending part of the average cost curve.) If, on the other hand, the differential earnings are *disallowed* as legitimate rent, or cost, of a resource scarce by nature, the average cost curve must stay in its place without promotion to the right. The adjudication of the case as one of imperfect pliopoly or non-pliopoly will condemn the average cost curve to remain at a leftish distance from the demand curve, exhibiting thereby a fuller or full (or in extreme cases even excessive degree of) utilization of capacity.[11] In other words, if we acquit the firm of the charge of making monopoly profit, we declare it guilty on the count of unused capacity; if we acquit it of unused capacity, we declare it guilty of reaping monopoly profits. It seems that we cannot escape from the curse of implicit theorizing.

There are two lessons we should have learned, or relearned, from this almost scholastic discourse: (1) Tangency between average cost and demand curves, or the absence of abnormal profit, must not be taken as a "proof" of the existence of perfect pliopoly. The conditions of entry must be examined separately because it is only on the basis of such an examination that all cost and rent elements can be fully evaluated. (2) If this whole line of reasoning is accepted, tangency between average cost and demand curves, or the absence of profit,—to the extent that they are brought about by increases in rents—is not an *effect* that would usually *result* from the condition of perfect pliopoly, but merely a repetitious *implication* that would be *contained* in the definition of scarcity rent, cost, and perfect pliopoly.

It is a matter of taste which interpretation of the tangency rule is considered more useful. Opponents of purely implicit theo-

[11] The firm will be of optimum size and will produce the optimum output if the marginal revenue curve passes through the lowest point of the long-run average cost curve (which, by definition, must be also the lowest point of the short-run average cost curve of the firm at its optimum size). This is so because the marginal cost curve must pass through that lowest point. Under conditions of differentiated polypoly (sloping demand curve) the marginal revenue curve can pass through the lowest point of the average cost curve only if the demand curve "is extremely elastic and also lies at a considerable distance above the cost curve." (See Fig. 19.) Under these circumstances it may cross the marginal cost curve even farther to the right and thus cause excessive utilization of capacity. The quoted clause is from a footnote in Chamberlin's *Theory of Monopolistic Competition,* p. 78.

rizing will prefer interpretations (1) or (4) with their more limited generality but truly empirical significance.

THE WASTES OF NEWCOMERS' COMPETITION

The significance of the empirical interpretations of the tangency rule for imperfect polypoly lies in the contention that perfect pliopoly—newcomers' competition—may operate as a force compelling firms to produce with unused capacity and unused economies and therefore *at higher costs* than if they were not under the pressure of newcomers' competition.

Product Variety at Higher Cost

The explanation, let us repeat, runs as follows: When profits (read: supernormal profits) exist in the industry, new firms will enter and produce similar products; the emergence of the new supply will reduce the sales possibilities of the existing firms; this will squeeze out their profits not merely by depressing selling prices, but partly by causing the firms to produce smaller outputs at higher unit costs. Indivisibilities of some of the resources needed in the industry make it impossible for the firms to produce the reduced outputs as cheaply as they could make larger outputs. Under such circumstances, the elimination of profits is not entirely a boon to the consumer; instead of forcing dissipation of profits by having them passed on to consumers in the form of reduced prices, newcomers' competition forces dissipation of profits in the wasteful defrayal of increased cost of unused capacity per unit of output. After the entry of the new firms, the total product of the industry, in all varieties and at all locations, will be produced by a larger number of firms than is compatible with the operation of firms of optimum size and with optimum use of capacity.

If the industry's output could be produced more cheaply by utilizing more fully the capacity of fewer firms, it is economically wasteful, so it is claimed, to have it produced at higher cost by a larger number of firms. The counterclaim is made that there is the offsetting advantage of a greater choice of varieties and locations in which the product is available to consumers. It is held, furthermore, that the consuming public as a whole prefers the greater choice at slightly higher prices to a smaller choice at lower prices; and that it gives evidence of this preference by its actions in the market. This last argument, however, is not tenable. One may say that the results of the market reflect the preferences of the consumers if they have chosen certain products from among all possible alternatives. But such a choice was not afforded the consumers in the case before us. They were not given an opportunity to choose between more standardized products at lower prices and more diversified products at higher prices. The individual producers of differentiated products do not offer their products at the lower prices. They do not make efforts to expand their business to such volumes as could be produced at lower unit cost, because they anticipate that their selling prices would come down faster than their unit costs. Hence, no one can tell what the consumers' choice would be if they had a chance to choose between cheap standard merchandise and more expensive varieties.

There are those who take it for granted that the public would decide in favor of the cheaper products. They are apt to consider the differentiation as a sheer waste that ought to be prevented by deliberate action of the government. Since newcomers' competition causes the waste of excess capacity, restrictions of entry appear to them as a logical remedy. Thus, the imperfections of polypoly (imperfect elasticity of demand for the product of the individual producer) are to be combined with apparently offsetting imperfections of pliopoly (imperfect movement of additional enterprise into the industry). Restrictions of output of existing firms are to be combatted by introducing restrictions of entry of new firms. This, in my opinion, is very bad policy—which we must discuss later at length.

At this point it is necessary to examine the exact nature of the higher cost of production which newcomers' competition may impose upon the many producers of differentiated products.

Nine Reasons for Higher Cost of Smaller Scale

The merely formal condition that a firm is operating in the phase of decreasing cost, and thus produces smaller outputs at higher unit costs, does not say anything about the actual technological or commercial conditions making for the higher costs. We can distinguish several different conditions resulting in decreasing cost. (Some of these conditions may cause decreasing marginal as well as average cost, others only decreasing average cost. The proposition under discussion refers to average cost.)

(1) Certain machines or apparatus needed for production may be of fixed size and best adapted to be worked with certain amounts of "variable factors," such as labor, material, or power; they may be usable also for operation below capacity, but only at a loss of efficiency in the sense that the physical output per unit of variable factor is smaller or, which is the same thing, that the input of variable factors per unit of physical output is greater. This is what is known as the "law of non-proportional outputs" or the "phase of increasing returns under the law of proportions." (The condition may give rise to increasing *marginal* physical productivity of the variable factors or, more likely in practice, only to increasing *average* physical productivity of the variable factors.) If the machine or apparatus (which through its indivisibility and inflexibility causes the decreasing cost of increasing production) is available in all sizes at the same cost relative to capacity, only short-run cost will be decreasing, while long-run cost may be constant. But if there is a certain minimum or optimum size of the machine or apparatus, the long-run cost of production must also be decreasing at least in a range of very small output volumes.

The condition is conveniently referred to as "decreasing cost due to increasing returns under the law of proportions." In practice, most firms have developed techniques enabling them to avoid operating their equipment under conditions of increasing returns.[12] Where they cannot avoid it, smaller production volumes would

[12] The reader will find a simple example of increasing returns under the law of proportions in the operation of coal furnaces for the heating systems of small homes on cool spring or autumn days when just a little heat is desired. More heat than the desired amount could be had at decreasing cost because more coal burnt in the fixed and indivisible furnace—which was built for larger heat outputs—would yield increasing physical returns. Incidentally, this is an example of "indivisibility in use" as distinguished from mere "indivisibility in acquisition."

necessitate inefficient operation of the indivisible and inflexible equipment and, therefore, higher unit cost.

(2) Certain materials needed for production may be purchased in larger lots more cheaply than in smaller lots. If the material is storable, bulk purchasing may be practicable even for small-scale production, but the cost of storage, especially the handling cost, would then be greater. In any event, quantity discounts, differentials in transportation cost for carload as against less-than-carload shipments, differentials in storage and handling cost, and similar cost advantages for large purchases and large shipments may result in "decreasing supply prices" to the firm. This may cause a condition of decreasing cost of production in a range of small output volumes and, therefore, higher unit cost of reduced outputs.

(3) Certain necessary means of production, especially skilled labor, may be imperfectly variable—"lumpy"—so that the smallest amount that can be had (such as one mechanic, engineer, greaser, or foreman) is sufficient for a certain range of output. This implies that the cost of these lumpy factors is imperfectly variable and therefore, when the cost of one unit is spread over increasing amounts of output, it decreases per unit of output. This may cause conditions of decreasing cost in a range of low outputs and, hence, higher unit cost of reduced outputs.

(4) Certain operations needed in the production process may be performed more efficiently if they can be broken down and subdivided into a series of small mechanical tasks, each assigned to a man specialized in its execution. The imperfect divisibility of the human unit limits the application of high degrees of subdivision of labor: the larger the scale of production, the more finely can given operations be subdivided for performance by specialized workers. This may result in conditions of decreasing cost up to a certain scale of operations and, hence, in higher unit cost of smaller-scale production.

(5) Certain more efficient methods, processes, or machines may be suitable only for production of larger outputs, while less efficient methods, processes, or machines have to be used for small-scale production. These economies of large-scale production are

usually due to indivisibilities of pieces of equipment that cannot be had, or cannot be practicably used, in sizes below certain relatively large minimum sizes. They may result in decreasing costs of production of typically long-run character, extending over substantial ranges of output. The higher unit cost of smaller firms is here a matter of the non-use of techniques which are economical only on a large scale.

(6) Certain machines, structures, or pieces of equipment can be had in various sizes but are relatively less expensive in large sizes. Machines such as electro-motors, diesel and steam engines, or units such as heating plants, are in smaller sizes more expensive relative to their productive capacity than they are in larger sizes. Decreasing costs of production of essentially long-run character may result. The higher unit cost of smaller firms is here, in contrast to all previous cases, a matter of higher machine cost, or "cost of capacity"—rather than labor or material cost—per unit of output.

(7) Certain necessary machines, structures, or pieces of equipment come only in large minimum sizes and their cost can be spread over a substantial range of possible production volumes. The decreasing cost due to these indivisibilities will for small outputs pertain to both long and short run. The higher unit cost of smaller-scale production is here a matter of unused productive capacity.

(8) No matter how great or small the long-run variability or divisibility of productive capacity is, in the short run the fixed overhead cost can be spread over smaller or larger outputs, resulting in decreasing average fixed cost and, for outputs "below capacity," also in decreasing average total cost per unit of output. In contrast to all previous cases, which referred either to the long run only or to both long and short run, the spreading of the overhead is only a short-run consideration; smaller outputs must "bear" a larger share of fixed cost per unit.

(9) A special case of a fixed resource whose cost may be spread over larger or smaller output volumes is the managerial capacity of the owner of the firm. Since management ordinarily is indivisible only in a one-man outfit, the case becomes pertinent chiefly in sole proprietorships. The "normal profit" due to the opportunity cost of the owner-manager's time is customarily included

in the long-run cost of production. It may result in decreasing cost and, thus, in higher unit costs of such outputs as fall considerably short of the owner's capacity.

The Significance of the Nine Points

The nine reasons given for the condition of decreasing costs are very different in their nature and significance. Some refer to the size of the firm, others to the output volume in a given firm; some, therefore, refer to the long run, others to the short run only; some relate to labor cost and material cost, others to machine cost, others again to management cost. The following recapitulation in the form of one-sentence propositions will facilitate a comparative evaluation:

Smaller-scale production or low production volumes may mean higher unit costs because

(1) certain machines work less efficiently at smaller utilization, so that larger amounts of labor, material, fuel, or energy are used per unit of output;

(2) higher prices must be paid for certain materials if purchased in smaller quantities;

(3) certain men in the crew must be employed even if insufficiently used for smaller outputs;

(4) labor in small-scale production cannot be so specialized (as for example through assembly line techniques) and hence not so efficient as in mass production;

(5) efficient methods and machines adapted for mass production are not suitable, and thus relatively more labor or fuel, etc., is needed, for smaller outputs;

(6) certain machines cost relatively more in smaller sizes, thus causing higher cost of capacity per unit of output;

(7) certain machines cannot be had in smaller sizes and their cost must be borne by smaller outputs;

(8) fixed overhead cost must be borne by smaller outputs;

(9) for normal profit—a long-run cost—to be earned by smaller outputs, higher profit margins per unit are required.

Four of the nine points relate to indivisibilities or imperfect divisibilities of machines; two of these result in higher labor (or material or energy) cost—points (1) and (5)—while the other two are reflected in higher machine cost per unit of output—points (6) and (7). Three other points relate to indivisibilities of human resources, either individuals or groups (teams) of men—points (3), (4), and (9), the former two resulting in higher labor cost, the last in higher management cost per unit of output. Indivisibilities in selling, purchasing, shipping or handling of materials may be behind point (2).

Only one point—(1)—has to do with "increasing returns under the law of proportions," some of the others with "economies under the law of scale." The higher labor cost (fuel cost, etc.,) in point (5) and the higher machine cost in points (6) and (7) are clearly in a relationship of substitutability for each other. As to the two cases of higher machine cost, point (6) constitutes a milder case of indivisibility than point (7), the latter suffering from the absolute limitation of a machine of minimum size, the former benefiting from the availability of below-optimum sizes.

A spreading of fixed or lumpy outlays over varying quantities of output is involved in four of the nine points—(3), (7), (8), and (9). One of these—point (8), the spreading of overhead costs—is pertinent only to short-run considerations and undoubtedly includes the results of some of the conditions that underlie the other three points. In these three the spreading effect relates to labor cost—in (3)—, to machine cost—in (7)—, and to management cost—in (9).

Higher unit costs under which individual firms operate are, as a rule, indications of higher social cost of the production of the goods and services concerned. This may, but need not mean higher prices to be paid by consumers. For there are situations in which the incidence is entirely upon one or more of the resources employed in the production, or upon the owners of the enterprises. It happens that the situation under discussion is one of this sort. The newcomers' competition that results in the creation of excess capacity (and thus in higher unit cost) is the outcome of the stimulus afforded by supernormal profits in the industry concerned, and it effects the dissipation of these profits partly in the form of higher cost. Since prices to consumers will not rise—although they will not fall as much as they "could"—the higher costs are not at the consumers' expense, but rather at the expense of monopoly profits. But since recipients of monopoly profits are also members of society and what they lose does not accrue to anybody—because the new fixed resources that enter the industry and create excess capacity would have earned normal profits anywhere—the consideration that consumers are spared the loss and that it falls entirely upon the "monopolists" does not do away with the fact that a social loss is involved.

Society pays higher unit cost for the smaller outputs produced by the individual monopolistic polypolists under the pressure of perfect pliopoly or, that is to say, for given amounts of output produced by an "unnecessarily" large number of producers operating at "unnecessarily" small scale. For an evaluation of the higher cost it would be desirable to know which of the listed points are quantitatively important and which are not. But very little can be said on this question on the basis of *a priori* reasoning and merely "casual empiricism."

It is highly unlikely that many firms are forced down into the inefficient range of "increasing returns under the law of proportions"—point (1). It is doubtful that the loss of quantity discounts —point (2)—can be an important factor. Only in very tiny establishments can the lumpiness of human labor play a significant role —point (3); yet, insufficient utilization of individual men in several service trades consisting of very small units may possibly add up to a substantial "waste." Whether mass production techniques could be used in many of the trades or industries concerned if these trades or industries were not pressed by pliopoly is more questionable; thus the waste of labor or energy under these headings—points (4) and (5)—is probably small. Use of relatively more expensive machinery of below-optimum size or insufficient utilization of machinery—points (6) and (7)—are certainly prevalent in many fields, but the quantitative importance cannot be assessed offhand. Insufficient utilization of managerial capacity— point (9)—occurs chiefly in trades in which establishments are typically operated by the owner (for example, automobile service stations, grocery and other retail stores). It is probable that "excess capacity" of owner-managers is the most prevalent of all decreasing cost cases resulting from the coexistence of pliopoly with imperfect polypoly.[13]

Empirical inquiry into these matters is badly needed. Cost studies in selected trades and industries might shed light on this complex of questions and permit us to proceed from pure speculation about the "wastes of competition" to a meaningful evaluation of the actual situation. Until empirical evidence to the contrary is forthcoming, this writer is inclined to take the "waste" story lightly; he remains unimpressed by the graphs which draftsmen chose to adorn with rather steeply declining cost curves.

Three Other Reasons of Higher Costs

In addition to the nine reasons that were given for conditions of decreasing cost, and thus for higher unit costs of smaller outputs, three other reasons can be found why differentiated polypolists possibly operate at higher cost if they are under heavy pliopolistic pressure. These additional reasons are not reflected in a negative slope but rather in a higher level of the average cost curve of the individual firm.

There is, first, a probability that under the pressure of newcomers' competition a producer will attempt to differentiate his product more ostentatiously from rival products and may for this purpose make expenditures he would not make without that pressure. It may well be that this differentiation does not constitute an acknowledged improvement of the product but is confined to increased advertising outlays and other selling efforts.[14]

There is, secondly, a probability that under the pressure of newcomers' competition and the consequent limitation in the

---

[13] In order to avoid any misunderstandings often occurring in discussions of "decreasing cost," it may be well to observe that (a) economies of large-scale industry which are external to (i.e., beyond the control of) the individual firms and (b) economies resulting from inventions, which change the state of technology, are not mentioned in the context, because they are not relevant to the problems under discussion.

[14] Chamberlin placed much emphasis on the distinction between the effects of selling costs and those of the negative slope of the cost curve and, therefore, stated that "under monopolistic competition prices are *two steps higher* than under pure competition." *Op. cit.*, p. 166. (Italics are mine.)

saleability of his particular product a producer will attempt to enlarge his production program in other directions and will thus substitute a policy of producing a larger line of products for a policy of specialization. Assume that real economies could be obtained by specialization. If each of the competing firms were allowed to specialize in a certain product, they all could then produce more cheaply than they can if they are compelled, so to speak, to make a full line of products. The coexistence of perfect pliopoly and imperfect polypoly results in this case, not in excess capacity, but instead in a "reduction of technical efficiency." [15]

We must not confuse this with joint production of technologically complementary products, which, of course, would be *more* rather than less efficient. The situation is different when products are combined in production, not because of technical complementarity, that is, not because joint production is cheaper, but only because producing them together is better than leaving capacity idle. Since newcomers stole some of the market of a producer who had been specializing in a particular product, he found himself with excess capacity, which he preferred to put to use by resorting to a diversification program. Thus there are, in

---

[15] This idea was advanced and elaborated by Nicholas Kaldor, *op. cit.*, pp. 46–49. The sequence of events may be sketched as follows: Assume a polypolist of a differentiated product utilizes his capacity fully for the article in which he has specialized. If he charges a price which maximizes his profits, this price will exceed his average cost and leave him with a supernormal profit. (Proof: (1) marginal cost is equal to average cost at the point of full-capacity output, (2) marginal cost is equal to marginal revenue at the most profitable output, (3) marginal revenue is below selling price if demand is less than infinitely elastic and, hence, (4) the price is higher than average cost. See Fig. 19.) The favorable profit position, under pliopoly, will attract newcomers. As the supply of the new rival products comes to the market, the demand for our polypolist's product will be reduced. He will reduce his output and will be faced with unused capacity. Other products, which had not appeared as technologically complementary as long as capacity was fully utilized for the product in which he had specialized, begin now to look as good stop-gaps for making some use of the otherwise idle capacity. Thus, our producer will include them in his production program. When he brings his new output to the market, he will encroach on the demand for products of other firms. This will result in excess capacity in these firms. They, in turn, will now wish to add new products to their lines. Thus, the economies of specialization may be lost under the pressure of perfect pliopoly upon a group of differentiated polypolists.

No Tangency of Sloping Demand Curve With Average Cost Curve

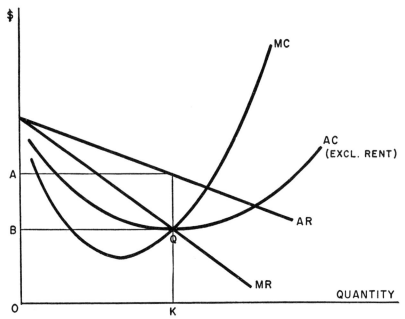

FIG. 19. Marginal Revenue Curve Happens to Pass Through the Lowest Point of Average Cost Curve (Without Rent), Output at Lowest-Cost Volume.

Since pliopoly is imperfect, average revenue may be above average cost without being reduced through newcomers' competition; since scarcity is artificial, rent is not regarded as cost and average cost not raised to average revenue. Conditions of demand will determine whether production is below capacity, at capacity, or above capacity volume. In Figure 19, the average revenue curve happens to be such that the marginal revenue curve passes through the lowest point—Q—of the average cost curve, where it must be intersected also by the marginal cost curve. Price will be *KP*, average monopoly profit *KQ*, total monopoly profit *BQPA*. Thus, the output at which profit is highest happens to be the lowest-cost output: the equilibrium of this imperfectly polypolistic firm shows no excess capacity.

this case, no gains from economies of joint production; there is, instead, a loss of the economies of specialization.[16]

The third of the reasons for higher costs due to newcomers' competition in an industry of imperfect polypolists would be the bidding up of prices of scarce resources which form a part, or are needed in the creation, of the additional capacity in the industry.

It would be an instance of double counting if these payments of higher prices for productive resources were treated as an additional item in the computation of the social cost of newcomers' competition. Excess capacity was most prominently listed in the evaluation of the so-called wastes of competition. The number of firms in the industry was increased beyond what would be needed for the efficient production of its output. This meant excess capacity in each firm and, of course, excess capacity in the industry as a whole. If in the creation of this excess capacity prices of resources in inelastic supply should be increased, this price increase does not constitute a separate item of social cost, but may at best be a factor in the quantitative appraisal of the cost of unused capacity. The higher resource prices, although they cause an upward shift in the cost curves of individual firms, represent for the industry as a whole merely indices for the valuation of any excess capacity that may have come into being with the competition from newcomers.

Weighing the Losses and Benefits

It was said before that no measurements have been attempted anywhere that would enable us to estimate the size of the social "waste" involved in the cost of excess capacity and in the cost of diversification (or sacrifice of the economies of specialization) which perfect pliopoly forces upon monopolistic polypolists. The counterbalancing benefits accruing to society from the pliopolistic

[16] Whether this reduction of efficiency will be at the expense of the consumer, or chiefly or only at the expense of profits cannot be said with any certainty. But, as was stated before, the new entries, to which the higher cost of the non-specialized production must be attributed, occur only upon the stimulus of supernormal profits; and the loss of specialization under the impact of pliopoly can therefore be presumed to constitute chiefly a dissipation of profits. Prices to consumers may be even lower than they would be without pliopoly.

pressures upon imperfectly polypolistic industries are not even conceivably subject to quantitative evaluation. Although these benefits are largely intangible, they are by no means negligible. Six major benefits may be listed: (1) greater variety in goods and services, (2) greater choice of sources of supply, (3) wider dispersion of economic power, (4) discipline for producers who become laggard under protection, (5) removal of very inefficient producers who can survive only when sheltered, and (6) safeguards against excessive prices to consumers.

That consumers prefer to have a greater variety of goods and services to choose from cannot be doubted. We have rejected the argument that the consumers' actions in the market are evidence of their preference being large enough to justify the higher cost. But greater variety is certainly worth something, even if it may not be worth all it costs. (We know neither how much it is worth nor how much it costs.)

A wide choice of sources of supply is a convenience which many consumers would not want to miss. Again it is true that we do not know how much it is worth to consumers that they can readily shift their patronage from one supplier to another and are able to allow their personal preferences for individual suppliers to influence their marketing decisions. A wide scope for the consumer's freedom of choice, his feeling that he does not depend on any particular source of supply is a great comfort, a psychic income that is surely worth something.

The wider dispersion of economic power which may be implied in an "unnecessarily" large number of "unnecessarily" small firms has economic and political implications.[17] Conscious efforts have often been undertaken by democratic governments to aid and promote small business even when such policies were rather costly

---

[17] We must not jump indiscriminately from an abstract economic model into the world of politics. The size of the "firm" in our industry model may be smaller under perfect than under imperfect pliopoly, but this "firm" may correspond to only a small department of a widely diversified real-world firm that belongs to hundreds of different industries. Thus we cannot blithely conclude from our theory that pliopoly will preserve "small business." But it is not unreasonable to assume as a general tendency that a maximum of freedom of entry would really work to keep actual firms smaller than they might be if protected from newcomers' competition.

or manifestly wasteful. The bias in favor of smaller business units may have a sound political objective related to the preservation of a socio-economic system most compatible with the widest scope of personal liberty. If pliopolistic pressures tend in the direction of smaller business units, they may be welcome, even at a cost, to a society which treasures liberal democracy and shuns concentrations of power.

That perfect newcomers' competition may be "wholesome discipline" for laggard producers presupposes some of them to be easy-going and indolent when protected from such competition and contented with the "satisfactory" profits they can make under protection, yet able to bestir themselves and to do a better job when hard pressed and compelled to fight to stay out of the red. This assumption is probably sound, although it is inconsistent with the general postulate that the businessman is always trying to maximize money profits. If he did try, his effort to produce efficiently should be as great under protection as under pressure.[18] In any event, it is agreed that the "input of effort" is variable and that efficiency under pressure is often increased. Thus, if the cost curve implies for each point a maximum of managerial effort, or a minimum of all costs that (eventually) have to be paid in money, a producer under protection from competitive pressure may be "off the curve": his performance may be such that he operates at costs higher than indicated by the course of the cost curve. If the pressure of pliopolistic competition forces producers to "hug" their cost curve when they would otherwise carelessly go above it, the argument about the wastes of competition is offset, if not reversed. Free entry of new competitors may force insiders losing some of their business to cut out the avoidable wastes of operation, even if it does force them into some unavoidable wastes of capacity.

Inefficiency due to lax management is one thing, inefficiency due to incompetent management and obsolete plant is another.

[18] No inconsistency between assumptions exists if the maximization principle is taken to apply to the businessman's total satisfaction, including pecuniary and non-pecuniary considerations. And, after all, the assumption that he tries to maximize money profits is used only because it simplifies most arguments without vitiating them. Where it does make an important difference the simplification must go.

(The former results in production costs higher than shown on the cost curves, the latter in production cost shown by higher cost curves.) The competitive pressures associated with free entry can remove both types of inefficiency: while they may cure the former, they may eliminate the latter by eliminating the incurable firms. The elimination of inefficient firms is one of the important positive contributions of pliopoly to the productivity of the economy, although individual hardship cases arising in this process may create social and political problems.[19] Where the new capacity created by newcomers takes the place of old capacity that could not be economically operated, and could not be operated on a paying basis except under protection against newcomers, the argument about the wasteful creation of excess capacity is out of place.

Producers who are neither laggard nor inefficient can earn super-normal profits if entry is barred. These monopoly profits are eliminated under pliopoly. Even if some monopoly profits may be dissipated in higher production costs—cost of excess capacity— the pressures that compel this dissipation are at the same time the most effective safeguard against excessive prices to consumers. In the absence of these pressures, costs to producers may be lower, but prices to consumers may be higher.

For all these reasons it is shortsighted, in my opinion, to recommend that the "wastes" be prevented through restraints on newcomers' competition in the hope that the imperfections of polypoly —differentiation of products—can somehow be "offset" by imperfections of pliopoly—artificial barriers to entering the industry.

IMPERFECT POLYPOLY AND IMPERFECT PLIOPOLY

The combination of imperfect polypoly with *imperfect* pliopoly seems in several respects more plausible than that with perfect pliopoly. For, first of all, the differentiation of products which ac-

[19] To the extent to which the newcomers are larger firms than the inefficient producers who are crowded out of the industry, the third argument above—concerning the importance of small business for the dispersion of economic control—is weakened. But we are talking about polypoly, which however imperfect, implies absence of power positions; and where no firm is important enough to affect any of its competitors, freedom of entry will more likely prevent than promote concentration of control.

counts for the imperfection of polypoly may make it also difficult to enter the industry with any prospects of success. There is, moreover, the argument that the same conditions that permit effective product differentiation will *necessarily* act as obstacles to effective newcomers' competition. Along different lines, it may be held that polypolistic industries are apt to develop organized pressure groups seeking and securing political support against unwelcome economic pressures of the pliopolistic type. Lastly, the point is made that individual firms may adopt business policies designed to ward off pliopolistic expansions of their industry.

Product Differentiation as a Barrier to Entry

It seems reasonably obvious that when the differentiation of the products of different producers within an industry is very considerable the difficulties of new firms entering the industry and offering closely similar products will be considerable too.

What is meant by "close similarity" of the product? Products need not be closely similar to one another in a technological sense in order to be rather close substitutes. New products physically quite "dissimilar" to existing ones may appear on the market, compete effectively for the same group of customers, and squeeze or eliminate the profits of the old firms in the "industry." Thus, whatever degree of "differentiation" in the sense of dissimilarity the existing firms may have achieved, they may nevertheless not be safe from newcomers competing through good substitutes. For this reason differentiation of products should be defined, not in any technological sense, but only in terms of consumer appeal and loyalty. What is meant by "considerable" or "effective" differentiation of products is that the competing firms have succeeded each in building up a clientele of its own. If the consumers' loyalty and attachment to the differentiated products is strong, it will be considered difficult and costly for outsiders to break into the market. The existence of supernormal profits of the insiders will then be compatible with meagre or unsatisfactory profit prospects for potential newcomers. No newcomers, then, will appear and the profits of the polypolistic insiders can endure.

Formulated in this way the argument seems foolproof, at least until the critical scrutiny is pressed further. It may be questioned whether product differentiation sufficiently effective to create strong consumer loyalties can exist in a polypolistic industry, that is, in an industry where individual firms consider themselves insignificant enough not to arouse rivals' reactions to their own actions. Where each firm has its own loyal customers, it will probably think of each expansion of its business as an inroad on some particular rival's trade; and it will consequently think of what its rivals might do in retaliation. In other words, market positions based on "considerable" differentiation of products will probably be oligopolistic in nature. If this reasoning is correct, it follows that the differentiation that is characteristic of positions of imperfect *polypoly* is not as a rule so decisive that it can be presumed to constitute also a natural barrier to entry.

There is, thus, no presumption that imperfect pliopoly is associated with imperfect polypoly because of the product differentiation which constitutes one of the criteria of the latter. All possibilities are open. Newcomers' competition may be alert, slow, or entirely excluded. If it is so alert that we can speak of perfect pliopoly, this need not imply the complete elimination of profits of each and every firm in the industry. According to the empirical interpretations given to the "tangency rule," differential rents of particular firms protected by relatively more effective differentiation of its products may well survive the invasion of the industry by newcomers.

A Common Cause for Both Imperfections

A neat syllogistic argument has been presented to prove that the imperfections of both polypoly and pliopoly go back to the same cause and must therefore be necessarily coexistent. The role of common cause is played by indivisibility.

If divisibility of resources, processes, and products were "perfect," there could be no economies of scale even at microscopically small business units and production volumes. Under these conditions there could be no noticeable product differentiation—for there could be millions of different firms each producing the minutest fraction of the total supply.[20] Thus, "indivisibility" is a logical prerequisite of product differentiation. "Indivisibility" is also an obstacle to entry. The inference seems to be that the same cause that prevents polypoly from being perfect prevents also pliopoly from being perfect.[21]

The snare in this inference is that the crucial indivisibilities are not of the same order of magnitude. The indivisibility necessary to permit product differentiation refers to very small scales of production, usually far below the customary ones. The indivisibility that will act as an obstacle to entry refers to relatively very large scales of production. To translate the difference into common sense terms we may use the following illustrations: The indivisibility behind differentiation lies in the fact that to operate a barber shop it takes at least one barber, perhaps only on part-time; in any event, the personal qualities of the barber and the location of his shop will differentiate him from all his competitors. This indivisibility, however, will not stand in the way of perfect entry into the trade.[22] Indivisibility apt to discourage potential newcomers from entering an industry is of a different dimension; it may lie in the fact that enormous amounts of capital may be needed to start a new business (of even the smallest size possible in the particular industry) and that the establishment of that new business

[20] Nicholas Kaldor is the champion of this notion and Edward H. Chamberlin the chief objector. It can be grasped best—as I have said earlier—with reference to locational differentiation: if there existed absolutely no minimum size of drug stores, there could be several hundreds of stores in each block, and locational differentiation would have disappeared. Chamberlin's objections are in part attributable to the fact that he thinks always of divisibility of *factors* of production and does not include the efficient *grouping* of factors (e.g., teams of six workers) in the concept of indivisibility. Perfect or imperfect divisibility of processes may have the same effects as perfect or imperfect divisibility of productive factors.

[21] "The same reason therefore which prevents competition from becoming 'perfect'—i.e., indivisibles—will also prevent the complete elimination of 'profits.' It will secure a 'monopolistic advantage' to anybody who is first in the field and merely by virtue of priority." Kaldor, *op. cit.*, p. 42.

[22] A qualification must be added: "provided there are already many barber shops in operation." In situations where only a few shops are operated, so that any addition amounts to a substantial expansion of the total supply, the indivisibility of the described dimension may be sufficient to act as a deterrent to entry. See above, Chapter 7.

might increase the total capacity of the industry by a substantial proportion.

Once it is recognized that the word indivisibility refers to very different things in the two contexts, it becomes clear that it is not "logically necessary" that imperfect polypoly and imperfect pliopoly should go together.

Political Interference with Entry

The link between imperfect polypoly and imperfect pliopoly—which could neither be shown to be "natural" nor to be "logical" —may yet exist: it may be "political" in nature.

Polypoly, a position and attitude typical of small business, will normally occur only in trades or industries in which large numbers of small enterprisers are engaged. Strongly organized in trade associations and businessmen's clubs these middle class groups, commanding votes, money, and social status, are often able to exercise considerable political pressure. They may prevail upon government to enact protective legislation designed to relieve their trades and industries of the economic pressures of "serious overcrowding," "entry of undesirable elements" or "disorderly competition from unqualified operators." Since perfect pliopoly always jeopardizes the profits in these trades or industries, regulation of entry is "called for" in order to "secure the maintenance of an 'adequate' supply at 'reasonable' prices and with 'fair' profit margins." These are the accepted phrases regularly invoked to justify legislation or adjudication under which restrictions on entry can be imposed by either governmental authorities or professional, industrial, or occupational organizations.[23]

The forms that the barriers and limitations of entry take will differ from trade to trade and from state to state. While their official justifications all run in terms of reasonableness, fairness, and

[23] In this connection it is interesting to note that the first writer who, to my knowledge, used the term polypoly meant by it that "too many sellers" were in the particular trade. This was Johann Joachim Becher in 1662, who in his *Politische Discurs* (Frankfurt: 3rd ed., 1688) called monopoly and polypoly the two chief enemies of a healthy economy (p. 110), the former because it excluded people from a trade, the latter because it ruined the people who overcrowded it. His remedy were the guilds and trade associations, to whom he wished to assign the task of regulating entry in such a way that incomes and

protection of the public, there is also the technical argument advanced by theoretical economists that limitations of entry would reduce the wastes of excess capacity. Since the nature and significance of these wastes were given ample discussion before, it remains here only to examine the combined effects which imperfect polypoly and imperfect pliopoly may have on the total output of an industry.

The Effects upon Total Output

Changes of the total output of an industry are conveniently analysed by considering separately the "firm effects" and the "industry effects," that is, by asking how the existing members of the industry are likely to change their output and what the output of new firms entering the industry will be. The *individual* polypolist will produce and sell more when his market is not encroached upon by rival products supplied by newcomers to his industry. Protected from this competition, he will find the demand for his product greater and his unit costs perhaps lower; thus there is little doubt that his output will be larger if pliopoly is restricted. But how will the total output of the *industry* be affected if larger outputs of individual firms are attained by limitations upon the number of firms? Is it possible to make a general statement concerning the differences in output produced by old firms compared with the outputs that would be produced by newcomers if such were admitted?

Under highly simplified assumptions a general statement on the combined effects can be made and it can shed light also on how the question has to be answered under conditions prevailing in reality and deviating from the simpler assumptions. It is not possible to proceed directly with an analysis based upon "realistic" assumptions, because the concept of total demand for the product is indispensable for the analysis; yet if it is a "total demand" for a variety of differentiated products that are neither sold at uniform prices nor purchased in fixed proportions, then the concept becomes

people in the trade would be "in the right proportion" (p. 115). Freedom of entry was, in Becher's opinion, a "foolish and pernicious" policy which permitted that "a thousand people try to live from a trade from which a hundred have had a fair and honest living, with the result that all thousand must be impoverished and eventually ruined" (p. 264). [Translation mine.]

too vague for our use. For this reason the analysis must, in a first approximation, abstract from differences in the demand for the products of the different firms as well as in their production cost; with this abstraction it becomes possible to postulate that all sellers in the industry will by independent considerations arrive at the *same selling price*—a postulate necessary in order to read off the "market demand" curve the total quantity that the public will buy at that price.

Our objective is to compare the effects of closed entry with those of unlimited entry. We therefore begin the analysis by assuming a situation in which entry is attractive: the firms in the industry are making profits. If entry is closed and each of the (almost identical) firms is optimally adjusted to the conditions which it faces, total output and price will be determined. Now we allow entry to take place and "see" what happens. It is assumed that total market demand does not change, and the cost curves of all firms also remain unchanged, in the process.

Newcomers open up shop and begin to produce. As their output reaches the market, the demand for the product of each of the old firms is reduced. These old firms will reduce their output. Will the aggregate reduction of the old firms' output be equal to, smaller, or greater than the output of the new firms? Having assumed uniform selling prices and a given total demand curve, we can expect that the magnitude of the contraction by old firms in relation to the volume of output of the new firms will show in the movement of the selling price. If the contraction by the old firms is exactly equal to the output of the new, selling price will not change; if the contraction is smaller, selling price must be lower; if the contraction is greater, selling price must be higher than before the industry was opened to newcomers.

Now we remember under what conditions an individual firm will find it preferable to raise its selling price in the face of a reduced demand for its product: it will do so (a) if it believes that at the former price the elasticity of the reduced demand is smaller than that of the old demand had been, and/or (b) if it operates under decreasing marginal cost so that smaller outputs account for higher marginal costs.[24] Where the reduction in the demand

[24] Joan Robinson, *The Economics of Imperfect Competition* (London: Macmillan, 1932), pp. 61–64.

for the product of a firm is caused by an increase in the number of competitors, the elasticity of demand is more likely to be increased —which would tend toward *lower* rather than higher prices. We have less *a priori* knowledge about marginal cost. If the firms have had excess capacity from the very start—which is not necessarily so since we started from a situation in which they were making attractive profits—their average cost was decreasing; this, however, is compatible with increasing, constant, or decreasing marginal cost. Even if it were decreasing, it would be doubtful whether it decreased fast enough to overcompensate for the increased elasticity of the reduced demand. Drastically decreasing marginal costs occur only for the first percentages of capacity use. Hence, we may regard it as improbable that the conditions will be favorable for a price increase to result from the newcomers' entry; it is more probable that the conditions are such that the price will be unchanged; and most probable that the price will be reduced. A lower price, however, implies under our assumptions that the aggregate output of the industry is greater than before entry was made possible; in other words, that the sum of the output reductions by the old firms falls short of the new output produced by the newcomers.

Limitations of entry, we conclude *a contrario*, are likely to result in smaller total production in spite of larger outputs of each individual firm. This conclusion was reached for an industry consisting of many firms which were all identical with respect to demand and cost conditions. If this assumption is dropped, the chief implication will be that some of the firms will have market positions superior to others, either because of an especially attached and loyal clientele, or because of greater efficiency in production, or for both reasons. Newcomers' competition will be much less destructive of the profits (differential rents) of these firms, while it may completely eliminate some less efficient producers. It thus appears that the more realistic assumptions provide a still stronger case against limitations of entry. For in these cases easy entry into the industry will, still more likely than in other cases, result in an increase in total production and a reduction of the level of prices.

Thus, that a high degree of pliopoly will create excess capacity in industries that are imperfectly polypolistic does not prevent it from continuing to act to eliminate inefficient producers, increase total output, and reduce prices. To combat perfect pliopoly as a creator of excess capacity is to be blind to its other effects or to the overriding importance of these effects.

Low Price Policy to Prevent Entry

The creation of obstacles to entry into a trade or industry by collective action of the polypolistic members or, on their behalf, by the government, should be clearly distinguished from actions which individual firms may take independently to attain the same purpose. A firm may pursue business policies designed to make it unattractive for outsiders to attempt an invasion of its market. For example, a firm may keep its prices lower than the competition of *existing* producers in the industry would call for; low enough to make the profit situation in the industry uninteresting to *potential* competitors.

This possibility has been mentioned in the literature as one of the ways in which the creation of excess capacity may be avoided in an industry in which the coexistence of imperfect polypoly and perfect pliopoly would normally lead to an equilibrium with excess capacity.[25] "Far-sighted" firms, practicing low-price policies, would ward off the appearance of newcomers in the industry.

The case may be both realistic and important, but it is mentioned under a wrong heading. It cannot occur under polypoly, no matter how imperfect; it belongs to the discussion of oligopoly. If a firm is so small that it is unconcerned about anything that its existing competitors might do in reaction to its own actions—because it expects that nobody will be affected by what it does—it will hardly find it worth while to formulate its price policy with a view to potential reactions of potential competitors. To sacrifice present profits to the objective of keeping newcomers away is a policy which an imperfect *monopolist* will find imperative and an *oligopolist* may find advisable. A *polypolist*, perfect or imperfect, cannot afford it.

[25] Kaldor, *op. cit.*, pp. 40–41, 46.

PART V—FEW SELLERS

CHAPTER 11

Characteristics and Classifications of Oligopoly

Terminology

The Characteristics of Oligopoly: The Monopoly Power of the Oligopolist · The Many and the Few · Objective Circumstances Behind Subjective Attitudes · The Emphasis on Price Policies · The Oligopoly Demand Curve · Split Personality

Classifications of Oligopoly: Alternative Principles of Classification · The Degree of Coordination · Fight, Truce and Peace

SOME TEN YEARS AGO it was still possible that men professionally concerned with economic questions had never heard the word oligopoly.[1] Since that time a special literature on oligopoly has grown up, with a steady stream of articles, theoretical and descriptive, in all economic journals and with a number of books devoted to the subject.

TERMINOLOGY

The idea of oligopoly is of course much older than the word. One of the earliest theoretical discussions appeared in 1838 in the

---

[1] The following exchange took place between an expert witness—P. B. Morehouse, testifying for the Federal Trade Commission—and a Committee member—Jerome N. Frank of the Temporary National Economic Committee: "*Mr. Morehouse:* . . . monopoly does not have to exist in one person. Nineteen competitors can still be nominally competitors and separate organizations and still have a monopoly. *Mr. Frank:* For educational purposes might it be desirable to get in the record the notion that the economists have invented the word 'oligopoly,' to describe what you are describing. *Mr. Morehouse:* I never heard the word before, but I think it is a good word." *Investigation of Concentration of Economic Power. Hearings before the Temporary National Economic Committee,* Part 5 (Washington: 1939), p. 1742.

work of the mathematical economist Cournot, who first analysed "competition between two producers" and then "competition among 3, 4, . . . n producers." [2] It is especially his duopoly analysis to which modern economic theorists find it necessary to refer whenever they analyse problems of non-collusive oligopoly.[3] Duopoly is generally regarded as a special case of oligopoly, or as "the leading species of a large genus." [4] The word duopoly was not coined by Cournot, but only later. It has been generally accepted and has held its ground against the linguistically preferable term dyopoly.[5]

Competition among a few sellers has been discussed under a number of different names. "Limited competition," "incomplete monopoly," "multiple monopoly," and "monopolistic competition" were among the terms used for the concept before the word oligopoly was generally accepted.[6] There was no need for separate

---

[2] Augustin Cournot, *Recherches sur les principes mathématiques de la théorie des richesses* (Paris, 1838). English translation by Nathaniel T. Bacon under the title *Researches into the Mathematical Principles of the Theory of Wealth* (New York: Macmillan, 1897, reprinted 1927). His analyses of duopoly and oligopoly begin on pp. 79 and 84, respectively, of the English edition.

[3] "Yet now, after more than a century, it still is difficult to see what is involved in an oligopoly theory without showing how the theory is related to Cournot's basic construction." William Fellner, *Competition Among the Few: Oligopoly and Similar Market Structures* (New York: Alfred A. Knopf, 1949), p. 57.

[4] N. Kaldor, "Market Imperfection and Excess Capacity," *Economica*, New Series, Vol. II (1935), p. 40.

[5] The linguistic objection to the word duopoly rests on the fact that the first half of the word is of a Latin, the second of a Greek root. The words monopoly and oligopoly are formed entirely from Greek roots. The analogous construction for two sellers would be *dyopoly*. This word is actually used by Heinrich von Stackelberg, *Marktform und Gleichgewicht* (Wien: Julius Springer, 1934) and by some of his followers.

[6] The term "limited competition" was used by the followers of Cournot, who spoke of unlimited competition when each of the producers supplied only an "inappreciable" part of the market. "Incomplete monopoly" was the term used by Karl Forchheimer, "Theoretisches zum unvollständigen Monopole," *Jahrbuch für Gesetzgebung, Verwaltung und Volkswirtschaft im Deutschen Reich*, 32. Jahrgang (1908), p. 8, who, however, was concerned with the case of one large seller sharing the market with many very small ones. "Multiple monopoly" was Knut Wicksell's term when he discussed "monopolists if their number is large" in his article "Mathematische Nationalökonomie," *Archiv für Sozialwissenschaften und Sozialpolitik*, 58. Band (1927), p. 273. A. C. Pigou, *The Economics of Welfare* (London: Macmillan, 2nd ed. 1924,

analyses and terms for intermediate models, although the term triopoly has been suggested for competition among three sellers.[7] It was felt that even duopoly models were important chiefly for the development of propositions which might hold for the general theory of oligopoly, but not as models needed for the interpretation of any "actual" duopoly situations in the real world. If much space in these chapters will be given to duopoly models it will be just for the reason that the exposition of classical duopoly theory is the best way of providing an understanding of certain concepts that have proved useful in the discussion of problems of oligopoly.

THE CHARACTERISTICS OF OLIGOPOLY

A good many things about the concept of oligopoly have been said in the preceding chapters of this book. A definition was offered and discussed, contrasts with other types of seller's behavior were examined, methodological observations about certain definitional conventions and decisions were made, and so on. A reader of a chapter on oligopoly has a right to find these more or less fundamental points conveniently before him, instead of being referred to different sections and paragraphs of earlier chapters. In recognition of this right we shall not mind repeating ourselves, summarizing some discussions and elaborating others.

4th ed. 1932) and F. Zeuthen, *Problems of Monopoly and Economic Warfare* (London: Routledge, 1930) used the term "monopolistic competition" for what is now generally called oligopoly. Erich Schneider, in his *Reine Theorie monopolistischer Wirtschaftsformen* (Tübingen: Mohr-Siebeck, 1932), proposed the term "polypoly" for competition among a few (p. 132), but later accepted the present terms with their present meanings.

The word oligopoly was probably first used by Karl Schlesinger, *Theorie der Geld-und Kreditwirtschaft* (Munich and Leipzig: Duncker & Humblot, 1914). He stated that "the laws of oligopolistic price formation have not yet been explored to any extent; in any event they could determine only the limits between which at given sets of data prices may move" (p. 18). It was, however, only the appearance of the books by Edward H. Chamberlin and Heinrich von Stackelberg in 1932 and 1934, respectively, which firmly established the word oligopoly in economic terminology.

[7] Melvin Warren Reder, *Studies in the Theory of Welfare Economics* (New York: Columbia University Press, 1947), p. 55. Reder did not present a model of triopoly but merely mentioned it along with duopoly and oligopoly in relation to the possibilities of welfare-increasing operations of the government.

The Monopoly Power of the Oligopolist

The categorical distinction made in this analysis between oligopoly and monopoly as different models or ideal types of "seller's attitudes" must not be allowed to lead us to the erroneous conclusion that oligopoly excludes monopoly in the other meanings in which the term is used. Thus, sellers who are not monopolists in the sense of this model analysis nevertheless have "monopoly power." The market position of an oligopolist as well as some of his business practices may be called "monopolistic"; and we may speak of the "degree of monopoly" that is expressed in the pricing and selling policies of the oligopolist.

It should not be too hard to keep these different meanings of the word monopoly in mind and to avoid confusion, but it is particularly important in discussions of the legal implications of "monopoly." Both section 1 and 2 of the Sherman Antitrust Act, for example, were essentially directed toward oligopoly problems: the prohibition of agreements and conspiracies in restraint of trade was designed to prevent collusive oligopoly; the prohibition of attempts to monopolize was designed not only to stop coercive oligopoly but also to keep competition among the few from being transformed into competition among still fewer.[8] Thus, probably in 99 per cent of all cases, it was the monopoly power of oligopolists, individually or collectively, which the law was supposed to check.

The Many and the Few

At least twice in earlier chapters we had occasion to dwell upon the difference between polypoly and oligopoly. This topic is again on the agenda at this point and our essential observations may bear repetition.[9]

It is a hopeless task to draw a line between situations of polypoly and oligopoly if the *number* of sellers is to be the criterion for the distinction. This is so despite the fact that the basic idea behind the words relates to numbers: *many* sellers and *few* sellers. But

[8] On the historical developments which caused the antitrust laws to fail miserably with respect to the last of these objectives, see Fritz Machlup, *The Political Economy of Monopoly: Business, Labor and Government Policies* (Baltimore: Johns Hopkins Press, 1952), Chapter 6.

[9] The earlier discussions were in Chapters 4, 5, and 6.

there is no borderline between many and few. In addition there is no way of defining unambiguously just who the many or the few are supposed to be: sellers of what? sellers where? Surely, the question is whether many or few sellers offer the "same" commodity or service in the "same" market. But ordinarily neither the sameness of the commodity or service nor the sameness of the market can be clearly established. Is it the same product if different brands or qualities are offered? Is it the same market if they are offered in the same city, in the same county, state, nation? It all depends—but on what? Does it depend on objectively discernible and measurable facts? The answer is no. And this settles the question. Whether there are many or few sellers offering a certain good in a certain market cannot be stated in any objective fashion, because neither many and few nor the good nor the market can be objectively delimited.

Not objectively in numbers then can we find the criterion for the distinction between polypoly and oligopoly, but rather in subjective attitudes, in the state of mind of the seller. The criterion is whether the seller, when he contemplates a decision or action that he might take concerning his selling prices, sales volumes, product qualities, selling efforts, or production capacity, is or is not conscious of what his competitors might think or do in reaction.

This rival-consciousness, or self-consciousness *vis-à-vis* competitors, contrasts oligopoly sharply with polypoly and also with monopoly as a type of seller's attitude. "Polypoly is the position where the seller believes that other sellers in the market would not care about what he does because there are too many for any one to feel or mind the effects of what he does; monopoly is the position where the seller believes that he does not have to care about what other sellers might do in reaction to what he does because what they sell is too different from what he sells." [10]

Objective Circumstances Behind Subjective Attitudes

Oligopoly is thus characterized by the state of mind of a seller *vis-à-vis* other sellers. Of course, the circumstances under which

[10] This formulation is reproduced from my paper on the "Evaluation of the Practical Significance of the Theory of Monopolistic Competition," *American Economic Review*, Vol. XXIX (1939), p. 232.

this mentality—the consciousness of possible reactions of rivals —is likely to exist can be described.

The following circumstances seem essential: The action of the seller must be conspicuous or at least noticeable; its effects upon competitors must be such that they mind; this minding will express itself either in attitudes of disapproval and resentment or in actions affecting the seller in a material way.

While these circumstances may be part of the thinking of the oligopolistic seller, they may be also subject to observation by an objective observer. For example, as an outside observer I can judge from objective appearances whether a price reduction by a certain seller is likely to be noticed by those who have been offering competing products to the same group of buyers; whether the price reduction is apt to affect adversely the business of these competitors; whether they are likely to resent such effects and would be able to attribute them to the action of the price cutter; and whether they are likely to respond to it by some counter-move which would be felt by the price cutter. Thus, the selection of a subjective attitude as the essential characteristic in the definition of oligopoly does not imply that it is impossible to diagnose a case from its appearance. To be sure, the appearance may be misleading and, therefore, it is preferable not to *define* in terms of appearance.

In no type of seller's attitude is the feeling of rivalry and competitiveness as prevalent as in some forms of oligopoly. Under perfect polypoly, as will be remembered, the feeling of rivalry is completely absent from the attitudes of the "pure competitors." Under imperfect polypoly a seller may be aware of the fact that he has competitors but, although he may watch them, he is not self-conscious about his own actions, because he has not the feeling of being watched by them. Since he is sure his actions cannot hurt any one of them and no one of them would ever "come back" at him for anything he might do, he will not have any particular "rival" or "rivals."

This is different under certain forms of oligopoly. The oligopolist usually thinks of certain firms as his rivals; he knows they are watching him or, at least, will notice his "competitive" actions; he believes he can hurt them or make them angry or cause them to take an action they would not take but for what he has done. And all this means that he will be very *conscious of being in competition,* actively or potentially. This being so, he cannot understand how economists can assert that oligopoly involves a *reduced* degree of competition or that "competition is *not so active* among a limited as among an unlimited number." [11] Economists who prefer to be understood by the practical man had better admit that what they regard as the "highest" degree of competition among the very many is not "active" competition at all but rather "passive" from the point of view of the competitor; whereas competition will be most "active" if a price war or promotional struggle develops among the few rivals in oligopolistic positions. But the point, again, is this: What the economist usually means when he speaks of the "degree" of competition or the "degree" of monopoly need not be correlated with the subjective attitude of the seller in market positions characterized as polypoly, oligopoly, or monopoly.

The Emphasis on Price Policies

We should guard against the rather common fallacies of defining or describing oligopoly (a) in terms of the geometric shape of the demand curve depicting the oligopolist's selling opportunities, (b) in terms of the mathematical relationships between his sales and the prices charged by his competitors, or (c) generally in terms of prices and price policies. While such descriptions may be perfectly adequate for particular forms of oligopoly or for introductory examples of the general problem of oligopoly, they are much too narrow for defining or circumscribing the concept.

The "case of the kinked demand curve," if it is a description or explanation of anything occurring in reality, is certainly only a very special case. We shall talk about it later; at this point we confine ourselves to a flat rejection of the idea that the kinky curve represents *the* demand curve under oligopoly. It is difficult to see how such a misunderstanding could have arisen. [12]

[11] John Stuart Mill, *Principles of Political Economy* (1st ed. 1848. 7th ed. 1871; London: Longmans, Green and Co., 1926, p. 932), Book V, Ch. X, § 4. (Italics are mine.)
[12] Paul M. Sweezy presented the kinky oligopoly demand curve as a hypothesis in his note "Demand under Conditions of Oligopoly," *Journal of Political Economy,* Vol. XLVII (1939), pp. 568–73. The same hypothesis was

The notion that cross-elasticities of demand may be sufficient for a definition of oligopoly is probably due to attempts to reduce the description of attitudes and mentalities to concise mathematical equations. But when one says that "oligopoly exists if any seller regards his sales as a function of at least one other price besides his own," [13] the distinction between differentiated polypoly and oligopoly is lost, since this supposedly characteristic dependence on other prices may hold, and is likely to hold, for several other kinds of sales function. If the sales volumes under polypoly are represented as functions of only the seller's own price, no more is meant than that other relevant prices are assumed to be given and unchanged as parameters; but no one means to deny or exclude the dependence of sales upon prices of other goods. What is characteristic for certain oligopoly situations—though not for all—is that other prices cannot be taken as parameters, but must themselves be taken as variables dependent on the price charged by the oligopolistic seller.[14]

But the most fundamental fallacy is the limitation of the concept of oligopoly to price determination and price policy. In a large number of oligopoly situations prices are only a small part, if any, of the considerations and actions of the members of the group concerned. Questions with respect to the quality of the products and services offered, or to the selling efforts made, by the oligopolistic sellers may be just as important, if not more so. Or it may be decisions regarding plant location and plant expansion that are the subjects of the analysis for which the model of

advanced independently by Hall and Hitch, "Price Theory and Business Behavior," *Oxford Economic Papers*, No. 2 (1939), pp. 12–45. Neither of the authors claimed that such a kinked demand curve was representative of all oligopoly situations. Yet, several text books presented it as such. See, e.g., Lorie Tarshis, *The Elements of Economics* (Boston: Houghton, Mifflin, 1947), pp. 142, 169, 181–84.

[13] Max Millikan, "Comments on the Duopoly-Oligopoly Problem" in "Report of the Detroit Meeting, December 27–30, 1938," *Econometrica*, Vol. VII (1939), p. 175.

[14] If the prices charged by competitors are uniquely determined functions of the price charged by the oligopolist, the partial dependence of his sales upon these other prices can be expressed within the function relating the sales to his own price. Thus in the sales function under oligopoly the prices charged by competitors could with more justification be excluded as separate variables than could be done under polypoly.

the oligopolistic seller is used. The disproportionately heavy emphasis on prices is justified only for didactic and illustrative purposes.

If the bulk of all theoretical analysis of oligopoly is in terms of selling prices, this need not imply that all theorists are victims of the fallacy of defining oligopoly in terms of price determination. The fact that prices are numerical quantities while quality differences cannot be quantified, the fact that most of the traditional tools of economic analysis refer to price-quantity relationships and that the demand curve is the most widely used tool in the theorist's box, can fully explain why theorists have preferred to discuss oligopoly in terms of prices, price changes, and demand curves. As long as they know that this emphasis is only a matter of our technique of analysis but is not in the nature of things, no harm is done.

The Oligopoly Demand Curve

There is no such thing as an oligopoly demand curve, or even a demand curve that can be said to be typical of oligopoly positions. A demand curve relates quantities saleable to prices charged, but it says neither in whose mind this relationship exists nor what are the considerations by which the relationship has been established. In particular, it does not say—even if we knew that the relationship in question existed in the mind of an individual seller imagining his selling opportunities—whether the seller assumes that his competitors will change their selling prices if he first changes his; indeed, it does not say whether or not the seller gives any thought to such possibilities, that is, whether or not he is an oligopolist.

Thus, no geometric finesse can reveal what type of mentality and attitude we assume the seller to have. If we assume he is an oligopolist, we shall have to say so, for we cannot show it by the kind of curve we draw. On the other hand, assuming a particular oligopolistic seller actually to relate in his mind the quantities he might sell with the prices he might charge, taking full account of the price changes with which his competitors might react to his own price changes, the curve depicting these price-quantity relations may have all sorts of shapes—it may be a straight horizontal line, a gently descending curve, a more steeply sloping continuous curve, a curve with drastically changing slopes, a curve with a conspicuous kink. And some parts of the curve may be good only for one-way movement, for example, for price reductions but not for price increases.

Assume a seller under non-cooperative oligopoly is pondering the effects of possible changes in his selling prices upon the quantities he might be able to sell: If he should cut his price by ten percent, will his competitors cut their prices? Perhaps not, but perhaps they will. If so, when? Perhaps immediately, perhaps only in a month, in two months. And by what percentage? Perhaps by only five percent, perhaps by fifteen, perhaps also by ten. Now, even if of all these possibilities the oligopolist should judge one particular course of events to be the most probable one, the resulting expectations cannot easily be translated into simple price-quantity relationships reducible to a simple demand curve. Let us see some of the difficulties in the use of the customary demand curve technique for the oligopolist's considerations.

This is, for example, what our oligopolist thinks would be the most probable outcome: If he continued to sell at his present price of $100, he would expect to sell 5000 tons a week. If he reduced his price to $90, he would expect his competitors not to take any action for two months, but then to reduce their prices also by ten percent. His sales would at first rise only slowly, but in the fourth week he would reach a volume of 7000 tons; average weekly sales for the two months might be 6500 tons. After the price cut by the other firms his sales volumes would level off to an average of 6000 tons a week.

How can these expectations be expressed in demand curves? Should we have different curves for every week? or should we have one curve for the average sales of the first two months and another curve for the time thereafter? or should all sales be averaged into one curve? We may choose whatever seems the easiest. Assume we decide in favor of two curves, one for the transition period, the other for the new "equilibrium." But are we ready to draw them? That our oligopolist has settled in his mind what would be the most probable course of events, does not mean that he can forget the other possibilities entirely. After all, there is a chance that the competitors cut their prices after only one month, or even after one week. And there is a chance that they cut by fifteen percent rather than ten. Of course, there is also the offsetting chance that they cut by only five percent. But the risk of a loss often weighs more heavily than the chance of an especially lucky outcome. In this case the most probable expectations must not be "counted on," but must be discounted; that is, the seller must calculate with safety margins. The demand curves corrected for uncertainty will not be the same as the uncorrected ones; and the corrections will depend on the optimistic or pessimistic outlook of the seller and on his aversion to risk.[15]

This was still a relatively "easy" case. Let us assume now that our oligopolist cannot decide which may be the most probable course of events; that he thinks his competitors may react to his 10 percent price cut (a) by leaving their prices unchanged, (b) by cutting them by 5 percent, (c) by cutting 10 percent or (d) by cutting 15 percent; that he judges the chances for these four possibilities to be just about equal; and that he expects his sales volume to gain in case (a) by 25 percent, in case (b) by 15 percent, in case (c) by 5 percent, and to drop by 5 percent in case (d). One may argue that an arithmetic average of these possible changes would represent his best judgment. In other words, his "expectation," on the basis of the average of the possible changes, would be for an increase in sales volume by ten percent as a result of his price cut by ten percent. If he judged the odds for the four possibilities to be different, the "average probable outcome" would be different because of the different weights given to each of the eventualities.[16] Further complications may be in-

---

[15] Exactly the same type of difficulties in representing a seller's expectations in the form of a demand curve exist for polypoly, only that there the number of uncertain variables is smaller.

[16] If the seller thought that there was a 40% chance for (a), a 10% chance for (b), a 40% chance for (c) and a 10% chance for (d), the weighted average expectation would be for his sales volume to increase by 13 percent: $(125 \times .4 + 115 \times .1 + 105 \times .4 + 95 \times .1 = 113)$.—According to the exponents of a recent revolution in mathematical economics, such a reduction of nonstatistical probabilities to a "mathematical expectation" is not a legitimate procedure. Uncontrollable variables "can be eliminated by the known procedures of the calculus of probabilities" only if they are "purely statistical phenomena"—which the alternatives expected by our seller are not. John

troduced if the expectations concerning the effects of each of the possible price cuts by the competitors upon his sales volume were also in terms of probability distributions, so that each of the four possibilities would call for weighted averaging of the probable effects. And on top of all this arises again the problem that different dispersions of probabilities may yield the same averages but will unquestionably be judged differently with regard to the risk involved. Hence, the averaging alone would not do without some correction for differences in the spreads between better and worse outcomes that also takes account of the seller's propensity to gamble, take risks, or play safe.

Some of us who are aware of all these difficulties develop so many inhibitions that we blush whenever we see a demand curve, and especially in an oligopoly problem. There is no need for blushing, however, if we are honest and do not misrepresent the nature of curve analysis. We must not present the curves as pictures of reality, but merely as auxiliary constructions helping us develop some general relationships which, through reasoning by analogy, may be useful in the explanation of more complicated phenomena. That few of the "real situations" are reducible to description in terms of geometric curves is irrelevant and need not restrict the "applicability" of curve analysis to the interpretation of these situations. On the other hand, nothing is farther from my mind than to claim that curve analysis is applicable to each and every problem. There may be many oligopoly problems for which curve analysis is of no use. This should neither induce us to discard entirely a technique which is so useful for many other problems, nor should it lead us to dispose of the particular problem as "irrelevant" merely because it cannot be treated by the customary technique.

Split Personality

One more reminder of an earlier observation may be in order before we feel sufficiently guarded against the worst snares in the analysis of oligopoly. We must bear in mind that one and the same

---

von Neumann and Oskar Morgenstern, *The Theory of Games and Economic Behavior* (Princeton: Princeton University Press, 2nd ed., 1947), p. 10.

firm may be at the same time a polypolist, an oligopolist, and a monopolist.

This is not due to a schizophrenic personality of the salesmen or the vice-presidents in charge of selling. Indeed, as soon as we remember that most firms in the real world sell more than one product, we realize that they may be in very different market positions with respect to the different products they offer. When a firm sells many different products we shall, more likely than not, need different ideal types of seller's attitude if we wish to interpret its selling policies. The firm may well act as an oligopolist in the sale of some of its products, but as polypolist or monopolist in the sale of others.

Even in the sale of one particular product the firm may have different attitudes at different times. Indeed, oscillations between polypoly and oligopoly may be possible in the course of seasonal or cyclical business fluctuations. A real "split personality" may exist—two types of attitude concerning the same product at the same time—if a separation of markets and the practice of price discrimination is possible, with some markets conditioning an oligopolistic state of mind, others a polypolistic one; or if different kinds of decision call for different types of consideration. For example, a producer may think as a short-run polypolist when he considers a decision of little consequence for the competitors in the short run; while he may think as an oligopolist when a decision is likely to affect the business for a long time. Or, occasionally the opposite may be true: he may reach investment decisions without giving much thought to his competitors' possible reactions, whereas he would not decide on the method of selling out his present large stock of finished goods without considering how they might react to it.

Classifications of Oligopoly

Hardly any generalizations could be made about the "economic consequences of oligopoly" or about the "causes of oligopoly" unless we first separated different types or kinds of oligopoly. In other words, a classification of oligopoly is needed.

Of course, an indefinite number of features or conditions could be named as conceivable bases for classification. The problem arises what to select in order to obtain a classification useful for purposes of economic analysis. Distinctions should be made wherever one finds differences suspected of "making a difference" sufficiently important within the chosen frame of reference. It is probably generally agreed that selling prices, output volumes, selling efforts, product qualities are among the major variables considered relevant for our purposes. Hence, the distinctions made in a classification of oligopoly may relate to differences likely to affect these major variables. It will also be agreed that the question of the sources of monopoly power and of the conditions responsible for oligopolistic situations is significant. Hence, a classification may be based on distinctions of the causes of oligopoly.

Alternative Principles of Classification

Let us survey the more important of the distinctions which various writers on oligopoly have proposed as relevant for purposes of economic analysis. We shall group them under convenient headings conveying the principles on which the distinction rests.

A. *Product Differentiation.* According to whether the products offered by the competing oligopolists are, in the minds of the buyers, perfectly or less than perfectly substitutable for each other, or whether it makes a difference to the buyers from which of the sellers they buy, "pure" or "undifferentiated" oligopoly is distinguished from "differentiated" oligopoly.[17] Another pair of terms for the same contrast of concepts is "perfect" versus "imperfect" oligopoly.[18] And even some highly unconventional terminology has been suggested for the same idea.[19]

B. *Entry into Industry.* Depending on whether new firms can freely and easily enter the industry if they regard it as a promising field of investment and enterprise, "open" oligopoly is distin-

[17] See, for example, Joe S. Bain, "Pricing in Monopoly and Oligopoly," *American Economic Review*, Vol. XXXIX (1949), p. 450; William Fellner, *op. cit.*, p. 69.

[18] Kenneth E. Boulding, *Economic Analysis* (New York: Harper, 2nd ed., 1948), p. 581.

[19] "Circular homeopoly" versus "circular heteropoly." Robert Triffin, *Monopolistic Competition and General Equilibrium Theory* (Cambridge: Harvard University Press, 1940), p. 143.

guished from "closed" oligopoly.[20] If the possibilities of entry of newcomers are assumed to be weighed by an oligopolist and to affect his decisions, many economists speak of "potential" competition.[21]

C. *Leadership.* Several distinctions and classificatory attempts are based on the existence of one or a few "dominant firms" in the industry, on the type of firms in positions of leaders or followers, on the ways in which the firms aspire to, or acquiesce in, positions of leadership or followership, and on their patterns of conduct in these roles. The case of one dominant firm faced with a large number of small firms which follow the leader—called "incomplete" or "partial monopoly" [22]—is contrasted with the case of a few big firms followed by a crowd of small ones—called "partial oligopoly" or "big-firm oligopoly"—and both are distinguished from "full oligopoly," where there are no firms accepting unconditional followership roles.[23] Other distinctions are based upon the preferences of the firms for the roles as leaders or followers, with the possibility of many different combinations depending on the "symmetrical" and "asymmetrical" aspirations to particular roles in the industry.[24] The significance of these distinctions lies in the probability that under symmetrical oligopoly, where, for example, each of the firms wants to be the leader and none a follower, they will attempt to fight it out. (If this involves a price war, the effects on prices are rather obvious.) Even under asymmetrical oligopoly, where, for example, one firm wants to lead and the others to follow, peaceful relations (and stability as long as given external condi-

[20] Walter Eucken, *Die Grundlagen der Nationalökonomie* (Bad Godesberg: H. Küpper, 1st ed., 1941), p. 128.

[21] For example, John M. Clark, "Toward a Concept of Workable Competition," *American Economic Review,* Vol. XXX (1940), p. 246; Bain, *op. cit.,* p. 451. On some popular exaggerations concerning the effectiveness of "potential" competition, see George J. Stigler, "Notes on the Theory of Duopoly," *The Journal of Political Economy,* Vol. XLVIII (1940), pp. 533 ff.

[22] Karl Forchheimer, *op. cit.;* A. J. Nichol, *Partial Monopoly and Price Leadership* (Philadelphia: Smith-Edwards, 1930), p. 29.

[23] Walter Eucken, *op. cit.,* p. 122; William Fellner, *op. cit.,* pp. 136–41.

[24] Heinrich von Stackelberg, *op. cit.,* p. 48. Alone for duopoly Stackelberg lists 16 combinations on this score. For cases of more than two competitors the number of possible combinations becomes formidable. For an explanatory discussion of symmetrical and asymmetrical duopoly positions see below, Chapter 12.

tions prevail) may be assured only in very particular constellations, except by means of collusion.

D. Collusion. The existence or non-existence of agreements among the sellers has often been taken as sufficient ground for a classification separating "collusive" from "non-collusive" oligopoly. It is necessary, however, to recognize that agreement is seldom complete (as to scope or compliance) and collusion is seldom completely absent. It is a long way and there is nowhere a sharp line between the lower degrees of collusion and the tighter organizations that some have chosen to regard as "collective monopolies." Assuming that higher degrees of collusion are a function of the maturity of the oligopolistic constellations, writers have distinguished between "immature" and "mature" oligopoly, or even among several stages between the "least mature oligopoly" and the "completely mature oligopoly." [25] In view of the various dispositions of oligopolists to compete aggressively, guardedly, or fraternally, "cut-throat competition" has been contrasted with "cautious competition," "considerate competition," and "cooperative competition." [26] Stressing a particular form of cooperative competition, "open-price oligopoly" has been distinguished from other species of oligopoly characterized by different pricing institutions.[27] The model of completely uncoordinated oligopoly has been set apart from all other types under the name of "true oligopoly." [28]

[25] The different stages of maturity were discussed by William Fellner, *op. cit.*, pp. 188–91. The distinction between immature and mature oligopoly was first proposed with different meaning by Gordon F. Bloom, "A Reconsideration of the Theory of Exploitation," *Quarterly Journal of Economics,* Vol. LV (1941), p. 426. Reprinted in *Readings on the Theory of Income Distribution* (Philadelphia: Blakiston, 1946), p. 260. Bloom saw immature oligopoly "where the oligopolist is still free to select the price which he intends to maintain thereafter," while in mature oligopoly price is "more or less given to him by the convention of the competitive relationships which have grown up in the market."

[26] John M. Cassels, "Monopolistic Competition and Economic Realism," *Canadian Journal of Economics and Political Science,* Vol. III (1937), p. 376.

[27] John M. Clark, *op. cit.*, p. 245. Open-price arrangements, "perfectly conformed to (rarely found)" constitute Clark's "first species of oligopoly," market-made prices characterize the "second main species," "uniform mill prices" set by spatially separated producers characterize a "third species of oligopoly."

[28] George J. Stigler, *op. cit.*, p. 533.

E. Fundamental Conditions. Distinctions of the fundamental conditions responsible for oligopolistic situations are made, not so much because the economic effects may be significantly different, but rather because governmental policies aiming at reduction of monopoly power and furtherance of competitive forces in the economy presuppose knowledge about the sources of monopoly power. Some structural conditions may be such that it is impossible to remove or alter them, or that one would not wish to do so. Institutional conditions, on the other hand, may be removable or controllable by appropriate governmental measures. A classification significant in the light of these considerations has distinguished oligopoly "based on real-cost advantages," oligopoly based on artificial, "monopolistic or institutional advantages," and "quasi-oligopolistic organization of an atomistic group by an outside agency." [29] Still other conditions of oligopolistic situations have been shown to lie in the existence of small subgroups of otherwise highly populated industries sectionalized through differences in quality or transportation cost. These subgroups may be either sharply delimited or chain-linked with one another.[30] The terms "sectional oligopoly" and "chain oligopoly" may be used to denote these two types.

The Degree of Coordination

This survey of classifications of oligopoly, though no doubt very incomplete, has probably demonstrated that no single classification could possibly serve all purposes. Cross-classifications may sometimes be helpful, although the number of possible combinations might become overwhelming. On the other hand, a problem under investigation may be aided by one classification while others are irrelevant. For example, those interested in public policy formation may find it important to know whether an existing big-firm oligopoly is based on definite real-cost advantages or rather on the exploitation of institutional privileges or on the use of coercive or oppressive practices. But they may not in the least be

[29] William Fellner, *op. cit.,* pp. 48–49.
[30] Edward H. Chamberlin, *The Theory of Monopolistic Competition* (Cambridge: Harvard University Press, 1931), p. 103.

interested in the symmetry or asymmetry of the leadership aspirations of the firms in question. A cross-classification according to leadership and collusion, however, may be significant. For there may be important differences in the effects of collusion without leadership, leadership without (a high degree of) collusion, and collusion enforced by leadership.[31]

More comprehensive and detailed classifications are sometimes helpful in conveying an impression of the range and gradation of the distinctions. For example, the degree of coordination between the actions and policies of the competing oligopolists is the underlying principle of the following classification:

    I. Completely coordinated oligopoly.

        1. Syndicated oligopoly (Centralized selling through a "syndicate," perhaps reinforced through pooling of revenue.)

        2. Organized oligopoly (Cartel, less tightly organized than syndicates, but involving agreement, explicit or only implied, about prices, quota, or other determinants of sales.)

    II. Incompletely coordinated oligopoly.

        3. Leadership oligopoly (Cartel without organization and agreement, based on tacit understanding and accepted leadership, resulting in concert of actions; may include also partial oligopoly with quasi-polypolistic sectors.)

        4. Cooperative oligopoly (Restraints imposed by "business ethics" and "realization of common interest," without organization, agreement, or leadership; may include also "considerate competition" and live-and-let-live policies.)

    III. Uncoordinated oligopoly.

The gradations within this classification could have been much finer, but there would have been still more overlapping of the different sub-types. As it is, the overlapping may be considerable. For example, strong leadership by a dominant firm may exist under organized oligopoly and even in the council of a syndicate.

The expression "incompletely coordinated" oligopoly can have several different meanings. The "incompleteness" may refer to

[31] See Fritz Machlup, *The Basing-Point System* (Philadelphia: Blackiston, 1949), pp. 129–34.

the reliability of the coordination and, thus, to the certainty with which the participants can each anticipate the conduct of the others. Or it could refer to the scope of the coordination, which, for example, may include price making but exclude selling effort or product quality. It was the former meaning of incomplete co-ordination that was referred to in Class II above. As to the non-price variables, we prefer to regard firms as being simultaneously in different classes of oligopoly with respect to different aspects of their competitive behavior. A firm may be a member of a strict price cartel, act as a cooperative oligopolist with respect to product quality, and perhaps compete aggressively without any caution in its selling efforts.

A high correlation between *organization* and *coordination* of conduct is implied in the proposed classification:

Class I: organized, completely coordinated;
Class II: unorganized, incompletely coordinated;
Class III: unorganized, uncoordinated.

This simplifies the classification but is probably at variance with reality. Qualifications and corrections will become necessary when we proceed to analyse the various types.

We shall not adopt the wide-spread habit of treating com-pletely coordinated oligopoly as "collective monopoly." In a cartel, however tight, policy determination is fundamentally different from that of a single-headed monopoly. As long as the income state-ments and balance sheets of the individual firms are separately evaluated by separate managements, the "common will" of the organized oligopolists is apt to differ from that of the management of a consolidated monopoly in otherwise identical situations. The council of a syndicate in deciding on its policies must take account of the individual sensibilities of all members and cultivate their continued loyalty. The management of a single monopoly is not so oriented with respect to the different departments of the con-solidated firm: there is no danger that they will quit or fail to re-new the arrangement next term.

Fight, Truce, and Peace

That arrangements among oligopolists may be temporary and sometimes rather precarious, that actions are often taken or poli-

cies pursued merely in order to maintain peace and avoid the outbreak of vigorous competition, that some oligopolists are willing
to stay in line only until further notice, that some are ready any
time for a showdown with their rivals, that others insist on fighting it out—all this suggests the use of another classification: *oligopoly in fight, oligopoly in truce, oligopoly in peace.*

Subdivisions of these distinctions between belligerent, quiescent, and peaceful oligopolies may be called for, particularly to
indicate whether the current state is an agreed, imposed, or spontaneous one. It may seem to be a spurious distinction between
spontaneous truce and spontaneous peace if objective criteria are
demanded. But it is the *animus* of the oligopolists that counts, not
any physical evidence, nor the *ex-post* duration of the absence of
fight. A spontaneous truce may turn out to be more durable than
any sort of peace. Truce or peace may be imposed from the outside, for example, by the government. Fight will probably always
be spontaneous. (It has been suggested, though, that an oligopolistic fight might also be imposed. And an agreed fight, I assume,
would be a sham battle to give the appearance of competition.)
The aims of an oligopolistic fight may be (a) to force the competitor out of the market, (b) to force him to cooperate, or (c) to
force him into a merger. (Needless to say, the best known name
for oligopoly in fight is cut-throat competition. Cut-throat competition can never occur under polypolistic conditions, it always
pre-supposes a fair degree of monopoly power on the part of some
of the competitors, and it is not competition for business but competition to subdue a rival.) [32]

Oligopoly in fight is of course uncoordinated oligopoly (apart
from arranged sham battles, if such exist). Oligopolies in truce
and in peace may be either uncoordinated or coordinated. But as
we shall see later, an oligopoly situation that is apt to lead to a
fight usually invites some degree of coordination as a means of
pacification.

Almost all theoretical analysis of oligopoly has been of uncoordinated oligopoly. This may be somewhat surprising because

---

[32] This is mentioned here because cut-throat competition is sometimes
so broadly defined or so loosely used as to include almost any kind of price
competition among sellers.

many analysts came to the conclusion that uncoordinated oligopoly cannot be stable, and that quiescent or peaceful oligopoly cannot be uncoordinated. Observation of the real world, however, suggests that oligopoly in fight is the exception and quiescent or peaceful oligopoly is the rule.

CHAPTER 12

Classical Duopoly Theories and Their Modern Extensions

Classical Duopoly Models: Mathematics, Geometry, and English · Assuming a Market Demand Schedule · The Cournot Model · The Bertrand Model · The Edgeworth Model

Comparisons of the Classical Models: Prices and Production · Expected Reactions of Rival · Own Reactions to Rival · Summary of Comparisons · Uniformity of Market Prices · Buyers' Indifference versus Inertia

Extensions of the Classical Models: Modifications of Assumptions · Product Differentiation · The Shape and Similarity of Cost Functions · Asymmetry of Attitudes · Guessing Definite Countermoves · Quasi-Collusive Behavior Patterns · More Variables: Product Quality and Sales Promotion · More Than Two Sellers

THE THEORY OF uncoordinated oligopoly is one of the oldest of all economic theories of competition and monopoly, or indeed of all theories of the conduct of the individual firm. The duopoly model presented by Cournot [1] in 1838 has served many economists not only as a model *in* the analysis of "competition among the few," but as a model *for* economic analysis *per se.* This particular duopoly model, however, was criticized in 1883 by the French mathematician Bertrand, who misunderstood Cournot's assumptions and misrepresented them grossly, but in so doing unwittingly offered a substitute model.[2] After Edgeworth in 1897 pub-

[1] Augustin Cournot, *Recherches sur les principes mathématiques de la théorie des richesses* (Paris, 1838). English translation by Nathaniel T. Bacon under the title *Researches into the Mathematical Principles of the Theory of Wealth* (New York: Macmillan, 1897, reprinted 1927).

[2] Joseph Bertrand, "Theorie Mathématique de la Richesse Sociale." *Journal des Savants* (Paris, September 1883), pp. 499–508. This was a joint review article of Leon Walras' book, published in 1883 under the title used in the review article, and of Cournot's book, published 45 years earlier but

lished, in an Italian journal, an article dealing with the subject and offering a third model,[3] duopoly theory began to receive wider attention from economic theorists.

CLASSICAL DUOPOLY MODELS

None of the three "classical" duopoly models is accepted today as much more than a school model on which to learn how to manœuvre some basic ideas of oligopoly analysis.[4] Familiarity with the classical models has become a kind of hall-mark of the education of an economic theorist, even if it helps him more in the comprehension of the traditional lingo than in the analysis of current economic problems.

Mathematics, Geometry, and English

Until this day, however, duopoly theory has remained rather "high-brow stuff," largely inaccessible to economists who can think much better in words than in functions and curves. The reason is

almost unnoticed until Walras called attention to it and paid homage to Cournot. Bertrand published word for word the same review of Walras' and Cournot's books in the *Bulletin des Sciences Mathématiques et Astronomiques*, 2nd series, Vol. VII (Paris, November 1883), Part I, pp. 293–303. The passage on Cournot's duopoly model is only about twenty lines long. It is somewhat farcical that one may credit Bertrand with proposing a "new model" for the analysis of the duopoly problem when in fact he was merely confused and believed he was criticizing Cournot's solution on the basis of Cournot's assumptions.

[3] F. Y. Edgeworth, "La teoria pura del monopolio," *Giornale degli Economisti*, Vol. XV (1897), pp. 13–31. Edgeworth had briefly dealt with the problem in his *Mathematical Psychics* (London, 1881). His Italian article was republished in English in Edgeworth's *Papers Relating to Political Economy* (London: Macmillan, 1925), Vol. I, pp. 111–42.

[4] See Fellner's statement quoted above in footnote 1, p. 916.—Similarly George J. Stigler, "Notes on the Theory of Duopoly," *Journal of Political Economy*, Vol. XLVIII (1940), p. 525: "The problem of duopoly may best be approached, following established precedent, by reproducing its first solution, that of Cournot."—Some writers give the Cournot model credit for more than that. Schneider calls the Cournot solution of the oligopoly problem "the ingenious solution, and the only one possible under its assumptions, of a central economic problem of eminent significance." Erich Schneider, *Reine Theorie monopolistischer Wirtschaftsformen* (Tübingen: Mohr-Siebeck, 1932), p. 175.

obvious: all three models, Cournot's, Bertrand's, and Edgeworth's, were mathematical in construction. And most economists who were good in mathematics have not bothered to translate the arguments into literary language.[5] At best, they offered rough translations from analytic into plain geometry. They usually avoided reasoning in words and simple arithmetic, apparently because it was too clumsy and could not yield results of general validity.

Yet, full comprehension of the working of the three classical duopoly models can hardly be achieved unless the reasoning is reduced to common-sense terms. Although some of the most competent economists have dealt with these models, their interpretations differ in significant details. The greatest difficulty seems to be in the task of ferreting out some of the implicit assumptions that underlie the operation of the models. Almost every new discussion of the subject succeeds in adding another previously hidden assumption to the list of explicit and tacit assumptions and working hypotheses. Most of these implications are far from obvious and cannot be clearly seen from the set of equations with which the models are described. The essence of the problem lies in a sequence of actions and reactions based on particular considerations on the part of the actors in question. Full comprehension requires rethinking of these considerations on the part of the student of the problem. It is necessary for each of us to imagine ourselves in the places of the duopolistic sellers—now Mr. A, now Mr. B, again Mr. A, and again Mr. B—and to ask ourselves what *we* in their places should do at each particular point in the process. Understanding rests on what I like to call "imagined introspection."

For this method of imagined introspection, curves or equations are poor substitutes. Sliding down along a smooth curve until it intersects another curve is a healthy mental exercise; and solving a set of simultaneous equations is too; but neither of these will ensure our understanding of the way a man makes up his mind when he ponders a business decision. (To be sure, sometimes we

[5] The most commendable of the few exceptions that I have come across is the work by A. J. Nichol. See "A Re-appraisal of Cournot's Theory of Duopoly Price," *Journal of Political Economy*, Vol. XLII (1934), pp. 80–105, and "Edgeworth's Theory of Duopoly Price," *The Economic Journal*, Vol. XLV (1935), pp. 51–66.

devise new mental tools for analysing business decisions which the businessman does not use himself and which he feels give the student a wrong impression of his way of reasoning. Constructs of this sort may be defended as long as they can satisfactorily explain what businessmen do and as long as they preserve the essential traits of the business process: the continual choosing among alternatives.) The operation of a duopoly model, if it is to be fully understood, must preserve in simulated exactitude the sequence of conscious decisions on the part of the duopolists introspectively imagined by the student of the problem. This, for most people, calls for thinking in words and figuring with numbers assumed for purposes of illustration.

Assuming a Market Demand Schedule

For a comparative demonstration of the Cournot, Bertrand, and Edgeworth models we shall choose a demand schedule representing the total market demand for a product offered by two, and only two, firms. The following schedule corresponds to a linear function (or straight-line demand curve) which would simplify the algebraic solutions but is of no relevance in the arithmetic treatment of the problem.[6]

At a price of	$1.30	the market would absorb	nil
" " " "	1.20	" " " "	100,000 units per week
" " " "	1.10	" " " "	200,000
" " " "	1.00	" " " "	300,000
" " " "	.90	" " " "	400,000
" " " "	.80	" " " "	500,000
" " " "	.70	" " " "	600,000
" " " "	.60	" " " "	700,000
" " " "	.50	" " " "	800,000
" " " "	.40	" " " "	900,000
" " " "	.30	" " " "	1,000,000
" " " "	.20	" " " "	1,100,000
" " " "	.10	" " " "	1,200,000
" " " "	0	" " " "	1,300,000

[6] The assumed schedule follows the function $p = 1.30 - 0.000001\ q$, where p is price and q is quantity demanded.

It is assumed that the smallest amount by which price can change is \$0.01 per unit. For each price reduction by 1 cent the quantity taken rises by 10,000 units.

While we assume this demand schedule to hold for all three models, and while we shall assume cost conditions also to be nearly the same in all three models, there will be some very conspicuous differences in other assumptions, which we shall be careful to point out.

The Cournot Model

The following assumptions are made, in the Cournot model, about our two sellers, A and B, and about the market in which they sell.

(1) The two sellers do not set or announce any prices. They sell their weekly output, no more and no less, to a mass of competing buyers and accept for it whatever price they can get. That is to say, the price is determined by the "impersonal forces of the market," owing to the fact that there is only one price at which the market can absorb the output that is currently offered for sale. There are no dealers in the market who would speculate by buying for stock or selling from stock.

(2) The two sellers are assumed to be totally uninformed about each other's policies: each believes that, regardless of his own actions and their effects on the market price, the other would go on producing the same output that he just happens to produce. This belief is absolutely unfounded because in fact each seller regularly adjusts his output, whenever the situation changes, in order to maximize his profits as he sees them in the light of his erroneous belief about the other seller's policy. No experience to the contrary will shake this belief; each will adhere to it religiously and make his own decisions—concerning his output volume—on that basis.[7]

(3) The two sellers, so ill-informed about each other's policy, are astoundingly well informed about the aggregate demand in the

---

[7] Justifying this assumption about the rather stupid beliefs of the two sellers about each other, Cournot said merely that "men cannot be supposed to be free from error and lack of forethought." *Researches*, p. 83.

market. Not only the omniscient economists know this demand schedule,—the two sellers know it also. This might be considered as a rather queer coincidence, because one cannot even say that they may have learned about the demand schedule by a trial-and-error method of output changes. For if they could learn by trial and error the exact reactions of the buyers in the market to the changes in output and the associated price changes, they surely could learn also each other's correct reactions to these changes. But since knowledge of the correct demand schedule is essential for Cournot's solution, we shall accept the assumption as "given" and shall not pause any longer to worry about it.

(4) The two sellers produce and sell a perfectly homogeneous product, in no way differentiated.

(5) The productive capacity of the two producers is not so limited as to influence their decisions. Each seller could actually produce any output that he might be interested in supplying.

(6) The two producers operate under similar cost conditions. The shape of the cost function is not relevant for the argument.[8] Each producer knows his own cost function thoroughly. For the sake of arithmetic simplicity we shall assume that both producers operate under constant cost for any output within the relevant range, in the amount of $0.10 per unit.

In order to simplify our arithmetic still further we are making two additional assumptions which are not relevant for the problem: that the smallest amount by which output can be changed is 10,000 units a week, and that a producer finding two alternative output volumes equally profitable will prefer to produce the smaller one.

We begin with a position of disequilibrium, be it that the demand had previously been different and has just become as in the assumed schedule, be it that the production cost had been much higher and has just been reduced to the assumed level, be it that the sellers had previously been misinformed about the market demand, or be it that they have been asleep and are just waking up to see whether there is anything to be done to improve their

---

[8] Cournot started his exposition with assuming the cost to be zero, but soon proceeded to the assumption of separate cost functions for each producer. *Op. cit.*, p. 85.

business. Each has been producing a weekly output of 250,000 units, which in the market as assumed in the schedule sells at $0.80 per unit. We start with A waking up to the fact that he could do better than he has been doing.

Period 1: Believing that B would go on producing 250,000 units regardless of what he himself might do, A sees the following possibilities:

My output	B's output	Total output	Market price	My total revenue	My total cost	My profit
250,000	250,000	500,000	.80	$200,000	$25,000	$175,000
300,000	250,000	550,000	.75	225,000	30,000	195,000
350,000	250,000	600,000	.70	245,000	35,000	210,000
400,000	250,000	650,000	.65	260,000	40,000	220,000
450,000	250,000	700,000	.60	270,000	45,000	225,000
460,000	250,000	710,000	.59	271,400	46,000	225,400
470,000	250,000	720,000	.58	272,600	47,000	**225,600**
480,000	250,000	730,000	.57	273,600	48,000	225,600
490,000	250,000	740,000	.56	274,400	49,000	225,400
500,000	250,000	750,000	.55	275,000	50,000	225,000
550,000	250,000	800,000	.50	275,000	55,000	220,000

Deciding in favor of the most profitable volume, A increases his output to 470,000 units. The total supply of 720,000 is absorbed by the market with a price decline to $0.58.

Period 2: Now B wakes up to the situation. Believing that A would go on producing 470,000 units regardless of what himself might do, B sees the following possibilities:

My output	A's output	Total output	Market price	My total revenue	My total cost	My profit
250,000	470,000	720,000	.58	$145,000	$25,000	$120,000
300,000	470,000	770,000	.53	159,000	30,000	129,000
350,000	470,000	820,000	.48	168,000	35,000	133,000
360,000	470,000	830,000	.47	169,200	36,000	**133,200**
370,000	470,000	840,000	.46	170,200	37,000	133,200
380,000	470,000	850,000	.45	171,000	38,000	133,000
400,000	470,000	870,000	.43	172,000	40,000	132,000
450,000	470,000	920,000	.38	171,000	45,000	126,000
470,000	470,000	940,000	.36	169,200	47,000	122,200

Deciding in favor of the optimal position, B increases his output to 360,000 units. Total supply is now 830,000 and the market price declines to $0.47.

Period 3: This change of the situation for A causes him to reconsider his last decision. Believing that B would go on producing 360,000 units regardless of what he himself might do, A canvasses the following apparent possibilities:

My output	B's output	Total output	Market price	My total revenue	My total cost	My profit
350,000	360,000	710,000	.59	$206,500	$35,000	$171,500
400,000	360,000	760,000	.54	216,000	40,000	176,000
410,000	360,000	770,000	.53	217,300	41,000	176,300
420,000	360,000	780,000	.52	218,400	42,000	**176,400**
430,000	360,000	790,000	.51	219,300	43,000	176,300
440,000	360,000	800,000	.50	220,000	44,000	176,000
450,000	360,000	810,000	.49	220,500	45,000	175,500
470,000	360,000	830,000	.47	220,900	47,000	173,900

Deciding in favor of the output that looks best to him, A reduces his production from 470,000 to 420,000 units. Total supply, therefore, is down to 780,000 and the market price rises from $0.47 to $0.52.

Period 4: Now B will reconsider his situation. Believing that A would go on producing 420,000 units regardless of what he himself might do, B compares the following possibilities:

My output	A's output	Total output	Market price	My total revenue	My total cost	My profit
350,000	420,000	770,000	.53	$185,500	$35,000	$150,500
360,000	420,000	780,000	.52	187,200	36,000	151,200
370,000	420,000	790,000	.51	188,700	37,000	151,700
380,000	420,000	800,000	.50	190,000	38,000	152,000
390,000	420,000	810,000	.49	191,100	39,000	**152,100**
400,000	420,000	820,000	.48	192,000	40,000	152,000
410,000	420,000	830,000	.47	192,700	41,000	151,700
420,000	420,000	840,000	.46	193,200	42,000	151,200

Deciding in favor of the volume which promises the greatest profit, B increases his output from 360,000 to 390,000 units. This raises total supply to 810,000 units and lowers the market price from $0.52 to $0.49.

Period 5: This change in the situation makes A think over the possibilities that are open to him. Believing that B would go on producing 390,000 units regardless of what he himself might do, A is confronted with these possibilities:

My output	B's output	Total output	Market price	My total revenue	My total cost	My profit
370,000	390,000	760,000	.54	$199,800	$37,000	$162,800
380,000	390,000	770,000	.53	201,400	38,000	163,400
390,000	390,000	780,000	.52	202,800	39,000	163,800
400,000	390,000	790,000	.51	204,000	40,000	**164,000**
410,000	390,000	800,000	.50	205,000	41,000	164,000
420,000	390,000	810,000	.49	205,800	42,000	163,800

Since the profit at his previous output of 420,000 units is not only smaller than it was before but also a little smaller than the profit at reduced production, A decides to cut his production to 400,000 units. This reduces total supply to 790,000 units, which sell in the market at a price of $0.51.

Period 6: B is now checking whether his production should be adjusted. Believing that A would go on producing 400,000 regardless of what he himself might do, B sees the following possibilities:

My output	A's output	Total output	Market price	My total revenue	My total cost	My profit
380,000	400,000	780,000	.52	$197,600	$38,000	$159,600
390,000	400,000	790,000	.51	198,900	39,000	159,900
400,000	400,000	800,000	.50	200,000	40,000	**160,000**
410,000	400,000	810,000	.49	200,900	41,000	159,900
420,000	400,000	820,000	.48	201,600	42,000	159,600

B realizes that an increase in his production seems warranted and he raises his output from 390,000 units to 400,000. This brings total supply in the market to 800,000 units and the price to $0.50.

Period 7: This is a slight change in A's position. But when he re-examines his possibilities, he finds that, although his profit is again less than before, he could not make more profit if he changed his output. The output which he has been producing is still the most profitable one and he continues to produce 400,000 units. (Thus, for once, B's belief that A would not change his output has proved correct!)

An equilibrium has been attained. Each of the producers makes half of the total market supply and neither of them has a desire to change it. Their combined output—800,000 units—is exactly two-thirds of the competitive output—1,200,000 units—the output at which the market price would be equal to the unit cost of production.[9]

The Bertrand Model

The Bertrand Model differs in several of the basic assumptions from the Cournot model.

(1) The competitors do not—as in Cournot—sell what they produce, but they produce what they sell. That is to say, they do not first decide on their output and then have to take whatever price can be got in the market, but they first name a price and then fill all the orders they receive.

(2) Speculation, hedging, advance orders, postponed deliveries are all excluded from the model. The sellers do not—as in Cournot—entertain any beliefs about fixed outputs produced by the competitor, but they have similarly erroneous and incorrigible beliefs about fixed prices charged by the competitor. In other words, each believes that, regardless of his own actions and their effects on the rival's business, the rival would go on charging the same price that he just happens to charge.

[9] This result can be generalized for all cases in which the demand function is linear and average cost is constant. In such cases the monopoly output will always be $\frac{1}{2}$, and the duopoly output $2 \times \frac{1}{3}$, i.e., $\frac{2}{3}$, of the competitive output. A similar generalization can be made for the price. Let us call "prohibitive price" the price at which the quantity in the linear demand function becomes zero; let us call "prohibitive net price" the excess of the prohibitive price over the average cost; likewise, let us call "monopoly net price" and "duopoly net price" the excess of monopoly price and duopoly price, respectively, over the (constant) average cost. Then we may state that—with a linear demand function—the monopoly net price will be $\frac{1}{2}$, and the duopoly net price $\frac{1}{3}$, of the prohibitive net price. In our illustration the prohibitive price is $1.30; the prohibitive net price $1.20; the monopoly net price $0.60, and the duopoly net price $0.40. Hence, the monopoly price is $0.70 and the duopoly price $0.50.

(3) It is not of the essence—as in Cournot—that the sellers "know" the "correct" demand schedule or have an identical notion about the market demand for their product. It is not even necessary for them to know that more can be sold at lower prices, for what matters really is that each knows he can conquer the whole market if he undercuts his competitor.

Other assumptions for the Bertrand model are the same as for the Cournot model (although their implications may be different). This goes particularly for the following:

(4) The product of the two sellers is homogeneous and not differentiated in any way. Thus, if one seller undercuts the other, he can attract the entire business of the latter. If both sellers charge the same price, buyers will pair themselves at random and each seller will serve half of the total market demand.

(5) The productive capacity of both producers is practically —that is, in the range of their practical considerations—unlimited.

(6) The cost conditions of both producers are identical; each knows his own cost. Both producers operate under constant (or decreasing) marginal cost. For our illustration we assume again that the cost is constant, at $0.10 per unit.

We begin with a situation analogous to the one prevailing at the beginning of the Cournot illustration: each producer has been charging $0.80 per unit and has been selling 250,000 units.

Period 1: A wakes up to the knowledge that he could do better than he has been doing. He finds that it would be most profitable to increase sales by cutting the price. Believing that B would go on charging $0.80 regardless of what he himself might do, A decides to cut his price to $0.70. The effect on his sales appears to be satisfactory: apart from the greater quantity—100,000 units—which the market absorbs at the lower price, A is getting all of B's business.

Period 2: As he is about to lose his entire business, B finds it imperative to reduce his price. Believing that A would go on charging $0.70 regardless of what he himself might do, B decides to cut his price to $0.69, at which we can attract all of A's business.[10]

[10] There was a reason for A, in the first period, to undercut B by ten cents and for B now to undercut only by one cent. The elasticity of demand was so high between $0.80 and $0.70 that the price cut would pay even for a

Period 3: Now A has to act if he wishes to stay in business. Believing that B would go on charging $0.69, regardless of his own price actions, A compares two alternatives: to cut by one cent in order to match B's price of $0.69—which would secure him half of the market—or to cut by two cents, that is, one cent below B's price—which would secure him the entire market. There is no doubt that the latter looks much more profitable, and thus A cuts his price to $0.68.

Period 4: B, of course, cannot afford to maintain his price. He might match A's price or underbid. Since he believes A would surely continue to charge $0.68, B cuts to $0.67.

Periods 5 to 60: Since each seller remains unshaken in his belief that, no matter what he does, his competitor will neither retaliate nor be at all influenced in his pricing, the price war will not stop until price reaches the floor: the cost of production. If the sellers thought that their competitor had higher costs or less financial stamina, they might temporarily even sell below marginal cost. But we shall assume that such thoughts are absent from our duopolists' thinking. By their mutual undercutting they had not intended to kill the rival, but only to get all his business. (The implication must have been that the rival would not mind losing his entire business, for otherwise he could not have been expected to maintain his price after being undercut.)

Period 61: B's price cut to $0.11 is depriving A of all his business. Hence A decides to cut his price to $0.10.

Period 62: At his price of $0.11, B would make no sales; at a price of $0.09 he could gain the entire market, but he would lose money; at a price of $0.10, the same as charged by A, B could get half of the market and cover all his costs. This is clearly his best bet. Thus, he cuts his price also to $0.10 and this time, for once, his belief that A would go on charging the same price regardless of B's price cut turns out to be fully correct.

Both producers are now selling at $0.10—their unit cost of

---

monopolist. $0.70 would be the perfect monopoly price. Below $0.70, however, the marginal revenue of a monopolistic seller would be smaller than the assumed marginal cost of ten cents: the expansion of sales from 600,000 to 610,000 units would increase revenue by only 9 cents per unit. Hence, the duopolist will cut his price as little as possible, just enough to conquer the market.

production—each producing 600,000 units. Neither of them wishes to cut the price further, because he would lose money on every part of his business. And neither of them dares to raise his price, because—believing that the other would go on charging the low price and would be capable of serving the whole market—he must fear losing his entire business. Thus, equilibrium has been attained.

The equilibrium output—1,200,000—the combined output of the two duopolists which neither of them has a desire to change, is exactly equal to the competitive output, the output at which the market price is equal to the unit cost of production.

The Edgeworth Model

The chief difference between the Edgeworth model and the Bertrand model lies in the assumption concerning the productive capacity of the two producers. In the Bertrand model each producer had virtually unlimited capacity to produce: he could take any amount of business and, likewise, he knew that his competitor could take any amount of business. In the Edgeworth model the capacity of each producer is limited such that neither producer can satisfy the entire market at the lower price ranges. Thus, neither of them would try to get more business than he could take and neither would fear that he lose all his business to a rival whose productive capacity was already fully, or almost fully, utilized.

The chief similarity between the Edgeworth and Bertrand models lies in the price-making mechanism and in the pricing policies. In both models prices are set by the sellers, they do not emerge through "competitive bidding" by the mass of buyers, and in both models each seller adheres to the firm belief—unshaken by any experience to the contrary—that his rival will stick to the announced price no matter what he himself might do and how this might affect the rival's sales.

We shall list the essential assumptions for the Edgeworth model in the same order as for the Cournot and Bertrand models:

(1) Each competitor announces his selling price, but he does not—as in Bertrand—accept any amount of business that should

be obtainable at that price; he accepts only as many orders as he can fill. As in Cournot and in Bertrand, there is no accumulation of inventories, no selling from inventories, no postponing of delivery, no advance selling for future delivery.

(2) Each competitor believes that, regardless of his own price changes and their effects upon the rival's business, the rival would maintain his price as announced, though not for any amount of orders, but only for such amounts as he can fill with his given productive capacity.

(3) It is not of the essence that both competitors "know" the demand schedule nor that their conjectures about the market demand are identical. But it simplifies the operation of the model if such an assumption is made, and it is herewith made for our demonstration.

(4) It is not essential for the products of the two competitors to be perfectly homogeneous. It does not affect the working of the model whether products are assumed to be completely alike or moderately differentiated—provided, however, that the smallest price differential is sufficient to switch an appreciable proportion of all customers from the higher-priced to the lower-priced product. For our illustration we shall assume that whatever preference any consumer should have for one of the producers or products can be completely overcome by a price differential of one cent.[11] Each seller anticipates that consumers will react to price changes by switching to the lower-priced product just as fast as they will react to price reductions by buying larger quantities.[12] The exact

[11] It can be shown that the outcome is almost the same if it is assumed that a producer, by slightly undercutting his rival, can attract only a fraction of the latter's customers. This was demonstrated by A. J. Nichol who, assuming that a price differential of one cent would switch *one-sixth* of the total amount demanded, obtained results very little different from those he got when he assumed that *all* customers switch. *Economic Journal*, Vol. XLV (1935), p. 63.

[12] It is not relevant to the problem whether or not these anticipations are correct, that is, whether consumers "in reality" react to changed prices with equal speed by transferring as by expanding and contracting their purchases. The sellers' anticipations is all that is needed for our present purposes.—The question of the comparative speed of the two kinds of buyer reaction was first discussed by F. Zeuthen, *Problems of Monopoly and Economic Warfare* (London: Routledge, 1930), p. 41. George Stigler—*op. cit.*, p. 526.—included equal speed of these reactions among the assumptions necessary for the Cournot model to which, however, it can hardly apply. For, in a market

distribution of buyers between the two producers when they charge the same price is not relevant for the outcome. For example, the inertia of customers may be just enough to make them stay with the seller from whom they have been buying until the other seller announces a lower price. Or the buyers may be so indifferent as to their source of supply that at equal prices they will buy at random, so that each seller can serve half of the total market demand. Although it makes no difference for the outcome, we shall for our illustration assume that sellers expect equal distribution of buyers when they charge equal prices.

(5) The productive capacity of each of the producers is fixed and its limits are within the range of outputs relevant for the producer's decisions. For the illustration chosen to demonstrate the operation of the model we shall assume that each firm has a capacity to produce 600,000 units a week.

(6) The cost conditions of both producers need not be identical but must be similar. Each producer knows his own cost and also his competitor's. Although the limitations of productive capacity would make it more reasonable to assume a U-shaped cost curve, we shall for the sake of simpler arithmetic again assume that the unit cost is constant—$0.10 per unit—up to an output volume of 600,000 units per week, and infinite for anything beyond this, which is another way of saying that output cannot be increased beyond that volume.[13]

---

organized in the way assumed for the Cournot model, the sellers have no "customers" whom they can lose, hold, or gain, and there are no seller-customer relationships of which either party is conscious. Sellers and buyers remain virtually anonymous, as they do, for example, in the New York Stock Exchange, where buyers hardly ever take notice of who the seller is from whom they are buying.

[13] The assumption of constant average cost of production implies either that the firm has no fixed overhead costs or that such costs are disregarded, and only variable costs considered, in the calculation of profit (or, more correctly, of quasi-rent). Edgeworth assumed zero cost up to capacity production and infinite cost from that point on. Cf. *Papers Relating to Political Economy*, Vol. I, p. 118. In a later note, on "The Mathematical Economics of Professor Amoroso," *Economic Journal*, Vol. XXXII (1922), pp. 400–407, Edgeworth accepted the assumptions of increasing cost which Luigi Amoroso had made in his *Lezioni di Economia Matematica* (Bologna: Zanichelli, 1921), but this did not change the outcome.

(7) An assumption, which had no equivalent in the Cournot and Bertrand models, must be made for the Edgeworth model, concerning the distribution of buyers among the sellers when prices are not equal and the low-price seller cannot satisfy the whole effective demand. It is easy to understand that a consumer who cannot get delivery from the cheaper source will turn to the more expensive one. But the aggregate quantity demanded is not immediately known from the assumed market demand schedule when some buyers are served at a lower price, others at a higher price. If the poorer or less eager buyers were steered to the cheaper seller, and the more eager ones to the high-price seller, total sales would be greater than if buyers happened to be grouped differently. This difficulty is avoided by the assumption that consumers are approximately alike in their desire for the product and in their ability to pay for it. If we assume for our illustration that there are altogether 1000 quasi-uniform consumers of the product, we shall know from the total market demand schedule the demand per consumer. This will permit us—and each of our sellers—to figure out how many buyers the low-price seller is able to serve before he is sold out and how many, therefore, will depend on the other source of supply. The total demand which these still unserved customers will have at various prices can then be easily calculated.[14]

We shall begin again with the disequilibrium situation where each producer charges $0.80 per unit and sells 250,000 units per week. For a number of steps the process will be the same as in the Bertrand model.

Period 1: A wakes up to the fact that he could do much better. Believing that B would stick to his price of $0.80 regardless of what he himself might do, he reasons that a price cut by 10 cents would allow him to increase his sales from 250,000 units to the

---

[14] These were Edgeworth's explicit assumptions. He assumed "the demand-curve [to] be the same for every consumer" (*Papers*, p. 118) and the low-price seller to serve the first customers "on a queue" until he is sold out (p. 120). A. J. Nichol argued that it was not necessary to assume all individual demands to be alike for, "in accordance with the law of large numbers, the total demand of each group tends to have the same general characteristics as the demand of the whole body of buyers, and in particular the same elasticity." *Op. cit.*, p. 56.

600,000 units which constitute his capacity output. He proceeds to do so.

Period 2: As he is about to lose his entire business, B finds it imperative to cut his selling price. Believing that A would not change his price of $0.70 regardless of what he himself might do, he finds that a price cut to $0.69 would secure him orders for his full capacity production. He announces this price cut.

Period 3: It is A's turn to take action. If he cuts his price to match B's, he can get half the market—sales of 305,000 units; if he cuts by one cent more, he can sell all the 600,000 that he can produce. Of course, he cuts to $0.68.

Period 4: A's price cut did not take all of B's business, but almost all: it left him with 33 customers, buying a little over 20,000 units. Believing that A would stick to the price of $0.68, B cuts to $0.67 and secures orders for his capacity output.

Periods 5 to 31: The price cutting goes on in much the same fashion. On the (erroneous) assumption that the rival would not react to a price cut, a price cut always looks as if it were the most profitable move to make. In Period 31, it is A who cuts his price to $0.40.

Period 32: We stop to look, not because the price cutting is to come to an end, but merely because we wish to examine the type of considerations on the basis of which the price cutting is continuing. The seller is not faced with a comparison between *no* business and *all* the business—as he was in the Bertrand model—but with a comparison between the business left over by the rival and the business he can handle. Thus, B realizes that A cannot serve the entire market,—total demand being for 900,000 units at a price of $0.40, while 600,000 is his capacity output. This means that A can serve only 667 customers, each buying 900 units; and that 333 customers are left for B and could be charged as high a price as B should find profitable to charge. Besides the choice of charging a monopoly price to the customers who depend entirely on his supply, B has two other choices: to match A's price and get a sales volume of half the demand, 450,000 units, or to undercut A and sell his capacity output, 600,000 units. As always, B believes that A would in any case stick to his current price of $0.40. How do his possibilities compare? This is how they look to B:

My price	Demand per customer	Number of customers	Sales	Total revenue	Total cost	Profits
.75	550	333	183,150	$137,362	$18,315	$119,047
.70	600	333	199,800	139,860	19,980	119,880
.65	650	333	216,450	140,692	21,645	119,047
.60	700	333	233,100	139,860	23,310	116,550
.55	750	333	249,750	137,362	24,975	112,387
.50	800	333	266,400	133,200	26,640	106,560
.45	850	333	283,050	127,372	28,305	99,067
.40	900	500	450,000	180,000	45,000	135,000
.39		capacity	600,000	234,000	60,000	**174,000**

It is quite obvious that the profits at even the best monopoly price—$0.70—compare rather poorly with the advantage of under-bidding A's price. Thus B cuts his price to $0.39.

Periods 33 to 37: The downward dance of the prices continues. In Period 37, A cuts his price to $0.34.

Period 38: Again we pause to make a check on the thought process by which B decides how he had best adjust himself to A's new price announcement of $0.34. As usual, he takes it for granted that this price will not be affected by any move on his part. At this price 960 units are demanded per customer; hence, A with his maximum production of 600,000 units can serve only 625 customers and the other 375 must buy from B. B could charge them any price between $0.35 and $1.29. Or he could match A's price of $0.34 and get a half-share of the market. Or, again, he could underbid A's price and sell his full capacity output. Comparing the expected results of these possibilities, B calculates like this:

My price	Demand per customer	Number of customers	Sales	Total revenue	Total cost	Profits
.71	590	375	221,250	$157,087	$22,125	$134,962
.70	600	375	225,000	157,500	22,500	135,000
.69	610	375	228,750	157,837	22,875	134,962
.60	700	375	262,500	157,500	26,250	131,250
.50	800	375	300,000	150,000	30,000	120,000
.40	900	375	337,500	135,000	33,750	101,250
.35	950	375	356,250	124,687	35,625	89,062
.34	960	500	480,000	163,200	48,000	115,200
.33		capacity	600,000	198,000	60,000	**138,000**

The margin between profits obtainable from charging a monopoly price to the customers not served by the competitor and profits obtainable from undercutting the competitor is getting closer. But the price cut is still preferable and B decides to cut his price to $0.33.

Period 39: Now A must reconsider his situation. Should he share the market by matching B's new price of $0.33? Should he secure orders for his full capacity output by cutting his price to $0.32? Or should he charge what the traffic will bear in the part of the market which B fails to serve? At B's price of $0.33 there is a demand for 970 units per customer. Only 618 customers, therefore, can place their orders with B before his production is sold out. The remaining 382 customers depend entirely on A. Believing that B's price of $0.33 will not be affected by his decision, A compares the following possibilities:

My price	Demand per customer	Number of customers	Sales	Total revenue	Total cost	Profits
.71	590	382	225,380	$160,019	$22,538	$137,481
.70	600	382	229,200	160,440	22,920	**137,520**
.69	610	382	233,020	160,783	23,302	137,481
.34	960	382	366,720	124,684	36,672	88,012
.33	970	485	470,450	155,248	47,045	108,203
.32		capacity	600,000	192,000	60,000	132,000

This time the decision will be against price cutting. There is a clear advantage in raising the price to the monopoly level. A boosts his price from $0.34 to $0.70.

Period 40: There is no doubt in B's mind about the desirability of a strong price boost on his part. The same 600,000 that he sells at a price of $0.33 he could sell also at a price of $0.69, which is one cent below A's price. At a price of $0.71 he could not sell a single unit of product. To match A's price of $0.70 and share the market with him is only about half as good as selling his capacity output at the highest price just below that of his rival. Thus B raises his price from $0.33 to $0.69.

Period 41: We are back where we were in Period 3, and A is faced with exactly the same situation. Since he makes exactly the same assumptions, he arrives also at the same decision and cuts his price to $0.68.

Period 42: A repetition of Period 4. B cuts to $0.67.

Periods 43 to 75: A repetition of Periods 5 to 37, ending with A cutting his price to $0.34.

Period 76: Just as in Period 38, B cuts his price to $0.33.

Period 77: Repeating his performance of Period 39, A raises his price to $0.70.

Period 78: As he had done in Period 40, B raises his price to $0.69.

Period 79: We are back again where we were in Periods 3 and 41, and we are embarking on more and more round-trips of the same sort.

There will be no equilibrium price nor an equilibrium output as long as our two producers adhere to their delusions about each other's reactions and as long as the other conditions hold as assumed. The price will oscillate in this queer fashion—gradually downwards, upwards in a jump—between a ceiling ($0.70), which is at the level of the perfect monopoly price, and a floor ($0.33), which is higher than the perfectly competitive price ($0.10). The combined supply by the duopolist producers will oscillate between a minimum (610,200 units) which is just a trifle larger than the perfect monopoly output (600,000 units) and a maximum (966,720 units) which is smaller than the competitive output (1,200,000 units).[15]

Only changes in our assumptions would alter the amplitude of the oscillations or end their continual repetition. "And so the system may dance down" and then again jump back, and "so perpetual motion is set up."[16]

COMPARISONS OF THE CLASSICAL MODELS

Now that we have seen how the three models work, let us compare the various solutions by recapitulating the prices and quantities arrived at in our illustrations.

[15] The minimum output is that of Period 3 or 41, before A cuts the price to $0.68, with B selling 600,000 units at $0.69 and A only 10,200 at $0.70. The maximum output is that of Period 39 or 77, before A raises the price to $0.70, with B selling 600,000 units at $0.33 and A 366,720 at $0.34.

[16] F. Y. Edgeworth, *op. cit.,* p. 121.

Prices and Production

	Price	Output
Perfect monopoly:	$0.70	600,000 units
Cournot duopoly:	0.50	800,000 "
Edgeworth duopoly: Oscillating between	0.70	610,200 "
and	0.33	966,720 "
Bertrand duopoly:	0.10	1,200,000 "
Perfect polypoly:	0.10	1,200,000 "

All three duopoly models yielded lower prices and larger outputs than would result from perfect monopoly. But it must be
borne in mind, not only that all these were models of uncoordinated duopoly—duopoly free from collusive actions and even of
cooperative attitudes—but also that they were based on patently
erroneous beliefs on the part of each seller with respect to the
policies of his rival. The consuming public would have to thank
these erroneous beliefs for being served larger quantities at lower
prices. Indeed, under the Bertrand duopoly the consumers fared
no worse than they would under perfect polypoly. The Cournot
result of a duopoly output exactly two-thirds of the competitive
output can, by mathematical reasoning, be shown to be the general solution for linear demand and constant cost.[17] The Edgeworth
result of oscillations in price and output can likewise be shown to
be general, but the exact upper and lower limits will depend on
the shapes of the demand and cost functions, where the latter is
understood to express the limits imposed by the given capacities
of the productive apparatus.

Expected Reactions of Rival

What we have called here the "erroneous beliefs" of the sellers
concerning their rival's reactions is sometimes called a "conjec-

[17] See above footnote 9 on p. 377. If the Cournot model is extended to
triopoly, the equilibrium output can be shown to be three-fourths of the competitive output. If n is the number of competitors, the undifferentiated oligopoly output produced under the Cournot assumptions will be $\dfrac{n}{n+1}$ of the
undifferentiated polypoly output. See Cournot, *op. cit.*, pp. 84 ff.

tural variation of zero," meaning that each seller believes or conjectures the variations in the rival's determination of his output
or price in reaction to his own variations to be zero.[18] "How and by
how much will my rival vary his output (price, quality, selling
effort, etc.) if I make a certain change in my output (price, quality, selling effort, etc.)?" This sort of question the oligopolist asks
himself before he decides about a change in one of these variables.
The answer he gives himself is his "conjecture" about the rival's
"variation" (adjustment, countermove) in response to his move. In
the Cournot model all conjectural variations refer to output. In
the Bertrand and Edgeworth models they refer to price. But in all
three models they are zero—because it is a zero variation which
each seller in stubborn regularity expects from his rival.

One might raise the objection that a conjectural variation of
zero makes the sellers in question ineligible for the title of duopolists or oligopolists, because according to our definition the
criterion of oligopoly was the state of mind of a seller concerned
about the possible reactions of his competitors. The sellers in the
three classical models seemed singularly unconcerned. They all
thought they had nothing to worry about, inasmuch as their competitor was not going to react at all to their moves. It is no doubt
possible to sustain this objection and to say that our classical
"oligopolists" behaved non-oligopolistically, and therefore were
not oligopolists, although they "should" have behaved very oligopolistically indeed. On the other hand it is perfectly legitimate to
overrule the objection and to say that the sellers in our models did
think things over and were concerned about their rival's possible
reaction—only that they were so hopelessly befuddled as to come
to the conclusion that the reactive variation (of output or price,
respectively) would be zero.

Own Reactions to Rival

The schedule of variations or adjustments which one seller
makes in reaction to variations or adjustments made by his competitor is often graphically represented by so-called reaction curves.

[18] See William Fellner, *op. cit.*, pp. 71 ff. The expression goes back to
Ragnar Frisch.

These curves refer not to the reaction expected of the competitor, but to the seller's reactions *to* the competitor's moves. Depending on which of the variables are subject to the adjusting variations, one speaks of price-reaction curves or output-reaction curves. For example, the output reaction curve of seller A in the Cournot model shows for each output of seller B the output A would decide to produce and put on the market; the output-reaction curve of seller B shows for each output of A the output B would decide to offer. These reaction curves and their intersection, if they do intersect, are meaningful aids in tracing the process of gradual adjustment leading to an equilibrium position—but only as long as there is no conjectural interdependence. If A discovered B's reaction curve and B also discovered A's, the curves would become inconsistent with each other.

The question of "leadership" in price or output variations is often raised in this connection. Our duopolists in all three models expect their competitor *not* to respond to their actions; they expect him neither to match their own variations nor to react in any other way. In other words, they expect him not to be a follower, but to make all his determinations independently of their moves. Thus, each expects the other to be a leader. On the other hand, each seller does in fact make adjustments to the changes in the situation that are caused by their competitor's actions. That is to say, each seller behaves as a follower. (Perhaps it should be stated that a "follower" in this sense need not match or imitate the leader's moves; the essential point is that he acts in reaction to them.) Thus, we find in the three classical models the peculiar constellation that each seller regularly acts as a follower, yet expects his competitor to be not a follower but a leader. This "symmetrical" striving for the position as follower, and the "symmetrical" imputation of the leadership position to the other seller are characteristic for the Cournot, Bertrand, and Edgeworth models.[19] It

[19] This was most strongly emphasized by Heinrich v. Stackelberg, *Marktform und Gleichgewicht* (Vienna: Springer, 1934), pp. 16–24, and was immediately accepted by most writers. For an exception see A. J. Nichol, *op. cit.*, p. 54, who described the Edgeworth process as one in which the leadership position was continually passing back and forth between the two sellers. Nichol gave the title "leader" to any seller taking a new action, even one de-

may be mentioned that these "symmetrical solutions" of the duopoly problem are now commonly rejected in favor of "asymmetrical solutions." [20]

Symmetry prevails in the classical models not only with regard to the sellers' attitudes, conjectures, and policies but also with
regard to their productive capacity and cost of production. Differences in capacity and cost would probably be forceful factors in
the removal of the inconsistent symmetry in the sellers' attitudes.
Inconsistent it is to the extreme. For it is clearly impossible for two
people continually to think that the *other* is the leader whom he
is following.[21] The inconsistency of the symmetry assumption is
not one in *logic*. For we have seen that the models can "work"
once the assumption is made, even if it is not easy to accept it in
the first place and to base on it, for the Cournot and Bertrand
solutions, an assertion of stability of the equilibrium attained. The
real inconsistency of the symmetry assumption is with our *experience*, which makes it difficult for us to imagine sensible people
sticking imperviously to delusions which are obviously exposed at
every step they make.

Summary of Comparisons

The following tabulation summarizes the similarities and differences between the three classical duopoly models:

---

scribed as an "adjustment." This does not appear to be a felicitous use of the
term.

[20] See especially Stackelberg, *op. cit.* Also R. F. Kahn, "The Problem of
Duopoly" *Economic Journal*, Vol. XLVII (1937), who stated (p. 10): "Asymmetry is the most obvious characteristic of the unique position of duopoly
equilibrium" to which his article was devoted. For a defense of a symmetrical
solution see Wassily Leontief, "Stackelberg on Monopolistic Competition,"
Journal of Political Economy, Vol. XLIV (1936), pp. 554–59.

[21] It reminds one of the old joke about the two drunks in an automobile,
each assuming that the other was doing the steering.

	Cournot	Bertrand	Edgeworth
"Variable" directly administered by each seller	output	price	price
"Variable" subject to conjectural variation	output	price	price
Degree of conjectural variation	zero	zero	zero
Attitude toward leadership and followership	symmetrical propensity to follow	symmetrical propensity to follow	symmetrical propensity to follow
Knowledge of aggregate demand	perfect knowledge	no accurate or identical knowledge required	no accurate or identical knowledge required
Productive capacities within the range of practical consideration	ample	ample	limited
Relative cost conditions	similar	identical	similar
Knowledge of competitor's cost conditions	not necessary	not necessary	necessary
Homogeneity of product	undifferentiated	undifferentiated	slight differentiation allowed
Uniformity of prices at which transactions take place	uniform	uniform	not uniform
Distribution of buyers at uniform prices	according to output produced	evenly divided	not relevant
Ultimate equilibrium position	stable	stable	oscillations
Output ratio to competitive output	⅔	1	oscillating between more than ½ and less than 1

Uniformity of Market Prices

Some comments are called for on the question of uniformity of prices in the market, because many confused ideas on this question have gained wide currency. I do not refer here to the arguments in legal proceedings as to whether price uniformity is a sign of competition or, instead, of collusion.[22] The issue relevant in our present discussion concerns the relationship between product differentiation and price uniformity, especially the question whether it is possible for two different prices to exist simultaneously in the market for a perfectly homogeneous product.

In the Cournot model there was naturally only one price in the market at any one time, because only one price was determined through the competitive bidding by a mass of buyers for the combined and undifferentiated output of the two producers. In the Bertrand model, where the producers named their prices, the announced prices were never identical during the 61 periods of downward bidding. But the existence of two different price quotations need not mean that buyers actually paid different prices; probably no transactions took place at the higher price. If the market is perfect, and the sellers and their products are not differentiated in any way, no sales will be made at the higher of two prices quoted by competing sellers, provided the seller quoting the lower price accepts orders from all comers and for any amounts. The assumption of a perfect market ruling out frictions of any sort was not stated above and thus it was left to the reader to decide whether the sales by one of the producers stopped abruptly and completely as soon as he was undercut by the other, or whether his sales merely dwindled and came to a gradual stop. But, for all practical purposes, transactions in the Bertrand model were only at the lowest quoted price, which therefore may be regarded as the only effective price in the market.

Not so in the Edgeworth model. Here the producer quoting the

[22] The presumption is that identical price quotations by several competing sellers are the result of overt or tacit collusion. For a discussion of this question see Fritz Machlup, *The Basing-Point System* (Philadelphia: Blakiston, 1949), pp. 95–99.

lower price did not accept orders for any amount of output, because his limited capacity would not permit him to do so. Would-be
buyers not served by him turned to the other source of supply and
placed their orders at a higher price. Hence, transactions took place
at two different prices at the same time. Our assumption allowed
for a moderate differentiation of the products, but this assumption
was not made with an eye to the two-price system; indeed, it would
not suffice to explain its existence since a proviso was made to the
effect that consumers' preferences for one product or the other
were not great enough to sustain a price differential. Is it then permissible to postulate that two different prices will be paid at the
same time for a practically homogeneous product?

There is of course the well known phenomenon of price discrimination in the sale of a homogeneous product. But price discrimination presupposes some sort of separability of the market,
either by different categories of buyers or by different qualities of
product. Where neither the product nor the buyers are differentiated, the coexistence of two prices in one market cannot be explained as an instance of conscious price discrimination.

An objection has been made to the effect that the producer
selling at the lower price is acting contrary to the economic postulate that all firms attempt to maximize their profits—for, if the same
product can be sold at a higher price, he would be able to increase
his profits by raising his price. This just is not so in the case before
us. Assuming that the rival will maintain his higher price, the low-
price seller is unquestionably maximizing his profit by selling more
cheaply. Only in this way can he sell his full capacity production;
if he matched the higher price of his competitor he would have to
be satisfied with the smaller sales volume which a half-share in the
market would give him. Under the assumptions of the Edgeworth
model, in nearly all phases of the process, it is not the low-price
seller but the high-price seller who is failing to maximize his profit.
And he quickly realizes this and attempts to correct the situation by
getting into the position of being the low-price seller himself. Indeed, with the exception of one short phase—Periods 39 and 40—
the Edgeworth process may be characterized as a struggle for the
position of the seller selling at the lower price, a struggle which

has the result that at any time two prices will coexist while both producers are active in the market.[23]

Another argument against the theoretical admissibility of the coexistence of two different prices for a homogeneous product has recourse to arbitrage activities of dealers. These dealers would always buy from the cheaper source and could profitably serve the potential customers of the high-price supplier. Thus the duopolists would gradually be pushed out of the market in which consumers buy their product, and dealers, making profits out of the difference in the prices at which the producers sell, would take over the market. This argument is meant to apply, of course, only to instances in which the product can be resold, but it is held that goods are resaleable in the vast majority of cases.[24] In actual fact, even where goods are "of such a kind" that they could be resold, oligopolists may, and often do, contrive to make the resale of their products impossible and to eliminate dealers from their markets. There are several industries where producers (of essentially resaleable goods) sell directly to consumers and deliberately exclude the "interference" of dealers. But quite apart from this question of fact, the dealer arbitrage argument cannot really answer the question of theory that is before us. The argument shows merely how the interference of middlemen can transform price inequality on the part of the producers into price uniformity for the ultimate consumers of the products. But this price equalization, achieved through arbitrage, need not do away with the inequality of prices charged by the duopolist producers.

The "paradox" of the coexistence of different prices for the undifferentiated products of the two sellers finds its explanation in the ambiguities of the concept of the perfect market. Some writers, associating nondifferentiation of products with the "perfect market," and "imperfection of the market" with differentiation of

[23] At any time after Period 2, to be exact; that is to say, whenever total demand exceeds the capacity of *one* seller.

[24] "It follows that a two-price system can only exist in the comparatively rare cases where the commodity is of such a kind that it cannot be resold. . . . It appears, therefore, that the possibility of a two-price system in a duopolist market can be considered as practically non-existent." Thorkil Kristensen, "A Note on Duopoly," *Review of Economic Studies,* Vol. VI (1938), p. 59.

the product, have created for themselves a paradox where none exists for those who look for other criteria when they speak of market perfection.[25] The principle "first come, first served" is certainly not one that is compatible with a perfect market. In a perfect market only the price bids, but not the place in the queue, can decide who is served and who is not. The fact that the low-price seller is "sold out" while more customers would like to place orders with him at the price he has asked, constitutes a definite imperfection of the market and is a sufficient explanation for the different price which some buyers pay *after* the first seller is sold out. Thus, strictly speaking, the two prices are not even simultaneous. First all transactions are only at the lower price; then, after this seller has disposed of his production, all further transactions take place at the higher price. By speaking of a "period," meaning the time for which the sales are made—for example, for the weekly production of the two sellers—we have been deluded into assuming a simultaneity of sales which was really excluded by the assumptions of the case.[26]

The market in the Edgeworth model is imperfect in that not all potential buyers have "access" to the seller who asks the lower price. This seller sells to customers selected by criteria other than their willingness and ability to pay, for example, selected by the order in which they arrive at the place of sale.[27] This imperfection of the market is an essential feature of the Edgeworth model.

Buyers' Indifference versus Inertia

The question of the distribution of buyers between the two sellers when they both charge the same price calls also for comment.

[25] See above, Chapter 4.
[26] See assumption 7 and footnote 14 on p. 383 above.
[27] Edgeworth himself once constructed a model of a perfect market for which he used the device of continuing "recontracting"—making only tentative contracts subject to change until no seller and no buyer finds any change to his advantage. In the market in which the weekly production of the two duopolists of the Edgeworth model is sold, there would be plenty of recontracts desired. But Edgeworth never said that his duopolists were selling in a perfect market.

In the Cournot model, there is of course no problem of buyer distribution. The output of the two sellers is indistinguishable and the buyers bid for it without being conscious from who they buy. One price emerges for the entire output of both producers and the number of customers that each of them serves depends on the quantity he has produced.

In the Edgeworth model, the problem of buyer distribution at uniform prices enters into the considerations of each seller when he compares the possibilities which are open to him. For, of course, one of these possibilities is always the matching of the price announced by the competitor. Hence, the seller must have some notion of the share in the market that he could obtain by matching the price, that is, of the way the customers would divide themselves between him and his rival. In our illustration we assumed that buyers would divide themselves evenly between the sellers who ask the same price. But we stated that other assumptions would not change the outcome. For example, we could have assumed that customers were expected to stay with the seller from whom they have been buying and to switch to the competing seller only when he asks a lower price than the former. The result of this expectation would considerably reduce the attractiveness of matching the competitor's price. While under the assumption made in our illustration a "price matcher" could hope to obtain half of the market, under the assumption that customers switch only when lured by a lower price a price matcher could not gain much at all. But, as we have seen in every single step of the Edgeworth process, price matching was never attractive enough to be seriously considered. Hence, it would not make any difference if it were even less attractive. To replace the assumption of "equal division of consumers among sellers quoting the same price" by the assumption of "consumer inertia to be overcome only by a lower price" would therefore not affect the working of the Edgeworth model.

This is not so for the Bertrand model, where we also assumed equal division of consumers among sellers quoting the same price. If we were to change this assumption in the Bertrand model, and stipulate that consumers were expected to stay with their source of supply until lured away by a lower price offer from the other seller, we should not be able to attain the stable equilibrium of the

Bertrand solution. After seller B had reduced his price to $0.10 and thereby gained the entire market, seller A could not have hoped to regain any part of it by merely matching B's price. On the other hand, A could not afford to cut below $0.10, since this was his production cost. Hence, A would have to withdraw completely and B would emerge temporarily as monopolist. Realizing that he had become a monopolist, B would raise his price—perhaps to the full monopoly price of $0.70—and A could then re-enter the market. The whole process of downward bidding would be repeated and the model would look much more like the Edgeworth model, despite the unlimited productive capacity of both producers.

From this instability the Bertrand model was saved only by the assumption that at a uniform price consumers would do half of their buying from each producer. Thus, while the price cutting was going on, the producers took turns in serving the entire market; but when the undercutting stopped and both were charging the same price, they shared the market equally, buyers dividing themselves evenly among the two suppliers.

Extensions of the Classical Models

We have said that the three classical models serve us nowadays chiefly as "school models" on which to practice manœuvring the basic ideas of oligopoly analysis. Perhaps this was too ungenerous and ungrateful an appraisal. For they have served as first approximations, as starting points for inquiries into important and very real problems, and gradual extensions of the original models have resulted in models of greater applicability. Some of the extensions, through modifications of the original assumptions, were made by the original designers, Cournot and Edgeworth. Other extensions were the work of early re-modelers, still others are of more recent design.

Modifications of Assumptions

It may be expedient to show the direction of these extensions first in tabular form and afterwards to single out some of the items for more detailed discussion.

Assumptions of original models	Extensions through modification of assumptions
Undifferentiated or highly substitutable products	Differentiated or imperfectly substitutable products
Linear cost functions	Non-linear cost functions
Identical or similar cost conditions	Different cost conditions (size)
Symmetrical preference for follower position	Asymmetrical preferences for leader and follower positions
Zero conjectural variation	Non-zero conjectural variation
Completely uncoordinated policies	Quasi-collusive behavior patterns
Output or price as the sole variables	Quality and promotion as other variables
Only two sellers: duopoly	More than two sellers: oligopoly

Product Differentiation

The step from perfectly homogeneous to differentiated products is often regarded as a crucial one. Many authors consider the difference important enough to be made the criterion of a class distinction between "perfect" and "imperfect," or "pure" and "differentiated" oligopoly.[28] We have seen, however, that the difference is not so essential once we assume the existence of other imperfections of the market. For the market of the Cournot model, where producers name no prices at all, product homogeneity is of course a necessary condition. But for the Edgeworth market, where one producer starts selling only after his rival's output is sold out, it makes little difference whether the products are homogeneous or differentiated. It is, therefore, not very much of an "extension" of

[28] The emphasis on this difference may be due to Chamberlin's fundamental dichotomy between "small numbers" and "product differentiation." When I stressed the difference in my 1937 classification—"Monopoly and Competition: A Classification of Market Positions," *American Economic Review*, Vol. XXVII (1937), p. 447—it was chiefly in order to maintain symmetry: since it was clearly necessary to distinguish polypoly with homogeneous products from polypoly with differentiated products it seemed natural to make the same distinction for oligopoly. The distinction is made by most writers. See above, Chapter 11.

the original model if it is modified to deal with imperfectly substitutable products.[29]

In two respects the assumption of product differentiation may really become significant and lead to results different from those obtained with homogeneous products. (1) Consumers' preferences for one of the products over its substitutes, or customers' loyalties to one source of supply, may be of such different strength that a small shading of price cannot produce large shifts of patronage. In such cases, price cutting will be less attractive even when each seller adheres to the belief that he may cut his price without fear of retaliation from his competitor. Thus, "gradualness in the shifting of customers from one merchant to another as their prices vary independently" may change the outcome of uncoordinated oligopolistic competition.[30] (2) The greater the differentiation of the products, the more reasonable becomes each seller's hope that his competitor(s) will be slow in retaliating for his price cutting. This point is significant in connection with other modifications of the original assumptions, especially those concerning the unreasonable belief of each seller in the unresponsiveness of his rival's price determination. Product differentiation can hardly make this belief entirely reasonable, but it can at least justify a hope that the retaliation to a price cut may be considerably delayed. This can explain the expectation of temporary gains large enough to warrant price action that would not seem warranted if the products were more substitutable and the rival's reaction therefore more rapid.[31]

Would it be gratuitous to remind the reader that product differentiation need not be physical differentiation of the products? Differentiation may rest on distance (transportation costs), terms of sale or delivery (e.g., terms of credit), patronage (e.g., personal preference for a seller) or merely imaginary differences (e.g., if a

[29] Edgeworth himself discussed the effects of a "diminution of the degree of correlation between the articles." *Op. cit.*, p. 121.

[30] Harold Hotelling, "Stability in Competition," *Economic Journal,* Vol XXXIX (1929), p. 44. Hotelling concludes that the instability of the Edgeworth solution "disappears when the quantity sold by each is considered as a continuous function of the differences in price." See, however, the criticism by Chamberlin, *Theory of Monopolistic Competition* (Cambridge: Harvard University Press, 5th ed., 1947), pp. 226–29.

[31] Kenneth E. Boulding, *Economic Analysis* (New York: Harper, 2nd ed 1948), pp. 588–89.

price differential makes otherwise identical products different in the eyes of uninformed consumers).

The Shape and Similarity of Cost Functions

The extension from linear cost functions [32] to non-linear ones was made by both Cournot and Edgeworth. It made no difference to the nature of their solutions.

Reasoning on the basis of an assumption of zero cost of production is often indicated for didactic reasons: it isolates the essential factors in the model. The use of linear cost functions, that is, the assumption of constant marginal and average variable costs, is advisable where numerical illustrations are to be handled with the smallest possible arithmetical effort. Otherwise, however, greatest possible generality of solutions is desired: hence, no limitation as to the shape of cost functions. But the extension from linearity to non-linearity of the cost functions does not involve any change in the results of oligopoly theory.

More strategic is the significance of extending oligopoly theory through the assumption of dissimilar cost conditions of the competing producers.

We have seen that the Bertrand model requires that the competitors produce under identical cost conditions, or the low-cost producer would end up as monopolist. The Cournot and Edgeworth models require that the competitors produce under similar cost conditions. The degree of dissimilarity still compatible with the solutions of the respective theories depends on the demand function. In general, where the cost conditions are too dissimilar, the high-cost producer would be pushed out of the market, leaving the low-cost producer as a monopolist. This would be so at least as long as the assumption of symmetrical stupidity, or symmetrical delusions about absence of rival's reactions, is maintained.

Drastically different cost conditions involve, however, large

[32] The "linearity" refers to the total cost curve rising as a straight line from the left to the right. This causes the marginal cost curve (and the average variable cost curve) to be a straight horizontal line. The average total cost curve will be a horizontal line only if the total cost curve starts from the origin; if it starts higher up, that is, if there are fixed costs, the average total cost curve will be hyperbolically decreasing.

differences in the size of the firms and in the share they have in the market. These differences are hardly compatible with the assumption of symmetrical preferences for the position as follower and symmetrical delusions about the leadership of the other. There are, besides monopoly through elimination of the weaker firm, two possible situations of uncoordinated oligopoly associated with substantial cost differences: asymmetrical oligopoly with reaction-conscious leader and follower firms, and the so-called partial monopoly, or quasi-oligopoly, where the dominant firm is a no-reaction-conscious leader and the weak firm a no-reaction-conscious follower.

Asymmetry of Attitudes

We have seen that all three classical models were based on the assumption of symmetrical attitudes of the sellers: each seller reacted to the actions of his competitor but expected no reactions to his own actions. In other words, each seller behaved as a "follower" in the sense of one who responds to the other's lead, and each believed that the other would not behave as a follower, but rather as a "leader" in the sense of one who does not respond.[33]

This symmetrical inferiority complex is not the only kind of symmetry that may exist in the sellers' opinions about each other. We shall make the acquaintance of the Bowley model, which is based on the assumption of a symmetrical superiority complex (or megalomania). At this point, however, we wish to discuss the extension of the models to asymmetrical attitudes. This is perhaps the most important of the extensions that later theorists have made of the classical models.

Symmetrical opinions of two sellers are, in most instances, incorrect opinions. For it is impossible for them to be correct if both have the *same* attitude *vis-à-vis* the other but expect the other to have the *opposite* attitude *vis-à-vis* him. Symmetrical duopoly in this sense implies one of two things: either the two sellers are of an incredible stupidity and chronic inability to revise opinions even when patently false and shown to be so at every step; or the two sellers are of an extraordinary stubbornness and unfaltering opti

[33] On other meanings of leadership see below, Chapter 15.

mism which makes them hope that the rival will stop behaving as he does and will start conforming to the expectation he has disappointed so consistently. No one can contend that conditions like these are never met in reality; but if they are, it will be much more in the nature of an exception than a rule. It is one of the merits of the symmetrical duopoly models that they show convincingly that symmetrical situations of this sort are likely to give way to asymmetrical ones—if not to one of the various forms of coordinated competition. The most probable solution is along the lines of cooperation among the competitors. If for any reason coordination cannot be obtained, the chances are that the outcome will be asymmetrical duopoly.

In contrast to the symmetrical situation, in which each seller makes the same mistake about the other, asymmetrical situations allow all participants to be right in their opinions about each other. If A acts responsively and regards B as unresponsive to his actions, and B acts unresponsively and regards A as responsive to B's actions, their actions and their expectations about the other's reactions may be mutually compatible. Of course, such "compatibility" can easily shade into "harmony" and, hence, "compatible asymmetry" into "coordination." But there is no harm speculating about the possibilities of absolutely uncoordinated compatibility. Indeed, such speculations are highly significant in view of the legal ban on collusion. More on this point will be said later.

Asymmetry is no guarantee of compatibility. For one must not think that every asymmetrical duopoly situation is such as to make the sellers' actions and expectations mutually compatible. If they are not, the solution is indeterminate, which most likely means that there will follow a series of steps on the part of the sellers designed to persuade, bluff, or compel the competitor into a change of his position and pattern of conduct.[34] Analysts are not yet agreed whether the terms and concepts of military science and warfare or those of the theory of games, such as chess or poker, are more suit-

---

[34] For a systematic catalogue of possible situations see Heinrich von Stackelberg, op. cit., pp. 45–48. Stackelberg derives various types of reaction curves from various types of equal-profit curves (profit indifference curves) and obtains sixteen possible combinations for the positions of two sellers pursuing either price or output policies. Stackelberg's exposition is entirely geometrical and not easily translatable into literary language.

able for explorations of situations of this type. But, in any event, the steps taken by the sellers in a situation which is characterized as "indeterminate" will eventually transform that situation into one of coordination or one of compatible asymmetry. (There is more to be said also on this question of oligopolistic indeterminacy, and we shall not too long defer saying it.)

Compatibility of the asymmetrical attitudes of the sellers will be greatly facilitated, without an indeterminate transition period, if the cost conditions and market shares of the firms are very different. In such situations, where a big and one or more small competitors face one another, the solution may, in extreme cases, lie in a virtual emancipation from rival-consciousness; in other cases, where the competing sellers are reaction-conscious, their "conjectural variations" may conform to the actual reactions along mutually acceptable lines. That is to say, each seller may expect his competitor to react in a certain way to his own actions; these expectations may prove correct, and the result of move and countermove may be such as to satisfy the participants that they could not do anything short of cooperation that would improve matters.

Guessing Definite Countermoves

In the classical models each seller guesses that his rival would make no countermove. These guesses, which of course are wrong (except in the ultimate step of the Cournot process), constitute what has been rather clumsily called "zero conjectural variation." Classical oligopoly theory was then extended to include cases of "non-zero conjectural variation." This unnecessarily awkward technical jargon merely means to convey the simple fact that each seller expects, and makes definite guesses about, the countermoves of his rival.

There is almost unanimous agreement about the need for this extension of the earlier theories. After all, it was somewhat embarrassing for economic theorists to insinuate by implication that in their models the businessmen were dumb, blind, and stubborn, and could never revise their incorrect anticipations about their rival's lack of response. Hence, the assumption had to be modified.

The new assumption was either that each seller's conjecture about his rival's reactions depended on his mood and intuition or that it depended on the rival's actual pattern of reaction which the seller has learned to judge correctly.[35]

The first kind of assumption does not permit determinate solutions unless we are told just what the moods and intuitions of the sellers are in each situation, what judgments are likely to result from particular moods and inclinations, and how they are apt to change as a result of disappointment. Perhaps it is not possible to make any statements on these matters; in this case we could do nothing better than to leave the outcome indeterminate. We might be able to say on what the exact outcome would depend, but if this "causal factor" could never be discerned independently from the outcome (that is, if the "cause" could be inferred only from the "effect") we would not be much helped by a statement specifying such an unascertainable element of explanation. On the other hand, it may be possible to work out a complete theory of the formation and successive revision of oligopolistic conjectures about rivals' reactions. If the successive revisions, however, are dictated by actual experience, there is a good chance that any assumption concerning the "development" of sellers' conjectures will merge with the second kind of assumption, namely, that the conjectures about a rival's reactions depend on the rival's actual pattern of reaction.

The second kind of assumption will permit determinate solutions if the correctly anticipated reactions of the competitors are

[35] Among the theorists inclined toward the first kind of assumption were A. C. Pigou, Joan Robinson, Edward H. Chamberlin, Roy Harrod; among those emphasizing that solutions of the duopoly problem had better be based on assumptions of seller's anticipations which prove to be correct were R. F. Kahn and George Stigler.

Pigou, for example, stated that the action of each seller "depends on his judgment of the policy which the other will pursue, and this judgment may be anything according to the mood of each and his expectation of success from a policy of bluff. As in a game of chess, each player's move is related to his reading of the psychology of his opponent and his guess as to that opponent's reply." *Economics of Welfare* (London: Macmillan, 4th ed., 1938), p. 268. Kahn, on the other hand, holds "that the *ultimate* position of equilibrium does not depend on the nature of firm's beliefs, which can be supposed to become rapidly revised if they start by being erroneous, but on what in fact happens." R. F. Kahn, "The Problem of Duopoly," *op. cit.*, p. 15.

compatible with each other. Some particular situations of mutual compatibility of reactions can be described even where the rivals' attitudes *vis-à-vis* each other are symmetrical. As a rule, however, symmetrical attitudes will prevent compatibility and, hence, an equilibrium solution. As an example of the indeterminacy of symmetrical duopoly with accurate knowledge of the rivals' reactions to each other's moves the Bowley model is often cited.[36] The characterization of this model as one based upon correct anticipations is, however, not justified. Indeed, the assumptions underlying the Bowley model are inconsistent and outright contradictory.

In this model it is assumed (1) that each of the two competing sellers "knows accurately" how his rival would react to any of his own moves, and (2) that the sellers have a symmetrical preference for the leadership position. Thus, each seller will try to set the pace; that is, each will determine his own price or output in a manner designed to yield maximum profits if the rival reacts in the "known" way. But, alas, if each expects the *other* to react while he himself acts not in response to the other's actions but rather in anticipation of the other's reactions, both must be disappointed. The so-called knowledge of how the rival *would* react *if* he reacted is of no use when in fact he does not react, but instead acts in the hope of himself eliciting the kind of reaction that he believes he can anticipate. If each stubbornly waits for the other to give in and start "reacting," they both will do rather poorly. They may proceed to try bluffing each other into the desired position or they may proceed to try forcing each other into submission by means of a price war. As an eventual outcome, one of them may revise his attitude and accept the position of a follower. Or, even more likely, they may come to an understanding and begin to cooperate.

The Bowley model, a model of "circular dependence," is clearly an extension of the classical models through substituting a nonzero for a zero "conjectural variation," that is, through assuming that the sellers always anticipate definite countermoves on the part of the rival instead of assuming that they anticipate no response. But the guesses of the Bowley duopolists are hardly more enlightened than the guesses of the classical duopolists, and the

[36] A. L. Bowley, *The Mathematical Groundwork of Economics* (Oxford: Oxford University Press, 1924), p. 38.

outcome of the operation of the Bowley model is not a bit more plausible.[37]

Two possible sets of correct and mutually compatible anticipations with symmetrical attitudes have been described: one, where each duopolist anticipates that his rival will match any price cut; another, where each duopolist anticipates that his rival will insist on maintaining his present share of the market.[38] These two cases lead to determinate and stable equilibrium solutions. The second case will lead to the perfect monopoly solution if the two sellers have the same cost conditions and share the market equally. The solution of the first case depends on the price ruling at the beginning of the process: if the price was initially higher, it will settle at the perfect monopoly level; if it was initially lower, it will stay where it was. Should each duopolist anticipate that his rival will match not only any price cut but also any price increase, the result, assuming identical cost conditions, will again be the perfect monopoly solution.

The question that arises with respect to these assumptions is whether they are really free of all elements of collusion. We shall argue that some degree of collusion is involved if competitors can with confidence form correct anticipations of the rival's reactions to their moves, especially if the firms in question are not of very different size and therefore not "predestined" to be leader or fol-

[37] Indeed, it is much less plausible, because the competitors not only must notice that their anticipations have been wrong but also that their profits are in effect minimized rather than maximized. One of the two sellers will sooner or later realize that he would greatly improve his position if he stopped waiting for his rival to become a follower and started being a follower himself. The other seller will of course accept such a switch with delight, for his anticipations, so consistently wrong up to this time, will now prove correct. The case would have transformed itself into an asymmetrical one. By a queer coincidence both sellers may simultaneously give up their leadership notions; if both turned into followers, expecting the other to lead, the Bowley case would transform itself into a Cournot or Edgeworth case. But then, again, one of them may go back to his assumed leadership position and asymmetry would thus be achieved. Several of these possibilities were described, by way of a critique of Stackelberg's theory of duopolistic indeterminacy, by Heinz Haller, "Der Erkenntniswert der Oligopoltheorien," *Jahrbücher für Nationalökonomie und Statistik*, Band 162 (1950), pp. 81–98.

[38] Both of these cases were proposed and analysed by George Stigler, "Notes on the Theory of Duopoly," *Journal of Political Economy*, Vol. XLVIII (1940), pp. 528–31.

lower in the determination of price or output. Only in clearly asymmetrical situations is it reasonable to assume that correct conjectures of mutually compatible reactions may have been formed without any elements of collusion.

Quasi-Collusive Behavior Patterns

The extension of the duopoly models from incorrect guessing to correct guessing raises the issue of collusion. For if a seller can confidently and correctly guess how his competitor will react to his moves, the "guess" is not much of a guess and the "competitor" not much of a competitor.

There are those who insist on keeping oligopoly theory free of all traces of coordination, collusion, cooperation, and quasi-collusive behavior; indeed they emphasize this by speaking of "true" duopoly and "true" oligopoly. It is probably a sound judgment that "the backbone of the theory of duopoly must be evolved on the assumption that no firm has any trust whatever in its competitors." [39] But we must realize that this theory will not get us very far. There is little doubt that most oligopoly in the real world is reinforced by a considerable admixture of collusiveness. Full-fledged collusion may possibly be less interesting as a subject of purely theoretical analysis. But lower degrees of collusion, behavior patterns characterized as quasi-collusive, are at least as interesting as the models of perfectly uncoordinated oligopoly, and are probably more significant. Thus, there is no excuse for resisting the extension of oligopoly models to include quasi-collusive and semi-collusive behavior patterns. We shall devote a part of the next chapter to the discussion of the forms and degrees of collusion.

More Variables: Product Quality and Sales Promotion

As long as the models dealt only with undifferentiated products, price and quantity of output were the only variables in the process. The extension of the models from undifferentiated to differentiated products opened the way for another extension: the addition of

[39] R. F. Kahn, *op. cit.*, p. 9.

more variables, such as product quality, sales promotion, and location.

Because the train of causation may run in either direction, from these variables to oligopoly and from oligopoly to these variables, we had better watch out lest we get on the wrong track in this discussion. Differences in product quality, advertising and other selling services, location and transport costs are all factors in "product differentiation" and often also effective forces in breaking down a large market of many sellers into several partial or regional markets with rivalry among only a few. This direction of causation—*differences* in quality, promotion, and location as causes of oligopoly—is not what we are concerned with at this point. Our present concern is with the opposite direction of causation: the influence of oligopoly upon *variations* which producers may consider and decide upon with respect to their product qualities, selling efforts, and plant location.

Producers may compete with each other not only by reducing the price of their product but also in many other ways, such as by improving the quality and appearance of the product, making it appear more desirable by means of advertising, adding services extended to their customers, moving closer to more of their customers. Accordingly one speaks of quality competition, service competition, promotional competition, and spatial competition as various forms of nonprice competition, and analyses the effects which certain oligopolistic positions are likely to have on them.

Spatial competition has been particularly attractive to economic theorists because, in contrast to quality, service, and advertising, the advantages and disadvantages of location to buyers as well as sellers could be exactly measured in terms of transport costs. This permitted a more elegant analysis of spatial competition,[40] the results of which could then be applied, through reasoning by analogy, to competitive variations of quality, services, and

[40] H. Hotelling, "Stability in Competition," *Economic Journal*, Vol. XXXIX (1929); F. Zeuthen, "Theoretical Remarks on Price Theory: Hotelling's Case with Variations," *Quarterly Journal of Economics*, Vol. XLVII (1933); A. P. Lerner and H. W. Singer, "Some Notes on Duopoly and Spatial Competition," *Journal of Political Economy*, Vol. XLV (1937); A. Smithies, "Optimum Location in Spatial Competition," *Journal of Political Economy*, Vol. XLIX (1941).

advertising. There is little direct application, however, of the theory of spatial or relocational competition because, as a rule, variations in producer's locations are not a simple matter. Ordinarily it is not possible for producers to pack up their equipment every other month and move elsewhere in reaction to similar relocational moves of their rivals. One writer, in an attempt to make his analysis of the producer's choice of a new location more realistic, made the explicit assumption that, "the buildings of B were burnt down." [41] Fully appreciating the advantages for the theorist which this sort of spatial competition has over competition through variations of quality and advertising, I shall dispense with the discussion of an analysis that can be made realistic only with the help of conflagrations and earthquakes conveniently destroying most of the industrial plants for each competitive move of the producers.

The chief significance of nonprice competition in oligopolistic positions lies in the fact that variations in quality and selling efforts are commonly used in lieu of variations of price and with a clearly implied message to the competitor that he too should refrain from competing through price. The variations of the nonprice variables are by nature limited in magnitude as well as frequency. Competitive quality improvements cannot possibly follow each other in as fast a succession as can competitive price reductions; nor are they likely to run to such amounts in terms of costs to producers (and benefits to consumers) as may a vigorous price war.

In addition to the natural limitations of competition through nonprice variables there may also be effective limitations in consequence of the oligopolistic climate or, more directly, in consequence of a closer understanding among the competitors. As a discerning student of the problem has found, "the presumption exists that quasi-agreements tend to become extended to these variables, as an oligopolistic constellation matures in time." [42]

These remarks will suffice at this place to indicate that the extension of the classical models to include other variables besides price and output, especially product quality and selling effort, is

[41] F. Zeuthen, *op. cit.*, p. 248.
[42] William Fellner, *Competition Among the Few: Oligopoly and Similar Market Structures* (New York: Knopf, 1949), p. 188.

of utmost importance and may justly claim the space for a more detailed discussion in another chapter.

More Than Two Sellers

The last of the modifications of assumptions which we listed among the extensions of the original classical models is that from two to several sellers. This extension did not have to wait for later writers; neither Cournot nor Edgeworth lost any time extending their theories from two to a larger number of competitors.

The question is raised by this extension whether, as the number of sellers is increased from two to a few, from a few to several, and from several to many, this increase involves a gradual deviation from the results of the theory of duopoly and oligopoly and a gradual approach to the results of the theory of polypoly. This, indeed, was Cournot's answer, whereas Edgeworth's position on this point was not clear and not quite consistent.[43]

Inasmuch as we have rejected the emphasis on mere numbers in developing and defining the concept of oligopoly and have looked to the seller's state of mind as our criterion, the question of the "gradual descent" to the solution of perfect polypoly is to us only a pseudo-problem.[44] The main reasons, however, for which we have rejected the emphasis on the numbers of sellers—the impossibility of delimiting their product and their market—need not hold for a pure construction in which it is simply *assumed* that the product is perfectly homogeneous and sold in a perfect market which is perfectly circumscribed. For such a model the Cournot extension from two to several and many sellers makes good sense, provided one grants that it makes sense to hold the sellers' attitudes constant and unvarying during the mental experiment. We must remember that the attitude of the Cournot sellers was definitely fixed: each believed that the competitor or competitors would not

[43] See Chamberlin, *op. cit.*, pp. 39 ff.; A. J. Nichol, *op. cit.*, pp. 57–62. Nichol points out that, on the basis of the assumptions of Edgeworth's model, "the range of oscillations increases with each increase in the number of competitors" (p. 60), but that "when competitors are numerous, prices tend also to fluctuate more infrequently, and when they rise, fall back again more rapidly to a lower level" (p. 61).

[44] This was convincingly pointed out by Chamberlin, *op. cit.*, p. 48.

respond to his actions. This unvarying attitude, no doubt, may fit well the typical seller in a market of very many sellers, but we have found it rather absurd to assume that it prevails where a seller finds himself *vis-à-vis* a few competitors. If sellers' attitudes cannot be assumed to be fixed, it is impossible to predict how price and total output would be affected if there were three sellers instead of two, four sellers instead of three, or sixteen instead of four.

The theories of duopolistic indeterminacy become theories of oligopolistic indeterminacy as the number of competitors increases beyond two. Indeed, it has been argued that the probability of equilibrium decreases as we move from models of two to models of more sellers.[45] The kind of mix-up and scramble that results from the circular dependence and inconsistent symmetrical preferences for leadership exhibited in the Bowley model may be still worse if more than two sellers are involved. The probability of more than one seller wanting to be the leader is indeed the greater the greater the number of competitors. And the probability of full compatibility of asymmetrical preferences becomes smaller with a larger number of competitors. Thus, the likelihood of unstable solutions and continued strife for better positions may well be greater rather than smaller if more sellers are in non-collusive competition—as long as there are not so many that they develop polypolistic attitudes.

The stress on sellers' attitudes as essential factors in oligopoly theory may be objected to by those who want to explain things by differences "of situation rather than of mentality." [46] Admittedly, it is a very commendable principle in the social sciences not to accept psychological propensities, preferences, and expectations as ultimate causes for the phenomena that are to be explained, but rather to look wherever possible for the "objective facts" behind the subjective determinants of action. This is often possible where the number of actors influenced by the same "objective facts" is very large. For in these cases, differences in the interpreta-

---

[45] Heinrich v. Stackelberg, *op. cit.*, pp. 22–24.

[46] R. F. Kahn, *op. cit.*, p. 11. Even more explicitly, Kahn looks for explanations of a difference in the outcome in "a difference not of belief but of fact, of technical conditions and market practice rather than of psychology" (p. 6).

tion of the facts by the actors will not weigh heavily in the out-come of the mass actions. This is an important element in the de-terminacy of polypolistic competition. Where, on the other hand, only a few actors are involved, deviations in the way they "see" the facts and are influenced by them will be very important, and it will not be possible to predict the outcome of their actions. Where there are only a few actors, differences in their "subjective make-up," in their thinking and their temperament, must not be disregarded. And this explains why the theory of oligopoly cannot be determinate as long as objective conditions are its only data.[47]

Strangely enough, this important reason why oligopoly theory needs more "psychological" data than are needed in the analysis of polypoly has often been overlooked. We shall bring this up again presently when we proceed to a discussion of oligopolistic indeterminacy. But now, winding up the discussion of the exten-sion of the analytical models to accommodate more than two competitors, we may conclude by saying that there is no *a priori* reason why competition among three or four sellers should be more "competitive" than competition among two. Where com-patible asymmetrical attitudes of the sellers lead to a leadership oligopoly, or where incompatible attitudes lead, after a period of strife, to organized oligopoly, the prices charged may easily be higher than they might be if only two sellers—or even only one—were in control of the entire productive capacity.

[47] Cf. Fritz Machlup, "Why Bother with Methodology?" *Economica*, New Series, Vol. III (1936), p. 42.

CHAPTER 13

Oligopolistic Indeterminacy and Collusion

Oligopolistic Indeterminacy: The General Meaning of Indeterminacy ·
Pure and Applied Economics · Anonymous Masses and the Conduct of
Individuals · Extra-Economic Factors · Position, Security, and Profit ·
Military Strategy and Games of Strategy · The Strong Sparing the Weak

The Forms and Degrees of Collusion: Coordination, Collusion, Cooperation · The Rationale of Collusion · The Degrees of Collusion · The Forms
of Collusion · Implicit Agreements to Agree, and Other Quasi-Agreements
· The Comprehensiveness of Collusion

Oligopoly and General Equilibrium: Polypolistic and Oligopolistic Expectations · The General Equilibrium Model

THE DISCUSSION of classical duopoly theories and their modern
extensions has left us with a strong impression that the outcome of uncoordinated oligopoly is indeterminate—or coordination by collusion. Indeterminacy and collusion will be the subjects
of this chapter.

OLICOPOLISTIC INDETERMINACY

What is "oligopolistic indeterminacy"? Is it merely a sophisticated word for a rather simple idea? or is the idea behind it very
intricate, if not mysterious? or is it perhaps a word standing in lieu
of an idea, a high-sounding phrase to cover up a void of thought?
Frankly, any one of these suspicions may prove true, for it is in a
variety of meanings that the word is being used. We feel obliged
to look behind the phrase, especially since the role which "oligopolistic indeterminacy" plays in the literature of the subject is very
much greater than has been indicated thus far.

The General Meaning of Indeterminacy

In a general way, economists speak of indeterminacy if not enough information is available to give a safe and unambiguous answer to a question before them. If they wish to solve a problem —for example, how the price of a certain commodity will change under certain conditions—but find that the data which are assumed to be "given" would permit of two or more (perhaps of an indefinite number of) answers, they will state that the problem has no determinate solution.[1] Such a statement does not mean that the problem is insoluble. It means only that more must be known before it can be solved.[2]

The realization that a problem has no determinate solution will not be disturbing in the least, if we know what additional data we need and how we can get them. Often it is clear that the additional data cannot be obtained. If this is merely a "practical" impossibility, the theorist will not be much worried. As far as he is concerned, the solution of his problem is determinate as soon as he assumes as given what in practical fact may not be known. It is really bad only if he must admit that the data in question cannot even "conceivably" be known. For then his model will not be operational either practically or conceivably. But this will rarely happen. Most things which we do not know are "conceivably knowable" even if we have no hope of ever knowing them in the world in which we live. Thus, if we find that a problem has no determinate solution, all we have to do is to make additional assumptions which will remove the indeterminacy.[3]

[1] Economists usually speak of indeterminacy where mathematicians would speak of a multiplicity of solutions.

[2] Depending on the number of additional independent variables they want to be given, economists sometimes say that the solution has still one or more "degrees of freedom." It will be determinate when enough is given to remove all "degrees of freedom." See Erich Schneider, *Einführung in die Wirtschaftstheorie, II. Teil, Wirtschaftspläne und wirtschaftliches Gleichgewicht in der Verkehrswirtschaft* (Tübingen: J. C. Mohr-Paul Siebeck, 1949), pp. 295 ff.

[3] The following types of indeterminacy—chiefly with regard to oligopoly analysis—may be conveniently distinguished:

(1) Two or more solutions, perhaps an infinite number of solutions, are compatible with the data assumed as given. We need more data to determine the outcome. The needed additional information may be about

Why, then, should we so often resort to the disclaimer of determinacy instead of filling out the gaps in our sets of data? There are at least two good reasons for it. First of all, the "missing" data may be of a nature entirely different from that of all other data assumed to be given. We may be reluctant to "mix" indiscriminately assumptions of too dissimilar or diverse character. Secondly, the problem for the solution of which more data are wanted may be very much like many other problems, which however are soluble without such additional data. We may be reluctant to furnish an extra supply of data to one problem when apparently very similar problems can do with less. Let us look more closely into both these reasons.

(a) external (environmental, objective) conditions, affecting the conduct of the actors concerned;

(b) subjective (inclinational, psychological) conditions, affecting the conduct of the actors; or

(c) external forces or interventions by third parties, including government, affecting the results of the conduct of the actors.

(2) Only one solution is compatible with the data assumed as given, but upon closer inspection it can be seen that there is only apparent determinacy due to the fact that one or more variables about which no explicit assumption is made are implicitly assumed to be zero. Knowing, however, that they cannot be zero, one realizes that the problem has not a uniquely determinate solution. If the magnitudes of these neglected variables are assumed to be known, other additional data may now be required for a determination of the outcome. [Example: Uncertainty implicitly assumed to be zero. If it is not zero, several more assumptions must be made.]

(3) The given sets of data result in a succession of merely tentative (provisional) solutions, each inherently unstable because whenever one actor attains equilibrium the equilibria of others are upset. The continuing shifts of positions may lead to oscillatory (or even explosive) movements which make the maintenance of the original assumptions impossible because they prove to be inconsistent with other, possibly implicit, assumptions. The problem can become determinate only through additional data concerning

(a) changes in the external conditions, brought about by the oscillatory (or explosive) movements and affecting the conduct of the actors concerned [Examples: plant deterioration, reduction of financial strength];

(b) changes in the subjective conditions, brought about by the movements and affecting conduct [Examples: tiredness, resignation]; or

(c) new external forces or interventions by third parties, including government, affecting the conduct of the actors or its result [Examples: government price control, buyers' cooperative movement].

This list is probably incomplete and perhaps unsystematic. The distinction between (a) and (c) may not be justified by any real differences.

Pure and Applied Economics

The question how far one should go in supplying additional assumptions in the analysis of particular economic problems has long been a matter of convention, if not fashion, among economists. A large number, perhaps a majority, of economists have adhered to the rule that "pure" theory should operate with a minimum of assumptions and that they must all be of the broadest, most general type. Anything else is "applied" theory, where many more assumptions, and assumptions of a more specific nature, are introduced. Needless to say, "concrete" problems approaching the complex situations prevalent in the real world ordinarily require a great many and very specific data for their solution and can, therefore, be accommodated only by applied economics. But even in a relatively general form, certain kinds of problems may not be soluble with the scant rations and the non-specific types of assumptions furnished in "pure" economics.

Depending on the various epistemological views, the propositions of "pure" theory have been interpreted alternatively as basic postulates of economic conduct, as fundamental assumptions of evident empirical validity, as ideal types of great explanatory value, as aprioristic truths inherent in the rationality of human thought, as logical inferences from useful tools of analysis. Accordingly, any problems not completely soluble in such terms were contrasted with propositions of pure theory, and the additional raw material required for the solutions was referred to as non-economic, more specific, less generally applicable, empirical, descriptive, or factual. It is on the basis of these methodological distinctions, much disputed although largely a matter of taste, that the comments of certain economists on oligopolistic indeterminacy within "pure economics" must be understood.[4]

---

[4] For example, Pareto said that "pure economics" cannot tell us anything about the continuing shifts of position of competing oligopolists and that we must turn to "the observation of facts," which may show us a large variety of actual solutions: cartel, trust, price leadership, cut-throat competition, live-and-let-live policies, etc. Vilfredo Pareto, *Manuel d'Economie Politique* (Paris: M. Giard, 2nd ed., 1927), pp. 601–602. In the same vein, Triffin said that "the limited tools of pure economics are powerless to yield by themselves a determinate solution," and that the actual solution is "an empirical question,

There is no need for us in this context to examine the different methodological positions of different schools of economics. (It is difficult, though, to resist the temptation on this occasion to criticize the notion that there is a difference in kind, rather than degree, in the logical nature of pure and applied economics and that the latter is empirical while the former is not. But we shall restrain ourselves.) The point here for us to focus on is that the line drawn between pure and applied economics can often explain what is meant by "indeterminacy" of the solution of a problem: it is indeterminate inside the line because the data needed to make the solution determinate may lie beyond the line.

Anonymous Masses and the Conduct of Individuals

Where thousands or even only hundreds of firms sell in the same market, we are usually able to do with much less information than if only a few sellers share the market. In the analysis of mass action, where each individual actor counts only a little, we need not know them intimately in order to explain the combined result. A very "anonymous" model (or ideal type) of the relevant kind of actor will suffice for an explanation of the process in question and its outcome. Not so when only a few people are involved; where each individual actor counts heavily, a much more intimate

---

and not a matter of logical deduction." Robert Triffin, *Monopolistic Competition and General Equilibrium Theory* (Cambridge: Harvard University Press, 1940), pp. 124–25. The following excellent statement by K. W. Rothschild characterizes different methodological positions towards oligopolistic indeterminacy: "But while thus the increasing acceptance of the indeterminateness of the problem was an advance towards a more realistic treatment of the subject, it was also a retreat from the former belief that price theory could be sufficiently developed to deal with all possible market phenomena. Indeed, the majority of these writers, once they have shown the inadequacy of the determinate solutions, take up an almost nihilistic attitude towards the theory of duopoly and oligopoly. They may, like Chamberlin, just add a short list of "uncertainties" to an artificial, determinate solution; or they may deny the possibility of a general theory covering industry under oligopolistic conditions and substitute for it voluminous case-studies describing the behavior pattern of particular industries; or oligopolistic industry is just viewed as a chaotic mess where practically anything may happen, and about which economic analysis has very little to say." K. W. Rothschild, "Price Theory and Oligopoly," *Economic Journal,* Vol. LVII (1947), p. 304.

knowledge about every one of them may be needed for an explanation of the combined result.

The important difference between ideal behavior-types (conduct models) of a high degree of "anonymity" and those of a high degree of "intimacy" has been developed in formal sociology.[5] It is related to the fact that analysis may deal with phenomena in very different strata of generality (in terms of particular conceptual schemes). The legitimacy of the reliance on the applicability of highly anonymous types may or may not be related also to the "law of large numbers," explaining the greater reliability of propositions about mass phenomena.[6]

This points to a very important difference between the theories of polypoly, on the one hand, and monopoly and oligopoly, on the other hand. Assume, for example, we knew perfectly well the cost conditions of every single plant in an industry and knew also the conditions of demand for its homogeneous product sold in large central markets. If there were, let us say, two hundred plants of approximately equal size and they were owned and operated by two hundred different capitalists, we could make a reasonably good prediction of the aggregate output that would be produced in the two hundred plants and of the price at which the product would be sold. There may be very odd characters among the two hundred producers; and some of them may be smart, others dumb; some lazy, others industrious; some venturous, others timid; some imaginative and optimistic, others pessimistic and pedestrian; some

[5] See Alfred Schütz, Der sinnhafte Aufbau der sozialen Welt (Vienna: Springer, 1932); Alfred Stonier and Karl Bode, "A New Approach to the Methodology of the Social Sciences," Economica, New Series, Vol. IV (1937), pp. 406–24; and my own article, "Why Bother with Methodology?", Economica, New Series, Vol. II (1936), p. 44.

[6] "It is a well known phenomenon in many branches of the exact and physical sciences that very great numbers are often easier to handle than those of medium size. . . . This is, of course, due to the excellent possibility of applying the laws of statistics and probabilities. . . ." John von Neumann and Oskar Morgenstern, The Theory of Games and Economic Behavior (Princeton: Princeton University Press, 2nd ed., 1947), p. 14. The authors warn, however, against premature reliance on this principle for generalizations in economics. While they "hope" that the principle will be found to apply there, they state: ". . . only after the theory for moderate numbers of participants has been satisfactorily developed will it be possible to decide whether extremely great numbers of participants simplify the situation." Ibid.

short-sighted, others far-sighted; some penny-pinchers, others spendthrifts; yet, we should not have to worry about these differences. There would be no need of knowing any of the sellers individually, because no one of them would make enough of a difference in the outcome. The most anonymous behavior type, the model of the perfect polypolist trying to make as much money as he can, would suffice for our analysis of the combined outcome. The more specific behavior types—and, of course, every one of the above mentioned fourteen personal qualities would represent another ideal type—would be of no use in improving our prediction.

Let us now assume that all two hundred plants are under unified control and the product is sold by a monopolist. Now to make a prediction of price and output—not merely a prediction of the decisions of an anonymous, "typical" monopolist, but rather a prediction of the real man acting in the real world—would call for a different method of analysis. We should have to know a good many of the personal qualities of the man, and about his background and experience, his friends and associates, his political ambitions, and perhaps also his digestive troubles; and even then we might not know half enough to come very close to the actual outcome.

The difficulties are not less but even more serious if the two hundred plants are divided among a few independent owners. What kind of people are they? If two or more of them are typical leaders, what kind of battle will they fight? Which of them will give in and after what length of time? How spiteful are they, or how complaisant? How much money have they to lose? Are they emotional or cool-headed? Are they good bluffers and good mind-readers? If we knew all this about our men, and a thousand other things too, we still should not know enough to make a prediction which—even if neither cost nor demand conditions had changed —would have a fifty percent chance of hitting the actual outcome with a twenty percent margin of error.

Have we exaggerated the differences in complexity between the analyses of polypolistic, monopolistic, and oligopolistic selling? The differences are so enormous if the comparisons are made, as we have done, in terms of predictions rather than merely explanations. This is probably not quite fair, since we are often satisfied to explain and do not always aspire to predict. Surely the explanatory value of a theory may be great even if its predictive value is small.[7] While the future may hold an infinite number of possibilities, the past has eliminated all but one. The reconstruction of the data which may have led to the actual outcome need no longer be encumbered with the infinite possible "solutions" that existed before the course of events unfolded itself. Looking backward we may select those givens which would make the operations of our theoretical model yield just the result that in actual fact has emerged from the operations of the real world. Thus, a theory which has merely the task of explaining, not of predicting, may be much less formidable and perfectly manageable. But even for this much more modest task the assumptions required for a model with only a few actors will nevertheless be much more numerous and much more specific than the assumptions required for a model in which a large number of actors are involved.

Extra-Economic Factors

If, in order to achieve determinacy, more specific assumptions are needed for a model schematizing the interactions among a few than for one schematizing the interactions among many, does this requirement for more detailed specification imply a departure from purely economic factors and the indiscriminate inclusion of non-economic ones?

To some extent the answer will depend on what one chooses to call an economic factor, and what a non-economic or extra-economic one. Are we dealing with an "economic" factor if we make assumptions about how great a man's ability is to estimate the production cost of an output he has not produced before? or about his confidence in his own ability to gauge the market and

---

[7] The meteorologists are much better in explaining why it rained yesterday than in predicting that it will rain tomorrow. The physicists may have a fully satisfactory explanation of all causes of an explosion last month, without being able to predict an explosion next month. And the physician may not be able to predict the death of a patient although he may afterwards explain what led to it. The economist's capacity to explain economic phenomena must not be judged by his small success in predicting them.

the elasticity of the demand? about a man's inclination to look far ahead into the distant future? a man's willingness to take risks? Is financial strength [8] an extra-economic factor? or the pride of leadership in an industry?

In a large measure, however, the factors that have to be introduced in order to make the outcome of oligopolistic competition determinate will be considered non-economic in almost any sort of classification. For example, assumptions about how much fun a man will get out of being in a good scrap with a competitor; how quickly a man will get tired and will acquiesce in a position he first vigorously rejected; how conscientiously a man, when he is in a pinch, will adhere to a gentlemen's agreement to maintain prices; how good a man's political connections are enabling him to bring off or to stop some governmental intervention in the industry. A thousand and one of such things may be the crucial factors in an oligopolistic situation. Disregard them—and the solution may be indeterminate.[9]

Does the realization of this mean that in order to analyse oligopoly we must psychoanalyse each member of each group? Does it mean that we should give up studying the "theory" of oligopoly and engage instead in a thousand different descriptive industry studies, considering each situation as a separate and unique one which has nothing in common with any other oligopoly situation? Indeed not. We have always known that no single science is self-sufficient or could explain a concrete situation of the real world fully to the last detail without recourse to theories, constructs, and models from many other fields of learning or every-day intelligence. Such is not the aim of scientific work in general or of economic analysis in particular or, in the present case, of the theory of oligopoly. All we want to say is what *can* be validly said about a general class of phenomena. Where the phenomena become so unique that they no longer fit into any class, we may still be interested—as we may be in something without equal or parallel

[8] Triffin lists "financial backing" among extraneous factors. *Op. cit.*, p. 71.

[9] Some of such factors may also be important in a polypolistic situation. But there they may merely affect and change the actual outcome, which is determinate in any event. Disregard them—and the solution will be *different*, but not indeterminate.

—but our interest is no longer that of generalizing scientists.[10] The theory of oligopoly must stop before it becomes too specific— that is, so specific that it applies only to unique cases—and even if it has not by that time arrived at complete determinacy.[11]

On the other hand, the theory of oligopoly must not stop too early, that is, it cannot be satisfied with the general assumption made for the economic analysis of the business firm, namely, that it will maximize its profits. This clearly is not enough. More is needed even for a rather general theory of oligopolistic behavior and, of course, still more for the theories of each of the main types of oligopoly which a classification chooses to distinguish. In exercising one's judgment about how far to go in introducing more specific assumptions, one should not be influenced by narrow partisanship to the "schools" of "abstract" versus "institutional" economics.[12] In the question of admitting additional assumptions into a theoretical model their relative usefulness should be the only decisive consideration. If an assumption seems to be in reasonable conformance with observation or reliable testimony in a large number of instances and with the findings of imagined intro-

[10] The very fact that students of supposedly purely descriptive case histories do not ordinarily publish within one book the unique cases of a melancholic mass murderer, a paraphlegmic concert violinist, a universal chess, track, and wrestling champion, and a guaranteed non-collusive oligopolist proves that they do recognize that even most unique cases somehow belong into general classes and that generalizations about types abstracting from all specific details are necessary and useful.

[11] In answer to an appeal for more empirical research into the thinking, prejudices, temperaments, intuitive judgment, and shrewd knowledge of entrepreneurs as a prerequisite of a proper analysis of price policy, K. W. Rothschild commented as follows: "But, surely, the peculiarities of price behaviour under oligopolistic conditions are not due to any peculiarities in the psychology of duopolists and oligopolists, but to the different economic environment in which they work. By all means let us have more research into the psychology of the business-man in all the various market situations, but the distinguishing feature of oligopolistic price theory cannot lie in additional psychological investigations, but in the provision of a framework which will show the actions of a "normal" business-man under the specific conditions of an oligopolistic environment." *Op. cit.*, p. 306.

[12] "The theory of oligopoly has been aptly described as a ticket of admission to institutional economics." Edward S. Mason, "Price and Production Policies of Large-Scale Enterprise," *American Economic Review*, Supplement, Vol. XXIX (1939), pp. 64–65.

spection, and if it modifies the operations of our models in a way as to achieve greater conformance with observed phenomena of the real world (and if this degree of conformance cannot be achieved with fewer or simpler assumptions) such assumption should be eligible for admission to our models no matter whether it is labeled "economic" or "extra-economic."

The "extra-economic" label might be hung either on the *motivation* of the oligopolistic seller's actions, or on the *nature* of their actions, or on some *outside influences* on these actions. The motivation may be one competing with the profit motive, which is commonly assumed to be the chief or sole guide of the actions of polypolistic sellers. The nature of the oligopolists' actions may be political—e.g., inducing an intervention by the government—or social—e.g., instigating other members of the trade to ostracize a rival—instead of strictly economic, that is, consisting (in our society) chiefly in selling, buying, offering, and bidding. The outside influences may, again, be governmental or corporative [13] policies.

Position, Security, and Profit

The "monistic" place given, in the theory of the firm, to the principle of profit maximization has been subject to severe criticism. Other motives are seen to be competing with the profit motive in entrepreneurial considerations. The desire for "position" and the quest for "security" are said to be on a par with the striving for maximum profits. Profit, security, and position are named as three separate objectives of the firm, one economic, the others "non-economic."

Two questions suggest themselves in connection with the proposed "inclusion of these 'non-economic' elements" [14] among the essential elements for an explanation of oligopolistic behavior and price: (1) To what extent are the two "non-economic" motives, the desires for position and security, separate from and independent of the profit motive? (2) To what extent is it true that the need for distinguishing position and security as separate motives

---

[13] "Corporative" are the policies of the trade associations.
[14] K. W. Rothschild, *op. cit.*, p. 319.

(or sub-motives) for the behavior of the firm arises in the theory of oligopoly, but not in the theories of polypoly and monopoly?

Taking the second question first, we can see immediately that attempts to improve a firm's *position* in the industry are foreign to polypolistic as well as to monopolistic behavior, because both the polypolist and the monopolist take their positions for granted. This is true regardless of whether "position" is defined by the seller's share in the total market for the products of the industry or, subjectively, by the importance he attaches to himself or by his feeling of being recognized as an important factor in his industry or line of business.[15] A seller is a polypolist if he considers himself too insignificant in the market to be recognized by any of the other sellers as an important factor in the market. A seller is a monopolist if he considers himself as the only one in the market and, thus, thinks of no one who would or would not recognize his importance. He is a perfect monopolist if he is not even afraid of any potential newcomer who might disturb the situation. In no event can he improve his position. The oligopolist, on the other hand, has, at any time, a certain share in the market and enjoys a certain recognition as an important factor in the industry. He may be bent upon improving his position, and he may fear to see it reduced. Position, thus, is a consideration that may count a good deal in the mental make-up of the oligopolist.

The same reasoning holds to a large extent for *security* as an objective of the firm. In polypoly the problem of security can hardly arise independently of the problem of maximum profit. The same policy which promises a maximum of money profits to the polypolist will also give him maximum security. The more money he makes, the more secure he will feel.[16] In perfect monopoly the seller feels absolutely safe; hence, he never needs to pass up any profit opportunities for the sake of his security. The imperfect monopolist is not in this happy situation. He does have to look out for his security and may have to forsake chances of juicier profits in order to safeguard his financial and market position,

---

[15] This is only one of several meanings of "position." Some writers use the term interchangeably or correlatively with "security"; to them the position which the seller desires is one of security. This "safe position" will be discussed presently.

[16] See above, Chapter 2, pp. 51–56.

chiefly against potential newcomer's competition, but also against government intervention or public opinion. This is even more so in the case of an oligopolist. The oligopolist must look out not only for potential newcomer's competition, potential government intervention, and potential public disapprobation, but in addition also for potential misunderstanding with, and retaliations from, his competitors. Indeed, we have made the concern with rival's reactions the characteristic of oligopoly and must certainly not fail to give it—and, in connection with it, the desire to avoid excessively costly conflict—a most prominent place in the explanation of oligopolistic behavior.

It remains to be seen, however, whether these security considerations can be clearly distinguished from profit considerations. This is, of course, nothing else but the first of the two questions raised above, namely, whether the security motive can be, and should be, distinguished from the profit motive.

There is a strong separatist movement agitating for the autonomy of the security motive.[17] It is admitted that, even under oligopoly, actions motivated by the desire for maximum security will in most instances be the same as actions motivated by the desire for maximum profit. But it is contended that there are instances in which "the two motives lead to conflicting patterns of behavior. Where profit maximization demands prices fluctuating with every change in revenue and cost conditions, security maximization may demand rigid prices; while profit maximization should tend to create firms of optimum size, security considerations will favor the oversized firm; again, where we should expect reserve funds to be invested in response to expected returns, we may find their practically unconditional reinvestment in their own firm." [18]

The separatist movement is opposed by those who campaign for maintaining the union of profit and security considerations under the banner of "long-run profits." If every price change may involve the risk of a price war cutting down the profits or even

---

[17] Rothschild declares that "the security motive must be given the same pride of place as has been occupied by the profit maximization principle for such a long time." *Op. cit.*, p. 309.

[18] *Ibid.*

turning them into losses, the avoidance of price changes can be fully explained in terms of long-run profits. If the oligopolist believes that a reserve of unused capacity, which he can threaten to utilize at any time, may help him maintain or even increase in the future his share in the market—be it in the form of agreed quotas or through silent acquiescence on the part of his competitors—his policy is perfectly explicable in terms of long-run money profits. Indeed, one may well insist that policies which fail to take account of all these factors should not properly be regarded as policies designed to maximize profits. For, after all, what sense can there be in calling "profit maximization" a course of action which *would* maximize profits only *if* half the facts of the situation were different from what they are? Is the separation of the security motive from the profit motive fundamentally anything but an arbitrary separation of some data from the rest of the data relevant in the situation?

The trouble with both the separatists and the unionists is that they fight for the universality and exclusive truthfulness of their respective points of view and fail to see that there can be many different models schematizing the same set of facts. Whether one model or another is "better" is often merely a matter of taste or habit of thought. That a separation of data is "arbitrary" is not a decisive criticism of the autonomy of the security motive. Likewise, that the merger of all pecuniary considerations under the name of long-run profit maximization may look "tautological" is not a decisive criticism of the subsumption of security considerations under the profit motive. One can deal with these considerations equally well whether they are treated under the heading of a separate security motive or as additional points under the all-inclusive profit motive. The main thing is that they are treated; under what heading they are treated is irrelevant.

There is much more justification in the demand for separating the firm's desire for "position" from the objective of maximum profits if position is merely a matter of vanity and conceit and not a means of making or safeguarding profits. In principle, of course, it is again true that it does not matter under what heading this sort of consideration is introduced in the analysis. But while the question of safe profits will hardly be overlooked when maximum profits are being discussed, there is a possibility that prestige considerations get lost in the shuffle. In order to guard against such an oversight one may well insist on a separate listing for the oligopolist's desire for position.

Military Strategy and Games of Strategy

It has been suggested that the analyst of oligopolistic behavior should study Clausewitz's *Principles of War*.[19] "There he will not only find numerous striking parallels between military and (oligopolistic) business strategy, but also a method of a *general* approach which . . . promises a more realistic treatment of the oligopoly problem."[20]

We should not deny that such a study can be highly suggestive. But what it probably would yield more than anything else is a metaphoric language of greater pungency. The oligopolists, in such a language, would "entrench themselves" in order "to hold what they hold"; they would "launch an offensive into rival territory"; they would "stick to the fortress of the quoted price" or have their "price surrounded by a variety of minor weapons," which may also "serve as tools for tactical manoeuvres in the enemy's territory" or "provide a defense in depth" against the enemy's attacks; they might hope for "a widening of the terrain," "proceed to new position," or plan "an attack on rival strongholds."[21]

Whether the treatment of oligopoly in terms of military strategy would yield much beyond a richer vocabulary and a larger stock of analogies is doubtful. The analogies might be most helpful to students of military science while sometimes confusing to civilian minds.

Of much greater force are the claims made for the application to the oligopoly problem of the mathematical theory of "games of strategy." Here the contention is not merely of strong analogies between the two spheres, that is, between economic and, in particular, oligopolistic behavior, on the one hand, and games of

[19] General Karl von Clausewitz, *Grundgedanken über Krieg und Kriegführung* (Leipzig: 1915).

[20] K. W. Rothschild, *op. cit.*, p. 307.

[21] All these quotations are from Rothschild's article.

strategy, on the other. The contention rather is "that the typical problems of economic behavior become strictly identical with the mathematical notions of suitable games of strategy." [22]

The crux of the problem of oligopoly as well as of any game of strategy (such as chess, poker, or bridge) is "the fact that every participant is influenced by the anticipated reactions of the others to his own measures, and that this is true for each of the participants." [23] Where "each participant attempts to maximize a function . . . of which he does not control all variables," the problem is not really a "maximum problem," not a "problem of the calculus of variations," but instead one of "combinatorics and set theory" of a very novel type.[24] A new concept of economic rationality evolves from this; it calls for provisos "for every possible conduct" of the other participants; that is, "its description must include rules of conduct for all conceivable situations—including those where 'the others' behaved irrationally." [25]

The essential difference between the customary theories of oligopoly and one in terms of the mathematical theory of games is this: in the customary theories it had to be assumed that each seller acted on the basis of *some* anticipations, however vague and uncertain, of his rivals' reactions to his own actions. In the theory of games each participant acts in such a way as to obtain a result that would be the best, or rather, least bad, in *any* event, including the most unfavorable counter-moves which the rivals may make to his move. In other words, the rational oligopolist, just as the player of a game of strategy, is supposed to adopt a "good strategy" securing him some minimum gain irrespective of what the rival or the rivals may do. Some of these good strategies are perfectly determinate. The theory of these strategies, therefore, partly overcomes the problem of duopolistic indeterminateness.

There are two kinds of good strategies: "pure strategies" and "mixed strategies." In the latter a player plays "several different strategies at random, so that only their probabilities are determined . . . By this device the opponent cannot possibly find out what the player's strategy is going to be, since the player does not

---

[22] John von Neumann and Oskar Morgenstern, *op. cit.*, p. 2.
[23] *Ibid.*, p. 13.
[24] *Ibid.*, pp. 11, 45.
[25] *Ibid.*, p. 32.

know it himself." [26] It is questionable, in my opinion, whether these mixed strategies are of great importance in oligopolistic behavior. An oligopolist, more often than not, will not mind if his competitors find out what his own strategy is; indeed he often prefers them to understand the intent of his moves because misunderstandings may lead to costly conflict.

The "good strategies" are not "permanently optimal." For example, if the opponent makes mistakes, adherence to the "good strategy" will involve failure to exploit these mistakes. That is to say, while the "good strategies are perfect from the defensive point of view, they will (in general) not get the maximum out of the opponent's (possible) mistakes,—i.e., they are not calculated for the offensive." [27] Whether or not this is a very serious matter, is hard to say.[28] In any case it leaves the competitors a choice between the "good strategies," which fail to exploit the opponents' mistakes, and such other strategies as may take full advantage of them. And thus, of course, the outcome is again indeterminate.

Among the most intriguing features of the theory of games is the problem of the formation of coalitions (combinations, alliances) among some players against others, with the implied problems of the distribution of the spoils, the threat of defection, the payment of compensations, and so forth. The whole "theory of games and economic behavior," however, has not yet been fully extended to cases of more than three or four participants. Since not only the sellers in an oligopolistic industry but also the buyers are regarded as players in this game of strategy, the number of participants in the market in question is much greater than the theory in its present form can "accommodate."

The Strong Sparing the Weak

There may be many good reasons for competitors in a coalition not to exploit their victories against non-members of the coali-

---

[26] *Ibid.*, p. 146.

[27] *Ibid.*, p. 164.

[28] Hans Brems believes that this is a serious weakness of the theory. See "Some Notes on the Structure of the Duopoly Problem," *Nordisk Tidskrift for Teknisk Økonomi*, Vol. XII (1948), p. 46.

tion too mercilessly.[29] And even apart from coalitions and combinations, a competitor may find that the elimination of a rival, however attractive from some (pecuniary) points of view, may not promise to be advantageous from other (likewise pecuniary) points of view.[30]

The problem of oligopolistic indeterminacy, however, is pointed up most effectively if the motives for a strong oligopolist to treat his weak competitors with leniency are non-pecuniary. One may easily visualize the situation in which a strong member of the industry—strong in terms of efficiency as well as financial resources —would find it both possible and profitable completely to eliminate his weaker competitors and nevertheless decides to spare them. Here are some possible reasons for the strong to favor the survival of the weak:

(1) He may not like to be regarded as a "killer" or "ruthless operator." (He may share this negative "ethical" evaluation of vigorous competition or he may merely wish to avoid the social disapproval that attaches to it.)

(2) He may not like to become a "monopolist" in the popular or legal sense. (He may share this negative evaluation of "monopoly" or merely wish to avoid the social disapproval that attaches to it and the danger of governmental action against him.)

(3) He may not like to make his management problem too complicated by removing the "check of competitive markets" upon the efficiency of the subdivisions of his company. (As long as each department of a firm can be compared with another firm, the head management has some standards of evaluating their efficiency. The ambition of department supervisors to operate more cheaply than the "competitors" may also be regarded as an aid to the management.)

(4) He may not like to miss the satisfaction of being the stronger one in a "competitive struggle." (Once he kills his weaker competitors, the fight is over; his work will be duller. As long as he keeps them alive, he can enjoy the feeling of being stronger, he can flex his muscles and be admired by the crowd.)

[29] Von Neumann and Morgenstern, *op. cit.*, p. 329.
[30] The Theory of Games and Economic Behavior is not entirely in terms of pecuniary gains, it accommodates gains in measurable utility.

There may be many other reasons besides these. I have mentioned them chiefly in order to add weight to the argument that "maximization of money profits" is not sufficient to determine or explain an oligopolist's policies. Of course, two of the reasons—avoidance of government action, and the problem of management —may have their pecuniary aspects and, thus, be part of profit maximizing. But, by and large, the motivation for the strong to spare the weak may not be pecuniary in nature and nothing is gained by including a "money equivalent" of non-pecuniary satisfaction and dissatisfaction in the hypothetical calculation of money profits. The point to bear in mind is that many such non-pecuniary considerations are probably of little or no significance in the analysis of polypolistic behavior, while they may be very important in the analysis of oligopolistic behavior. The extent to which we choose to disregard or to take account of them will materially affect the determinacy of oligopoly theory.

The Forms and Degrees of Collusion

Several times we have used the terms "collusive," "coordinated," and "cooperative" oligopoly as if they were fully equivalent and interchangeable; at other places we have used them with slight shadings of meaning. Before we proceed to a more detailed discussion of the forms and degrees of collusion, we had better clarify the semantic relationships between collusion, coordination, and cooperation in selling.

Coordination, Collusion, Cooperation

Since coordination is combined action in the production of a particular result, it requires collusion, cooperation, or coercion. We may omit the separate listing of coercion if we note that collusion or cooperation may be either voluntary or under pressure. Thus, we can state that coordinated oligopoly implies collusion (or cooperation). This statement, however, is not reversible. Not all collusion achieves coordination. Some collusive attempts may be so feeble that they will not succeed in producing even imperfectly coordinated oligopoly. There may be a slight degree of collusion in uncoordinated oligopoly. Ordinarily, of course, collusive oligopoly will produce some measure of coordination.

More arbitrariness is involved in the use of the words collusion and cooperation. From the ethical and legal points of view the difference seems to be considerable; but there may be only a slight difference, if any, from the point of view of economics.[31] The most expedient way of using these words in connection with competition in selling is to say that cooperative selling is collusive selling with the idea in the seller's mind that it is the nice thing to do (and perhaps even legal), while the concept of collusive selling also comprises certain kinds of "considerate" or "cautious" competition that fall short of cooperation as well as more elaborate schemes going beyond mere cooperation. In other words, we propose to use the term collusion for the wider concept which includes cooperation. But there is nothing sacrosanct about this terminological decision. It would be just as well to use collusive and cooperative oligopoly as interchangeable words with identical meaning.

Sensitive readers may accuse us of attempting to use loaded words, since "collusion" is sometimes used with an undertone of condemnation and with an allusion to deceit, fraud, or trickery. Let us make it absolutely clear that no ethical connotation is here intended and that the word as used in economic analysis is meant to be neutral as to ethical judgments and unprejudicial as to legal consequences.[32] The word has been used so long in economics that one would be needlessly fussy if, on account of any ethical

---

[31] "To be charged with 'collusion' sounds rather bad. Besides suggesting legal sanctions, it connotes a severe moral opprobrium. But the word can be replaced by an equivalent and the opprobrious connotation disappears. Call it 'cooperation' and the frown of the moralist gives place to an approving nod.

"Is collusive and cooperative conduct really the same thing with respect to the competitive relationships between businessmen? The literal meanings of the Latin verbs from which the adjectives are derived are 'to play together' and 'to work together,' respectively. The former has acquired a derogatory, the latter a commendatory connotation in everyday language as well as in the law. In the economics of competitive behavior the differences tend to disappear because the effects of 'collusive' and 'cooperative' conduct on the part of competitors may be the same. If competitors 'cooperate' in pricing their products, they engage in 'collusion.'" Fritz Machlup, *The Basing-Point System* (Philadelphia: Blakiston, 1949), p. 34.

[32] For a discussion of the "ethics of law violation" and the "ethics of restraint of competition" see Fritz Machlup, *op. cit.*, pp. 32–41.

connotations, one tried to do without it, particularly since it is less ambiguous in its economic meaning than most other terms are.

We should renounce also the connotation of secrecy which sometimes attaches to the term collusion. To be sure, there are many forms of collusion which are essentially tacit and implicit. It is true also that in countries where restraints of trade are illegal the secrecy of collusive attempts may be essential. But there are many countries where cartels are not unlawful and are even fostered by the state. The collusion behind the most perfectly co-ordinated oligopolies is often open and official. Collusion, as the word is used in this book, ranges from the most tender forms of understanding without contact or communication to the most formal and elaborate compacts or treaties.

We shall avoid speaking of "independence of action" as indicating "the absence of agreement or of 'tacit' agreement." [33] The word independence has been used in so many different meanings that misunderstandings are bound to arise if one continues to use it in the discussion of oligopolistic behavior.[34]

The Rationale of Collusion

Unlimited competition may be a fine thing from the point of view of the political philosopher speculating about the welfare of the people, but it surely is a nuisance from the point of view

---

[33] Chamberlin, *The Theory of Monopolistic Competition* (Cambridge: Harvard University Press, 5th ed., 1947), p. 47.

[34] The statement "seller A is *independent* of seller B" may have any of the following eight meanings, and probably more:

1. A is not linked to B through corporate ties, not under the same ownership or control.

2. A is not obligated to B by contract, not bound by any direct or indirect agreement.

3. A does not feel committed to B under any implied understanding or moral code.

4. A is not animated by a will to cooperate with B or to avoid his displeasure.

5. A is not under B's pressure, coercive power, authority, or leadership.

6. A is not under B's influence exercised through advice or suggestion.

7. A is not conscious of any possible repercussions of B's possible reactions to his actions.

8. A is not aware of any effects of B's prices or sales on his sales.

of most businessmen. There may be a few hardy individualists among them who enjoy vigorous competition—as long as they are stronger than their opponents, can take pride in their success, and make enough money for comfort. But those who are losing ground and those who are losing money, or fear that they may lose, and all those who prefer an easy life to one of strain and strife—the majority, I dare say—regard unrestrained competition as an uncivilized way of doing business, unnecessarily costly of nervous energy and money, and disruptive of friendly relations with their fellow men.

"Vigorous competition" among oligopolists has been defined as the behavior of sellers "if and when they take active steps to expand their share of the market or defend themselves against other sellers' attempts to expand their shares." [35] Such reciprocal attempts to steal business from each other involve sacrifices to the sellers in the form of lower prices or higher costs depending on whether it is price competition, quality competition, or promotional competition to which they resort. These sacrifices are felt to be "unnecessary" from the point of view of the group of competitors taken as a whole; they certainly reduce their combined profits.

If all the productive resources of the industry were united under single control, the policy aiming at highest possible profits would be "monopolistic policy" and the profits attained would be "monopoly profits." If the productive resources are not under single control, the most perfectly coordinated oligopoly could pursue a policy *approaching* the monopolistic policy, and could hope to attain profits *approaching* the potential monopoly profits. Deviations are unavoidable chiefly because of these four factors: (1) different judgments about present and future market and cost conditions, necessitating compromises among the different managements; (2) different cost conditions in different plants owned by different firms, necessitating different allocation of the business within the industry; (3) the cost of administering the various compromises and the payments of compensations and bribes among the members of the groups; and (4) the deliberate sacrifice of the optimal group policies (i.e., of policies designed to attain a

[35] Hans Brems, "Cartels and Competition," *Weltwirtschaftliches Archiv.*, Vol. 66 (1951), p. 54.

maximum of the combined profits of the group) in favor of policies benefiting particular members or subgroups of members.

It is possible, for purposes of theorizing, always to start with the hypothetical assumption that the maximization of the combined profits of the group is the paramount objective of all oligopolistic policy, and then to take account of all the factors which in any particular constellation prevent such a policy from being pursued and which, thus, limit the attainment of the goal under particular conditions.[36] The traditional approach, on the other hand, begins with the considerations and actions of the individual seller in the historical situation in which he finds himself, striving to maximize his own profits but realizing that this may call for self-restraint or for agreed or imposed restraint in order to avoid the useless ("ruinous") competitive tug of war. Where the acceptance of the historical situation takes too much of the developed pattern of collusion as a datum—and thus leaves too much of the oligopolistic behavior unexplained—one will have to retrace some of the steps and show the dynamic evolution of the collusive-oligopolistic situation. This kind of analysis emphasizes the departure and deviation from uncoordinated competition and the attainment of such degree of coordination as the collusive conduct of the individual sellers makes possible. (This approach is, in a sense, the exact opposite of the one that starts from the most perfect coordination and then corrects the full-monopoly-results for deviations due to any obstacles standing in the way of the attainment of the highest forms and degrees of collusion.)

In any event, the rationale of collusion is clear no matter whether it is high-powered collusion aiming at maximization of the combined profits of the group or collusion of a lowly form and modest degree aiming at prevention of the worst losses from "reckless price-cutting."

The Degrees of Collusion

As we have said repeatedly, and probably to the dismay of lawyers to whom collusion is either present or absent, for the economist the question of collusion in oligopolistic competition

[36] This is the procedure which Fellner adopted for his analysis of oligopoly.

usually is not one of "whether" but of "how much." It is rather difficult to visualize or construct plausible models of oligopoly in which the sellers continue for a long time to act without the least bit of collusion. Complete absence of collusion implies "that no firm has any trust whatever in its competitors," [37] that is, the firm may try to guess the competitors' reactions to its actions, but it may never expect particular reactions with any confidence.[38] In actual fact, however, oligopolists in most instances think they know pretty well what reactions they can expect from their competitors and, moreover, their expectations ordinarily prove correct.

One may call it the "first degree of collusion" if a seller has reason to trust his competitors not to initiate a price cut independently unless their volume of business falls below a subsistence minimum; thus, unless business is extraordinarily slack, he can expect that his own refusal to accept lower prices will keep the others from cutting.[39] One may call it a case of "collusion of the second degree" if a seller has reason to trust his competitors not to start selling without provocation in the territory (or to the customer group) which he considers his own market unless their business volume falls below a subsistence minimum; thus, unless business is terribly bad, he can expect that his own refusal to accept orders from their territory will keep them from entering his. Similar expectations, based on a certain amount of confidence that his competitors will, for the time being, restrain various of their competitive impulses, may constitute other, though still relatively low, degrees of collusion.

Somewhat higher degrees of collusion might leave off the reservations concerning very bad business, or might add expectations of more positive behavior than mere abstention from starting

---

William Fellner, *Competition Among the Few: Oligopoly and Similar Market Structures* (New York: Knopf, 1949), pp. 120–232. He characterizes his theory as one of "limited joint maximization" (p. 198).

[37] R. F. Kahn, "The Problem of Duopoly," *Economic Journal*, Vol. XLVII (1937), p. 9.

[38] This is the reason for applying the "theory of games" to noncollusive oligopoly.

[39] This is an adaptation from Kahn (*op. cit.*, 9) who was the first to speak of the "first degree of collusion," but did not include the "escape clause" for very bad times. Without such an escape clause the collusion is already of a somewhat higher degree.

unprovoked vigorous competition. For example, where the product comes in several qualities, shapes, calipers, etc., for which different prices must be asked, or where discriminatory prices are charged, mere maintenance of some "average" level of prices will hardly be enough; it may be necessary, in order to allow the expectations to be (a) sufficiently specific and (b) sufficiently confident, to develop a system of informing the competitors (a) of the prices that will be quoted to potential buyers and (b) of the prices that were charged to actual buyers. Schemes providing this intelligence among the competitors constitute a much higher degree of collusion.

I shall not attempt to construct a roster of all degrees of collusion, ranging, say, from one to one hundred. Merely in order to indicate the general idea, I shall call it the "39th degree of collusion" if a seller has reason to trust his competitors to announce a list of the prices they are going to quote to any potential buyers or to specific groups of buyers, and not to recede from these prices without giving him advance notice in some form, provided he adheres to the same code of behavior. This, of course, is what in our classification was called an open-price oligopoly. A scheme providing only *ex post* information on orders, without implied promise of price maintenance or of quota restrictions, would constitute a somewhat lower degree of collusion, whereas a combination of such *ex post* reporting with an open-price system would be a substantially higher degree. It is, say, the "68th degree of collusion" if a seller has reason to trust his competitors to announce a list of their prices, not to recede from these prices without advance notice, and to report all sales and selling prices to the statistical service of their trade association.[40]

[40] Attempts have been made to describe and justify open-price oligopoly in terms of the "perfect information" which it provides as a necessary ingredient of perfect competition—since in a perfect market full knowledge of all offers and bids is required. When the number of both sellers and buyers is very large, publicity of bids and offers will indeed be an aid to competition. For example, publicity of the momentary prices asked by the mass of sellers will allow the shiftability of buyers, and the elasticity of their demand for each seller's wares, to be greatly increased. Things are different where the number of sellers is not very large. Here open prices become a monopolistic device, instrumental in the suppression of price competition, in the operation of price leadership, and in the sellers' confidence in the maintenance of the an-

Still higher degrees of collusion would add expectations of price followership in the case of price increases by one of the sellers, either within limits or, better still, without limits. It would be a similarly high degree of collusion if a seller could expect each of his competitors not to exceed his sales quota without paying an agreed penalty. The "100th degree of collusion" is realized if a member of a syndicate has reason to trust the other members not even to make preparations for leaving the syndicate and not to break any of its rules as long as he himself remains faithful; he can thus expect that his own refusal to break away from the syndicate and to break its rules will keep the others from defection and contravention.

The Forms of Collusion

The differences in the degree of collusion which we discussed were chiefly in the *contents* of the expectations regarding the competitors' conduct. Under collusive oligopoly a seller "has reason" to trust his competitors to do this or that, or to refrain from doing one thing or another. What is the basis for this confidence? What gives the seller reason to expect certain behavior on the part of his competitors? To answer these questions is to describe the *forms* collusion can take.

There is a strong tendency for non-collusive oligopoly to develop into collusive oligopoly, and for collusion of lower degrees to develop into collusion of higher degrees.[41] No such tendency is recognizable for the form of collusion; the forms which particular industries have chosen for their collusive ties show no general

---

nounced prices by the competitors as long as he himself complies. The downward price-elasticity of demand is thereby so effectively reduced that price cutting becomes unattractive.

[41] Competitive behavior in non-collusive oligopoly will usually "invite retaliation, and the fear of retaliation invites self-restraint. The self-restraint, in turn, is apt to lead to some sort of understanding between the oligopolists; and collusive oligopoly . . . will be the outcome. For this reason it is rather unlikely that oligopoly would remain noncollusive for a long time. When each oligopolist has to guess the others' reactions and to practice self-restraint in order to avoid unpleasant competition, they all will be inclined to make the restraint a little more dependable and replace the vague guessing of the others' price quotations by safe knowledge." Fritz Machlup, *op. cit.*, p. 177.

tendency to become more highly developed. Indeed, the form of collusion is not correlated with the degree of collusion. That is to say, the form of collusion is not the predominant factor in determining either the *contents* of the expectations which sellers entertain regarding the behavior of their rivals or the *confidence* with which they entertain these expectations. Collusion of a relatively high degree may be most informal, based on nothing but tacit understanding. On the other hand, a rather elaborate apparatus is sometimes established to accomplish collusion of a relatively low degree. This lack of positive correlation between form and degree is due chiefly to the presence of other essential variables, especially the number of cooperating firms in the group.

A naive idea has long assumed that collusion necessarily involves "agreement" or, at least, communication among the "conspirators." This view is now commonly rejected in economic analysis as well as in law.[42] There are many possible forms of collusion requiring no direct contact and no direct communication among the participants. Even indirect communication may be dispensable. We shall see that in some of the forms described here either direct contact or communication or both are absent.

Tradition or consistent usage constitutes the "first form of collusion." The individual seller has reason to trust his competitors to act in a certain way if they have always done so or if they have done so consistently for a long time. A consistent pattern of conduct adhered to over long periods of time, especially a pattern of responses to the competitors' actions, permits the competitors to expect continued adherence to the same pattern.

Informal expressions of opinions about the fairness of certain practices or about the ethics of the trade, with the implication that one will adhere to these standards of fairness, constitute a second form of collusion. (If the facts of both the first and the second forms are combined, a higher form of collusion results.) Informal talk among the sales agents of the competing firms acquainting

---

[42] The official rejection of the doctrine requiring evidence of communication among the participants of collusion was pronounced by the Supreme Court of the United States in the Tobacco Case and reiterated in the Cement Case. *American Tobacco Co. et al.* v. *United States*, 328 U.S. 781 (1946); *Federal Trade Commission* v. *Cement Institute et al.*, 333 U.S. 683 (1948).

one another with the policies of their principals may establish collusion in a third form. A fourth form is through announcements by trade associations of which the sellers are members and whose declarations they approve explicitly or through actual compliance. A fifth form is through announcements by the firms themselves with the implication that they will adhere to the announced policy. Participation by the firms in trade association meetings, with the implication that its code of practices and recommendations of policy will be accepted, is a sixth form of collusion. None of these six forms of collusion includes "agreement"; at best they involve "understanding." But, it should be obvious, the most informal, impersonal understanding will often achieve far better compliance than the most formal and pretentious covenant.

A simple form of collusion for which neither direct contact nor communication among the participants is required, is the use of the same sales agent (or sales agents for particular territories). All possible degrees of collusion, from the lowest to the highest, can be achieved through this form. If the firms want it, syndicated oligopoly can be achieved in this very simple and "innocent" form of collusion. In this case, of course, the agency agreements between each producer and the sales agent are really a way of circumventing the need for formal agreements among the producers; but agreement among them, voluntary or imposed, is of course a prerequisite of syndicated oligopoly if it is to last for longer periods.

There is a great variety of form in collusion based on explicit agreement. The least formal is the gentlemen's agreement, purely oral, with no minutes, no correspondence, no record whatever. Then there are the gentlemen's agreements with minutes of meetings, however cryptic, or with memoranda on some complicated points. Written agreements come next, first those concluded by each producer "separately" with a central agency or trade association, then those among the producers themselves, either in the form of simple correspondence or in the form of formal contracts. In countries with antitrust laws contracts must take the form of patent license agreements. In other countries they may be "straight" cartel contracts. They may provide sanctions for contravention, penalties for sales above quota, etc. And, in a still tighter form, they sometimes provide for the deposition of collateral as security for the payment of fines assessed in the case of violations. The "highest" of all forms of collusion may be seen in governmental orders and in private contracts with governmental stipulations for sanctions in the event of contravention.

Full descriptions of many of the higher forms of collusion have appeared in the (already impressive, but still growing) literature on national and international cartels.[43] The number of variations in cartel organization is rather large, as one should expect realizing how different are the structures of different industries and the legal institutions of different countries, and how great is the ingenuity of business leaders and corporation lawyers. The following generalizations suggest themselves to the observer:

1. If the group of firms is rather large and not subdivided in sectional or chain oligopolies, relatively more elaborate forms of collusion may be required in order to achieve relatively low degrees of collusion. Conversely, if the group is small,[44] very elementary forms of collusion may suffice to achieve collusion of relatively high degrees.

2. For any given group of firms it is probably easier to achieve a higher degree of collusion by a more elaborate form of collusion.[45]

3. In contrast to what has been found concerning the degree of collusion, there is no tendency for "lower" forms of collusion to develop into "higher" forms. On the contrary, if competitors have been cooperating for some time, they may be able to dispense with much of the formality and apparatus previously employed and may maintain the same, or even a higher, degree of collusion with a much lower form of collusion.

---

[43] Corwin D. Edwards, *Economic and Political Aspects of International Cartels*, Subcommittee on War Mobilization of the Senate Committee on Military Affairs, 78th Congress, 2nd Session (Washington: 1944); Ervin Hexner, *International Cartels* (Chapel Hill: University of North Carolina Press, 1945); George W. Stocking and Myron W. Watkins, *Cartels or Competition?* (New York: Twentieth Century Fund, 1948).

[44] Relevant is only the size of the group of close competitors "as seen by the individual seller," not in the "objective" sense of a census definition.

[45] "Coördination is likely to be tighter under explicit cartel agreements than under quasi-agreements." William Fellner, *op. cit.*, p. 230. This statement is valid only for a given group of firms. Otherwise it would be contradicted by our first proposition.

Implicit Agreements to Agree, and Other Quasi-Agreements

The possible informality of collusion is a fact fundamental for the understanding of business conduct. It was probably only because of the illegality of collusion in the United States and its legality elsewhere that the stress has usually been on formal agreements, of which material evidence could be produced. The often astounding parallelism of conduct on the part of supposedly competing sellers, the manifestly common pattern of action in the market, was frequently explained by the phenomenon of leadership, as if leadership were an *alternative* to collusion. Leadership, ordinarily, *implies* collusion, although it may be informal collusion. Leadership usually is based, if not on explicit agreement, on "quasi-agreement" [46] or, in particular, on an implicit "agreement to agree." [47]

The same people who under the pressure of antitrust investigation and prosecution explained the uniformity or parallelism of action in the market as an outcome of leadership oligopoly have sometimes tried to explain it *also* as an outcome of unrestricted price competition forcing selling prices to an identical level and making it impossible for any one of the competitors to sell at a higher price. This naive (but nevertheless often successful) attempt to confuse is self-contradictory because unrestricted price competition and price leadership are mutually exclusive.[48] What defendants charged with collusion should attempt to demonstrate is the absence of any agreement, contact, communication, direct or indirect, recent or past; they should attempt to prove that the

---

[46] William Fellner, *op. cit.*, pp. 120–36.

[47] Carl Kaysen, "Collusion under the Sherman Act," *Quarterly Journal of Economics*, Vol. LXV (1951), p. 268.

[48] According to Chamberlin, if there is "a dominant competitor to whose prices all others adapt themselves, recognizing that therein lies their greatest ultimate gain," the result is the same as "if there were no competition at all." *Op. cit.*, p. 50. The attempt to explain identical prices as the result of unrestricted price competition fallaciously identifies selling prices with quoted prices. Under price competition, quotations by different sellers will at first be very different, and only after some "shopping around and active higgling" can a uniform market price emerge. Under price leadership, as under most techniques of collusive pricing, the price quoted by any seller is immediately identical with that announced by the leader.

basis of the parallelism of action in the market is not an explicit but only an implicit agreement to agree, not an agreement but merely a quasi-agreement that has developed without communication among the competitors and without any history of organized collusion.[49]

In countries where "price fixing" is illegal and in industries where several products, qualities, shapes, calipers, etc., are sold at different prices or where varying transportation costs are somehow reflected in price differentials, agreements to agree are not only a great convenience, they are indeed indispensable for collusive oligopoly to be workable. It would be impossible for the competitors to get together on each price, each price differential, each price change. An agreement to agree makes such continuous consultation unnecessary; it substitutes *one* agreement for thousands of agreements. This one agreement may last, with interruptions or without, for years or decades, without any need for further communication among the oligopolists. And even this one basic agreement need not be explicit, but may be implied, may be a mere quasi-agreement. To be sure, in complicated cases, this is not very likely. If in such cases satisfactory coordination is achieved without apparent communication, one may assume that organized collusion, with direct communication among the participants and with some machinery for the dissemination of the necessary information, will have existed at some time in the past. The original conclusion of the agreement to agree then was explicit and only

[49] Kaysen offers this lucid explanation for the agreement to agree: "The basis of such an 'agreement' is the recognition by each seller that it may be better for him to follow a single judgment of the changing market situation, even though it is not his own and he sometimes disagrees with it, than to engage in the struggle which could arise if each seller attempted to enforce his own views. Thus each seller sacrifices his exercise of independent judgment in the market; in return he gains a much greater degree of certainty as to what his rivals will do. The 'agreement to agree' may result in the appearance of a single leader whose actions other sellers follow, or it may operate through a changing succession of leaders. Long continued uniformity of action, extended through a variety of situations amid changing circumstances, can therefore be taken as a basis for inferring, with a high degree of certainty, the existence of at least an 'agreement to agree'." In a footnote Kaysen adds the qualification: "It is not inconceivable that a situation could exist in which each of a group of sellers, with the appropriate exception, trusted the judgment of one of their number better than his own, and uniformity thus would be consistent with true independence. But it is hardly likely." *Op. cit.*, pp. 268–69.

its continuation is implicit. Compliance is the most effective way of continuing or renewing a past agreement.

Under leadership oligopoly each price and each price change may then be interpreted as being the subject of a quasi-agreement based on a lasting agreement to agree, which in turn may or may not be a quasi-agreement. Quasi-agreements, of course, are not only involved in leadership oligopoly but frequently form the basis for cooperative oligopoly with lower degrees of collusion. For example, schemes of peaceful division of the market or of peaceful sharing of the market often rest on quasi-agreements.[50]

Division of markets exists if sellers avoid selling to customers "reserved" to their competitors. Market sharing exists if sellers avoid selling more than a certain share of the total sales of the group of competitors. These divisions or shares may go back to an explicit agreement or may be merely a matter of custom, observed because of a quasi-agreement among the oligopolists. The following synthetic statement may correctly picture the way of thinking of each part to such a quasi-agreement: "If I go out and try to get a bigger share of the business, it will hurt the others. They will surely hit back. This won't do us any good. If I steal some of their customers, they will steal some of mine, and we'll all be worse off in the end. They know this just as well as I do, 'cause they are not any dumber than I am. So if I don't do anything that will hurt them, they won't do anything to hurt me. We all pull our punches, if we punch at all. And this is surely the best way for every single one of us." [51]

The Comprehensiveness of Collusion

Besides price making, market allocation, production and sales quotas, collusion may also comprise coordination concerning prod-

[50] I am not trying here to give aid and comfort to defendants charged with unlawful combination in restraint of trade. When I say that such schemes of dividing the market or sharing the market may rest on quasi-agreements only rather than on explicit collusion, I am not trying to give an impression that this is *likely* to be the case in many instances. Nor am I saying that collusion is lawful when it rests only on quasi-agreements.

[51] This is my own formulation, but I am sure that similar statements could be found in testimonies before official investigating committees or in answers to private investigators.

uct quality, credit terms, special services, and promotional efforts. The comprehensiveness of coordination is really an aspect of the degree of collusion; the highest degrees of collusion comprise all variables that may be relevant in the competitive efforts of the sellers. But, although we have said a good many things about the degrees of collusion, we have to add some observations on the question of the inclusion or exclusion of the "nonprice variables," the question of complete or incomplete coverage of collusion, and therefore the scope of oligopolistic nonprice competition.

Partially qualifying an earlier statement, we must note that the form of collusion seems to have a rather direct bearing upon the comprehensiveness of the oligopolistic coordination. While formal cartel contracts often extend to the nonprice variables of competition, collusion based on quasi-agreements is typically confined to price making, market allocation, and market sharing. This may have several reasons. First of all, tacit understandings must needs be simple and thus cannot include complicated arrangements about quality improvements or advertising expenditures. Secondly, competitors are not so anxious to restrain quality competition or promotional competition, because they do not fear that these will become cutthroat. Thirdly, the ostentatious practice of nonprice competition may be used as a symbol of the taboo on price competition. Fourthly, the competitors may prefer, at least under certain conditions, to leave open some outlets for their future competitive ambitions.[52]

OLIGOPOLY AND GENERAL EQUILIBRIUM

After all that has been said about oligopolistic indeterminacy and collusion we may be reasonably satisfied that oligopoly will not fit into a workable model of the general equilibrium of the

[52] "While oligopolistic firms typically live in a state of quasi-agreement, quasi-agreements do not typically cover the entire range of the market variables. The main reason for this appears to be that the relative strength of the participating firms is apt to change, and, if quasi-agreements included no outlets, the pressure exerted by the firms whose relative strength has increased would, in most cases, soon destroy the existing arrangements." William Fellner, op. cit., p. 183.

economy. A few remarks about the significance of this incompatibility may be in order.

Polypolistic and Oligopolistic Expectations

When we discussed polypoly we found that even our model of perfect polypoly required additional restrictions in order to permit the traditional elegance of the general equilibrium model: one had to assume that every seller expected every current market price to remain unchanged. Alternatively, general equilibrium analysis would have to be encumbered with additional "expectations functions" telling us the price expectations of each seller and how they would change when other things changed.

The next step was to inquire whether models of imperfect polypoly might be accommodated within a general equilibrium model of the whole economy without disrupting it. The answer was that the price expectations functions would have to be replaced by sales expectations functions of each seller, with all the complicated elasticity estimates and their changes due to all possible variations of other things. If it could be done, it would probably not be worth the trouble, because a general equilibrium model loses in usefulness whenever it loses in simplicity.

The additional assumptions that would be needed to make the conduct of oligopolistic sellers determinate were shown (in this chapter) to be unmanageable for anything but special cases. Hence they are certainly unmanageable within a general equilibrium model. This does not mean that everything that happens in an economy with oligopoly prevalent happens haphazardly and without reason. But it does mean that there is no use trying to play with a model crammed so full of special assumptions that both its lucidity and its generality are lost.

The General Equilibrium Model

There are those who are so firmly convinced of the supremacy of general equilibrium analysis in economics that they deny the prevalence of oligopoly in the economy or the relevance of oligopoly models in economic theory. There are others who are so convinced of the prevalence of oligopoly and of the necessity of recognizing it in the basic assumptions of economic theory that they deny the usefulness of general equilibrium analysis. Both these absolutist views are purblind. They fail to grasp the methodological principle that different aspects of reality can often be most advantageously clarified by models whose basic assumptions are mutually contradictory.[53]

General equilibrium models do not serve the same purpose and therefore need not include the same assumptions as the conduct models of individual decision-makers. The purpose of general equilibrium models is to depict the interdependence between the various parts of the economy, to show how any single change in any of the data affects everything else through a long chain of repercussions. The nature of these repercussions and of the interrelationships between variations of different magnitudes is elucidated the more clearly the fewer the variables and the simpler their interconnections. Nothing is gained by introducing "realistic" complications into such a model (except perhaps some admiration for the mathematical virtuosity of the exhibitor of the model).

There is thus no reason for decrying the incompatibility of oligopoly theory and general equilibrium analysis. The value of neither is diminished by the realization that they cannot be merged.

---

[53] Successive use of contradictory assumptions is made all the time in economics (as well as in other fields). Economists assume at one moment that all factors are mobile, then that they are not; that all factors and products and processes are perfectly divisible, then that many are indivisible; that the products made by a group of firms are homogeneous, then that they are differentiated; that all firms are equally efficient, then that some are superior to others; that transport costs are zero, then that they are significant; that technology is given and unchanged and known and open to all, then that it advances but is known and open to all, then that it advances but that the new knowledge is reserved to particular firms; that the capital stock remains unchanged, then that it increases; that uncertainty is absent, then that uncertainty exists but results in the same discounts everywhere, then that uncertainty is different in different ventures; and so forth. For more comprehensive models, especially for general equilibrium models, only the simplest assumptions are suitable—perfect mobility, divisibility, homogeneity, certainty, given technology and capital stock, etc.—, while for less comprehensive models more complex assumptions are practicable.

CHAPTER 14

Oligopolistic Nonprice Competition and Price Rigidity

Oligopolistic Nonprice Competition: The Nonprice Variables · Some Important Distinctions · Limits to the Practice of Nonprice Competition · The Significance of Oligopolistic Quality Competition · Determination of Outlay for Nonprice Competition

Oligopolistic Price Rigidity: The Concept of Price Rigidity · General Causes of Price Rigidity · Reasons Applying to Oligopoly Only · The Kink Theory of Price Rigidity

THE EXTENSION OF oligopoly theory to the "nonprice variables" of selling policy, and the question of the possible inclusion of these variables in collusive arrangements, have made us aware of the desirability of a more detailed discussion of oligopolistic nonprice competition. This discussion will, with almost logical force, lead us into an examination of the problem of oligopolistic price rigidity.

OLIGOPOLISTIC NONPRICE COMPETITION

We shall ask the following questions concerning oligopolistic nonprice competition: Can useful distinctions be made among the various nonprice variables of competitive selling? What are the inherent limitations on the use of different forms of competition in different industries? How valid and how significant is the distinction between polypolistic and oligopolistic nonprice competition? Can one for oligopoly situations arrive at valid generalizations regarding the determination of nonprice variables under given conditions?

The Nonprice Variables

In order to simplify classification and analysis the number of nonprice variables of competitive selling is customarily reduced to two: quality and promotion. In a good many instances, however, the distinction between better quality and greater selling effort is rather tenuous. (This was pointed out earlier, in Chapter 6, when "polypolistic competition through selling effort" was discussed.) Many things done by the seller to increase the appeal of his product to the buying public could be regarded with equal justification as improvement of quality or as increase in selling effort.[1]

This is largely true for the various activities of sellers that come under the heading of service to the customer. Firms may, for example, provide free consultation or engineering service to their clients; as a result of a study of the customer's needs the product may be more serviceable than one chosen without such service. Likewise, firms sometimes provide repair service which customers may regard as essentially contributing to the usefulness of the product (not because the service is free or less expensive, but because it is more reliable). Now, one may prefer to distinguish "service competition" as a type of its own, but nothing would be lost if the performance of these services were to be grouped either with quality competition or with promotional competition.

But while some of the competitive exertions could be classified either as better quality or as better promotion, there are others that could be called neither, at least not if their real nature is to be disclosed. The granting of better credit terms could be viewed as a deduction from the selling price if nothing else were involved but the saving of interest on the part of the customers. In fact, however, competition through credit terms usually means that firms extend credit to customers who might not be able to secure credit elsewhere. This sort of qualitative credit policy cannot be so easily "quantified"; to treat it merely as an aspect of price com-

---

[1] For example, if a product is sold in better containers, does this represent better quality or better promotion? The distinction will not do "as soon as we come to differences of color and design, fashion and style, to the things which satisfy and appeal, flatter and distinguish, to the matters which make buying more agreeable and convenient . . ." (p. 182, above).

petition may be more misleading than helpful; [2] to treat it as a form of promotional competition, along with advertising and better salesmanship, is to hide significant differences. It is probably best to recognize competition through credit terms as a separate form of nonprice competition.

The same is true for certain forms of competition through systematic freight absorption. Freight absorption by a seller may be just another form of price competition when it results in reduced delivered prices to the buyer. Sometimes, however, the sellers adhere to a system of quoting identical delivered prices, that is, to a system that excludes price competition. Under such a system a seller, honor-bound to eschew lowering delivered prices, can obtain additional business only by increasing his sales efforts, securing orders from far-away customers and absorbing the cost of shipping the product over the longer distances. Another seller, losing the orders of near-by customers but faithfully refraining from reducing delivered prices, can make up for his loss of business by selling to distant customers whom his competitor might supply at much smaller transport costs. The sellers, in this case, compete by paying for unnecessary transportation. The buyers do not get any benefit from this "competition through added mileage." [3]

Although the sellers' mill-net prices are reduced in consequence of this competition through added mileage, it is different from price competition in that prices paid by the buyers are not reduced. Although the sellers absorb the cost of transportation services to the buyers, this is different from "service competition" in that the buyers do not obtain any services they would not have obtained without the cross-hauling of the competitors' products. The case comes closest to that of competition through counterbalancing advertising, where the efforts of each seller neutralize one another. But while in both cases the benefit to the buyers is nil and the cost to the sellers may be considerable, and while in

[2] This does not mean that we must abandon geometric devices whenever we deal with cases that include selling for credit. We can, of course, elucidate *certain aspects* of these problems by the usual curve analysis, no less than for problems of quality improvement and selling effort. The risk of "bad debts" and the loss of interest could be treated as deductions from the revenue curves.

[3] Fritz Machlup, *The Basing-Point System* (Philadelphia: Blakiston, 1949), pp. 192–93.

both cases productive resources are wasted, there is at least a chance that competitive advertising increases the aggregate demand for the product; there is probably no chance that competitive cross-hauling can do the same.

Some Important Distinctions

Mention should be made again of the problem of "spatial competition," because this may erroneously be taken for a special form of oligopolistic competition, different from price competition as well as from any of the forms of nonprice competition here discussed. As the term has been employed in the literature, "spatial competition" is chiefly a problem in the theory of location, that is, an attempt to explain the choice of location under non-collusive oligopoly. As was said above (pp. 409–10), the model of spatial competition is used also as an aid in the analysis of oligopolistic quality competition, under the assumption that locational differentiation, which is measurable in terms of transportation cost, can serve as an analogy for quality differentiation, which is not measurable. But is "spatial competition" really competition, that is, part of a seller's effort to obtain more business at the expense of other sellers? As a strategy for reducing transportation cost with a view to lowering delivered prices to customers the search for the "best" location may be subservient to price competition. But in itself it is not competition at all. It is merely "getting into a position" enabling the seller to compete more effectively *if* he wants to compete.

There are many other actions that sometimes are called competitive but in fact are merely designed to improve, maintain, or restore the capacity to compete. "Competitive" efforts to increase productive efficiency and reduce production costs, "competitive" research and engineering work aiming at the development of cheaper or better products are partly an *effect* of competition from others and partly *preparation* for competition with others, but they are not themselves competitive actions.

Besides such actions as a firm may take to increase its competitive potential there are actions it may take to reduce the competitive potential of its rivals. A firm may try to put obstacles in the way of its competitors, reducing their productive efficiency or their financial strength or blocking an increase in their capacity to compete. Such actions are really designed to ward off price reductions or quality improvements by competitors; hence, they are designed to reduce competition. If every action against a competitor is called competitive, an important difference is lost sight of: the difference between a seller inducing buyers to switch their trade to him, and a seller preventing competitors from holding out inducements to buyers to attract their trade.[4] It is confusing if competition is given so wide a meaning that it includes interferences with competition.

Limits to the Practice of Nonprice Competition

When we say that competing sellers have a choice between price competition and nonprice competition, and among various forms of nonprice competition, we must not forget that the scope of the choice may be wide or narrow depending on circumstances beyond the control of the sellers.

The extent to which *quality competition* can be practiced in an industry depends largely on technological factors, that is, on how a product is made and for what it is used. The range of possible variations in quality will as a rule be greater for products made out of many component parts or ingredients than for products that combine fewer things. The number of possible combinations increases in geometric progression as the number of component parts increases. This explains, for example, why there can be more quality differences in automobiles than in window glass.[5] The range of variations, furthermore, is likely to be greater for products

---

[4] There are useful analogies in sports: for example, one might win a race by running faster or by keeping competitors from running fast; should both be called "competing"? There are, of course, some competitive sports with rules that permit "interferences."

[5] There is of course the arbitrary decision whether plate glass and window glass, milk bottles and beer bottles, etc., are different products or different qualities. Within each kind of glass container there is, according to a witness before a congressional committee, little "competition as to quality" because the possible differences in quality are small. *Investigation of Concentration of Economic Power. Hearings before the Temporary National Economic Committee*, Part 2 (Washington: 1939), pp. 548–49.

in the production of which precision, skill, or taste are essential. This explains, for example, why quality differences in wrist watches are usually greater than in gas stoves, and why the differences in ladies' dresses are greater than in jute bags.

Despite these "rules" we may find most remarkable ranges of quality differences in goods made out of relatively few component parts or ingredients or with relatively little precision, skill, or taste. Even with non-synthetic, non-composite materials more or less careful sorting and grading may cause significant differences in "quality." Fabrics that look identical to the layman may differ in a number of ways: the better grades may be washable, non-shrinking, non-fading, waterproof, holding shape, etc. Paper board may be more or less suited for various kinds of processing, such as bending, shaping, folding, grooving, pasting, printing, waterproofing, etc.[6]

Needless to say, quality competition has a much wider scope if we consider developing technology than if we consider only existing technology. In static analysis, therefore, the scope is narrower than in a dynamic analysis in which technology may be assumed to advance with time. This, however, is true for practically all forms of competition, and for price competition no less than for nonprice competition. For if new technology allows producers to manufacture their products by improved processes, it enables them to offer their products more cheaply. The impression that the scope of quality competition is naturally so much wider than that of price competition is due to the prevalence of static analysis in the economics of competition. In a *given* state of technical knowledge there are probably many different qualities in which a producer may choose to offer his product; but for each product quality there is only one cheapest way of producing it. Static analysis is thus apt to lead to an underestimation of the inherent

---

[6] Book paper is only one of many different types of paper. But even within this type one can distinguish "40 product classes, 12 grades, 33 finishes, . . . 8 colors, . . . and 19 types of packing." Combining this with the different sizes, trims, and quantity classes, "a meticulous specification of product would distinguish between 170 and 180 million possible products in the book paper industry." Committee on Price Determination for the Conference on Price Research, *Cost Behavior and Price Policy* (New York: National Bureau of Economic Research, 1943), p. 333.

scope of price competition. (If in actual fact, despite advancing technology, price competition in many fields is so much less in evidence than nonprice competition, this need not indicate that the inherent scope of price competition is so much narrower; it may mean merely that oligopolistic sellers choose not to make use of its potentialities.)

It is easy to understand why the possibilities of *competition through advertising* are considerably different in different fields. The effectiveness of newspaper and radio advertising in the sales promotion for consumers goods is probably very much greater than for producers goods. The number of buyers of consumers goods reached by the large advertising media is greater and their technological judgment is more naive. Industrial users will ordinarily rely more heavily on mechanical or chemical testing devices than on claims which suppliers make for their materials or appliances in papers, magazines, or over the radio. And while the majority of all newspaper readers and radio listeners are potential buyers of advertised consumers goods, only a small minority may be buyers of advertised producers goods. In general it would be only in trade journals or through selective mailing of circulars that printed advertisements of producers goods would promise to be an economical way of sales promotion.

Of course, not all advertising is sales promotion and not all sales promotion is competition. Sales promotion is competitive only if the seller expects by means of it to draw business away from an identifiable group of competing sellers, if not from identified particular rivals. And not a small part of all advertising is designed to advance the "public relations" of the advertisers rather than their sales. Much expensive radio time is taken up by sponsors who wish to court the favor of the broad public, not in order to sell more product, but in order to win the people's support or avoid antagonism in issues involving governmental controls or other matters of public policy affecting their activities.[7]

[7] It is highly unlikely that the "Railroad Hour" can persuade many radio listeners to travel by railroad. And it is hardly believable that anybody would get telephone service just because he has listened to the "Telephone Hour." (Indeed, in the post-war years the telephone company was unable to meet the demand and may have offered radio entertainment partly to maintain its good will with frustrated would-be customers who might be getting impa-

We might turn to other kinds of selling efforts and again observe that the scope of this form of competition is different in different fields.[8] But there is no need of pursuing the theme any further. It should be clear by now that the choice between alternative methods of competitive selling is limited by technological conditions or other circumstances beyond the control of the sellers. There may still be plenty of leeway for the sellers, but the differences between industries make it impossible to take the form of competition that prevails in a particular industry as a sufficient basis from which to infer the competitive position of the sellers.

The Significance of Oligopolistic Quality Competition

The situation of the ladies garments industry, in which the sellers adhere to certain "price lines," but compete by offering "better values" at fixed prices, was characterized (in Chapter 6) as polypolistic quality competition. There are many other industries in which competition takes place chiefly through offering better values at given prices, but where the situation must be characterized as oligopolistic quality competition. How valid is this distinction and what, if anything, is its practical significance?

Although inadequate information makes it difficult to apply the distinction to every concrete situation, it is, I submit, a valid and significant distinction. It does make a difference whether a seller can make his decisions about changes in product quality, or in his selling methods, free from any concern about rivals' retaliations or whether he feels that every move on his part is likely to result in counter-moves by his rivals with effects which he cannot afford to neglect.

Just as an oligopolist in fear of retaliation will often refrain from reducing his selling prices although he would otherwise find

---

tient.) Likewise, it would be difficult to explain the radio entertainment sponsored by the United States Steel Corporation as a competitive selling effort. Many examples could be added of radio time and newspaper and magazine space bought by large corporations for the sake of public relations, not as a part of their sales promotion programs.

[8] For example, we could find that individual cellophane wrappings might aid the sale of chocolate candies but would not be recommended in the sale of coal to industrial users.

such reduction useful, he may refrain from improving his product quality if he expects this step to be countered and neutralized by a similar step on the part of his rivals. This possibility has been seized upon as an "argument" by advocates of strong patent protection, who say that such protection relieves the oligopolist from the fear of quick imitation by competitors and hence allows him to introduce improvements he would not introduce without protection. This is a gross exaggeration, to say the least. An improvement in the quality of a product may be the result of (1) rather obvious additions or improvements of parts or ingredients, which are not patentable and can be imitated easily with little delay; (2) less obvious but non-patentable combinations of known technologies, which can be imitated by rivals after some experimentation; (3) the use of newly invented technology, protected by patents, but easily matched by different though equivalent improvements of the qualities offered by rivals; or (4) the use of newly invented technology, protected by patents and not likely to be matched by anything that can produce an equivalent quality improvement by rivals. Now, where oligopolistic inhibitions prevent producers from offering a product of better quality, it could be only with regard to the last of these four kinds of improvements that the inhibitions might be removed by the existence of a strong patent system. And surely this fourth kind of quality improvement is rather exceptional, almost all improvements falling into the first three categories. The theory of oligopolistic quality competition does not yield a strong argument for the advocacy of a strong patent system. To the extent to which patents keep a few existing firms protected from newcomers one might even come to the opposite conclusion.

That quality improvements are occurring in an industry does not prove that quality competition among the firms concerned is unrestricted. (After all, one can also observe occasional price reductions in an industry in which price competition is restricted.) If firms now and then improve their products, this need not mean that they are under no restraints in competing in this fashion. They may have oligopolistic inhibitions, or may be under collusive restrictions, and may nevertheless be free or bold enough at times to offer better values. On the other hand, it is possible that firms may be oligopolists with regard to price policies and polypolists with regard to quality improvements. This may not be a very likely story if the sellers are very few. But where cooperative efforts have succeeded in creating oligopolistic abstinence from price competition among a relatively large number of sellers—oligopolistic because observance implies that each seller is concerned about what the others would say or think of him if he were to start chiseling—the sellers may be entirely uninhibited in competing through the quality of their products or services.

Although it may be the exception rather than the rule, collusion does sometimes extend to quality competition. Examples of restrictions of quality competition under collusive oligopoly can be more readily furnished from countries where cartels are under no legal or moral ban. Thus we know that the hotel industry in Switzerland in recent years has been regulating all major improvements of service; the trade association keeps tab on its members lest some uncooperative innkeeper install a few more bathrooms without raising his rates. Similarly, it is reported that the Swiss watch industry polices the quality improvements proposed by all manufacturers.[9] In the United States we obtain information on such matters only when a cartel is prosecuted. Thus we learnt that the cartel in incandescent electric lamps enforced a standardization program which prevented producers from making lamps of longer service life and from "engaging in a competitive way in proving detailed superiority of individual brands."[10] We also learnt that the cement industry had excluded quality competition through the adoption of standardized minimum specifications and the practice of not accepting specifications calling for better qualities.[11] This did not mean that firms were forbidden to make better cement, but they could not publicly brag about it or mention it in confirming their orders.

[9] Both the hotel and the watch industries are able to enforce the restrictions owing to Federal laws enacted for the benefit of these industries.

[10] *United States* v. *General Electric Co.*, 82 Fed. Supp. 753 (1949). See George W. Stocking and Myron W. Watkins, *Cartels in Action* (New York: Twentieth Century Fund, 1946), pp. 359–62.

[11] *United States before the Federal Trade Commission, in the Matter of the Cement Institute, et al.* Docket No. 3167. Brief in Support of the Complaint, Part II, pp. 414–22.

It remains to point to the possibility that quality competition may be used in some industries as a device to keep alive a sentiment against the use of price competition. A firm maintaining its old prices but offering "better values" may try thereby to demonstrate to its rivals that it continues to believe in the "ethics of the industry" which interdicts price competition but permits nonprice competition. Every act of nonprice competition may be used as a "sign" directed toward the competitors, telling them, as it were: "You see, I will not cut prices; I confine myself to these more civilized ways of competing! I trust you will do likewise."

Nonprice competition of predominantly symbolic significance is probably to be found frequently in the form of advertising. The implied message of the advertiser to his competitors is again: "You see, I compete only in this nice way." But it may mean even more than this, namely: "You see, I am advertising my prices and I shall stick to them. I trust you will too." In other words, oligopolistic nonprice competition may be more in the nature of a manœuvre to avoid price competition than a manœuvre to compete for customers and increase sales at the expense of competitors.

Determination of Outlay for Nonprice Competition

What with all the non-competitive purposes of oligopolistic nonprice competition, one may wonder whether it is possible to arrive at generalizations about the determination of the improvements in quality, service, or selling effort that oligopolists may find it "most profitable" to make under given conditions. It was possible to derive certain generalizations about polypolistic quality competition and polypolistic selling efforts. (See Chapter 6.) Can it be done for oligopolistic competition?

After what was said about oligopolistic indeterminacy it should be obvious that no general theory of outlay determination for the nonprice variables in oligopolistic competition can be formulated.[12] It may be possible to formulate special theories that make very specific assumptions regarding the exact way of thinking of every

---

[12] Just as oligopolists in fight may reduce prices even if marginal revenue is painfully negative, they may increase selling costs far beyond the point where such increases can bring any additional business at all.

one of the oligopolists in the group. Perhaps it would be interesting to try the construction of such models. But their applicability would be so restricted that we shall not take the time to do it.

It is easy, however, to demonstrate that certain very widespread types of oligopolistic cooperation will restrict nonprice competition together with price competition even if no explicit understanding exists with regard to either. For example, a division of the market (market allocation) or sharing of the market (quota restrictions) will reduce a seller's efforts to expand his sales at the expense of his "competitors." If it is understood, for example, that a producer must not exceed a certain percentage of the total sales of the industry, he will be less anxious to spend extra money to improve the quality of his product. This will hold no matter in what form the understanding was made, whether by formal cartel organization, by informal gentlemen's agreement, or by patent license contract,—with one qualification: since formal cartel agreements have to be renewed from time to time, individual members might make somewhat greater competitive efforts in order to be stronger for prospective renegotiations of the quota or other terms.[13]

In the absence of market division and market sharing, agreements fixing the selling prices but leaving other competitive measures unrestricted will sometimes permit competitive wars to be waged with all possible weapons except price cutting. Oligopolists in fight have resorted to the most costly free-gift campaigns—which, after all, are indirect ways of price cutting—while they continued to respect the ban on direct price cutting.[14] In at least one famous instance, an agreement which had not only fixed prices

[13] This would be another instance of the apparent paradox that competition may be more effectively restricted by gentlemen's agreements than by formal covenants.

[14] In 1933 a free-gift war among British cigarette producers was ended when the smaller firms asked for a truce after the powerful Imperial Tobacco Company intimated, according to the London *Economist*, "that there would be nothing half-hearted in the waging of hostilities." The *Economist* commented as follows: "If the 'war' is thus to terminate, the chief benefits may accrue to the 'combine' companies, rather than the smaller firms. The latter found the 'free gift' a powerful weapon for encroachment on the combine's territory, since it enabled them to indulge in real price-cutting, while remaining nominally within the bounds of price agreements." *The Economist*, Vol. CXVII (August 26, 1933), p. 418.

but also restricted selling efforts was violated and repudiated with respect to the latter, and a reckless competitive war developed causing huge selling expenses to the participants.[15] Of course, where promotional competition takes largely the form of gifts to buyers, the distinction between it and price competition will from certain points of view become less significant.[16]

OLIGOPOLISTIC PRICE RIGIDITY

Price rigidity is not always due to oligopoly, and oligopoly does not always result in price rigidity. Oligopolies in fight may produce those extreme price variations that are the conspicuous feature of price wars; and other unstable oligopoly situations may produce price swings such as those exhibited by the Edgeworth model. Price rigidity, on the other hand, may exist under monopoly as well as under oligopoly, and even under polypoly if prices are controlled by governmental dictates. Thus, one may speak of

[15] Reference is made to the circulation war between the four national morning newspapers in England, especially between the *Daily Herald* and *Daily Express*. Both these papers managed within a few months to increase their circulations from about 1,650,000 to over 2,000,000 each. Prior to March 1933 an agreement had fixed prices, restricted the amounts to be spent on door-to-door canvassing, and forbidden the offer of gifts in return for subscriptions. Hostilities opened when the *Herald* advertised in Sunday papers and weeklies an offer of a 16-volume set of Dickens for 96 coupons clipped from successive issues of the *Herald* plus 11 shillings in cash. The *Express* countered with a bigger and better Dickens, and soon the papers were offering not only series of classics, encyclopaedias, high prizes for crossword puzzles and for correct forecasts of results in racing and popularity tests, but also free insurance policies, toys, cameras, cutlery, hosiery, underwear, mangles, tea sets, etc. Most of these gifts were presented by teams of door-to-door canvassers for subscriptions; loud posters and special stunts supported the campaigns. For descriptions of this selling war and estimates of its cost see *The Economist*, Vol. CXVII (July 15, 1933), pp. 119–20, and subsequent issues of the same year.

[16] The price is reduced by the value of the gift. This point of view, however, overlooks (a) that the cost of the gift to the seller may be less than its value to the buyer (because the retailer's mark-up or distribution cost are cut out), (b) that the cost of the gift per unit of the product sold may be a fraction of the smallest monetary unit and therefore less than the smallest possible price reduction (provided the product is sold in small quantities) and (c) that buyers may not be rational and may be more impressed by the "free gift" than by an equivalent price reduction.

authoritarian price rigidity and of monopolistic price rigidity besides oligopolistic price rigidity.

The Concept of Price Rigidity

But before we go into the question why prices are rigid, we had better first pause to reflect on the meaning of rigid prices. For it is neither clear what is meant by rigid nor what is meant by price.

I have elsewhere dealt with price flexibility in connection with the problem of measuring the degree of monopoly.[17] Indexes of price flexibility were calculated by several research groups; as a rule they were based on two kinds of observation: the frequency of price change per unit of time and the amplitude of change. These data showed that some prices changed more (more often and more sharply) than others: and the prices that changed most were called "flexible" and the ones that changed least were called "rigid."

This procedure implies the heroic assumption that the same cause for change existed for all prices. For the assumption that actual change reflects changeability presupposes that the same forces have been operating everywhere and have met with different degrees of resistance. Something is rigid if it resists change or movement. But where there is no *cause* for change the *absence* of change does not reflect *resistance* to change. Hence, some prices may conceivably be stable without being rigid; if basic conditions changed, these prices would change accordingly. Some prices have changed much and are therefore called relatively *flexible;* but there may have been ample cause for these prices to change to an even greater extent and more frequently. Other prices have changed little and are therefore called *rigid;* but there may have been no reason for more change and these prices might have changed very sensitively if there had been changes in the underlying conditions.

[17] Fritz Machlup, *The Political Economy of Monopoly: Business, Labor and Government Policies* (Baltimore: Johns Hopkins Press, 1952), Chapter 12.—For a good discussion of various concepts of price flexibility see also Edward S. Mason, "Price Inflexibility," *Review of Economic Statistics,* Vol. XX (1938), pp. 53–64.

The usual working hypothesis for research on price flexibility has been that there is, at least over a long period of time, plenty of cause for change. Demand as well as cost conditions are continually in flux.[18] Hence, the presumption is strong that unchanging prices are rigid prices. Perfectly stable prices can safely be regarded as rigid.[19]

All this has presupposed that we know what we mean by price. Is it a list price or a price corrected for extras added and for secret rebates deducted? Is it a price for an unchanged product or for a product of changing quality or with changing specifications? As to the former question, there is probably no doubt that conceptually we mean the actual price, not a fictitious list price, even if we cannot know that which the people concerned try to keep secret. Nor can we find a very satisfactory way of dealing with the difference between prices paid by the buyers and prices received by the sellers, what with transportation charges, excise taxes, agents' commissions, and similar expenses defrayed by the sellers.

Probably more serious is the question about quality and specification of the product. Take for example the "customary prices" such as the five-cent price for chocolate bars or the unvarying price lines for women's dresses. Should these be regarded as stable prices although the commodities sold at these prices may vary in quantity and quality? Surely, "one dollar's worth" of cheese cannot be called a "stable price" of cheese if what you get for the dollar changes frequently. Where the quantity of product that is sold for a fixed amount of money is varied, we may easily compute the prices and price changes for a fixed quantity of product. But

---

[18] This may be an occasion to point out that rigid pricing rules, for example, the so-called "full-cost principle" of pricing, might lead to highly flexible prices. See George Katona, *Psychological Analysis of Economic Behavior* (New York: McGraw-Hill, 1951), p. 231.—The prevalence of rigid prices in certain industries contradicts the assertion of the prevalence of full-cost pricing.

[19] Examples of the most extreme cases of price stability can be found in the history of the glass container industry, a group of collusive oligopolies organized as patent cartels. The list price of milk bottles remained unchanged from November 1924 to January 1931, and again from November 1933 to April 1938. *Investigation of Concentration of Economic Power. Hearings before the Temporary National Economic Committee*, Part 2 (Washington: 1939), p. 534.

what if it is the quality that is varied? Is there a difference in kind or only in degree between variations in quantity and variations in quality of a product offered at a given price? Suppose that bakers add another ounce to the loaf of bread they sell at a "rigid" price, and also another ounce of some ingredient to the cake they sell at a "rigid" price. One may be tempted to argue that if the offering of a heavier loaf of bread for the same money is regarded as a *de facto* price variation, the offering of a better cake for the same money should also be so regarded. In other words, one may want to argue that quality variations at unchanged prices, no less than quantity variations at unchanged prices, should be sufficient to save a case in question from being labeled as one of price inflexibility.

To yield to this temptation would lead to confusion. A variation of the quantity sold at a given amount of money is not "equivalent" to a change in price, but *is* a change in price, provided the different relevant expressions of quantity vary proportionally.[20] But a change in the quality of a product sold at a given amount of money cannot for our purposes reasonably be identified with a price change. One may of course say that the two are "equivalent" from certain points of view, but they are surely not the same thing and had better be kept apart when the problem of price flexibility is discussed. If the change in quality is very great, one may even prefer to speak of different products, one product having been discontinued and another introduced as a (superior or inferior) substitute. If the change in quality is not very great, it should be mentioned as a change in quality, not as a change in the "adjusted price" of the product, at least for purposes of analysis of sellers' conduct.

In summary, for an analysis of price rigidity, price should be strictly defined with reference to the "product," and rigidity should be defined in terms of resistance to changing a price in response to changes in cost or market conditions. Since rigidity and flexibility are only relative, one needs a standard of comparison. This standard is sometimes found in a theoretical "standard model" con-

---

[20] Where this is not so, an apparently quantitative variation may constitute a variation of quality. For example, where weight, square measures, and cubic contents vary in different proportions because of differences in substance, thickness or shape, it will as a rule be preferable to speak of different qualities.

structed for the purpose. Prices are called rigid if they fail to adjust themselves to changed cost or market conditions with the same rapidity and to the same extent as they would in the theoretical standard model.

General Causes of Price Rigidity

The standard model for the discussion of price flexibility has often been conceived as that of a perfect market with perfect polypoly and perfect polypsony. Sellers and buyers under such circumstances adjust the quantities offered and demanded, accepting prices as given and outside their control; and the frequency of price changes depends then on the organization of the market. Prices may be in continual flux during the daily business hours, or they may be set—by appointed clerks of the "exchange"—once every hour, once every weekday, or perhaps once every "Monday." [21]

Apart from these "market-made" prices there are "negotiated" prices, "buyer-made" prices, and "seller-made" prices. If one does not take market-made prices as the standard for the discussion of price rigidity, a model with seller-made prices will be most suitable for our purposes. It will be a model in which there is nothing that would keep the seller from adjusting his selling prices to changes in (objectively ascertained) cost or market conditions.

Price inflexibility in this sense may arise for two general kinds of reasons: (1) Sellers in particular positions or situations may not notice, or may not be impressed by, changes in cost or market conditions in the same way as would the seller in the standard model. (2) Adjustments of prices to changed cost or market conditions may involve greater costs (smaller benefits) to sellers in particular positions or situations than to the seller in the standard model. An example of the first kind would be the neutralization of a change in demand (under conditions of increasing cost of production) by a parallel change in the elasticity of demand as seen by a seller in a monopolistic position.[22] An example of the

[21] J. R. Hicks, *Value and Capital* (London: Oxford University Press, 1939), p. 122.
[22] It is doubtful and controversial whether the elasticity considerations of sellers in monopolistic positions can be generalized to explain price rigidity. If

second kind would be the high cost of price alterations by a seller of a nationally advertised product.

The cost of change is certainly the most effective and most general cause of price rigidity. The cost of adjusting prices to changes in cost or market conditions must be compared with the benefits to be derived from the adjustment, which in turn will depend on the extent to which conditions have changed and on the time for which they are expected to last. Expensive adjustments will be avoided if the changes in the underlying conditions are relatively small or expected to last only a relatively short time. Adjustments to such temporary changes may require two price changes and, if their cost is high, the adjustments will not pay.

What are the expenses involved in changing the selling prices? To alter the price of a nationally advertised branded good which for years has been offered at the same price may be a serious operation, costly in good will apart from all other expenses. Wherever a firm offers a large variety of commodities in an elaborate price list or through an elaborate sales organization, every price change gives rise to considerable cost and trouble. Where distributors, dealers, or processors keep stocks and, according to trade practice, have to be indemnified for inventory losses or otherwise placated, a price reduction may be an extremely costly affair for the producer. The great difficulties of changing the traditional prices for

---

every increase in demand were associated with an upward revision of the elasticity estimates by the sellers, the increased elasticity might offset the effects of increasing cost of production. Likewise, if a smaller output could be produced at lower cost but every reduction in demand were associated with a downward revision of elasticity estimates by the sellers, no net change in selling price might be indicated. See Joan Robinson, *The Economics of Imperfect Competition* (London: Macmillan, 1932), pp. 62 ff. On the other hand, there is Harrod's "law of diminishing elasticity of demand," asserting that price elasticities may change inversely with income and, hence, demand. See R. F. Harrod, *The Trade Cycle* (London: Oxford University Press, 1936), pp. 17–22. This "law" has been seriously questioned, e.g., by John D. Sumner, "A Note on Cyclical Changes in Demand Elasticity," *American Economic Review*, Vol. XXX (1940), pp. 300–308. But Scitovsky believes that Harrod's "law" will "hold good more often than its opposite" and that consequently shifts in demand will "enhance the flexibility of the monopolist's price." T. de Scitovsky, "Prices under Monopoly and Competition," *Journal of Political Economy*, Vol. XLIX (1941), pp. 672, 674.

the traditional quantities of traditional qualities of bottled beverages (such as Coca Cola and Pepsi Cola) have been widely discussed in recent years.

A special cause of rigidity is present wherever price changes require the approval of some authority, whether this be an authority within an industry (trade association, board, or syndicate) or a governmental authority (regulatory commission). Any authority responsible to people with divergent interests normally has a hard time making up "its" mind; and to leave things as they are is ordinarily easier than to make a change. If a seller has to convince the authority of the desirability or appropriateness of every price change he wishes to make, many of these changes will not be made, partly because approval will be denied, partly because the seller will not care to go to the trouble of pleading his cause. (The requirement of approval for a price change may amount to a large increase in the cost of change.) Even if he expected to be successful in convincing the authority of the appropriateness of a particular price change, he might have misgivings concerning the future: perhaps he might later want to change prices back to their present level or thereabouts and might then be unable to persuade the authority to permit him to do so. Rather than run this risk he may prefer to leave prices as they are.

In discussions of price inflexibility "long-run considerations" of the sellers are sometimes referred to as "reasons for rigidity." If these long-run considerations, based on the developments of demand or cost which the seller expects, call for no change in prices, should one speak of price rigidity? One might argue that there is in this case no resistance to change, but simply no cause for change: In the light of the demand and cost conditions which the seller expects for the future, it would not be the best policy for him to change his prices; he would want to make a change only *if* he were near-sighted or *if* he neglected to look that far ahead. To argue in this fashion, however, is to "define away" what one seeks to explain. Consistent procedure is to consult the "standard model" constructed for the sake of comparison. If the seller in this model is inclined to take a shorter view and to adjust to passing changes, while certain sellers under given circumstances are wont to take a longer view and to pass over changes in conditions they believe to be of relatively brief duration, these circumstances deserve to be mentioned among the causes of price rigidity.

Take for example the frequent case of a seller who fears that a temporary price reduction in adjustment to a temporary decline of demand may spoil his customers and cause trouble when he later restores his present prices. This "cost of price change" does not exist for a more competitive seller. He "has no such problems; paying little or no heed to his own influence on present price, he will worry even less about influencing the future demand for his produce." [23] If price adjustments involve a cost to sellers in certain positions but not to sellers differently situated, this difference may be taken as a cause of rigidity.

The cost of a price change—or of two changes in the case of adjustments to temporary conditions—may be regarded as an investment that will be undertaken only if it more than pays for itself.[24] Treatment of the cost of price alteration as an investment helps us to bear in mind that purely short-run considerations, concentrating on variations of prime costs, are not appropriate when new overhead or investment costs are to be incurred. Investment always raises the question of the period of amortization of the outlay.

Some resistance to price alteration derives from oligopolistic market positions and would not exist if the sellers were not oligopolists. To these strictly oligopolistic price rigidities we shall now turn.

[23] Tibor de Scitovsky, *op. cit.*, p. 675.

[24] While it is always possible to include the cost of price change into the calculation of marginal revenue and marginal cost, it may be too complicated to attempt it. One must certainly avoid merging the cost of price change—no matter how it is allocated and transformed into a per-unit charge—with the cost of production. In the case of price reductions it is conceivable that the cost of change could be allocated to the additional output sold as a result of the change, but for price increases the cost of change can only be set against the additional revenue on a reduced output and its combination with the marginal values would be confusing. Just as the calculations that underlie an investment decision will be separate from calculations behind price decisions even if they are closely linked with each other, the costs of price changes can be treated as separate items and as such compared with the results of the calculations of revenue and cost at various prices.

Reasons Applying to Oligopoly Only

Under completely coordinated oligopoly, price making is a "collective" task and the individual firm will sometimes play only a very indirect role in the price making process. Under incompletely coordinated oligopoly, the individual firm remains its own price maker but is supposed to "play the game" in accordance with the adopted scheme or to "observe the ethics of the trade." Under uncoordinated oligopoly, the seller is "free" in his price policy except that he is wary of rival's reactions to his moves. Thus, depending on how prices are set and by whom, the strictly oligopolistic resistance to price alterations will undoubtedly be of very different kinds. The discussion of oligopolistic price rigidity has suffered because analysts were sometimes preoccupied with only one type of oligopoly and forgot the others.

Under completely coordinated oligopoly, prices for the products of the members are set by a special meeting or body—syndicate, council, board, committee—in which the individual firms are directly or indirectly represented. One might think, and several economists have done so, that this centralized price making is equivalent to price determination by a perfect monopolist. (In other words, one might take the maximization of the joint profits as the fundamental working hypothesis.[25]) But in fact there are important differences between individual and collective price making. There is an element of politics in all group deliberations. This political element becomes particularly significant in considerations of a representative body, considerations which will typically include the question how to secure the continued loyalty and support of the constituency.[26] Under these circumstances

[25] William Fellner, *Competition Among the Few: Oligopoly and Similar Market Structures* (New York: Knopf, 1949), pp. 120–232.

[26] Where the number of firms is too large to permit price setting in a meeting of all members, the participation of an individual member firm in the price making process will depend on the "position" of the firm in the industry and on the personal qualities of its managers. On the one extreme is the firm that runs the whole show and can make its own views stick. On the other extreme is the firm that can do no more than try to get the ear of some council members, or to campaign for a change in the personnel of the council, or to talk about breaking away or not renewing its membership when the agreement expires.

quick and frequent decisions are most unlikely—and this makes
it likely that prices will be rigid under syndicated or organized
oligopoly. The probability of price rigidity is especially great if
the price-setting body—be it a meeting of all members or a committee only—has a hard job of reconciling different points of view.
If each decision is a compromise of divergent interests reached
after long and difficult negotiations, the tendency will be not to
reopen the question unless conditions change most drastically. It
will be considered more politic to pass over some of the changes
that would be large enough to induce a single-headed monopoly
to alter its prices.

Under incompletely coordinated oligopoly, prices are not set by
agreement, and each firm has always the alternative of conforming or not conforming with the standard of conduct with which it is
supposed to conform. Normally oligopolists prefer peaceful cooperation to costly fights and this implies that they avoid all moves
that might initiate vigorous price competition. This does not mean
that prices are never changed; but it does imply that prices will
not be changed for minor causes. Of course, it will make a difference whether a price cutter can reasonably hope that his action
will remain secret or whether everything must be done openly or
is apt to come out in the open. Where a group of firms is anxious
not to disturb a situation of order and cooperation, prices will not
be changed under many conditions that would otherwise have
induced changes.

In contrast to oligopoly positions that involve some degree of
coordination, the seller under uncoordinated oligopoly has no
reason to trust his competitors to abstain from competing for a
larger share in the market through price cutting or otherwise. But
although he cannot guess whether and where they will initiate a
price cut independently of his actions, he can guess with a good
deal of confidence that they would not let him get away if he
undertook to cut prices, but would fight back by following suit. On
the other hand, he might be quite uncertain as to whether they
would follow him also if he were to raise his prices. This difference
in expected response *may* be a strong reason against initiating any
price changes—at least as long as cost and demand conditions do
not substantially change. Whether or not real price rigidity—re-

sistance to change despite cause for change—can be explained in this fashion is a controversial question.

The Kink Theory of Price Rigidity

The difference in the response which an oligopolist may expect on the part of his rivals to his price cuts, on the one hand, and his price boosts, on the other, will be reflected in the demand curve depicting the expected sales at various prices. If the seller's price reductions are imitated by his rivals but his price increases are not, his price increases would lose him much more business than his price reductions would gain him. In other words, the "downward elasticity" of demand, in this case, is smaller than the "upward elasticity," and the demand curve has a kink at the current price.[27] The sharper the kink, that is, the greater the difference in elasticity, the greater will be the resistance to a price change even in the face of important changes in the conditions confronting the seller.[28]

If the downward elasticity of demand is smaller than unity, the seller will never think of reducing the price, no matter how much his production costs fall. For the gross proceeds of his sales would decline if he lowered his price; in more technical language, his marginal revenue would become negative. (See Fig. 20.) But even if the downward elasticity is still above unity, the discontinuity of the marginal revenue curve may be big enough to make the current price the best possible price with considerable leeway for, or insensitiveness to, changes in cost. (See Fig. 21.) And any changes in the total demand for the product may be reflected in sideway shifts of the demand curve, perhaps with moderate changes in elasticities, but without moving the kink away from the given price, which therefore is rigid also with regard to changes in demand. (See Fig. 22.)

The theory of the kinky oligopoly demand curve does not apply

[27] Paul M. Sweezy, "Demand Under Conditions of Oligopoly," *Journal of Political Economy,* Vol. XLVII (1939), pp. 568–73; R. L. Hall and C. J. Hitch, "Price Theory and Business Behavior," *Oxford Economic Papers,* No. 2 (1939), pp. 12–45.

[28] M. Bronfenbrenner, "Applications of the Discontinuous Oligopoly Demand Curve," *Journal of Political Economy,* Vol. XLVIII (1940), pp. 420–27.

OLIGOPOLY AND KINKED DEMAND CURVES

Price Insensitivity to Changes in Cost or Demand

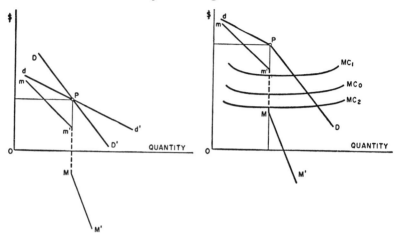

FIG. 20. No Price Reduction at Any Cost: Downward Elasticity Below Unity.

FIG. 21. No Price Change Despite Large Changes in Cost and Elasticity Above Unity.

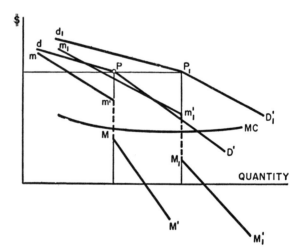

FIG. 22. No Price Change Despite Large Change in Demand.

In Figure 20, *dd'* is the sales curve if rivals do not change their prices, and *DD'* is the sales curve if rivals do change their prices in response to price

to a seller who believes that his competitors would follow his price increases as well as his price reductions; in other words, it does not apply to a price leader. Nor does it apply to a seller who believes that his price cutting would remain secret and, thus, that his competitors would not meet his reduced prices.[29]

The theory does apply chiefly to members of informal minimum-price cartels, to small-fry participants in open-price agreements, to followers in leadership oligopolies, and to sellers within a loose group of firms cooperating in stamping out chiseling. All these are instances of more or less *coordinated* oligopoly and the kink theory explains merely why non-leaders avoid initiating price changes. The price policies of the cartel leaders or of the individual price leaders are not explained by the kink theory. The question now is whether the theory may apply also to occasional situations of *uncoordinated* oligopoly. It has been fairly generally assumed that it does. But there is a serious difficulty. What the theory attempts to explain is the *consistent* maintenance of prices by the firms in question, but such consistency will regularly transform the oligopoly into a collusive one. For if the firms continue to hold their prices stable for long periods, they thereby indicate to their competitors that they believe in price maintenance and can be expected to remain peaceful and to refrain from aggressive price competition.

The kink theory has been seriously misunderstood by some who have believed it can demonstrate that oligopoly prices are insensitive to all increases in production cost. This demonstration, however, holds only with regard to those cost increases that are confined to the firm in question and do not extend to its competitors. If the firm knows that the rivals' costs also increase, the entire demand curve (with its kink) will be shifted upwards and selling

[29] Paul M. Sweezy, *op. cit.*, p. 571.

---

changes of this oligopolist. In all three graphs, dPD' and $d_1P_1D_1'$ are sales curves if rivals are expected to imitate price reductions but not price increases; and $mm'MM'$ and $m_1m_1'M_1M_1'$ are the marginal revenue curves corresponding to these sales curves. MC_0, MC_1 and MC_2 are three different marginal cost curves, in Figure 21, not affecting the price charged by the firm. MC is the marginal cost curve in Figure 22, where the sideway shift of the sales curve does not affect the price charged.

prices will be raised. Thus, contrary to the hopes of some labor economists, the kink theory cannot be used to "prove" that product prices will not rise under oligopoly when wage rates in the industry are increased under trade-union pressure.

Even apart from this misunderstanding the significance of the kink theory has probably been exaggerated. Most of the reasons for price rigidity under oligopoly can be expressed more simply and more generally: the seller's fear of costly cut-throat competition, his awareness of the danger of retaliation, his inclination to let others take the lead, the difficulty of agreeing on the right price and the preference for avoiding the cost and trouble of reopening difficult questions. The kinky demand curve picturing the selling opportunities seen by the oligopolist reflects only some of these reasons. Perhaps it has become so popular because it can help explain price stability without explicit reference to collusion, and this is comforting to all who are afraid of the antitrust laws.[30]

[30] In a critical analysis and empirical test of the kink theory, Stigler cast considerable doubt on its validity. See George J. Stigler, "The Kinky Oligopoly Demand Curve and Rigid Prices," *Journal of Political Economy*, Vol. LV (1947), pp. 432–49. However, some of his interpretations are questionable. For example: "According to the kink theory, there will be no kink when the oligopolists enter into explicit collusion; and hence prices would be expected to become more flexible. All empirical evidence contradicts this implication." (*Op. cit.*, p. 443.) Stigler holds that "there will be no kink" under explicit collusion because "there is no kink in a monopolist's demand curve." (*Op. cit.*, p. 435.) But explicit collusion may imply a monopolist's demand curve for the group of oligopolists as a whole when they fix a price, not for the individual oligopolist when he considers whether or not he should stick to it. Apart from this, it need not follow that "prices would be expected to become more flexible" under collusion; collusion may result in rigid prices for reasons about which the kink theory is silent. Indeed, the adherents of the kink theory probably took it for granted that collusion resulted in price rigidity; they merely wished to show why prices could be rigid even under non-collusive oligopoly.

CHAPTER 15

Organized Oligopoly, Leadership Oligopoly, Unorganized Oligopoly

Organized Oligopoly: Types of Organized Oligopoly · Approximation to Monopoly Policy · The Policy of a Syndicate · The Policies of a Price Cartel and Its Members · Member's Conduct Under Given Cartel Rules · Member's Conduct With an Eye to Renegotiations · The Theory of Cartel Negotiations · The Cartel Government

Leadership Oligopoly: Different Concepts of Leadership · The Qualifications of the Leader · "Partial Monopoly" and "Partial Oligopoly" · Rotating and Divided Leadership

Unorganized Oligopoly: Unorganized Cooperation · Types of Uncoordinated Oligopoly · Fighting Oligopoly · Hyper-Competitive Oligopoly · Chain Oligopoly · Guessing-Game Oligopoly

Historical Trends: Speculative Clues · Historical Clues

W HEN WE PROPOSED a classification of oligopoly according to the degree of coordination we distinguished, in descending order, syndicated oligopoly, organized oligopoly, leadership oligopoly, cooperative oligopoly, and uncoordinated oligopoly. The first two were characterized by the existence of an agreement among the firms and of some organization for its implementation. We shall discuss them here under the heading of *organized* oligopoly. The other three are *unorganized,* but we shall devote a separate section to *leadership* oligopoly because leadership is often secretly organized and, even when it is not, it may achieve a high degree of coordination.

ORGANIZED OLIGOPOLY

We did not mean the classes and types distinguished to be mutually exclusive in every respect. Higher degrees of coordina-

[475]

tion may include some of the characteristics of lower degrees. Syndicated oligopoly is certainly always organized; and organized oligopoly may involve leadership in several of its aspects.

Types of Organized Oligopoly

The criterion of organized oligopoly lies in the existence either of an agreement among the oligopolists or of joint activities (relating to sales and marketing) carried on directly or through any "organs" or agencies. The agreement need not be in writing; the joint activities may consist merely in meetings, discussions, or other communications; and the organs or agencies may be trade associations, institutes, statistical services and reports, joint sales representatives, or any other aids in coordinating the selling policies of the firms concerned.

Elsewhere I have given descriptions of several kinds of organized oligopoly: syndicates, central sales agencies, average-price cartels, profit pools, market-sharing agreements (quota cartels), allocations of markets, restrictive patent license contracts, basing-point systems, open-price associations, price-fixing agreements, organized price leadership, etc.[1] All these organized reductions of competition—cartels, in short—are unlawful in the United States insofar as the courts have understood their nature.

The degree of organization, measured by the number of "organs" or the complexity of the apparatus employed, is not correlated with the degree of coordination that it achieves. And the degree of coordination, in turn, is not correlated with the degree of approximation to perfect monopoly.

Approximation to Monopoly Policy

A higher degree of coordination implies greater reliability of individual performance securing a concert of action in a collective design. Increased reliability need not, however, secure a closer approximation to the "ideal" goal of complete monopoly. Indeed,

[1] Fritz Machlup, *The Political Economy of Monopoly: Business, Labor and Government Policies* (Baltimore: Johns Hopkins Press, 1952), Chapters 4 and 5.

it is conceivable that the ideal objective of a maximization of the joint profits of a group of oligopolists is more closely approximated by the much less coordinated conduct of individual sellers without any organization whatever or at least without any central plan, direction, or guidance.

For example, a simple division of the market, which the sellers may continue to respect merely because they believe in the inherent ethics of the "customary" scheme, can create a collection of several complete monopolies, each fully exploited by a sole seller in the territory or sectional market. The aggregate profits of this "group of monopolists" would probably be lower than the profits of a single monopolist serving all the territories or sectional markets, but probably still higher than the joint profits of a group of oligopolists selling exclusively through a central agency. The profitability of such a thoroughly coordinated oligopoly is likely to suffer from the fact that the syndicate as a rule cannot afford to neglect the conflicting particular interests of its members and cannot devise an inexpensive system of compensations that would induce members to waive their particular interests in order to pursue only the collective interest. Thus, all actions by any of the members, officers, or agents of the organized oligopoly may be fully coordinated and yet the results would fall short of those attainable under uncoordinated selling in territorially divided markets and, by a still more substantial margin, fall short of the results attainable by a single-headed monopoly.

Perhaps it would be well to recall the chief reasons why the profitability of a single-headed monopoly is superior to that of any kind of organized oligopoly. There is, first of all, the possibility of outsider's competition—a danger to which a perfect monopoly, by definition, is not exposed. There is, furthermore, the great probability that the production costs of different cartel members are very different and that the cartel does not have the control over cost which a single producer can exercise, transferring business from less efficient to more efficient plants and perhaps closing down the least efficient ones. And, finally, there is the necessity of compromise between conflicting interests and the likelihood that the compromise would seriously diverge from the collective optimum.

The Policy of a Syndicate

Syndicates for the centralized sale of the production of all members of the group are established only where the coordination of individual members' actions cannot be reliably achieved when they sell their products themselves, and where their products are sufficiently standardized to permit centralized sale.[2] Syndicated oligopoly achieves coordination by prohibiting its members from selling their products except to or through the syndicate. Only the syndicate can quote prices, submit bids, and accept orders.

The policy determination of the syndicate will differ in several respects from the policy determination of a single monopolist. There is, first of all, the problem of "marginal cost." An individual producer, selling his own product and weighing the desirability of securing additional business through price concessions or greater selling efforts, will have an eye on the cost of his additional output. A syndicate selling for a group of producers cannot weigh the desirability of securing additional business in the same way inasmuch as sales are to be made for different firms whose cost of production may greatly differ from one another. The syndicate, anxious to avoid dissatisfaction and defection on the part of its members, will be guided chiefly by considerations such as how far ahead or behind it is in filling any sales quota agreed upon or confidently expected by the firms. The marginal cost to the producer who might be awarded additional orders is perhaps much higher than the marginal cost of the same total output if produced by the industry in the most economical way. The syndicate of the industry may be uninformed about the marginal cost to the industry as a whole as well as about the marginal cost to the individual members. It is merely through suggestions, requests, or complaints coming to the

---

[2] The following conditions favor the formation of a selling cartel: (1) The number of producers is too large to permit reliable enforcement of fixed prices if the selling is left to the individual members. In other words, centralized selling is the only way of keeping individual sellers from chiseling in secret. (2) Producers can somehow be assured that they will not lose all personal contact with customers when their products are sold through the syndicate. Otherwise they fear that they will be too much handicapped in case the cartel is terminated. (3) Individual products are standardized, if not homogeneous. Quality differences can be objectively evaluated and price differentials determined accordingly.

syndicate from particular members that their cost considerations are impressed upon those who decide on selling policy.

The "marginal revenue" problem is similarly complex. Members may have divergent views about the sales possibilities of the syndicate and even the officers of the syndicate may disagree among themselves. The "judgment" that prevails may be a compromise which no one regards as "correct." And the results of the compromise, the proceeds from marginal sales, may not become marginal revenue for any one of the members, inasmuch as the rules about profit pooling or average-revenue computing may distribute any additional revenue in the most artificial ways.[3] Thus, the additional revenue to the group as a whole will be different from the additional revenue going to those firms to which additional business is assigned.

Now, all this does not mean that no principles can be found by which to explain policy decisions of selling cartels; it only means that the explanation cannot be based on a simple calculus of "joint profit maximization." The basic consideration for the syndicate is not the highest aggregate profit of the group but the best reconciliation of group interests and individual member interests. (To repeat, this task is more *political* than economic in nature.) And this implies that the marginal-revenue-marginal-cost ideas of the individual members cannot be entirely neglected. A member whose marginal cost is well below the price that he gets from or through the syndicate will surely clamor for more business. A member whose marginal cost is above the price that he gets will probably clamor for higher prices. The conflict between more sales and higher prices will be aired in the meetings of the cartel members as well as in the executive committee of the syndicate. The reconciliation of this conflict may be sought through special premiums or bonuses paid to individual members, through changes in the sales quota, or through promises of future adjustments.

To these generalities probably little can be added as a general theory of syndicate pricing, although a multitude of special models can be constructed to demonstrate the working of the different varieties in which the selling cartels may be organized and oper-

[3] For a general description of arrangements of this sort see Fritz Machlup, *op. cit.*, Chapter 4, p. 97.

ated. The important implications which outsiders' and newcomers' competition may have for the policies of syndicates will be dealt with later.

The Policies of a Price Cartel and Its Members

While for a *selling cartel* the views and actions of the members are relevant only to the extent to which they influence the views and actions of the officers of the syndicate, the operation of a *price cartel* is constantly affected by the conduct of its members. Hence, models demonstrating how a price cartel works must have two parts: one showing how the price decisions of the cartel are reached, the other showing how the decisions of an individual member are reached, that is, mainly his decisions regarding observance or non-observance of the fixed cartel price list, and regarding output determination, order acceptance, and nonprice variables. Needless to say, there will be an interdependence between cartel decisions and member performance, an interdependence which can be described in static or dynamic terms. Cartel decisions will be influenced in two ways: once "politically" through the members' participation in negotiations, discussions, resolutions, elections of officers, and through the members' requests, complaints, and threats of secession; and again "economically" through the members' conduct in the market. Members' decisions also will fall into two categories: those in which the cartel agreement and the cartel decisions are taken as given and the best possible adjustments are made to them; and those in which the future possibilities of influencing cartel decisions and of altering the cartel agreement are considered.[4]

It may be helpful to present more systematically the outlines of a theory of cartel operation. Such a theory must analyse

(I) the conduct of the cartel member

(1) confronted with given cartel agreements and cartel

[4] One of the few authors who have systematically analysed the conduct of cartel members is Hans Brems in an article on "Cartels and Competition," *Weltwirtschaftliches Archiv*, Vol. 66 (1951) and in two mimeographed papers presented at Harvard University in 1947. In his article he distinguishes between "the effect of an established cartel agreement" and "the effect of prospective cartel negotiations." *Op. cit.*, pp. 59 and 64.

decisions,—chiefly: fixed selling prices, fixed sales quota, fixed fines and compensations, etc.,

(2) with an eye to possible changes of cartel agreements and cartel decisions,—chiefly: changes in prices, quota, fines, compensations, etc.;

(II) the conduct of the cartel government

(1) confronted with given member performance,—chiefly: observance or non-observance of fixed prices, sales above or below quota, secret sales, total production, etc.,

(2) with an eye to possible changes in member performance,—chiefly: possible changes of agreements, threatened secession of member, etc.

Where the cartel cannot arrange for protection from outsiders' and newcomers' competition—for example, through exclusive patent agreements or through governmental restrictions of entry into the industry—the theory of cartel operation will have to include an analysis of the effects of pliopoly. For, undoubtedly, the emergence of new firms will affect cartel policy in essential aspects.[5] We shall provisionally assume that the oligopoly is closed to newcomers, and shall defer the discussion of entry until later, as we are going to devote a separate chapter to the subject.

The relatively best developed part of cartel theory is, as one may well have expected, the one to which customary techniques of analysis could be applied. Graphical analysis as employed in the theory of the firm (designed to explain price and output determination) has proved applicable to the problem of the individual cartel member's conduct under given cartel agreements and cartel decisions.

Member's Conduct Under Given Cartel Rules

Some cartel members are willing to consider non-observance of the cartel rules as an alternative open to them, especially if it

---

[5] It was chiefly in connection with the problem of entry that a recent writer on cartel theory said "that the cartel model is the most fruitful approach to economic analysis of our real world." Don Patinkin, "Multiple-Plant Firms, Cartels, and Imperfect Competition," *Quarterly Journal of Economics,* Vol. LXI (1947), p. 203.

looks very attractive. Others are so honest that they feel they have no choice than to stick to the collusive agreement no matter what it costs. Each type can be represented by an appropriately drawn "demand curve"—a curve depicting the sales possibilities as the cartel member sees them. If a cartel has fixed the price as well as the quality of the product and has ruled out all extra selling efforts on the part of the members, the sales curve (average revenue curve) of a faithful member will be a horizontal straight line breaking off at the largest quantity he can sell under the circumstances. The sales curve of an "open-minded" member under the same conditions may be a stepped curve or a normally tilted curve of a steepness depending on the risks he would run of being found out as a price cutter and penalized as a violator of the agreement. (See Fig. 23.)

It is instructive to demonstrate the effects of various kinds of cartel agreements upon the conduct of members abiding by the rules but trying to make the best possible adjustment to them. Some of the results are not immediately obvious, although they become so upon inspection. Consider, for example, the effects the "percentage-quota" restrictions under a price and quota cartel will tend to have upon total output produced. These quotas are fixed percentages of the as yet unknown total sales of the entire industry. If one abstracts from the effects of prospective quota renegotiations, it can be shown that such a quota system, enforced by a system of fines collected from producers who exceed their quotas and of compensations paid to producers who fall behind their quotas, will not restrict total production directly but only through the level of the fines and compensations. Since every increase in output sold involves either a loss of compensation collectable if below the quota or a penalty payable if above the quota, the marginal revenue of the cartel member is reduced by the amounts of compensation or fine per unit of output. It is this reduction of marginal revenue which induces the firms to cut down the volume of production, and it is the rate of compensations and fines which determines the extent of the output restriction.[6] (See Fig. 24.) The very same reduction of marginal revenue through a

---

[6] Hans Brems, *Some Notes on the Theory of Cartels, Holding Companies, Mergers, et al.* (Cambridge, Mass., 1947, mimeographed), p. 10.

I. *Total, Average, and Marginal Revenue of a Secret Price Cutter*

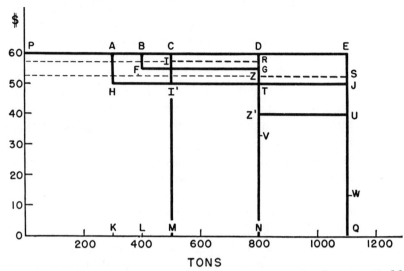

FIG. 23. Secret Rebates on Cartel Price at Risk of Fines Yield
Increased Sales With Reduced Average and Marginal Revenue.

The following assumptions are made about the sales opportunities of a
cartel member willing to violate the agreement:

(a) He could sell 500 tons, or OM, at the fixed cartel price of $60, or OP.
This would yield a gross revenue of $30,000, or $OMCP$, and an average as
well as marginal revenue of $60, or MC.

(b) If he offered to selected customers a secret rebate of $5, or DG, he
could sell 800 tons, or ON,—half of it, OL, at the regular price and the other
half, LN, subject to the rebate. His gross revenue would be $48,000 minus
$2,000, that is $46,000, or $ONGFBP$. If there were no risk involved, average
revenue would be $57.50, or NR, and marginal revenue—since the extra
300 tons sold would add $16,000 to the total proceeds—would be $53.33
per ton. If he figured with a risk premium of $6,000 for possible fines and
expenses in the event his contravention is discovered, his total revenue net
of this premium would be $40,000, average revenue $50, or NT, and marginal revenue $33.33, or NV.

(c) If he offered to a larger group of selected customers a secret rebate
of $10, or EJ, he could sell 1100 tons, or OQ,—300 tons, or OK, at the regular
price, and 800 tons, or KQ, subject to the rebate. His gross revenue would
be $66,000 minus $8,000, that is, $58,000, or $OQJHAP$. Neglecting all risks,
his average revenue would be $52.73, or QS, and his marginal revenue—
since the additional 300 tons sold would add $12,000 to the total proceeds
—would be $40 per ton, or QU. If he figures with a risk premium of $14,000,
his total revenue net of this premium would be $44,000, average revenue
$40, or QU, and marginal revenue $13.33 per ton, or QW.

(d) The resulting average revenues without regard to risk are shown
on the stepped curve $PCIRZS$; the average revenues net of risk premiums are
shown on the stepped curve $PCI'TZ'U$.

system of fines and compensations in a percentage-quota cartel will also reduce the incentives to make competitive outlays for quality improvement or sales promotion.

There are of course other ways of enforcing quota agreements among cartel members. Sellers who exceed their quotas may find themselves faced with patent suits (in the case of patent cartels), with increased duties under tariffs (in the case of international cartels) or with legal sanctions (in the case of cartels or "commodity agreements" supported by the state). In some of these and similar cases the sanctions for above-quota sales are more or less analogous to specific fines and have corresponding effects on total sales. Where there are penalties for above-quota sales but no compensations for unused quotas a prompt reporting and information system will be needed to induce members to "hold back" when they are "ahead" in selling.

Should we conclude that if percentage-quota restrictions were not enforced by any system of penalties they would have no effect upon output produced or upon outlays for nonprice competition? Such a conclusion would be based on an implicit assumption that in the absence of penalties a member of a quota cartel or market-sharing club would not care in the least whether or not he exceeded his agreed relative share in the market. Such an assumption would surely be unwarranted. Even when the observance of an understanding is not aided by sanctions expressed in dollars and cents, the sanctions implied in an honor code have an effect equivalent to that of some pecuniary consideration. The magnitude of this effect will depend on the honorableness and compunction of the individual member,—though some of us should shy at the suggestion that the money equivalent of a marginal prick of conscience be measured and expressed by distances between points along the ordinates of a pretty graph!

Where the products offered by the oligopolists are perfectly homogeneous, it is possible to implement a percentage-quota system by an agreed obligation for any member selling more than his quota to buy at the cartel price a quantity equal to his excess sales from members who had sold less than their quotas. Such a system —which, of course, is rather exceptional—reduces the net marginal revenue of excess sales to zero and, hence, no member who expects

II. *Output Reduction Due to Sanctions for Excess Sales*

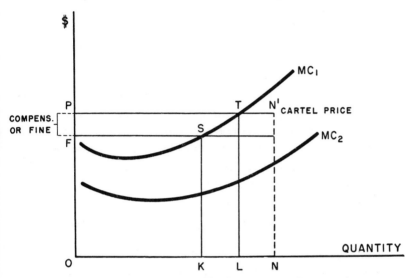

FIG. 24. Compensations for Unfilled Quota and Fines for Excess Sales Reduce Marginal Revenue and Therefore the Output of the Cartel Member.

It is assumed that the cartel agreement fixes the selling price at OP and allocates to the member a percentage-quota of aggregate sales, with a compensation of PF per unit for unfilled parts of the quota and a fine in the same amount for sales in excess of the quota. The member finds that he would be able to sell ON of his product at the cartel price, but he cannot know in advance whether this would be more or less than the percentage share that he is allowed in the market. If his marginal cost is as shown by MC_1, he would, in the absence of any sanctions for excess sales, produce an output OL, this being the output for which his marginal cost would equal his marginal revenue, LT $(= OP)$. If he must, however, figure on losing an amount of PF per unit on additional sales—either by foregoing compensation for unfilled quota or by paying fines for exceeding the quota—his marginal revenue is lowered to OF and his output to OK, where his marginal cost equals marginal revenue, KS $(= OF)$. Hence, an output reduction by KL is effected by the system of fines and compensations.

If his marginal cost were much lower, say, MC_2, sanctions in the amount stipulated would be ineffective in restricting production; he would produce ON, that is, all he could sell at the cartel price. In this case, the cartel price *per se* would set the limit to sales and production. It is assumed that this firm is faithful to the cartel rules.

the cartel and its quota distribution to continue will have any incentive to push his sales. For if he sold nothing at all in the market, his competitors would have to buy from him as much of his product as he is permitted to sell under the quota agreement.[7]

The purchase of cartelized product from other cartel members must not be confused with purchases of cartel quotas from other members. Purchase and sale of quotas are a common feature of cartels where the products are not exactly homogeneous, where the fines for excess sales are different in amount per unit from the compensations for unfilled quotas, or where the direct contact with as many customers as possible is highly valued by members who are apprehensive of a possible termination of the cartel and of an outbreak of vigorous competition.[8]

Member's Conduct With an Eye to Renegotiations

Most quota agreements, whether they fix the quotas in absolute quantities or as percentage shares of total sales, are based on past sales or present capacity or both. A firm that has supplied, say, 25 percent of the market on an average over the past few years will feel that it has a right to a share of at least that much when quotas for the next years are negotiated. A firm whose productive capacity

---

[7] An example of such a cartel was the International Aniline Convention. See Alfred Plummer, *International Combines in Modern Industry* (New York: Pitman, 2nd ed., 1938), pp. 163–64.

[8] Brems, *Some Notes* etc., pp. 14–18. The purchase of cartel quotas occurs also in selling cartels. There the chief reasons for such transactions among members are differences in production cost and, if the products are heterogeneous, the possibility of developing customer preferences for the qualities offered by members who doubt that the cartel will last. In selling cartels with absolute (rather than relative) quotas the syndicate may find it difficult to fill the quotas of particular members and may decide to buy them as a kind of shut-down compensation (similar to unemployment benefits). Since the purchase price of these quotas must be paid out of general sales proceeds, it will reduce the average net revenue per unit of product sold. The syndicate obviously figures that this reduction would be smaller than one resulting from an attempt to increase sales and fill all quotas. As an example of a syndicate's shut-down policy the German potash cartel may be cited, which in 1928 operated only 60 out of 229 plants. Benjamin Bruce Wallace and Lynn Ramsay Edminster, *International Control of Raw Materials* (Washington: Brookings Institution, 1930), p. 93.

is, say, 25 percent of the total capacity of the industry will feel justified in demanding a 25 percent quota of total sales. If an agreement is to be reached, a compromise will be needed because some firms probably have larger shares of past sales than of present capacity, while the reverse is true for others.

If a compromise is reached and quotas are agreed for the next few years—perhaps on the basis of relative bargaining power, perhaps on the basis of a formula which makes uniform allowance for both principles—some members may count on obtaining larger quotas later when the renewal of the agreement is negotiated. Especially if total demand is increasing—so that unchanged relative shares could be supplied only if some members increased their productive facilities, and the unchanged capacity of other members would be more fully utilized or even overtaxed if the relative shares remained the same—certain members will hope that the next quota distribution will be changed in their favor. To strengthen their case for such renegotiations they may adopt policies which they would not pursue if the cartel agreement with its present quota distribution were unchangeable for many more years.

Broadly speaking, three lines of policy are followed by a cartel member intent upon increasing his quota at the next renewal of the agreement. (1) In order to demonstrate that his quota has been too small, a cartel member may deliberately exceed his quota and pay the stipulated fines, or buy unfilled quotas from other members, even when it is not profitable to do so under given revenue and cost conditions. (2) In order to prove that his present quota would leave him with too much unused capacity, he may expand his productive facilities beyond the capacity called for by the growth of the demand for the industry's product, and beyond the capacity he could hope to utilize even if he were to obtain the larger quota that he is aiming for. (3) In order to be in a strong enough position for the renegotiations to threaten other members with non-renewal if they refused him an increase in the quota, he may improve his product and his productive facilities in preparedness for vigorous competition through quality and price.

These policies, if pursued by several members of the cartel, may have significant effects upon the supply of the cartelized product in both the long and the short run. (1) If the quotas are not fixed in absolute quantities but as percentage shares of total sales, the propensity of some members to increase their output even in the face of fines and negative marginal profits may result in a greater pressure than would exist otherwise and therefore in a lower cartel price. (2) The "overexpansion" of productive facilities may eventually influence the members in favor of a cartel price policy facilitating the sale of outputs corresponding more nearly to the built-up capacities. (Even with large excess capacity, total output then may be greater than it would be were it not for the expansions undertaken in view of quota renegotiations.) (3) The reductions in production cost achieved through improvements in technical facilities may also eventually induce members to press for larger sales and, therefore, for lower cartel prices. While the time lag of these price reductions behind the cost reductions may be considerable, quality improvements may accrue to the benefit of the consumer without delay.

Advocates of "orderly competition" (i.e., organized oligopoly) will be quick to seize upon these arguments to prove that competition is not eliminated by cartels and that competitive tendencies to increase outputs, expand productive capacities, reduce prices and improve qualities remain effective under a price-and-quota-cartel. The answer to this is of course that these effects must be attributed to the competition for higher quotas at the expiration of the existing agreement and to the possibility that it might not be renewed. The restriction of output that is inherent in the observance of a fixed price and in the desire to avoid the sanctions connected with an agreed quota is only partly—and perhaps only for a small part—offset by the cartel members' preparedness policies. The reduction of the incentive to improve the product under a quota cartel is only to some extent offset by the desire to be prepared if the cartel should become defunct. None of the policies which the cartel member may adopt in view of prospective renegotiations of the agreement would be followed if the agreement were permanent. Only the instability and possible breakdown of the established "order" secures the relaxation of its restrictive effects.

The Theory of Cartel Negotiations

The theories of the cartel member's conduct in the light of existing agreements and of prospective negotiations should be supplemented by the theory of cartel negotiations. Not only is such a theory not available in well developed form,[9] but unfortunately we do not even have any descriptive accounts. This is not surprising. After all, cartel negotiations in the United States constitute criminal conspiracy and we cannot expect the "conspirators" kindly to furnish detailed memoirs about their considerations and activities so that economists may learn and district attorneys may prosecute. Even in countries in which cartels are legal, cartel negotiations are usually secret.

The Cartel Government

Depending on the number of members and their personalities, cartels are governed by direct democracy, by representative democracy, by an oligarchy, or by a czar.

Where there are only a handful of members, consent by each is probably required for every decision and the cartel is "run" by all its members. In this case there will be little difference between negotiations of the cartel agreement—the "constitution," so to speak, of the cartel—and negotiations of particular cartel decisions —single "acts," such as changes of price lists. For very small groups, therefore, one may prefer not to distinguish between the conduct of the members and the conduct of the cartel government, although the distinction in my opinion may still serve a good purpose. For there are fundamental differences between decisions of individuals orientated toward their own interests and group decisions reached by negotiation, compromise, and agreement. Even when only two people get together, there will usually be a whiff of "government" in their joint decisions.

Delegation of decision-making power to a group smaller than the group of members will ordinarily occur when the cartel in-

---

[9] Hans Brems was brave enough to make a try. He built upon the principles of duopoly theory and the familiar contract curves. See his article, "On the Theory of Price Agreements," *Quarterly Journal of Economics*, Vol. LXV (1951), pp. 252–62.

cludes more persons than can conveniently get together for a cup of coffee around a table to thrash out all questions of mutual interest. The "critical number" of cartel members will depend, however, less on the size of the conference table than on the personalities involved. Of course, the most fundamental decisions, such as the distribution of quotas, will almost never be left to a governing body that does not include all members. (Even this is sometimes done when the state organizes the cartel or forces producers to accept an orderly-marketing scheme.) On the other hand, trivial matters, such as the adoption of uniform "small print" conditions of delivery for sales contracts, will more often than not be entrusted to a small committee. The fixing of prices may be a matter for direct democracy or for delegation to a committee, depending on how many members there are who jealously guard their "sovereignty."

Government by an oligarchy or by a czar will, ordinarily, be found in organized oligopolies only where the group of members is so large as to be unwieldy and consists partly of people who allow themselves to be dominated (or cannot help it). Cartels with thirty or forty members will rarely remain democratic, and sometimes even start out with a good deal of coercion. The pressures need not come from the strongest competitors, they may come from important customers, from suppliers of strategic materials, or from suppliers of finance. In some European countries the moral suasion or coercive power of the national government may be behind the organization of the cartel and its internal government.

The principles of cartel management are still to be written. But we cannot expect that any such study will draw much on American experience. There may be thousands of cartels operating in the United States, but information is unavailable. The members may not even know that this technical term applies to them. They may know only that they have an agreement with their competitors, that they discuss certain marketing problems with them, that they handle some matters of mutual interest through their trade association, institute or club, and that they had better not talk about it to outsiders lest the Antitrust Division get wise to it and make trouble.

LEADERSHIP OLIGOPOLY

The words "leadership oligopoly" may suggest such different things as leadership in organized oligopoly, organized price leadership, and unorganized price leadership.

Leadership in organized oligopoly is a problem of cartel management and member conduct; it may relate to all matters regulated by the cartel, not only to price making. It is a problem of politics and sociology as well as economics, and the little that is known about it was alluded to in the preceding section. *Organized price leadership* is a simple type of cartel; its organization may be confined to a tacit agreement that all members follow the price changes announced by a leader, though there may be more machinery to it, such as systematic recording and reporting services. *Unorganized price leadership* rests on no agreement and employs no machinery whatever. What will be said here on organized and unorganized leadership oligopoly will supplement what I have said elsewhere on the subject of price leadership.[10]

Different Concepts of Leadership

Leadership is essentially established by the conduct of the followers. Thus, the simplest concept of leadership contains only two elements: our observation that certain persons behave regularly and essentially in the same way that we observe in one who precedes them; and, second, our interpretative construction, based on some of these persons' admissions or on other clues, that the sameness of behavior is deliberate in the sense that they themselves observe the behavior of the "leader" and follow his example.

This is a rather extensive definition; it omits, among other attributes, the subjective interpretation by the leader himself. One may prefer a narrower concept of leadership, adding as further attributes the leader's knowledge that he is being followed, and his expectation that his behavior will produce similar behavior on the part of the others; and perhaps also, as a fourth attribute, some de-

---

[10] Fritz Machlup, *op. cit.*, Chapter 5.

liberate conduct on the part of the leader designed to secure continued followership.

This so much narrower concept of leadership with its four elements—(1) the objective observation of the same behavior in one who precedes and in others who follow, (2) the subjective interpretation by the followers, (3) the subjective interpretation by the leader, (4) deliberate actions by the leader to secure his position as a leader—does not fit all kinds of leadership in oligopoly. One may want a concept of leadership in which the first and fourth elements are not required. When, for instance, the leader leads not by example but by advice or persuasion, there will be no observable leader-follower sequence of behavior. (And if the persons in question do not like to be observed, they may well from time to time arrange that the "lead" is given only by word of mouth or some other sign and the sequence of observable behavior is reversed.) Deliberate action on the part of the leader to secure his leadership position is often unnecessary and this fourth element, therefore, need not be in the picture at all.

An analysis of leadership in any of these meanings will as a rule proceed in two directions: first, what kind of behavior does it—the existence of "leadership"—produce in those who are led; and second, what kind of behavior or position does it presuppose for him who leads? Classifications of leadership may rest on the findings of either of these inquiries.

An entirely different concept of leadership was discussed in connection with classical duopoly theory. Some modern expositors of this theory interpreted a seller's attitude of responsiveness to his competitor's action as "followership" even if his response was not imitation. Conversely, "lack of response" was called "leadership" and, thus, a seller expecting his competitor not to respond to his action was described as regarding his competitor as a "leader." (See above pp. 390–91, 402–08.) The idea, in speaking of leadership where no one leads, no one imitates and no one follows, is apparently that a "leader" is one who is independent enough not to care about what anybody else is doing. But this idea is so far from the other connotations of leadership that it would probably be wiser not to insist on using the same term to denote it.[11]

[11] It may be helpful to list different kinds of constellations that have been

The Qualifications of the Leader

What is there in the leader's position, personality, or conduct that makes followers accept his lead?

One may begin answering this question by stating that the seller whose prices are matched, or whose price changes are followed, by other sellers may be a "dominant" firm, a "barometric" firm, or an "appointed" firm.[12] The appointed price leader occupies this position on the basis of an explicit or implicit agreement among the sellers under organized oligopoly. The leadership position of the dominant firm need not imply any understanding between this firm and its followers, but ordinarily it will have become conventionalized by a mutual understanding, and it may have even become part of an organized oligopoly. The barometric firm may be price leader without being leader through domination or leader by appointment. This seller's price changes are followed by others because they regard him as a good judge of market conditions, a barometer, so to speak, registering reliably the changes of the market weather.

The expression "dominant firm" may mean so many things that it will be preferable to break this type down into several sub-types.

---

regarded as instances of leadership in matters of oligopolistic price making: Seller A is a leader in that

(1) seller B usually matches A's price;

(2) seller B usually responds to A's price changes by changing his price so that the differential remains approximately the same;

(3) seller B usually responds to A's price changes by changing his price in the same direction;

(4) seller B usually responds to A's price changes by changing his price in a way expected by A;

(5) seller B usually responds to A's price changes by changing his price, no matter how;

(6) seller B usually charges the price that A tells him to charge;

(7) seller A usually does not respond to any price changes by seller B.

We shall confine our further discussion to the first three of these leadership cases.

[12] The first two distinctions were made by George J. Stigler, "The Kinky Oligopoly Demand Curve and Rigid Prices," *Journal of Political Economy*, Vol. LV (1947), p. 445. He was dealing only with price leadership without collusion. The dominant firm may, of course, be the leader also in organized price leadership. But in order to take account of price leaders in collusive situations who are not dominant firms, I have added the "appointed" firm to Stigler's list.

A firm may be called dominant—in connection with price policy—when it is

(a) so large compared with all other firms in the industry that it is not seriously affected by the actions of the small ones and allows them to do as they please;

(b) so powerful compared with the smaller firms and so intent upon dictating the price policy in the industry that it is inclined to use its power to make the smaller firms conform with its wishes;

(c) so much larger than most other firms in the industry that the latter, anxious to avoid vigorous competition, prefer to accept its policy, even if they do not expect that the large firm would try to impose its will on them;

(d) the largest firm in the industry and recognized as being naturally better equipped than others to judge the market conditions and to set prices in the best interest of the whole industry.

In the last of these four meanings the dominant firm becomes the same as the barometric firm and also, if the situation becomes conventional in the industry, the same as the appointed firm under organized oligopoly. Likewise, in the second and third meanings, the dominant firm becomes, if the situation continues for some time, a sort of cartel leader. It makes no real difference whether it established itself as dominant firm and price leader by exercising its power to inflict damage on firms which failed to follow its lead [13] or whether the other firms in the industry recognized the leadership simply because they had found that they fared better in the position of followers free from costly price competition. In any case, if price leadership has become customary in an industry, an understanding among the parties is implied. And if it is more than a vague understanding, if it is an agreement of some sort, explicit

[13] Many instances could be cited to illustrate the case of leadership enforced by power and intimidation. For example, it is reported that the price leadership behind the basing-point system in the salt industry was established in such fashion: "There is some evidence to the effect that this uniformity in published prices resulted from a definite fear on the part of smaller producers of disastrous reprisals if they disturbed the prices established by the larger, more powerful producers." National Recovery Administration, Division of Review, *Manufacturers Control of Distribution: A Study of Trade Practice Provisions in Selected National Recovery Administration Codes.* Work Materials No. 62. (Washington: 1936), p. 83.

or implicit, or if it is aided by any kind of organized action, the situation will be one of organized oligopoly. For example, if the leader, directly or through some "organs" or agencies, takes pains to keep his competitors fully informed about his exact price list or pricing technique, one must assume that he wants them to follow his lead, and if they actually do it, the presumption of organized oligopoly is hardly refutable.

"Partial Monopoly" and "Partial Oligopoly"

In the first of the listed meanings the dominant firm may be considered as a quasi-monopolist, and its small competitors as quasi-polypolists. The situation can best be visualized if we imagine that there is one large firm supplying something like 90 percent of the total, and several small firms each supplying between one and three percent of the total. The position of these small firms can be considered as quasi-perfect polypoly because at any given price —equal to or a trifle below that fixed by the large firm—they can sell all they care to sell. (See Chapter 6.) The position of the large firm has been called "incomplete monopoly" [14] or "partial monopoly." [15] This seller's price leadership is not explained by his personality or conduct, but by the position of the small sellers, each of whom is so insignificant in the market that he cannot pursue any price "policy" and must accept the price as "given."

The large seller is a quasi-monopolist in that he can set a "monopoly price" in the manner described by simple monopoly theory, his sales curve being his estimate of the total market demand minus the "competitive output" of the small firms. For any given total market demand the quasi-monopoly price will be lower the larger the aggregate productive capacity of the follower firms, because the elasticity of the net sales curve of the large firm will be the

[14] Karl Forchheimer, "Theoretisches zum unvollständigen Monopole," *Jahrbuch für Gesetzgebung, Verwaltung und Volkswirtschaft im Deutschen Reich*, Vol. 32 (1908), pp. 1–12.

[15] A. J. Nichol, *Partial Monopoly and Price Leadership* (Philadelphia: Smith-Edwards Co., 1930); F. Zeuthen, *Problems of Monopoly and Economic Warfare* (London: Routledge, 1930), pp. 17–23; George J. Stigler, "Notes on the Theory of Duopoly," *Journal of Political Economy*, Vol. XLVIII (1940), p. 522; Walter Eucken, *Die Grundlagen der Nationalökonomie* (Bad Godesberg: H. Küpper, 1941), p. 122.

more drastically increased the more its net sales are reduced owing to the competitors' supply.[16] If the marginal cost of the small firms and, hence, the "competitive supply" are elastic, that is, if the small firms produce more at higher prices than at lower prices, the net sales curve of the large firm will be still more elastic and its "monopoly price" accordingly lower.[17] (See Fig. 25.)

While this situation of "competition among the few" puts the large seller in a position of quasi-monopoly and the small sellers in positions of quasi-perfect polypoly—and no one, therefore, in a position of oligopoly in the strict sense of our definition—we may find situations in which two or more large firms share the market that is left after several very small firms have disposed of their competitive output. The small firms may again be quasi-perfect polypolists, but the large firms will now be real oligopolists. Because some of the firms in this industry act perfectly polypolistically, the situation is sometimes characterized as one of "partial oligopoly." [18]

The existence of price leadership under partial oligopoly cannot be explained quite so simply as under partial monopoly. The very small firms, of course, will follow the leader because they have no choice in the matter; they cannot raise the price, since they would have no sales, and they will not reduce the price, since they can sell all they care to sell anyway. The larger firms, however, do have a choice and, if they follow the leader, they do so for a reason. In all probability they have decided that it is best for all if price policy is coordinated. In other words, price leadership is probably organized for a part of this industry and unorganized for the rest. For the conduct of the larger followers the position,

---

[16] If given quantities (supplied by the small competitors) are deducted from a given demand curve, the resulting net sales curve will be more to the left and hence more elastic at any given price.

[17] Karl Forchheimer, *op. cit.*, p. 10.

[18] Walter Eucken, *op. cit.*, p. 122; William Fellner, *Competition Among the Few: Oligopoly and Similar Market Structures* (New York: Knopf, 1949), pp. 136–41. The small firms, says Fellner, are "unaware of their mutual influence on one another" (p. 136). "The situation will be that of partial oligopoly because price, output, profits, and so forth, will depend on the deliberate behavior of the big firms, which are aware of their individual influence, as well as on the competitive forces emanating from the area of small firms" (p. 138).

Elasticity of Demand for Large Firm's Output Increases With the Size and Elasticity of Supply from Small Competitors

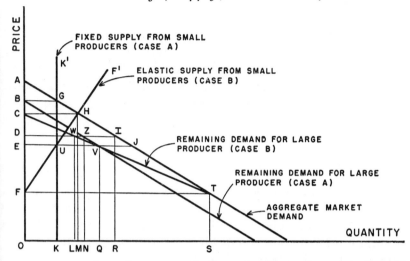

Fig. 25. Fixed or Elastic Supply from Small Producers Deducted from Aggregate Demand Leaves More Elastic Demand for Output of Large Firm.

If small producers act as quasi-perfect polypolists, the large firm may count on the demand left over after the competitors sell their entire supply. If that supply is OK and perfectly inelastic (Case A), the demand remaining after deducting OK (= BG) from the aggregate demand will begin at price OB and will be more elastic (at given prices) than the aggregate demand. If the supply from the small firms is elastic—so that (in Case B) at price OE the same quantity OK will come forth, but larger quantities at higher prices and only smaller quantities at lower prices (and none at or below the price OF)—the demand left over for the large firm will be still more elastic (up to the quantity FT, where it will become identical with the aggregate demand). For example, at a price OD, the elasticity of demand is larger in point W (Case B) than in point Z (Case A), where, in turn, it is larger than in point I (Total Market). This is demonstrated geometrically by the fact that $\frac{OD}{DC} > \frac{OD}{DB} > \frac{OD}{DA}$. The implication is obvious: lower prices will be charged and larger quantities sold when the elasticity of demand is greater.

the personality, or the conduct of the leader may have been of importance, while nothing but their own size is needed to explain why the small firms are followers.

It is interesting to speculate about the comparative prices and outputs under partial monopoly, partial oligopoly, and complete oligopoly, coordinated or uncoordinated. The easiest comparison is that between the results of partial monopoly and coordinated oligopoly: the coordinated selling policy of the oligopolists is oriented towards the aggregate demand for their combined product, the elasticity of which is obviously smaller than the "left-over demand" confronting the partial monopolist. Hence, if cost conditions are not too different, one may expect prices to be higher and outputs lower under coordinated oligopoly than under partial monopoly.

Under uncoordinated oligopoly the outcome is uncertain. Fear of price wars and aversion to price competition may well result in still higher prices and accordingly smaller outputs; under other circumstances prices might be lower and outputs larger; and there are no *a priori* reasons for holding the one outcome to be more probable than the other.

The comparison between the results of partial monopoly and partial oligopoly is even more speculative. Let us assume that the cost conditions are the same under both situations and that the number and size of the small competitors who act quasi-polypolistically are also the same; the only difference being that in the one case it is one big firm, in the other case two or more firms, who can serve the market demand that is left over after the supply of the small sellers is disposed of. Now, if the two or more partial oligopolists could achieve perfect coordination, they would of course fix the same price as would a partial monopolist. But, since "joint profit maximization" is so very unlikely, the result will probably be different; if the same fear of price war and aversion to price competition prevails that we mentioned before, the price under partial oligopoly may well be higher, and the output smaller, than under partial monopoly; other attitudes and dispositions may lead to the opposite result.

A slight alteration of assumptions may make the higher-price solution for the partial-oligopoly case more probable than the lower-price solution. In the previous comparison we assumed that the number and size of the small quasi-polypolists were the same in both situations so that the combined market share of the partial oligopolists was the same as the market share of the partial monopolist. This comparison might be relevant for an industry in which a dissolution of the firm possessing the partial monopoly had forced this firm to split up into two or more separate parts. But the comparison between partial monopoly and partial oligopoly may also be of interest for a case in which partial oligopoly has developed through a relatively greater rate of growth of some of the small competitors, who would thereby have transformed themselves from quasi-perfect polypolists into oligopolists. The supply from firms continuing to act as quasi-perfect polypolists would then be relatively smaller than in the other situation, and the combined productive capacity and market share of the partial oligopolists together would be relatively greater than that of the partial monopolist. In other words, the left-over demand confronting the larger firms under partial oligopoly would be relatively larger and less elastic than that faced by the big firm under partial monopoly and, therefore, would invite higher seller prices.

Needless to say, I know of no empirical evidence to support these conclusions. They are merely deductions from "plausible assumptions," and one may prefer not to trust them. But if they could be trusted, they would have very interesting policy implications. For example, it would follow that an industry with four firms would probably produce more, and sell more cheaply, if the shares of the firms in the market were something like 80, 8, 7, and 5 percent than it would, under otherwise similar conditions, with the market shares something like 40, 33, 22, and 5 percent. For in the former case 20 percent of the market would be supplied by quasi-perfect polypolists, while only 5 percent would be so supplied in the latter case. If this is correct, one would have to reject the idea that an industry can be made "more competitive" by fostering the growth of the small producers and strengthening their so-called "competitive position" vis-à-vis the big firm. As long as the small fry feel so insignificant that they sell all they can profitably produce, the big firm is faced with a more elastic demand, and will set prices accordingly lower. If a small producer grows so much that he gets the feeling that he "counts" in the market, he develops a sense of responsibility for "orderly marketing"—and high-price oligopoly may emerge.

Rotating and Divided Leadership

The idea that unorganized price leadership is very common even where the followers are not of atomistic smallness is probably an outgrowth of defense arguments in antitrust cases. The defense frequently denied the charges of collusion and tried to explain the challenged price-making conduct of the defendants as instances of unorganized price leadership. In most cases, however, a thorough investigation succeeded in uncovering evidence of organized oligopoly. Of course, when the group of oligopolists is small and essential communications among them can be oral, it is easy to remove incriminating traces of collusion.

Since exactly simultaneous price changes by competing sellers suggest prior agreements among them, they prefer to make or announce the changes with slight time lags. Price leadership in the strict sense of the word implies such lags. But since perfect consistency in the procedure may again look too systematic and thus suggest a standing agreement or understanding, prudent members of price leadership organizations may arrange for varying time lags and for either rotating leadership or divided leadership.

Rotating leadership has the advantage for the sellers that outside observers will have nothing they can point to as indicative of any system, scheme, or arrangement among the sellers in question. Divided leadership, likewise, may be quite inconspicuous if the differences between the various types of product for which different firms act as leaders are familiar only to the expert in the field. Where the field itself is divided among producers in such a way that only two or three of them share the market in each type of product, price leadership will naturally go to the "leading" producer of each type of product. Such a system of divided price leadership was practiced for many years in the American glass container industry, a well organized patent license cartel which included division of fields, division of territories, and quotas, in addition to "price leadership." [19]

Nevertheless there may be instances of unorganized price leadership. It certainly is easy to construct plausible models to explain how they would work. Yet, through the insight which personal business experience has given me and in view of the evidence produced in court cases in which firms long insisted that leadership was unorganized, I am persuaded that not the models of unorganized but rather those of organized leadership correspond more closely to the greater number of observed cases in the world of business.

UNORGANIZED OLIGOPOLY

Some degree of coordination of selling policy—in exceptional cases even a high degree—can be achieved in an industry by unorganized leadership or unorganized cooperation. In the absence of leadership or cooperation, unorganized oligopoly can only be uncoordinated oligopoly.

Unorganized Cooperation

Much of what is described as unorganized cooperation in various trades is in fact secretly organized cooperation; and organized

[19] *Investigation in the Concentration of Economic Power. Hearings before the Temporary National Economic Committee,* Part 2 (Washington, 1939). As a witness before the Committee the president of Owens-Illinois Glass Co. testified: "But Thatcher [another producer of glass containers] sets a price on milk bottles and Ball does on certain lines and we do on certain lines and Hazel do on certain lines" (p. 530). The vice president of Hazel-Atlas Glass Co. stated: "Hazel-Atlas Glass Co. initiates the prices covering wide-mouthed container ware, and the Hazel-Atlas price list for ware of this class constitutes the recognized market price in the industry" (p. 547). "As to prices on proprietary and prescription ware we adopt the schedules of the Owens-Illinois Glass Co. and make their prices ours. The same conditions . . . apply in connection of our liquor ware lists and our beer bottle lists. We are relatively small operators in these lines, and follow the market as established by the leaders in these branches of the industry . . . for similar reasons we adopt the prices as published by the Ball Bros. Co. as our prices for fruit jars, jelly glasses, and fruit jar tops . . . We initiate our own prices on opal ware for the cosmetic and drug trade . . . we have only one competitor in that line . . ." (p. 548).

cooperation among competitors constitutes a cartel. But, there can be no doubt, unorganized cooperation does exist.

Moreover, oligopolistic conduct that is cooperative without being supported by any existing organization, agreement or leadership may have had such support in the past. The inhibitions and self-restraints that constitute the cooperative attitudes of the sellers sometimes develop in a period in which restraints are imposed upon them by leaders or by organized control. For example, during emergency periods—serious depressions, wars—restrictions upon competitive efforts are frequently organized and create a mentality of relaxed competition that continues after the enforcement of the restrictions has been discontinued. Especially where trade associations participate in the implementation of emergency controls, a lasting climate of cooperation, or at least of relaxed competition, tends to remain.[20] In antitrust cases in which the last evidence of explicit collusion is of a time long ago, the courts are faced with the question whether this organized restraint in the past can still be regarded as the basis of cooperation *now* practiced within an industry. Is it organized or unorganized cooperation if present practice has had organized support until several years ago but none since? The economic theorist, unlike the lawyer, is not pressed for an answer to this question.[21]

Personal and social contacts among the sellers will often facilitate cooperation and weaken competition. It is not easy to make every effort to steal customers from a friend with whom one

[20] Many of the restrictions contained in the "codes of fair competition" under the National Industrial Recovery Act of 1933 have become part of the "ethics" of the industries concerned. However, it is not known how many of these "ethical" rules continued to have the secret organized support of trade associations. (In several European countries war time controls established under war emergency programs have been officially continued as permanent voluntary institutions of the various trades and industries.)

[21] The fact that I always suspect cooperation to be "organized" may give the impression that I regard cooperation somehow as "less natural" than competition. I do not hold such a view. An attitude of unmitigated competition is not "more natural" than an attitude of friendly cooperation. Without making any anthropological pretensions I submit that the spirit of competition can survive only if it is (artificially) fostered by society. Thus, competition must also be "organized" in the sense that interferences with and restraints of price and quality competition in any lines of business must be deliberately prevented.

played billiards yesterday and will drink cocktails tomorrow. Where local producers sell in a local market they will most likely belong to the same club, same church, or same social group and will feel constrained to pull their punches when they compete for business. In the discussion of organized oligopoly, meetings of the competing sellers were enumerated among the joint actions designed to achieve some coordination of the oligopolists' conduct. One may now say that there is no great difference between a "cocktail party" at which competitors meet and talk shop and a "meeting" at which competitors talk shop and drink cocktails.[22] But there is enough of a difference to permit a line to be drawn between the primarily social and the primarily business character of such meetings, and between the unorganized or organized nature of the cooperative attitudes of the sellers involved.

Again, there is the question of the trade journal fostering a kind of *esprit de corps* among the people in the trade. If the journal is the organ of the trade association or institute of which the firms are members, the publicity that it gives to the desirability of certain practices is surely part of organized activity to achieve coordination of sellers' conduct. But if the journal is run by an independent publisher or editor, and if it does not through the publication of price announcements, production and sales statistics, or similar reports, aid in the execution of collusive schemes, but confines itself to the general propaganda of anti-competitive business ethics, this journalistic activity standing by itself would hardly be enough to warrant a judgment of "organized" cooperation in the industry.

In many industries, it is reported, so-called live-and-let-live policies on the part of the competing firms are prevalent. Although this is in many instances merely a euphemistic way of speaking of the existence of collusion in these industries, non-collusive relaxations of competition may and do occur, especially where

[22] From time to time and place to place the kind of drinks served at such parties seems to change more than the shop talk. "In 1802, at a meeting of [Welsh] ironmasters . . . members agreed . . . [that] each new member had also to provide a bowl of punch for the gathering . . . prices were fixed for foundry and forge pigs and for bar iron each quarter from 1803 onwards." Thomas Southcliffe Ashton, *Iron and Steel in the Industrial Revolution* (London: Longmans, Green, 1924), pp. 177–78.

entry of newcomers is difficult. The general propensity to take it easy and to be a good fellow is apt to get stronger if existing firms are not constantly threatened by newcomers' competition. If the group of oligopolists remains unchanged for a long time, the members may become increasingly considerate of one another. "Considerate competition" may be the result, characterizing the conduct of sellers under unorganized though not uncoordinated oligopoly.

Types of Uncoordinated Oligopoly

The large number of different ways in which oligopoly can be coordinated makes it impossible to formulate a general theory of coordinated oligopoly that would be more than a few empty generalities. It has sometimes been held, however, that one could formulate a general theory of *uncoordinated* oligopoly. But, as we have learnt from the survey of classical duopoly theory, all these supposedly general theories proved to be special theories of very limited applicability. This is not surprising once it becomes clear that there are also several types of uncoordinated oligopoly differing from one another in significant respects.

We shall select four types of uncoordinated oligopoly for discussion: fighting oligopoly, hyper-competitive oligopoly, chain oligopoly, and guessing-game oligopoly. These names may or may not be self-explanatory; but we shall forthwith proceed to descriptions.

Fighting Oligopoly

Although it is sometimes difficult to distinguish a seller who competes for business from one who competes in order to hurt a rival, it is necessary to make the distinction. The differences between vigorous competition and belligerent competition, between price competition and price war, are significant even if it takes an analysis of motivation to make the proper identifications in any concrete case.

Even plainly belligerent conduct—actions designed to hurt a rival although they also hurt the actor himself—may have different motives worth distinguishing. One seller may wish to hurt another just out of an irritation or resentment, a mere act of temper; or in a playful mood "for the fun of fighting"; or deliberately in order to "teach him a lesson"; or planfully in order to force him to do what he would not willingly do; or in a studied attempt to "finish" him, to get rid of him. All these and other motives may spur oligopolists into wars or fights. Sometimes, perhaps, a seller knows that he cannot really hurt his rival, but he may be out to spite him. At other times a careful evaluation of the opponent's strength and designs precedes the outbreak of hostilities.

Economists, mainly concerned with "rational" behavior, have had little to say about fights motivated by emotional outbreaks or by the fun of sparring. They were chiefly interested in rational causes of oligopolistic warfare and a heroic attempt was made to develop a theory based on a model analysis of all market positions and attitudes that are likely to involve duopolists in warfare.[23] The limitation to two sellers was necessary because the chosen technique of analysis, two-dimensional graphs, cannot handle more, and perhaps also because the number of possible combinations for more than two would be forbidding. The technique employs "mutual reaction curves" derived from "profit-indifference maps." The latter consist of curves showing all combinations of the two sellers' "variables"—either prices or quantities of output—which yield equal profits. From such maps one can find the points of maximum profit for a seller adjusting his price (or output) to that of the rival or inducing his rival to adjust to him. The juxtaposition of the resulting reaction curves show then whether the constellation is compatible or incompatible. Mutually incompatible situations are likely to lead to fight.

From the fact that a catalogue of all possible constellations includes many more incompatible than compatible ones, a political conclusion has been drawn in favor of a corporative state that would settle the otherwise unsettled market conflicts.[24] But surely one cannot deduce the probability of oligopolistic fight—and the need to avoid or settle them by government fiat—from a catalogue of possibilities. The relevance of the various models to the explana-

[23] Heinrich von Stackelberg, *Marktform und Gleichgewicht* (Vienna: Springer, 1934), pp. 45 ff. See above, Chapter 12, pp. 402–04.

[24] Stackelberg published his book in 1934, one year after the Nazis had come into power. In fairness it should be mentioned that Stackelberg later left Germany and became very critical of the National-Socialist regime.

tion of actual situations has not been shown and it is hard to say whether many fights among oligopolists have arisen out of constellations similar to those pictured by the mutually incompatible reaction curves constructed by the theory in question.[25]

With due respect for the intellectual effort involved in formulating a general theory of the rational *causes* of oligopolistic warfare, I believe that at this juncture we could learn more by a series of individual case studies. The same is true with respect to the principles of the *conduct* of oligopolistic warfare. Of course, often these wars are so primitive that not much theorizing is needed for the analysis of the strategies employed. For example, there is nothing complicated in a price war fought by successive jabs of simple price slashing, where each seller offers his product at a single price to any buyer.[26] Warfare by reckless advertising and give-away campaigns is similarly simple.[27] More complicated is the analysis of oligopolistic warfare when it employs local price cutting or similar schemes of price discrimination. But not enough of the theory of discriminatory price making has been expounded in this book to equip us for such an analysis here. I shall leave it for extensive treatment elsewhere.[28]

Hyper-Competitive Oligopoly

With the exception of oligopoly in fight, which obviously results in lower prices to consumers and in larger sales, oligopoly is

[25] Fellner, who devotes a chapter of his book to the exposition and criticism of Stackelberg's theory, calls it "the most mature product growing out of the preceding stages of development," but nonetheless rejects it as basically faulty. William Fellner, *op. cit.*, p. 119.

[26] The following news item (1951) illustrates a case of simple price war: "Corvallis, Ore., Oct. 20 (AP)—Bread sold at a penny a loaf today and the only catch was a one-loaf-to-a-customer limit.

"It was the result of a price war that started yesterday. The pound and a half loaf, normally 23 cents for most brands, started going down when local grocers matched a lower chain store price.

"By nightfall the price was 10 cents.

"This morning, two stores listed it at 1 cent."—A price war of this kind, however, is probably largely emotional, rather than rational.

[27] For an illustration see above, p. 461 n.

[28] My monograph on "The Economics of Price Discrimination," which has been under preparation for several years, will contain a detailed analysis of discriminatory pricing for all sorts of purposes.

commonly understood to imply inhibitions and restrictions on a
seller's propensity or freedom to resort to price reductions when
he wants more business. There is a type of oligopoly, however,
besides belligerent oligopoly, which produces results very close
to or beyond the "competitive norm." That is, selling prices may
be below, and sales quantities above, what they would be if
sellers were in polypolistic positions. This is what the name "hyper-
competitive" oligopoly is supposed to express.

This type of oligopoly can exist in an industry composed of a
considerable number of independent firms—none of them dominant—producing a little differentiated product. Each seller considers himself one of a small group of firms producing very closely
substitutable qualities. They sell in an unorganized and somewhat
imperfect market where transactions are secret and "knowledge"
is based more on rumors than on information; each seller is eager
to increase his business and is insensitive to what their rivals think
of him, though of course conscious of their response to his aggressive selling; but this consciousness does not inhibit him because
he always believes the others are more eager and more aggressive
than he; and he is always confirmed in this belief by customers who
play one seller against the other. Typically, it is easy for newcomers to enter the industry and some of the insiders are rugged
individualists and non-conformers; cooperation among the insiders
is therefore impossible.

The situation would be close to polypoly were it not for the fact
that each seller is conscious of a few others whose products are
the most highly substitutable for his own. The kind of grouping
creates "sectional oligopolies" within an industry of "many firms."
Within each group the firms watch one another and are conscious
of being watched. But the result is not any restraint in selling
effort or in price competition, but merely an attempt to keep things
secret—which can be exploited by sharp buyers who do not mind
telling stories about wonderful bargains offered by certain competitors. An oligopolist under such circumstances is less concerned
about what his rivals might do if he accepts a big order at a low
price than about what they might do if he hesitates and waits for
another hour. In other words, he cares first of all about getting
enough orders and, therefore, is more afraid that his rivals will

start taking lower prices and steal his business than that they might retaliate for his own price concessions.

Most businessmen dislike situations of this sort and refer to them as demoralized markets, unhealthy, chaotic. Especially during depressions firms in hyper-competitive oligopoly positions will suffer severely, most of them selling below cost and being heavily "in the red." Attempts will be made to organize such an industry into a cartel, but these attempts are apt to fail or to be only temporarily successful if some insiders persist in being individualists and if the industry continues to be open to newcomers' competition. If governments are not willing to assist in the cartelization of these industries, the only dependable way to convert such hyper-competitive oligopolies into coordinated ones is through merger, reducing the number of firms and creating dominating positions.

Economists are not agreed on the evaluation of hyper-competitive conditions. Some are inclined to side with the businessmen in condemning the conditions as unhealthy. Others find no reason for such condemnation, but on the contrary recognize that this kind of oligopoly is the only one that is not restrictive in its effects upon production and investment.

Chain Oligopoly

The oligopoly type just discussed owes its competitive nature largely to the fact that it exists within an industry of relatively many firms; the firms in question are oligopolistic because they are members of smaller subgroups of an industry sectionalized through quality differences. Where such industry subgroups are chain-linked with one another one may speak of a "chain oligopoly." [29]

Chain oligopolies exist within highly populated industries where firms find themselves surrounded by "a few neighbors," close to them in space or because of an especially high degree of similarity of the quality of their products. There may be hundreds of thousands of firms in the industry, but only some compete for exactly the same clientele and only the particularly close ones—

[29] Chamberlin was, to my knowledge, the first to describe this kind of relationship. Edward Hastings Chamberlin, *The Theory of Monopolistic Competition* (Cambridge: Harvard University Press, 1931), p. 103.

in terms of location or quality—may be conscious of each other's reactions. For example, seller M may be an oligopolist *vis-à-vis* sellers L and N, while L is oligopolist *vis-à-vis* K and M, and so forth in chain fashion. Thus, every seller is a member of an oligopolistic subgroup within an industry of many sellers, but each of these subgroups has a different composition because everybody has different "neighbors."

If the industry becomes more densely settled, both the number of sellers regarded as close rivals and the number of sellers noticed as competitors may increase. The larger the group of sellers who are directly affected by the competitive actions of an individual seller and must therefore be expected to react to them, the less important will each seller become, and the oligopolistic interdependences will give place to more anonymous, polypolistic relationships. It is also possible that hyper-competitive conduct will develop, depending chiefly on the personalities involved. Indeed, it is conceivable that in some parts of the network of chain-linked oligopolies sellers act hyper-competitively, but in other parts with great caution and restraint. In some parts, their conduct may be coordinated and even organized; while they may be fighting elsewhere. In other words, it is not possible to deduce the kind of competitive conduct from the chain-structure of the market.

In a sense, chain-structure of markets is a very general phenomenon, but need not result in chain oligopoly. Unless the market is perfect, as on an organized exchange, there will usually be faster responses and repercussions among neighboring firms than among distant ones. If one observes price movements in large produce markets one can notice how price reductions spread gradually from stall to stall. Such chain reactions need not be of an oligopolistic nature. Chain-linking may be the basic structure of a polypolistic market as it responds to stimuli whose first impact is local.

Guessing-Game Oligopoly

Where a group is quite small in number and stable in composition, the sellers as a rule will have learned to live with each other and their market conduct will have become coordinated.

This is why uncoordinated oligopoly is rare. Where it prevails it is largely due to the existence of a few stubborn characters in the group. As they mellow or die, coordination will grow up or will be organized. But while they are still around and steadfastly refuse to "play ball" or even to act according to a stable pattern, oligopoly takes the form of a guessing game, each seller trying to guess what the rival may do in reaction to his actions.

Classical and neo-classical oligopoly models were essentially of this type, but the assumed "guessing" was rather silly, as we have shown at length (Chapter 12). Consistently wrong guessing was the working principle of the models, leading either to an equilibrium position or to continuous oscillations. But when consistently correct guessing is substituted as the basic principle, the model becomes one of coordinated oligopoly. If therefore neither consistently wrong guessing nor consistently right guessing is acceptable for a theory of uncoordinated oligopoly, and since such a theory cannot well be based on an assumption that guesses and actions are haphazard and random, this is clearly a place for trying to work with the "theory of games." [30]

The fundamental idea behind the theory of games is to drop the assumption that a player (or seller) acts on the basis of *some* anticipations of his opponents' reactions to his own actions, and to substitute the assumption that he acts in a way that will give him some minimum gain irrespective of how his opponents may react. The trouble with this new assumption is that it excludes the possibility of action on "strong hunches" and of the exploitation of the opponents' obvious mistakes.[31] It is perhaps possible to relax the assumption in order to admit the inclusion of these alternative possibilities under particular circumstances—even if this spoils the purity of the theory.

In any event, we must bear in mind that, although guessing-game oligopoly is intellectually the most rewarding to theorize about, it is probably the least important in practice. The modern penchant for playing safe has left little room for a kind of competition among a few firms where each has to make uncertain guesses

[30] John von Neumann and Oskar Morgenstern, *The Theory of Games and Economic Behavior* (Princeton: Princeton University Press, 1945.)
[31] See above, Chapter 13, pp. 428–30.

of how its rivals would react to its own actions; each usually knows what to expect from the others and avoids acting in an unexpected way.

HISTORICAL TRENDS

Has oligopoly become more prevalent in the course of time? Economists have certainly become increasingly aware of this form of seller's competition and have devoted to its discussion an increasing share of their published work. There are many who hold that the history of economic thought is to a large extent a reflection of the course of economic history, because the practical problems of the day always impress themselves upon the economists' attention. From this it might be concluded that oligopoly has gained in importance relative to polypoly. But should one conclude from the present vogue of electron theory in physics that there are now more electrons than there used to be, or from the modern theory of genetics that genes must have spread a great deal during recent centuries? No indeed, the increased attention to oligopoly theory in economics need not indicate anything about economic developments in the real world.

Speculative Clues

It is not easy, incidentally, to give exact meaning to statements that oligopoly has become more prevalent or less prevalent. Is it implied that the number of oligopolistic firms has changed relative to the total number of firms? Or, since a firm may sometimes act oligopolistically and sometimes polypolistically, that the number of oligopolistic business decisions has changed relative to the total number of decisions? Or, since some firms are big and others small, and some decisions relate to large transactions and others to modest ones, should one try to compare the money values of product sold by oligopolists with the total of all sales in the economy? Needless to say, with available information we could not conclusively demonstrate whether oligopoly in any of these meanings has grown or declined.

A highly speculative argument was offered above in the discussion of "the rise or decline of polypoly" (Chapter 6). It was argued there that, owing to increased urbanization, greater density of rural settlement, and improvement of transportation, the growth of markets may have exceeded the growth of the business unit, with the result that the number of sellers competing for the same clientele may in many fields be greater now than it was in earlier times. Even an absolute reduction of the number of firms in an "industry" in the census use of the term may be consistent with a finding that more firms than before compete in the "same market." For example, in each of thousands of relatively isolated towns two or three local firms may have been in oligopolistic competition; gradually, the size of the firm may have grown so much that only fifty firms may now be in the industry; but cheap transportation may have created a truly national market and these fifty firms now serve the nation where previously many thousands produced the same product, but each served only its own locality; hence, fifty firms, not only two or three firms as in earlier times, would now compete with one another.

This argument may apply, though we cannot be certain, to a good many industries if we think of a long time span—say, two hundred years, perhaps even one hundred years. It is doubtful whether it applies in any large measure to the last fifty or sixty years. For during this time there have not been any drastic reductions in transport cost [32] or other developments notably reducing the barriers between local or regional markets, while the size of the business firm has grown enormously. Thus, a plausible case may be made for the thesis that oligopoly, after having become less prevalent (in any of the meanings referred to) during most of the nineteenth century, has again become more prevalent since the 1880's.

Historical Clues

According to a "crude interpretation of economic history . . . an original system of free competition has been metamorphosed

[32] Perhaps we should qualify this statement with reference to highway transport and the cheapening of short-distance and medium-distance hauling by truck.

into a new system of industrial monopoly," [33] and some who adhered to this notion of a decline of competition as a historical trend made the mistake of dating the beginning of the combination movement as of the last part of the nineteenth century.[34] In fact there is ample evidence that competition in early capitalism was largely oligopolistic in nature and, indeed, that there was organized oligopoly all over the place.[35]

There is also evidence for the hypothesis that the improvements in transportation weakened or destroyed some of the schemes of oligopolistic coordination. (For example, some of the regional coal combinations in England broke up when coal from other regions became cheaper to haul and could then compete with the cartelized product.)[36] Sometimes it was possible to fuse regional cartels into national ones, but often the number of independent firms was too large to permit nationwide coordination. It took an increase in the size of firms and a reduction in their number for the group of competitors again to become small enough for effective coordination of their selling.

While the cartel form of oligopolistic selling is neither of recent origin nor probably of greater prevalence now than 150 years ago, the technique of corporate merger is unquestionably a creation of the last decades of the nineteenth century. This technique must have immensely aided any resurgence of oligopoly and has probably increased the frequency of dominance and leadership. We have not enough historical information about the size distribution of firms in the past to tell whether dominance played any great role in the oligopolies of earlier times. It is conceivable that in those times there were "relative giants" dominating their small

[33] Thomas Southcliffe Ashton, *Iron and Steel in the Industrial Revolution* (London: Longmans, Green, 1924), p. 185.

[34] "By many writers the combination movement has been treated as a new-born product of the late nineteenth century . . . Nothing could be more false." Ashton, *op. cit.*, p. 184.

[35] Ashton names the following among the industries which had cartels, or "regulative associations," in England around the year 1800: coal, iron, steel, nails, files, tools, copper, silverplating, cutlery, pottery, book selling; some of these had existed since the seventeenth century. For example, he cites a 1665 agreement regulating the sales of iron bars (*ibid.*, p. 162).

[36] Hermann Levy, *Monopolies, Cartels and Trusts in British Industry* (London: Macmillan, 1927), pp. 120 ff.

competitors. I have the impression, however, that in many industries firms then were more nearly equal in size than they are now and that big-firm oligopoly is actually a product of the merger movement under modern corporation laws.[37]

[37] As late as 1914 it was possible for empirical investigators of the size of business firms to arrive at the conclusion—on the basis of statistical data from the textile industries in Europe and America—that "generally speaking, there would seem to exist in industries, . . . under given sets of conditions, typical or representative magnitudes to which businesses tend to grow . . . ," and that the dispersion of the size of firms "seems to embody an appreciable or substantial degree of regularity in each case." At that time, however, "the vast majority of firms [were] housed in one building." S. J. Chapman and T. S. Ashton, "The Sizes of Businesses, Mainly in the Textile Industries," *Journal of the Royal Statistical Society,* Vol. LXXVII (1914), pp. 512, 514, 516.

PART VI—FEW BUT MORE SELLERS

CHAPTER 16

Oligopoly and Pliopoly Combined

Combined Effects and Interaction: Pliopoly Affecting Oligopoly · Oligopoly Affecting Pliopoly

Free Entry, Gluts, and Oligopolistic Control: Free Entry Without Entrants · Cartels as Children of Depression · Restriction Warranted in Overexpanded Industries?

Oligopoly, Entry, and Excess Capacity: Cartels in Open Industries · Mergers and Concentration in Open Industries · The Essential Differences

The Threat of Potential Competition: How to Keep Them Away · Sacrificing Short-Run Profits · Sectional and Chain Oligopoly

REPEATEDLY WHILE dealing with oligopoly in the preceding chapters we referred to newcomers' competition but postponed a full discussion of the problems connected with the possibility of new competitors joining a group of only a few sellers. Now we shall inquire into this subject—into the combined effects of and interactions between oligopoly in its various forms and pliopoly in its various degrees.

COMBINED EFFECTS AND INTERACTION

In combining or synthesizing the theory of oligopoly with the theory of pliopoly after having discussed each separately we follow the example set at an earlier stage, where we combined polypoly and pliopoly theories after separate analyses. We found this procedure useful in that it brought usually blurred causal connections into a sharper focus.

When we combined the models of (perfect or imperfect) polypoly with the models of (perfect or imperfect) pliopoly we were able to derive certain effects that could not be obtained without that combination. These effects concerned such things as output volumes and productive capacity, production costs and profits. Similar effects can be derived from a combination of oligopoly and pliopoly models. We shall again obtain conclusions about output, capacity, costs, and profits, conclusions which are particularly illuminating in the case of organized oligopoly, in the case of cartelized industries struggling with ever-increasing excess capacity. But the combination of oligopoly and pliopoly models yields more than that. It shows not merely how the two combined affect other things, but also how they affect each other. For, as we shall see, pliopoly can change the kind and nature of oligopoly, and oligopoly can change the degree of pliopoly.

Pliopoly Affecting Oligopoly

If directly competing sellers are few, oligopoly results. If oligopolistic conduct secures higher than "normal" profits, entry into the industry becomes attractive. If pliopoly prevails, newcomers will appear and the number of sellers increases. Sellers may still be few, but there will be more than before. If the process goes on, pliopoly may transform oligopoly into polypoly. If the process stops before that, as it well may, the group of sellers will nevertheless be enlarged and the chances for coordinating their conduct diminished.

A relatively stable composition of the small group of sellers is important if the oligopolists are to achieve a high degree of coordination. If pliopoly works and newcomers join the group, established confidences may be disturbed, elaborate schemes disrupted, accepted usages and patterns of conduct disregarded. The form and performance of oligopoly may be effectively altered by the working of pliopoly.

A modicum of satisfaction with the results achieved is necessary for the continued functioning of organized oligopoly, for the survival of a cartel. If pliopoly is not kept in check and outsiders in increasing number take advantage of the output restrictions by insiders, the latter will not for long sustain the sacrifices imposed by the cartel rules. The cartel will break down as a result of pliopolistic competition.

A succession of mergers may have reduced the number of firms in an industry and established the leadership of a dominant concern. If pliopoly is not curbed and newcomers keep entering, the relative dominance of the large concern may conceivably be reduced enough to reduce the effectiveness of its leadership. The operation of pliopoly may bring about an increasing demoralization among the members of a leadership oligopoly.

We could easily add to this list of influences of pliopoly upon oligopoly. We could also modify it by changing the signs, so to speak, and enumerate some of the influences which the curbing of pliopoly may have upon oligopoly. For example, the suspension of pliopoly by government fiat may give oligopoly a chance to get organized, or organize more tightly; or it may allow looser groups of oligopolists to develop stricter "ethics," restraining the competitive ambitions of the members of the group.

Oligopoly Affecting Pliopoly

No one knows and appreciates the effects of pliopoly upon oligopoly better than the oligopolists themselves. And, needless to say, they are prepared to do all they can to suspend or restrict pliopoly.[1]

Oligopolists may use political influence to get the government to close or restrict new entry into their fields. Or they may use existing instruments of exclusion, such as patents, to close their fields to newcomers. This may be done through closed patent pools, through accumulation of vast numbers of patents in the hands of one concern, through harassing patent litigation to frighten away all potential newcomers.

Oligopolists may discourage potential newcomers through periodic price wars or through pricing techniques that make it impossible for a newcomer to calculate with any half-way certain net receipt.

Oligopolists may contrive to restrict or bar access to necessary means of production; they may make it difficult, excessively expensive, or impossible for would-be newcomers to obtain strategic

---

[1] For a survey and description of business practices designed to restrict entry in an industry see Fritz Machlup, *The Political Economy of Monopoly: Business, Labor and Government Policies* (Baltimore: Johns Hopkins Press, 1952), Chapter 4. In the text above I shall confine myself to the briefest digest of that survey.

materials, necessary machinery, transportation services, or financial accommodation, or to make use of existing distribution channels. A most effective exclusion of newcomers is achieved by allocation of "scarce resources" according to "requirements in the past."

Oligopolists may make it more difficult to enter their fields as they increase the minimum size of the efficient unit of operation. This can be done far beyond technological requirements by organizational devices, chiefly related to marketing. National advertising,[2] the distribution system, and servicing and repair organizations may have such effects.

No polypolist could succeed in doing any of these things, nor would he go out of his way to do them if he could. Since he would have only a trivial share in any benefit to be attained, he would not be prepared to make the necessary effort. Oligopolists, on the other hand, have the incentive and may have the power to contrive to control pliopoly.

FREE ENTRY, GLUTS, AND OLIGOPOLISTIC CONTROL

Having indicated how pliopoly affects oligopoly, having stated that free entry tends to weaken or destroy oligopolistic control, we must make an important qualification to explain why free entry does not always prevent lastingly successful cartelization or merger.

Free Entry Without Entrants

That entry is free does not mean that entry takes place all the time. Free entry means that a newcomer may enter if he likes to enter. But whether he likes to enter depends on how attractive it is to do so. Pliopoly is the likelihood of the emergence of newcomers in a field in which supernormal profits can be made. When business is bad and no profits can be made, no newcomers will appear even if the doors are wide open. Thus, even where pliopoly is perfect it will not be effective while the industry is "in the red."

---

[2] For a most interesting case study describing, among other things, how advertising outlays may operate as a device of exclusion of newcomers see William H. Nicholls, *Price Policies in the Cigarette Industry* (Nashville: Vanderbilt University Press, 1951).

Two conclusions can be drawn from this. The first refers to seriously overexpanded industries.[3] Oligopolistic coordination of such industries by cartels or by dominant concerns can achieve a lasting improvement of the earnings positions of the firms without raising the profit rates on new investment to such levels as would attract newcomers. In other words, cartels and mergers in depressed industries will not be exposed to the pressures of newcomers' competition even if entry remains open.

The second conclusion refers to industries which are only temporarily depressed. In these industries it may be possible for a cartel or for merger-grown concerns to use the time while no newcomers are attracted to take measures that will block entry when it again becomes attractive to enter. Thus, while pliopoly is still unrestricted the scheme of oligopolistic coordination may succeed under the protection, as it were, of the depression, and by the time the depression is over the insiders may have managed to shut the doors to potential newcomers.

These propositions throw some light on the problems of the origin, success, and justification of organized oligopoly.

Cartels as Children of Depression

It is a widely accepted theory that cartelization and sometimes also combination by merger are a consequence of depressed business. A series of bad years with severe losses—whether due to general depression or to gluts in particular markets or to overexpansion of particular industries—will "foster" the establishment of organizations to achieve oligopolistic control.[4]

---

[3] "Overexpansion" of an industry implies a disproportion between its productive facilities and the long-run demand for its products. Overexpanded industries must not be confused with industries suffering from temporary reductions in demand, nor with "decreasing-cost industries" where productive facilities would not be smaller even if demand had been correctly foreseen. Hence, the connotations of overexpansion are (1) that it would be impossible to sell at cost anything approaching the capacity output of the industry, (2) that this condition is likely to last a long time, if not forever, (perhaps for the entire normal amortization period of the equipment) and (3) that this condition would not have arisen if long-run demand had not been greatly overestimated.

[4] "There can hardly be any doubt that periods of heavy trade depressions

Statistical data show that most cartels were formed during depression periods and most mergers were executed during prosperity.[5] It is not hard to explain why prosperity is more conducive than depression to the promotion of corporate mergers. But what is the explanation of the fact that cartels are more likely to be established during depression than during prosperity?

It is usually assumed that competing sellers under the pressure of heavy losses may agree to give up the independence of action which they would not otherwise be willing to surrender. Does this assumption presuppose that loss avoidance is a stronger incentive than profit anticipation? It is perhaps plausible to assume that the avoidance of a two million loss means more to a firm than a two million increase of its profits—plausible at least if credit or equity capital are not in infinitely elastic supply. But the pecuniary success that can be expected from a monopolistic combination may be much greater in good times than in bad. For example, in depression cartelization may promise to do away with a firm's two million loss; while in prosperity it may promise to bring a ten million profit. In such a case the incentive to combine and strengthen the coordinating power of the oligopoly may not be smaller during prosperity than during depression, and an opportunity to combine would be utilized or passed up in either period with equal likelihood. The crucial point, missing thus far in the argument, is that profit and loss do not fully convey the real importance which the decision to cartelize may have for a firm whose real alternatives may be failure or survival. It may be argued with much force that no amount of prospective profits will

---

were especially instrumental in fostering the cartel movement." Karl Pribram, *Cartel Problems: An Analysis of Collective Monopolies in Europe With American Application* (Washington: Brookings Institution, 1935), p. 21. While Pribram agrees that, unlike these "collective monopolies," "unified combinations" through trusts and mergers are usually products of prosperity, he states that "under specific conditions certain types of unified combinations have been fostered by depressed markets." *Ibid.*, p. 22.

[5] One may stress that it takes time to establish a cartel or execute a merger and that, because of the "gestation period," a combination born in prosperity may have been conceived in depression and *vice versa*. In many instances it may be possible to ascertain the time when the particular moves were initiated, and it will probably remain true that more cartels were initiated during depression and more mergers during prosperity than the other way around.

persuade a rugged individualist to give up his independence of action, but that a serious threat of bankruptcy will.

This explains why depression increases the incentive to cartelize. An additional reason for the frequency of cartel formation in depression periods may be that depression increases also the practicability of cartelization—and this is explained by what we have found concerning "free entry without entrants." When entry is free and business is good, cartelization increases profits to a level at which newcomers actually appear, and the cartel, no matter how well organized, will not long be able to withstand the loss of business to newly established outsiders who take advantage of the restrictions of sales by the members. But when business is bad, cartels may go a long way in improving the profit-and-loss accounts of the firms concerned—and yet no newcomers will appear on the scene. Hence, the cartels may operate undisturbed from new entrants. The upshot of all this is that, quite apart from the incentive to cartelize, the ability to cartelize and the chances of the cartel to survive are greater in depression than in prosperity.[6]

Experienced promoters of cartels must know that cartelization in "open industries" is safe from newcomers' competition only as long as business is not too good. Hence, it will be their best policy to establish cartels when business is bad and to use the time while nobody enters to provide for restrictions on entry that will enable the cartel to survive and enjoy eventual prosperity. In other words, the open door to the industry makes it difficult to start a cartel and succeed in keeping it together when business is prospering; the time to start it is when business is slow; then perhaps the door can be closed before a crowd arrives to enter.

Restriction Warranted in Overexpanded Industries?

One of our earlier conclusions was that organized restriction may succeed in improving earnings in overexpanded open indus-

---

[6] I owe much to discussions with Edith Penrose, who first suggested this idea and then saved me from overstating it.—Incidentally, in periods of overemployment pliopoly may also be ineffective—or rather suspended—because labor or materials may not be available to potential entrants. Hence such periods (especially war years) might also be favorable for the formation of cartels.

tries undisturbed by newcomers. Such an improvement in the earnings of the firms in the industry is often welcomed not only by the vested interests but also by supposed guardians of the public interest, who argue that restrictive schemes of this sort are socially beneficial in that they involve, not extraordinary profits, but merely the avoidance of losses and of selling below cost. I venture to digress briefly from the subject matter of this chapter to comment on the controversial question whether restriction is warranted in overexpanded industries.

In depressed industries (or, more generally, in depressed years) the losses and the cost calculations of the firms concerned are mostly based on fallacious accounting in that the capital losses on excess capacity and the fixed cost of unused equipment are charged to current operations,—a practice justified perhaps if the accounts are to show the solvency of the firms, but not if they are to show the profitability of the use of existing resources. Sunk investment in excess capacity may be regarded as lost forever if there is no hope of ever using it, or not as lost if such hope still exists, but in no case is it right to "tax" the consumer in order to recover an investment in equipment that is not used for producing what he consumes.[7] To include depreciation of unused assets or interest charges on debts incurred for their acquisition in the cost of current output is wrong accounting, social as well as private. Correct accounting may well demonstrate that the depression losses reflect neither losses on current production nor selling below cost.

In some instances the depression losses are even greater than the investment cost of unused capacity, that is, the depreciation and interest for *used* capital equipment cannot be earned either. Marginal costs of production under such circumstances are below average cost even if the latter does not include the fixed cost of unused capacity. The question essential for a social appraisal of price policy is whether the productive resources in the economy are more efficiently used if prices in depressed industries cover only the marginal cost of output or if they are raised—by means of oligopolistic coordination or otherwise—to cover average cost.

---

[7] The consumer is here said to be "taxed" inasmuch as he is made to pay a cartel price in excess of the competitive price and this is "justified" by the high cost of unused equipment.

Most economists answer this question in favor of marginal cost pricing, provided the user cost of equipment [8] is duly included in marginal cost. On the basis of this answer, any scheme enabling the industry to earn "full cost" when it could not do so under unrestricted competition is likely to lead to an uneconomic use (or non-use) of resources and thus is injurious to the national interest.

The same idea can be expressed in a different, perhaps less technical fashion. Anything abundant, that is, anything of which there is more than people wish to use, has no economic value. Buildings or machines which cannot be used in the production for which they are designed nor for any other purposes now or later have no value (no matter how much has been invested in their construction). If it is expected that they may become useful again in the future, they have value. The actual use of productive equipment will of course depend on what price is charged for its use. If its use now may preclude or reduce its use later and if its use later may be worth something, the cost of present use is determined by the opportunity foregone in the future. If the present use of existing equipment does not encroach upon any alternative use now or later, its economic cost is nil. If nevertheless a charge for its use is made and its present use thereby restricted—because consumers cannot buy as much at higher prices—resources are being wasted. Hence, if selling prices under unrestricted competition do not cover any charges for abundant productive capacity, a more economical use of resources is attained than if under oligopolistic arrangements selling prices are raised to cover such charges.[9]

OLIGOPOLY, ENTRY, AND EXCESS CAPACITY

Our general assumption has been that the coordination of oligopoly can be successful if pliopoly is ineffective or restricted,

[8] "User cost" is Keynes' expression denoting the difference in maintenance outlay and depreciation between using and not-using one's capital equipment. John Maynard Keynes, *The General Theory of Employment, Interest and Money* (London: Macmillan, 1936), pp. 66–73.

[9] There are, admittedly, more sides to this difficult question, theoretical as well as political. The comments above were only intended to point to the most fundamental issues involved.

but will fail if pliopoly is unrestricted and effective. These are oversimplifications. To realize this we need only to recall that even perfect pliopoly may take time to be effective. It follows that the coordination of oligopoly may continue for a considerable time, and be reasonably successful, despite the pressure of pliopoly. Moreover it is conceivable that, even if oligopolistic coordinators are unable to block entry into their industries, nevertheless a more or less precarious equilibrium is reached in which the coordinating scheme is to some extent maintained. Let us examine these possibilities of temporary or lasting oligopolistic control in industries where entry remains open.

We shall deal separately with cartels and with merger and leadership in open industries. For, although cartels are most easily established in industries in which by means of mergers the number of firms was reduced and positions of dominance were created, and although therefore in reality corporate combination, domination, and cartelization are usually intermingled, analysis means separation. Hence we shall first assume cartelization as the method of coordinating the selling policies in an industry in which there are no dominant firms. Then we shall assume corporate merger, concentration, and domination without cartelization as the method of coordination. The combined method of control through cartels which include merger-grown dominant firms will not require much more discussion.

Cartels in Open Industries

The formation of a cartel, limiting or eliminating price competition among sellers, is likely to result in higher selling prices regardless of whether sales are centralized or decentralized and whether outputs are restricted directly through quota rules (with penalties for excessive sales) or only indirectly as a result of the observance of minimum price rules.[10] If cartel participation is one hundred percent or nearly so, the increased prices will increase the total profits of the member firms, for total production costs will be re-

---

[10] Once the cartel is in operation, there may be periods during which prices, largely because of oligopolistic rigidity, are lower than they would be under competition. We shall ignore this in the discussion in the text because over time cartel prices will be higher than competitive prices.

duced (even though the average cost per unit of the reduced output is higher than before) and total sales proceeds for the reduced output will be reduced by less than total cost, or unchanged, or even increased, according as the elasticity of the demand for the product of the industry is greater than, equal to, or smaller than unity. This increase in profits is, after all, the prime objective of the cartel.

Assume now that entry into the industry is free and the cartelists find no way of restricting it; and that new firms can produce as efficiently as the old and, selling at the increased prices, can make nice money on their investment.[11] Entering firms may either join the cartel (as the members would surely prefer) or remain outsiders (as they themselves would prefer). As outsiders they have the advantage of getting the same selling prices as the cartel members, or perhaps just a shade less, without sharing in the expenses of the cartel and without having to restrict output. Thus they can utilize their capacity and sell all they care to produce, while the members of the cartel must see their sales further reduced. As the number of outsiders increases, the cartel members will find themselves "holding the umbrella" over the outsiders and getting increasingly wet feet. For as long as prices are maintained and newcomers can count on selling their output, the business of the cartel members will continue to shrink while outsiders get an increasing share of the market.

The cartel will not be able to survive unless newcomers can be made to join up (or unless they cannot produce as cheaply as the insiders, perhaps because they have no access to certain materials, facilities, or processes exclusively available to cartel members through "monopoly controls" of some sort). Various methods can be used for making newcomers join the cartel. Governments often lend a hand in accomplishing this even where they may not be willing to close the industry to newcomers altogether.[12] Sometimes

---

[11] Needless to say, "new" firms in an industry are usually firms extending their areas of operations, that is, they are old firms in other industries.

[12] In Germany and other European countries both kinds of government aid to cartels have been very common. The most radical measure is the prohibition of all new investment in an industry. The German cement cartel was protected in this way not only from potential newcomers but also from ambitious insiders. In other instances, certificates of convenience and neces-

advantages may be associated with membership in the cartel, for example, the availability of licences under patents for improved technological processes. If the cartel enjoys neither government aid in forcing newcomers to join nor any monopoly privileges in which it can let them share if they join, it may try to bribe newcomers into joining, for example, by giving them preferential treatment of some sort (at the expense of older cartel members) or it may attempt to coerce them by harassing them through price raids, litigation, or other strategems of economic warfare. Let us assume then that, one way or other, newcomers can be made to join the cartel and accept its restrictive arrangements; hence, that a newcomer cannot merrily sell his full capacity output at the generous cartel price, but that he too must leave a part of his productive potential unutilized.

With every new entry the industry will find its average cost (inclusive of the fixed cost on total investment) increased as any given amount of output will be burdened with greater investment costs. Thus, even if the cartel and all members stick to the high prices, profits will fall steadily as excess capacity increases and total cost is swelled by the rising burden. Eventually the profits, which the cartel had first made possible, will be completely absorbed by the cost of idle capacity. This will mean either that every member operates with large unused productive facilities or that some members shut down completely and are paid compensation by the other members. According to our assumption, every newcomer must join the cartel and share in the cost of idle capacity, either by accepting a quota far below his own capacity or by contributing to the compensations paid to others. Under these conditions new entry will no longer be attractive and an industry equilibrium—with average cost equal to price—is attained.[13]

---

sity were required before new firms could enter an industry but the newcomer usually was committed to join the restrictive schemes of the insiders. In the last ten years, governmental allocations of "strategic" materials or of "scarce" foreign exchange have been used for the purpose of closing an industry to newcomers or compelling them to accept the existing cartel arrangements. This is done most simply by giving trade associations the task of, or a guiding voice in, screening the material requirements of the members of the industry.

[13] This process of equilibration through gradual cost increase is demonstrated in detail and with the use of graphical and algebraic reasoning in Don

This equilibrium of the industry is characterized by an amount of excess capacity to which several "forces" may have contributed. First, there may have been excess capacity even before the cartel was established (indeed, this may have been one of the factors behind the efforts to form the cartel). Second, the output restriction effected by the cartel must have implied (unless total demand increased) a reduced utilization of the existing capacity. Third, (unless the cartel agreement ruled it out and members were confident regarding the stability of the cartel arrangements and the given distribution of the shares in the market) members may have added to their productive facilities (in a hope of increasing their market shares when the arrangements come up for renegotiation). Fourth, the capacity of the industry was still further increased by the newcomers (which eventually raised the excess capacity to the point where its cost made further entries unattractive).[14]

This equilibrium, however, is essentially unstable because for every one of the firms marginal cost of production is far below average cost and, of course, below the marginal revenue obtainable by violating the cartel rules. In other words, contraventions are exceedingly tempting, particularly since the no-profit situation of the industry probably means that some firms make losses. And if some weaker characters cannot resist the temptation and some stronger ones get angry, many others will get fed up—and the cartel breaks down. But this need not happen. It may be that there are no weak characters in the industry and everybody keeps faith; or that although some break faith, the others are generous or wise and forgive them their trespassing; or that although some start chiseling and others get angry and hit back, the breach is healed and the cartel can go on, however precariously.

These then are our conclusions with regard to the success or failure of cartels under the pressure of free entry:

Patinkin, "Multiple-Plant Firms, Cartels, and Imperfect Competition," *Quarterly Journal of Economics*, Vol. LXI (1947), pp. 173–205.—It should be noted that the assumption on which this industry equilibrium is based—that newcomers must share in the burden of all excess capacity—is not realistic. If the assumption is dropped, collapse of the cartel is the only solution.

[14] "Although there are more plants in the cartel than under long-run competitive equilibrium, the industry output is less and the cost and price higher, with a very low (normal) rate of profit." Don Patinkin, *op. cit.*, p. 199.

(1) If entry cannot be restricted, if newcomers cannot be made to join the cartel, and if the cartel members have no special advantages over outsiders (for example, through exclusive use of unique facilities, patented inventions, or superior materials) the cartel cannot maintain prices that secure (supernormal) profits; if it tries, the number of outsiders will increase and the cartel will collapse.

(2) If entry cannot be restricted but newcomers can be made to join the cartel and share in all costs of idle capacity, the cartel will be able to maintain prices that are profitable at the outset; but excess capacity and total cost will steadily increase until profits are eliminated; the cartel will either collapse or continue a precarious existence.

Mergers and Concentration in Open Industries

Does it make a difference if corporate merger rather than cartelization achieves the coordination or unification of the selling activities of an industry that can be freely entered? To find the answer we shall start out with the assumption of a corporate merger attaining one hundred percent concentration of the industry, just as we earlier assumed a cartel with one hundred percent participation at the outset. As in the case of cartel control, we assume (provisionally) that there are no legal prohibitions of merger or domination.

A corporate combine comprising all the firms in the industry transforms oligopoly into monopoly. There is no longer a problem of "coordinating" the selling policies and activities of several firms, no problem of compromising, cheating, chiseling, disciplining, holding in line. Only one seller is left, and he can do what he thinks is best.

New entry recreates oligopoly, which in the first instance probably—if the new firm is a relatively small firm—will take the form of "partial monopoly." Just as the ousiders vis-à-vis the cartel, the newcomers will act as quasi-polypolists vis-à-vis the big concern. But there will be a difference in the chances of the continued independence of the newcomers. In contradistinction to the cartel, the corporate combine will have a much better chance of absorbing a small independent; and the independent will find it profitable to sell out to the combine. For, unlike the cartel, the corporate combine has something to offer, namely, a fat price for the stock or the assets of the new firm. And should the independent hold out, the large corporation has much better opportunities than the cartel to make life uncomfortable for him. Aggressive action by a cartel is not easy to organize, what with members likely to resist extra expenses, to quarrel about methods, and to resent and prevent overtures made to outsiders willing to yield. No such problems exist for the large concern; unhampered by disagreement, it can move swiftly, whether it is to exchange blows with a recalcitrant independent or to exchange stock with one who has come around and is willing to be taken over.

Of course, if the concern uses only its big purse and generous terms to buy out the new independents, more and more newcomers will appear on the scene. For every one whose business is acquired by the concern, two more may arrive, ready to compete or to be bought out. Thus, it will be important for the concern to administer rough treatment to any newcomers and "prepare" them for a merger in which they give up their assets cheaply. But even so, the productive capacity of the industry is likely to grow ahead of demand and, similar to the cartel burdened with increasing membership, increasing excess capacity, and increasing fixed cost, the concern may have to acquire many more plants than it will wish to operate. Only a very aggressive policy, threatening so severe a punishment to newcomers that none dare to come, can save the concern from a growth of excess capacity that would eventually put it in the red. Even then dissolution would be unlikely.[15]

That the big combine is able to swallow up every newcomer that appears on the scene presupposes that there are no laws to prevent it and that all newcomers are small firms. Of course, a "new firm" in this industry may be in fact an old firm expanding its field of activities and too big and strong to be swallowed. Perhaps prices, in an oligopolistic guessing game, will now be lowered sufficiently to make further entry unattractive. This, after all, is what the big

[15] There have been cases where bankruptcy, or reorganization on the brink of bankruptcy, caused a split-up of a corporate combine and restored subsidiaries to independence. But such cases are rare.

combine would in any case be forced to do if it did not succeed in frightening small potential entrants away from the field.

The introduction and enforcement of antitrust laws may affect the development in two respects: it may become more difficult for the corporate combine—which we must assume was formed before the antitrust laws began to be enforced—to use predatory methods of competition to get rid of independents; and it may become unlawful for the combine to absorb them. The continued growth of the giant corporation by acquisition of newcomers will be ruled out.

Now, if entry remains free, the degree of concentration in the industry is likely to fall gradually—in the sense that an increasing number of firms will share in the total capacity of the industry, and the share of the largest firm will decline. The large concern's share in the market is likely to decline even a little faster than its share in the total productive capacity of the industry, because most of the output restriction necessary for maintaining "satisfactory" selling prices will have to be effected by the large firm.[16] In the beginning, when the newcomers serve only a small portion of the market, they can utilize their capacity fully, while the large firm will have to carry the entire burden of excess capacity. As the number and size of newcomers increases, oligopoly in the industry will assume other forms. But, and herein lies the biggest difference between the corporate combine and the cartel, even if the profitability of the combine is much reduced, there is little or no danger of its falling apart. A cartel without dominant firm would surely go to pieces if 30 or 40 percent of the market were served by outsiders. A corporate combine which has lost 30 or 40 percent of the market to newcomers may be less profitable than it used to be, but it will not be a "failure" in any other respect.

A firm of this size will probably be the recognized leader in the industry. The larger ones among the other firms will begin to cooperate with the dominant firm. They will assume some share

---

[16] This conclusion rests on the assumption of equal efficiency, equal product qualities, and given demand. If the large concern is more efficient than its smaller competitors, if its products are superior in quality, or if total demand is expanding at least as fast as the capacity of the industry, the large concern will not have to restrict its output relatively more than the others, and may even restrict it less.

of responsibility for output restriction (for the sake of price maintenance) and perhaps also for entry restriction. And herein lies another difference between the corporate combine and the cartel: in an industry dominated by a large corporation sharing the market with a few others, a climate unattractive to potential newcomers can be created. Quite apart from any special pricing or distribution techniques which the firms may develop and which may make entry for newcomers a hazardous gamble even while the insiders make high profits, the large firms become so firmly entrenched in the markets that any expectations potential newcomers may have of succeeding in breaking into the market and in conquering enough sales to make it worth while grow dim and dimmer. Especially where the industry caters to the ultimate consumer and the products can be branded, trade-marked and nationally advertised, consumer acceptance is attained only by large expenditures made over several years.[17] Thus, from the outside, the prospects for high returns on investment appear under a dark cloud of uncertainty. While the insiders are "in the pink," potential newcomers may stay out for fear they would be "in the red" if they entered the industry. Entry under these circumstances will stop considerably short of the point where the profits of insiders are pushed down to normal.[18]

Insofar as potential newcomers to industries dominated by large firms are discouraged in this manner, an eventual "industry equilibrium" with supernormal profits to insiders will not be characterized by as much excess capacity as the equilibrium in cartelized industries with open entry. There will probably be excess capacity due to output restriction and perhaps also due to expansion of productive facilities by oligopolists bent upon maintaining or improving their "position" in the industry; but the contribution which new entry makes to excess capacity will typically be smaller than in open industries in which oligopoly is organized without the aid of large corporate combines.

[17] The difference in this respect between the cartel case and the concentration case should be clear: in the former the number of different qualities and brands is much larger and obtaining the acceptance of a new one would not be a serious problem.

[18] See above Chapter 8, pp. 261 ff. See also Fritz Machlup, *The Basing-Point System* (Philadelphia: Blakiston, 1949), p. 167.

The Essential Differences

Among the differences between cartelization and merger-made concentration we ought to single out for repeated emphasis the capacity of the corporate combine to stand up under a pliopolistic pressure under which a cartel would surely collapse. But the most essential of all differences is probably the end-effect of the inter-action between pliopoly and oligopoly. In the absence of government support, several years of pliopoly is likely to destroy a cartel in an industry without big-firm dominance; on the other hand, several years of big-firm dominance in an industry is likely to destroy pliopoly.

Assume, for example, that an industry of some twenty independent firms of similar strength and efficiency, and without any barriers against newcomers, can be "united" either by cartelization or by merger. What will be the most likely developments in each of these alternative cases? After a few years of pliopoly at work, the cartel, which originally had one hundred percent participation, would be struggling with several outsiders and would have a hard time of it. After a few more years, the cartel would have fallen apart and the industry would be hyper-competitive, saddled with huge costs of idle capacity. In the alternative case, the corporate combine, which originally controlled one hundred percent of the capacity of the industry, would have lost its monopoly and would share the market with a few competitors. After several years of big-firm oligopoly, further entry would have become impractical and the positions of the firms would have become more or less stabilized.

Thus, things look bad for small-firm cartels under the pressure of newcomers' competition—unless governments are willing to help. In many countries they are willing. In order to allow small-firm cartels to survive, the state must intervene and check further entry into the overcrowded industries.

THE THREAT OF POTENTIAL COMPETITION

Let us recall to mind that we have defined pliopoly as the "probability" of new entry into an industry where supernormal profits are made, and that this probability may be seen ("objec-tively") by the disinterested economist or ("subjectively") by someone with a personal interest in the matter, for example, by a large seller whose business would be seriously affected by actual newcomers' competition.

How to Keep Them Away

How will a large seller's conduct be influenced by the realiza-tion that the probability of newcomers' competition is high? This is how he might formulate his own considerations:

"If people see how much money is made in this field, they will want to enter it. This would be bad for me. What can I do about it? I might try to do something that will

(a) make it impossible for them to enter this field, no matter how much they would want to enter it;

(b) cause extra expenses to newcomers to this field, so that they will not want to enter it although they see how much money is made by those who are in it;

(c) give extra advantages to those now in the field but not to newcomers, so that they will less eagerly want to enter the field although they see how much money is made by those in it;

(d) indicate to them that their entry would decisively alter, through price slashing and cost boosting, the possibilities of making money in the field, so that they would not want to enter it although they see how much money is made by those in it;

(e) prevent them from seeing how much money is made in this field, so that they would not want to enter it;

(f) reduce the profits made in this field, so that nobody would want to enter it."

Skills along various lines—politics, law, technology, organiza-tion, marketing, finance, publicity, accounting, and others—are needed to carry out most of these policies, for example, to secure (a) prohibitions of entry, (b) high costs of entry, (c) advantages to insiders, (d) threats to outsiders, or (e) concealment of profits. These policies may not look equally effective; some may be entirely impracticable in particular situations; some may involve expenses to the insider and therefore a reduction in his profits. But as long as any of these policies appears practicable and not too costly, an insider will prefer it to the last policy, (f), the outright sacrifice of profits.

Sacrificing Short-Run Profits

The sacrifice of short-run profits for fear of potential newcomers' competition (and as a means of averting actual entry and the loss of long-run profits which such entry would entail) is ordinarily assumed to take the form of lower prices charged for the products of the oligopolists. Alternatively, these oligopolists might pay higher factor costs or engage in more extravagant selling costs than they would in the absence of such fear.[19]

Many economists take it for granted that potential competition will induce sellers to resort to a policy of lower prices. There are those who regard an entry-conscious price policy as oligopolistic policy and find no essential difference between anticipations of reactions of *existing* competitors and of *potential* competitors. The fact that the established firms set prices such as to discourage potential entrants and that potential entrants in turn may take into account the possible effects of their entry upon the prices of the established firms is considered as "a special sort of oligopolistic interdependence."[20] On the other side are those who find that there is a categoric difference between oligopolistic competition among existing sellers and potential competition from newcomers. Emphasis is placed on the fact that the former is likely to result in higher prices—as a means of avoiding competitive price reductions

[19] Thus, "established collusive firms might extend selling costs beyond the point of industry profit maximization in order to discourage entry, so that the threat of entry could cause increased cost rather than reduced prices." Joe S. Bain, "A Note on Pricing in Monopoly and Oligopoly," *American Economic Review*, Vol. XXXIX (1949), pp. 463–64. Probably no one has thought that insiders would try to "fool" potential entrants by foregoing profits through deliberately inefficient production. Yet Triffin finds it necessary to point out that such a method of sacrificing profits "is dangerous as it makes the task easier for the competitor who does not let himself be fooled by the absence of profit" in the established firms. Robert Triffin, *Monopolistic Competition and General Equilibrium Theory* (Cambridge: Harvard University Press, 1940), p. 122.

[20] Bain, *op. cit.*, p. 452; similarly Triffin, *op. cit.*, p. 123.

—but the latter, contrariwise, in lower prices—as a means of avoiding the appearance of new competitors.[21]

This theory of the price reducing effects of potential competition has some fascinating implications in connection with uncoordinated oligopoly. Such an oligopolist appears to be on the horns of a dilemma: low prices might induce his actual competitors to start competing vigorously or even belligerently; high prices might induce potential competitors to appear on the scene and claim a share in the market. His only hope is that his existing rivals share his fear of potential newcomers and have the same notions as he has concerning the prices that will be just low enough to be unattractive to those who might consider entering the field.

If the sellers in the industry are in collusion, they can exchange ideas about the prices which would be low enough to discourage or high enough to attract potential newcomers. For a formal treatment of the problem the concept of a "limit price" has been proposed, defined as the "highest common price which the established sellers believe they can charge without inducing at least one increment of entry." [22] The estimate of the "limit price" becomes an important factor in the price policy of the organized oligopolists. An estimate of the consequences of entry will be another such factor. After all, if charging the limit price involves a sacrifice of short-run profits, this sacrifice made to avert the danger of new entries must be compared with the importance of the threatened long-run loss of net revenue that would result if sales were lost to new competitors. These estimates—the limit price and the loss comparison—are needed in addition to the usual data—the estimates of cost and of demand—if the best price policy of the organized oligopolists is to be determined.

Whether this policy is the "best" not only *ex ante* but also *ex post* will depend of course on whether all estimates are "correct."

[21] "If a producer takes into account the consequences of his policy on his *existing* competitors, this will probably induce him to charge a higher price than otherwise (will make his 'imagined demand curve' less elastic). But if he takes *potential* competition into account, this will probably induce him to charge a price lower than otherwise (make his imagined demand curve more elastic)." Nicholas Kaldor, "Market Imperfection and Excess Capacity," *Economica*, New Series, Vol. II (1935), p. 40.

[22] Bain, *op. cit.*, p. 454.

With respect to the limit price, this would imply that the potential entrant is really decisively influenced by the prices that are being charged by the established firms, that he regards a certain price as the critical one for his decision to enter or not to enter the field, and that the firms within the field make a correct estimate of that critical price. If the existing sellers find it most profitable actually to charge the price they consider the limit price, and if they do not overestimate it, there is a good chance—depending on relative cost conditions—that a situation will be stabilized at which, without actual entries occurring, selling price is kept below and output above what they would be in the absence of potential competition.[23]

However, the theory of the price reducing effect of potential competition, this "time-honored limitation on monopoly power," [24] is not universally accepted. Indeed, it cannot reasonably be accepted except on the assumption that all other methods of keeping newcomers away have proved impractical or more costly. And in many situations a policy of "implicit threats to newcomers" should be a practical as well as less costly, and therefore preferred, alternative to the policy of sacrificing short-run profits. Rather than keep prices so low that no profits are made by the insiders and none expected by potential newcomers, it is better for the insiders to make all the profits they can make, but let it be known that they will slash prices if a newcomer should actually start establishing himself. It is on the basis of this argument that at least one writer concluded "that potential competition does not in general exert any influence on duopoly (or monopoly) price." [25]

[23] *Ibid.*, pp. 454–63. Bain concludes that "a vigorous threat of entry which at an appropriate time is anticipated and forestalled . . . may serve to keep firms producing at outputs which give a fairly close approximation to optimum average cost" (p. 459).

[24] George J. Stigler, "Notes on the Theory of Duopoly," *Journal of Political Economy*, Vol. XLVIII (1940), p. 533.

[25] Stigler, *op. cit.*, p. 534.—One can recognize a policy of latent threats to newcomers as a practical alternative to a low-price policy, and yet need not conclude that potential newcomers' competition is without influence on prices. Fellner, for example, states: "Constantly foregoing some of the potential profits need not be the cheapest nor the most effective method of keeping out possible newcomers. The alternative is to acquire the reputation of adopting an aggressive attitude whenever attempts are made at entering the industry. Nevertheless, it is likely that the menace of newcomers . . . fre-

This conclusion probably goes much too far. There will be many instances in which the oligopolists cannot rely on the effectiveness of the policy of the latent threat to newcomers, nor on any other method of keeping them away when high profits lure them. In these instances the existing firms will want to be cautious and avoid showing profits that incite the envy and appetite of others. If high short-run profits are seen as a possible danger to the stability of a situation that permits the making of secure long-run profits at a more modest rate, most businessmen will forego the former to safeguard the latter. In this sense potential newcomers' competition undoubtedly exerts a restraining influence on price making and profit taking by oligopolistic sellers.[26]

Sectional and Chain Oligopoly

The question of potential newcomers' competition and of entry into the industry is very different if the industry consists of a large number of sellers who act oligopolistically only in relation to a small number of firms which are in more direct competition with one another because their products are closest substitutes. These small subgroups of oligopolistic sellers within a highly populated industry may be either clearly delimited or overlapping, that is, oligopoly may be sectional or chain-linked.

New entry into such an industry may be of vital importance to the few firms with whom the newcomer will directly compete owing to the location or product quality that he selects. But to the mass of other sellers in the industry the new competition will mean little. The fact that another newcomer has arrived will go unnoticed by all but his closest rivals.

Under such circumstances the *potential* appearance of newcomers will not be a great issue in the price and selling policies

---

quently [does] set limits to the exploitation of short-run profit opportunities." William Fellner, *Competition Among the Few: Oligopoly and Similar Market Structures* (New York: Knopf, 1949), p. 162. Likewise on p. 310: "Even where entry does not materialize, the threat of entry at the cost-of-production price of potential rivals would set narrower limits to the exploitation of oligopoly power."

[26] For further comments on the effects of potential competition see Chapter 17.

of the firms. Potential competition from newcomers to the industry will hardly be more important to any one seller in a subgroup of the industry than the permanent and anonymous competition from sellers outside the same subgroup but already inside the industry. The presence of these firms and their indirect and impersonal competition acts as permanent limitation on the price policies of each seller in the industry. No additional limitations to the exercise of oligopoly power can be attributed to the influence of potential competition from newcomers.[27]

[27] This follows from our definitions of industry and subgroup. We speak of "industry" only because the products of its members are significantly competitive with one another even if the producers are in different subgroups.

PART VII—ONE SELLER

Monopoly

MOST OF THE WORK relevant to the interpretation of "real" conduct of sellers can be done with the various polypoly and oligopoly models; monopoly models are largely show pieces. They are wanted primarily to complete the collection. Anybody with a systematic mind would feel that there was something missing if the collection contained models with "many sellers" and models with "few sellers," but no models with "only one seller."

THE CHARACTERISTICS OF MONOPOLY

The judgment that "monopoly" rarely occurs in the real world is not inconsistent with the judgment that "monopoly" is all-pervading, ubiquitous, for the two propositions refer to different meanings of monopoly. Monopoly in the sense of a deviation from the models of perfect polypoly and perfect pliopoly exists well-nigh everywhere; almost every seller's position in the market has some monopolistic features in this sense. But monopoly in the sense of a position without polypolistic and oligopolistic elements is rare.

This "infrequency" of monopoly in the real world is of course the result of the way we have constructed our models and have chosen to label them. We might have used different labels or different constructions with the result that appraisals of the real world would seem different. This is stressed here merely as a warning against unwarranted conclusions from propositions containing terms that may be used with different connotations.

The Definition

Monopoly, in this analysis of seller's conduct, is defined as the market position of a seller who knows neither any individuals nor any particular groups of other sellers with whom he is in competition. (If such competition is potential in the sense that it may only arise under certain conditions and if it is taken into account in the considerations and conduct of the seller, his position is one of imperfect monopoly. Monopoly may be imperfect also for other reasons besides potential competition, as we shall see later.)

This definition is intended to contrast monopoly with polypoly, oligopoly, and pliopoly. The seller in a position of *polypoly* knows no individuals whom he would regard as rivals but he considers himself as a member of a group of sellers offering products that are heavily competing with each other. The seller in a position of *oligopoly* regards certain other sellers as his rivals (although he may cooperate with them in a peaceful regulation of the market). Where *pliopoly* is present, the group of sellers offering competing products—if such a group has existed—is likely to grow when the production of these products seems attractive, or—where no group has existed—rivals begin to appear on the scene. The seller in a position of perfect *monopoly* does not consider himself as a member of a group of producers of competing products, does not consider anybody as his competitor, and does not consider it necessary to restrain himself in his policies for fear of newcomers' competition.

"Pure Monopoly"

The concept of monopoly as a position without any elements of oligopoly—and, of course, without elements of polypoly—has been termed *"pure"* monopoly because it "defines a limiting case, not a typical one." [1] This adjectival qualification would be helpful were it not for the fact that "pure monopoly" has meant so many other things to other writers.

For example, the expression "pure monopoly" has been used to indicate the absence of monopsony elements.[2] It has also been used to denote the hypothetical case of one monopolist controlling the supply of all the goods in existence.[3] Again it has been used as a symmetrical countertype for pure competition, pure monopoly being characterized by zero elasticity of demand in contrast to the infinite elasticity of demand which is characteristic of pure competition.[4] With all these and probably many more different meanings of "pure monopoly," the term has lost its usefulness.[5]

[1] Robert Triffin, *Monopolistic Competition and General Equilibrium Theory* (Cambridge: Harvard University Press, 1940), p. 133.

[2] Abba P. Lerner, "The Concept of Monopoly and the Measurement of Monopoly Power," *Review of Economic Studies*, Vol. I (1934), p. 161, n. 2.

[3] Edward Hastings Chamberlin, *The Theory of Monopolistic Competition* (Cambridge: Harvard University Press, 1931), p. 63. This position of only one seller, who sells everything, was called "absolute monopoly" by Piero Sraffa, "The Laws of Return Under Competitive Conditions," *Economic Journal*, Vol. XXXVI (1926), p. 545. But the expression "absolute monopoly" was again used by Kaldor to denote the situation "when no other producer is able to produce a completely identical product at any cost." Nicholas Kaldor, "Market Imperfection and Excess Capacity," *Economica*, New Series, Vol. II (1935), p. 44.

[4] John D. Sumner in his lectures at the University of Buffalo. It was understood, of course, that the assumption of zero elasticity of demand was incompatible with the assumption of profit maximization. No price would maximize profits if always a higher price could be obtained without any loss of sales. The symmetry is only apparent, for the perfectly horizontal demand curve pictures a possible case, while the perfectly vertical demand curve does not.

[5] This was recognized by Triffin, who therefore (*op. cit.*, p. 144n) proposed a new term, *heremopoly*, using the Greek *heremos*, meaning lone, solitary. This is a good term, but has not been accepted. With a little more courage I would have adopted it in lieu of "monopoly as a type of seller's conduct."

Cross-Elasticity of Demand

It has been proposed to define all market positions in terms of the cross-elasticities of demand between the product in question and other products. A seller, according to this proposal, is a monopolist if the cross-elasticity of demand between his product and every other product offered in the market is zero.[6]

If this criterion is meant as an objective one, that is, if the estimate of the elasticity is to be made by a disinterested observer, monopoly cannot exist at all, except perhaps as a sheer accident of a momentary constellation. The cross-elasticity of demand for a good, the relative change in the quantity demanded divided by the relative change in the price of another good, is the combined result of the "substitution effect" and the "income effect" of that price change.[7] In order for the cross-elasticity to be zero with respect to every single product in the market, every positive substitution effect would have to be exactly compensated by a negative income effect, and every negative substitution effect (complementarity) by a positive income effect,—clearly an absurd condition. Or every substitution effect would have to be zero and likewise every income effect,—which is equally absurd.[8]

Understood as a subjective consideration of the seller, the criterion of zero cross-elasticity of demand is valid. The monopolist thinks of no other product sold in the market whose price reduction would significantly reduce his sales or whose price increase would significantly increase his sales; nor does he, when he deliberates on the effects of his own price changes, think of any particular sellers to whom he might lose or from whom he might gain

[6] Triffin, *op. cit.*, p. 103.

[7] J. R. Hicks, *Value and Capital* (London: Oxford University Press, 1938), pp. 31–32.

[8] Assume that all substitution effects were actually zero, that is, that there were no good or service in the market whose price change would induce people with unchanged real income to buy more or less of the product offered by the "monopolist." There would remain the fact that the price change of *some* good or service would affect the real income of *some* people, who then, being richer or poorer in consequence of the price change, might buy more or less of the product offered by the seller—who thereby would have lost the title of a "monopolist."

any business. Hence, cross-elasticities of demand do not enter his considerations; they are zero from his point of view.[9]

As always, one must have certain prices, price ranges, or price relations in mind when one speaks of particular demand elasticities. The cross-elasticity of demand may be of very different magnitudes at different price relations and, hence, when making an estimate of the elasticity, one obviously thinks of the currently existing price relations. If we now say that the cross-elasticity of demand between two products is zero, it may refer only to the given price relation, while at others the cross-elasticities may be positive. Where this is the case, the monopoly position exists only within certain price ranges and is therefore an imperfect one. Perfect monopoly means that the seller does not reckon with positive cross-elasticities of demand at *any* price relations.

Instances of Monopoly

It is difficult to think of concrete instances of monopoly in the narrow sense of the word discussed in this chapter. The sole seller in an industry according to census classification is, more likely than not, an oligopolist or an imperfect polypolist in that he competes directly either with particular firms listed in another industry or with large numbers of firms in another industry (in the census sense). For example, when there was only one producer of aluminum in the United States, it is quite likely that he found himself in an oligopolistic relationship with the tin cartel, with copper producers, or with the sellers of other non-ferrous metals. And if there were only one producer of a certain type of steel furniture, he might be an imperfect polypolist in view of the large number of manufacturers of furniture of various other materials.

Actual instances of monopoly can probably be found in indus-

[9] "If no particularly marked substitutability between a seller's product and other products is obvious; if, instead, the substitutability is so widely dispersed over goods and services 'in general' that one will not find it worth while to single out any of them as close substitutes; then we can say that our seller has no competitor, that he is a monopolist. In brief, a monopolist is a seller who competes for the consumer's dollar but does not know either the individuals or the products that he competes with." Quoted from Chapter 4, above, p. 113. In this statement substitutability is understood in the wider sense, hence, roughly equivalent to cross-elasticity of demand.

tries which are composed of very many firms as far as the whole country is concerned, but which sell only in local markets. The only moving-picture theatre in an isolated town may be a case in point. (On the other hand, the only legitimate theatre in a larger city might be an oligopolist in relation to moving-picture theatres.) We do not know how frequent such instances of monopoly are. They are more likely to be found in small towns than in large cities, and more likely in services than in goods.

THE ABSENCE OF PLIOPOLY

"Absence of polypoly and oligopoly means that the seller is the only one in the market; absence of pliopoly means that he is likely to remain the only one." This we said when the model of the monopolist was first introduced (Chapter 4, p. 112). We have yet to justify why the expectation that the position will last for some time should be an integral part of the model, that is, why ephemeral positions of "no competitors" are not here regarded as monopoly positions.

Temporary versus Lasting Positions

While all economic processes take place over time, it is sometimes useful in analysis to abstract from the lapse of time. Sometimes, for example, the momentary situation in the course of a continuing movement may, for very special problems and purposes, be described as a temporary "state of rest." For some problems and purposes, however, this abstraction from the time element is more misleading than helpful. The problem of entry, of the emergence of newcomers to an industry which has become attractive because of the promise of (supernormal) profits, is one of these problems. For it the lapse of time is of the essence. The invasion of a profitable field by newcomers takes time even if it is not held up by special obstructions. The fiction of "*instantaneous entry*" has little or no didactic or analytical value, and a model of perfect newcomers' competition that requires instantaneous entry usually confuses the issue. The clock time or calendar time that it takes newcomers to start business will probably be different in the manufacturing of airplane engines and in the production of knit-goods; it will undoubtedly take longer to establish a new continuous-strip steel mill than a new hot-dog stand. But if a field that has become profitable is *open* to entry, the time it takes newcomers to get started should not by itself be regarded as a criterion of a deviation from "perfect competition"; otherwise the analysis of the real world, the differentiation between open and closed fields, the discussion of removable barriers against entry, become unnecessarily hazy. If the position of a seller who is without competition today but will in all probability have competitors tomorrow is called one of monopoly, we are apt to lose sight of an essential feature of monopoly: the possibility of positive profits in a position of stable equilibrium.

This does not mean that the concept of a temporary monopoly is banned from our analysis. The producer of a newly invented gadget may at the moment be without competitor; if no patent nor any other protective barrier keeps imitators and makers of substitutes away, he will still enjoy his "headstart"; if a patent or some other specific device or circumstance protects him for a number of years from competitors, he has a "temporary monopoly"; if the protection is of such a nature that its termination is so indefinite that it cannot be expected with any degree of confidence, he has a "lasting monopoly." The important point here is that the character of each situation can only be understood with reference to the probable future expected by actors and observers under the circumstances.

The innovator, by definition, has a headstart and he will be able to exploit it as long as others do not catch up with him. If his lead should in fact last a considerable time because others are *slow*, or hesitant, there is no reason to characterize it as a monopoly. If, however, his lead continues because others are *slowed down* and thus prevented from catching up, we speak of a monopoly, temporary or lasting, depending on what it is that interferes with the would-be competitors. Just as there is in a track race a difference between the lead of one who runs faster and the lead of one whose competitors are slowed down by interference. And such interference may be temporary or lasting.

Natural versus Artificial Obstacles

It must be admitted, of course, that no clear lines can be drawn to mark these differences. Are the measures which an innovator takes to keep his new methods secret part of his natural lead or rather an interference with the competition of imitators? Are laws against bribery or industrial espionage in the nature of interferences with competition and, hence, instrumental in the creation of monopoly positions? It is not really important whether these questions are answered one way or another. There will be borderline cases wherever distinctions are made, for analytical purposes as well as for political.

The distinction between "natural" and "artificial" is inherently tenuous with regard to all social phenomena. There are schools of social thought according to which almost everything social is institutional and, hence, not natural. On the other hand, there is no use denying that some institutions are more deeply rooted in human thinking than others, and hence may be regarded as more natural and less artificial; others can be traced to particular acts of kings and legislators, or can be attributed to particular historical developments, political movements, or even individual actions, and can therefore be safely characterized as artificial.

A convenient test—mental, of course, rather than practical—is to pose the question whether the barrier that protects the position of the sole seller is removable by social action. If it could be removed but is not, one cannot regard the barrier as a natural one: it is condoned, if not erected, by society and the position which it protects is truly monopolistic. (It need not be one of monopoly in the strict sense used in this chapter, but may be one of oligopoly.)

The absence of pliopoly may be due, apart from artificial barriers against newcomers, to serious indivisibilities of production units. There are products for which the entire demand (or local demand) can be met by a single establishment—not merely the quantity demanded at current prices, but even the demand that would become effective at prices below the current ones (though still covering the long-run marginal cost of production). In this case it would be technology that is the basis of a sheltered position, allowing the owner of the first unit in the business to make monopoly profits which are relatively safe from inroads by newcomers. (See Chapter 7, pp. 231–33.) As long as demand does not grow to permit the establishment of additional production units of large size, and technology does not change to permit the establishment of additional production units of smaller size, a position of stable equilibrium may be created with the first producer remaining the only one.[10]

Subjective versus Objective Judgments

In our discussion of pliopoly we emphasized that the existence of pliopoly was primarily a probability estimate by the (objective) observer, who on the basis of his appraisal of the pertinent facts judged the ease with which newcomers would enter a particular industry if it became profitable. When the presence or absence (or the degree) of pliopoly was discussed in connection with polypoly positions, the (subjective) judgments of the people already in the field were held to be irrelevant. In connection with oligopoly positions, however, the (subjective) judgments of the individual sellers concerning the ease of entry into their field could be quite important as a consideration in the formation of business policies. In connection with monopoly there can be no question that the (subjective) judgment of the monopolist concerning the vulnerability of his position is an essential factor.

If in the economist's judgment a high degree of pliopoly exists, he need not be much concerned about whether or not the seller himself shares this judgment. To be sure, the seller might behave differently if he thought he was a monopolist from the way he would behave if he knew that he was not. But this would not be interesting to the economist knowing that the whole situation was ephemeral. It does not matter how the man acts in a situation which is liable to change presently in any case.

The subjective judgment matters a great deal if in the economist's judgment pliopoly is absent, or the degree of pliopoly is low. For in this case, where the seller is likely to remain for a long time

[10] The indivisibility may be a matter of cost or of quality of service. Duplication of facilities would be regarded as wasteful in either case. Examples: electricity, telephone, etc.

without competitors, much will depend on his conduct, and his conduct will surely depend on what he himself thinks about the situation. At least three typical cases should be distinguished: (1) He thinks that he is absolutely safe. (2) He thinks that he is not safe at all, that competitors may at any moment appear on the scene and spoil his business. (3) He thinks that he is reasonably safe as long as he is cautious and moderate in his policies.

In the first case his policies will be influenced by his long-term expectations with regard to the growth of the market and the change of technology; *long-run* considerations will dominate his decisions. In the second case he will not take a long view, for he expects that the imminent invasion of his field by competitors will affect his business more significantly than any long-run developments of demand or technology; *short-run* considerations will dominate his decisions, he will try to "make hay while the sun shines." In the third case he will not be free to make the most of his monopoly position, either in the short or in the long run; his is an *imperfect monopoly,* a position that cannot be fully exploited lest it be lost.

LONG-RANGE MONOPOLY POLICIES

Conduct models of monopolists are either very general and "empty," so that they have little predictive value, or they are so specific that they apply only to special cases and again have little predictive value unless one is able to identify the concrete cases in advance. In other words, few safe generalizations can be made about the business policies of monopolists; too much depends on their personal idiosyncracies, foresight, preferences, temperaments, and even moods of the moment. We may assume, however, that the expectations of the monopolists concerning the security of their position will be sufficiently significant in the formation of their policies to call for the construction of a model of the *confident* long-range monopolist.

Perfect Monopoly and the Confident Monopolist

We are speaking here of a perfect monopoly, that is, of a monopoly position which, not endangered by "potential" competition or any other limiting anticipations, gives the seller enough of a feeling of security to make him unconcerned about safeguarding his position. He feels no need of restraint in his policies; his decisions about price, quality, terms of sale, etc., are not influenced by any thoughts that newcomers' competition, government action, or other relevant reaction, may be provoked by his conduct.

It does not follow from these assumptions that a perfect monopolist whose position is secure in the long run will always try to "maximize his money profits." We may be sure that his confidence in the long-run security of his position well-nigh excludes the possibility that "*short-run* profit maximization" is at all relevant in the formation of his policies. Long-run demand and long-run cost, anticipations of future developments, will underlie his decisions. And there is nothing that compels us to assume that the long-range monopoly policies will be dominated by the desire to maximize long-run *money* profits. A businessman exposed to heavy competition may feel constrained to watch his profit-and-loss account more than anything else, simply because he cannot afford to do otherwise. But a perfect monopolist sure of his position and confident of his profits can well afford to pursue other objectives.

Non-Profit Objectives

This freedom in the motives of the monopolist is the main reason for the unpredictability of monopoly policies. For example, the men in charge may be anxious to maintain or increase their prestige as patriots or social-minded citizens and may forego considerable amounts of money profits for the sake of public acclaim. Or they may entertain some pet theories with regard to the social significance of low prices, high wages and pensions, quality improvements, technological innovations, radio programs, and similar matters affecting cost or revenue adversely from the point of view of money profits. Here lie some of the origins of the widespread slogan that "there are good as well as bad monopolies." But there is no way of telling what these monopolists will do. It is not possible, for example, to state with any degree of confidence whether the long-range policies of the perfect monopolist will be favorable or unfavorable to technological advance, just as it is impossible to predict for what kinds of fancies rich men will spend their money. There is nothing inherent in the position of perfect monopolists that would make them predisposed to spend their profits for research and development, nor is there anything that would keep them from doing so. No amount of case studies will furnish evidence on which to base generalizations valid for other monopolists or even the same ones at other times.

Despite all these degrees of freedom in the model as constructed, there is sense in working (and exercising) with special models demonstrating the principles of price and output determination of the perfect monopolist bent on maximizing money profits. These models can explain *some* of the conduct of monopolists, or *some* of the differences between the decisions of a monopolist and of other types of sellers. One must not expect them to do more than this.

SHORT-RANGE MONOPOLY POLICIES

The concern with short-run profit maximization, which some economists have mistaken for a "general principle" of the theory of price and output determination by the individual firm, may be the real thing in that peculiar type of monopoly where the monopolist does not expect to enjoy his position for very long. The model of such a "pessimistic monopolist" has fewer degrees of freedom than the model of the "confident monopolist," that is, it will yield much more definite results. On the other hand, there is some doubt about the applicability of the model: how can we know just when a seller whose position we judge to be that of a monopolist does not believe it will last? The type probably exists, but can we spot him in reality? Will we recognize him when we see him?

The Pessimistic Monopolist

Let us recall that the type before us is that of a man suffering from a kind of inferiority complex: he is a monopolist whose position we regard as safe—because we find the probability of newcomers invading his bailiwick to be very small—but who himself is convinced that newcomers' competition will arise any moment and will spoil his business. His judgment and our judgment disagree. If he should be right, the case would be without great social significance, because his monopoly would be all over. But if we are right, his conduct is apt to be rather unfortunate from the point of view of society.

There is of course the possibility that after some time, when his pessimistic expectations have proved to be unwarranted or at least exaggerated, he acquires the confidence in the durability of his monopoly position which would allow him to pay more attention to long-run considerations and even to pursue non-profit objectives. But, as a rule, a pessimist does not change merely because the expected dire events fail to become reality; normally he will continue to expect them with even greater apprehension. The emergence of competition may have been delayed but, as he sees it, it cannot be delayed much longer. And so he will continue to play the short run and try to make as much money as he can make in a short time.

Pessimism, Optimism, and Progress

For the pessimistic monopolist we can plausibly generalize that open avenues of technological advance will remain untried. Investment in industrial research, development, and innovation will not appear promising in view of the supposedly imminent advent of competition. Inventions will be suppressed if the time for the amortization of the required new investments seems too short.

If we are permitted to digress for a moment, we may point to the possibility of the opposite error, the over-optimistic entrepreneur who underestimates the actual degree of pliopoly and overestimates the safe period. He need not be an actual monopolist, nor even imagine that he is one; it suffices that he believes it will take his competitors—imitators or makers of substitutes—longer than it actually does to start competing with him. This optimism is the best promoter of technical progress. Progress calls for both innovation and imitation. If firms anticipate rapid imitation, they will not risk expensive innovations. But if imitation is rapid while the firms expect it to be slow, society will get the benefit of innovation as well as of rapid imitation.[11]

[11] The disparagers of perfect competition are badly mistaken if they regard perfect competition as inimical to progress. Of course, if they define

To buy innovation by paying with unnecessarily long delays of imitation is a poor bargain for society to make. Imitation always and necessarily lags behind innovation. It will be the best deal from the point of view of society if innovators optimistically overestimate this lag. If they expect the lag to be longer than it actually is, innovation will be enhanced and imitation will not be delayed. That it may create this socially wholesome illusion on the part of innovators is the strongest justification for a well-designed patent system.

Let us return to our pessimistic monopolist and make sure that we do not confuse him with the seller in a position of imperfect monopoly. The latter hopes to maintain his position if he is cautious in his policy, particularly if he avoids appearing too prosperous, and perhaps also if he tries to make his position secure by introducing new technology. The pessimistic monopolist does not believe moderation in his price policies would avert competition nor that he could avert it by technical innovations. Since he expects competitors to break in in any event, he sees no sense in moderation in pricing and no sense in risking large investments. There is sense only in exploiting his position while he can. He will not want to pass up profit opportunities which he thinks will be gone before long.

From the point of view of society, pessimistic monopolists are the worst possible type. *Confident* monopolists may after all be "do-gooders" and, although there is no presumption that policies which people believe to be "good for society" really turn out to be so, there is at least a chance that they are. Moreover, the attention which confident monopolists are apt to pay to expected long-run developments, especially to the long-term growth of demand, may to some extent offset the essentially restrictive effects of monopolistic business operation. Sellers under *imperfect* monopoly are somehow limited in exploiting their position lest they invite its termination. But the *pessimistic* monopolists have nothing that would keep them from pursuing the most restrictive policies.

---

it as *instantaneous* entry of newcomers, it obviously follows that "perfect competition is not only impossible but inferior"—as we read in Joseph A. Schumpeter, *Capitalism, Socialism and Democracy* (New York: Harper, 1943), p. 106. But such a model of perfect competition serves no purpose except to confuse the issue. Instantaneous entry of newcomers, instantaneous appearance of imitators, is not only impossible but nonsensical.

IMPERFECT MONOPOLY

A monopoly position which is conditionally threatened by new-comers' competition, government sanctions, organized public re-action, or reactions of an opponent in bilateral monopoly is called imperfect monopoly. The threat is assumed to be conditional upon certain circumstances, such as "excessive" prices or "inordinately high" profits, that is, it can be averted by adequate policies on the part of the monopolist. These policies may relate to selling prices, product quality, technological research, development and inno-vation, or public relations. Some of these policies imply positive actions which the monopolist would not take if his position were perfectly secure; others imply that he refrains from doing what he would like to do if nothing threatened his monopoly position. The upshot of this is that he does not feel free to use his monopoly position in all ways he would deem desirable, but must impose certain restraints on his freedom of action if he wishes to maintain his monopoly or avoid other undesired consequences.

Potential Competition

While the imperfect monopolist, like any monopolist, is not in actual competition with any existing firms or products on the market, he may feel under the pressure of potential competition. He may fear such competition will arise under certain circum-stances, for example,

(1) if his prices are too high,
(2) if his profits are too large,
(3) if his product quality is too low,
(4) if improvements in his technology or organization are too slow.

There is a logical correlation between the confinement of a monopoly position within a particular *price* zone, the anticipation of competition becoming effective as the selling price is raised above a certain limit, and the fact, previously mentioned, that cross-elasticities of demand may be zero within a certain range of price relations, but may become positive from a certain point on. This potential competition of the conditional monopolist may be with

(a) a large group of existing sellers of a potentially competing product marketed in very large quantities (relative to the monopolist's output);

(b) a few individual existing sellers of existing, potentially competing products; or

(c) newcomers not yet in the market, that is, not yet producing the potentially competing products, but expected to emerge on the basis of known technological conditions.

In other words, beyond the safe price zone of the monopolist may begin (a) an area of potential polypoly, (b) an area of potential oligopoly, or (c) an area in which a high degree of pliopoly is likely to prevail, leading to either polypolistic or oligopolistic competition.

Illustrations of the first two cases, (a) and (b), will readily be found in fields in which a sole producer in a country enjoys protection behind tariffs which exclude foreign competition as long as the difference between domestic and foreign prices falls short of the sum of transport costs and import duties. Depending on the size of the world market relative to the domestic market it will be either polypoly or oligopoly which is contiguous to the safe zone of monopoly prices. Other illustrations may be found in fields in which a product may be without economically practical substitutes within a certain price range, but may be confronted with such substitutes when it becomes too expensive.[12] There may, incidentally, be also a lower price limit to the monopoly zone, in that the product may become an economically practical substitute for other things when it becomes sufficiently inexpensive; that is to say, at low prices the product may qualify for uses for which it will not be taken at higher prices. Depending on the circumstances, the potential competition in the high or in the low price ranges may be polypolistic or oligopolistic. (See Fig. 26.) Indeed, it would be possible that on the one side of the safe zone lies polypolistic competition while oligopolistic competition lies on the other.

[12] In all these instances the geometrical device of the kinked demand curve may be employed to picture the situation: above a certain price, competition of foreign or domestic substitute products would make the sales curve of the imperfect monopolist highly elastic.

A Price Zone Safe From Competition Bordered by Zones of Potential Competition

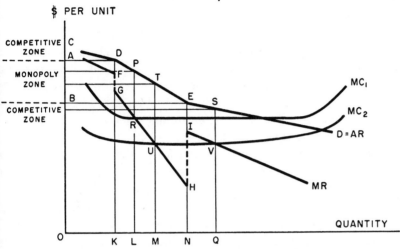

Fig. 26. Average Revenue Curve With Abrupt Changes to Greater Elasticities at Upper and Lower Limit Prices; the Corresponding Marginal Revenue Curve and Two Alternative Marginal Cost Curves.

Between selling price *OA* as an upper limit and *OB* as a lower limit the firm is assumed to be without actual or potential competitor. Above *OA*, however, it would run into severe competition, and would lose its market completely at price *OC*. Below *OB*, its product would become a good substitute for different goods, supplied by "another industry." The abrupt change in elasticity at *D* and *E* shows in a corresponding drop or jump, respectively, of the marginal revenue curve.

If marginal cost is as shown by the curve MC₁, the intersection of this curve, at *R*, with the marginal revenue curve indicates *OL* as the most profitable output and *LP* as the selling price of our imperfect monopolist. If marginal cost were lower, say as in MC₂, there would be a question, indicated by the two points of intersection, *U* and *V*, of invading the lower competitive zone with a price *QS*. But, if price discrimination is not possible, it will be better policy to remain in the monopoly zone and charge the price *MT*, since total profits will obviously be larger than they would be with the larger output sold at the lower price. (This can be most conveniently seen by comparing the little triangles below and above MC₂ for the additional sales *MQ*.)

The third case, (c), refers to pliopolistic developments in which the leading role is not played by any particular group of existing producers of a competing product but by firms expected to start out new in the business. On the basis of existing technological conditions it may be known that at a certain cost certain products may be so processed or fabricated that they become close substitutes for the hitherto monopolized product. If this fabrication or processing does not pay until the product can be sold at a certain price, it is only at this price that the potential competition need be expected. Perhaps moderate conversions of productive facilities are needed for the new production. These plant conversions may not pay below a certain selling price of the product. As the price rises above that limit, conversions must be expected and, thus, competition. What was said in the preceding chapter about the "limit price"—which is supposed to avert newcomers' competition—is valid for monopoly as well as collusive oligopoly.

There is no essential difference between the safe price zone and the safe *profit* zone. Where it is not potential competition from abroad or from given substitute products, or from given products or production facilities technologically linked with the monopolized product, price limits as such will not be relevant to the conditional emergence of competition. The termination of the (imperfect) monopoly may then be conditional upon a conspicuously attractive profit rate. Perhaps in view of special uncertainties, drastic indivisibilities, or other obstacles to newcomers' competition, certain supernormal profit rates as calculated by an insider would not be sufficient to entice outsiders to enter the field. The insider may be quite safe in his monopoly position until profits rise to a level where the temptation becomes irresistible. He may be apprehensive of this and avoid policies that would result in excessively juicy profits. This apprehension and avoidance of overly attractive profits need not result in low prices to consumers. It may just as well lead to great generosity in the expense account, particularly in wage bargaining; the imperfect monopolist may be inclined to give his workers a cut of his monopoly profits. By sharing the monopoly earnings with the workers, he reduces the attractiveness of the business to outsiders, and thus keeps free from competition. Of course, this is true only if the high wage rates would apply also to a newcomer. A cost increase that would not automatically apply to a newcomer would not discourage potential entrants, but instead might encourage them.

The possibility that the maintenance of a position of monopoly may depend on the maintenance of a certain *quality* of the product is logically related to what was said above about zones of relative prices within which substitution may be economically impractical. Just as an increase in the price of a product for which the seller has an imperfect monopoly may move it from a safe monopoly zone into a zone of polypolistic or oligopolistic competition, a deterioration of its quality may change the position of the seller from one of imperfect monopoly into one of polypoly or oligopoly. For in a certain quality and at given price relations the product may have no practical substitute; deteriorate the quality and, at the same price relations, substitution becomes practical. Needless to say, the monopolist confronted with the potential competition of producers of inferior substitutes will have more inhibitions about skimping on the quality of his product than a perfect monopolist would have.

The restraints which the imperfection of monopoly imposes on the monopolist's policies with regard to price, profit, and quality are all of a negative sort: he has to shy away from doing what he might do if he were perfectly safe from newcomers' competition. These restraints are, moreover, based on "static" considerations: he reasons on the basis of given cost-price relationships and of a given state of technology. There is a different kind of influence emanating from the threat of newcomers' competition, an influence of a positive sort and based on "dynamic" considerations: the monopolist feels constrained to do what he might not do if his position were perfectly secure, for he reasons that the state of technology advances with time and that cost conditions are apt to change accordingly. He concludes that he can maintain his monopoly position only if he stays "ahead of the game" by continually improving his *technological* or *organizational* methods of operation. In order to do this he may have to spend much money for research, development and pioneering work and introduce innovations which might not look profitable if his monopoly position were not threatened by outside-innovators.

Distinctions and Differences

Is there any difference between a monopolist taking account of potential competition and an oligopolist taking account of potential reactions on the part of his actual competitors? There are certainly close similarities between the two types: in both cases the seller anticipates reactions to his own actions; these are reactions of other sellers offering goods in competition, actual or potential, with his products; and these reactions can be averted by his desisting from certain actions. Some economists consider these similarities to be sufficiently close to warrant classification of potential competition as a kind of oligopolistic competition.[13]

Differences may be seen in the following points: (1) The seller under imperfect monopoly is sure to be free from competition as long as he does not exceed certain limits in his policies, limits that may leave him considerable scope for pursuing genuine monopoly policies; the oligopolist has rarely such a "free zone" for his policies, but must anticipate responses by his competitors to almost any moves he makes. (2) The oligopolist has his competitors always well identified, has observed their ways of doing business and their typical responses to his actions; the monopolist faced with potential competition *may* know the firms who would become his competitors if he allowed himself to step out of his safe zone, but they are not currently his competitors; and, of course, he may not know them but may merely be aware of their existence and general capacity to produce. (3) The oligopolist taking account of the reactions of his rivals to his policy may be hesitant to reduce his prices, while the monopolist taking account of potential competition will be more hesitant to raise his prices.[14] (4) The potential competition which makes the seller's position one of

---

[13] The effects which a seller expects his own prices to have upon the decisions of firms outside his industry to enter or not to enter the field have been treated as instances of "oligopolistic interdependence," instances in which in response to price or output decisions of one firm (insider), other firms (outsiders) vary their prices or output—only that in this "extreme case" they "pass from an output of zero to a positive one." Robert Triffin, *op. cit.*, p. 123. A similar remark by Joe S. Bain was cited above, Chapter 16, p. 536.

[14] See above Chapter 16, pp. 536–37.

imperfect monopoly need not be oligopolistic competition but may be, as was said before, polypolistic competition with a large number of sellers, a relatively "anonymous" group with no feelings of potential rivalry *vis-à-vis* any particular firms.

I submit that these differences are significant and that potential competition should not be regarded as oligopolistic competition. I realize that others may find that the differences are not essential enough to warrant a distinction; but this is usually so in borderline cases. It will always be possible to construct other ideal types or models that draw the dividing lines differently and thus comprise in one class the specimens or instances which fall into different classes in accordance with the distinctions one has chosen to adopt.

Potential Government Sanctions and Organized Reaction

We turn to another species of imperfect monopoly, where the limitations upon the monopolist's policies are caused by a threat of government sanctions or of organized public reaction in the case of "misuse of monopoly power" or excessive "price gouging" or "profiteering."

Government sanctions may be of many different varieties, ranging from formal antitrust proceedings, investigations with awkward publicity, or informal moral suasion, to the introduction of official price regulation or merely to the application of higher tax rates.[15] Similarly, organized public reaction to unpopular policies of the monopolist may take a variety of forms, ranging from social ostracism of the men in charge to boycott of the products they sell.

No separate analysis is needed to understand the nature of the consequent limitations in the monopolist's policies. The mono-

[15] It is a question of convenience how tax provisions should be treated in economic analysis. Sometimes one may take full account of all tax provisions by adding taxes to cost, sometimes by deducting them from revenue; sometimes neither of these techniques will do and one may employ other constructions, such as "limitations to the monopolist's policies." Graduated income taxes and excess profits taxes cannot be taken care of in the cost and revenue curves of customary price theory (because the two curves would become interdependent) but algebraic treatment remains easily manageable. Only in very special cases will it be preferable to treat tax provisions as instances of limitations to the monopolist's policies.

polist will be anxious to avoid raising his selling price, increasing his profits, or lowering his quality where this would mean risking dire consequences. Whether these dire consequences are government sanctions that are burdensome or troublesome to the monopolist, or organized public reaction injurious to his business or his public standing, or the appearance of competition as previously discussed, the effect upon his conduct is much the same: he avoids stepping outside the zone—of prices, profits, quality—in which he believes to be safe. The threat of sanctions keeps him within bounds.

It would be a highly worth-while task to evaluate the effectiveness of different kinds of government measures in terms of the checks they produce on the conduct of monopolists. This chapter, however, is not the place for such an inquiry. But since one so easily prejudges the issue, a warning may not be out of place: one must not assume that every restraint or limitation on the policies of a monopolist works in the public interest. The effects of imperfect monopoly need not be more beneficial or less harmful to the welfare of the public than the effects of perfect monopoly. For example, a monopolist may for fear of sanctions avoid raising his price and may find himself compelled to resort to rationing; yet, the allocation of the "scarce" output among favored customers may be much more injurious to the public than the charging of an unashamed monopoly price might be.

Restraints Due to Bilateral Monopoly

A different sort of limiting influence on the policy formation of a monopolist can be found in situations in which the monopolist's conduct in selling the monopolized product is likely to affect his bargaining position in another market. In his decisions he will take account of how his conduct may affect his bargaining position.

Bargaining is a matter of bilateral monopoly and similar market situations (that is, of situations where a monopsonist or oligopsonist buys from a monopolist or an oligopolist). One may, of course, regard bilateral monopoly *per se* as an instance of imperfect monopoly. Monopolist M is surely limited in his selling policies by the reactions he anticipates on the part of his cus-

tomer, monopsonist N. But these limitations are of a more complicated nature and are better dealt with separately. The analysis
of bilateral monopoly requires subtle techniques. It calls for the
construction of conduct models that are somewhat akin to those
needed in the analysis of non-collusive oligopoly. The exposition
and discussion of the theory of bilateral monopoly must be deferred to another occasion. At the moment we are dealing only with
the limitations which the existence of bilateral monopoly may impose on the monopolist's policies regarding other markets in which
he operates.

In the case of imperfect monopoly before us we are interested
in the policy of a monopolist who sells to a large number of customers competing for his output and who therefore does not have
to bargain with them. But he feels constrained to observe certain
limits in his selling policies because he fears his bargaining position in selling another product or in buying a productive factor
would be adversely affected should he overstep these limits. Monopolist M may, for example, be limited in his selling policies, not
by the reactions of his customers, but by the reactions he anticipates on the part of monopolist L, from whom he buys some of
his means of production. To offer a concrete example, our monopolist may avoid exploiting his monopoly in selling his product
because he fears reactions on the part of the trade-union leaders
with whom he must bargain about the wages he pays to his workers.

The trade-union leaders may not care so much about the selling prices of the monopolist with whom they bargain about wage
rates as they care about his profits. Their wage policies will often
depend on the employer's profits. And since the latter will know
that increased profits may provoke union demands for, and in-
sistence on, higher wage rates, he will not fail to consider the
possible effects of higher selling prices upon his profits and, indirectly, on the union's wage policy. If he could be sure of stable
market conditions, the knowledge that any profit increase obtained through an increase in selling prices would soon be can-
celed by a wage increase to be granted to the union need not discourage him from going ahead with the price increase. For, after
all, he will usually be interested more in keeping his workers happy

than his consumers and, thus, he would not mind squeezing the consumers for the benefit of his workers. However, there is no certainty that market conditions remain stable and, while consumers' demand may easily go up and down, union wage rates will not go down as easily as they go up. Consequently, a profit increase due to the exploitation of a merely temporary market situation would lead to a permanent increase in wages that would be a heavy burden later if the market should slacken. The monopolist will draw the appropriate conclusion and pass up the opportunity of getting the "most profitable" prices from the consumers. In other words, his freedom of action as a monopolist in the sale of his product is limited by his fear of reactions on the labor front.

JOINT SUPPLY, RELATED DEMAND, DISCRIMINATORY PRICING

The generalizations arrived at in this and all previous chapters have deliberately disregarded some unquestionable "facts" of the real world of business: that most firms produce more than one product; that the demands for many of these joint products are interrelated; and that many sellers in monopolistic positions charge discriminatory prices.

The simplifications made possible in the analysis of sellers' conduct by assuming *a single-product firm selling at a single price* were great. Many insights have been gained that are useful even where multi-product firms sell at discriminatory prices. But for that matter we may not legitimately continue to disregard the problems of joint supply, related demand, and discriminatory pricing. Yet this book has probably now reached, if not surpassed, the optimum size for its sale in a competitive market and I shall, therefore, defer further analysis to another volume.

Index

Absolute monopoly, 545n
Accounting, cost, 252, 256; data, 16, 18, 25, 39; losses fallacious, 524-25; profits, 13, 17-18, 218-19, 222, 238-39, 253, 256; versus economic concepts, 252-54
Advertising, and cost of price change, 466; and oligopoly, 409, 446; and pliopoly, 330; as barrier to entry, 233, 263, 520, 533; as public relations, 455; counterbalancing, 451; limits to, 455-56; through high wages, 49n; to appeal to customer, 83; to avert price competition, 459; to increase product differentiation, 96, 149; versus quality improvement, 182-83; warfare by reckless, 461n, 506
Agreement to agree, 443-45
Alchian, Armen A., 54n
American Tobacco Company et al. versus U.S., 440n
Amoroso, Luigi, 382n
Annual wages, 221n
Anonymous masses versus individuals, 418-21
Antitrust prosecution, 350, 443, 474, 532, 563
Applied versus pure economics, 6, 78, 417-18
Appointed price leader, 493-95
Apriorism, 417
Arbitrage, 155n, 395
Arnold, Thurman W., 167n
Artificial, barriers to entry, 114-15, 550-51; delay of adjustment, 220; immobility, 238-39; indivisibility, 221n, 233, 263, 319; scarcity, 257, 266, 267-69, 299, 302, 319; versus natural, 550
Ashton, Thomas Southcliffe, 503n, 513n, 514n
Asymmetry of attitudes, 361, 402-08, 412
Atomistic competition, 81, 91
Automobile analogies, driving at night, 46n; drunks driving, 391n; overtaking, 44-46; parking, 42n; speed versus safety, 53; ulterior motives, 53
Average cost, above marginal cost, 64; and business conduct, 43; and price

making, 60-78; below price, 302; calculation of, 19-22, 60-61; curve tangent to demand curve, 276, 306, 311-22; decreasing, 306, 311, 323-30, 343; definition of long run, 293-94; equal to price, 306, 311; including rent, 288-92; made identical with price, 288; production at minimum, 292-99; raised through cost of excess capacity, 528; raised through newcomers' entry, 330-33
Average-cost pricing, 60-78, 463n, 524-25
Average revenue, at fixed prices, 65n, 179-81; calculation of, 19; computed by cartel, 476, 479; differentiation, discrimination and, 14; from sales over time, 60; in lieu of demand curve, 38n; net of quality cost differentials, 179-82; net of selling cost, 97, 189-97

Bacon, Nathaniel T., 348n, 368n
Bain, Joe S., 266n, 360n, 361n, 536n, 537n, 538n, 562n
Barometric firm, 493
Basing-point system, 451n, 476, 494n
Becher, Johann Joachim, 86n, 340-41n
Benham, Frederic, 105n
Bertrand, Joseph, 368, 369n
Bertrand model, 370, 377-80, 387-98
Bilateral monopoly, 564-66
Black-market prices, 50n
Bloom, Gordon F., 362n
Bode, Karl, 419n
Boulding, Kenneth E., 104n, 116n, 360n, 400n
Bowley, A. L., 406n
Bowley model, 402, 406-07, 412
Break-even chart, 76-77
Brems, Hans, 430n, 435n, 480n, 482n, 486n, 489n
Bronfenbrenner, M., 471n
Burns, Arthur Robert, 116n
Business ethics, and price maintenance, 66; emergency controls perpetuated in, 502; reflected in testimonies and replies, 59; restraining competition, 364; see also Ethics

567

or in acquisition, 231, 324n; of management, 151, 326, 329-30; of resources, 143, 151-52, 221n; or lumpiness, 231; scale and decreasing costs, 143, 322, 328-29, 338-40; technological, 233
Industry, concept of, 102, 112, 130, 213-17; declining, 223-25; group of product sellers or factor buyers, 130, 214-15, 287; growth of, 149; in definition of monopoly, 547
Inferiority complex, 402, 554
Inflation, and full-cost theory, 74
Innovation, 549, 550, 555-56, 561
Institutional economics, 5, 423
Institutions, as source of monopoly, 363; changeability of, 12, 267-68, 550; creating indivisibility, 221n, 319; creating scarcity, 267, 319; in social sciences, 550; of perfect market, 118-24; reducing mobility, 238-39; regarding prices, 162-63
Interest, as production cost, 17; on bonds, 248, 250; on equity capital, 18, 23, 250; versus rent for owned resources, 253
Internal economies, 152, 319-21, 323-30
International Aniline Convention, 486n
International cartels, 442, 484, 486n
Interviews, 58-59, 68-70, 137, 203
Inventions, 330n, 457, 555
Investment, a long-run decision, 40, 101, 150; cost of price change, 468; for management's benefit, 50; indivisibility and, 235; normal return on, 75; of retained earnings, 27, 426; opportunity, 251, 260; scarce funds for, 143, 235n; sunk, 255

Joint costs, 19-25
Joint products, in model of the firm, 29; in narrow sense, 21, 23-24; regarded in simple model, 566; to utilize capacity, 331
Joint profit maximization, 436, 469, 477, 479, 498
Joint sales agency, 441, 476

Kahn, Richard F., 391n, 405n, 408n, 412n, 437n
Kaldor, Nicholas, 104n, 152n, 216n, 317n, 331n, 339n, 344n, 348n, 537n, 545n
Kant, Immanuel, 78n

Katona, George, 42n, 50n, 59n, 69n, 463n
Kaysen, Carl, 443n, 444n
Keim, Walter G., 167n
Keynes, John Maynard, 525n
Kinked curve, 100, 129, 353, 471-74, 558n
Knight, Frank H., vii, 104n, 120n, 226n, 227n, 228n, 229n
Knowledge, of offers and bids, 118, 119-20; of rivals' price quotations, 438; of supply and demand, 119-20; of the future, 104n, 120, 229
Kristensen, Thorkil, 395n

Law of large numbers, 419
Law of proportions, 324, 328-29
Law of scale, 328
Leadership, as failure to respond, 390-91, 402-08, 492; concepts of, 491-93; in oligopoly, 361, 364, 413, 443, 491-501; of dominant firm, 532-34; symmetrical or asymmetrical attitudes towards, 361, 390-91, 401, 402-08; usually implies collusion, 443; with or without collusion, 364
Leadership oligopoly, 364, 413, 443, 491-501, 519
Leontief, Wassily, 391n
Lerner, Abba P., 194n, 202n, 409n, 545n
Lester, Richard A., 41n, 45n
Levy, Hermann, 513n
LIFO, 18n
Limit price, 537, 560
Limited competition, 348
Linearity, of cost function, 401; of demand function, 371, 377n
Location, and central markets, 153-56; and spatial competition, 409-10, 452; greater choice of, 322-23; of products, 14, 153-58; of resources, 12
Locational differentiation, 153-58, 322-23, 409
Long-run cost, 40, 142-43, 150, 243, 292-95
Long-run profits, 41, 426-28, 536-40, 552-56, 565-66
Lumpiness, 231-36, 325

Machlup, Fritz, 10n, 31n, 59n, 87n, 111n, 125n, 130n, 156n, 226n, 227n, 350n, 351n, 364n, 393n, 399n, 413n, 419n, 433n, 439n, 451n, 462n, 476n, 479n, 491n, 506n, 519n, 533n

578   INDEX